1856

Daniel C. McCallum
On October 5, 1841, two American passenger trains collided head-on, making it clear that one boss could not watch everything. A well-defined organizational structure was needed, and McCallum developed the organization chart to show that structure

1887

Woodrow Wilson
While still a practicing political scientist, Wilson called for public administration to focus on effectiveness and efficiency—not just personnel reform

Frederic Taylor
The "Father of Scientific Management" recognized the need for labor-management cooperation, for controlling costs, and analyzing work methods

Max Weber
Defined fully the bureaucratic form of organization

Elton Mayo
Conducted the famous management study at the Hawthorne Works of the Western Electric Company near Chicago which examined the relationship between work environment and productivity. These studies were the genesis of the human relations school of management thought

30

Mary Parker Follet
Developed a management philosophy based on individual motivation and group problem solving — a forerunner of the participatory management idea

Luther Gulick
Lyndall Urwick
Provided the definitive statement of the "principles" approach to management: planning, organizing, staffing, directing, coordinating, reporting, and budgeting (in short, POSDCORB)

Chester I. Barnard
Viewed organizations as cooperative systems in which the "functions of the executive" (title of his classic work) were to maintain a balance between the needs of the organization and the needs of the individual and to establish effective communications

Robert K. Merton
Proclaimed that bureaucracy, which Weber [1922] had defined so systematically, had a number of dysfunctions (that is, characteristics that lead to inefficiency)

Abraham H. Maslow
Developed a theory of human motivation in which men and women moved up or down a needs hierarchy, as each level was satisfied or threatened

Managing the
Public Sector

To my wife,
Yolanda Blandón Starling

Preface

One of my great joys in revising *Managing the Public Sector* has been the comments from students and professors who used earlier editions of the book. Their questions and suggestions, together with my own continuing work on the problems of public administration, have led me to make several important changes in this third edition:

- A greater recognition of the profound interrelationship between the public and private sectors.
- A more streamlined discussion of the major themes animating modern public administration.
- The addition of cases at the end of each chapter.
- An expanded discussion of key issues surrounding what is perhaps the most neglected topic in American public administration: defense management.

In addition to these strategic changes, I have rewritten most of the text and updated every chapter extensively. This third edition takes into account important recent research by scholars and the latest experiences of practitioners. The new material includes such topics as the long-range implications of Reagan's New Federalism, the real danger of large deficits, the politics of tax reform, the role of microcomputers in government, up-to-date assessments of efforts at budget and personnel reform by Congress, the concept of organizational culture and its relationship to public personnel management, and recent court cases involving affirmative action and comparable pay for comparable worth.

Despite these many and substantial changes, the original approach and purpose of *Managing the Public Sector* remain the same. The operative word in the title is still *managing.* To many authorities, and surely most of the American public, the most acute need facing government in the decades ahead will be better management. But "better management" means more than the improvement of basic personnel, budgeting, and administrative practices. It means greater attention to modern analytical, behavioral, and informational techniques that are required to manage any large-scale enterprise successfully.

But an introduction to public administration must provide more than an exposure to such business school topics as management-by-objectives, accrual and cost accounting, microeconomic analysis, decision theory, and job redesign. Otherwise, this book would hardly be necessary—after all, a clutch of business school textbooks are available on all of these topics. No, an introduction to public administration must in at least two ways go beyond an inventory of management techniques. It must, first, place these techniques in the context of the public sector. And by *public sector,* I refer not only to governmental jurisdictions but also to other nonprofit institutions such as hospitals, foundations, and universities.

Second, an introduction must make crystal clear the highly political environment of American public administration. While I am sympathetic to the notion that the environment of private sector management is becoming increasingly similar to that of public sector management, I still see fundamental, and perhaps irreducible, differences. To cite only one: In the private sector, objectives are usually given—they are treated as problems to be solved. In contrast, the public sector's objectives are far less certain, far more debatable. Indeed, the public administrator often participates in the process of determining those objectives. In finding a place for the management expert, we cannot afford to toss out the political scientist.

Besides the strong, though not exclusive, emphasis on management, this book is unusual in avoiding potted summaries of what individual scholars have said. Instead, it provides organizing assumptions, concepts, and definitions that underlie any systematic inquiry and give a field coherence. To provide this coherence, the book builds around three major themes: the sociopolitical environment of public administration (Part I), the management of governmental programs (Part II), and the management of financial and human resources (Part III). The trio forms an integrated whole that attempts to reconcile the current thinking on administrative theory.

The body of this book provides concrete techniques that can be applied in any organization at any level. Whenever possible, I have used examples drawn from experience to illustrate the theories and strategies described.

Taking this tack forces the introduction of the real problems of public policy. For example: What is the best transportation system for Seattle? What approach should Florida take to managing its coastal zone? Who really benefits from the current federal tax structure? What should be done about the projected imbalances in the financing of the social security system? Because the public administrator cannot duck these kinds of questions, this book does not.

I should like to conclude on a brief pedagogical note. To ease the reader's journey into what may be entirely unfamiliar territory, I have taken several steps. Chapter titles and formats were carefully drawn to provide a clear and balanced view of the subject. Lists of new terms were placed at the end of each chapter; connective summaries, throughout. I have attempted to make the theoretical parts as clear-cut, short, and relevant as possible.

The philosopher and mathematician, Alfred North Whitehead (1929:13) once said, "A merely well-informed man is the most useless bore on God's earth." He added: "Above all things we must beware of what I will call 'inert ideas'—that is to say, ideas that are merely received into the mind without being utilized, or tested, or thrown into fresh combinations." To battle the pestilence of inert ideas, I have added to the end of each chapter a set of problems designed not for review but for critical, analytical thinking. These problems are an integral part of the book. They help attain what surely must be our ultimate objective: to improve the quality of thinking about the management of the public sector.

Acknowledgments

For help in preparing this third edition, I must express my deepest thanks to Roger Durand of the University of Houston–Clear Lake and James I. Scheiner, Secretary of Revenue for Pennsylvania. I also wish to thank Ross A. Webber of the Wharton School, University of Pennsylvania and Thomas L. Wheeler of the University of South Florida for use of their materials in Chapters 10 and 11. I also wish to thank Professors David N. Ammons of North Texas State University, Rufus Browning of San Francisco State University, Larry Elowitz of Georgia College, and Robert W. Kweit of the University of North Dakota for many valuable suggestions. And I must thank the many instructors and practitioners who took the time to send me useful suggestions based on their experiences with earlier editions. As before, I will greatly appreciate comments from those who use this new book.

All told, I found writing this edition to be a renewed management education for myself. I can only hope that I have made the way a little easier for others.

January 1986

GROVER STARLING
School of Business and Public Administration
University of Houston-Clear Lake
Houston, Texas 77058

Contents

Preface vii
End-of-Chapter Cases xvii
List of Figures xviii
List of Tables xx

1 *What is Public Administration?* 1
Who Public Administrators Are 1
What Public Administrators Do 5
What Public Administrators Need to Know 7
The Environment 7
Policy Analysis 9
Managerial Processes 10
Analytical Tools 12
Individual, Group, and Organizational Behavior 12
The Approach of This Book 12
Two Splits in the Field of Management 13
How Do Public and Private Management Differ? 14
How Do Management Theory and Practice Differ? 19

Part I *Political Management* (4 chapters)
2 *The Politics of Administration* 33
Introduction 33
On the Folly of Separating Politics from Administration 34
The Case of A. J. Cervantes 34
The Case of Jimmy Carter 34
Politics and Administration: A Historical Perspective 35
Administration in the Field of Policy Determination 36
Formulation of Policy 37
Implementation of Policy 39

Administration in the Force Field of Politics   44
The Legislative Connection   47
The Political Appointee Connection   49
The Client Connection   52
The Cognate Agency Connection   53
Media and Other Forces   54
Political Competency   55
Resources   56
Costs   62
Strategies   63

3   *Intergovernmental Relations   77*
Introduction   77
Federalism and IGR Compared   78
The Evolution of the Intergovernmental System   79
The Era of Dual Federalism (Until 1933)   79
The Era of Cooperative Federalism (1933-1960)   80
The Era of "Creative" Federalism (1960-1968)   80
Nixon's New Federalism (1968-1980)   82
Reagan's New Federalism, 1981 to Present   85
A Model for the Intergovernmental System   88
Intergovernmental Cooperation and Coordination   90
Federal→State   90
State→Local   91
State↔State   98
Local↔Local   99
Administrative Implications of IGR   100
Behavioral Patterns   100
Innovation   102
Diversity   103
Grantsmanship, Strings, and Priorities   104
Organization   105

4   *Administrative Responsibility and Ethics   114*
Introduction   114
The Ideal of Administrative Responsibility   115
Responsiveness   115
Flexibility   117
Competence   119
Due Process   119
Accountability   123
Honesty   124
Pitfalls on the Way to Responsibility   125
Collusion   125
Coercion and Nannyism   126
Distortion   127
Elitism   131

External and Internal Controls   133
    Judicial Control   136
    Citizen Participation   139
    Professional Codes   141
    Representative Bureaucracy   143
    Public Interest   144
    Ethical Analysis   145

Part II *Program Management* (4 chapters)

5 *Planning   165*
Introduction   165
Critical Definitions   166
    A Variety of Meanings   166
    Policy, Plans, Programs   168
The Formal Planning Model   170
    Premises   171
    Policy Planning   173
    Medium-Range Planning   175
    Programming   178
    Evaluation   179
Reconciling the Formal Model with the Realities of Planning   180
    Strengths and Weaknesses of the Formal Planning Model   180
    A New Synthesis: Logical Incrementalism   183
Forecasting—A Critical Planning Ingredient   186
    What Is a Forecast?   187
    Expert Forecasting   187
    Trend Extrapolation   188
    Leading Indicators   190
    Impact Assessment   191

6 *Decision Making   201*
Introduction   201
Identifying the Problem (or Opportunity)   201
Gathering Facts   203
    Framing a Decision   203
    Consulting People   205
Making the Decision: Five Analytical Techniques   206
    Cost-Benefit Analysis   207
    Multiobjective Models   213
    Decision Analysis   215
    Systems Analysis   217
    Operations Research (OR)   222
    The Perry Mason Syndrome, or Why You Need to
        Understand Analytical Techniques Even if You
        Do Not Use Them   224
Making the Decision: Alternatives to the Analytical Approach   225

7 *Implementation and Evaluation*   240
Introduction   240
                                    A. Implementation   241
Understanding the Process   241
    Complexity of Joint Action   242
    A System of Games   244
Toward More Effective Implementation   245
    Start Thinking about It Early   245
    Scheduling Models   247
    Expediters, Incentives, and Participation   250
    Communication   252
    Management by Objectives   256
                                    B. Evaluation   259
Why Evaluation?   259
    Evaluation for Policymakers   260
    Evaluation for Program Managers   263
How to Evaluate   264
    Find Goals   264
    Translate Goals into Measurable Indicators   265
    Collect Data   267
    Compare Data   267
    The Ordeal of Termination   269
The Role of Computers in Program Planning,
        Implementation, and Evaluation   271
    The Information Gap   271
    The Information Technology Package   273
    The Technology   274
    Four Fallacies about Computers   277

8 *Organizing*   295
Introduction   295
Five Types of Organizations   296
    The Leader/Follower Organization   297
    Mosaic Organization   299
    Pyramidal Organization   299
    The Pathology of the Pyramid   305
    The Bennis Critique   312
    Conglomerate Organization   313
    Organic Organization   315
Organizations of the Future: Three Forerunners   317
    The Systems Structure   317
    Task Force   318
    Matrix Organization   319
The Process of Organizational Design   321
The Organization Chart: A Few Cautionary Remarks   321
    Three Critical Steps   322
    Design Criteria   326

The Politics of Reorganization   *328*
  Rationale   *328*
  Realities   *328*

Part III *Resources Management* (3 Chapters)

9 *Public Financial Administration*   *345*
  Introduction   *345*
  Functions of Federal Fiscal Policy   *346*
    The Allocation Function   *347*
    Distribution Function   *348*
    Stabilization Function   *349*
  Assumptions behind Fiscal Policy   *350*
    The Traditional View   *350*
    The Supply-Side View   *351*
    Assessment of Reagan Fiscal Policy   *352*
  Meeting the Costs of Government   *352*
    Tax Structures   *354*
    Sources of Revenue   *356*
    Who Pays?   *358*
  How Government Spends   *359*
    Expenditure Structure   *359*
    Tax Expenditures   *360*
  The Changing Role of the Budget   *362*
    Line-Item Budgeting   *363*
    Performance Budgeting   *363*
    Program Budgeting   *365*
    Zero-Based Budgeting   *366*
    Capital Budgeting   *367*
    The Future of Public Budgeting   *369*
  The Federal Budget Cycle   *370*
    Executive Formulation and Transmittal (Phase I)   *371*
    Congressional Authorization and Appropriation (Phase II)   *373*
    Budget Execution and Control (Phase III)   *377*
    Review and Audit (Phase IV)   *377*
  State and Local Budgeting   *378*

---

10 *Organizational Behavior*   *398*
  Introduction   *398*
  Behavioral Approaches to Management   *399*
    Hawthorne Studies   *399*
    Maslow's Hierarchy of Needs   *401*
    After Maslow   *408*
    Douglas McGregor: Theory X and Theory Y   *410*
    Chris Argyris: Personality and Organization   *410*
  Three Ideas for Achieving Greater Worker Productivity   *411*
    Job Design   *411*
    Participative Management   *413*

The Theory Z Organization   **415**
Keeping Things in Balance   **415**
Contingency Approaches to Management   **417**
The Concept of Leadership   **417**
Can Leadership Traits Be Identified?   **418**
Using the Contingency Approach   **421**
Managing Your Most Important Resource   **425**
Managing Short-Term Time   **426**
Managing Long-Term Conditions that Waste Time   **430**
Transcending Time and Moving up the Career Ladder   **433**

11   *Human Resources Management*   **443**
Introduction   **443**
The Goals and Structure of Personnel Systems   **444**
The Aims of Public Personnel   **444**
The Structure of Public Personnel   **446**
A Framework for Analysis   **448**
Five Basic Functions of a Public Personnel System   **448**
Staffing   **448**
Classification and Compensation   **452**
Training and Management Development   **455**
Advancement   **460**
Discipline and Grievances   **461**
Organizational Culture   **464**
Toward a Definition   **464**
Two Case Studies in Organizational Culture   **464**
The Legal Environment of Human Resources Management   **467**
The Hatch Act   **467**
The Occupational Safety and Health Act (OSHA) of 1970   **467**
Civil Service Reform Act of 1978   **469**
Laws at the Grassroots   **470**
The Legal Environment of Labor-Management Relations   **471**
Legal Cornerstones   **471**
The Collective Bargaining Process   **475**
Impasse Procedures   **478**
Laws concerning Discrimination   **479**
Title VII: The Cornerstone   **479**
Developing an Affirmative Action Plan   **481**
Recent Developments   **482**

Part IV   *Looking Ahead* (1 Chapter)
12   *Looking Ahead—Trends and Challenges*   **501**
Introduction   **501**
Advances in Electronics and Telecommunications   **502**
The Office of the Future   **502**
Implications   **503**
Globalization   **505**
One More Time: The Concept of the Global Village   **505**

A "New Comparative Administration"   ***505***
Forging an "Urban Foreign Policy"   ***506***
Demographic Change   ***506***
Pig in a Python   ***506***
Implications   ***507***
The Productivity Challenge   ***509***
The Meaning of Productivity   ***509***
The Importance of Productivity   ***509***
Productivity as a State of Mind   ***510***
Barriers to Productivity   ***511***
Effective Productivity Management Efforts Tend to
    Include Seven Elements   ***515***
Specific Strategies for Improving Productivity   ***516***
Client Behavior   ***517***
Volunteers   ***517***
Technology   ***518***
Infrastructure   ***519***
Incentives   ***520***
Privatization   ***520***
Public-Private Partnership: A Challenge for
    Urban Communities   ***524***
Redefining Urban Management   ***524***
Private-Sector Contributions   ***525***
Collaborative Efforts   ***526***
Public-Private Cooperation: A Challenge for America   ***528***
The Problem: The Changing Structure of
    the Private Sector   ***528***
Current Federal Policies toward Industry   ***530***
Alternative Industrial Policy Strategies   ***531***
A Final Word   ***536***

Bibliography   ***541***

Index   *i*

End-of-Chapter Cases

1.1 Ruckelshaus Tries to Turn Around the
       Environmental Protection Agency   **23**
2.1 Closing Sydenham Hospital   **72**
3.1 Washington State Develops a Cutback Strategy   **109**
4.1 Controlling Biomedical Technology   **156**
4.2 Eldridge's Complaint   **159**
4.3 Relocating a State School   **162**
5.1 What Is the Purpose of the Peace Corps?   **197**
6.1 The Structure of a Government Decision   **233**

7.1   Communicating and Implementing the Inchon Decision   285
7.2   American Social Policy, 1965–1985: Losing Ground?   290
8.1   Senator Judson Blair's Office   332
8.2   Restructing the Pentagon   338
9.1   Formulating the Reagan Tax Plan   389
10.1 Sanitation Workers at the Gate   438
10.2 Fred the Great   439
10.3 Diane Wilson and Steve Carmichael   440
11.1 Three Ways to Fire an Employee   492
11.2 Gardner City Police Department   496

List of Figures

1-1   Classified Advertisements for Qualified Public
      Administrators   8
1-2   The Environment and Tasks of the Public
      Administrator   14
1-3   Relative Time Spent on Three Core Management
      Elements in Public and Private Sectors   15
2-1   Parallel Codification of Legislation and Regulation
      Legislation Is Implemented by Federal Agencies as
      Rules and Regulations   40
2-2   Pictorial Representation of Political Field
      Surrounding a Single Public Administrator   45
3-1   Federal Grant-in-Aid to State and Local Governments   81
3-2   Grants as Percentage of State and Local Receipts   82
3-3   Map of the United States Showing Federal
      Administrative Regions   84
3-4   Illustrative Operating Structure for a
      Federal Aid Program   90
3-5   A Model of the American Intergovernmental System   92
4-1   Different Approaches to Market Segmentation   119
4-2   Judicial Control of a Federal Agency or Commission   137
5-1   Objectives for the Fiscal Year, Charlotte, North
      Carolina: Law Enforcement Administration   169
5-2   Basic Planning Model   171
5-3   How Specific Should Goals Be?   182
5-4   The "Logical Incremental" Planning Model   186
5-5   Progress in the Mile Run   189
5-6   Trend Extrapolation Dilemmas   190
5-7   Seven Major Steps in Making a Technology
      Assessment   193
6-1   Generic and Unique Problems, or Why Effective
      Administrators Make Few Decisions   202

6-2	A Decision Tree	**216**
6-3	Model of Criminal Justice System	**219**
6-4	A Global Simulation	**221**
6-1A	Graph of Diet Problem	**237**
6-2A	Graph of Range Management Problem	**238**
7-1	Gantt Bar Chart	**247**
7-2	PERT Network	**248**
7-3	Quasi-Experimental Analysis for the Effect of Specific Course Work, Including Control Series Design	**267**
7-4	Connecticut Traffic Fatalities	**269**
8-1	The Seven Organizational Concepts	**298**
8-2	Line and Functional Authority	**305**
8-3	Memorandum—Department of Health, Education, and Welfare	**313**
8-4	Matrix Organization	**320**
9-1	Total Revenue by Major Financial Sectors for the Federal Government and for State and Local Governments	**354**
9-2	Expenditure by Major Financial Sectors for the Federal Government and for State and Local Governments	**359**
9-3	Four Ways to Prepare a Budget	**368**
9-4	Major Steps in the Budget Process	**371**
9-5	State and Local Budget Process	**380**
10-1	Maslow's Hierarchy of Needs	**403**
10-2	Comparison of Satisfiers and Dissatisfiers	**412**
10-3	Leadership Styles	**421**
10-4	Stress at Work	**431**
10-5	Yerkes-Dodson Law	**432**
11-1	Framework for Analyzing Human Resources Management	**449**
11-2	Dangerous Jobs (Three-Year Injury Rates in Selected Public and Private Sector Jobs, 1974–1976)	**468**
11-3	The Collective Bargaining Process	**476**
12-1	The Environment and Tasks of the Public Administrator	**502**

List of Tables

3-1	The Haves and Have-Nots of U.S. Cities: U.S. Cities Most (and least) in Need of Federal Support, 1980	83
3-2	States with Most and Least Local Discretionary Authority	95
4-1	From Which Level of Government Do You Feel You Get the Most for Your Money—Federal, State, or Local?	118
4-2	American Society for Public Administration Code of Ethics	142
5-1	Extrapolating World Records in Track	189
6-1	Major Categories of Costs and Benefits for Irrigation Project	208
6-2	Hypothetical Cost-Benefit Study	210
7-1	Alternative Governmental Mechanisms for Pollution Control	251
8-1	Characteristics of Mechanistic and Organic Organizations	316
9-1	Comparison of Revenue Sources	357
9-2	Who Bears the Tax Burden?	358
9-3	"Uncontrollables" in the Federal Budget	373
10-1	The Less Effective and More Effective Versions of the Four Basic Management Styles	424
11-1	White-Collar Civilian Employment in the Federal Government, by Sex and Grade: 1970 to 1983	456
11-2	Description of Exercises Used at the Assessment Center	459
11-3	Laws, Executive Orders, and Court Decisions on Discrimination	483
12-1	Illustrative Set of Output Measures, Qualitative Factors, and Local Condition Factors in Local Government	510
12-2	Milestones toward Deregulation	533

1

What Is Public Administration?

Is There A Difference Between Being An Administrator And Being A Manager?

> Even more important than winning the election is governing the nation. That is the test of a political party—the acid, final test. When the tumult and the shouting die, when the bands are gone and the lights are dimmed, there is the stark reality of responsibility. . . .
> *Adlai Stevenson, 1952*

What Are The Functions Of An Administrator? A Manager?
How Does A Public Organization Differ From A Private Organization?

Traditionally, public administration is thought of as the accomplishing side of government. It is supposed to comprise all those activities involved in carrying out the policies of elected officials and some activities associated with the development of those policies. Public administration is, as the Stevenson quote suggests, all that comes after the last campaign promise and the election night cheer.

Stevenson's is a fine definition, as far as it goes. But in this book we shall use a broader definition of public administration: _the process by which resources are marshaled and then used to cope with the problems facing a political community._ It is the aim of this introductory chapter to make this definition clear, as well as to show why the traditional one will not do. Perhaps the easiest way to begin is by meeting a few public administrators.

Who Public Administrators Are

In Detroit, Michigan, a man sits behind his desk in a blue, three-piece suit. He talks of computers, half-billion dollar budgets, in-service training requirements, construction projects, and cost effectiveness analysis. He is not an advertising executive, an investment counselor, or a production manager; he is a county executive.

William Lucas oversees operations in Wayne County, a sprawling 615-square miles of industrial facilities with a population of 2.4 million. When Lucas became chief administrative official in 1983, the

1

Bill Lucas has drawn high praise for his management of Wayne County government. He already claims a larger constituency than all but two black elected officials, Mayors Washington of Chicago and Bradley of Los Angeles. (Photo courtesy of William Lucas, County Executive, County of Wayne)

county government was "a shambles, plagued by woeful mismanagement, sky-high budget deficits, fractious infighting, cronyism, and other assorted ills" (Perkins, 1985). He moved quickly to balance the budget, eliminate the county's deficit, reduce payroll costs and health care outlays, privatize the county-run hospital, and rein in the bureaucracy. William Lucas is also a public administrator, one of a new breed of men and women effecting fundamental changes on some of the oldest governmental institutions in the English-speaking world. (The county developed in England from the shire, a unit of local government that originated in the Saxon settlements of the fifth century.)

Five hundred miles east of Wayne County, in Washington, D.C., a woman oversees the nation's air traffic controllers, testifies with ease before Congress on such matters as federal liability in offshore oil spills, and commands an armed service (the U.S. Coast Guard). Elizabeth Hanford Dole is secretary of the transportation department, a huge bureaucracy with 102,000 employees and a budget of $28 billion.

Like Lucas, Dole faced some tough initial assignments. These included getting a gasoline tax increase, keeping planes flying and starting to rebuild the air-traffic control system after the controllers' walkout in August 1981, and gaining congressional backing for the sale of the government-owned Consolidated Rail Corporation to private interests.

At her office, the first thing Dole sees in the reception area each morning are imposing portraits of the seven male secretaries of transportation who preceded her. Of the seven she is among the most activist oriented, a woman who makes safety her first priority. If one major air disaster is traced to the negligence of her department, her promising career could be seriously damaged. But, no matter what the pressures, Elizabeth Dole has cultivated a reputation as strong-minded, politically astute, and a judicious decision maker. Reporters and associates also regard her as a hard worker.

> She often comes on like a dewy magnolia blossom, but her drive and ambition have long been focused like a laser. How else to explain a Harvard-trained lawyer who not only graduated from Duke University Phi Beta Kappa but also was president of the student government council and chosen May Queen? These days on the campaign trail, Dole might take a 20-pound working "packet" of DOT materials with her. Thirty-year-old staffers complain she exhausts them, and the pace rarely lets up. (Orth, 1984)

Lucas and Dole illustrate at least one important thing about who public administrators are; namely, individuals who are found at all levels of government—urban/local, state/regional, national, and international. But as used in this text, the term *public administrator* has an even broader meaning. Specifically, it refers to those individuals employed not only by government but also by service institutions, such as hospitals and universities. It also refers to individuals employed by the many quasi-governmental institutions that have proliferated in the last 10 or 15 years. Among these quasi-governmental institutions, we might include research institutes (e.g., Rand), foundations (e.g., the Ford Foundation), laboratories (e.g., the Jet Propulsion Laboratory in Pasadena, California), museums (e.g., the Metropolitan Museum of Art in New York City), and federally chartered corporations (e.g., Amtrak). We shall refer to this broad spectrum of institutions—governmental,

Modernizing U.S. air traffic control is a top priority for Secretary Dole. (Photo courtesy of Elizabeth Dole, U.S. Secretary of Transportation)

The Public Sector in Perspective

We need early in our inquiry to put the size and importance of the public sector in proper perspective. Conventional wisdom says that the private sector creates five out of six jobs. While that may have been true in 1929, it is nowhere near the mark today. How can conventional wisdom be so wrong? Part of the problem is that many of the quasi-governmental institutions noted on page 3 are classified as private sector enterprises. I would suggest further that categorizing the production of military aircraft by Lockheed Corporation and nuclear submarines by General Dynamics Corporation as private sector activities obscures the true size of the public sector.

To comprehend the actual dimensions of the public sector, Eli Ginzberg and George J. Vojta in a *Scientific American* article (1981) count not only the people on the public payroll but also the people who are employed because of government purchases or grants. It makes a difference. Counting only those on the government payroll, employment rose from 11 million in 1962 to 25.3 million in 1983. (Most of the increase came at the state and local levels of government.) But when the wider view is taken, Ginzberg and Vojta found that the public sector accounted for more than a third of the total employment and nearly a third of the gross national product (i.e., all the goods and services produced by the American economy in a year).

Another bit of conventional wisdom about the public sector runs like this: the rapid expansion of employment and expenditure in the public sector is at a cost to the "productive" side of the economy, that is, to the private sector. This is at best a half truth. Consider: Government expenditures for agricultural research were crucial for the enormous productivity gains in farming, and expenditures on highways contributed to the prolonged prosperity of the automobile industry. In short, the public sector performs a large number of functions that are of critical importance to the health of the private sector.

"None of these functions is more important," Ginzberg and Vojta write, "than the acknowledged responsibility and role of the not-for-profit sector in *the nurturing and enhancement of the country's human capital*" (981:2; emphasis added). What would the U.S./electronics and petrochemical industries be like in the absence of governmental expenditures for the education of highly specialized personnel?

service, and quasi-governmental—as the *public* sector (see accompanying box).

Now let us meet another individual—Peter Ueberroth, who was in 1979 president of the nonprofit Los Angeles Olympic Organizing Committee (LAOOC). How he staffed, financed, and managed the 1984 Olympics is a story not without interest to students of public administration.

In 1978, the International Olympic Committee awarded the 1984 games to the city of Los Angeles after Mayor Tom Bradley suggested that the city make a bid. To protect the taxpayers, the Los Angeles City

Council required that LAOOC contract with the city for those municipal services necessary to the games and prohibited the city from spending its general tax dollars on direct Olympic services (Remy & Lawson,
1984).

Ueberroth's challenge was probably even greater than those facing
County Executive Lucas and Secretary Dole—namely, to open an
office for an organization that had no assets and build it into an
organization capable of running a two-week sports and cultural event
the size of nine Super Bowls. Ueberroth, then 42 years old, knew that
his best chance to get financing was from the television networks. He
designed a bold blind-bidding contest that yielded $225 million from
ABC. Then he began negotiating contracts with the largest corporations. Colleagues say that his "reverse salesmanship"—earnestly
seeming to take the other person's side—was awesome to watch.

As revenue began to increase, building international goodwill became Ueberroth's new priority. In attempting to cultivate the various
national ministers of sport, Ueberroth discovered that the political
power of athletics and athletic officials around the world was considerable. When foreign officials occasionally asked if he might help change
some aspect of U.S. foreign policy, Ueberroth had to explain that sports
officials in this country do not have that kind of influence.

His management style throughout was to delegate authority and
responsibility. The man who actually ran the games, Harry Usher says
leadership and inspiration, not operations, are Ueberroth's managerial
talents. If someone faltered, however, Ueberroth did not hesitate to
take charge. To build unity, Ueberroth encouraged staff members to
lunch at the cafeteria in the converted hangar that served as the
committee's main office. When he saw a staff member not using all of
his or her skills, Ueberroth, always the teacher, showed his annoyance;
conversely, when someone performed well, he was exhilarated. When
the three Olympic villages opened for the athletes two weeks before
the games, he seemed everywhere at once with an electronic gadget on
his hip that delivered printed, urgent messages to him. He particularly
sought out the 29 different police forces involved in the games. In
working with the police, Ueberroth's priority was not equipment but
attitude: "The law-enforcement people were so upbeat," he explained,
"and that affected everyone" (*Time*, January 7, 1985).

What Public Administrators Do

Based on the three brief profiles above, we can already make a few
generalizations. We know, for example, that all are more than just
competent administrators and program managers who ensure effective performance. They are also astute politicians and decision
makers. Further, as we saw clearly in the case of Bill Lucas—who had
to develop a set of strategies to meet the fiscal problems of Wayne

In 1979, Peter Ueberroth hired Harry Usher as general manager of the 1984 Olympics and then set out to hire a staff that would ultimately grow to more than 60,000. He set up an administrative structure that was flexible enough to move from planning to operations. In 1985, President Reagan asked him to serve on a committee to mobilize the private sector in causes all the way from world hunger to urban blight. (Heinz Kluetmeier/*Sports Illustrated*)

County—they can also be *policy formulators*. As we know from Elizabeth Dole's vigorous pursuit of safety, they can be *reformers* as well. And from Dole's ability to choose among competing interests and reconcile all parties to the outcome in tough issues involving mass transit, airport policy, shipping, and highway safety, we know public administrators must also play the role of *interest broker*.

Perhaps in Peter Ueberroth we saw most vividly the role of *public relations expert* (building support for the games) and *leader* (commanding attention and stimulating subordinates). To boost morale during the games, he wore a different uniform each day: a bus driver's suit, a kitchen staffer's whites, a blue and gold usher's shirt. Recently, staffers, when driving into the Department of Transportation garage, were startled to encounter a well-tailored woman at the entrance holding a stop sign and checking to see if occupants had their seat belts buckled. The inspector: Elizabeth Dole.

Ueberroth also provides an excellent example of a role some think is likely to become increasingly important for public administrators: *crisis manager*. Remembering the violence in Munich in 1972 and the financial disaster in Montreal in 1976, Ueberroth reasoned that the 1984 games could be a real test. He was not mistaken. When the Soviet Union announced its boycott, Ueberroth and his staff were ready.

Their immediate concern was to prevent other countries from following the Soviet lead. Experienced envoys quickly flew to assigned countries; Ueberroth went to Cuba. There Fidel Castro told him that, while he had to follow the Soviet lead, he would not pressure other Latin American countries to stay away.

Another role—one likely to be increasingly important in the years ahead—is _private sector partner_, helping to set up arrangements that permit government to cooperate better with business in areas of agreed upon social priority. We already have a number of illustrations of this role besides the Los Angeles Organizing Committee: the liquid metal fast breeder reactor program, the Connecticut Resource (Solid Waste) Recovery Authority, the program to make the Island of Hawaii energy self-sufficient, various aerospace programs (e.g., Apollo and Space Shuttle), deregulation of communications and transportation, and programs to enhance the nation's human resources through education and research grants.

The functional areas in which public administrators are involved are even more varied than the roles they may perform. In addition to general management (Lucas), transportation (Dole), and sports and cultural affairs (Ueberroth), public administrators might find themselves involved in such areas as community development, business regulation, educational administration, environmental management, international development administration, human resources and employment, national security and arms control, space law, personnel, health care service administration, medical research, public works administration, and housing.

In sum, the challenge of a career in public administration today is as broad and exciting as contemporary life itself (see Figure 1-1).

But the question what public administrators do raises still another question: What basic knowledge and skills must public administrators have to perform the functions and fulfill the roles outlined above? Mark this question well, for it points us squarely in the direction of the subject of this book.

What Public Administrators Need to Know

The National Association of Schools of Public Affairs and Administration (NASPAA) recommends that public administration programs in colleges and universities cover five subject matter areas: _(a)_ the political, social, and economic environment; _(b)_ policy analysis; _(c)_ managerial processes; _(d)_ analytical tools; and _(e)_ individual, group, and organizational behavior.

The Environment

The first axiom of administration might be that organizations do not operate in vacuums. And this axiom applies not only to the public

Figure 1-1

Classified Advertisements for Qualified Public Administrators

ASSISTANT COUNTY MANAGER
($52,000-$70,000)
Pima County, Arizona
(Tucson)

Pima County is looking for an energetic, enthusiastic and proven executive level manager to participate in the active administration of the County's operations. The successful candidate will have a Master's degree in Public Administration or Business Administration from an accredited college or university and 8 years of progressively responsible administrative and managerial experience in a medium to large size organization, including at least 3 years at the executive level of management. Submit a resume to the attention of:
Director, Pima County, Human Resources Department, 7th floor, 131 W. Congress St., Tucson, AZ 85701 by May 17, 1985.
Pima County is an equal opportunity employer
Minorities, handicapped and women are encouraged to apply

PIMA COUNTY GOVERNMENT

National Science Foundation

The National Science Foundation, Division of Social and Economic Sciences, is seeking candidates for the position of Associate Program Director, Political Science Program, Political and Policy Science Section. This is a rotational assignment for 1 or 2 years and is expected from the competitive civil service at the EC-13/14 grade range (equivalent to GS-13/14), $33,586 to $51,596 per annum. Appointment period beginning mid-summer 1982. Candidates should have a Ph.D. or equivalent experience and at least 5 years of scientific research experience beyond the Ph.D. in political science/public administration. Responsibilities include all aspects of proposal development, review and evaluation, grant and program administration. Candidates should submit a curriculum vitae to the ...

Consulting Opportunities in Developing Countries

Clapp and Mayne, Inc.'s roster for consultants interested in work in developing countries is being reopened. At least three years' relevant work experience in developing countries is recommended. We are particularly interested in candidates with experience in the Caribbean and Latin America, fluency in Spanish or French, and graduate degrees. In early 1984 we will submit proposals for short-term assistance in Development Administration, Rural Development, Customs Administration, and other projects involving data processing, tax administration, training, project design, and evaluation. Please send a resume of professional qualifications.

Management Opportunity

The Washington Metropolitan Area Transit Authority seeks an experienced manager for the following key position:

Director of Human Resources

Responsible for planning, implementing, coordinating, directing and monitoring an imaginative, aggressive, communications-oriented human resources program. Will provide leadership and directon to a staff of 50 involved in the management of the personnel (employment, classification, training, and medical services) and labor relations (labor negotiatons, administration, and interpretaton of various labor agreements) programs. Bachelor's Degree and extensive diversified executive level experience in a large organization managing a results-oriented human resources program which includes the broad spectrum of personnel and labor relations functions. Sensitivity to human resource needs and demonstrated success in addressing those needs are required. Closing date: July 23, 1982.

The Washington Metropolitan Area Transit Authority offers a comprehensive benefits program including deferred compensation and salary level commensurate with experience. If you seek the opportunity to manage transportation activities and grow with our organization, please send your resume, in confidence, including salary requirement and position for which you are applying to
Assista

GAO Evaluators and Accountants

The US General Accounting Office opens its Spring 1985 recruiting cycle Feb. 18-April 12 for entry-level Evaluators and Accountants. Positions available in 15 GAO locations for college graduates with academic background or experience in Public Administration, Accounting, Business Administration and Computer Science. Demonstrated knowledge in analytical reasoning, interviewing, written and oral communication, interpersonal and teamwork abilities required. Salary range $17,824-$21,804 plus benefits. Write or call for required application package. Applications must be received by April 12, 1985.

Accounting Office
cruitment Program

State Court Administrator

State Court Administrator—Oregon Judicial Department, Salem, Oregon. The State Court Administrator, under the direction of the Chief Justice of the Supreme Court, is responsible for the administration and management of a state-funded court system. Responsibilities include the following: administration of a statewide personnel plan (1300 employees); preparation and legislative presentation of the Judicial Department budget ($133 million for the 1983-85 Biennium); fiscal operations and accounting procedures; provide management assistance to support trial court operations; collect and compile statistical and other data relating to the courts; preparation of court-related legislation; provide legislative liaison services for the Judicial Department; in-service education and training for judges and non-judge staff; act as court administrator for the Supreme Court and Court of Appeals; court system planning; provide liaison services to State Bar Association and State Executive Department; public relations; annual report. Applicants must have a significant amount of increasingly responsible management level experience. Preference may be given to applicants with management level experience in court administration.
Salary: open
Send resume, including academic and work-related history and salary inforamtion to:
Personnel Director
Judicial Department -
Supreme Court Building
Salem, OR 97310
Resumes must be received by November 1, 1983.

City Manager
Hartford, Connecticut

ty of Hartford seeks applications from public adors to head this capital City's municipal administra-

ty of Hartford operates under the Council/Manager vernment with the City Manager being appointed by member City Council. The salary range of $60,000 to is negotiable, commensurate with previous salary nd experience.

d is located midway between Boston and New York, a of 18 square miles, a population of 136,000 and is f its insurance and banking industries. The City's ation has a reputation for professionalism and the ncil wishes to continue this tradition.

ty's government operates with a current general over 218 million dollars and employs 2,300 full time es who provide the full range of municipal services in y environment. Hartford has an expanding economic l enjoys the active participation of both neighbord the business community in the conduct of its

bly, applicants should have a Masters Degree in ministration, or a similar field, and at least four (4) extensive, increasingly responsible experience in nt. Applicants may apply by sending a detailed City of Hartford, ███████████
06103 by April 16, 1984.

President
Public Technology, Inc.
Washington, DC

Public interest organization which assists local governments seek solutions to urban problems through research, information sharing and technology transfer, seeks entrepreneurial administrator with proven leadership and financial management skills to head 47 member staff; $3.6 million annual budget. Marketing, sales, and membership services experience desirable; working knowledge of local government essential. Responsible to 7-member Board for self-supporting income generation and productive services to national membership. Salary negotiable, dependent upon qualifications and experience. Submit resume at once, in confidence, to: ███

100 Waukegan Road, Lake Bluff, IL 60044.
EEO/AA

8

sector but also to the private. For that reason, few graduate level business curriculums today fail to require courses such as business environment or business and society. Nevertheless, it is in the public sector that the axiom becomes the most crucial to competent administration.

To say that organizations do not operate in vacuums implies much. For example, public administrators should have knowledge of the cultural and social mores and patterns of the locale within which their organization operates; moreover, they should have tolerance for this diversity. Public administrators should also have knowledge of the physical environment, particularly when their organization has responsibility for technological projects. Further, they should have knowledge of economic processes and institutions. In an era of increasing concern about pollution, energy, inflation, and the quality of life, the reason for the last two requirements should be obvious.

What other knowledge does the competent public administrator need to have about the environment? Perhaps the most obvious is knowledge of governmental institutions, powers, processes, and relationships. The last item can be especially vexing, for the United States has a political system composed of not one but thousands of jurisdictions. Unfortunately, political knowledge alone is not enough; good administrators must also have political skills—skills to analyze and interpret political, social, and economic trends; skills to evaluate the consequences of administrative actions; and skills to persuade and bargain and thereby further their organization's objective. To put it bluntly: It behooves those people who possess great technical and managerial talent to be skilled politicians. I think society suffers a great loss when outstandingly talented people are so inept in their political skills that they can only contribute a small fraction of their talents.

Finally, administrators cannot—must not—ignore the political values of society. In the United States at least, among these values we would include the democratic tradition, constitutionalism, the rule of law, ethics, citizen participation, and responsiveness (i.e., prompt acquiescence by government to popular demands for policy change).

Policy Analysis

The term responsiveness suggests that public administrators are, like elected officials, very much involved in the process of making policy (that is, deciding on broad courses of action). This is quite true. Therefore, public administrators need to be able to think through their alternatives as carefully as possible. Policy analysis is a relatively new approach and method, drawing on both political science and economics, for doing just that.

What exactly does the policy analyst look for? Certainly one of the most important items is whether the problem is correctly defined.

Another important item concerns the costs, benefits, and impacts of alternative policies. Do the benefits exceed the costs? What effect, if any, will the contemplated action have on the environment? What is the distribution of the costs and benefits of a policy? Further, the analysis should look for internal consistency in, and establish priorities among, the policy objectives. Nor should political feasibility, that is, the prospects for enactment or implementation of a chosen policy, be overlooked.

The foregoing provides only a glimpse at a few of the many components of policy analysis. Nonetheless, the reason why NASPAA chose to include this subject on their list should be clear enough. The days have passed when government could launch expensive new policies with little or no regard to consequences and feasibility. Today, administrators as well as their political leaders must think before acting. At least on this point, public opinion seems unequivocal.

Managerial Processes

The third subject area, administrative process, probably requires less explanation than the preceding two.* After all, it is fairly self-evident that after a policy has been decided upon, somebody must be concerned with carrying it out—making it work. This means that organizations must be designed, work assigned, progress monitored, efficiency maintained, and money spent.

To dismiss these activities as mundane would be a grave mistake. Today, we see a growing concern over the managerial process of the public sector. One study finds that 59 percent of federal personnel are engaged in activities "in which the tendencies toward business management are most pronounced" (McCurdy, 1978:575). Peter Drucker (1974:8), a distinguished management consultant, thinks that managing the service institution is likely to be the frontier of management for the rest of the century. "The management of the nonbusiness institutions will indeed be a growing concern from now on. Their

---

* NASPAA uses the term *administrative process* along with *managerial process.* Unfortunately, a quick trip to the dictionary will do little to untangle the two terms. But *administration* does seem to have a more subtle and extended series of meanings than *management.* "It is more usually found in the public sector than the private and, in general, carries an implication not of ultimate sovereign control, but of directing and coordinating things on behalf of other people or authorities" (Baker, 1972:12). The term *management,* on the other hand, usually carries a rather different flavor. Drucker (1973) views *management* primarily in terms of a fairly specific set of tasks: to perform the function for the sake of which the institution exists; to make work productive and the worker achieving; to manage the institution's social impacts. But in coordinating complex situations where no criteria really exist, *administration* is probably a more appropriate word. It is also slightly more embracing in that it includes a lot of preparatory and supportive work for higher-level decision making (for example, all those activities referred to as *policy analysis* above). For consistency, we shall use the term *administrator* when referring to public sector managers.

management may well become the central management problem—simply because the lack of management of the public-service institutions is such a glaring weakness, whether municipal water department or graduate university."

While this line of thinking is a cornerstone of *Managing the Public Sector*, its hue is entirely negative. This need not be. Positive justifications for the importance of management to the public sector are not hard to make. Indeed, to Jean-Jacques Servan-Schreiber, a French journalist, "Management is, all things considered, the most creative of all arts. It is the art of arts. Because it is the organizer of talent."

Now, no one can prove such a statement right or wrong. But at least consider this:

One of the most striking things about the science fiction of the pre-Apollo era is the virtual absence of any reference to, or appreciation of, the purely managerial complexities involved in a moon landing. Robert A. Heinlein's *Destination Moon*, a 1950 milestone in the history of science fiction motion pictures, is an obvious—and by no means isolated—example. Space flight seemed to require only two ingredients: a dauntless protagonist and a brilliant scientist. (Three ingredients, if one counts the latter's pulchritudinous daughter.)

Yet the most important thing about the Apollo mission was not the technology, which had been in existence for some time, but the extraordinary organizational structure. What was this structure? In reporting on their four years of intensive study, Sayles and Chandler (1971) pointed out that, at its peak, NASA sought contributions from 20,000 different organizations. The key to making NASA's structure work rested upon creating an effective communications network that engulfed anyone who could conceivably influence or implement the decision and that also contained various "management councils" composed of coequal associates to share progress and problems.

Why did science fiction writers fail to see the emergence of management as one of the pivotal events of our time? I think the answer is that rarely, if ever, has a human activity developed as rapidly as management. But the rate of development should not be surprising, for today every developed country has become a society of institutions, and institutions require management. Indeed, every major social task—economic performance, health care, education, conservation, scientific research, and so on—is today entrusted to big organizations, managed by their own managements. This situation contrasts sharply to the society at the turn of the century. The emergence of big government and big business hardly needs elaboration, but interestingly, other institutions have grown much faster. Before 1914, no university in the world had much more than 6,000 students; today, the State University of New York has well over 200,000. Similarly, the hospital has grown from a humble institution for the poor to a gigantic health care complex.

Analytical Tools

In carrying out the managerial tasks noted above, the competent administrator uses, when possible, analytical tools. The idea here is not to make all general administrators "computer experts" or "management science experts" but to introduce them to the bare essentials necessary to make effective use of these tools. The focus needs to be upon the role of analysis in managerial decision making, upon the strengths and limitations of the quantitative approach, and upon the systems aspect of decision making.

While analytical tools really became installed and refined in government during the McNamara dynasty at the Pentagon (1961–1968), the idea of using analytical tools to improve management is hardly new. Double-entry bookkeeping, for example, began in the Renaissance. Today, however, the number and sophistication of double-entry bookkeeping systems have grown—to understate considerably.

Roughly, we may divide these modern tools into three classes: first are quantitative and logical approaches to decision making; second, systems and procedures analysis; and third, computer-based management information systems. When judiciously used, these tools can provide the public administrator with a better understanding of the risks involved in a certain decision, of the most economical way to use resources, and of exactly what resources are available.

Individual, Group, and Organizational Behavior

Finally, NASPAA recommended that public administrators have some knowledge about how individuals behave in an organizational setting. In particular, competent administrators should be able to motivate and lead. They also must be able to interact effectively with superiors and peers. It is in this subject area that public administration has drawn most heavily upon behavioral sciences such as psychology. Like the analytical tools noted above, the behavioral sciences can improve the performance of an administrator in the managerial process.

The Approach of This Book

These five subject areas—environment, policy analysis, managerial processes, analytical tools, and behavior—not only answer the question of what public administrators need to know but also highlight what lies in the chapters ahead. But we shall not follow NASPAA in lockstep; considerable rerouting will be necessary. To see why this is so, let us consider just one change.

The chief reason why policy analysis and analytical tools have not been more widely used in the public sector is that public administrators, by and large, have failed to take managerial responsibility for them. They have not done so because they have viewed policy analysis and analytical tools not as a *part of the task of managing* but as separate bodies of knowledge, perhaps best left to the experts. As a partial solution to this state of affairs, I have tried to blend both subjects into the chapters of the book that deal with the management of governmental programs. The chart below attempts to show at a glance how three parts of this book relate to NASPAA's five subjects.

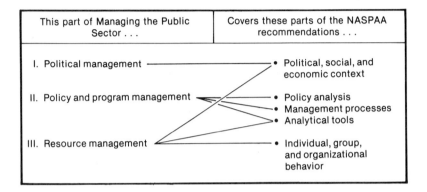

This part of Managing the Public Sector . . .	Covers these parts of the NASPAA recommendations . . .
I. Political management	• Political, social, and economic context
II. Policy and program management	• Policy analysis • Management processes • Analytical tools
III. Resource management	• Individual, group, and organizational behavior

As shown in the table above, and in greater detail in Figure 1-2 (on the following page), this book builds around three major themes: *political management* (i.e., operating in an environment in which groups have common or overlapping claims concerning the distribution of goods and services), *program management* (i.e., formulation and implementation of public policy), and *resources management* (especially financial and human resources). Ultimately, what it attempts to accomplish is twofold: *(a)* to reconcile the current thinking on administrative theory and then *(b)* to reconcile that theoretical thinking with the everyday problems of the administrator who stands on the firing line. The operative word is *to reconcile*, and it merits emphasis.

To reconcile, as used in *(a)* does not mean merely to tie together—in a more or less neat package (usually called a survey)—all the facts, hypotheses, and opinions that happen to be in good currency among the theoreticians of administration. It means instead to inventory systematically the current state of the art; then, to eliminate mercilessly all that is dated, mediocre, irrelevant, or redundant; and last, to present the balance in as clear, concise, and consistent a manner as possible.

Two Splits in the Field of Management

We have considered who public administrators are, what they do, and what they need to know. But we still have not adequately addressed

Figure 1–2
The Environment and Tasks of the Public Administrator

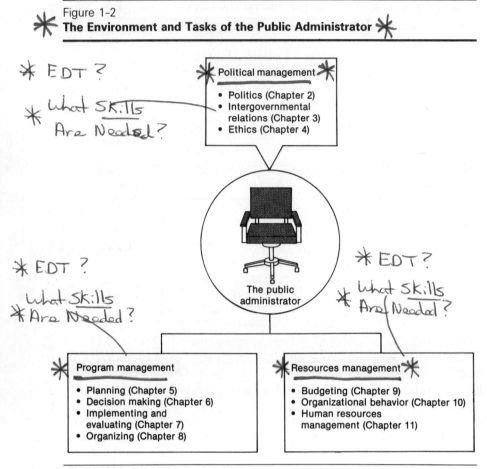

Handwritten annotations:
✻ EDT?
✻ What Skills Are Needed?

✻ EDT?
What Skills ✻ Are Needed?

✻ EDT?
✻ What Skills Are Needed?

Political management
- Politics (Chapter 2)
- Intergovernmental relations (Chapter 3)
- Ethics (Chapter 4)

The public administrator

Program management
- Planning (Chapter 5)
- Decision making (Chapter 6)
- Implementing and evaluating (Chapter 7)
- Organizing (Chapter 8)

Resources management
- Budgeting (Chapter 9)
- Organizational behavior (Chapter 10)
- Human resources management (Chapter 11)

Note: Chapter 12 (not shown above) deals with future trends and issues of concern to public administrators.

the question posed in the chapter title; in fact, we have only scratched the surface. The purpose of this concluding section is to probe more deeply the nature of managerial work.

The field of management has long been marked by two conflicts. The first concerns the differences between public administration and business administration; the second concerns differences between theory and practice.

How Do Public and Private Management Differ?

At one level of abstraction, we can say that the three core management functions noted earlier—political management, policy and program management, and resources management—are common to both public administration and business administration.* So far so good. But when we begin to consider the relative importance of these functions, significant differences emerge (see Figure 1-3). Moreover, based on the reflections of individuals who have operated in both the public and the private sector, we must conclude that the execution of these three functions is much more difficult in the public sector. Why should this be?

Figure 1-3
Relative Time Spent on Three Core Management Elements in Public and Private Sectors

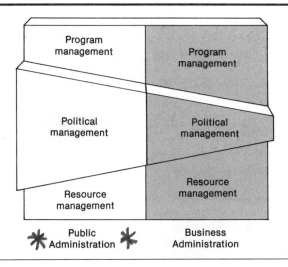

Different Purposes.   Both public and private organizations use resources (inputs) to produce goods and services (outputs). In a business enterprise, profit provides not only a purpose but also an overall measure of both *effectiveness* (i.e., the extent to which outputs accomplish objectives) and *efficiency* (i.e., the ratio of output to input). In a public

---

* For those who doubt that business executives must be skilled *political* managers, Copley Place in Boston might provide an illuminating case study. The largest construction project in Boston's 353-year history, Copley Place represents a national breakthrough in intense, open consultation by a private developer and the city neighborhoods that his project would affect. The state government insisted that the construction firm "win" its right to a long-term lease by first negotiating an agreement with representations of the affluent Back Bay and the economically, racially diverse South End. The $550 million project represents not only a complex engineering feat but a virtuoso political performance.

sector organization, however, outputs are hard to quantify. The Constitution is just not much help: Congress is to provide "for the common defense and general welfare"; the president is to recommend "such Measures as he shall judge necessary and expedient."

Without a single broad measure of performance, it becomes difficult for governments to delegate important decisions to lower-level managers to the same extent that a business firm can. Moreover, the absence of this measure of performance makes comparison between alternative investments difficult. For example, should the cancer detection program or the school lunch program be funded the extra $10 million? How many main battle tanks equal one guided missile frigate? To save whales should we prohibit Eskimos from slaughtering them, even though their entire culture is built around the whale? If the national speed limit were reduced to 20 miles per hour, the carnage on U.S. highways would be virtually eliminated. Are 30,000 lives worth millions of hours of additional travel time? At this point, the student of public administration is inclined to scream, "Where is the bottom line around here?" Do not be too discouraged, however. As we shall see in Chapter 6, there *are* performance measures in the public sector—we just have to look a little longer and harder for them.

In short, business managers look for profitability while public administrators are more concerned with noneconomic factors—namely, the problems of the political community, the issue of who gets what. This focus helps to explain why I would categorize the men and women who run an organization like the Ford Foundation as essentially public administrators. Over the years, the foundation has invested heavily in agricultural research overseas and educational reform at home, tried to influence the policies of the United States and other governments, supported scholars, revitalized blighted neighborhoods, and given substantial backing to the civil rights movement.

It also helps to explain why I would categorize Peter Ueberroth's service as president of the LAOOC as public administration; his purpose was not the same as when he ran an airline. Actually, he could be quite imperious with those working for LAOOC whose motivation did not seem appropriate to him. One day in the cafeteria he stopped to talk to some women having lunch. The chat was pleasantly routine until one of the women asked about possible salary increases. Ueberroth, the unsalaried volunteer, turned cold and said angrily: "You shouldn't be working here if you don't understand what we're trying to do" (*Time*, January 7, 1985).

Different Structures.   The second fundamental difference between business administration and public administration is that *responsibility in the latter is blurred*. In other words, government does not give complete authority for government policy to any one individual or institution. Let us hope that the Pod People from the far side of the

Great Nebula in Andromeda do not land in Washington, asking to be taken to our leader. It would be embarrassing.

As a consequence of the blurred authority, agency heads, unlike their counterparts in industry, cannot set the level of their agencies' budgets. Rather, budgets must be submitted to department heads, who submit them in turn to the Office of Management and Budget, which submits them in turn to the president, who in turn submits them to Congress. Then things really get complicated.

Needless to say, the time lag in this process makes quick responses to new problems and opportunities—not to mention long-range planning—difficult. Unlike their industrial counterparts, agency heads lack full power to hire and fire. Finally, any planning that public administrations engage in must be shared with legislative bodies, city councils, or governing boards.

Here is how a former president of a life insurance company who became the head of the Small Business Administration explained the difference:

> At the average company, I would report to only one person—the chairman of the board. Here, in addition to the president, I must report to 535 people. Dealing with Congress takes over 40 percent of my time.
>
> In business, I wouldn't have to show up for a week and everything would run smoothly. In government, I can be gone for just a day, and I come back to emergencies. It's difficult to organize well enough to let the ship sail for a few hours alone. (A. Vernon Weaver, quoted in *U.S. News & World Report,* September 25, 1978.)

Different Incentives.   The third fundamental difference you may have experienced personally. Because public sector organizations receive a significant amount of financial support from sources other than their clients, *the incentive is to satisfy those who provide resources.* In fact, some agencies even view additional clients not as an opportunity but as an additional strain on resources. In contrast, the very survival of a business hinges on its ability to get and retain customers. And that is why the attendants at McDonald's are more polite to you than the better educated, better paid bureaucrats at the Immigration and Naturalization Service.

Different Settings.   Fourth, public administration could almost be described as *business administration in a fishbowl.* The press and the public feel that they have a right to know everything that goes on in a public agency, and the Freedom of Information Act makes sure that they can find out if they want to. To quote another businessman-turned-bureaucrat:

> My biggest surprise here is how government is ruled by leakage. Employees use the press and Congress to accomplish their goals instead of meeting the issue head-on in an honest fashion. I know that if I make a decision

against someone, that person will be on the phone to Congress and the press within an hour. It astounds me how reporters are willing to take as gospel anything that a low-level employee says. They never check with me to see if it's true. (W. Michael Blumenthal, *Fortune*, January 29, 1979.)

In the chapter that follows, you will see the multiple external forces that play on the public administrator. For example, every public administrator is ultimately under some *elected official*, whose chief concern is likely to center on short-run results rather than on long-run investments. The solar power satellite, which would beam solar energy to earth, may or may not be a good idea. But this much is certain: Few politicians are going to be interested in a multibillion-dollar project that will take 30 years to yield dividends to voters.

In the federal government, a completely new top-management team is possible every four years. Between elections, assistant secretaries average less than two years in their job—not much longer than the time required to find the cafeteria. In contrast, business managers tend to stay with a firm longer and thereby provide continuity. Some authorities argue that one of the strengths of the Japanese management system is that managers tend to stay with a company for a lifetime.

The purpose of the foregoing analysis has been to enumerate four major reasons why public administration tends to be more difficult than business administration. (I freely admit all exceptions to this generalization.) But it would be wrong to say that we are dealing with two separate and distinct categories of management (Figure 1-3 should have already dispelled that notion.) A more useful way to conclude would be by recognizing that different organizations are managed in different ways. The crucial question then is not whether they are public or private, *but how they are doing.* Federal agencies like NASA and the Securities and Exchange Commission, and cities like Dallas, Texas, and Scottsdale, Arizona, are extremely well managed; they are far ahead of many private sector organizations in adopting advanced management practices.

Let us also recognize the *interdependence of the two sectors.* While the public sector is dependent on business for resources (especially revenue and the performance of some activities through contracts), the reverse is equally true. Let me be very specific here. California is the richest state in the union—and not merely because of its factories, thriving crops, and private affluence. Little of this would have been possible had it not been for government action. Despite its great natural advantages, California has depended on public investment perhaps more than any other state. If government had not spent billions on irrigation, crops would not have grown. If governors like Earl Warren, Pat Brown, and Ronald Reagan had not built up that great intellectual resource, the University of California, agribusiness, Silicon Valley, and other high-tech industries would not have flourished.

✳ *How Do Management Theory and Practice Differ?* ✳

Is the manager a technician whose practice consists of applying the principles and methods derived from management science to the everyday problems of his or her organization? Or, is the manager a craftsman, a practitioner of an art of managing that cannot be reduced to explicit rules and theories? The view that managers are technicians dates from the early decades of the 20th century when the idea of professional management first arose. The other view, that managers are craftsmen, has an even longer history, management having been understood as an art, a matter of skill and wisdom, long before it began to be understood as a body of techniques. The fact that the first view has gained steady recognition in no way lessens our need to examine the second.

Origins of Management Science.   Attempts to make management a science have a venerable history, now almost a century old. In the 1880s Frederick Taylor, a self-taught American engineer, began to study work systematically. The *scientific management* concepts that Taylor pioneered were based on the notion that, in any undertaking, scientific analysis would lead to the discovery of the "one best way" of carrying out each operation. With this hypothesis, the scientific management of work became the key to productivity. Taylor's aim, however, was not merely to increase productivity in the service of higher profits but actually to free the worker from the burden of heavy toil—a point often forgotten when Taylor is mentioned today. *Fayol's Administrative Functions:*

The mood of "Taylorism" helped to create the <u>*administrative science movement*</u>. The idea of this movement was that if you look coldly at the facts for a long enough time, soon you will begin to see principles that tell you how to administer. The origins of this approach could perhaps be traced as far back as 1908, the year in which Henry Fayol's classic *Administration Industrielle et Generale* appeared. <u>Fayol</u>, who had a long and successful career as a general manager in French mining and engineering, argued in a lofty, almost Napoleonic vein that the <u>administrative function may be subdivided into five elements or processes</u>—<u>foresight, organization, command, coordination, and control.</u>

 ✳ *Gulick's Functions*

In the United States, <u>Luther Gulick</u> began to develop Fayol's analysis of administrative functions and in 1937 put forth the <u>POSDCORB</u> formula. <u>This snappy anagram stood for the seven principles of administration: planning, organizing, staffing, directing, coordinating, reporting, and budgeting.</u> As Gulick (1937:191,195) put it: "At the present time administration is more an art than science; in fact there are those who assert dogmatically that it can never be anything else. They draw no hope from the fact that metallurgy, for example, was completely an art several centuries before it became primarily a science. . . . [Several] factors played their part in the conquest of the natural world by exact science, and may be counted upon again to advance scientific knowledge and control in the world of human affairs."

World War II gave enormous impetus to the management science movement because of the rise in prestige of science and technology and because of the birth of a new discipline: operations research (see Chapter 6 for details). This discipline, often referred to as OR, grew out of the use of applied mathematics to solve problems of submarine search and bomb tracking. After the war, men like Robert S. McNamara, secretary of defense from 1961 to 1968, helped export OR to industry and government. In the post-World War II era, management science reached maturity.

Problems Persist.   Despite the increasing prestige of management science and technique, many managers remain aware of important areas of practice for which management theory provides little help: interpreting the external environment's response to the action of one's organization, diagnosing signs of trouble within an organization, negotiating with hostile interest groups, and so forth. It is commonplace for experienced executives like George P. Shultz, the president of Bechtel Group Inc. who became secretary of state in 1982, to muse about their jobs in tentative ways: "Well, issues emerge. You can't always predict what they are going to be. However, I think it's important to try to set your own strategy as much as you can, and identify, and have work going on, and so on" (Gwertzman, 1983:32). His watchwords are not those of the scientific management movement: "ready both ways," "advance the process," "the long haul."

Several distinguished management theorists have noted this nonrational dimension of managing. As early as 1938, in an essay called "Mind in Everyday Affairs," Chester Barnard distinguished "thinking process" from "nonlogical processes," which cannot be expressed in words or as reasoning, and thus only become manifest by a judgment, decision, or action. Barnard recognized that mental processes consist of both the nonlogical and the logical; he believed that an effective manager has access to either mode, as the situation demands.

More recently, a Canadian professor of management, Henry Mintzberg (1973:30), caused a considerable stir with studies of the actual behavior of top managers that revealed a virtual absence of the methods that managers are "supposed to" use. He found the workday of a typical executive *intense.* "The mail (average of 36 pieces per day), telephone calls (average of five per day), and meetings (average of eight) accounted for almost every minute from the moment these executives entered their offices in the morning until they departed in the evenings. . . . When free time appeared, ever-present subordinates quickly usurped it." Mintzberg also found the workday highly *fragmented* and *varied,* with frequent interruptions and tasks involving many different types of activities, each needing to be completed quickly. According to Mintzberg (1973:30), the manager's job is *open-ended.*

There are really no tangible mileposts where one can stop and say, "Now my job is finished." The engineer finishes the design of a casting on a certain day; the lawyer wins or loses a case at some moment in time. The manager must always keep going, never sure when he or she has succeeded, never sure when the whole organization may come down because of some miscalculation. As a result, the manager is a person with a perpetual preoccupation. The manager can never be free to forget the job, and never has the pleasure of knowing, even temporarily, that there is nothing else to do.

What It All Means. Mintzberg's picture of management practice is quite different from the one suggested by Gulick's principles. Fortunately, the two views are not irreconcilable.

In management, as in other fields, the term *art* has a twofold meaning. It may mean intuitive judgment and skill, the feeling for phenomena (e.g., subtleties and nuances of conversation) and for action (e.g., the importance of ceremony). But it may also mean an ability to analyze problems for which intuition gives no immediate answer. When managers analyze such problems, they should be able to bring to bear on them some organized body of knowledge. And here is where theory comes in. The primary purpose of any theory is to clarify concepts and ideas that have become, as it were, confused and entangled. Thus, theory can help managers in their search for solutions.

Any good description of the art of managing—whether of the public or the private sector—must consider both aspects of a manager's job; that is, it must try to capture the flavor of management with all its subtleties and nuances as well as present theories that will help managers think on their feet when they are puzzled. The key to success in both cases is to focus unremittingly on real problems faced by real administrators.

Nailing Down the Main Points

1. Traditionally, public administration is thought of as the accomplishing side of government. It is supposed to comprise all those activities involved in carrying out the policies of elected officials and some activities associated with the development of those policies. This book broadens the definition of public administration: the process by which resources are marshaled and then used to cope with the problems facing a political community. Public administrators are therefore found at all levels of government as well as in a wide variety of nonbusiness institutions.

2. The National Association of schools of Public Affairs and Administration recommends that the study of public administration cover five basic subject areas: *(a)* the political, social, and economic environment; *(b)* policy analysis; *(c)* managerial processes; *(d)* analytical tools; and *(e)* individual, group, and organizational behavior.

3. Competent administrators are sensitive to the environment of their organization and are able to analyze problems. For the latter, policy analysis and many new analytical tools are proving to be quite useful.

4. In the decades ahead, the management of public sector institutions will likely become the central management problem facing society.

5. This book builds around three themes: political management (i.e., operating in an environment in which groups have common or overlapping claims concerning the distribution of goods and services), program management, (i.e., formulation and implementation of public policy), and resources management (especially financial and human resources).

6. Public administration differs from business administration in four respects—purpose, structure, incentive, and setting. More specifically, the purpose of public administration is often to produce public goods (things like clean air that can be shared by many members of a political community), rather than private goods (things like skateboards that can be individually owned and enjoyed). At other times, its purpose might be to produce justice; seldom, if ever, will it seek profit.

7. While management theory sometimes bears little resemblance to management practice, theory can help managers who face problems for which their intuition provides little direction. To describe the art of management in the public sector, both aspects—the intuitive and the rational—must be considered. Above all, the description must center on problems faced by *practicing managers*.

Concepts for Review

administrative science movement
analytical tools
interdependence of the two sectors
managerial processes

policy analysis
public administration
public sector
scientific management

Problems

1. Alvin Toffler (1980) argues that six guiding principles, which lent a distinctive stamp to Western industrial society, are under attack. These principles are standardization, specialization, synchronization (i.e., work carefully organized in time), concentration (in population, work, education, energy, and economic organization), maximization ("a kind of Texas infatuation with bigness and growth"), and centralization (of management, of government, of the economy, and of banks). Do you agree with Toffler? If so, what will be the new "guiding principles," and how will they affect public administration in the United States? If you do not agree with Toffler, support your position with examples and logical analysis.

2. How separate do you think politics is from administration? This chapter suggested ways in which the job of public administrator differs from that of the business executive. How are they alike?

3. Do you agree or disagree with the Servan-Schreiber quote on page 11?

4. Present to the class a report on one of the individuals listed in t
   papers of this book. What relevance, if any, does this individual ﾠ
   contemporary public administration?

5. Is business really better run than government? Read one of the following
   books and report your conclusions.

   Ken Auletta, *The Art of Corporate Success: The Story of Schlumberger*
   (New York: G.P. Putnam's Sons, 1984).

   Tracy Kidder, *The Soul of a New Machine* (Boston: Little, Brown, 1981).

   Lee Iacocca, *Iacocca* (New York: Bantam Books, 1984).

   Michael Moritz, *The Little Kingdom: The Private Story of Apple Computer* (New York: William Morrow, 1984).

   John J. Nance, *Splash of Colors: The Self-Destruction of Braniff International* (New York: William Morrow, 1984).

   John Newhouse, *The Sporty Game* (New York: Alfred A. Knopf, 1982).

   Robert Sobel, *IBM: Colossus in Transition* (New York: Bantam Books, 1983).

   J. Patrick Wright, *On a Clear Day You Can See General Motors* (New York: Avon Books, 1979).

   Brock Yates, *The Decline and Fall of the American Automobile Industry* (New York: Random House, 1984).

 6. Sometimes professionals such as physicians and engineers become administrators. Suppose one of these professionals-as-administrators comes home and his wife asks, "What sort of day did you have?" He replies, "It was a complete waste of time. I spent three hours with the Community Mental Health Board and then two hours with the assistant commissioner of hospitals discussing our affiliation contract. Then I spent the lunch hour with the site visit team to lend my weight to a member of the department whose research application's being reviewed. Then an hour mediating between the service group and the teaching group about a program, and on, and on, and on. A complete waste of time." What is your reaction to this comment?

Case 1.1
Ruckelshaus Tries to Turn Around the Environmental Protection Agency

"Dead in the Water"

One cannot help seeing the plaque on the wall as you enter the U.S. Environmental Protection Agency (EPA) building in Washington, D.C. On it the agency's mission is inscribed: "To protect the public from environmental hazards" (see Exhibit 1). That mission was sidetracked in 1983 when 12 high officials were fired or resigned; a contempt of Congress charge was filed against Anne McGill Burford, the administrator of the EPA, and Rita Lavelle, head of the agency's hazardous-waste cleanup program, was convicted of perjury. As one top administrator observed, the agency was "dead in the water" for most of 1983.

Exhibit 1
Environmental Protection Agency

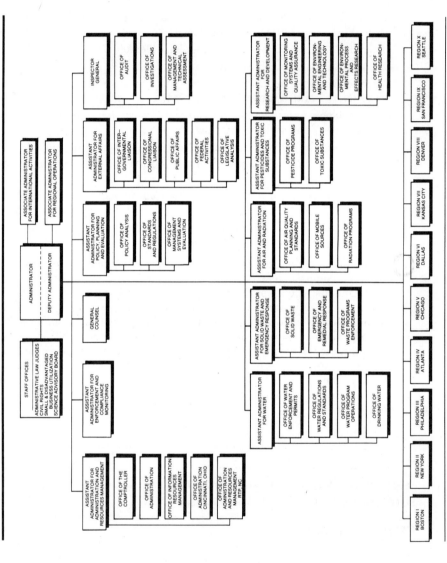

Source: *The U.S. Government Manual 1984/85*, p. 841.

Morale had gotten so bad that some loyal, hard-working employees were even ashamed to admit to friends or neighbors that they worked at the agency. Suspicions at EPA headquarters were so intense that a few civil-service employees, after almost everyone else had gone home for the evening, began surreptitiously posting satirical memos attacking administration policies and picking through wastebaskets to find documents spelling out actions taken by their Reagan-appointed bosses. Agency managers even considered installing closed-circuit television cameras in the halls to catch the late-night culprits, but eventually dropped the idea. "There's a bizarre quality to the whole place," a lobbyist for a major chemical company said. "It's turned into a never-never land of rumor, innuendo, and constant bureaucratic upheaval."

The extent of the agency's morale problems can be seen in other ways. Burford distrusted the bureaucracy from the beginning. She tended to isolate herself with a few trusted lieutenants picked more for their conservative, probusiness philosophy than for managerial or political experience.

Against this backdrop, President Reagan turned to William D. Ruckelshaus, the man who guided the EPA through its first four years (1970–73), to restore the prestige and sense of urgency the agency originally had. Nowhere was the appointment greeted with more enthusiasm than inside the EPA.

Tasks

But Ruckelshaus's job would not be easy. The scientific and regulatory issues that the agency had to handle were more complex in 1983 than they had been in 1973. Furthermore, the Reagan administration had cut the agency's budget by $400 million from the $1.35-billion level of 1981 when Reagan took office; and during that period the number of employees had dropped from 14,000 to 11,500.

Ruckelshaus needed to move rapidly to improve the agency's morale and

In March 1983, William Ruckelshaus was given a hero's welcome by EPA employees and former colleagues after President Reagan named him to take over the troubled agency. (Photos by Vanessa Barnes-Hillian—*Washington Post*)

determine its policy direction. Here are the most controversial and pressing issues the new administrator faced:

- Personnel: Ruckelshaus faced a formidable task in filling the vacant slots.
- Legislation: Perhaps the biggest task that faced Ruckelshaus was finding a way to end the two-year-old deadlock on the administration's legislative priorities. The White House had sought but failed to push legislation through Congress to roll back environmental standards and give states and companies more authority to determine how and when expensive pollution controls would be installed. Perhaps it was already too late for the EPA to have much say in what would happen to clean-air, clean-water, and toxic-waste legislation in 1983.
- Enforcement: During 1981, the EPA's enforcement operations were reorganized every few months. The result: Litigation to force companies to clean up pollution virtually came to a halt. Many lawmakers contended that enforcement offices were seriously understaffed; cases routinely sat around for as long as a year without any action.
- International: The EPA was under increasing pressure from the Canadian government and others to crack down on what apparently causes "acid rain" by limiting emissions from power plants and factories, primarily in the Midwest. The Reagan administration strongly opposed such moves, but Congress could have required additional pollution controls unless the administration came up with its own plan quickly.
- Regulatory: Ruckelshaus faced a long list of complex, politically explosive decisions that had been put on hold. The new appointee, for example, had to decide whether to cut off tens of millions of dollars in federal aid and impose other sanctions on counties and cities that had not complied with clean-air requirements. He also had to (1) issue rules to protect underground water supplies from toxic chemicals; (2) change some of the standards historically used by the government to measure air quality; and (3) determine whether treated sewage and other wastes should be dumped into the oceans instead of landfills. A new policy to assess public health risks posed by potential carcinogens was also pending.
- Political: Almost simultaneously Ruckelshaus had to decontaminate the scandal that had toppled his predecessor Anne Burford and stop it from spreading to the White House doors; deal with a hostile Congress that had ordered investigators from six subcommittees to look into the EPA's handling of efforts to clean up the nation's most toxic chemical-waste dumps; mend fences with outraged environmentalists, who accused the Reagan administration of trying to destroy the progress the nation had made in cleaning up its air and water; and come to terms with industry officials, who complained that the agency had lost its efficiency.

Strategy and Tactics

When Ruckelshaus took over as head of the embattled EPA, he followed many of the time-tested rules of thumb that had helped him survive tough periods in the past. (When he left the EPA in 1973, he became acting director of the FBI. Later, he became deputy attorney general and emerged as one of the few Nixon administration heroes of the Watergate scandal.) Among these "rules," we can note the following:

1. Public officials should think of everything they say or do, even behind closed doors, "as if it were on a billboard." "If you look up and what you see embarrasses you or gives the slightest appearance of impropriety, then don't do it or don't say it."
2. "The best politics is good government: If you start horsing around in areas where the public's health is concerned, you're going to get in trouble."
3. Minimize political miscalculations, assure a sense of calm and serious analysis in the organization, and continue to meet with environmentalists after being confirmed by Congress.
4. When staffing a regulatory agency, "it is probably better if you can find people who are not subject to the charge [of being too close to industry]." If you want people who you can put to work immediately, look to government first, not industry. (This is in sharp contrast to the previous political leadership. Anne McGill Burford had virtually no federal background, and many people in Washington have said that her unfamiliarity with the capitol labyrinth is what brought her to grief.)
5. Perceptions are important. Ruckelshaus thought that the Reagan administration had initially misread its mandate from the public on environmental laws, that it had "confused" the public's wish to improve the way the goals of protecting the environment and public health were achieved with a desire to change those goals. As a result, the administration initially sought to change some of the goals through deregulation. This, he thought, caused the "perception" that the administration was hostile to environmental and public health regulation.
6. Sometimes a "high purpose" of a public executive's office is to "educate" the public. The public cannot be totally protected from environmental hazards—even by statute. Therefore, explain what the actual risks of chemicals and other pollutants are as well as the costs of regulating them. "We fool ourselves if we think we can have zero risks," he said, adding that that was what many of the environmental statutes required. He said failure to educate the public was a result of "the denial of reality by congressional fiat."
7. Goals in one area of public policy (e.g., protecting health and environment) must be assessed in the light of other social goals (e.g., more jobs and economic growth).
8. Develop a consistent approach to the management and assessment of risk. His formula was deceptively simple: Obtain the best scientific analysis to determine just how much of a threat to health or environment is posed by some new substance or process. Building on these findings and the analysis of the risks, costs, and benefits of various options for reducing or eliminating the danger, decide what to do about it. To make the ultimate choice more widely acceptable, bring the affected groups into the decision-making process and try to inform the public about the problem.

Managing Internal Components

Ruckelshaus's management style was based on a belief in the quality and dedication of EPA employees. In his opinion, a lot of people within the agency had become discouraged about how environmental laws and rules were working in practice and had ideas about change—as did senior members of the Reagan administration. But the Reagan administration was suspicious and failed to realize that these bureaucrats had, like the rest of the country, changed their views about regulation.

Accordingly, Ruckelshaus allowed much more participation in decision making. For example:

- One EPA official recalls how the agency decided what to do after traces of the cancer-causing pesticide EDB were discovered in some foods in Florida. "We had to bring extra chairs into [Ruckelshaus's] office in the EDB meetings. It was wall-to-wall people, including all the permanent employees involved—real knockdown, drag-outs."
- Immediately after taking office, Ruckelshaus formed a number of task forces to examine the EPA's policies and options in such areas as groundwater protection, dioxin contamination, and acid rain, as well as the agency's budget and its problems with federal and state programs. All had tight deadlines for reporting back to Ruckelshaus.

But Ruckelshaus could be tough when the need arose. For example, when the Environmental Protection Agency's top pollution prosecutors gathered in Alexandria, Virginia, in January 1984 for a conference, they got a tongue lashing. After he took over the EPA, Ruckelshaus told agency employees that he expected to find a "bunch of tigers" itching to go aggressively after violators of federal clean-air and clean-water laws. "But on the basis of what I see here in the past few months, there may be more pussycats in the tank than tigers."

Ruckelshaus knew he would never improve agency morale if he merely sat in Washington mending political fences. Therefore, his first three months as head of the EPA, he visited almost all the agency's regional offices to give staff pep rallies. At every stop, he also made it a point to meet with local environmentalists. This practice is known as "touching all the bases."

Managing External Constituents

To revive a foundering government agency required more than good internal operation. Ruckelshaus had to launch a first-rate public relations offensive. His first step was bold and in sharp contrast to the policy of Anne Burford. He opened the agency's doors to all—environmentalists, journalists, and industrial executives—to dispel any notion that EPA officials preferred to hear only polluters' pleadings. He even made public his daily appointment book.

Here is how he dealt with other key constituents:

- Congress: To placate congressional critics, Ruckelshaus made frequent trips to Capitol Hill where he personally visited with key legislators. He proposed a budget increase—even when there was a real question about whether the agency could absorb it—partly to appease congressional critics.
- White House: Environmental groups were not pleased with Ruckelshaus's ability to influence the White House to accept acid rain and toxic waste legislation. Ruckelshaus repeatedly had to battle with the Office of Budget and Management (OMB) when attempting to issue EPA regulations.
- Citizens: In a much publicized action in Tacoma, Washington, Ruckelshaus asked local residents to help the EPA decide on the acceptable level of arsenic emissions from a copper smelter that, if closed down, would have

cost the community 575 jobs. Ruckelshaus wanted people to know that the EPA's scientific information was often imprecise, especially about lethal toxic chemicals that the agency was only beginning to deal with. The public hearings were not a "rationalization for inaction," he insisted. Rather, he wanted the public to "share with me the vexing nature of environmental decisions. Even if all of the people do not agree with the final decision, at least they will understand we did the best we could. And gaining public acceptance of our decisions is very important."

- Industry: Another problem that faced Ruckelshaus was how to get responsible parties to come up with the money to pay for waste-site cleanups. Some chemical companies whose wastes were deposited at dumps wanted, he said, to "negotiate until the world looks level." But the EPA slowly gained in the process of forcing the chemical industry to clean up hazardous dumps. Cleanup settlements—under which a company agrees to spend a specified amount of money to clean up a waste site—amounted to $107 million in fiscal year 1984 and $91 million in fiscal year 1983, compared to $49 million in 1982 and $31 million in 1981.

To summarize, if Ruckelshaus was the White Knight in 1983, then he was a knight without armor or horse. Surrounding him were many dragons: environmental groups, headline-hunting politicians, scientists, complex technical regulations, the Chemical Manufacturers Association, the American Petroleum Institute, administration budget cutters, waste disposal firms hungry for contracts, sometimes the EPA's own regional offices, the states, and a growing number of disenchanted taxpayers. "It is frustrating," Ruckelshaus said. "There's a lot of history behind these squabbles. It takes time."

Epilogue

In November 1984, the White House announced the resignation of William D. Ruckelshaus. There was almost uniform agreement that he had turned a foundering, dispirited agency into a well-managed organization where a reinvigorated bureaucracy was again confident that its efforts to carry out the environmental laws were supported by the agency's head. Perhaps the most telling commentary on his 18-month tenure was the reaction of many environmental groups. Spokesmen for groups that had been his severest critics expressed dismay and anxiety over his departure; in the end, no doubt to their own surprise, they concluded that they would miss him.

EPA employees gave Ruckelshaus an affectionate send-off, with a standing ovation before and after his speech and cheers in between. A hand-lettered sign, hung from the proscenium of the auditorium's stage, said "Thanks Bill!"

Ruckelshaus had a few words for Lee M. Thomas, who was selected as the next chief of the agency at his suggestion. "You get two days in the sun at the EPA," he said, "once when you come and once when you leave. Every day in between it rains on you."

Case Questions

1. Can you identify examples of political management, program management, and resource management in the case?

2. What differences and similarities can you suggest between the skills and knowledge inherent in the job of EPA administrator and the job of managing a corporation. (In terms of number of employees, the EPA would rank about 350 among the largest U.S. corporations; in terms of budget, about 445.)

Case References

"An Old Hand Tries to Clean Up Mess at EPA," *U.S. News & World Report,* April 4, 1983; Andy Pasztor, "In Seeking to Put EPA in Order, Ruckelshaus Is Facing a Tough Job," *The Wall Street Journal,* April 29, 1983; Andy Pasztor, "Lots of Controversial Issues Await at EPA as Ruckelshaus Hearings Get Underway," *The Wall Street Journal,* May 4, 1983; "Ruckelshaus Vows to End EPA's 'Abuses' of Power," *The Wall Street Journal,* May 5, 1983; Andy Pasztor, "Ruckelshaus Seeks Boost in EPA Budget," *The Wall Street Journal,* June 15, 1983; Lawrence Mosher, "Ruckelshaus Is Seen as His Own Man in Battle to Renew Clean Air Act," *National Journal,* July 16, 1983; Philip Shabecoff, "Environmental Groups Now Offer Some Praise," *New York Times,* July 19, 1983; Philip Shabecoff, "Ruckelshaus Says Administration Misread Mandate on Environment," *New York Times,* July 27, 1983; "The Environmental Impact of the EPA's New Mr. Fix-It," *Business Week,* August 22, 1983; Alan L. Oten, "Can EPA Be Made Rational," *The Wall Street Journal,* October 19, 1983; "Clearing the Air at EPA," *Time,* December 5, 1983; Andy Pasztor, "Ruckelshaus Criticized by All Sides as Honeymoon at EPA Nears End," *The Wall Street Journal,* April 6, 1984; Guy Darst, "Ruckelshaus Gets Praise for Raising Morale at EPA," *Houston Chronicle,* May 20, 1984; Nicholas C. Chriss, "EPA Defining, Assessing Waste Risks," *Houston Chronicle,* May 31, 1984; Nicholas C. Chriss, "Shakeup Sidetracked EPA," *Houston Chronicle,* May 31, 1984; Philip Shabecoff, "Après Ruckelshaus le Deluge?" *New York Times,* December 3, 1984; Philip Shabecoff, "Ruckelshaus Says EPA Is Improved," *New York Times,* December 7, 1984; Michele Perrault, "Ruckelshaus, Thwarted," *New York Times,* December 11, 1984.

PART I

Political Management

2

The Politics of Administration

Introduction

Today administrators cannot ignore the political environment of their agencies. In the first place, these administrators are involved both in the formulation and implementation of public policy. Because policy decisions so profoundly influence who gets what, this involvement in policy inevitably involves them in politics. In the second place, they must deal on a day-to-day basis not only with their immediate supervisors but also with all kinds of external groups and publics. As a result, administrators find themselves in a kind of political force field. Competent administrators do not turn their backs on these matters, however. "The lifeblood of administration is power. Its attainment, maintenance, increase, dissipation, and loss are subjects the practitioners can ill afford to neglect" (Long, 1949:257).

In this chapter, we begin with a couple of examples designed to show how difficult it is for public administrators to ignore the political realm. We then see how the issue of separating politics from administration was debated among the early students of public administration.

That brings us to the heart of the chapter, which can be highlighted with three questions: How is the public administrator involved in the policymaking process? What are the relationships between the administrator and external political forces? And, how can the administrator be more skillful politically?

On the Folly of Separating Politics from Administration

The Case of A. J. Cervantes

In the 1960s, the voters of St. Louis twice elected as mayor a successful insurance executive. His name was A. J. Cervantes, and his message to the voters was plain: "Put government back into the hands of men who know the meaning of the tax dollar, the balanced budget, business methods, and a successful city."

In retrospect, what does Mr. Cervantes (1973:19–20) think about this notion—still quite popular—that businessmen can restore life to American cities?" As one becomes more involved in governing a large city, one learns that in many cases business methods cannot be translated into political reality." To take a word from business, let us consider a couple of his "practical" examples:

St. Louis has a number of recreation programs operating in school playgrounds and parks. Some programs have many participants, others few. Again, good management would say close those programs that have relatively few participants. But this would mean that some neighborhoods would have no programs for those who would use the facilities. Recreation centers must be reasonably close to everyone, so all of them stay open.

St. Louis needs a new, modern airport suitable for the needs of the 21st century. Federal officials and airlines agree that the best location would be in Illinois, just across the river from St. Louis. Jobs would be created, the area's economy given a boost, and the city's tax base improved. But Missouri interests—union and business—want the contracts and jobs that would flow from the new airport. Even though Missouri does not have a site or funds for the land, they would block the Illinois airport. Would a good manager turn down an investment opportunity because one group of workers or subcontractors received the benefits rather than another? Not one who wanted to survive. Yet political reality forced other government leaders to oppose the Illinois site.

The Case of Jimmy Carter

Before his election in 1976, Jimmy Carter devoted little attention to thinking about major national issues. Until he began his race for the White House, his life had been devoted chiefly to managing a peanut warehouse, serving on community planning boards, and taking care of state business (such as highway construction). Therefore, when he entered the Oval Office, he had to put himself in seclusion and study the issues, from arms control to the federal tax system to U.S. African policy.

This he seemed to enjoy. As Martin Schram wrote: "His was the clockwork presidency. He was chief engineer and operating officer of the United States of America. His role, as he seemed to see it, was to study it all and then engineer the very best program a country could want, send it up to Capitol Hill for enactment, and then wait to sign the measure after congressional enactment" (*Washington Post*, October 27, 1980).

While this approach has a certain aesthetic appeal, it is no way to run a government. Political realities spill over fact sheets and reports; they bend position papers, break option papers, and obliterate multicolor flip charts.

The consequences of this approach can be seen in Carter's attempts to reorganize the government. He seemed to ignore the fact that every department and agency was connected to a powerful outside interest. So he proceeded as if he were a student at Harvard Business School facing a Friday deadline on his solution to a management problem. Concentrating on the details, he ignored pursuading, cultivating, even counting key congressional committee leaders. What communication he did have with congressional leadership centered on the economic and managerial advantages of his "solution"—not why each senator and representative should want to do it for the sake of his or her own career.

Once his plan had taken shape, Carter then turned the awesome responsibility of shepherding it through Congress to an aide. As Schram reports, the aide met alone with Carter on his first visit to the White House but after that consulted with the president mainly by memorandums.

In sharp contrast, Carter's successor, Ronald Reagan, made several dramatic trips to Capitol Hill. Another important contrast was that Reagan knew that priorities had to be set and political strength had to be husbanded for principal goals rather than dissipated on peripheral schemes. Consequently, Reagan focused his persuasive powers on selling his economic policy, whereas Carter dumped a desktop full of major policy proposals on Congress in his first year.

The irony in the Carter record is that a man who had displayed considerable persuasive powers and charm during his 1976 presidential campaign left those vital attributes at the doorstep of the White House. The job of chief executive was a job for an engineer, not a politician. Or so he thought.

Politics and Administration: A Historical Perspective

The point of the preceding examples is obvious. Purely administrative matters can seldom be separated from politics. Yet, interestingly enough, this view, which most experts now articulate with such verve, could not always be found in the literature of public administration. In fact, for several decades, its antithesis prevailed.

"The field of administration is a field of business," a young academic in the Progressive movement of the 1800s once argued. "It is removed," he continued, "from the hurry and strife of politics." An incredible observation, perhaps; but its author, Woodrow Wilson (1887), did not stand alone. For example, F. Goodnow, often termed the "father of American public administration," and W. F. Willoughby, another early pioneer in the field, also had little trouble dividing government into two functions: political decision and administrative execution. Unlike Wilson and Carter, Goodnow and Willoughby had the good fortune of never having to carry such views into the White House.*

Unfortunately, it was not until the end of World War II that these difficulties in politics-administration separation began to be widely recognized. Fritz Morstein Marx's *The Elements of Public Administration* (1946) pointed out the involvement of administrators in policy formation, in the use of discretionary power, and in the general political process. The following year, Waldo (1948:121) put the debate into sharp focus: "The disagreement is not generally with politics-administration itself; only with the spirit of rigid separatism. In some measure, this is an advance into realism. In some measure, it flows from a feeling of strength and security, a feeling that the processes and the study of administration have matured, that they no longer need be isolated from the germs of politics. Administration can even think about invading the field of politics, the field of policy determination."

Feelings of strength and security, invasions into the fields of politics and policy determination—all heady stuff indeed. But has the debate, which we have quickly traced from Wilson, been ended by venial rhetoric or, as Professor Waldo suggests, increased realism? The next two sections address this question.

Our approach will be analytic in that we divide the issue into two components. First, we consider the degree to which administration has entered the field of policy determination; second, we consider the degree to which it has entered the field of politics.

Administration in the Field of Policy Determination

We all recall the neat textbook diagrams in Government 101 outlining how a bill becomes a law, that very logical process by which legislative bodies make *policy*. (By *policy*, I mean here simply laws that are, in scope and impact, major attempts to solve problems or to seize opportunities. Chapter 5 will provide a more rigorous—but not dissimilar—definition of *policy*.) In the process, we were told, the chief executive is the chief legislator, since most major policies—roughly 80 percent over the last two decades—originate with him. Further, we learned

---

* This statement might sound like I am implying that Wilson (generally considered one of America's better presidents) was not as good a politician in the White House as he should have been. Well I am. The best proof is Wilson's inept handling of Senate Republicans and refusal to compromise on the Treaty of Versailles.

that members of Congress submit bills, which must pass through committee, onto the floor and the other chamber, and (prior to a presidential signature) probably to a conference committee. Things were so simple.

The foregoing interpretation of the policymaking process is not so much wrong as it is misleading. In the first place, administrators frequently participate in the process. Chief executives rarely make decisions about issues not presented to them. The issues and solutions, therefore, sometimes bubble up from the echelon of planners just above the career administrators and just below the political appointees of the cabinet and subcabinet.

In the second place, administrative decisions may, in effect, produce policy. For example, the choice of new weapon systems, of new state highway routes, of solar energy programs, of the level of price support for agricultural commodities are all choices likely to be influenced greatly by administrators. In sum, administrative agencies are influential in both the formulation and implementation of public policy. This fact is quite important. And at least one political scientist suggested a redefinition of public administration in terms of policymaking: "Public administration is that organized and purposeful interaction of society which, within law, systematically formulates and applies policies of government agencies" (Boyer, 1964). Without necessarily subscribing to this definition, we might at least take a closer look at what the formulation and implementation of policy involves.

✳ Formulation of Policy ✳

More than is realized, agencies themselves provide a productive source of new ideas. In some instances, an administrative agency may conceive of its function largely as accommodating the needs of some interest group, which is representing its specialized clientele (farmers, truckers, bankers, and so on). Thus, the policy proposal is really designed to further those interests.

Such is not always the case. NASA alone proposed to go to the moon. "Operating pretty much in a political vacuum in terms of policy guidance, and basing their choice on what constituted a rational technical program of manned space flight development, NASA planners chose a lunar-landing objective fully two years before President Kennedy announced his choice of the lunar landing as a national goal." And without the Kennedy decision in 1961, NASA no doubt would have continued pressing for the lunar decision (see Lambright, 1976:195).

Perhaps a more typical pattern of policy formulation can be seen in the War on Poverty. The initial work in formulating the antipoverty policy was handled in 1963 by a task force drawn from the Council of Economic Advisors and the Bureau of the Budget (now the Office of

Management and Budget). No attempt was made to devise specific programs. Then, in early November, the chairman of the council requested that the major departments and agencies submit suggestions for a legislative program. "The result was a veritable flood of proposals, featuring many of their favorite ideas—job training and employment programs from Labor, rural development from Agriculture, education and welfare services from Health, Education and Welfare, and so on. The council-bureau task force was now confronted with the necessity of selecting from among the many proposals presented concerning how to do this and develop an integrated war on poverty for $500 million" (Anderson, 1975:73).

About this time, the CEA–BOB task force began favoring a program featuring a limited number of direct grants to help localities develop their own antipoverty program. Not surprisingly, the departments and agencies were unhappy about this proposal, which would have meant loss of control over their own funds and programs.

The situation changed suddenly in early February 1964, when President Johnson appointed Sargent Shriver to plan the War on Poverty. Recognizing that the broad-based and multifaceted War on Poverty enjoyed wide support among the administrative agencies, "Shriver assembled a new task force of volunteers and others on loan from their departments and agencies. Included were people from the Departments of Labor, Agriculture, Defense, and HEW, the Bureau of the Budget, the Small Business Administration, and other agencies. Some concerned intellectuals were also involved. All ideas and proposals were reconsidered. Scores of businessmen, union officials, mayors, welfare officials, and others were consulted or asked for suggestions" (Anderson, 1975:74). Within a few weeks a legislative proposal was developed, and by March, President Johnson was able to submit to Congress his bill for the Economic Opportunity Act.

Agencies also become involved in policy formulation when they recommend to the legislature amendments to existing laws. A large part—perhaps the major portion—of modern legislation is proposed by administrative agencies. This should not be surprising. Agencies are closest to where the action is and therefore are more likely to see imperfection and incompleteness in the laws. Indeed, legislatures *expect* that those who deal continuously with problems will suggest improvements.

In concluding this discussion of the role of the administrator in policy formulation, we ought to note its negative aspect. Bureaucracy *stops* far more policy than it formulates. Is this a bad thing? One close observer of Washington thinks not.

> As an entity the bureaucracy is no better equipped to manufacture grand designs for government programs than carpenters, electricians, and plumbers are to be architects. But if an architect attempted to build a house, the

results might well be disastrous. What the White House identifies as bureaucracy's inherent deficiencies are often its strengths. Effective functioning of the governmental machine requires a high degree of stability, uniformity, and awareness of the impact of new policies, regulations, and procedures on the affected public. (Seidman, 1980:76)

Implementation of Policy

The formulation of policy ends when the policy becomes law. The annual product of Congress appears in the *Statutes at Large* and the collection of all statutes of the nation still in force appears in the U.S. Code.

Now, the implementation begins. In Chapter 7, we shall look at this process from a management perspective, but here our perspective is political. Our aim: to lay bare the ways in which administrative decisions may implement policy. We shall note four: (1) rule making, (2) adjudication, (3) law enforcement, and (4) program operations.

Rule Making. Administrative rule making is the establishment of *prospective rules*, that is, agency statements of general applicability and future effect that concern the rights of private parties. These guidelines have the force and effect of law.

Under the requirements of the *Federal Administrative Procedure Act of 1946* (APA), general notice of proposed rule making must be published in the *Federal Register* (Figure 2–1). The *Register*, published five days a week, also contains the latest presidential orders and rules adopted by agencies, and a great variety of official notices. Items range from the results of mileage tests on model autos to a notice that the Mississippi conservation director was granted a federal permit to "capture and transport alligators" in that state and move them "to more advantageous locations."

Notices of proposed rules must indicate clearly where the proceedings are to be held, under what legal authority rules are being proposed, and the substance of the proposed rules. After such notice is given, interested parties are to be provided with the opportunity to participate in the rule-making proceedings through the presentation of written data. At the discretion of the agency, oral presentation may be permitted. Unless notice or hearing is required by the statutes governing the agency's operation, notice of rule making can be withheld if the agency considers it to be "impracticable, unnecessary, or contrary to public interest." While this could potentially exclude many proceedings from public participation, agencies do in practice attempt to conform to the spirit of the APA.

A typical hearing might involve an Environmental Protection Agency official discussing proposals to curtail hydrocarbon emission in a city. These might range from controversial (e.g., gasoline rationing and limiting car travel) to mild (e.g., establishing car pools and installation of vapor recovery systems at service stations). In any event, the

Figure 2-1
Parallel Codification of Legislation and Regulation

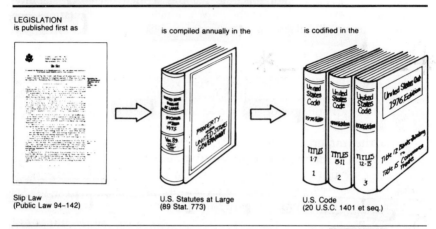

LEGISLATION
is published first as

is compiled annually in the

is codified in the

Slip Law
(Public Law 94–142)

U.S. Statutes at Large
(89 Stat. 773)

U.S. Code
(20 U.S.C. 1401 et seq.)

Legislation Is Implemented by Federal Agencies as Rules and Regulations

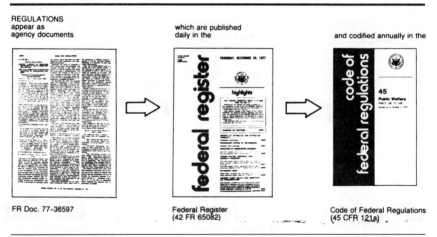

REGULATIONS
appear as
agency documents

which are published
daily in the

and codified annually in the

FR Doc. 77–36597

Federal Register
(42 FR 65082)

Code of Federal Regulations
(45 CFR 121a)

The *Federal Register,* widely considered to be one of Washington's most unreadable publications, has recently been made more readable and useful to ordinary citizens. Its front pages now feature brief highlights of the day's contents. Further, agencies have been required to summarize their rules in language that nonexperts can understand.

agency comes up with the final proposals. A well-publicized hearing occurred in 1979, shortly after the nuclear incident at the Three Mile Island power plant in Pennsylvania. The Nuclear Regulatory Commission and several other agencies reviewed existing rules and formed new ones to improve nuclear power plant safety.

Those who wish to change or repeal rules are given the opportunity of petition by the APA, although changes and repeal rules on this basis have been extremely rare. Actually, no effective way to compel an agency to alter its policies exists—short of recourse to a superior agency, to the courts, or to the Congress.

In sum, rule making by more than 100 agencies is a continual national activity. Collectively, the volume of rules to a substantial extent is policy. Rule making involves modifying existing policies as well as adopting new ones: The Department of Agriculture describes the labeling requirements for pesticides one day; the Food and Drug Administration prescribes safe levels of pesticide residues on plants the next; and an agency in the Interior Department sets a different standard of pesticide toxicity for fish and fowl on another occasion. Moreover, as we shall see in the next chapter, these vertical negotiations with Washington are crisscrossed with horizontal negotiations at the state and local levels. Not without reason did Bailey (1966:17) once refer to this process of policy refinement, communications, and compliance as kaleidoscopic.

Adjudication. Another important way in which agencies implement policy is through their adjudicative powers, granted to them by Congress. Adjudication differs from rule making in that it applies only to the specific parties involved in a controversy before the agency. Administrative orders have retroactive effect, unlike prospective rule making. In other words, the parties involved do not know how the policy is going to be applied until after the order is issued, giving the agency decision a retroactive effect like a courtroom decision. Deciding policy through adjudication necessarily means that it will be decided on a case-by-case basis. And while the rule of *stare decisis* (i.e., requiring precedent to be followed) does not prevail, over time these cases can mark out public policy and indicate the kinds of practices prohibited.

Essentially, administrative adjudication involves two kinds of cases—accusatory, in which one party is charged with a violation of law, and nonaccusatory, in which a party has applied for permission (say, to offer transportation over a certain route). If the charge in an accusatory case proves true, the agency can impose a fine, revoke a license, or direct the accused to cease and desist.

The Administrative Procedures Act of 1946 laid a firm foundation for transforming the agency's hearing officer from a traffic cop into a genuine adjudicator. In 1972, the Civil Service Commission conferred upon these officials the coveted title of administrative law judge (ALJ).

Critics of administrative adjudication argue that the emphasis on trial-type procedures is incompatible with effective rule making. Proceeding case by case can lead to inordinate delay and an incoherent set of policies. Defenders argue that developing coherent policies and standards—not reviewing every decision of an ALJ—is the task of the commission that heads the regulatory agency.

"So that's where it goes! Well, I'd like to thank you fellows for bringing this to my attention."

Agencies may also influence public policy by the vigor or laxity with which they enforce the law. (Drawing by Stevenson: © 1970 *The New Yorker Magazine, Inc.*)

Law Enforcement. Agencies may also implement policy by the vigor or laxity with which they enforce the law. The obvious example is, of course, whether the highway patrol gives you a ticket or a warning. Less obvious, but more relevant to policymaking, is the following.

The Hepburn Act of 1906 authorized the Interstate Commerce Commission to regulate rates charged by pipeline companies, but the commission took no action by itself until 1934. It did not complete a pipeline rate proceeding until 1948, and even then no action resulted. "Since then, the ICC has continued to do little to carry out this authorization, essentially substituting a policy of no regulation for the legislatively declared policy of regulation" (Anderson, 1975:117).

Program Operations. Much of an agency's day-to-day operations is not *directly* concerned with rule making, adjudication, or law enforcement. The agency simply administers a program, which means it distributes certain benefits and services, makes loans, provides insurance, constructs dams, and so forth. But the kinds of decisions an agency makes in administering the programs for which it has been given responsibility can, over time, help determine policy. And the more general the language the more this is true. Indeed, some legislative grants of authority to administrators are very broad, for example, the delegation of authority to agencies to make "reasonable" policies for the protection of public health or to eliminate "unfair" trade practices. (What is reasonable? Unfair?) To get a better idea of just how much delegation can be contained in certain legislation, let us go back to the Economic Opportunity Act for a moment.

Policymakers in the executive branch carefully crafted the bill to grant great discretion to the administrator. The content of the program and the definition of the community were left vague. The new Office of Economic Opportunity would "establish procedures which facilitate effective participation of the states." Formulas for dividing the funds among states and communities were broad. Finally, the act gave the local community the option to designate either a "public or private nonprofit agency" to administer a community action program provided that the program "was developed, conducted, and administered with *maximum feasible participation* of the . . . groups served." If there were international contests for ambiguity, the three words that I have italicized would be world-class material. As Harold Seidman (1980:186–87) writes:

> "Citizen participation" is a very slippery term and means very different things to different people. If participation is measured by the number of people who vote for . . . community action boards, it rests on a very narrow base. Many so-called representatives of the poor were elected by as little as 1 percent of the eligible voters. Citizen participation can be and has been used as a means for transferring power from officials who have at least some

political responsibility to the community at large, to self-perpetuating local cliques, or the bureaucracy. It can operate in ways that provide nominal citizen participation but minimal citizen influence and maximum citizen frustration. Fifty-three percent of the funds appropriated for the community action program in 1968 were earmarked for national purposes devised by the Office of Economic Opportunity in Washington, not by the local citizenry.

B Administration in the Force Field of Politics

In the preceding section, we saw how profoundly administrators can influence the formulation and implementation of policy. In this section, we see how public administrators must operate every day in a kind of political force field.

Great pictorial convenience results from the use of the field concept. Consider a single isolated administrator in Figure 2–2. What is the political field surrounding him or her? If arrows are drawn from the administrator through certain individuals and institutions, the resulting porcupine quills provide a two-dimensional picture of the political field. We may attach arrowheads to the radiating lines to indicate the various directions of force being exerted on the administrator.

The lines constructed in this way are called, as in physics, lines of force. They provide a convenient picture of the administrator's political field. Actually, they do even more than this: The thickness and

"Isn't it about time we issued some new guidelines for something?"
Since it is impossible for legislatures to give specific guidelines to implement public policy, broad grants of authority have been given to agencies. (Drawing by Alan Dunn, © 1968 *The New Yorker Magazine, Inc.*)

Figure 2-2
**Pictorial Representation of Political Field Surrounding
a Single Public Administrator**

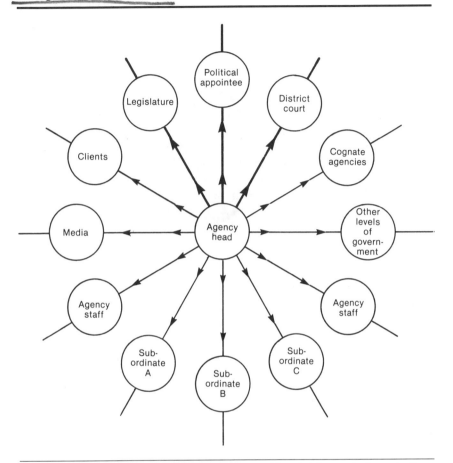

The straight lines radiating in all directions from the public administrator indicate the lines of force that constitute his or her daily political environment. While the lines do not quite extend on to infinity, they are likely to extend well beyond any specific individual or constitution appearing in the surrounding circles. For example, beyond the political appointee may be a chief executive or board of directors; beyond the legislators, the voters; beyond a district court, the Supreme Court; beyond subordinate A, still other subordinates (it seems that everybody within a public agency feels that he or she has a legitimate piece of the action and must be involved); beyond a client, an interest group or trade association; and so on.

number of the arrows can provide a picture of the strength of a particular field.

To understand the concept of political field is not difficult. The real problem is to understand why this concept is useful. The essential fact to appreciate about a field is that it shatters the older notion of a public administrator sitting at the apex of a *hierarchy*.

The concept of hierarchy is based on the distinction between the role of superior and subordinate. The former is expected to exercise *authority* over the latter. In other words, the superior has the power to make decisions that will guide the actions of the subordinate. In most organizations, of course, this relationship is carried much further by making one subordinate the superior of another subordinate. The resulting configuration is often shown as a pyramid. The tremendous potential of the pyramidal form for bringing larger numbers of subordinates under central authority should not go unnoticed. Consider a pyramid with only nine levels of administrators and six subordinates for each administrator at the upper eight levels. Under such an arrangement, one executive could exercise formal authority over 2,015,539 people.

In recent years, as observations and insights increased, it became apparent that the single hierarchical picture, especially when applied to public agencies, was inadequate. Why? It is based on the assumption that each subordinate has only one direct supervisor. At the national level, for example, the president is certainly subject to the authority of both the voters and Congress. In that sense, there is an overhead hierarchy.

This phenomenon of multiple subordination is probably even more widespread at levels below the chief executive offices. Thus, Figure 2–2 shows the administrator not sitting on a pyramid but in a political field. The next several subsections elaborate lines of force at the national level. Before turning to these linkages, a couple of points regarding Figure 2–2 need to be made.

First, technically speaking, what we have in Figure 2–2 is a *model*. A *model* is a simplified representation of some part of reality. It is usually simplified because reality is too complex to copy exactly and because, for the modeler's purposes, much of the complexity is irrelevant. On the other hand, no model can cover satisfactorily as many specific cases as the modeler might wish. For example, several agencies have more independence than suggested by our model in Figure 2–2. The Veterans Administration is such an agency. Veterans organizations, such as the Veterans of Foreign Wars and the American Legion, feel their interests are best served by not subordinating the VA within an executive department.

Second, as drawn, the model refers explicitly to the governmental administrator, but it could be easily redrawn for the university president or hospital administrator. Let us consider for a moment the former. When asked to reflect on how their jobs have changed, university presidents invariably reply that they must woo and satisfy new external constituencies. State legislators and federal bureaucracies are becoming increasingly important sources of money for private as well

as public institutions. And along with public money comes new requirements, such as federal affirmative action plans (discussed in
Chapter 11). As a former executive of International Business Ma-
chines—who now runs a college—puts it: The college president's job
is now closer to that of a big city mayor than a business executive. "He
has a lot of shared power arrangements. It's like getting people to agree
on the need to revive the downtown area" (Fiske, 1975).

The Legislative Connection

One important means by which Congress exercises formal authority
over agencies is by setting policy, a process already discussed in this
chapter. To that earlier discussion, one point might be added. To the
extent that congressional power is fragmented, the programs administered by a federal agency are fragmented. Thus, the chaotic character
of social programs can often be traced to congressional sources—
specifically, the conflicts between congressional authorization and the
appropriations committees, the desire of legislators to author their
own pet bills regardless of the narrow structure of the categories found
in each, the tendency to legislate redundant programs in order to
remain popular with constituents, and the poularity of latching onto
faddish ideas that seem popular to the public at the expense of more
essential programs that are not in vogue. (Richardson, 1973)

Some legislation has a pervasive influence on the operations of
agencies. *The Freedom of Information Act (FOIA) of 1966*, sunset
laws, and sunshine laws are prime examples. FOIA gave any person the
right to request information from agencies and to file action in federal
court if the request was denied. With an estimated 6 billion files, the
U.S. federal government is the largest single creator and collector of
information in the world. This vast storehouse includes the well-
known files of the FBI and CIA, information on almost every type of
product and service the government purchases, safety reports on products it regulates, compliance reports on laws it administered, and
written records of official communication and action. The purpose of
the 1966 act was, in brief, to give the public the right to know what
their government knows (with certain specific exceptions such as
national security and law enforcement investigatory records), and to
have the data upon which decision making is based. In 1975, over a
presidential veto, Congress passed a number of changes to the act to
make it more effective; in particular, they required a reply by agencies
to any request within 10 working days and limited duplicating charges
to actual costs.

Sunset laws provide that an agency is automatically abolished, or
self-destructs, after a period of years (perhaps 7 or 10) unless the
legislature passes a law extending it. Thirty-five states already have
such laws but sunset legislation has been proposed only at the federal
level. Another reform is *sunshine laws*, which require that meetings be

held in the open—in the sunshine—so that all can see what is happening.

A second means by which Congress exercises control over agencies is the appropriations process. A case study in the extent to which the power of the purse can undermine attempts to cope with major national problems such as hunger is provided by Nick Kotz's (1969) vivid portrait of Jamie Whitten, chairman of the House Appropriations Subcommittee on Agriculture. Whitten exercises his power shrewdly. His appropriations subcommittee doles out funds for every item in the department's $7 billion budget, and it does not take long for Washington bureaucrats to realize that the chairman's wrath can destroy precious projects and throw hundreds of people out of jobs. As Kotz writes:

> The key to this phenomenal power—which goes beyond that of budget control—lies in Whitten's network of informants within the department and his skills in directing their activities and operations. Executive branch officials learn to protect their own jobs, adjusting their loyalties to the legislative branch in a way the Founding Fathers may never have envisioned.

A third means by which Congress controls agencies is *oversight*. At its best, oversight involves continuing, systematic congressional checking on the performance of the executive branch—how well government programs are working, how honestly or efficiently or faithfully the laws are being administered. By and large, though, oversight has been infrequent and slipshod. The reasons are political: There is just more political mileage in running errands for constituents and more satisfaction in passing new laws. Tough oversight, on the other hand, can make enemies among congressional colleagues or powerful interest groups.

Still, some members of Congress practice oversight with a vengeance. Senator William Proxmire is perhaps the best known watchdog of the bureaucracy. Among his examples of waste have been the supersonic transport plane, federal limousines, and National Science Foundation grants. Each month he gives his own Golden Fleece Award for what he feels is the greatest waste of the taxpayer's money. The March 1980 award went to the National Institute for Mental Health for funding a study of why bowlers, hockey fans, and pedestrians smile. In September 1981, it went to the Commerce Department's Economic Development Administration which had provided Bedford, Indiana, a $200,000 grant to build a limestone model of the Great Pyramid of Egypt. While some of his awards are no doubt deserved, others show an ignorance of science. Studying the sex habits of the Australian toad might bring congressional guffaws, but medical researchers know that generic research is no more laughable than birth defects and that the frogs, the research, and the defects are all related.

Legislative oversight is strengthened by the General Accounting Office (GAO), an operating staff arm of Congress created in 1921 and originally designed to postaudit government expenditures. Since 1950, the GAO has been moving into what might be called management audits. These audits are policy oriented, seeking to determine what the basis for agency decisions and actions were. (See Chapter 9 for fuller discussion of the GAO's new role.)

As the accompanying box suggests, the multifarious role of Congress in the execution of policy is not without its critics.

The Political Appointee Connection

For a number of reasons, national administration tends to be fragmented. First, agencies form alliances with legislative subcommittees and outside interest groups; this enables, and indeed encourages, them to pursue independent policy courses. We shall discuss these triple alliances later in the chapter. Second, if the president or his appointees can be at cross-purposes with agencies over the *ends* of policy, so too can they be over the *means*. For example, in attempting to attain policy goals, presidents are often driven to economize and to reorganize—two activities that invariably upset some agency interests. Third, agencies have a tendency to become resistant to change due to strong ties to traditional policies and the professional orientation of careerists. Finally, the average tenure of political appointees is only 18 months.

Not surprisingly, presidents wanting to be effective have increasingly circumvented large bureaucracies either by using their own staffs or setting up new agencies. Arthur M. Schlesinger, Jr. (1965:406) reports that President John F. Kennedy well understood the difficulty of converting a tradition ridden bureaucracy into a mechanism for providing information and making decisions. Nevertheless, it was a constant puzzle to him that the State Department remained so formless and impenetrable. He would say, "Damn it, Bundy (one of Kennedy's advisors) and I get more done in one day in the White House than they do in six months in the State Department." Giving State an instruction, he remarked, is like dropping it in the dead-letter box. "They never have any ideas over there," he complained, "and never come up with anything new." "The State Department is a bowl of jelly," he told *Time* in the summer of 1961. "It's got all those people over there who are constantly smiling. I think we need to smile less and be tougher."

Yet the president and his appointees do not stand helpless. In addition to his formidable command over the public attention and his power to appoint key administrators (discussed in Chapter 11), the president has the Office of Management and Budget (OMB). The largest of the executive office components, the OMB has two main functions. The first is preparation of the budget, a process examined in detail in

The Cost of Congressional Micromanagement

For more than a decade the Agriculture Department has been prevented by Congress from even studying potential savings from the consolidation of Forest Service regional offices. Since 1981 the Veterans Administration has needed congressional approval for any personnel actions affecting as few as three employees. Congressional committees have established *floors* rather than ceilings on agency employment, and one committee even dictates the size and style of calendars on the walls of agency offices.

What these examples illustrate is the tendency of Congress in recent years to expand the scope of its oversight of the executive branch far beyond matters of program and policy. Congress has assumed the role of bureaucratic manager while seeking to preserve the status quo of government in size, structure, and personnel, regardless of the resulting inefficiencies and costs. The costs to the taxpayers are in the hundreds of millions of dollars.

This trend can be traced back, at least partly, to 1973–75, when Congress adopted "reform" measures that increased both the number and power of subcommittees. What emerged were new legislative fiefdoms and an explosion in the number of committee staffers, from 918 House committee employees in 1973 to 1,937 in 1980.

Former Representative James Collins (R., Texas), who spent years resisting "the era of subcommittee government," predicted that these new

congressional staffers (many of whom earn $50,000 and more a year) would justify their jobs "by continually inventing new ways to spend the American tax dollars." They have done that and more—rapidly increasing their power at all levels of operation.

From 1970 to 1980 the number of agency reporting requirements imposed by law by House committees surged from 759 to more than 1,500. Though Congress is entitled to information from agencies on federal programs, many of these requirements produce useless, unread reports.

The compulsion of congressional committees to micromanage the structure of agency operations has been reinforced by what we call the "parochial imperative," a desire of individual lawmakers to protect federal facilities and federal jobs in their districts no matter what the cost or effect on national priorities. The fate of recommendations in three GAO reports underscores our point. In 1978 the GAO concluded that the Department of Housing and Urban Development should consolidate its field offices and that the Customs Service should reduce regional offices from nine to six, to achieve higher efficiencies and savings. In 1979 the GAO urged the Agriculture Department to make similar consolidations with its nearly 17,000 field offices.

When HUD attempted to implement a nationwide office reorganization, one aspect of which would have transferred most HUD personnel from the Topeka,

Chapter 9. The second is *legislative clearance*. Before an agency can submit new legislation to Congress, that legislation must be cleared by OMB to ensure that it is consistent with the goals and policies of the administration. In recent years, OMB has begun to take on a third

Kan., office to another state, Senator Robert Dole (R., Kan.) intervened with a legislative prohibition that has to date prevented any changes. Senator Dole said he acted because "this reorganization is disrupting the lives of countless HUD employees."

Border state senators led by Senator Dennis DeConcini (D., Ariz.) similarly blocked the Treasury Department from consolidating Customs Service regions or transferring any personnel. The Agriculture Department fared even worse. Already restrained by a 1972 ban on consolidation within the Forest Service, the department was further shackled by Representative Jack Hightower (D., Texas) when it tried to close a Food Safety and Inspection Service training center in his district, and by Senator Lawton Chiles (D., Fla.) when it tried to close two Agricultural Research Service stations in his state.

Representative Gerry Studds (D., Mass.) got into the personnel-management act by adding language to the Coast Guard's 1982 authorization bill requiring the agency's maintenance of at least 5,484 civilian employees through fiscal 1983 and 1984. That same year Congress wrote into law personnel floors for specific offices in the Energy Department, and designated their responsibilities. The assistant secretary for conservation and renewables was allocated 352 employees, all but 18 designated. The assistant secretary for fossil energy was ordered to maintain 530 employees in the Morgantown, West Virginia, and Pittsburgh energy-technology centers,

with 160 employees of the Economic Regulatory Administration designated by law as auditors.

This picture of massive congressional micromanagement of the federal government does not result from any master scheme hatched by House and Senate leaders. It is a mosaic created by hundreds of individual actions, each unrelated to the others, but cumulatively representing a broad assault on the separation of powers of the legislative and executive branches.

Congress's parochial imperative compels its members to serve specific and limited groups of voters. Only the president is charged with national responsibility for operation of the federal government, and his only constitutional defense against intrusions into the executive branch is the veto. But micromanagement language usually constitutes only a minuscule part of multibillion-dollar spending measures, forcing the president to veto an entire bill just to purge it of intrusive language.

The only hope for ending a practice that is emasculating the ability of any president to direct and, through his appointed officials, to control the federal government is some form of an *item veto.* Governors in 43 states already have that power, and a Gallup Poll taken in 1983 found 67 percent of those surveyed in favor of extending it to the federal level.

When the only defense against a swarm of mosquitoes is a .357 Magnum, one is rendered rather effectively defenseless. It is time to give presidents an effective mosquito repellent.

function: the coordination and evaluation of executive branch programs. Chapter 7 will be devoted to a few of the management techniques executives at all strata of government have available to gain better control over the bureaucracy.

Problems associated with the bureaucracy should not be overstated.

Well-run corporations like IBM and Delta have long known that challenging, training, and trusting employees is critical to their success. The belief that government employees will not respond to changes in management's policy, while private-sector employees will, is simply unfounded. Rather, workers in both sectors tend to behave the way management expects them to behave.

Two of Washington's most successful managers, former Transportation Secretary Drew Lewis and General Services Administrator Jerry Carmen, have used management philosophies that come as close to the IBM-Delta model as any that can be found in government. Both have gotten exactly what they expected from their bureaucrats: loyalty and results.

- Lewis had to make large, budget-driven cutbacks in urban mass transit and hazardous materials-transportation safety programs. Instead of prejudging an entrenched bureaucracy's intentions and then proceeding to pick a fight, he relied on career civil servants, who had strong emotional commitments to their programs, to implement the reductions. They were loyal and highly effective in executing their boss's policies.
- Carmen is known for having shaken up the General Services Administration. But he has been effective, according to key associates, because of the tough-minded respect he accords his bureaucrats. He has filled some slots formerly reserved for political appointees with career civil servants. When one high-ranking career employee complained about a GSA program, Carmen let him hold a news conference to vent his views, and then put him in charge of a program to fix it.

In contrast, Anne Gorsuch Burford (Case 1.1) had an us-versus-them attitude toward her EPA post, and quickly set about trying to control her bureaucracy. The result was exactly what should have been expected: a bureaucracy that undermined her and her program. The reason for Lewis's and Carmen's successes and Burford's failure is not a matter of ideological harmony on the one hand and discord on the other; it is the way they managed their people (Christensen, 1984).

The Client Connection

One important way in which interest groups interact with agencies is by contributing members to the advisory groups used during the policymaking process. Not surprisingly, the interaction between agencies and interest groups involves more than advising.

Top administrators are quite sensitive to the dominant interest groups they represent. Nowhere is this more evident than with the federal regulatory agencies. As one Justice Department deputy assistant attorney general put it: In general, there are "incredible love affairs going on between the regulators and the regulated." As a result, critics say, the agencies often condone or even champion monopolistic practices and rubberstamp higher prices for everything from airline tickets, to natural gas, to telephone calls. Regulators, on the other hand, say that they are not unduly influenced and that they cannot be insulated from the regulated if they do their jobs right.

But every agency has its own constituency that helps it do battle (especially around budget time). The Department of Defense has contractors, the Environmental Protection Agency has the Sierra Club, the Foreign Aid Agency has the League of Women Voters, the Labor Department has the unions, the Department of Housing and Urban Development has the National League of Cities, and so on.

To find an explanation for such cozy ties is not hard. As already indicated, agencies need outside support for their programs; thus, a symbiotic relationship emerges. How does it work? Say an agency develops a long-range plan that would, among other things, bring certain benefits to a particular industry. Given this set of circumstances, it would hardly be surprising to find some private industry, say, to sponsor a conference to promote the plan. Another obvious reason for friendly relationships is that some administrators come from the industry they regulate or support. Moreover, commissioners and top administrators often need interest group support to get and keep appointments, and, once in office, they sometimes feel it necessary to curry favor with interest groups to help win renomination.

The Cognate Agency Connection

According to the *Oxford English Dictionary*, *cognate* means "kindred, related, connected, having affinity." In considering how government goes about attacking national problems (e.g., decay of city, pollution, regional economic development, and work force development), the expression *cognate agencies* seems a handy way of indicating that seldom will only one agency be involved.

> The problem of the cities belongs in the Federal Housing Administration because of its special concern with urban housing. It belongs to the Department of Commerce because of the role of the cities in economic development. It belongs in the Department of Health, Education and Welfare because of the city as a focus for health, education, and welfare services. It belongs in the Department of Agriculture because the city consumes the nation's agricultural products. It belongs in the Department of Interior because the city is a center for the consumption, distribution, and the use of natural resources." (Schon, 1971:166)

Such a situation breeds not only management problems (e.g., interagency coordination) but also political ones. Agencies compete for specific programs: the Bureau of Reclamation versus the Army Corps of Engineers, the Federal Reserve Board versus the Treasury Department, the air force versus the navy, the Soil Conservation Service versus the Agricultural Extension Service, and so on. In the area of solar energy policy, no less than 15 agencies compete. In the new area of genetic engineering (see Case 4.1), the National Institutes of Health, EPA, the Department of Agriculture, FDA, and assorted elements of the White House are all jockeying for position.

But is all this jurisdictional and mission overlap, which breeds so much interagency conflict, entirely bad? The problems are clear enough. Agencies become rigid and uncompromising. The results, at best, can be wasted time and money—at worst, policy stalemates in the face of critical problems. Careful. More might be involved here than economy and efficiency. Does not this duplication and overlap provide greater access to and representation of different views and interests? Might not the duplication of mission management and information gathering by cognate agencies provide backups and corrective forces for errors and bad judgments?

Indeed, some would suggest that agencies should have not one but several paths through which policy may be formed and then implemented. Like an electric current in a parallel circuit, formulation and administration of policy in an agency should be able to flow through more than one branch. Thus, the chance for error to be fatal to an agency's policy and administrative responsibilities is lessened. The agency is far less vulnerable to administrative sabotage, while far more capable of policy initiation.

Media and Other Forces

Suppose one day the president asks his secretary of the treasury to develop an economic policy toward Japan. Almost immediately, scores of people swing into action. The House Ways and Means Committee, the Senate Finance Committee, and virtually every member on them and every staff member will have an opinion and seek to exert influence. Also, the Foreign Relations Committee, the oversight committees, and then the interest groups, business, the unions, the State Department, Commerce Department, OMB, Council of Economic Advisers (and not only the top people, but all their staff) will be mobilized.

Remember, all the president said was "develop me an economic policy toward Japan" to his secretary of the treasury. Why is there no limit to the number of people who get in on the act? Why will the secretary of the treasury, who has been assigned lead responsibility, soon find others—who have not been assigned anything—discussing and negotiating Japanese trade policy? Why, in short, are so many, so quickly in the loop? To a large extent, the news media explains the phenomenon. All the people mentioned above, you may be sure, are reading the *Washington Post* and the *New York Times*. Much of what they know about new initiatives in trade policy comes from reading the newspapers.

Many would defend the large amount of time and money spent on assembling and disseminating the news on the basis of the public's right to know and as a means by which top administrators can learn about the operations of their programs at the grass roots. Cynics would say the media distorts—or, at least, reshapes—the process.

The media reshapes (perhaps a better word than *distorts*) the administrative process in several subtle ways. First, it allows for the disclosure of information—concerning, for example, what the secretary of the treasury is about to recommend on American trade policy toward Japan—through unofficial channels. Of course, not all such disclosures are considered improper by public administrators. For administrators who wish to see something in print but would rather not be on record as formally committed to a particular policy, there is the "authorized leak." Richard Neustadt (quoted in Safire, 1978:369) endorses this tactic. "The class of confidential communication commonly called leaks plays, in my opinion, a vital role in the functioning of our democracy. A *leak* is, in essence, an appeal to public opinion. Leaks generally do not occur in dictatorships."

Reputations in government depend on the press. Glowing press clippings, while at the head of an agency, can be a decisive factor in an admininstrator's promotion to positions of greater responsibility. Charles Peters (1980:22) writes: "A cabinet secretary can become apoplectic when a leading columnist suggests he is losing his clout with the president. . . . As long as power depends on the appearance of being listened to by the president, and as long as newspapers are the primary conveyors of that appearance, high officials will always make time for reporters."

Finally, what can be said about the remaining components in Figure 2-2? Well, a lot. In fact, we shall devote all of the next chapter to the circle labeled "other levels of government" and two chapters (10 and 11) to the circles labeled either "agency staff" or "subordinate." The role of the courts and the media will be explored further in Chapter 4.

Political Competency

Our discussion has ranged far beyond the pleas of Woodrow Wilson and others for a separation of politics and administration. As we have seen, the administrator is placed squarely in the policymaking process. Further, day-to-day events force administrators to operate in a field crisscrossed by political forces generated by overhead authority (Congress and president), client groups, cognate agencies, other levels of government, and the media. The greater the number of these forces, the more time and energy a public administrator tends to spend on power-oriented behavior.

What follows is neither an essay on realpolitik nor revelations on the political art—the former would be improper, the latter presumptuous. This concluding section only attempts to introduce a few basic political concepts that are highly pertinent to good administration. And by good administration, we simply mean administration that can mobilize support for its programs and, in short, get things done. "There is no more forlorn spectacle in the administrative world than an agency and a program possessed of statutory life, armed with executive orders, sustained in the courts, yet stricken with paralysis and deprived of power. An object of contempt to its enemies and of despair to its friends" (Long, 1949:257).

But what are these concepts so pertinent to good administration? Recall for a moment the case of Mr. Cervantes, the former mayor of St. Louis, cited at the start of this chapter. If he had decided to attempt to get the airport built in Illinois, then what basic *political* considerations would have been involved? First, he probably would have wanted to assess his strength—or, to put it in the political vernacular, his clout— to see if he should even try. Assuming he did have sufficient political strength, he would then probably have asked himself: Does my objective really merit such an expenditure of political capital?

Let us be clear on the meaning of this second question. If it is financially possible for me to buy a Mercedes 450 SEL, it does not necessarily follow that I should. Where else could I have invested my limited capital? How much would I have left for future contingencies?

But we shall assume Cervantes is in a better position than the author. Therefore, he decides that he has the political capital *and* that the price (in terms of allies lost, and so on) is not too high. Now he must consider the specific strategies and tactics he must use to attain his objective. In sum, what we have done in this example is simply suggest that the administrator must sometimes think through three political questions concerning resources, costs, and strategy.

Resources

Essentially, the administrator's political resources appear in one of three forms: external support, professionalism, and leadership. The prudent administrator assesses each before attempting any major political act.

External Support. One of the more enduring sources of bureaucratic power is the phenomenon of the *subsystem* or *triple alliance.* Agencies ally themselves with congressional committees and interest groups. Examples are legion: agriculture committees, the American Farm Bureau Federation, and agencies within the Department of Agriculture; subcommittees on Indian Affairs, the Association on American Indian Affairs, and the Bureau of Indian Affairs; the House Agriculture Committee, the sugar industry, and the Sugar Division of the Department of Agriculture; and so forth. The most immediate consequence of the alliance is that agencies are able to take less seriously supervision by superiors in the executive branch. The two examples below highlight other aspects of the alliance—how it can work and how it can fail to work:

> In the early 1960s, both the president's Science Advisory Committee (PSAC) and the air force were unhappy about the amounts of money NASA was receiving. The basic scientists, who were on PSAC to advise the president, were unhappy because so large a proportion of the nation's scientific talent was being devoted to a spectacular political purpose rather than basic research. Similarly, the air force (a cognate agency in this case) was unhappy because it would have preferred rocket development to be kept as the means toward air force ends. But, and this is the crucial point, neither the air force nor the basic scientists were able to dent the alliance that NASA had forged with applied scientists and relevant congressional committees.

> In 1952, Samuel P. Huntington (1952:461–509) analyzed the causes of the decline of the Interstate Commerce Commission in terms of its alliance with the railroads. Huntington concluded that the commission had tied itself too closely with the railroads. Consequently, nonrailroad interest groups (water, motor, and air carriers) blocked the extension of commission power into their field. The ICC was thus unable to expand its basis of support. (Reed, 1978:54)

Thus, administrators in assessing their own strength, must at the same time assess the strength of their support. But the size alone is not enough; also important are the dispersion and unity of the constituency. For example, the strength of the secretary of interior increased with the establishment of the Bureau of Outdoor Recreation, which broadened the department's base from just the western states to the urban Northeast (Rourke 1969:65). For similar reasons, state university systems try to establish satellite campuses in as many state senatorial districts as possible. Regarding the importance of unity, one need only compare the influence of the large, loosely knit consumer movement with the relatively small, tightly knit National Rifle Association.

Professionalism. The second source of agency power is *professionalism*. In defining a *profession*, we shall follow Frederick G. Mosher (1968:106): a reasonably clear-cut occupational field that ordinarily requires higher education, at least through the bachelor's level, and offers a lifetime career to its members. As society becomes more specialized and dominated by technological concerns, we can surely expect to see more individuals fitting this description in government agencies. The consequences of this trend are twofold.

Professionals within an organization are obviously in an excellent position to mobilize the support of relevant external professional organizations. Actually, the arrangement is reciprocal, for each profession tends to stake its territory within the appropriate government agency—for example, the medical profession in the Food and Drug Administration.

Another consequence of professionalism is that, within the agency, professionals tend to form a kind of elite with substantial control over operations. At least three elements form the base of this power, which can override political control from the top.

Full-time attention to a problem.
Specialization develops expertise by breaking the function, issue, or problem into subparts.
Monopolization of information.

③ Leadership. Thus far, we have looked at the political resources of the administrator in terms of interest groups and professional elites. Now we want to consider the political resources that individual administrators themselves can generate.

If leadership is the process by which one person successfully influences another, then power is the means by which he or she does it. Over the years, students of human behavior have identified eight important bases of individual power.

Coercive Power derives from a leader's ability to threaten punishment and deliver penalties. Its strength depends on two factors. First is the magnitude of punishment, real or imagined, that the leader controls. Second is the other party's estimate of the probability that the leader will in fact mete out punishment (e.g., undesirable work assignments, reprimands, and dismissal) if necessary.

Connection Power derives from a leader's personal ties with important persons inside or outside an organization. When a junior aide on the president's staff telephones a senior cabinet member and begins by saying "This is the White House calling," he is using connection powers.

Expert Power derives from a leader's reputation for special knowledge, expertise, or skill in a given area. Lobbyists, who maintain their credibility with members of the legislature, find this kind of power far more effective than the preceding two. House Speaker Thomas P. (Tip) O'Neill provides us with a good illustration of how David Stockman, who was director of the Office of Management and Budget from 1981 to 1985, used expert power. "Every time a Cabinet secretary comes up here, he brings a battery of assistants and refers everything to them," said House Speaker O'Neill. "This guy comes in all by himself and ticks them off boom, boom. I've never seen anybody who knows the operation like this kid—he's something else, believe me" (*Newsweek,* February 16, 1981). After his infamous interview—which was inconsistent with what he had been telling Congress—Stockman's expert power was largely eroded. Congress could no longer believe him, so he ceased to be the Reagan administration's chief economic spokesman.

Dependence Power derives from a people's perception that they are dependent on the leader either for help or protection. Leaders create dependence through finding and acquiring resources (e.g., authority to make certain decisions, access to important people) that others need for their jobs.

Obligation Power derives from a leader's efforts to do favors for people who they expect will feel an obligation to return those favors and to develop true friendships with those on whom they depend. (Kotter, 1977:129–30)

Legitimate Power derives from the formal position held by the leader. In recent years, textbooks on the president have tended to emphasize a theory of presidential power based on persuasion. Richard M. Pious (1979) attacks this bit of perceived wisdom. Ability to persuade, he argues, affects power at the margins but does not determine its use or set its limits. The key to understanding presidential power, Pious says, "is to concentrate on the constitutional authority that the president asserts unilaterally through various rules of constitutional construction and interpretation in order to resolve crises or important issues facing the nation." Based on personal interviews with operating managers at all levels of government, I am inclined to think there is some truth in this. Although persuasion is an important tool, it has limits. To make it work requires time and people who listen; but both are sometimes absent.

Referent Power derives from the identification of others with the leader. This identification can be established if the leader is greatly liked, admired, or respected. Kotter (1977:131) writes: "Managers develop power based on others' idealized views of them in a number of ways. They try to look and behave in ways that others respect. They go out of their way to be visible to their employees and to give speeches about their organizational goals, values, and ideas." When Martin Luther King gave his famous "I Have a Dream" speech, he was fostering the listener's subconscious identification with his dream.

Reward Power derives from the leader's ability to make followers believe that their compliance will lead to pay, promotion, recognition, or other rewards. In a particularly sophisticated application of reward power, when General George Patton asked his troops how they would answer when their grandchildren ask them what they did in the war, he suggested that they could either say they shoveled manure in the states—or they rode through Europe with Patton's Third Army.

According to John Kotter, managers who successfully exercise power tend to share a number of characteristics. They are sensitive to what others consider legitimate uses of power and the "obligation of power." Consequently, they know when, where, and with whom to use the various types of power. And, they do not rely on any one type of power.

They use all their resources to develop still more power. In effect,

The Good, the Bad, and the Ugly:
Three Approaches to Political Competency

Laird (Wide World Photos)

Waterman (Wide World Photos)

Hoover (Wide World Photos)

The Complete Politician

An article in the August 1979 issue of the *Armed Forces Journal* reported on a poll of the Defense Department press corps on the effectiveness of the 14 secretaries. Melvin Laird, who served from 1969 to 1973, had the highest rating from the 15 or so reporters who cover the Pentagon. He was endorsed as the most effective, likeable, trustworthy, strong, and forthcoming. He was the only secretary of defense who won nothing but positive comments.

Harold Brown, widely lauded as one of Jimmy Carter's better cabinet choices, was rated third best. James Schlesinger, Laird's successor, was rated second best—"effective but arrogant." The three worst defense secretaries were Robert McNamara (1961–68), Clark Clifford (1968–69), and Donald Rumsfeld (1975–77).

The secret of Laird's success was that he was a professional politician and knew his subject thoroughly before taking office. This is the way Henry Kissinger (1979) described Laird's ability to accomplish with verve and goodwill what President Nixon "performed with grim determination and inward resentment":

Laird liked to win, but unlike Nixon, derived no great pleasure from seeing someone else lose. There was about him a buoyancy and a rascally good humor that made working with him as satisfying as it could on occasion be maddening.

Laird acted on the assumption that he had a constitutional right to seek to outsmart and outmaneuver anyone with whom his office brought him into contact. I eventually learned that it was safest to begin a battle with Laird by closing off all of his bureaucratic or congressional escape routes, provided I could figure them out. Only then would I broach substance. But even with such tactics, I lost as often as I won. John Ehrlichman considered mine a cowardly procedure and decided he would teach me how to deal with Laird. Following the best administrative theory of White House predominance, Ehrlichman, without troubling to touch any bureaucratic or congressional bases, transmitted a direct order to Laird to relinquish some army-owned land in Hawaii for a national park. Laird treated this clumsy procedure the way a matador handles the lunges of a bull. He accelerated his plan to use the land for two army recreation hotels. Using his old congressional connections, he put a bill through the Congress that neatly overrode the directive, all the time protesting that he would carry out any White House orders permitted by the Congress. The hotels are still there under Army control; the national park is still a planner's dream. Ehrlichman learned the hard way that there are dimensions of political science not taught at universities and that being right on substance does not always guarantee success in Washington.

Administrative Self-Restraint

Alan Waterman was the first director of the National Science Foundation (NSF), serving from 1950 to 1963. To him the agency's supreme objective was to serve the needs of the scientific community. The single-minded pursuit of this objective led Waterman largely to ignore national bureaucratic politics. In a word, Waterman followed a strategy of self-restraint.

NSF was born when a number of federal research organizations already existed. In addition to the Office of Naval Research, already a major source of funds for the scientific community, the National Institutes of Health were entrenched in life sciences, and the navy, the air force, and the Atomic Energy Commission were active in the physical sciences. Where would NSF fit in? To Waterman the answer was obvious: where others did not. As a result, NSF was placed in the position of supporting research that was least relevant to any mission-oriented goal. "NSF avoided expansion of jurisdiction into applied areas, even when there was little competition from other agencies" (Lambright, 1976:143).

Since NSF under Waterman did not want to enlarge its jurisdiction, it could hardly hope to enlarge its constituency. But "by moving into applied areas, NSF might have built a broader, more applied constituency to go along with the performers. It might have used its direct access to the president as a means to gain his support and that of his broad national clientele." As for Congress, NSF "might have enlarged its legislative constituency by distributing grants with an eye to geographical spread and congressional support (Lambright, 1976:144).

The Truth about Hoover

Above I suggested that Laird effectively acquired and held influence in Congress. So too did J. Edgar Hoover, but in a very different way. Hoover seemed to benefit from the general suspicion in Congress that he knew about some skeletons in the closet.

Apparently, these general suspicions were not without foundation. For only three years after his death, congressional and journalistic scrutiny, as well as the writings of his once fearful agents, began to reveal a rather dark picture of the man who built the Federal Bureau of Investigation into one of the world's most reputable police organizations through 48 years as its director. In the new picture, Hoover is seen as a "shrewd bureaucratic genius who cared less about crime than about perpetuating his crime-busting image. With his acute public relations sense, he managed to obscure his bureau's failings while magnifying its sometimes successes. Even his fervent anti-Communism has been cast into doubt; some former aides insist that he knew the party was never a genuine internal threat to the nation but a useful, popular target to ensure financial and public support for the FBI" (*Time*, 1975).

In a 1975 cover story, *Time* reported that Hoover did in fact use information compiled by his agents to build political support for the bureau. For example:

> Hoover went to one senator with the revelation that his daughter was using hard drugs. Hoover agreed to keep the matter quiet—and thereby earned the senator's lasting gratitude.
>
> When Hoover discovered that one Congressman was a homosexual, he visited the legislator to assure him that this news would never leak from the FBI—and this made a new friend for the bureau.

they invest in power. For example: "by asking a person to do him two important favors, a manager might be able to finish his construction program one day ahead of schedule. That request may cost him most of the obligation-based power he has over that person, but in return he may significantly increase his perceived expertise as a manager of construction projects in the eyes of everyone in his organization" (Kotter, 1977:136). That is, when the leader has more power, the follower need not have less. Studies by Likert (1961) and Tannenbaum (1968) indicate that in organizations where there is a greater amount of power at all levels, the organization is likely to be more effective and the members more satisfied.

 ## Costs

Since *cost* is an economic term, we might do well to discuss political cost in essentially economic terms and, in so doing, perhaps achieve a little more rigor.

Virtually every important administrative action has an indirect cost; the economists call such indirect or secondary impacts *externalities* or spillovers. David Halberstam (1969:302–3), a Pulitzer Prize-winning journalist, provides the following incident from the Kennedy years:

> In 1962 [Secretary of Defense] McNamara came charging into the White House ready to save millions on the budget by closing certain naval bases. All the statistics were there. Close this base, save this many dollars. Close that one and save that much more. All obsolete. All fat. Each base figured to the fraction of the penny. Kennedy interrupted him and said, "Bob, you're going to close the Brooklyn Navy Yard, with 26,000 people, and they're going to be out of work and go across the street and draw unemployment, and you better figure that into the cost. That's going to cost us something and they're going to be awfully mad at me, and we better figure that in too.

I believe it was Paul H. Appleby who remarked that the four questions every administrator should always ask before making an important decision are: Who is going to be glad? How glad? Who is going to be mad? And how mad?

Agency administrators can also go into debt. If they use top-level support, it is quite likely that higher officials will later demand bureau backing for other administration programs or demand influence in bureau policy in return. Presidents too sometimes go into the red. As

Richard Neustadt (1960:31) suggests, when Truman dismissed General MacArthur he "exhausted his credit"; as a consequence, he was unable to make his case with Congress, court, and public in a steel strike that came the next year.

Strategies

Top administrators have a wide range of strategies available for dealing with the agency's political environment. And all administrators may safely assume that, either voluntarily or otherwise, they will become involved in these strategies. To ignore them, therefore, is to ignore a very big part of day-to-day administration. For purposes of discussion, we shall classify them rather broadly as (1) cooperation, (2) competition, and (3) conflict.

Cooperation. Cooperation is based on the idea that two groups can share compatible goals without one having to completely give in to the other. All parties can be winners, though some more than others. In the language of game theory, a cooperative strategy means the parties are engaged in a *variable-sum game* in which both parties win.

Cooperative strategies come in many varieties. *Persuasion*, for example, is a variety of cooperation, and its essence was stated precisely by Richard Neustadt (1960:46) as follows: To induce someone to believe that what you want of them is what their own appraisal of their own responsibilities requires them to do in their own self-interest. As one aide to President Eisenhower put it: "The people . . . [in Congress] don't do what they might *like* to do, they do what they think they have to do in their own interest as they see it."

Another variety of cooperation is *bargaining*, that is, the negotiation of an agreement for the exchange of goods, services, or other resources. Universities bargain the name of a hall in return for the donor's contribution. The attorney general's antitrust division signs consent decrees with firms that promise not to pursue actions further without first admitting guilt.

To add precision to our analysis, we draw a distinction between two bargaining techniques. *Compromise*, the first, usually results from bargaining over a single isolated issue when the outcome is one of more or less. Examples would include such matters as busing distances or boundaries, hiring and promotion requirements in government employment, amounts of public housing for ghetto areas; trade-offs between environmental and energy needs; and types of learning programs for the unemployed. Quite clearly, compromise is widely regarded as a positive value in the American political system, but it can lead to ludicrous solutions. In 1961, the director of defense research and engineering had to negotiate between the air force and navy for the requirements for a fighter to be used by both. The navy argued for a wing span of 56 feet; the air force, 90 feet. Solution? Seventy-three feet, of course.

With the second bargaining technique, _logrolling_, we are concerned with more than one issue. Logrolling, therefore, involves reciprocity of support for different items of interest to each bargainer. For example, a governor's task force on welfare, in return for the support of a powerful adviser to the governor, might be willing to let that adviser's office develop some other plan that would properly belong with the task force. Or when a top administrator from the Department of Labor concedes something to a representative of the U.S. Treasury, he or she can often expect a concession at some later date. Observes Charles Lindblom (1968:96), "He has stored up a stock of goodwill on which he can later draw."

In addition to persuasion and bargaining, we might consider the coalition as a variety of cooperation. _Coalition_ involves a combination of two or more organizations for a specific purpose. A good example is provided by the "Mohole" project, which sought to develop new technology that would allow an anchored drilling ship to penetrate the Earth's mantle (see Greenberg 1967:Chapter 9). The original group of sponsoring scientists was concerned with maximizing the scientific returns from the drilling. The contractor understandably sought to confine the project as nearly as possible to a straightforward engineering task. Meanwhile, the President's Office of Science and Technology was concerned with the international and prestige aspects of the success or failure of the project. The National Academy leadership was concerned with preserving the prestige of science, free from controversy. The National Science Foundation sought to sustain the impetus of an important project in earth sciences, but at the same time to support orderly progress in all other fields of science it was sponsoring. Similarly, today we see a coalition of NASA, air force, and contractors backing the space shuttle program.

What do we know about the art of coalition building? The first thing good administrators have learned is that, because of the speed of communication, a proposal can be tested by feinting. The proposal is released by a "reliable source" as a trial balloon before it is officially made. This gives the agency an opportunity to test the different responses that might occur if such a proposal is actually made. Then, if opposition develops or support fails to develop it can either be modified or dropped.

Good administrators have learned too that clarity—sometimes but not always—is essential; in other words, if a coalition is to form around a proposal, then that proposal must be as unambiguous as possible. For example, one of the central difficulties of the negative income tax proposal (which would guarantee a minimum income to all Americans), lay in not communicating to the public, to the press, and to Congress exactly how it would work. The National Institutes of Health provides an example of how such ambiguity might be eliminated. In 1955, the NIH National Microbiological Institute was renamed the National Institute of Allergy and Infectious Diseases. No longer would they be handicapped because "no one died of micro-biology" (Seidman, 1980:36).

Good administrators have learned the advantage of linking—or re-packaging—their agency's proposal with the goals of other agencies and political authorities. Advocates of the nuclear plane in 1953 were successful in linking this proposal in an unmistakable way to a high-priority defense need. Similarly, President Johnson increased the coalition backing the Elementary and Secondary Education Act of 1965 by linking the proposal of federal aid to public schools to his antipoverty program. By the late 1970s, NASA was linking its programs to environment and energy concerns, and in the 1980s, it was linking its programs to defense concerns.

Competition.   In the last few pages, we have discussed the various forms that a cooperative strategy might take. Now we turn to the second classification of strategy: _competition._ Competition may be defined as a struggle between two or more parties with a third party mediating. Often, in competitive situations, the winnings of one competitor are equaled by the losses of the other. A simple example is when a project is transferred from one agency to another. Game theorists call this kind of competitive situation a _zero-sum game._

What can an administrator do in a zero-sum situation? While the alternatives are no doubt many, we shall consider only two examples. In the early 1960s, it became apparent to the air force as well as the navy that the new defense secretary, McNamara, was going to choose a single plane, with certain modifications, for both services. The plane would be a modification of either the air force's TFX or the navy's F-4. Under these conditions, the air force immediately and successfully launched a campaign emphasizing the flexibility of _its_ plane; at the same time, it glossed over how well the TFX would suit its special needs (Coulam, 1975:1–38).

Administrators sometimes can co-opt their adversaries. The classic example of co-optation is the way in which the Tennessee Valley Authority (TVA) adapted its goals so that it would survive. Philip Selznick (1949) defines _co-optation_ as "the process of absorbing new elements into the leadership, as the policy determining structure of an organization, as a means of averting threats to its stability or existence." Co-optation deliberately seeks participation as a means of gaining public agreement to agency programs. In his study of TVA strategy, Selznick tells how potential opposition from the community and regional groups were brought into the TVA's decision-making process.

Finally, awarding lucrative government contracts can provide an enormously flexible way for an agency to co-opt legislators (see drawing at the top of page 66). Companies are simply selected in the districts of key legislative constituents. "Locational politics can be used by the agency to enlarge the program's geographical, legislative clientele" (Lambright, 1976:48–49). Similarly, certain federal agencies

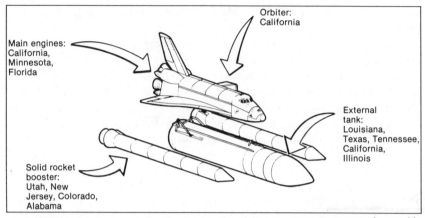

Orbiter: California

Main engines: California, Minnesota, Florida

External tank: Louisiana, Texas, Tennessee, California, Illinois

Solid rocket booster: Utah, New Jersey, Colorado, Alabama

At last! A spacecraft absolutely impervious to attack: It has components manufactured in 300 of the 435 congressional districts. (Only major contractors are shown above.)

seek to co-opt the scientific community by appointing scientists to advisory boards and giving research grants.

③ Conflict. While cooperation and competition are essentially peaceful and governed by formal rules and informal normative constraints, _conflict_ involves situations where actors pursue goals that are fundamentally incompatible. It also can involve attitudes not unlike that of Metternich at the Congress of Vienna. Upon hearing of the death of the Russian ambassador, Metternich is said to have asked, "What could have been the motive?" While these situations and attitudes do not flourish in the American political system, they nonetheless exist.

Consider the case of John Kennedy and U.S. Steel. On Tuesday, April 10, 1962, President Kennedy was surprised to note that his appointment calendar included a 5:45 P.M. appointment with Roger Blough, U.S. Steel chairman. The purpose of the Blough visit was to hand the president a press release announcing a $6-a-ton price increase. The president was stunned. He felt his whole fight against inflation was being reduced to tatters. Above all, he felt duped. The man seated on the sofa next to his rocking chair had personally, knowingly, accepted his help in securing from the workers a contract that _would not_ lead to an increase in prices. Although being challenged in an area where he had few weapons, the president would not accept this _fait accompli_ without a fight. His main strategy was to divide and conquer; more specifically, he focused his efforts on the Inland Steel Company of Chicago in order to obtain an agreement that they would not follow U.S. Steel's lead. He also followed other courses of action. In brief, he got Senator Kefauver and the Justice Department to begin investigating steel activities, used a press conference to sway public opinion, and made implied threats to cancel certain defense contracts.

Within a period of 72 hours, Blough capitulated before the onslaught. What this event had shown was the ability of the chief executive "to mobilize and concentrate every talent and tool he possessed and could borrow to prevent a serious blow to his program, his prestige, and his office" (Sorensen, 1965:516).

Conflict, of course, occurs at less lofty levels, and does not always end in a government victory. Journalist Tom Wolfe (1970:22–23) gives us a vivid picture of how ghetto youth and militants can intimidate the bureaucrats at city hall and in the local Office of Economic Opportunity. Wolfe calls the practice "mau-mauing." One man named Chaser, Wolfe relates, almost gave classes in mau-mauing.

> Then Chaser would say, "Now when we get there, I want you to come down front and stare at the man and don't say nothing. You just glare. No matter what he says. He'll try to get you to agree with him. He'll say, 'Ain't that right?' and 'You know what I mean?' and he wants you to say yes or nod your head . . . see . . . it's part of his psychological jiveass. But you don't say nothing. You just glare . . . see. . . . Then some of the other brothers will get up on that stage behind him, like there's no more room or like they just gathering around. Then you brothers up there behind him, you start letting him have it. . . . He starts thinking, 'Oh God! Those bad cats are in front of me, they all around me, they behind me. I'm surrounded.' That shakes 'em up.
>
> "And then when one of the brothers is up talking, another brother comes up and whispers something in his ear, like this," and Chaser cups his hand around his mouth like he's whispering something. "And the brother stops talking, like he's listening, and the man thinks, 'What's he saying? What kind of unbelievable s—— are they planning now?' The brother, he's not saying anything. He's just moving his lips. It's a tactic . . . you know. . . . And at the end I'll slap my hand down on the desk—whop—and everybody gets up, like one man, and walks out of there. And that really shakes 'em up. They see that the people are unified, and disciplined, and mad, and tired of talking and ready for walking, and that shakes 'em up." (Reprinted with the permission of Farrar, Straus & Giroux, Inc., from *Radical Chic & Mau-Mauing the Flak Catchers* by Tom Wolfe. Copyright © 1970 by Tom Wolfe.)

In conflict situations, the astute administrator needs to keep several things in mind. First is the ever-present danger of *escalation*. This process is characterized by each side in the conflict repeatedly increasing the intensity of the conflict; if continued with a constant rate of increments, the process is likely to get out of control and end in violence. Suppose that a minor incident occurs in which a black citizen is challenged or wronged by a white police officer and a fracas results. Black witnesses spread the word. As rumors circulate, the hostilities involved become exaggerated. People react angrily and a demonstration takes place, which leads to looting and destruction. The police are ordered to contain what is now a riot; this attempt at control increases the anger of the blacks. Snipers begin to fire at the police and firefighters. The national guard is brought in and shoots into the crowd. There are 34 dead, as in the Watts riot in Los Angeles. As a result, great resentment spreads, which in turn results in more clandestine attacks, more arson and rioting, and more attacks against the police. The police respond with armored trucks partrolling the streets, and more heavy-handed repression. In short, we have a spiral of bloodshed.

Besides attempting to stop the escalation process before it gets out of hand, the administrator should remember in conflict situations to avoid humiliation of the interests that lose out in the policy clash; where an adversary has no honorable path of retreat, conflict can become quite protracted.

Timing and forbearance are also important. In the steel price dispute, Kennedy realized that he had to act swiftly, before a parade of companies, rushing to imitate U.S. Steel's increase, began. But one must also know when to stop pressing the attack, how to avoid overkill. Benjamin Disraeli recognized this factor when he said, "Next to knowing when to seize an advantage, the most important thing in life is to know when to forego an advantage."

Last, and most important, the administrator needs to know that conflict situations do not require backroom politics; rather, they can be managed with forthrightness and even a certain dignity. Indeed, even in the ultimate of conflicts—war—men and women still have this option. The following letter (Churchill, 1959:508) to the Japanese ambassador illustrates my point.

Sir,

On the evening of December 7th His Majesty's Government in the United Kingdom learned that Japanese forces without previous warning either in the form of a declaration of war or of an ultimatum with a conditional declaration of war had attempted a landing on the coast of Malaya and bombed Singapore and Hong Kong.

In view of these wanton acts of unprovoked aggression committed in flagrant violation of International Law and particularly of Article I of the Third Hague Convention relative to the opening of hostilities, to which both Japan and the United Kingdom are parties, His Majesty's Ambassador at Tokyo has been instructed to inform the Imperial Japanese Government in the name of His Majesty's Government in the United Kingdom that a state of war exists between our two countries.

I have the honour to be, with high consideration,

Sir,

Your obedient servant,

WINSTON S. CHURCHILL

As Churchill (1959:508) noted in his *Memoirs:* "Some people did not like this ceremonial style. But after all when you have to kill a man it costs nothing to be polite."

Nailing Down the Main Points

1. Public administrators have learned that to separate administration from politics is impossible; the two are inextricably intertwined. Specifically, today's administrators are intimately involved in policymaking as well as the day-to-day play of politics.

2. Administrators frequently participate in formulation of public policy by making proposals that further their client's interests, originate entirely with the agency, or suggest improvements on existing legislation. Nevertheless, bureaucracy *stops* far more policy proposals than it starts.

3. Implementation of policy begins where formulation ends. Administrative decisions can be crucial in this stage of the policymaking process.

4. Legislative bodies exercise authority over agencies by approving or authorizing the programs that the agencies must administer, by appropriating funds for those programs, and by checking on the agencies' performance (oversight). Thus, the entire policy planning cycle may be thought of as a four-step process:

PROBLEM OR NEED RECOGNIZED
↓
POLICY FORMULATION
↓
APPROVAL OR AUTHORIZATION
↓
IMPLEMENTATION

5. Control by the chief executive officer is made difficult by the alliances the agency may form with legislators and clients. Nonetheless, at the national level, the president possesses formidable tools to control agencies: public opinion, appointment power, budget preparation, and legislative clearance. In recent years, presidents have used the Office of Management and Budget for the coordination and evaluation of agency activities. Significantly, many governors have adapted this approach.

6. In addition to the varying degrees of control exercised over the agency by legislatures and chief executives, agencies need to consider three other external political bodies: clients, cognate agencies, and the media. While agencies supposedly regulate these clients, critics charge that, in reality, the relationships become too cozy. Since several agencies can become involved in one policy area, administrators need to consider these cognate agencies when surveying their own political environment. Finally, the media shapes the administrative processes in several subtle ways.

7. The political resources available to an administrator flow from three chief sources: external support, professionalism, and leadership. In assessing the political consequences of their actions, administrators need to consider, in addition to the resources available, the *political* costs involved.

8. In dealing with the environment, administrators have three broad strategies available: cooperation, competition, and conflict. While a cooperative strategy might be preferred, administrators should recognize that they can frequently become embroiled in competition or conflict.

Concepts for Review

authority	item veto
bargaining	leak
bases of power	legislative clearance
clients	logrolling
coalition	persuasion
cognate agencies	policy
congressional oversight	policymaking, policy formulation,
cooperation, competition, and	and policy implementation
conflict	political force field
co-optation	politics administration debate
escalation	professionalism
externalities	prospective rules
Federal Administrative Procedures	rule making, adjudication, law en-
Act	forcement, and program operations
Federal Register	*stare decisis*
Freedom of Information Act	subsystem politics or triple alliances
General Accounting Office	sunset laws
hierarchies	variable-sum game and zero-sum
	game

Problems

1. An especially important skill in political management is negotiating. According to expert negotiators, some of the following statements are true and some are false. Which do you think are true and which false? Explain.
   a. People are basically the same.
   b. Do not make things personal.
   c. Do your negotiating before a public meeting if possible.
   d. Do not give ultimatums.
   e. If you want something, a face-to-face meeting(s) is better than a telephone call(s).
   f. After a meeting, it is better if the other party writes the memo of understanding than if you write it.
   g. Don't be afraid to ask the other party for help during a negotiation.

2. Discuss the possibility and implications of citizen participation being overwhelmed during hearings on controversial issues by expert testimony from government and industry representatives. Can you find examples in the local newspapers?

3. Look up a major national act in either the *Statutes at Large* or the *Congressional Quarterly Weekly Report,* and then attempt to find applicable executive agency decrees relevant to it in either the *Federal*

Register or the *Bureau of National Affairs Reports.* Do you think the law has been perverted to serve the goals of those who enforce it?

4. "The successful executive will readily accede to congressional participation in areas where its committees or members have a proper concern," writes former NASA chief James E. Webb. Is Mr. Webb naive?

5. "TVA has lost much of its national constituency," Senator Howard H. Baker has remarked. Using recent periodicals, analyze the TVA's political position and outline a plan to rebuild it.

6. Given the prevalence of logrolling, why might an administrator want to keep his preferences unclear? What do you think the effect of a ban on logrolling would be?

7. Assess the possibility of the adoption in your city of free-fare bus service or some issue of your choice. Consider the possibility in terms of *(a)* possible allies, *(b)* probable opponents, *(c)* distribution of resources among the activities, *(d)* legal constraints, and *(e)* alternative strategies for achieving it. Begin by completing the following table:

Actors: list the names of all relevant groups or individuals	(A) Political power: rate each actor on a scale from 1 (weak) to 3 (strong)	(B) Position: rate each actor on a scale from -3 (strongly oppose issue) to $+3$ (strongly favor issue)	(C) Relative importance: rate each actor on a scale from 1 (low priority) to 3 (high priority)	A × B × C
Total				

8. What externalities were involved in the two decisions faced by Mayor Cervantes?

9. "Expertise," Harold J. Laski said, "sacrifices the insight of commonsense to the intensity of experience." Discuss.

10. In general, what forms of power are associated with different sexes, age groups, social strata, and economic groups?

11. Can you see any link between the American party system, which is fairly weak in comparison to that of other Western nations, and the political activism of administrators?

12. "Vote trading and arm twisting are effective when the issue is not that big, when it isn't a glaring national issue. But it doesn't work when you've got the full focus of national attention on it." Do you agree or disagree? Support your answer with recent examples.

13. Redraw Figure 2-2 with a college president in the center. Can you redraw it for a union leader as well? A hospital administrator? What do you think it would look like for the chief executive of a multinational corporation? Be specific.

14. What kinds of power do even "powerless" people have?

15. Recall situations in which you eagerly or reluctantly did what someone told you to do. What types of powers were used in each case? What types of power do you feel most comfortable and most awkward exercising?

16. An interesting approach to increasing political strategy skills was suggested by Arnold J. Meltsner in "Political Feasibility and Policy Analysis," *Public Administration Review*, November–December 1972, pp. 859–67. As a way of getting started, Meltsner suggested the following broad categories about which the analyst should gather information for the policy issue under consideration: (1) actors, (2) motivation, (3) beliefs, (4) resources, (5) sites, and (6) exchanges. Read this article, select an issue, and try to apply his approach.

Case 2.1
Closing Sydenham Hospital

Unlike other major cities, which have at most 1 municipal hospital, New York City has 17. The smallest of them, Sydenham, was built in the heart of Harlem in 1925. By the 1950s, with modern medicine requiring ever-more space, Sydenham had fallen seriously behind the other city hospitals in providing quality health care. When mayors began to recommend closing it, the Harlem leadership protested vigorously. Sydenham, they argued, was not only a hospital but a cultural landmark.

Nevertheless, in January 1980, the New York Health and Hospitals Corporation (HHC) voted to proceed with the closing of Sydenham. Not surprisingly, the vote caused a furor among blacks as well as Hispanic residents of the area. Fifty percent of New York City Council members urged Mayor Ed Koch to drop all plans to close the hospital. Representative Charles B. Rangel called Koch the most repressive mayor in the city's history, and immediately petitioned the Justice Department to block closing, pending investigation by the Office of Civil Rights into charges that the situation would deprive minorities of health care. (Seven months later, the office would conclude that there was no violation of civil rights laws.)

The Politics and Economics of Health Care

Retrenchment has been a common theme in municipal government for nearly a decade, especially in New York City (see Exhibit 1). It was in this context that Mayor Koch decided to close Sydenham. The mayor argued that (a) alternative uses of the hospital were fiscally unsound, (b) federal funds to keep it open would not be sought because the hospital would need $10 million in repairs to bring it into compliance with building codes, and (c) the hospital's patient load could be handled by four other hospitals in the area.

The core economic issue to Koch was empty beds. Sydenham, which had 119 beds, had only 70 or so patients in them because the people of Harlem knew that the care they got at Sydenham was not as good as the care they could get at any of six hospitals between 4 and 12 blocks away. Yet the cost of a bed remained high—$250 to $300 per night—even when it was empty.

Koch's political strategy was simple. According to the experts, two hospitals, Sydenham and Metropolitan, both located in Harlem, met the criteria for closing. So Koch announced that he would close both. Eventually, it became clear to Koch that if both hospitals were closed his administration would lose political support for his other programs. He believed that by not prematurely indicating a surrender at Metropolitan, he would be in a better position to get federal aid to keep it open. After all, President Carter was running for reelection.

Exhibit 1
City of New York Expenditures, Fiscal Years 1975, 1978, 1982
(Dollars in Millions)

	Amount		
	1975	**1978**	**1982**
Debt service	$1,896.0	$2,184.0	$1,879.7
Public assistance	1,203.3	1.368.9	1,356.3
Health services	1,007.3	1,052.6	1,271.4
Social services	1,019.6	1,314.6	1,708.5
Housing	169.7	128.5	333.8
Infrastructure projects	893.5	352.7	733.7
Other development programs	3.3	6.8	38.1
Transportation	270.5	374.9	492.0
Education	2,982.2	3,139.6	4,141.4
Criminal justice	1,324.4	1,411.0	1,737.2
General government	1,571.0	1,765.5	2,670.0
Total	$12,340.8	$13,099.1	$16,370.8

Source: Adapted from Annual Reports of the Comptroller of the City of New York as reported in Charles Brecher and Raymond D. Horton, "Expenditures," in *Setting Municipal Priorities, 1984*, Brecher and Horton, eds. (New York: New York University Press, 1983), pp. 68-96.

The $42 Million Solution

On March 2, 1980, Mayor Koch and his staff began to put his plan into action. They submitted a $42 million proposal to the U.S. Department of Health, Education and Welfare (HEW)—now the Department of Health and Human Services—calling for federal financing to keep Sydenham and Metropolitan Hospitals open. Under the plan, New York City would have had no financial responsibility to Sydenham after October 1.

On March 29, HEW rejected the proposal, saying that it was too similar to a $30 million rescue of a Brooklyn hospital the previous fall; the department could not justify financing two parallel projects in the same city.

Koch spent the next few weeks urging HEW to save Metropolitan. He warned that unless help came, he would decide the hospital's future on his own. High officials in HEW then began suspecting that Koch preferred to close Metropolitan, thereby saving the hospital's annual $30 million deficit and placing the blame on the department. HEW Secretary Patricia R. Harris found herself spending much of April denying Koch's assertions that she was blocking plans to keep the two hospitals open.

By mid-June an agreement was reached in which the federal government would help fund Metropolitan for at least three years and Sydenham would become, on October 1, a community-operated drug, alcohol, and mental health facility financed by medicaid funds. At a White House ceremony, Representative Rangel offered Koch stained praise.

Koch Sends in the Police

At about 10 P.M. on the evening of September 15, Mayor Koch received a call while having dinner in Chinatown. About 60 demonstrators, he was told, had taken over Sydenham. The media wanted a response.

Koch detailed a response over the phone and the next day held a press conference to tell his side of the story. He said that he would not order the police to forcibly evict the demonstrators but he refused to accede to their demand that the city negotiate if it wanted to end their occupation. On September 21, some 30 people, including 10 police officers, were injured when demonstrations outside the hospital became violent.

The next day, Koch met with representatives from the Coalition to Save Sydenham. He agreed to postpone the deadline for closing for two weeks to allow more time for the coalition to seek funds to keep Sydenham open as a voluntary general hospital.

Meanwhile, the demonstrators continued their sit-in. Gradually, their numbers thinned to nine. For the next week nothing happened except that the city continuously pulled the plugs on them. First no lights; then no food—except what was supplied by the police; next no telephone; and then no visual contact with the outside. Koch felt that efforts on behalf of the protesters by local politicians during this period were just last-minute posturings. But he wondered: When would it end? As long as the demonstrators were allowed to occupy center stage, the orderly phasing out of Sydenham and the transfer of its employees could not take place.

On Wednesday afternoon, September 24, the Intelligence Division of the N.Y. Police Department advised Mayor Koch that members of the Communist party, white agitators, and others looking for a confrontation might bring guns into the community. Working through Charlie Rangel, Koch let the sit-ins know that if they

Cops under assault defending Sydenham Hospital from the mob that was bent on forcibly taking it over. (Wide World)

would leave, the city would waive criminal and civil sanctions. But they remained adamant.

Koch knew that on Saturday, September 26, there would be a huge demonstration. Therefore, he ordered the police to act; at 2 A.M. on the day of the demonstration, the police moved in.

Citicaid

On the afternoon of September 26, Sydenham Hospital, for the first time in nearly 60 years, stood empty. It was ringed with police barriers, and a large contingent of police officers remained on the scene. But the hospital was closed.

Meanwhile, posturing by elected officials continued. For example, Governor Carey, in a surprise move on the day of the huge demonstration, promised to help Harlem community leaders with a plan to convert Sydenham into a private hospital, and to help get federal funds to carry out that plan. But the die was cast. Sydenham closed on November 24, and the protracted fight between Koch and community, religious, and political groups had finally come to an end.

All the news, however, was not bad for Harlem that fall. In October, Koch announced that $108 million would be spent over the next five years to provide comprehensive health care in Harlem. The new program, designated "Citicaid," would cover indigents who were eligible for medicaid and 17,000 others who were too poor to afford Blue Cross, did not receive it as an employee benefit, and were not destitute enough to qualify for medicaid. The federal government would pay 50 percent, New York State 17 percent, and the city 33 percent. It would be the nation's largest publicly operated health maintenance organization (HMO) in an urban setting.

Case Questions
1. What are Mayor Koch's strengths and weaknesses as a political manager?
2. What was he trying to achieve?
3. What would you have done differently? (Note that the case says nothing about what happened after the police moved in on the morning of September 26.)
4. What is your assessment of what Koch termed "political posturing?"

Case References
Charles Brecher and Raymond D. Horton, *Setting Municipal Priorities, 1982* (New York: Russell Sage Foundation, 1981); Edward I. Koch, *Mayor* (New York: Warner Books, 1984); Karen Gerard, *American Survivors: Cities and Other Scenes* (New York: Harcourt Brace Jovanovich, 1984); *New York Times:* January 22, 1980, February 18, 1980, February 20, 1980, March 1, 1980, March 11, 1980, March 13, 1980, March 30, 1980, April 30, 1980, May 16, 1980, May 30, 1980, June 4, 1980, June 20, 1980, July 13, 1980, September 21, 1980, September 23, 1980, September 24, 1980, September 26, 1980, September 27, 1980, September 28, 1980, October 1, 1980, October 2, 1980, November 21, 1980; *New York Daily News,* September 27, 1980.

3

Intergovernmental Relations

Introduction

In Chapter 2, we began sketching the environment of American public administration. Now we add to our palette and attempt a brighter, truer sketch of that environment.

You will recall that Figure 2-2, contained one line of force labeled "other levels of government." This suggests that today's administrator works in a context of *intergovernmental relations (IGR)* as well as interagency relations. And by intergovernmental relations, we mean all those activities occurring between governmental units of all types and levels within the United States.

Because the subject of our investigation is so vast, the temptation is simply to plunge in and swim indiscriminately from one island of fact to another, until we emerge at the end dripping with irrelevant details. Let us, therefore, resolve to set an objective and then plot as straight a course as possible toward it.

Simply stated, the aim of this chapter is to explain how intergovernmental relations affect the job of managing the public sector. But before we can deal directly with that topic, three preliminary steps are essential. First, we must be clear on what the term *intergovernmental relations* means and how it differs from the concept of federalism. Second, it is useful to see how intergovernmental relations have evolved; only then can we assess Reagan's New Federalism. Third, we shall sketch a dynamic model of the intergovernmental system.

Then, in the last section, we shall address the central issue of the chapter—the administrative implications of intergovernmental relations.

Federalism and IGR Compared

Some might say that IGR is just another word for *federalism*. But that would not be accurate.

What then is federalism? In its most formal sense, a federal system (such as the United States, Canada, Switzerland, and West Germany) stands in contrast to a unitary or centralized system (such as France or Great Britain). A federal system divides power between the central government and regional governments (states, provinces, cantons, and lands); each government, central or regional, is legally supreme in its own area of jurisdiction. Thus, in the United States, the federal government controls external affairs, regulates interstate commerce, and establishes rules for immigration and naturalization. But the Constitution reserves certain powers for the states: control of elections, local governments, and public health, safety, and morals. Although some powers are shared between governments—taxing and spending for the general welfare, defining and punishing crimes, and so forth—the traditional or "layer cake" model of federalism assumes that functions appropriate to each level can be defined with reasonable precision and should be kept independent.

Morton Grodzin and Daniel J. Elazar (1966) reject this model of the federal system, preferring a *marble cake model.* According to Grodzin and Elazar, separation of functions is both impractical and undesirable when governments operate in the same area, serve the same clients, and seek comparable goals.

Models should simplify, but layer cakes and marble cakes is going a little too far. We need a more accurate picture of how governments operate together in the same program area. That is, what are the *relationships* among administrators in the federal system? We also need to recognize that there are many more governments involved than the concept of federalism implies.

A major deficiency of federalism as a descriptive model is that it tends to recognize mainly national-state and interstate relations but to ignore national-local, state-local, national-state-local, and interlocal relations. In contrast, "IGR includes as proper objects of study all the permutations and combinations of relations among the units of government in the American system" (Wright, 1974:2). And *local*, as used here, means not only the 3,041 counties, 19,076 cities, villages, and boroughs, 16,734 townships, but also the paragovernments for special purposes. Among these paragovernments are 14,851 school districts and 28,588 other special districts for sewerage and water supply, natural resources, health, utilities, and the like (U.S. Bureau of Census, *Census of Governments, 1982*). Also worth noting here are metropolitan area *councils of government* (COGs), consisting of one member from each local government in a given region. COGs, now numbering over 300, serve as a forum for airing problems and exploring ways of cooperating; many are regional planning commissions.

To sum up: While the term *federalism* perhaps helps us distinguish between one general class of government and another class (called unitary), it does not provide the best approach to understanding the kinds of knowledge (useful to administrators) highlighted earlier. For the public administrator at least, the preferable term then is *intergovernmental relations.*

The Evolution of the Intergovernmental System

Talk about the evolution of the intergovernmental system may offend bureaucrats in Washington, a city where a feeling of national dominance and self-importance always seems to be in vogue. It may bore the life out of many journalists, who tend to be preoccupied with what is current rather than long-range historical changes in the relationship among national, state, and local governments and agencies. Nevertheless, the relationship of states to the federal government is the cardinal question of our constitutional system. "It cannot be settled," Woodrow Wilson once wrote, "by the opinion of any one generation, because it is a question of growth, and every new successive stage of our political and economic development gives it a new aspect, makes it a new question." Wilson could not have been more right. As we shall see in this section, IGR have changed greatly since the early 19th century. These changes are closely linked to the overall growth of government in American society. As public administration has come to play a larger and larger role in our lives, the links between the different levels of the federal system have become both tighter and more complex.

The Era of Dual Federalism (Until 1933)

The two-term presidency of Andrew Jackson (1829–37) marked a renewed emphasis on states' rights. During the period, when emerging economic interests sought subsidies or tax breaks, they were likely to go to their state government. But, when these interests wanted protection from competition by cheap imports, they had to go to the national government.

Certain political developments reinforced this arrangement, often characterized as *dual federalism.* As the vote was extended to new groups, business elite, who were interested in a more centralized government, lost influence to farmers and workers, who were less interested in a strong national government.

Roughly speaking, we can say that this era lasted until the New Deal years of the 1930s, despite the fact that cooperation between national and state governments in areas such as railroad construction and banking existed before and during Franklin Roosevelt's administration. Not until the New Deal did the idea really take hold that the national government and the states were complementary parts of a single governmental mechanism for coping with problems.

The Era of Cooperative Federalism (1933–1960)

The Great Depression of the 1930s led to several new and important changes in IGR. The Social Security Act of 1935, for example, included national grants for state and local unemployment as well as welfare programs; the Housing Act of 1937 was the first instance of national involvement in local public housing. During this era of *cooperative federalism*, intergovernmental relations became more centralized in Washington, and the role of federal dollars became more important.

Without question, the national government had given money to states since its creation; in fact, the first such *grants-in-aid* were used to pay the debts the states had incurred during the American Revolution. In 1802, Congress passed a law providing that revenue from the sale of federal lands be shared with states. Since the early 1800s, however, the tendency has been for the national government to give money for specific purposes. Such *categorical grants* require that funds be spent for particular programs in particular ways (in other words, "with strings attached").

The Era of "Creative" Federalism (1960–1968)

If the great growth in national aid to state and local government began with Franklin Roosevelt's New Deal in 1933, then it is fair to say that the most explosive period of such growth occurred during Lyndon Johnson's Great Society (1963–1968). The number of grant programs grew at an astounding pace—from about 50 in 1961 to some 420 by the time Johnson left office. These programs included legislative landmarks—medicaid, the Elementary and Secondary Education Act, and the Model Cities program—as well as smaller initiatives tailored to the interests of narrower constituencies. As Figure 3–1 shows, federal aid to states and localities in this period almost doubled—from $7.9 billion in fiscal year 1962 to $13.0 billion in fiscal year 1966. Johnson called his program "Creative Federalism." Scholars disagree as to the inventive merit, the insight, and the imagination that went into the design of some of these programs, but none dispute Johnson's creation of many new categorical grant programs.

Creative federalism was a turning point in the development of the intergovernmental system for several reasons (Howitt, 1984:7–12).

- The federal government had become a far more significant presence in the daily lives of state and local administrators and in the delivery of government services to citizens.
- Creative federalism raised practical and philosophical questions.

Figure 3–1
Federal Grants-in-Aid to State and Local Governments

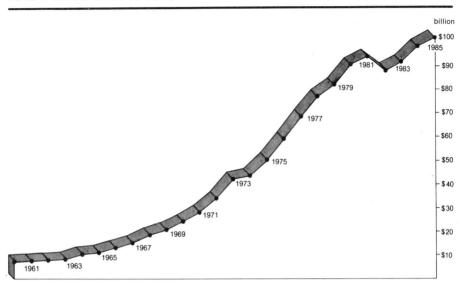

Source: Advisory Commission on Intergovernmental Relations, *Significant Features of Fiscal Federalism, 1983–84* (Washington, D.C.: Government Printing Office, 1984).

Did the individual programs created in Washington work as intended when implemented in dozens, hundreds, or thousands of state and local sites? What were the limits of purposeful government intervention in the social, economic, and political lives of its citizens? Could sweeping national purposes actually be effectively achieved by planned government activity? Should they be?

- The intergovernmental system became more difficult to manage. Federal administrators now had to manage a larger number of separate programs, work with many more governmental units, and oversee the expenditure of increasing amounts of money. Moreover, because Congress had prescribed the goals and means of the programs in greater detail (to avoid problems like those associated with the community action program discussed in the last chapter), they were more complex than their predecessors' programs.

- Because new programs involved *project grants* for which state and local governments had to compete with other states and localities, federal administrators had more discretion in, and responsibility for, choosing recipients.

- State and local officials found it increasingly difficult to keep track of all the programs for which they might be eligible.

- Since grants frequently went directly to the agencies that ran federal programs, chief executives like governors and mayors found they had less power.

• Because governors, mayors, and other state and municipal officials had a growing financial stake in intergovernmental aid (see Figure 3–2), creative federalism developed a strong constituency that was prepared, when necessary, to lobby for the programs.

President Nixon, who came into office in 1968, recognized these political realities and crafted his new policy for intergovernmental relations accordingly.

Nixon's New Federalism (1968–1980)

Revenue Sharing.   In a message to Congress on February 4, 1971, President Nixon noted that most federal assistance takes the form of "highly restricted programs of categorical grants-in-aid. . . . The ma-

---

Figure 3-2
Grants as Percentage of State and Local Receipts

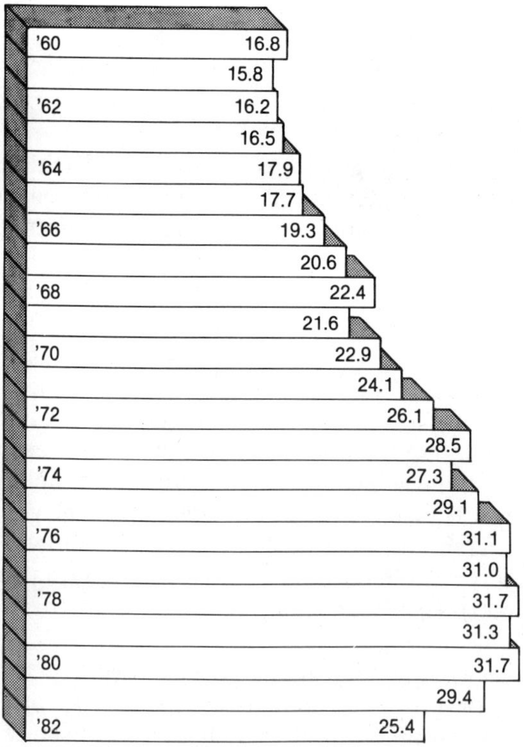

Year	Percentage
'60	16.8
	15.8
'62	16.2
	16.5
'64	17.9
	17.7
'66	19.3
	20.6
'68	22.4
	21.6
'70	22.9
	24.1
'72	26.1
	28.5
'74	27.3
	29.1
'76	31.1
	31.0
'78	31.7
	31.3
'80	31.7
	29.4
'82	25.4

Source: Advisory Commission on Intergovernmental Relations, *Significant Features of Fiscal Federalism, 1983–84* (Washington, D.C.: Government Printing Office, 1984).

jor difficulty is that states and localities are not free to spend these funds on their own needs as they see them. The money is spent instead for the things Washington wants and in the way Washington orders. . . . State and local governments need federal . . . money to spend, but they also need greater freedom in spending it."

To effect this policy, Nixon proposed both *general revenue sharing* in which states and localities would receive funds with virtually no restrictions on how they might be used, and *special revenue sharing* in which existing categorical programs would be consolidated into a broad-purpose or *block grant* in a particular policy area like education with relatively few restrictions on its use. Ultimately, Congress adopted several block grant compromises, such as the Comprehensive Employment and Training Act of 1973 (CETA), but let the special revenue-sharing proposals languish in committee. Congress also continued to enact new categorical programs—despite the objectives of the Nixon administration. As Figures 3-1 and 3-2 show, the federal government's fiscal commitment to the intergovernmental system continued to lumber upward and onward under Nixon and later under Gerald R. Ford.

According to many specialists in intergovernmental relations, two things were wrong with revenue sharing. First, most of the money was expected to be used for buildings, sewers, and other construction projects. But, with no strings attached, cities often simply put the money

Table 3-1
The Haves and Have-Nots of U.S. Cities: U.S. Cities Most (and least) in Need of Federal Support, 1980*

Greatest Need	Least Need
1980	**1980**
Newark, New Jersey	Tulsa, Oklahoma
Detroit, Michigan	San Jose, California
Atlanta, Georgia	Wichita, Kansas
Cleveland, Ohio	Houston, Texas
Baltimore, Maryland	Virginia Beach, Virginia
Buffalo, New York	Seattle, Washington
Philadelphia, Pennsylvania	Honolulu, Hawaii
New York, New York	Austin, Texas
Chicago, Illinois	Charlotte, North Carolina
St. Louis, Missouri	Denver, Colorado

* The ranking, which included the 53 largest cities, was determined by calculating the number of people living below the poverty level, net change, and real growth in per capita income from the 1979 and 1980 unemployment rate.

Source: Joint Economic Committee, National Urban Policy Advisory Committee, 1984.

Figure 3-3
Map of the United States Showing Federal Administrative Regions

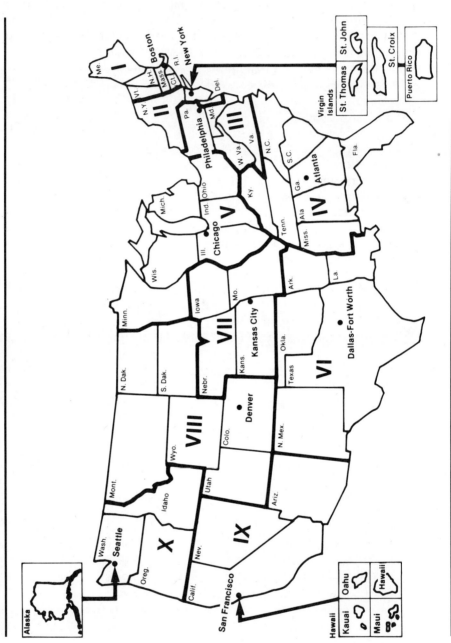

Source: U.S. Bureau of Census, 1974.

functions as police, fire fighters, and even golf courses. Second, in the political struggle over the funds, nearly every city got *some* revenue. A compromise formula based on population, tax base, and per capita income led to a thin, scattershot dispersal of money. The recipients included not only poor cities like Newark and Detroit but also affluent communities like Palm Springs, California, Vail, Colorado, and Greenwich, Connecticut. Table 3-1 (page 83), provides a list of the 10 cities most in need of special support along with a list of the 10 cities least in need, according to a report issued by the Joint Economic Committee of the U.S. Congress.

Management Improvements. Revenue sharing was not the only thrust in the New Federalism. Nixon also wanted to improve organizational arrangements, a task he assigned to his Office of Management and Budget (OMB).

Among the specific tools OMB used (and continues to use) is *Circular A-95*, which established a Project Notification and Review System under which "clearinghouses" at state, regional, and metropolitan levels are to receive notification by governments in their jurisdiction that they intend to apply for federal aid before doing so. The clearinghouses perform two functions subsequent to such notification: (1) they transmit this information to other governmental entities in the affected area and solicit comments; and (2) they screen the applications for conformity with established state, regional, and local planning. (The COGs, noted earlier in this chapter, often fulfill this screening role.)

To promote better communication and coordination among different levels of government, President Nixon created the *Federal Regional Council*, composed of the regional directors of major agencies in each of the 10 administrative regions that he established (see Figure 3-3). To foster coordination at an intermediate level between agency headquarters in Washington and state and local levels, these councils seek to integrate programs managed by the different agencies within their regions. Since the establishment of such councils, the time needed to process grant requests for federal funding has been reduced by half.

President Carter's domestic program (1977–80) focused on urban problems and better management, but most observers found his approach of only limited effectiveness. In light of what was to come, the Carter administration may be seen as a transition period between an era of expansion and an era of cutback.

Reagan's New Federalism, 1981 to Present

As the foregoing survey demonstrates, every president since Lyndon Johnson has expressed a philosophy of federalism for his domestic program: Lyndon Johnson called for a creative federalism; Richard into their general budgets, spending it on such traditionally local Nixon advanced his new federalism; and Jimmy Carter had a strong federalism concept embedded in his 1978 national urban program.

But no president entered the White House with firmer views or stronger campaign commitments about intergovernmental relations than Ronald Reagan.

> As governor of California during the late 1960s and early 1970s, Reagan had watched with dismay—politically and philosophically—as President Johnson's Great Society programs had grown in number and scale, bringing the federal government increasingly into policy matters that had been largely, if not exclusively, the province of state and local authorities. As governor, too, he had chafed at federal intrusions into his own state's affairs—quarreling, most notably, with the Office of Economic Opportunity over California's rural legal assistance program. These experiences, as well as his underlying conservative political views, led Reagan to make reform of the intergovernmental system one of the earliest and highest priorities of his presidency. (Howitt, 1984:15)

More specifically, Reagan, like Nixon and Ford, sought to enhance the role of states as opposed to localities. How successful was he?

Analysis.   In his 1982 State of the Union message, Mr. Reagan proposed a wide-ranging plan to "turn back" federal functions to, or "swap" them with, the states. The essence of this plan was that fiscal and administrative responsibility for welfare programs would be turned over to the states, with the federal government assuming responsibility for the medicaid programs currently run by the states. All of this was to have been combined with an elaborate restructuring of taxes and grants. This plan was not well received in Congress.

Conventional wisdom holds that the Reagan administration has been highly successful in cutting domestic spending and increasing defense spending, but has failed in its federalism agenda. Richard P. Nathan and Fred C. Doolittle of Princeton University believe that this view is mistaken. They argue that the Reagan administration's domestic cuts, while significant in some areas, tend to be seen as overly important. And they maintain that Reagan's federalism reform efforts—which have nearly disappeared from the public consciousness—are turning out to have substantial impact. (The following discussion is based on Nathan & Doolittle, 1984.)

To provide a better understanding of the changes in federal aid levels under President Reagan, Nathan and Doolittle divide them into the following three main types of grant programs:

- *Entitlement programs*, such as welfare and food stamps, where the payment of benefits is administered by states and localities. Here we find the biggest cuts—cuts that hit immediately and have stayed in place.
- *Operating programs* under which the federal government provides grants to state and local governments in areas such as

education, public health, and other social services. While cuts were also made here, the states gained new authority to set program priorities and distribute funds.

- *Capital programs* in which the federal government provides grants to states and localities for public facilities such as highways. Although capital grants were initially slated for large cuts under Reagan, Congress increased funding for these programs.

In sum, President Reagan has had a measurable but not substantial effect on spending *levels*. But the effect he has had on the *structure* of domestic spending is quite another matter—one that merits a closer look.

The changes made to date by Reagan have increased the states' influence. States are allowed more discretion under the present block grant arrangement. For example, Reagan's Job Training Partnership Act of 1982 assigned the lead policy and management role to the states. The Reagan administration has also (1) reduced regulatory and administrative oversight in many federal programs; (2) made changes in medicaid that enhance the power of the states to cut and control costs; and (3) rejected many proposed programs which, in its opinion, are designed only to throw money at domestic problems. Overall, Nathan and Doolittle are impressed that the Reagan era has seen such a resurgence in the role of state governments. The character and degree of this resurgence vary with the states, but in a large and well-established political system like that of the United States, such a shift is notable and important.

In addition to the states' enlarged role vis-à-vis Washington, Nathan and Doolittle detect a similar increase in their role relative to local governments. Local governments are increasingly turning to their state capitols as it becomes clear that the federal government is pulling back in domestic areas. Finally, these authors note major changes in the role and importance of nonprofit community groups, especially those that provide social services. With the exception of programs for the hungry, these groups (many began during Lyndon Johnson's "War on Poverty") are losing out under Reagan.

The Politics of Revenue Sharing.   Because of the large federal deficit, it is unlikely that these structural changes in federal-state, state-local relationships, and in the role of nonprofit organizations will be easily reversed. As Reagan told the National Governor's Association in 1985, "There's simply no justification for the federal government, which is running a deficit, to be borrowing money to be spent by state and local governments, some of which are now running surpluses"* (*Time*, March 11, 1985). And there's the rub.

---

* Essentially, this statement is correct. In 1979 and 1980, the balance for the 50 states was a surplus of over $11 billion. In 1984 and 1985, it was over $6 billion and $5 billion. But, only 16 states had balances of more than 5 percent of general-fund spending in 1985. The other 34 states remained vulnerable to any downturn in the economy.

(Bob Englehart, *The Hartford Courant*)

Because they shared Reagan's concern about the federal deficit, the governors, 34 of whom were Democrats in 1985, did not object to the revenue cuts. But they can hardly be called idle spectators in the fight over revenue sharing. The governors know that if the cities continue to lose their federal revenue, mayors will turn to them in an effort to make up the differences. Many governors contend that their state surpluses are small relative to their budgets. To give more help to the cities, the governors say, they will have to raise taxes—hardly a politically attractive alternative. Democratic governors, in particular, complain that if Reagan will not take the unpopular steps of raising federal taxes and freezing Social Security benefits—as well as holding down military spending—it is unfair to expect the states to raise money once again.

Still, there is a deeper argument over revenue sharing than the matter of whether the president or the governors possess the most political courage. It centers on the old question of just which governmental functions should be national, and financed by all taxpayers, and which are primarily local and should be funded locally. It is unlikely that the question will be resolved any time soon.

A Model for the Intergovernmental System

Let us see if we can tie together a little better what has just been said about IGR. To construct a model of today's intergovernmental system, we must first isolate the elements. These are:

1. The three major levels of government: national, state, and local.

2. The governors, mayors, county executives, and other officeholders who are responsible for running state and local governments and who offer advice and press requests before the executive and legislative branches of government. This lobbying activity can be carried out either individually or collectively, through organizations like the National Governors Conference, the Council of State Governments, the U.S. Conference of Mayors, the National League of Cities, the National Association of Counties, the International City Managers Association, and the National Legislative Conference.

3. The thousands of professionals in government and nonprofit organizations who are responsible for administering these programs. Because these professionals are program specialists, we can categorize them by program area—education, energy, poverty, health, transportation, and so forth. Within each program

The intergovernmental lobby at work. In a 1985 appearance connected with the National Governors Association, Governor Cuomo of New York, with the help of a computer printout, testifies before Congress on crime. (From left: Governor James J. Blanchard of Michigan, Senator Alfonse M. D'Amato of New York and Governor Michael N. Castle of Delaware.) Governor Cuomo told the hearing, "We have a right to expect the Federal Government to protect us from foreign drugs the way it protects us from foreign missiles." At an earlier meeting, held at the White House, the executive committee of the National Governors Association criticized the Reagan administration for proposing cuts in such programs while refusing to curtail spending for the military and individual benefit programs like social security. (*New York Times*, February 26, 1985, p. 18. Photo Paul Hosefros/NYT Pictures)

Figure 3-4
Illustrative Operating Structure for a Federal Aid Program

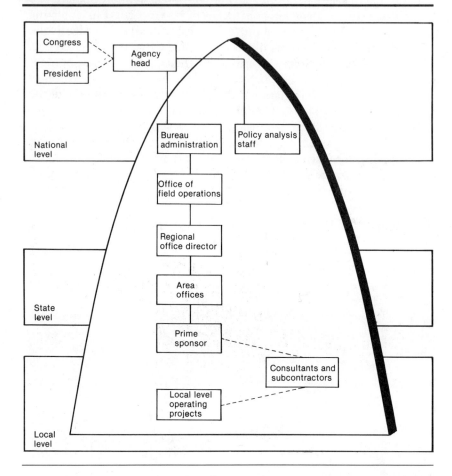

we can see a kind of bureaucratic or cone-like arrangement. Figure 3-4 provides a highly simplified picture of what an operating structure for a typical federal program might look like.

Figure 3-5 on page 92 suggests how these three elements—levels of government, executive officers, and professionals—fit together. The next section will show you how they work.

Intergovernmental Cooperation and Coordination

Federal→State

The great unasked question in this chapter is why the federal government, especially under President Johnson, became so heavily involved in areas traditionally left to the states. What were the driving forces? Answers are not hard to find, though assessing their relative importance is another matter.

First, there is the pressure brought to bear on Washington by sundry interest groups, the program specialists and professionals (Figure 3–4), and the intergovernmental lobby (Figure 3–5). Second are political considerations: presidential commitments made in the heat of an election campaign and congressional entrepreneurship (a phenomenon one cynic referred to as "spend, spend, elect, elect"). A third reason— one that had much more merit yesterday than it does today—is the inadequacy of state and local revenue sources.

Fourth is the regional nature of some problems. For example, cleanup of groundwater that has been polluted by pesticides, solvents, and other toxic chemicals seems a problem demanding federal-state cooperation. Groundwater, which is drinking water for almost half the population, does not respect state boundaries—the Ogalalla Aquinfer, for example, covers parts of seven High Plains states. Some states, Massachusetts, Connecticut, Florida, and Arizona among them, have begun to control their water supplies effectively on their own. But groundwater regulation in many states is rudimentary—critics would say a joke.

Finally, federal action has been predicated on the unwillingness of states to assist their localities. Politicians, administrators, journalists, and citizens hold widely divergent opinions of the states' willingness and ability to govern. The states have been labeled by some observers as the "dark continents," "fallen arches," or "old gray mares" of the federal system. Governors Bruce Babbitt of Arizona, a Democrat, and Richard A. Snelling of Vermont, a Republican, provide a quite different perspective. See box on pages 93–94.

State →Local

Dillon's Rule. All units of local government are public corporations created under the authority of state law to provide services that, presumably, could not adequately be provided by the private sector. *Dillon's rule,* which declares that local jurisdictions are the creatures of the state and may exercise only those powers expressly granted them by the state, has been a guiding doctrine for more than a century. But after creating local units, states tenaciously try to keep them under control.

Although some states have departments to coordinate state and local affairs, administrative relations between the city and the state are generally conducted on a functional basis. Thus, the state department of education supervises the activities of local school districts and the state department of health, the activities of local health departments.

State bureaucracies have several techniques of supervision. First, they can simply require reports from local communities. Reports warn the state agency when trouble spots (e.g., excessive debts) begin to appear. Second, state agencies can, as the federal government does for

Figure 3–5
A Model of the American Intergovernmental System

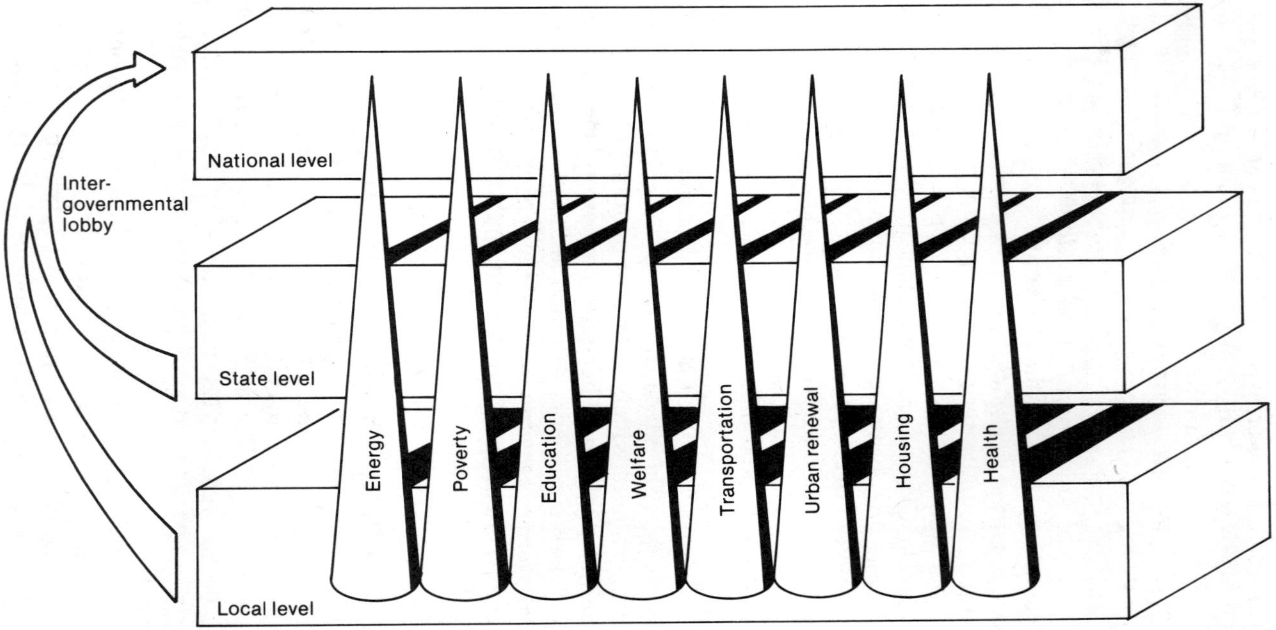

How Competent Are the State Governments?

A leading spokesman for the states and local governments is Governor Bruce Babbitt of Arizona. A former civil rights lawyer, he says he supports states' rights not because he believes less government is better but because, as an activist Harvard-educated governor, he sees the parent system as dysfunctional.

Babbitt stands the competency question on its head by asking whether a central government can effectively manage so many activities.

> Political philosophy aside, it is hard to see why a national Congress, responsible for governing a continental nation, should be involved in formulating programs for rat control, humanities grants for town hall debates on capital punishment, sculpture commissions for local art museums, educating displaced homemakers, training for use of the metric system, jellyfish control, bike paths, and police disability grants.
>
> It is long past time for Congress to dust off the *Federalist Papers,* reread the Constitution, and, occasionally, ask . . . , "Is this truly a national concern?" Congress ought to be worrying about arms control and defense instead of the potholes in the street. We might have both an increased chance of survival and better streets. (*New Republic,* January 24, 1981)

He does concede that supporting states' rights lacks respectability because it was for many years the rallying cry of those who supported racial segregation.

> The reason I think we are always rowing upstream is because of what happened in 1960. The concept of state sovereignty was identified with the denial of civil rights and racism. In the public mind there has been that connotation ever since. The popular image, when you start talking about the rules of the game, is that they are reactionary. That's historical fact. (*Houston Chronicle,* February 26, 1984)

Governor Bruce Babbitt of Arizona
(Jerry Jacka Photography)

Governor Richard A. Snelling of Vermont, who headed the National Governors Association, is a sharp critic of those who attack the competence and compassion of state and local governments. In a reply to one such critic, Snelling made the following points:

- State and local governments have changed tremendously since the 1960s, as any objective analysis would disclose. Reapportionment has cured our worst faults, and no patron of federal power can any longer claim automatic moral superiority for the Congress in terms of representing the people. Indeed, while blacks, for example, remain under-represented at all levels of government, they are a larger percentage of state legislators than of Congress, and in many cities they dominate important government offices.

  Similarly, a forthcoming study of the states authorized by Congress . . . concludes that the "structurally and procedurally stronger, more accountable, assertive states of today, performing a major intergovernmental management and financing role, bear little resemblance to the generally poorly organized and equipped and unresponsive entities of a quarter-century ago."

- While no one knows the exact number of state and local employees who are paid with federal funds to administer federal programs, the *National Journal* estimated, in a carefully researched article in 1979, that the number was 5 million. . . .

  Far from accelerating state and local government growth, President Reagan's initiatives offer the hope of trimming our bureaucracies. Most governors and mayors believe that with additional flexibility, they could transfer some employees from unproductive and needlessly complex federal paper work to direct provision of services or even, ultimately, to jobs in the private sector.

- From John Kennedy's modest beginnings, Congress developed a compulsion to solve every problem brought to its attention by creating a new federal program, and when it began to run out of resources in the 1970s, it stepped up its spending of state and local funds through the imposition of simplistic but costly mandates.

- Today state governments spend a larger share of their resources than does the federal government (even when defense is excluded) to meet the needs of the most unfortunate members of our society—the poor, the handicapped, the mentally ill and retarded, the socially maladjusted, and lawbreakers. Yet the states are criticized by those who do not have to carry these burdens to the same degree.

  The governors believe that we can no longer afford—either fiscally or politically—to have every level of government involved in the delivery of the entire range of public services. While the state and federal governments will continue to share responsibility for some major functions, we have offered to exchange a greater state role in such areas as education, law enforcement, and community and economic development for a greater federal role in income security programs, whose costs are tied so closely to the performance of the economy. (All quotes are excerpted from *The Wall Street Journal,* October 30, 1981. Reprinted by permission of *The Wall Street Journal.* © Dow Jones & Company, Inc. 1985. All rights reserved.)

them, furnish advice and information. Third, with larger budgets and more specialized equipment and personnel, the state can provide technical aid. Finally, if all else fails, the state can use its coercive power. For example, it can grant or withhold permits for certain things (e.g., to dump raw sewage into a stream under prescribed conditions); issue orders (e.g., to prescribe the standards for water supply purification); withhold grants-in-aid; require prior permission from a state agency; and appoint certain local officials or remove them.

Cities and the New Federalism. Most mayors seem to have accepted the reality of Reagan's new federalism, described earlier in this chapter. Thus, they are giving up their long and arduous effort to obtain more money from the federal government and are instead seeking to expand authority that would permit them to increase their own revenue and carry out their own initiatives as they see fit. This new drive for authority is being made chiefly before the state legislatures, which hold the constitutional power to decide the extent of local

Table 3-2
States with Most and Least Local Discretionary Authority

Rank	State	State's Strength as Fiscal Partner	
1 (most)	Oregon	State strong fiscal partner	
2	Maine	State strong fiscal partner	
3	North Carolina	State dominant fiscal partner	
4	Connecticut	State strong fiscal partner	
47	South Dakota	State junior fiscal partner	
48	New Mexico	State dominant fiscal partner	
49	West Virginia	State dominant fiscal partner	
50 (least)	Idaho	State strong fiscal partner	

* Index was computed by assigning weights to each of four types of authority: financial, functions, personnel, and structure.

Source: Advisory Commission on Intergovernmental Relations, *Measuring Local Discretionary Authority* (Washington, D.C.: Government Printing Office, 1981).

autonomy (see Table 3–2). Cities are struggling to exert their own authority in a variety of ways.

- Columbus, Ohio, is one city seeking greater flexibility in providing services. Columbus and surrounding Franklin County have already combined their court systems and their jails, saving money for both governments.
- Chicago has been involved in a political tug-of-war with the state and suburban governments over the control of mass transit and other services performed by a variety of agencies, many of them set up outside the city.

- Seattle has been fighting the Washington legislature on a law that prohibited it from levying a hotel and motel tax. Boston has been opposing the requirement that its bond issues for capital improvements be approved by the Massachusetts legislature.
- In New Jersey, the cities are seeking to change state laws so that they may spend more. In California, where local governments were stripped of much of their authority to raise property taxes by the enactment of Proposition 13 in 1978, the cities are seeking authority to assess or to increase other kinds of taxes (examples from *Houston Chronicle,* February 26, 1984).

Local officials have also joined with the states to persuade the federal courts to restore some of the powers lost to Washington through 50 years of centralization. And well they might. Taking the rare step of overruling one of its own recent precedents, the Supreme Court, on February 18, 1985, significantly enhanced the power of the federal government to regulate state activities that had been considered immune from federal courts. The Court ruled, five to four, that federal minimum wage and hour standards cover employees of publicly owned mass transit systems. As important as this decision is for state and local employees, the Court went even further: it seriously eroded the theoretical underpinnings of what has been known as the new federalism—namely, the belief that the Constitution gives the states special protections and sets affirmative limits on the federal government's power to interfere in their affairs.

Counties and Special Districts.   Cities are not, of course, the only significant actors at the local level. The populations of the once-powerful cities have spilled over municipal boundaries into the counties. County officials administer a range of federal and state programs, and in many metropolitan areas the county executive spends more money and serves far more people than the mayor of the central city.

County officials are more influential with state governments than their counterparts in the cities. They also tend to be more conservative and have better access to the Reagan White House.

In addition to cities and counties are the new special entities that have been created to provide such services as transportation, parks, libraries, hospitals, fire protection, and others that were previously handled by general governments. From 1977 to 1982, the Census Bureau reported, the number of such special purpose districts increased by 2,626—to 28,588. Cities have increasingly set up such districts to serve as separate entities with substantial fiscal independence because they are no longer able to provide these services through general taxes. This has happened even though the authority of the city governments was diminished in the process.

Enterprise Zones.   According to several studies, most cities are still struggling to provide basic services and make their communities liv-

In the 1960s, Jane Jacobs, a commentator on the economic development of cities, wrote: "The overwhelming fact about cities is that if they do not maintain self-generating economies, they will ultimately stagnate and decline. . . . Cities, individually, must generate their own economic bases, and cities, taken collectively, must generate the innovations that make developing economies possible." A decade later two congressmen—conservative Republican, Jack Kemp, and liberal Democrat, Robert Garcia (above)—introduced a bill that would use tax credits to corporations to reduce urban decay. Garcia represents New York City's impoverished South Bronx. (*Newsweek*—Robert R. McElroy. Copyright 1981 by Newsweek, Inc. All rights by permission.)

able. Yet it is on the municipal level that change has been most pronounced in recent years.

One new way of saving central cities was the creation of *enterprise zones*. The concept is fairly straightforward: remove most zoning, taxation, and federal and local business regulations from carefully defined central-city districts. Presumably, these actions encourage new industrial and commercial development, including jobs, in those same areas.

Diverse political and economic groups seemed to show a strong interest in the concept. The reason is that, given tight pressures on the federal budget, the zoning-taxation approach offers a practical, low-cost method of attempting to lure business back into central-city areas. Not surprisingly, Reagan made enterprise zones one of the cornerstones of his urban political agenda. But support for the special zones goes beyond only the Republican party. In fact, a version of the concept in the House of Representatives is cosponsored by conservative Upstate New York Republican Jack Kemp and liberal Democrat Robert Garcia, whose district encompasses the South Bronx, one of the most blighted urban areas in the United States.

State⟷State

The Founding Fathers attempted to provide mechanisms to facilitate cooperation between the states. For instance, Article 1, Section 10 of the Constitution permits states to enter into *compacts* or agreements (with the consent of Congress). The Crime Compact of 1934, which allows parole officers to cooperate across state lines with a minimum of red tape, is now subscribed to by all states. States lacking adequate facilities make compacts with other states to help them with professional education, welfare, tuberculosis, and mental illness.

As state officials have come to realize that problems, such as transportation, energy, pollution, water resources, and fishing, burst across state boundaries, the number of compacts has risen accordingly. Whereas there were only 24 compacts before the turn of the century, today over 170 are in existence.

One of the most notable and largest interstate agencies established by an interstate compact was the Port of New York Authority. Established in 1921 by New York and New Jersey, the authority constricts and operates bridges, tunnels, terminal facilities, and airports.

The Founding Fathers did not foresee the variety of conflicts that would arise between the states. We cannot hope to categorize all the conflicting forces here, but a few can be briefly noted. The growth of Spanish-speaking populations in several southwestern states has lead some political analysts to expect a situation in the 1990s similar to that which Canada experienced in the 1970s and 1980s with its French-speaking citizens. Around 1990, the majority of California will be Hispanic. Will it become an American Quebec?

More in the present, energy-producing states want more control over their resources and resent the fact that an oil refinery has not been built on the East Coast since 1957. Will they become "energy colonies" to the industrial Northeast? And New England does not appreciate its little gift from Ohio—acid rain.

Another source of conflict involves how the federal pie is divided. The Northeast-Midwest Congressional Coalition released an elaborate report on the last decade's shift of wealth and population from North to South. Felix Rohatyn, New York City's financial wizard, claims that this flow threatens the social and economic stability of the United States.

As these few examples should suggest, what the mass media used to simplify as a Sunbelt-Frostbelt fight is a much more complicated regional pattern. Moreover, the rhetoric about the Sunbelt-Frostbelt fight has been superseded by new economic realities. The New England portion of the supposedly stagnant North has embarked on an impressive boom. The southeastern portion of the supposedly flourishing Sunbelt has run into economic trouble.

Local⟷Local

Given the interrelationship of society due to modern transportation and communication technology, and given the great number of local governments, it is no surprise to learn that local administrators are meeting with increasing frequency. This subsection examines two ways in which these administrators can work out their problems together: *cooperative arrangements* and *regional councils*.

One of the oldest forms of interlocal cooperation is an agreement between two or more adjacent units. A 1972 national survey of nearly 6,000 incorporated municipalities revealed that, of the 2,248 responding, 61 percent had entered into formal or informal agreements for the provision of services to their citizens by other government units or private firms. As population increases, local governmental units—especially the smaller ones—will surely tend to turn over the administration of some of their programs (e.g., water supply) to other local units on a contractual basis.

The basis of informal arrangements, unlike contracts, consists of personal relations among operating officials. Just as the Council of State Governments helps bring state officials together, state associations of municipal officers facilitate cooperation on common problems.

Efforts to merge the government of the central city with surrounding governments—and thereby put government on a more rational administrative basis—have a long, intricate, often checkered history. These efforts seldom end in success. Yet the need for a more regional basis of administration remains.

As a partial solution to the fragmented character of metropolitan areas, the early 1970s witnessed the rapid growth of regional councils. These councils include councils of government, regional planning commissions, and economic development districts. The membership directory of the National Association of Regional Councils lists more than 600 such councils.

Much of the pressure for the creation of this fourth layer of government, as some refer to it, comes in part from federal legislation that recognizes that in metropolitan areas everything connects with everything else, that an action in one community affects another community. Consequently, applications for federal grants and loans must be first reviewed by some *areawide* agency.

As you will recall, in 1969, the Office of Management and Budget published its *Circular A-95*, which encouraged intergovernmental planning for a wide variety of federal programs. Today, regional councils serve as clearinghouses for the review of proposed projects within their region. Among the possible improvement projects that a council might first review and then comment upon are airports, water supply and distribution systems, sewage and waste treatment plants, highway and transportation facilities, labor force programs, education systems, and criminal justice systems. For prospective applicants, councils generally maintain catalogs of federal and state assistance programs and help applicants fold their local plans into regionwide planning.

By the early 1980s, numerous cities were losing political power and autonomy to rising county governments dominated by suburbanites. While signs of this trend were evident throughout the United States, the cities of the industrial Middle West (such as Cleveland, Detroit, and Louisville) led the way in giving up to the counties their control over city functions—sewers, jails, mass transit, and so forth.

An explanation for this trend is not hard to find. The federal system has failed to establish metropolitan government to deal with large concentrations of people; and cities, for the most part, have been unable to expand. Thus, counties, with their healthy tax base (which includes all of the suburbs), have gained power by default.

Administrative Implications of IGR

It takes no long-run patience or spinning of fine webs to capture and assess the consequences of the complex relationships described in this chapter for administration. In this closing section, therefore, we shall do no more than highlight a few of them.

Behavioral Patterns

The Problem Defined. Intergovernmental relations pose distinctive challenges for the public administrator. One reason these new behavior patterns are difficult to learn is that they simply have not been anticipated. As we observed in Chapter 1, much of management education is concerned with planning programs, analyzing problems, and motivating employees. Therefore, it is hardly surprising that inexperienced managers often view time spent coordinating with other organizations as evidence that they are not doing their real job, that they are spinning their wheels. (Recall Problem 6 in Chapter 1.)

Another factor that makes interacting with outsiders more complex, less automatic, and more difficult is the absence of interpersonal understanding and shared values that members of the same organization are likely to have, especially when they have worked together for a long period of time. Such people

> learn to adopt comfortable routines of easy give-and-take to exchange ideas and help. The comfortable perfection of this reaches its zenith in the hospital operating room or on the athletic playing field. Hardly a full sentence is spoken to obtain coordination; just a glance, a muttered word, or wink communicates all the other persons need to know to adjust their behavior to yours. It is only when people are irregular in their contacts that they must explain and expound in lengthy and often discomforting detail. (Sayles, 1979: 76–77)

When something has not been anticipated and requires approval and consensus, interrelationships mushroom. These relationships multiply quickly because most do not lend themselves to yes or no answers. Assume, for example, that administrator A in one jurisdiction wants something from administrator B in another: an approval, a change in schedule, or some aid. Rather than giving a simple yes or no answer, B is likely to say "Well, that depends," or "I'll have to run that by C."

While the nature of most relationships between administrator and subordinate is relatively clear-cut, the nature of relationships in the intergovernmental system is usually ambiguous. For example, confronted with a wildcat strike by the tugboat union, Mayor Edward I. Koch of New York turned to the coast guard for help in pulling garbage scows; it seemed like the reasonable thing to do.

> I knew the Admiral—Vice Admiral Robert I. Price, a big, craggy-looking guy. I recalled welcoming him to New York when he received his appointment. As I am thinking about the way he looks, I am thinking, he's a real tough guy. This assignment won't be too big for him. He's probably over there on Governors Island just waiting for the phone to ring.
>
> But nothing could have been further from the mark. My people called him and, as they told it to me, he became very vague and made statements to them about strikebreaking. . . . He actually said the coast guard wasn't going to help us. I was amazed by that. Really amazed. (Koch, 1985: 124–25)

Koch's next step was to phone Jack Watson, President Carter's special assistant for intergovernmental relations. Watson asked for a little time: 24 hours. (Remember: One seldom gets a quick yes or no in these kind of relationships.) Sometime later, Watson called Koch back to suggest that he now give the admiral a call. Koch and Price speak at around midnight. It is clear to Koch, from the tone of the voice at the other end of the telephone, that Price is still opposed to helping him. (The following dialogue is based on Koch, 1985:126.)

Koch: Admiral, that is not a request. It is an order. You are going to carry it out, aren't you? That is an order from the White House.

Price: Oh yes, we will be carrying it out. But what I was really calling about is how we can work this out. We will need police protection.

Koch: Admiral, I don't believe you need police protection, but if you tell me you do we will provide you with it. But what we need is help pulling the garbage scows. And my hope is that you are going to be cooperative. And I want to tell you further, Admiral, I don't think you were very helpful in this situation when you said that you would not engage in scabbing or union busting. What do you think your function is if not to serve the people of this city or country in time of emergency? You think it was scabbing when the state of New York called in the national guard to run the prisons when the prison guards' union struck? And, as it happens, you are not even involved in a situation where the union objects to your presence. What is going on here? And even if it did object, wouldn't it be your function to carry out your orders?

How to Manage External Relationships. Administrators want to know when and how to manage their numerous external contacts. Do they call the White House as Koch did, or do they try to work around the problem? Whom exactly do they want to see once thay have decided to start "touching bases," as Ruckelshaus did in Case 1.1?

Explicit guidance in this area is difficult. The ideas about negotiation and persuasion, presented at the end of the last chapter, are certainly relevant. In fact, I would only add one point to that discussion.

Administrators should recognize the true nature of an overture to them from some external source. Some communications are mandated; these should cause relatively little difficulty. Other intergovernmental negotiations are aimed at reducing uncertainty: for example, the federal Social Security Administration seeks an agreement from state administrators of the Disability Insurance Benefit program that claimants have an attending physician's medical report confirming their disability. A third type of overture is a power play, that is, efforts on the part of A to gain more influence over B merely for the sake of expanding his or her power base. Administrators should be careful not to mistake an effort to reduce uncertainty for a power play.

Innovation

Unlike a unitary system, the American intergovernmental system outlined in this chapter probably provides a higher capacity for experimentation and innovation in policy as well as administration. Much of the domestic policy enacted by Congress reflects the pioneering legislative experience of particular states. For example, Montana's Reclamation Act of 1972 served as the model for the Federal Surface Mine and Reclamation Act of 1977. Similarly, the larger cities and counties of a state can be important innovators of policies later applied statewide. As John Naisbitt (1984:111-14) points out in his best-seller *Megatrends*, the states are no longer waiting for federal leadership— they are initiating local solutions to national problems.

> In addition, the states have upgraded tax systems and modernized legislatures as well as the executive branch (partly the result of federal legislation and federal court decisions). Better qualified, more public-spirited representatives are being elected to state office. This new breed of state officials, in turn, are surrounding themselves with more professional legislative staffs.

Even more impressive to Naisbitt is the fact that the states are "reviving their traditional function as the laboratories of democracy, experimenting with society's most intractable problems." For example:

- Alaska, Nevada, Texas, and Arizona have neutralized the FDA's federal authority by legalizing the controversial drug Laetrile.

- Six Minnesota counties joined together to manage a 200-mile stretch of land along the Mississippi River in order to keep the federal government from declaring it a federally managed wildlife and scenic river.
- Seven states levied additional gasoline taxes in mid-1980, after Congress rejected former President Carter's proposal of a 10-cent-per-gallon fee on oil imports.
- Georgia, Alabama, Kentucky, Virginia, Indiana, New York, and Pennsylvania thought the Justice Department was moving too slowly in an investigation of organized crime, so the states joined together to investigate loansharking, bribery, extortion, and kickbacks in the coal industry.
- Ten eastern states sought a Law Enforcement Assistance Administration grant to share information and chase illegal dumpers of hazardous waste across state lines.
- Ohio, Michigan, Illinois, Indiana, Kentucky, Pennsylvania, and West Virginia are considering building a 150-mile-per-hour train. The plan is significant not only for its pioneering new technology, but also because it raises the question of whether interstate transportation is an exclusively federal concern.
- While Congress has yet to act on the Garcia-Kemp enterprise zone legislation (see pp. 96–98), 21 states have now enacted such legislation.

Diversity

To say that the United States is a large and diverse nation surely must be one of the hoariest platitudes around. Yet federal administrators cannot ignore it. When a federal agency suggests legislation it must be sensitive to the regional biases in Congress. Assuming passage, the agency then must be sensitive to the different claimants within state boundaries when administering the policy.

Daniel Elazar (1972:106–7) captured some of this diversity by mapping the United States in terms of three political cultures. He identified three pure types: moralistic, individualistic, and traditionalistic. *Moralistic* political culture views government as a positive instrument with which the general welfare is secured and in which politics is seen as righteous activity. The *individualistic* culture stresses limitations on government and the centrality of private concerns. It views governmental bureaucracy as a fetter on private affairs, but also as a resource that public officials can use to further their own goals. *Traditionalistic* culture desires that government maintain existing relationships, and that politics be the caretaker of established interests. It opposes all governmental activities except those necessary to maintain the existing power structure.

While every state is more or less a mixture of these three political cultures, Elazar finds the following three states exhibiting a particular culture to a considerable degree: Wisconsin—moralistic; Wyoming—individualistic; Mississippi—traditionalistic.

I strongly suspect that regional, local, ethnic, social, and religious groups are making the United States less uniform. The needs and conditions of one part of the country are not those of another. Public administrators in the federal government might benefit from following a policy business managers call market segmentation, instead of trying to treat the nation as a more or less homogeneous whole. See Chapter 4 for more about market segmentation.

Uniform economic and social policies stamped out in Washington like so many license plates can sometimes produce a gross misallocation of resources. When it comes to helping cities, the national government is afflicted by what might be called the "pork paradox" and "printout politics."

The pork paradox refers to the fact that targeting a meaningful amount of money on some parts of the country requires obtaining congressional support from others. That is, one must engage in "pork-barrel politics." But to obtain that wider support requires spreading the money so broadly that the original purpose is in jeopardy—hence, the paradox. The Model Cities program of the 1960s was a case in point. It began as a demonstration of the effect of very large amounts of money and talent on poverty and decay in three big sick cities. But eventually it was directed to 36 cities, then 63, and ultimately 150. A lot of money targeted on a few places was turned into a little money for a lot of places.

The case of Winter Park, Florida, illuminates another problem in the distribution of funds, "printout politics." When this affluent community applied for a $900,000 federal grant, it got $2.65 million. The unexpected windfall amounted to more than $100 for every man, woman, and child in this city of 23,000, or more than one half the city's annual budget of about $5 million. It also carried a condition that the money had to be spent within 28 days. But the grant, "a planning target for spending" in Economic Development Administration jargon, resulted from a very logical computer formula. The size of someone's request on an application has nothing to do with the money that is appropriated. The money is allocated according to a formula. (In this case, the formula was based on a comparison between 1970 and 1976 unemployment and labor force figures.)

Grantsmanship, Strings, and Priorities

If the federal administrator must seek accommodations with the various interests at the state and local level, then the reverse is equally true. Consider, for example, the proliferation of federal grants, which gives rise to the grantsmanship perspective.

Buried in hundreds of spots all over Washington are piles of money—federal grants that cities can use to buy buses, to repair streets, or to establish health clinics. To obtain it, writes Shafer (1976), a "locality must learn where the money is and then figure out how to qualify for it. None of that is easy, for the federal aid system has grown into an overlapping and confusing maze of more than 1,000 grant, loan programs, and subsidy arrangements." "Many state and local officials don't learn about the assistance available or learn of it too late to apply," according to a report by the General Accounting Office. Shafer reports that about 20 states and more than 50 cities have Washington representatives.

Often these federal funds are dispensed on very attractive matching terms. Economically and politically, it is hard for a mayor to say no to an $8 million federal grant, when the city needs to supply only $2 million. Unfortunately, the $2 million out of the city's treasury might not go to a real priority. Furthermore, the annual federal grant cycle, and delays in processing applications, interjects a high degree of uncertainty into state and local planning efforts.

But, even assuming the project is for a priority item, it comes to the mayor with strings attached. Among the bewildering array of requirements applied to most federal aid programs are these: equal employment opportunities for women and minorities, rights for the handicapped, civil service merit rules, citizen participation, historic preservation and environmental impact statements. Neal R. Peirce (1980) writes: "It's almost impossible to argue against the right or protection sought in each case—all seem desirable, some essential. But the cumulative mass so impedes grants that the whole process is often slowed to a snail's pace."

Thus, in order to get federal funds for a new library, university presidents must struggle with lengthy applications. For example, Washington might want to know how the proposed project "may affect energy sources by introducing or deleting electromagnetic wave sources which may alter manmade or natural structures or the physiology, behavior patterns, and/or activities of 10 percent of a human, animal, or plant population." The questions go on and on, but you get the idea.

Organization

Jurisdictional fragmentation obstructs delivery of services. A private organization has few restrictions on the organization of its operations other than the logic of profit or survival. Not so in the public sector.

A *Standard Metropolitan Statistical Area* (SMSA) is defined as an integrated economic and social unit with a large population nucleus. Generally consisting of a central city with a population of at least 50,000, and the metropolitan area around it, it may include two or more central cities in one area, although generally within one state. In any case, "an integrated economic and social unit" does seem to imply a certain commonality of interest between the central city and the suburbs around it. In short, the SMSA provides a logical basis for administration.

In reality, however, the SMSAs are incredibly fragmental. In 1971, 243 SMSAs harbored some 20,000 units of government. (In 1980, the census bureau reported 284 SMSAs.) To bring the problem into sharper focus, the Chicago metropolitan area may be taken as an example. As of the early 1970s, it was composed of 6 counties, 114 townships, 250 municipalities, 327 school districts, and 501 special purpose districts. For this metropolitan area, there were 1,198 separate units of government. This represented one local government for every three square miles, or one for every 5,550 inhabitants. Not surprisingly, some of these governments have quite limited functions, such as mosquito abatement or street lighting.

The Houston SMSA might be given as a second example. There, eight governmental agencies try to enforce protection programs for the environment. The eight agencies are involved only in monitoring, regulating, and carrying out pollution abatement programs.* But a swarm of additional agencies has an interest and some authority in environmental programs. Among these we might include the U.S. Corps of Engineers, the U.S. Coast Guard, the attorney general's office, the department of health, the Parks and Wildlife Department, the General Land Office, the agricultural departments of the state, various river authorities, the Harris County district attorney and county attorney, and planning agencies such as the Houston Galveston Area Council and the Houston City Planning Division.

Administratively, this overlap and fragmentation is expensive, confusing, and inefficient. But more macabre examples are available—firemen watching houses burn just outside their jurisdiction and police from one town arresting the plainclothes detectives of another. We need not go on.

In sum, the complexity of intergovernmental relations, like the forces of politics, makes the task of managing the public sector a little more arduous. And, despite major innovations such as the new federalism, I suspect that this will remain true.

Nailing Down the Main Points

1. *Intergovernmental relations* is a more satisfactory term than federalism to describe the complete governmental structure in the United States. Federalism places too much emphasis on separation of federal, state, and

---

* Houston's eight environmental control agencies are the Environmental Protection Agency, Texas Water Control Board, Texas Air Control Board, Gulf Coast Waste Disposal Authority, Harris County Pollution Control Department, Air Pollution Division, the Water Pollution Control Division of the City Health Department, and the Waste Water Treatment Division of the City Public Works Department.

local government and not enough on the intermediate levels of government.

2. The relationship of states to the federal government is the cardinal question of our constitutional system. As Wilson pointed out, every successive stage in the political development of the United States gives IGR a new aspect. The period to 1932 may be termed of the era of dual federalism; 1933–60, the era of creative federalism; 1961–68, Nixon's New Federalism; and 1981 to the present, Reagan's New Federalism.

3. Federal grants to states take many forms. Many programs since 1960 establish project grants, rather than distribute funds to states automatically according to a set formula. This approach, most popular during creative federalism (1960–1968), leads to a management mess as the number of grants begins to increase. To alleviate some of this management mess, the federal government began to distribute a portion of the income tax to the states each year with little restriction on how it might be spent. This approach was called revenue sharing, and it was a key element of Nixon's new federalism.

4. Reagan's new federalism gave more responsibility back to the states and began to reduce revenue sharing.

5. The key elements in a model of the IGR system are the three major levels of government, state and local executives and their lobbying organizations, and the thousands of professionals that work in various program "cones."

6. Given the thousands of jurisdictions in the United States, the number of possible and actual intergovernmental relationships is staggering. States and communities constantly vie for grants. States form compacts among themselves, and tenaciously try to keep their cities under control. And cities try to work out their mutual problems through a myriad of cooperative arrangements and some 600 regional councils.

7. These complex relations, not surprisingly, affect the job of the public administrator. The relationships in the cone, for example, lead to smoother relations among like-minded professionals *within* the cone, but often result in conflict between these professional program administrators and the elected policymakers on the outside. The variety of governments in the United States leads to increased opportunity for experimentation and hence cross-fertilization. But the variety of political cultures and the jurisdictional fragmentation within the United States can lead, especially at the national level, to greater complexity in program design and administration. Meanwhile, at the local level, administrators find that accepting federal grants can mean more red tape.

Concepts for Review

block grant	Dillon's rule
Circular A-95	dual federalism
cooperative arrangements	Federal Regional Council
cooperative federalism	federal regions
councils of government	federalism
creative federalism	free enterprise zones

general revenue and special revenue-
sharing grant
grants-in-aid, categorical, and project
grant
intergovernmental lobby
intergovernmental relations
interstate compacts

layer cake and marble cake, models
new federalism
political cultures
program cones
regional councils
Standard Metropolitan Statistical
Area

Problems

1. Alvin Toffler (1980:414) writes:

A political system must not only be able to make and enforce decisions; it must operate on the right scale, it must be able too integrate disparate policies, it must be able to make decisions at the right speed, and it must both reflect and respond to the diversity of society. If it fails on any of these points it courts disaster. Our problems are no longer a matter of "left-wing" or "right-wing," "strong leadership" or "weak." The decision system itself has become a menace.

The truly astonishing fact today is that our governments continue to function at all. No corporation president would try to run a large company with a table of organization first sketched by the quill pen of some eighteenth-century ancestor whose sole managerial experience consisted of running a farm. No sane pilot would attempt to fly a supersonic jet with the antique navigation and control instruments available to Blériot or Lindbergh. Yet this is approximately what we are trying to do politically.

Do you think Toffler overstates the problem? What do you think the optimum size of a city would be? What do you think are the most important factors determining the quality of urban life? (Hint: The Advisory Commission on Intergovernmental Relations suggests four criteria that should provide the basic guidelines in reassigning functions to governmental units: economic efficiency, equality, political accountability, and administrative effectiveness.)

2. By 1985, three states (New York, New Jersey, and Illinois) had already adopted mandatory seat belt laws. Thirty other states were considering such measures. This sudden surge of legislative activity was not entirely spontaneous in the several capitols. It was the direct consequence of a federal regulation handed down by the secretary of transportation in July 1984. This is how it works: Commencing in September 1989, all cars sold in the United States must be equipped either with air bags or with automatic seat belts—unless states that together contain two thirds of the U.S. population enact mandatory seat belt laws by April 1, 1989. If enough states fall in line, the air-bag requirement will be nullified. Does the regulation amount to a form of blackmail?

3. Some observers think that the policies coordinated by *Circular A–95* have established the potential for evolving a new level of government. Why do you think they think that? Assuming they are correct, do you view this new level as a good or bad thing? Why?

4. Write an essay on whether revenue sharing should be continued.

5. Actually, the areas of federal control are relatively few, compared to those of states and their subdivisions. List those areas in which you think federal policy control is essential. (For example, some would argue that state and local radio stations could not operate effectively unless they were coordinated with commercial stations.)

6. Some of the major social and economic innovations in the United States have begun with small-scale experiments on the state level. Wyoming, for example, permitted women's suffrage 50 years before the 19th Amendment. Can you think of others? What current state experiments might one day be taken up by the federal government?

7. President Reagan's budget for fiscal year 1986 would authorize $2.4 billion in grants to localities to build local sewerage systems. It also contains $161 million for grants from and administration of the National Endowment for the Arts. The grants go to local symphonies, opera companies, choral groups, and troupes of players. Is building local sewer lines a federal responsibility? Is a performance of La Bohême in Bartlesville, Oklahoma, a federal responsibility? Justify your answer.

8. How do you think business executives view centralizing power in Washington rather than decentralizing it via the 50 states?

Case 3.1
Washington State Develops a Cutback Strategy

Alan Gibbs and the Department of Social and Health Services (DSHS)

In February 1981, while Congress debated President Reagan's proposal to restructure grant-in-aid programs for state and local government, Dr. John Beare sat in Alan Gibbs's new office in a white sandstone building in Olympia, Washington. Gibbs, secretary of social and health services, had asked his director of the Health Services Division to see him about the tight fiscal situation they faced.

In a nutshell, this was the problem confronting Gibbs's huge department. The state's economic recession had caused the Aid to Families with Dependent Children (AFDC) program for unemployed parents and medicaid caseloads to rise sharply. If President Reagan's proposal were adopted, Washington State might lose about $110 million in federal aid over the 1981 to 1983 budget period. About 45 percent of the department's funds came from the federal government. (This flow, along with the other major relationship discussed in this case, can be seen in Exhibit 1.)

Gibbs, as an experienced public administrator, knew several things about a situation like this one.

Point One: Budgets tend to get cut at the last minute in an arbitrary manner (e.g., "The governor's office just called and said *all* programs must be slashed by 17 percent").

Point Two: It is better to establish priorities *and then* switch state money around to make up for federal reductions in high priority areas.

Point Three: Because an analytical approach must begin immediately, various interest groups have time to mobilize and defend any cuts in their areas.

Point Four: Only if the people involved—both inside and outside your department—are kept informed of what you are doing can you ever hope to convince them that you are making fair and sensible cuts.

Exhibit 1
Chart of IGR and in Washington State's Welfare Program

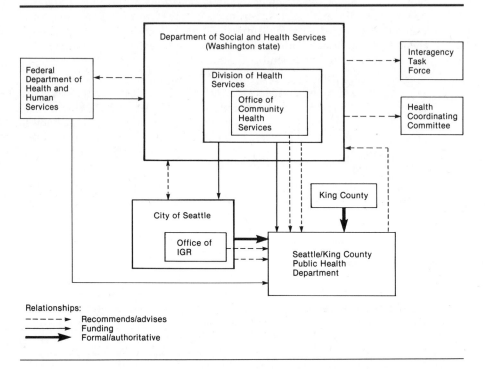

Relationships:
- ----- ► Recommends/advises
- ――――► Funding
- ━━━━► Formal/authoritative

Beare and other staff members agreed with Gibbs's analysis, and they immediately went to work developing a cutback plan. After two months of hard work, Gibbs felt they were ready to go public. The following were some of the actions he took:

- Distributed a memo to state and local officials and interested citizens explaining the need for careful planning of cutbacks and consulted personally with important constituencies like the statewide Health Coordinating Committee.
- Established an interagency task force to keep other governmental bodies in the state informed (and so he could get early warning of possible political opposition).
- Made himself accessible to people who wanted to express their views on the budget and consulted personally with all program managers.

Charles Royer and the City of Seattle

Charles Royer, the mayor of Washington's largest city, had two concerns during this period. First, Royer was concerned that a program that had taken a generation to create might suddenly vanish and that continued uncertainty could "sabotage the machinery of government at every level." He was also concerned "that those few resources which are made available to the states be used fairly to meet the needs of urban populations. Our country simply cannot afford to have so many of its people without jobs and without hope."

Second, Royer was wary of what DSHS might do to Seattle. For several years, the Office of Community Health Services had felt that Seattle was receiving too large a share of federal maternal and child health funds (Seattle had 12 percent of the state's population but received 46 percent of the state's share of these funds). Royer suspected that Dr. Robert Leahy, director of the office, was more than a little attracted to Reagan's promise of "flexibility" in the administration of block grants.

With these two concerns in mind, Mayor Royer turned to William Stafford, head of the city's Office of Intergovernmental Relations. Their aim was simple: to keep influential members of Congress informed on Royer's views about the Reagan budget and block grants and to continue to lobby through the National League of Cities and the U.S. Conference of Mayors.

Royer and Stafford also sought help from Jill Marsden, director of the Seattle/King County Public Health Department. This organization, administered jointly by the city and the county, received most of its funds from DSHS. Therefore, Marsden had a keen interest in the "priorities" Gibbs and his staff might establish. Meanwhile, she and her staff had their own analysis of priorities and possible cuts.

On June 1, Royer, Stafford, and Marsden got some bad news. DSHS was thinking about cutting maternal and child health programs in the county by 31 percent while reducing programs in other jurisdictions by about 25 percent. About one month later, Marsden was asked to comment on a document received from John Beare's DSHS Division of Health Services. By sending this document, Beare had gotten ahead of Gibbs's timetable; Gibbs had wanted to first obtain agreement on general principles.

The document divided up 69 programs into the following four categories of need:

- Essential—(e.g., immunization).
- High—(e.g., crippled children services).
- Medium—(e.g., water supply operations).
- Eliminate—(e.g., swimming pools).

In setting these priorities, the division used five criteria: (1) community protection, (2) long-term consequences, (3) benefits to clients, (4) appropriateness of division intervention, and (5) effectiveness. Unfortunately, there was no elaboration of what the criteria meant or how the rankings were arrived at.

Marsden, in consternation, wrote Secretary Gibbs, pointing out that a high proportion of the county's population consisted of socially and economically disadvantaged people who "depend on the public sector for health care." (Howitt, 1984:54) She demanded a detailed explanation of the grounds on which the Division of Health Services was planning to make its cuts. A few weeks later, Mayor Royer would also complain to Gibbs about the state's objective to provide minimum levels of service. Although this *seems* rational, he argued, it is "patently inequitable" because it siphons off money from major cities to jurisdictions that make no real effort to support the needy. (Ibid:64)

Later in July, Gibbs issued a DSHS "program perspective," which outlined in general form the department's program objectives, and solicited public comments on it. Surprisingly, controversy was minimal. Gibbs also requested that each manager in his department establish his or her own priorities. (This process is similar to zero-based budgeting; see Chapter 9.)

By early September, the time had come for Gibbs and his senior staff to decide where the budget would be cut.

Epilogue

After the Reagan administration pushed through deep cuts in federal domestic programs for 1982, many states reacted by making cuts of their own. Some states increased spending for some programs to offset the administration reductions, but overall the restorations were "low." In most cases, money was replaced in single-purpose programs like child health care rather than with general assistance programs.

Only three states—Missouri, Ohio, and Texas—joined Washington in making no effort to replace federal cuts. And even at that, the state still had a substantial average payment per person in the country's largest cash welfare program, AFDC (see Exhibit 2).

Exhibit 2
Aid to Families with Dependent Children, 1983

State	Average Payment per Person	State	Average Payment per Person
Alabama	$ 39.45	Nebraska	110.54
Alaska	227.04	Nevada	69.82
Arizona	77.22	New Hampshire	104.19
Arkansas	45.04	New Jersey	104.49
California	157.54	New Mexico	75.06
Colorado	96.85	New York	132.88
Connecticut	141.57	North Carolina	73.16
Delaware	85.63	North Dakota	113.25
District of Columbia	107.00	Ohio	85.75
Florida	70.97	Oklahoma	88.87
Georgia	65.75	Oregon	113.24
Hawaii	131.87	Pennsylvania	105.54
Idaho	94.28	Rhode Island	124.67
Illinois	93.48	South Carolina	47.12
Indiana	73.79	South Dakota	87.45
Iowa	116.82	Tennessee	44.33
Kansas	105.05	Texas	42.41
Kentucky	69.26	Utah	118.08
Louisiana	55.41	Vermont	142.12
Maine	107.95	Virginia	87.33
Maryland	97.26	Washington	150.47
Massachusetts	135.31	West Virginia	59.41
Michigan	125.52	Wisconsin	148.63
Minnesota	154.89	Wyoming	121.34
Mississippi	31.20	Guam	65.07
Missouri	85.95	Puerto Rico	29.07
Montana	110.09	Virgin Islands	66.60

Source: U.S. Social Security Administration, *Social Security Bulletin*, monthly.

The cuts had a sizable impact on larger cities like Seattle. The cities found themselves obligated to provide shelter and social services for those taken off the welfare rolls at a time when their own treasuries were depleted by the recession.

The range of federal programs before 1982 had brought a degree of uniformity to regions, states, and communities, and the federal government had provided a minimum level of assistance, or "floor," for citizens everywhere. Although the Reagan cuts and policies that took effect in 1982 were limited, they made social services more diverse. Differences between states such as Washington and Texas, between cities within regions, and between cities and suburbs as a result of the Reagan initiatives were widened.

Case Questions

1. Based on this case, what generalizations can you make about administration in an environment of IGR?
2. What do you think of Gibbs's strategy? Why do you think he emphasized public participation?
3. How reasonable were the objections of Royer and Marsden?
4. At the heart of the debate over revenue sharing are profound disagreements over the role and responsibility of government. Conservatives firmly believe that the people who spend the money ought to raise the revenue; otherwise, there will be a lack of political accountability. Liberals say that political accountability often fails to serve the interests of those who have the least power—the poor and members of racial and ethnic minorities. What do you say?

Case References

The principal basis for this case was Arnold M. Howitt, "The Maternal and Child Health Block Grant in Washington State and Seattle," which appears in his *Managing Federalism: Studies in Intergovernmental Relations,* (Washington, D.C.: CQ Press, 1984), pp. 39–70. In addition, the following materials were helpful in preparing this case: Richard P. Nathan and Fred C. Doolittle, *The Consequencs of Cuts* (Princeton, N.J.: Princeton University Press, 1984); Robert Pear, "In Revenue Sharing, Cities Prefer the Old Federalism," *New York Times,* December 19, 1982; Arthur Wiese, "Coalition Presents Gloomy Assessment of Urban Conditions," *Houston Chronicle,* May 14, 1982.

4

Administrative Responsibility and Ethics

Introduction

In the last chapter, we saw how intergovernmental relations complicates even further the already complicated core function of political management. In that chapter, you might recall, our concerns were fairly concrete—block grants, National Governors Association, Councils of Government, and so forth. In this chapter, I want to consider several matters more abstract in nature but also affecting political management. One such matter is the dominant values of the society in which the administrator works.

By values we simply mean things or relationships that people would like to have or to enjoy. Obviously, we cannot—and fortunately we need not—consider the entire complex of values held by American society. We need concern ourselves only with those values that are relevant to administration. What might these be? Most Americans would agree, I think, that government should be responsive, flexible, consistent, stable, honest, prudent, lawful, and accountable. In this chapter, we shall use the word *responsibility* as a collective term for values like these, for qualities people would like to see in their government.

In the first section, we shall attempt to spell out how several of these values relate to public administration. In doing so, we should be, in effect, helping to explain what the ideal of responsibility has come to stand for in the literature of public administration. To speak of an ideal implies an existence not in the actual world but in the mind; it suggests a perfection exceeding what is possible in reality. So it is with the ideal of administrative responsibility. Our discussion, therefore, would be quite incomplete if we did not consider a few of the pitfalls on the road to administrative responsibility in the actual world of governmental administration. Among those pitfalls discussed in the second section of this chapter are coercion, collusion, distortion, and elitism.

James Madison and the Founding Fathers knew that administrative responsibility could not be assumed. They knew too that some thought must be given to its protection.

> If men were angels, no government would be necessary. If angels were to govern men neither external nor internal controls on government would be necessary. In framing a government which is to be administered by men over men, the greatest difficulty lies in this: you must first enable the government to control the governed; and in the next place to oblige it to control itself. A dependence on the people is, no doubt, the primary control on the government; but experience has taught mankind the necessity of auxiliary precautions. (Federalist Paper No. 51)

Going on the assumption that angels still do not govern, we shall conclude this chapter by giving some thought to external and internal controls designed to help ensure administrative responsibility. Particular emphasis will be placed on ethical analysis as a means toward that end.

The Ideal of Administrative Responsibility

While neither exhaustive nor definitive, the following subsections do cover most of the values implied when the term *administrative responsibility* is used. (For this approach to defining responsibility, I am indebted to Gilbert, 1959.)

Responsiveness

This term refers to the prompt acquiescence by an organization to the popular demands for policy change. Responsiveness can also mean that government does more than merely react to popular demands. In some cases, it can mean that government takes initiatives in the proposal of solutions for problems and even in the definitions of problems.

In an effort to determine what people regard as the most significant criticism of the federal bureaucracy, David A. Brown and his students at George Washington University polled 1,470 persons to get their views. The most frequently heard criticism was that bureaucracy is "slow, ponderous; incapable of taking immediate action" (*Public Administration Times*, January 1981).

In fact, organizations might even be classified according to their level of organizational responsiveness. Philip Kotler (1975:40–43) finds four types. First is the unresponsive organization that (a) does nothing to measure the needs, perceptions, preferences, or satisfaction of its constituent publics, and (b) even makes it difficult for them to make inquiries, complaints, or suggestions. The prevailing attitude seems to be "we know what is best." Organizations facing a high and continuous demand for customer needs (such as hospitals) often fall into this category.

Second is the casually responsive organization that *does* show an interest in learning about constituent needs and complaints. Thus, as American universities began to experience a decline in student applications in the early 1970s, they began to listen more to students and to encourage faculty-student committees.

Third is the highly responsive organization that uses systematic information collection procedures (e.g., formal opinion surveys and consumer panels); creates formal systems to facilitate complaints and suggestions (e.g., comment cards); and where called for, takes steps to adjust services and procedures. Kotler reports that large firms such as Sears, Roebuck and Co., Procter & Gamble, General Mills, Inc., and GE have gone farthest in adopting these characteristics. Sears, for example, uses information from its surveys to chart an attitude index to see if there are *developing* problems requiring attention. Universities, municipalities, and hospitals tend to be rather casual about these matters, although in later chapters a few exceptions are noted (see page 380, for example).

Fourth is the fully responsive organization that overcomes the "us and them" attitude of most organizations by accepting its publics as voting members. Examples of organizations that are seen, in principle at least, as existing for and serving the interest of their constituents are churches and trade unions. Kotler thinks that once the principles of a fully responsive organization are fulfilled, then the members will be ready to lend their support and energy. Consider the case of a Canadian university that was searching for ways to build a more active alumni association. "Just sending out newsletters about the school did not suffice to build up alumni pride or interest. It developed the idea of conferring membership status to its alumni, with certain privileges and voting rights on certain issues. Suddenly this group became alive with interest in the school. This gesture proved very meaningful to the alumni, who had hitherto felt that the university was simply using them for their money" (Kotler, 1975:43).

Public administrators sincerely interested in the responsiveness of their agencies might find it useful to think of clients as consumers. What this means in practice is that all an agency's efforts should be focused on satisfying consumer needs—instead of producing a good or service and then trying to find a buyer. When an agency tries to find out what the consumer wants and then to produce that good or service consistent with that, we say it has a marketing (as opposed to a selling) orientation.

Regarding the responsiveness of public administrators, what might be said? Contrary to cliché, a University of Michigan research team reported in 1975 that administrators are reasonably responsive. After surveying 1,431 persons, the team concluded, "Americans like the bureaucrats *they* deal with pretty well." Similarly, a recent poll conducted by the Advisory Commission on Intergovernmental Relations (ACIR) found that for seven major federal programs, in almost every instance, the most frequent rating by the clients was "very satisfied." ACIR also found that local government for the first time surpassed both federal and state government as the level of government from which people get the most for their money (Table 4–1 on the following page). This support might indicate Reagan's new federalism is achieving one of its goals—getting people to turn to local government first for solutions to their problems.

Flexibility

In the formulation and implementation of policy (see Chapter 2), administrators should not ignore individual groups, local concerns, or situational differences relevant to the attainment of policy goals.

One of the first steps facing an organization is to define the boundaries of a policy's market. "Any market consisting of more than one member will have a structure insofar as the members have different needs, perceptions, and preferences. In most cases, the organization cannot serve the whole market with equal facility and must make a choice among the parts it will serve" (Kotler, 1975:94). In certain cases, such as poverty or public health programs, the choices become exceedingly difficult, analytically as well as politically.

Figure 4–1 attempts to illustrate some of the difficulty involved. Figure 4–1A shows a hypothetical market consisting of six persons who share some need in common; no segmentation is required. Figure 4–1B shows the opposite case: Here the organization has decided to see each of the six members of this market as being different. But few organizations find it worthwhile to study every individual member and then customize and service to each member's need. Instead, organizations generally search for broad groupings that can be approached as segments. The organization can then choose to deal with all these segments or concentrate on one or a few of them (Kotler, 1975:101–2). In Figure 4–1C, the organization has taken this approach and used income class as the basis for *market segmentation.*

Of course, many other variables could have been used other than income. The most important fall into three major classes: geographic (by region, county size, climate, and so on), demographic (by age, sex, race, and so on), and psychographic (usage rate, benefits sought, lifestyle, and so on). When governments ignore these kind of complexities in the formulation and implementation of policy, they tend to fail the standard of flexibility and thereby become a little less responsive.

Table 4-1

From Which Level of Government Do You Feel You Get the Most for Your Money—Federal, State, or Local? *(Percent of U.S. Public)*

	May 1984	May 1983	May 1982	Sept. 1981	May 1980	May 1979	May 1978	May 1977	March 1976	May 1975	April 1974	May 1973	March 1972
Federal	24	31	35	30	33	29	35	36	36	38	29	35	39
Local	35	31	28	33	26	33	26	26	25	25	28	25	26
State	27	20	20	25	22	22	20	20	20	20	24	18	18
Don't know	14	19	17	14	19	16	19	18	19	17	19	22	17

Source: Advisory Commission on Intergovernmental Relations, *P. A. Times*, August 1, 1984.

Figure 4-1
Different Approaches to Market Segmentation

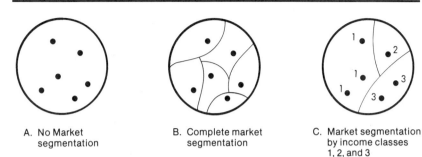

A. No Market   B. Complete market   C. Market segmentation
   segmentation   segmentation   by income classes
                                                 1, 2, and 3

Source: Adapted from Kotler (1975:101).

The concept of client as consumer is potentially a very powerful one in the attainment of responsiveness and flexibility. The box gives you some idea of how a public agency might build on it.

Competence

Administrative responsibility also requires that the formulation and implementation of public policy should be guided by recognized objective standards, where they are available. Administrative action should be prudent rather than hasty and should display care for the consequence rather than negligence. Such action should also be efficient (i.e., carried out with minimum waste) and effective (i.e., accomplish its objectives). One character in the film *Electra Glide in Blue* capsulated this value when he said, "The worst form of corruption is incompetency."

Due Process

To the lawyer, *due process* connotes something sufficiently special that it cannot be *completely* encompassed in any other term. The concept of due process is stated for the federal courts in the 5th Amendment and for the state courts in the 14th. It assumes that no citizen should "be deprived of life, liberty, or property without due process of law." In short, it is an assurance that the government will be administered by laws, not by the arbitrary will of people who condemn without a public hearing.

While the concept of due process originally applied to criminal law, it was later extended to administration. Today, thanks largely to the Administrative Procedures Act of 1946, it serves as a major limitation on administrative discretion. Thus agencies must have jurisdiction over the matters with which they deal; must give fair hearings to all persons affected by their rulings; must give adequate notice of such

Designing a Marketing Mix for a Public Sector Organization

Once a public administrator has identified the market segments, he or she can begin to design a full-fledged marketing program responsive to human needs. It is convenient to refer to the components of such a program in terms of four Ps—product, price, promotion, and placement. Below we shall discuss a few of the public sector decisions associated with each component.

Consumer Attitudes toward the Product

The crucial point about a consumer's attitude toward any good or service an organization might provide is that it is a mixture of the evaluation of a variety of features. For example, whether a high school student decides to attend a particular college depends on several features: cost, distance from home, number of friends enrolled, and so forth. Of course, the student will weigh (or value) each of these features differently and hold opinions about the probability that the college does in fact offer each of these features. The following formula represents the attitude structure of a citizen toward mass transit:

Overall attitude = (Strength of belief that city transit system is *fast*) (importance of speed) + (Strength of belief system is *safe*) (importance of safety) + (Strength of belief that system is *clean*) (importance of cleanliness) + . . . + (strength of belief that system is *economical*) (importance of economy)

How can such models help college presidents, directors of city transportation authorities, or hospital administrators (who find physicians are always recommending somebody else's hospital to their patients)? They tell the administrator what is most affecting consumer's attitudes. The col-

lege administrator may be placing too much emphasis on a winning football team when national rankings do not influence applicants—which is what he thought.

Pricing the Service

What should NASA charge private companies to carry payloads weighing up to 200 pounds and occupying less than 5 cubic feet into orbit aboard the space shuttle? What should a college charge for tuition? A power company for electricity? A highway commission for tolls?

The answer depends to a large degree on whether the service is new. The NASA example above, known as the "gateway special," is an innovative service to promote the shuttle. Because the shuttle's payload bay is so spacious, there will be incidental room on a space-available basis for NASA to tuck away small research packages with its larger cargoes. The user pays several thousand dollars for a shuttle trip. The gateway special is not designed to balance the federal budget but to provide an inexpensive (and hence enticing) way for people to get involved with the shuttle possibility. In the language of marketing, we call this penetration pricing.

But NASA is also interested in recovering a certain amount of the costs incurred in building the shuttle. Therefore, it also follows a cost-recovery pricing policy. Given a sufficient number of customers, operations could be amortized in 12 years.

Among the other pricing strategies a public sector organization might follow are no-fare (e.g., to get people to ride buses rather than automobiles), profit maximization (e.g., tickets to a charity ball), cost-plus (e.g., gift shop at museum), variable (e.g., charge more for electricity during peak periods), and discriminatory (e.g., charge higher tuition to out of state students).

Promotion

To promote a service, the agency must communicate with the consumer. As with pricing policies, several strategies are available.

Advertising probably comes first to mind, though its effectiveness is widely overestimated. Witness television commercials for the 55-mile-per-hour speed limit to reduce the average speed on the highway. Nevertheless, the federal government is one of the nation's top 20 advertisers, with outlays rivaling those of such business giants as Coca-Cola and Procter & Gamble. In one year, government advertising costs totaled $200 million.

Market segmentation can help. For example, a small private university in Minnesota might develop three brochures rather than one for prospective students. For inquiries from the West, one brochure might emphasize the winter sports; for inquiries from the East, the teaching excellence; and for inquiries from within Minnesota, the opportunity to go to a national rather than regional university. The crux of the recruitment problem the army faces appears to be attracting bright young men and women who can handle increasingly sophisticated technology. To target this market segment, perhaps the advertising should emphasize the opportunities for additional education at a quality university rather than the glories of surfing off the coast of Diego Garcia.

Public sector organization can also communicate with customers directly through personal selling. For example, the administrator of a new hospital might try to visit every physician in the area to explain the hospital's services.

Remember, you're among friends.

SMOKEY

Only you can prevent forest fires.

The federal government is one of the largest advertisers in the United States but still spends only about a third of what Procter & Gamble does. The U.S. Forest Service's Smokey the Bear (above) is now as recognizable a symbol as AT&T's bell—though one might question why his poster gets placed in Brooklyn subway stations. The U.S. Army demands that its ads be realistic and accurate. To get women to sign up for the Soviet military, recruiters purloined the "Be All that You Can Be" slogan. In Russian, it comes out as "*Byt vsyo shto moyhno byt.*" (Used by permission of the USDA Forest Service.)

Another promotional technique is in the form of incentives, either in cash or kind. In the 1960s, the U.S. Soil Conservation Service offered cash payments to farmers to encourage them to adopt conservation practices. In India, the Ministry of Health and Family Planning offered transistor radios to men undergoing sterilization after having two or three children (Deshpande, 1979:391).

Finally, publicity involves stimulating demand for a service or product by planting significant and favorable news about it in the mass media. Because it is not paid for by the sponsor, it has a higher level of credibility than advertising.

trains, or use satellite communication to remoter locations.

Evaluating Consumer Satisfaction
Last, public administrators should mea-

The fourth component in the marketing mix is placement, that is, how the agency plans to make its products or services available and accessible to customers. Avoidable inconveniences should be rooted out. (From *The Wall Street Journal,* with permission of Cartoon Features Syndicate.)

Placement

Within cost constraints, a public sector organization should try to make consumer access to the product or service as easy as possible. Hospitals and medical societies can use cable television or prerecorded radio messages to provide useful information to customers. Blood banks can be set up in neighborhood stations to get donations. Subsidized meals can be distributed to disadvantaged and elderly people by having volunteers drive their own cars. Universities can set up ranch campuses, provide courses on commuter

sure directly consumer satisfaction or dissatisfaction. To go by level of use, number of clients, or number of public hearings will not do.

As pointed out earlier, successful marketing must be responsive to consumer wants and needs. Instead of writing a better regulation or developing a new service under the assumption that an appreciation of it, or market for it, will develop later, an agency must consciously try to meet consumer requirements. In this context, public opinion polls and other survey research techniques might help.

hearings well in advance of the dates when they are held; and must allow any interested persons to appear. Their officers must be impartial, with no personal interest in the questions upon which they decide. Moreover, their decisions must be based upon substantial evidence. In the orders they issue, specific findings of the law and fact must be set forth. The persons affected by such orders must be permitted counsel and given an opportunity to appeal. This is due process in the *procedural* sense of the term.

Case 4.2, "Eldridge's Complaint," discusses in some detail what one man felt was an unfair and arbitrary process of decision making by the Social Security Administration. It presents a classic example of how the essential values of the administrative process (e.g., efficiency) can come into conflict with the values of the judicial process (e.g., equity and due process).

Accountability

A good synonym for this term is *answerability*. The organization must be answerable to someone or something outside themselves. When things go wrong, someone must be held responsible. Unfortunately, a frequently heard charge is that government is faceless and that, consequently, affixing blame is difficult.

Immediately after British troops retook the Falkland Islands from Argentina on June 14, 1982, British Foreign Secretary Lord Carrington resigned his position in Margaret Thatcher's Conservative government. He did so because of the failure of British diplomacy to prevent, and of British intelligence services to anticipate, the Argentine invasion that cost the nation lives, territory, and international embarrassment. Although the recapture of the Falklands proved in time to be a political plus for the Thatcher government (and for British morale), Lord Carrington's action was judged appropriate and was not reversed.

Carrington's action provides an interesting contrast to what happened after the October 23, 1983, bombing of the marine barracks at the Beirut airport in Lebanon. Although the bombing was a severe setback to American interests in the region and standard in the world, no one resigned, no one was disciplined, and no one was fired. President Reagan said no one should have been because "I accepted responsibility." He spoke those words as he flew to Palm Springs for a vacation, which makes one wonder how much he meant them.

The failure is not just personal; it is systemic, particularly in the U.S. government where the whole concept of accountability tends to be muddled.

Accountability can also refer to the managerial processes of "direction and control." One of the best-known illustrations of control in the federal bureaucracy came from President Franklin D. Roosevelt. Roosevelt reportedly had this exchange with one of his aides (cited in Sherrill, 1974:203):

When I woke up this morning, the first thing I saw was a headline in the *New York Times* to the effect that our navy was going to spend $2 billion on a shipbuilding program. Here I am, the commander in chief of the navy having to read about that for the first time in the press. Do you know what I said to that?

(Aide): "No, Mr. President."

I said: "Jesus Chr-rist!"

Honesty

When the values of Americans are surveyed, honesty inevitably ranks either at the top or quite close to it. Not surprisingly, governments have devoted considerable effort to enforcing it—although disagreeing widely on the means.

One dimension of honesty is candor. As used here, *candor* refers to the notion that policymaking and administration should be at some stage open to public scrutiny. Gilbert (1959:376) elaborates:

The political and governmental system in general should reach and decide the merits of issues rather than obscure them through personal or pro-

Reagan and national security advisers at Sunday morning meeting after a powerful bomb, detonated by the driver of a truck, exploded at the headquarters building occupied by U.S. troops in Beirut, Lebanon, resulting in the deaths of 241 men, mostly marines. Fixing blame on the U.S. government is not, however, easy (see text). (Bill Fitz-Patrick/The White House)

cedural obfuscation. A further requirement might include that of reasoned justification of governmental decisions. Though logically three separate notions, they are lumped together here since they all have presumed value for public discussion, education, and the sense of individual "responsibility" for public policy.

Some theorists believe that total candor can "overheat" the political system. Certainly, many of the newer decision-making techniques (see Chapter 6) require that the merits of an issue be made explicit, that the risks of each alternative be justified, and that all costs be identified. To that extent, these analytical techniques can increase the probability of open conflict.

In an earlier age, these kinds of issues were lost in a murky sea of political wheeling and dealing or technical jargon. Then it was harder for outside groups and individuals to see exactly how they would be affected by the outcome of the process. Today greater candor in government seems worth a little political conflict to most Americans.

Pitfalls on the Way to Responsibility

In the opening section, we distinguished six values or concerns generally linked to the ideal of administrative responsibility. They were responsiveness, flexibility, competence, due process, accountability, and honesty. But as T. S. Eliot reminds us: "Between the idea/and the reality/Between the motion/and the act/Falls the Shadow." In this section, therefore, we must pause to consider how far the practice of public administration is from realizing the theory of administrative responsibility. Our discussion centers around four major shortcomings: collusion, coercion, distortion, and elitism.

Collusion

In Chapter 2, we saw much policymaking taking place in the political subsystems composed of congressional subcommittees, relevant agencies, and special interest groups. All too often these subsystems are impervious to higher political officials such as the president or more representative bodies such as the entire Congress, who would appear to have a broader perspective and more clearly represent the public interest.

Collusion in some instances might be too strong a word, since frequently agencies, over time, come to see certain special interests as their "clients." Hence, the agency comes to feel it has a *legitimate* responsibility to protect that interest.

Possibilities for collusion are not limited to national government. One can easily identify a number of areas that have potential opportunity for corruption and that should be carefully watched by local officials: contracting out of municipal services, purchase of supplies, awarding of liquor licenses and construction permits, and so forth.

Courage in government takes many forms. President Kennedy's *Profiles in Courage*, for example, dealt with a rather dramatic form: abiding by principle in an unpopular cause. In public administration, however, courage is more frequently required to avoid small favors. As Washington once told a friend seeking an appointment: "You are welcome to my house; you are welcome to my heart . . . my personal feelings have nothing to do with the present case. I am not George Washington, but president of the United States. As George Washington, I would do anything in my power for you. As president, I can do nothing." (quoted in Appleby, 1952:130.)

Coercion and Nannyism

A second pitfall on the road to administrative responsibility is coercion. And how it emerges is itself interesting. Democracy cannot exist without a modicum of consensus. (The modern administrative state has yet to adopt the principle of George Barnard Shaw's friend: Do whatever you want, as long as you don't scare the horses.) Consequently, the administrative state has what some observers might call an alarming number of programs and techniques for dealing with those who fail to share in the consensus, who dissent from it, and who, in some instances, advocate covertly or overtly its destruction. Among these sometimes coercive programs and techniques, we might include loyalty oaths, restriction on speech and assembly, lie detector tests, wiretapping, data banks, and behavior modification drugs. These activities are not always easily reconciled with the value of due process.

A milder form of coercion might be called "nannyism." The motive here is not the desire for consensus but the desire to protect—or, more accurately, to overprotect. In this sense, the administrative state becomes a kind of nanny.

Frequently cited examples of this phenomenon are the Federal Trade Commission (FTC) and the Food and Drug Administration (FDA). Some think that the FTC had, by the end of the 1970s, become a kind of "national nanny."

An FTC administrative judge challenged pitching star Vida Blue's pitches for drinking milk because blacks often have trouble digesting milk. The commission proposed a truth-in-menu rule that might mean, for example, that no restaurant could offer as Maryland crab any crustacean that had crawled into Delaware. The agency intensified a holy war against breakfast cereal companies; it has proposed breaking them up and banning ads for presweetened cereals from Saturday morning's TV cartoon shows. An FTC-proposed rule warned that such ads were enticing children to "surreptitiously" sneak cereals into Mom's shopping cart. Washington wags quipped that the FTC would soon ban peanut butter because it stuck to the roof of the mouth. (*Time*, December 3, 1979)

The FDA tries to protect consumers by restricting their freedom of choice. Under present law, no new drug or medical device can be made available for sale until it has been officially approved as "safe and effective" by the FDA. Unapproved products like the mechanical heart can be used only in investigational studies when they have been previously cleared by the FDA on application by physicians or their sponsor through a complex approval procedure. Due to lack of FDA approval, numerous cases have been reported where patients have been unable to obtain investigational drugs, even when suffering from debilitating conditions like arthritis, multiple sclerosis, and cancer.

In theory, the purpose of the FDA regulation is to protect consumers from undue risk. In fact, however, no evidence has ever been produced demonstrating a need for the complex approval procedures. In one study, experts expressed disagreement with FDA decisions in half the approval cases surveyed. The approval system was set up in 1962 after the thalidomide disaster when it was found that more than two million doses of the infamous drug had been distributed to doctors on a promotional basis. Nevertheless, the net toll of thalidomide-caused birth defects in the United States was 10, a tragic cost, but one that was probably far exceeded by the harm resulting from subsequent over-regulation. (Gieringer, 1985).

Distortion

Public relations is the management function that assesses public attitudes, identifies the policies of an organization with the public interest, and then executes a program of action to earn public understanding and acceptance. Thus, the purposes of an agency's public relations program are to inform and to constructively influence the public. And with both, the risk of distortion needs to be recognized.

Informing the public. The importance of keeping the public informed can not be overemphasized. An informed public is an essential ingredient of democracy.

Yet, in practice, some policymakers have found an easy justification for both secrecy and deception. Ordinary citizens, they believe, cannot understand complex decisions like the following:

Do aerosol cans affect the ozone content of the stratosphere?

Does underground nuclear bomb testing produce serious earthquakes and tidal waves?

Are we spending too much on nuclear energy research and not enough on solar energy?

Is our level of defense spending really adequate in comparison with the Soviet Union?

What should we do about the economy? What is the proper trade-off between inflation and unemployment?

The apparent inability of the people to understand these complex problems gives the policymakers—so the argument runs—a kind of "right to deception." Consider the case of the Atomic Energy Commission (now the Nuclear Regulatory Commission), which for at least 10 years repeatedly sought to suppress studies by its own scientists that found nuclear reactors were more dangerous than was officially acknowledged. One key study, which was suppressed, found that if a major reactor accident did occur, nearly 45,000 persons could be killed and the disaster could cover an area possibly the size of Pennsylvania (Burnham, 1974).

Public administrators need not resort to outright suppression of information. In 1980, then Secretary of Health and Human Services, Patricia R. Harris tried a little "newspeak." Students of George Orwell's *1984* will recall that in his fictional state, language was used to obfuscate any undesirable aspects of government operations the ruling bureaucratic class did not care to have publicized. After an inspector general's report found a lot of fraud, waste, and abuse at HHS, Harris called an executive staff meeting. She then eliminated all fraud, waste, and abuse by the simple expedient of ordering that the phrase "fraud, waste, and abuse" be eliminated and replaced throughout the department with the words "program misuse and management inefficiency."

As Walter Lippmann noted many years earlier, it is sophistry to think that in a free country certain people have some sort of inalienable or constitutional rights to deceive their fellow humans like this. "There is no more right to deceive than there is a right to swindle, to cheat, or to pick pockets."

Influencing the Public.   The second objective in a public relations program, besides simply providing information, is to influence the public. As we said in Chapter 2, the effective administrators are the ones who can attain their agencies' goals. This task, in turn, frequently *requires* the mobilization of public support. I can cite no better authority on the importance of honest communication than Abraham Lincoln: "In this and like communities public sentiment is everything. With public sentiment nothing can fail; without it nothing can succeed." In a few instances, the agency must actually *persuade* the public to take certain action—for example, participate in immunization programs, use seat belts, and stop smoking.

No official of the federal government has the words *public relations* in his or her title. A survey conducted in 1979 turned up nearly 5,000 government "information specialists" in 47 federal agencies and commissions.

> Though official estimates put their numbers near 20,000, every audit to find the true extent of federal public relations has fizzled because the publicity network is so widespread and the identities and activities of many of those involved are disguised by vague titles. The federal government spends at least $2.5 billion annually on attempts to influence the way people think. (*U.S. News & World Report*, August 27, 1979)

Critics contend that, in one sense, all of what these information specialists do is propaganda. A task force of the Commission on Federal Paperwork concluded: "The timed release or manipulation of information by an agency has developed into almost a fine-art form, most effectively employed by the Defense Department and related national-security agencies that report real or contrived threats or gaps at budget hearings to justify defense funding." Nevertheless, reporters need these press releases to keep the public informed. As columnist Joseph Kraft explains:

> In the typical Washington situation, news is not nosed out by keen reporters and then purveyed to the public. It is manufactured inside the government, by various interested parties for purposes of their own, and then put out to the press in ways and at times that suit the sources. That is how it happens that when the president prepares a message on crime, all the leading columnists suddenly become concerned with crime. That is even how it happens that when the Air Force budget comes up for consideration, some new plane will streak across the continent in record time. (*U.S. News & World Report*, August 27, 1979)

Public relations operations at the local level, while obviously smaller in scope, are basically no different. Public relations at the local level is not, however, the sole responsibility of community relations officers. The chief administrator certainly has an important role too. "The city manager has an inescapable obligation for public relations, an obligation that is just as compelling as his responsibilities for sound public finance, effective personnel systems, and other areas of management. He must instigate training for employees in all areas of public relations. . . . It is the city manager's job, using all means available to fashion improvement in the image of the city. He sets the pace for the entire municipality" (Desmond L. Anderson, quoted in Fowles, 1974:282).

Like the chief administrator, the employee in municipal government has a public relations role. Supervisors should make sure that the rank and file are given a preliminary orientation and then kept up-to-date about the activities of their government. If not, it is unlikely they will be able to answer accurately questions from the public and thus avoid the negative feelings generated by the dreaded runaround.

Increasingly, public administrators at all levels are finding it necessary to talk to the media—a task for which they are seldom trained. Moreover, such interviews usually occur after something has gone wrong. Dan Rather (quoted in Dickson, 1978:159) has given one rule that may be of help: "Stick with one of three responses: (a) I know and I can tell you, (b) I know and I can't tell you, and (c) I don't know." But there are other points worth bearing in mind:

- Use short, concise answers. *Reason*: Much reporting has to be short and snappy. Long complicated answers can lead to contradictions or revelations you do not wish to make.
- Remain calm and pleasant. *Reason*: Most good journalists are aggressive, but you are not obligated to be.
- Have a prepared statement and adhere to it. *Reason*: Same as the above two.
- Avoid humor. *Reason*: It frequently backfires.

Shortcomings in Public Sector Advertising and Publicity.   After a two-year study of press officers in government, Stephen Hess (1984) says one of the best he found was Linda Gosden, who worked in 1982 for Drew Lewis, then secretary of transportation. Gosden had an understanding of the news business, but more important, she had the respect and the ear of their chief. Hess thinks this situation is the exception. To the extent that public administrators are heavily dependent on the media—their first and most effective line of communication with the taxpayers—this is somewhat surprising.

Hess (1984) writes, "To serve effectively as an honest advocate for a political executive and his policies, a press secretary must be in the loop." That means being a part of the inner circle and a party to debates that lead to decisions. And, for the most part, Hess found that even senior press officers are not "in the loop."

Another problem is that most government public relations programs emphasize information dissemination when they ought to be also providing their chiefs with infiltered information from the field.

A third problem is lack of planning. In its evaluation of public affairs activities at HEW, the GAO (1979) recommended that the department set criteria to enable managers to evaluate the soundness of such programs before funding them. Among its key recommendations concerning standards to be applied to public affairs programs were: "Does the campaign have clear and meaningful objectives?" "Has the intended audience been precisely targeted?" "What mix of information channels (media, community elements, professional organizations, and so on) are to be utilized?" "Specifically, how is the effectiveness of the campaign to be evaluated—by behavior change, attitude change, dissemination of information?"

Elitism

In addition to the pitfalls of collusion, coercion, and distortion, there is yet another on the road to the administrative responsibility. And its recognition here is no revelation, for a number of observers have pointed to the ever-present possibility of the emergence of a faceless amoral elite of experts who run the government. The threat such a group poses to the ideal of administrative responsibility comes in many guises.

In 1954 the French sociologist, Jacques Ellul (1964:275) argued that the use of technique—that is, any complex of standardized means for attaining predetermined results—subverts democracy and tends to create a new aristocracy.

> In the administrative domain, the intervention of a technique of organization and mechanism results in the creation . . . of two classes very far removed from one another. The first, numerically, small, understands the means to conceive, organize, direct, and control: the second, infinitely more numerous, is composed of mere executants. The latter are hacks who understand nothing of the complicated techniques they are carrying out. It is not conceivable that the normal operation of democracy would be acceptable to those who exercise this technical monopoly: which, moreover, is a hidden monopoly in the sense that its practitioners are unknown to the masses.

Joining into the spirit of things, Theodore Roszak (1973:35–36) argued that technology is an "extraordinarily potent means of subverting democracy from within its own ideals and institutions. It is a citadel of expertise dominating the high ground of urban-industrial society, exercising control over a social system that is utterly beholden to technicians and scientists for its survival and prosperity."

One need not really strain to such lengths to make the simple point that expertise and elites can threaten the values of administrative responsibility. The emergence of professionalism in government and the insensitivity of bureaucratic elites to minorities are issues of today, not tomorrow. Indeed, art critic Robert Hughes (1980:105) thinks the architectural style of many public buildings is itself symbolic of this elitism: "clear and regular on the outside, and let the passing eye deduce nothing of what goes on inside." (See photo.)

The growth of professionalism raises at least four major concerns. First, certain elite professions (e.g., law, medicine, and science) tend to dominate the governance of many bureaus and other public agencies. Second, at the expense of general government agencies such as the civil service, professional groups dominate in matters of recruitment, selection, and advancement. Third, professional specializations are becoming narrower. Fourth, organized public employees in professional and subprofessional fields constantly press for changes in public policy

According to art critic Robert Hughes (1980:108), one of the scariest examples of architecture of state power is the seat of government for New York State, the Albany Mall. "As Nelson Rockefeller's monument, it has a Roman coarseness and a more than Roman size: a stone plateau, modeled on the ceremonial buildings of Brasilia and, if possible, even uglier than they. It is designed for one purpose and achieves it perfectly: it expresses the centralization of power." The rich surface and splendid embellishments of the original capitol (center) make the South Mall, the tower on the left, and the giant bowl on the right, appear all the more brutish, bland, and out of control. (Freelance Photographers Guild)

related to their particular fields of endeavor and thereby infringe upon the prerogatives of elective and appointed officials.

According to Frederick C. Mosher (1968:132–33), the trend toward professionalism inside or outside of government will not soon be reversed or even slowed. The best check on professionalism, therefore, appears to be the educational process through which the professionals are produced and later refreshed (in continuing educational programs). This process can, Mosher suggests, be studied and conceivably changed. "The needs for broadening, for humanizing, and in some fields for lengthening professional education programs may in the long run prove more crucial to governmental response to societal problems than any amount of civil service reform."

The litmus test of the responsiveness and flexibility of a government might be how well it treats those at the bottom of the social order. To survey the contemporary circumstances of minorities and to examine the minority-related programs of the last two decades are objectives beyond the scope of a work of this kind. But to consider briefly how the cultures of Mexican-Americans and blacks differ from that of the dominant society could be fruitful if it leads to a somewhat better appreciation of the many viewpoints of the various segments of the population in the United States.

Unfortunately, too many administrators have not given consideration to these matters. They tend to view other groups strictly in terms of their own culture, a tendency sociologists call *ethnocentricism*. Regardless of the label, it smacks of insensitive, elitism and retards the values of responsiveness and flexibility, since the thrust for racial identity in certain segments of the population is ignored. (See box.)

External and Internal Controls

A multitude of measures have been taken to avoid the pitfalls of collusion, coercion, distortion, and elitism. As a simple framework for discussion, these measures are divided into four main categories: internal formal, internal informal, external formal, and external informal. No writers advocate exclusive reliance upon any *one* of these four. There is, then, no school of thought to be found *entirely* within any one of the cells in the diagram below, or in either the vertical or horizontal columns (adapted with slight modification from Gilbert, 1959:382):

	Internal	**External**
Formal	Chief executive officer	Legislature
		Courts
Informal	Professional codes	Interest group representation
	Representative bureaucracy	Citizen participation
	Public interest	Media
	Ethical analysis	

Of course, use of the four descriptive categories entails difficulties of definition and classification; but on balance, it does seem a helpful means of distinguishing and analyzing various institutional approaches and proposals for ensuring administrative responsibility. The distinction between formal and informal, though not always easy to draw, is roughly this: Informal relationships are those not explicitly provided for in the Constitution. The distinction between internal and external is that between (a) the executive branch of government and the top executives who head it, and (b) the rest of society and its political apparatus.

Since the internal formal measures available to a president were touched on in a previous chapter and will be further developed in Part II, nothing need be said here. Likewise, the external formal measures available to Congress (e.g., oversight) and the external informal influence by interest groups and media were noted in Chapter 2 and should require no reiteration. This leaves us with six topics to consider: the

Elitism, Ethnocentrism, and Administration

Roughly, the worldview of nearly all nonminority Americans has the following values, assumptions, and preferences:

Individualistic: It is natural for individuals to compete and to seek to satisfy themselves through material gain.

Faustian: It is natural for man to struggle against and master nature.

Objective: Problems and situations are to be analyzed by means of tangible evidence ("hard facts") and the scientific method.

In contrast, the Mexican-American worldview has at least some roots in the Indian worldview that places individualism on a social rather than economic basis and considers human life inextricably bound up with nature. In addition to this affinity with their Indian forbears, Mexican-Americans want to recapture their unique Spanish-Indian heritage and thereby make "*la Raza*" an effective political force. Writes Armando Rendon in *Chicano Manifesto* (1971:46): "Our ideals, our way of looking at life, our traditions, our sense of brotherhood and human dignity, and the deep love and trust among our own are truths and principles which have prevailed in spite of the gringo, who would rather have us remade in his image and likeness: materialistic, cultureless, colorless, monolingual, and racist. Some Mexican-Americans have sold out and become agringados . . . like the Anglo in almost every respect. Perhaps, that has been their way of survival, but it has been at the expense of their self-respect and of their people's dignity."

Unlike Mexican-Americans, who tend to envision a multiminority cultural pluralism, blacks emphasize black culture as a prelude to a more far-reaching social change. Blacks, however, are equally sensitive to the necessity of maintaining one's identity.

For more than 40 years, anthropologist Edward T. Hall (1976) has interpreted other cultures for business and government. According to Hall, some cultures are high-context, others low-context. In the former category, Hall includes Chinese, Japanese, Arab, and American black cultures; in the latter, white western cultures, which certainly includes middle-class America. One of the most salient differences between the two is found in communication: In high-context cultures, less information is carried in the verbal part of a message since more is in the context (e.g., social status of sender). In low-context cultures, *words* carry most of the information; messages are quite explicit.

"Since much of culture operates outside our awareness, frequently we don't even know that we know. We pick them up in the cradle. We unconsciously learn what to notice and what not to notice, how to divide time and space, how to walk and talk and use our bodies, how to behave as men and women, how to relate to other people, how to handle responsibility. . . . What we think of as 'mind' is really internalized culture" (Hall, 1976:74). These different assumptions work to make misunderstanding between people likely and destructive. Hall gives specifics:

> Take the matter of the way we listen or show that we are paying attention when someone is talking. I once got a young black draftsman a job with an architectural firm, where he almost got fired. He did his work well but his employer complained about his attitude. This mystified me until

This building mural in a Hispanic section of Chicago symbolizes the importance of localism, the family, and the neighborhood as primary forms of association. (Chicago Tribune Photo. Used with permission.)

once when I was talking to him and noticed I wasn't getting any feedback. He just sat there, quietly drawing. Finally I said, "Are you listening?" He said, "Man, if you're in the room, I'm listening. You listen with your ears." In their own mode, interacting with each other, ethnic blacks who know each other don't feel they have to look at each other while talking. They don't nod their heads or make little noises to show that they're listening the way whites do. (Hall, 1976:74)

Blacks also pay more attention than we do to nonverbal behavior. I once ran an experiment in which one black filmed another in a job interview. Each time something significant happened, the watching black started the camera. When I looked at those films, I couldn't believe my eyes. Nothing was happening! Or so I thought. It turned out that my camera operator was catching—and identifying—body signals as minor as the movement of a thumb, which foreshadowed an intention to speak. Whites aren't so finely tuned. (Hall, 1976:97)

Administrators are apt to make high-context ethnic neighborhoods as slums, and classify them for renewal because they do not see the order behind what appears to be disorder.

> Live, vital, cohesive ethnic communities are destroyed. To make way for a university in Chicago, planners wiped out a Greek and Italian neighborhood, over strong protests. The scars haven't healed yet. It is important to stress that when you scatter such a community, you're doing more than tearing down buildings; you're destroying most of what gives life meaning, particularly for people who are deeply involved with each other. The displaced people grieve for their homes as if they had lost children and parents. To low-context whites, one neighborhood is much like the next. To high-context people, it is something else again. (Hall, 1976:97)

And what does all this mean for the public administrator? First, most governmental programs designed to aid minorities are based on the dominant worldview. To participate in these programs as a route to progress, minorities must perforce cast aside part of their very identity. Thus they are placed in a dilemma—the implications of which can be fully measured by income and employment statistics. While it is unlikely that public administrators can easily resolve the dilemma, it is inexcusable for them not to recognize it.

courts, citizen participation, professional codes, representative bureaucracy, public interest, and ethical analysis.

Judicial Control

A Model of the Administrative Process. Many, particularly members of the legal professions, hold that one of the principal arrangements designed to monitor administrative decisions that affect individuals, private organizations, and local communities, is the national court system. After exhausting administrative remedies, individuals in many cases have the opportunity to obtain a judicial review of administrative decisions (see Figure 4-2).

Various parties—Aunt Beth, Engulf & Devour Corporation, Dean Wormley—make demands on the agency that must first pass through an *informal* screening process. The purpose of this step, which comes before any formal hearing, is to resolve a problem in as economical and flexible a manner as possible. A problem here may involve nothing more than answering a telephone call ("Where is my social security check?" "What do you mean I underpaid my taxes by $735?"). Or it may involve much larger issues ("May we merge with GM?" "Does our prospectus for a security system look OK?"). Even these more complex issues can often be negotiated and resolved congenially.

What triggers *formal* adjudication under APA? For the formal hearing provisions of the APA to come into play, an agency's authorizing statute must require it. If the statue is vague on this point, the courts will look to the legislative history (i.e., what members of Congress had in mind) and, of course, ensure that constitutional due process governs.

Figure 4-2
Judicial Control of a Federal Agency or Commission

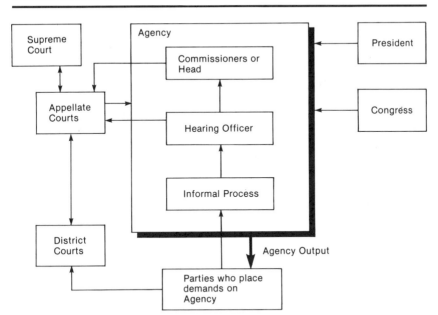

Sometimes the courts favor administrative discretion; other times they favor the benefits of fairness. It all depends.

In cases requiring a more formal process, an administrative law judge generally reviews the evidence and makes preliminary conclusions as to the disposition of the issue. If an appeal is needed, it will usually be an administrative appeal in which the record is examined by other agency officials. Eventually, a final decision is reached. The decision may concern claims and benefits, licenses, rules, rates, routes, or sanctions (for noncompliance). These, in effect, are the output of the administrative agency and they can have a considerable effect on the involved parties.

Thus, some form of review of agency decisions can be sought in the courts. This review may occur after the administrative procedures have been exhausted; if a case presents important legal questions, there may be appeals leading to the Supreme Court. In Case 4.2, at the end of this chapter, the party circumvented the administrative process by taking his grievance directly to court. The court may set aside any agency action that entailed abuse of discretion, excess of statutory or constitutional authority, improper proceedings, or an action unwarranted by the facts.

Congress appears in the model (Figure 4-2) because it can define and limit the authority of the agency through law. The president appears because he can issue specific policy directives and executive orders to the agency.

The Importance of Judicial Control. Arguably, the most rapidly expanding control over administration in recent years has been the courts. But it has also been extended to prison administration (size of cells and number of prisoners per cell), education policy (routes for buses and content of curriculum), and on to technical areas like automobile safety standards and resource management. In 1979, for example, the Supreme Court ruled that the Federal Communications Commission had no authority to require cable television operators to allow free access to a portion of their broadcast facilities and, in another case the same year, the court ruled that the Securities and Exchange Commission had no jurisdiction over private pension plans. Clearly, the Supreme Court can be a powerful constriction on the authority of regulatory commissions. A cynic might say that the very thought of the government making a decision without first asking judicial permission seems today almost unconstitutional.

But this power is not limited to federal agencies. Sovereign states and independent school districts are also affected. In the state of Alabama, Frank Johnson, a U.S. district judge, in effect, helps run the state. He supervises the operations of the prisons, mental hospitals, highway patrol, and other state institutions. In the Boston school district, District Judge W. Arthur Garrity, Jr. helps run things. Then Superintendent of Schools Robert Wood (1981) recalls:

> The scope of the court's intervention . . . was simply staggering and quickly went beyond remedies for specific legal grievances such as classroom segregation. During the first 18 months I was superintendent, the court held 30 hearings, and considered 109 items to assure compliance with more than 200 orders outstanding. Virtually every administrative appointment, and even decisions about curriculum, had to be approved in court-ordered proceedings. The court even held hearings about whether a particular school's auditorium needed roofing.

Needless to say, many of these administrative and curricular details exceed the traditional authority of lawyers and judges.

State courts also challenge what public executives can do. For example, in 1984, a state judge in New York declared unconstitutional an order by Mayor Koch forbidding discrimination against homosexuals by private companies and other groups that do business with New York City. The judge ruled that the mayor had usurped the power of the New York City Council and had impermissibly invaded the legislative domain by extending employment protection to homosexuals.

What are the limitations to judicial control? The first point to recognize is that responsibility is always after the fact; that is to say, all that courts can do is alleviate or punish wrongs that have already occurred.

A second point about judicial control is that the Supreme Court and its individual members tend to support federal agencies more frequently than they oppose them. In other words, research suggests that the outlook is not altogether promising for individuals who choose to control agency action in court. It is likely that at state and local levels, where judges tend to construe the powers of government more narrowly, that this pattern would hold to a lesser degree.

Our third point is speculative. The rise of public interest lawyers and a post-Watergate climate of "litigious paranoia" have probably brought the courts into public administration more than at any other time in U.S. history. Harlan Cleveland suggested that the ultimate effect of this phenomenon might be to cause every public agency to write down all its procedures, to put greater power in the hands of lawyers, and to generate in consequence jerky and arthritic administrative procedures.

Fourth, at a time when courts already face huge backlogs of cases, one wonders whether it is even physically possible for them to involve themselves in so many aspects of administration. Of particular concern is judicial decision making in cases involving scientific, technological, and managerial expertise.

Finally, and perhaps most fundamentally, do courts really need to decide whether an agency has "failed to consider all relevant factors" or has "abused its discretion" in writing a regulation on how to label peanut butter? A more useful division of labor might be for the people's representatives to monitor these matters, while courts concentrate on checking on bureaucrats who are accountable in no other way. Assuming agencies are under *political* control, judges can concentrate on their original job of protecting the Bill of Rights. They can let others worry about the hydrogenated vegetable oil in Skippy peanut butter.

Citizen Participation

When William F. Buckley, Jr. wrote that he would rather entrust his governance to the first hundred persons listed in the Cambridge telephone directory than to the faculty of Harvard College, he was simply stating the basic philosophy behind including the citizenry in the public decision-making process. Other observers maintain that citizens, as customers of government, are naturally more responsive to public needs than government officials. It might even be put forth as a tentative proposition that the poorest moral performances and the least accountability by government are generally associated with conditions in which few citizens have any influence. For these reasons, among others, it is not surprising to see government at all levels trying to formalize the participation of citizens in the administrative process.

The most common forms that institutionalized citizen participation assume are the citizen committee as an advisory group, the citizen group as a governing group in a specific policy area, and the idea of neighborhood government, where citizens have direct responsibility in a number of policy areas. Citizens' advisory committees often play important roles in the policymaking process described in Chapter 2.

Advisory groups, as used here, refer to the over 1,200 boards, commissions, and committees found within federal executive departments, their regional or district subdivisions, and within units of local government. These advisory committees involve more than 20,000 people and cover nearly every imaginable topic—from the President's Council on Energy Research and Development to the Agriculture Department's committee on hog cholera eradication.

Local governments create advisory committees on subjects ranging from community planning and police reform to mass transit and air pollution control. Administrators use these bodies to obtain information, advice, and opinions from representatives of affected interests, as this input may aid them in making informed policy decisions.

A limitation of citizen participation is that it can take the more politicized form of self-serving actions. The objective here is less to advise government than it is to win in the political marketplace. In the following example, Curtis Ventriss (1985:437) raises the issues of whether the extension of participatory democracy into the social sphere might result in antisocial consequences as well as whether participatory democracy itself is any guarantee that citizens will be accountable to the broader common interest. Ventriss asks us to assume

> that a community exists in which all members freely participate in the decisions that affect their immediate lives. Let us further assume that this community is relatively homogeneous in its ethnic and economic makeup (e.g., a white middle-income community). One of the decisions facing this community is a proposal by the local housing authority to build a low-income housing project in the area. The residents fear the building of this project for two reasons: it would reduce property values, and it might increase crime in the community. After a lengthy and open discussion, the citizens categorically reject the project. Their perceived fears, let us say, are primarily racially motivated, and thus, by direct participatory processes the project is declared politically dead.

What other limitations to citizen participation might we note? First, it could be argued that some public administrators see the participatory movement as a way to rid themselves of insoluble problems. Given an intractable problem one need only hoist the banner of participatory democracy while transferring responsibility elsewhere. Second, by bringing highly dissatisfied groups into the administrative process, administrators may be able to pacify (or co-opt) them. Third, citizen participation can be used as a vehicle by which a bureaucracy builds a clientele. This technique could be used, for instance, with environmental programs, which have no natural interest group. Enterprising administrators need only form a task force, composed of highly influential citizens, and they would have the nucleus of an effective citizens lobby for their pet programs.

Professional Codes

The remainder of this chapter devotes itself to consideration of the so-called internal-informal controls to ensure administrative responsibility. The first of these is the use of professional codes—a device that can be traced back *at least* to the Hippocratic Oath, which has guided the practice of medicine for more than 2,000 years. Next to physicians, lawyers probably have the most stringent set of professional requirements to be found. Interestingly, with few exceptions, the Watergate culprits were lawyers.

Three reasons might be suggested to explain why professional codes have such limited usefulnesss. To make these more concrete you might want to ask yourself how they might apply to Table 4–2.

First, the scope of activities of an administrator seldom limits itself to one profession; inevitably, questions arise that are outside the code's purview. Similarly, the administrator often finds his or her code in conflict with other loyalties (such as a particular client or geographic region, political leader, social class or union).

A second reason for the limitations of professional codes derives from the wording of these guidelines. If too general, they are useless as a guide to action. If specific enough to serve as a guide to action, they might be so numerous, so detailed, as to be unworkable on a day-to-day basis.

Third, to the extent that many codes posit obedience to authority in one form or another, it could be argued that they are inherently weak, possibly even dangerous. Fortunately, we need not rehash the Watergate affair to make the point that obedience to authority can be a self-defeating component in a code of ethics. Rather, let us consider the famous series of experiments on human beings begun in 1960 by Stanley Milgram (1974) at Yale University. (The experiments themselves are worthy of Kafka.)

The participants were led to believe that the purpose of the research project was the "scientific study of memory and learning." By a series of manipulations the participant was chosen to be the "teacher." Next, a fake "learner" was then taken to an adjacent room, strapped into a chair, and manacled with electrodes. Enter a supervisor dressed in a gray technician coat who tells the "teacher" to administer a verbal learning test to the man in the next room. Whenever an incorrect answer is given, the "teacher" is to give the "learner" an electric shock from the "shock generator."

Table 4–2
American Society for Public Administration Code of Ethics

The American Society for Public Administration (ASPA) exists to advance the science, processes, and art of public administration. ASPA encourages professionalism and improved quality of service at all levels of government, education, and the not-for-profit private sectors. ASPA contributes to the analysis, understanding and resolution of public issues by providing programs, services, policy studies, conferences, and publications.

ASPA members share with their neighbors all of the responsibilities and rights of citizenship in a democratic society. However, the mission and goals of ASPA call every member to additional dedication and commitment. Certain principles and moral standards must guide the conduct of ASPA members not merely in preventing wrong, in pursuing right through timely and energetic execution of responsibilities.

To this end, we, the members of the Society, recognizing the critical role of conscience in choosing among courses of action and taking into account the moral ambiguities of life, commit ourselves to:

1. Demonstrate the highest standards of personal integrity, truthfulness, honesty, and fortitude in all our public activities in order to inspire public confidence and trust in public institutions.
2. Serve the public with respect, concern, courtesy, and responsiveness, recognizing that service to the public is beyond service to oneself.
3. Strive for personal professional excellence and encourage the professional development of our associates and those seeking to enter the field of public administration.
4. Approach our organization and operational duties with a positive attitude and constructively support open communication, creativity, dedication, and compassion.
5. Serve in such a way that we do not realize undue personal gain from the performance of our official duties.
6. Avoid any interest or activity which is in conflict with the conduct of our official duties.
7. Respect and protect the privileged information to which we have access in the course of official duties.
8. Exercise whatever discretionary authority we have under law to promote the public interest.
9. Accept as a personal duty the responsibility to keep up to date on emerging issues and to administer the public's business with professional competence, fairness, and impartiality, efficiency, and effectiveness.
10. Support, implement, and promote merit employment and programs of affirmative action to assure equal opportunity by our recruitment, selection, and advancement of qualified persons from all elements of society.
11. Eliminate all forms of illegal discrimination, fraud, and mismanagement of public funds, and support colleagues if they are in difficulty because of responsible efforts to correct such discrimination, fraud, mismanagement or abuse.
12. Respect, support, study, and when necessary, work to improve federal and state constitutions, and other laws which define the relationships among public agencies, employees, clients and all citizens.

Approved by National Council April 8, 1984.

The results of this experiment were surprising and disturbing, for no one refused and walked out of this "Eichmann experiment." In fact, nearly two thirds of the "teachers," who represented a broad cross section of the occupational community, kept pressing away to 450 volts—despite the well-rehearsed shouts and screams of the "learner." The results, to state the obvious, were not what was expected: The autonomy of human beings proved astoundingly low. (Another interesting aspect of this experiment, which we can only mention parenthetically, concerns the professional ethics of a psychologist who, like Milgram, manipulates and deceives his subjects.)

Representative Bureaucracy

A representative bureaucracy is, roughly speaking, one that represents its society; that is, the percentage of each minority group in the government approximates the percentage of that group in the entire population. The assumption is, of course, that by hiring more members of some ethnic group, the representation of that group's attitudes within the bureaucracy is enhanced. This representation can be either passive or active (the distinction is Mosher's; 1968:12). Passive representation focuses on the source of origin of civil servants and the degree to which their backgrounds mirror the total society. Active representation denotes situations where the administrator presses for the interests and desires of those whom he or she is presumed to represent—whether the whole people or some segment of the people.

Does ethnic representation lead to active representation of that group's interest in the bureaucracy? Frank Thompson (1976:576–601), after a rather thorough review of studies on the question, concludes probably not, although the data are quite inclusive.

Consider these findings:

One study of black and white police in 15 core cities found that the black police viewed ghetto dwellers more positively. They more readily perceived ghetto residents as honest, industrious, respectable, and religious. Other data reveal that black police are more likely to view black citizens as mistreated by the police.

A study of Model City workers in Atlanta revealed that black professionals and paraprofessionals were more likely than white coworkers to perceive their clients as having "positive attitudes." But black welfare workers in 15 cities concluded—to a greater degree than their white colleagues—that black clients did not do enough to improve themselves and that black clients were especially arrogant.

Similarly, another study of law enforcement personnel in core cities showed that race had little effect on whether police engaged in such potentially controversial practices as searching without a warrant, breaking up loitering groups, and stopping and frisking.

Indeed, an analysis of black police in New York City uncovered a "Cossack" disposition. When black police worked with white ones, some of them tended to view black offenders as an embarrassment and treat them harshly. In the words of one black officer, "I have treated many Negroes in a way I wouldn't treat a dog. I am harder on a Negro that commits an infraction than a white person" (cited in Thompson, 1976:591).

Anthony Downs (1967:233) suggests this explanation for the weak link between ethnic representation and substantive representation: "Officials . . . have no strong incentives to employ representative values in making decisions. The pressure on them to seek representative goals is much weaker than the pressure of their own personal goals or those of their bureaus. . . . Neither do officials face reelection, thus having to account for or justify their policies. This lack of any enforcement mechanism further reduces the probability that officials will behave in [a] representative way."

A number of other explanations might be offered: Officials may lack authority to do very much; formal organizational sanction and peer group pressure may reduce gestures of sympathy by public servants from certain ethnic groups (one "gets ahead by going along"); and uncertainty may exist regarding just what the "proper ethnic perspective" is (Thompson, 1976:589–90).

Public Interest

Given the limitations involved in professional codes and representative bureaucracy as internal informal approaches to administrative responsibility, some posit the concept of the *public interest* as a guide to making administrative decisions. According to this view, the administrator should make decisions based on the best interests of some collective, overarching community or national good rather than on the narrower interest of some small self-serving group.

To discern clearly the public interests is no easy task. Walter Lippmann (1955:42), as lucid a thinker as one is likely to encounter on the subject, could give no better answer than this:

There is no point in toying with any notion of an imaginary plebiscite to discern the public interest. We cannot know what we ourselves will be thinking five years hence much less what infants now in the cradle will be thinking when they go into the polling booth. Yet their interests, as we observe them today, are within the public interest. Living adults share, we must believe, the same public interest. For them, however, the public interest is mixed with, and is often at odds with, their private and special interests. Put this way, we can say, I suggest, that the public interest may be presumed to be what men would choose if they saw clearly, thought rationally, acted disinterestedly and benevolently.

Quite a tall order. But even if the public official could see with this clarity, rationality, and objectivity, would it really be enough? How does one distinguish qualitatively between aggregated private interests (e.g., public opinion polls) and genuine common concerns? How does one distinguish between the various types of public: reasonable and long-range versus passionate and temporary?

During the late 1960s and early 1970s, a number of scholars began advocating a *new public administration*. While their aims lacked sharp focus, a few tendencies were clear enough. They charged that mainstream public administration in the United States had become too status quo oriented. In particular, the mainstream denied social justice to the disadvantaged members of society. The purpose of public administration should be, therefore, the realization of social equity.

This redefinition of the public interest raises several questions. Why should this particular doctrine (social equity) be adopted over others (e.g., freedom)? The answer seems to derive more from revelation than reason. How does one implement social equity—to what extent should Peter be robbed to pay Paul, and who is Peter and who is Paul? Finally, what are the implications for representative government? Should un-elected administrators "correct" the "wrong" decisions of elected officials? By what authority?

The main point about the new public administration is not that it provided a satisfactory definition of public administration but that it caused some rethinking about the nature and scope of the field. Never again would public administration be viewed as purely a matter of efficiency and economy in program execution. Nor would it continue to blithely ignore the needs of clients. Finally, and perhaps most importantly, students of public administration began to talk about ethics.

Ethical Analysis

Taking what has been said in the chapter about judicial control, citizen participation, professional codes, and the public interest, along with our earlier reflections on executive and legislative control of the bureaucracy and interest group activities in administrative policymaking, one tentative conclusion is possible: The quest for more responsible administration is a never-ending one. By way of conclusion, I want to focus upon some traditional as well as recent work in the field of ethics. Our immodest goal: to develop a more workable framework of moral choice for the public administrator.

Ethics is the systematic study of values. Before considering the very practical question of why ethical training can help a public administrator, I want to deal briefly with the commonly heard objection that ethics cannot be taught. Most of the resistance to ethics stems from the assumption that no one can say that certain attitudes are really true and others really false. Those who hold this view reject the philosophy and spirit of Plato, Aristotle, Buddha, Christ, Confucius, and Jefferson. They insist that, since there is neither traditional morality nor practical reason to guide us, the right solution to any moral problem "depends on the situation." This insistence is known as situation ethics and was a hallmark of the Nixon White House. John Ehrlichman, who accepted situation ethics when he was President Nixon's domestic policy chief, today rejects it: "The White House should lead in setting standards, morality, and goals. But when you are facing reelection, you look at the polls. When one is not elected, one defers to the guy who is. I never felt I had the right to substitute my judgment for his [Nixon's]" (quoted in *Time*, December 1, 1975).

A more recent practitioner of this moral relativism is the Reverend Jesse Jackson. For example, when Louis Farrakhan publicly threatened the life of a reporter who had disclosed Jackson's "Hymie" slur, Jackson characterized the episode as a "conflict" between "two very able professionals caught in a cycle that could be damaging to their career." Charles Krauthammer (1984) called Jackson's characterization the lanaguage of moral equivalence.

> "Two professionals"—each guy just doing his job—cleverly places the two men on the same moral plane. "Caught"—passive victims, both men done to and not doing—neatly removes any notion of guilt or responsibility. "In a cycle"—no beginning and no end—insinuates an indeterminateness in the relationship between the two men: Someone may have started this, but who can tell and what does it matter? (Nor is this the first time Jackson has pressed the cycle image into dubious service. Remember his "cycle of pain" in Lebanon, as if Navy Lieutenant Robert Goodman, the flyer for the American peace-keeping force that had lost more than 250 men to terrorist attack, and President Hafez Assad, who had at least acquiesced in that attack, were equal partners in crime?) Having framed the issue in these terms, Jackson proceeded to the logical conclusion: he proposed a meeting between Farrakhan and the reporter, offering himself as mediator.

Why Study Ethics?   There are several practical reasons for studying ethics. First, the study of ethics can help public administrators arrive at decisions more quickly. When confronted with decisions involving conflicting values, the individual who has thought through and clarified his or her own values does not lose time wondering what to do. Such an individual can act more swiftly and assuredly. Consider these two examples:

- Beleaguered by the developing Watergate scandals, President Nixon's counsel, John Dean, produced an "enemies list" and told the Internal Revenue Service (IRS) to harass everyone on it. The IRS asked then Secretary of Treasury Shultz what to do. He remembers the episode well. "I felt," he says, "that this was something we had no business doing. So I just told the IRS, 'Do nothing.'" Soon afterward, an IRS computer kicked out Nixon's tax return for audit. Again, the IRS asked Shultz what to do. "It was an easy question to answer," he recalls. "I said, 'Go audit the president's tax return.'" Nixon was furious. He called Shultz and ordered him to find out by the next morning how many other presidents had had their taxes audited. "The answer was that every recent president had his tax return audited." Mr. Shultz says. "Some have been assessed for back taxes. That is because they were wealthy men and had complicated returns, including President Nixon" (Gwertzman, 1983:15).

• When former Secretary of State Cyrus R. Vance examined President Carter's plan to rescue the 53 hostages in Iran in 1980, he judged the mission profoundly ill-advised. He could have dodged and bluffed his way through questions of whether he supported Carter's move. Or he could have swallowed his conscience and simply stood up like John Ehrlichman. (Situation ethics is a well-traveled road in Washington.) Or he could have done what he did. Vance said that presidents must have secretaries of state who can support them publicly, and then he resigned, solely over the issue of the mission. Vance did not wait to see how the mission turned out. He saw values in conflict—namely, his ideal of American foreign policy and his loyalty to Carter—and acted swiftly.

A second reason for studying ethics is that it leads to greater consistency in decision making. Administrators who are capable of this are seen by subordinates as fair; they avoid the charge of treating employees unequally.

Third, the study of ethics can reveal the value dimensions of a decision that would otherwise seem value free. For example, consider a fairly straightforward decision involving the U.S. Postal Services' money order operation. The original question is: How could the service make money orders more profitable? But then a different question might be raised: *Should* they be made more profitable, never mind how? Behind the second question is the recognition that money orders are used primarily by lower-income Americans who do not have checking accounts.

Fourth, the study of ethics can help public administrators make more reflective judgments—ones that can be defended in public. Generally, Americans feel awkward talking about values, as if such talk is something that "real men" do not do. Yet the public and the media continue to clamor for the very qualities that we are reluctant to talk about (honor, enterprise, justice, good faith, mercy, magnanimity, duty, beneficence, and the like). We laugh at virtue and are shocked to find knaves in our midst.

Moral conflicts are often inevitable and difficult. One golden value often must be brutally sacrificed so that another may be realized. Sometimes one value might carry more than one meaning, and the two meanings conflict. Equality is such a value. Does it mean equality of opportunity or equality of results?

The dangers of flimsy and slipshod arguments arising when one moves from ethical principles to their application in the world of administration are plentiful. A classic case of these dangers involves a great liberal hero, Ernest Fitzgerald, who was fired during the Nixon administration for giving information to the Congress. More specifically, Fitzgerald, who was a cost analyst in the Pentagon, exposed cost overruns on the C-5A aircraft.

A less famous *whistleblower* is David Sullivan. In 1979, Sullivan was fired by the CIA for giving information to an aide of Senator Henry Jackson. More specifically, Sullivan provided information that was useful to those who opposed the Strategic Arms Limitation Treaty. Though liberals had vigorously defended Fitzgerald and argued for years about the need for Congress to inform itself about the Pentagon, no liberal attacked Sullivan's summary firing. How might we be a little more systematic in our ethical analysis?

Some Avenues for Ethical Analysis.   The public administrator inevitably faces decisions that have a significant ethical dimension. Sometimes the right course is obvious. (Perhaps the cases of Shultz and Vance are examples of such situations.) At other times the right course of action is less clear.

- How far should administrators go in trumpeting the merits of their agencies?
- What do you do if you learn that a 58-year-old employee, who has been a solid performer, lied about his age or education on his resume?
- Must all decision making be in the open all the time?
- Should Mayor Koch have closed the Sydenham Hospital (Case 2.1)?
- Should President Reagan have fired and refused to rehire the air traffic controllers (Chapter 11)?
- How far may one go in discriminating against whites and males in order to meet affirmative action goals?
- Should regulatory agency employees take jobs with industries they have been regulating?
- What kinds of dress standards (e.g., ties, Mohawks, shorts, and so on) are appropriate—if any?
- Should employees ever be polygraphed? What about employees in the CIA or nursing homes?
- When and how do you fire a marginal employee (Case 11.1)?
- How does an administrator handle office romances, especially when one or both are married to someone else?

In situations like these, which involve both internal and external relationships, administrators seek and need a more or less orderly way of thinking through the ethical implications of a decision—an approach and a language for assessing alternatives from a moral perspective. While a rigorous review of the many ways philosophers have sought to organize what we are calling ethical analysis is beyond the scope of this book, it is possible to briefly sketch three of the more important views.

Contractarianism One of the most influential ethical views in American society is contractarianism. The central idea is that there are certain rights that should not be taken away (e.g., "life, liberty, and the pursuit of happiness") and contractual limitations on what A can do to B. The emphasis here is on the rights of the individual.

In an administrative setting, contractarian reasoning manifests itself in concerns about the implications of a decision concerning the rights of an employee and clients and the fair treatment of minorities.

One modern articulate advocate of this view is Robert Nozick (1974) who asserts that "The holdings of a person are just if he is entitled to them by the principles of justice in acquisition and transfer."

Stakeholder Analysis This approach is based on the early 19th century idea of utilitarianism. Rather than use inalienable rights and contractual limitations to limit the decision maker's power, the standard of value is applied by the principle of utility, which holds that the greatest happiness of the greatest number is the measure of right and wrong.

While this view continues to have influence, it is not always practical. What do we mean by happiness—*anything* that might give an individual pleasure? And how is happiness to be measured in a vast heterogenious population?

Thus, in stakeholder analysis, the aims are relatively modest. First, identify all groups that will be appreciably affected by the decision, and then think through how they are affected. Adversely or positively— and *how* adversely or positively? At this point, one can begin to make a rough summation of the pluses and the minuses. Only if the pluses outweigh the minuses is the decision right. This approach may seem like common sense masquerading as philosophical insight, but the fact is that decisions *are* commonly made without any attempt to identify *all* potentially affected groups (the obvious ones are easy), or to think through all the implications (again, the obvious ones are easy).

Obligation to Rules, Principles, or Right Reason The third approach to ethical analysis comes in many versions. But the central idea is not hard to state: In making difficult choices one should adhere to some rule or principle; for example, "do unto others as you would have them do unto you."

John Rawls provides a recent example of this approach. Rawls asks us to imagine rational, mutually disinterested individuals meeting. But in this hypothetical situation, rather than making specific decisions, people choose the first principles of a conception of justice. And these principles are operational; that is, they can serve to regulate all subsequent decision making.

But what are these principles they agree to? Rawls maintains that persons in this initial situation:

would choose two rather different principles: The first requires equality in the assignment or basic rights and duties, while the second holds that social and economic inequalities . . . are just only if they result in compensating benefits for everyone, and in particular for the least advantaged members of society. These principles rule out justifying institutions on the ground that the hardships of some are offset by a greater good in the aggregate. It may be expedient but it is not just that some should have less in order that others may prosper. But there is no injustice in the greater benefits earned by a few provided that the situation of persons not so fortunate is thereby improved. (Rawls, 1970)

According to Rawls, these principles are, in essence, a rigorous statement of the traditional Anglo-Saxon concept of fairness. But according to his critics, Rawls's principles are more the application of the handicapper's art to humanity. Compensatory equalization of this sort was the theme of Aristophanes' *Ecclesiazusae*, a play in which the dirty old men of Athens are compensated for their natural handicap by going to the head of the line for access to girls. A the same time, crones have first call on young men—the most cronish first of all.

Another problem with Rawls's theory of justice, at least from the standpoint of the public decision maker, is that it is inflexible and, as such, reduces autonomy. This objection is raised by Walter Kaufmann, who like Rawls, is a professor of philosophy capable of original thought. "Invocations of justice," he writes, "help to blind a moral agent to the full range of his choices. Thus they keep people from realizing the extent of their autonomy." Kaufmann continues: "We can point to examples of love and honesty, courage and humanity. We do not know in the same way what justice is. . . . We cannot point to concrete examples. Solomon's celebrated judgment illustrates his legendary wisdom rather than his justice. What made his judgement so remarkable was that *he managed to get at the facts*" [Emphasis added.] (Kaufmann, 1973:4).

What Kaufmann seems to be saying here can be illustrated by a recent example. Not long ago, the Wampanoag Indian tribe filed a lawsuit against the town of Mashpee, Massachusetts (example from McIntyre, 1984:153–54). The tribe claimed that their tribal lands had been illegally and unconstitutionally appropriated, and they wanted them returned. As the case moved slowly through the court system, property values in Mashpee dropped drastically. In this type of situation, what is just?

Robert Nozick would be of little help since the problem in Mashpee concerns a period of time in which we do not exactly know who had a just title by "acquisition and transfer." Nor would John Rawls help since we do not know which is the least advantaged group in Mashpee. That will depend on the outcome of the case; if the tribe wins, it will be the richest group in town, but for now it is the poorest.

Nonetheless, the tribal claimants have devised a solution that seems to take Kaufmann's approach, namely, all properties of one acre or less on which a dwelling house stands shall be exempted from the suit. Strictly speaking, this solution does not represent the application of a rule; rather, it is the result of rough-and-ready reasoning involving a consideration of all salient facts (e.g., the proportion of the land claimed that comprises such properties and the number of people affected if the size of the property exempted were fixed at one acre rather than more or less).

As Kaufmann sees it, in our time one concept of integrity, which is closely linked with justice, is being replaced by another, which is associated with individual autonomy and honesty. As used here, honesty does not mean only sincerity, credibility, or frankness; rather, it is as justice was to the Greeks, the *sum* of the virtues. Surely, says Kaufmann, that is what we mean when we refer to Abraham Lincoln as "Honest Abe"—not that he could never tell a lie (that was George Washington) but that he was virtuous.

Again Kaufmann: "High standards of honesty mean that one has a conscience about what one says and what one believes. They mean that one takes some trouble to determine what speaks for and against a view, what the alternatives are, what speaks for and against each, and what alternatives are preferable on these grounds. This is the heart of rationality, the essence of the scientific method, and the meaning of intellectual integrity" (1973:178).

But the newer concept of integrity requires on additional quality: Practice must be integrated with theory. To live in accordance with the new integrity thus requires self-confidence and courage; one must be able to *apply* the canon to the most important questions one faces. Rather than bow to authority, one decides for himself or herself.

Can the New Integrity Work?   The question can only be addressed by considering additional cases drawn from the world of administration.

- Early in 1975 William T. Coleman Jr. became transportation secretary. As his style of decision making began to emerge, it became obvious that Coleman was a post-Watergate example of a man of independence, accepting responsibility. He approached decisions like a judge; that is, he tried to get all the facts and then actually wrote an opinion explaining his decision in an open way. For example, when deciding on a proposed superhighway through the Virginia suburbs, he took the unusual step of personally holding a four-hour public hearing in which both sides gave their arguments. The following year, he faced an even tougher decision: whether the controversial Concorde airplane should be allowed flights into the United States. Taking careful measure of the complex—often conflicting—values of technology, the environment, and world politics, he reached a cautiously balanced decision that established a limited test period for the flights under carefully controlled conditions (Karr, 1975; Lewis, 1975).

William T. Coleman Jr., President Ford's transportation secretary, holding a copy of his opinion on the Concorde in Washington. (*The New York Times*/Teresa Zabala)

Typically, the decision was accompanied by a cogently reasoned explanation running 61 pages (*New York Times*, February 17, 1976).

- Harlan Cleveland (1975) has had a rich experience as a public executive—foreign aid administrator, magazine publisher, university president, political executive in Washington, and ambassador abroad. His reflections on public administration, therefore, are worth considering. First, he disposes of the notion that any one set of principles is going to be much of a guide: "Wise sayings from Mencius and Aristotle, the Bible, and the Founding Fathers, not to mention our own parents, may likewise be useful but hardly controlling: with a little help from a concordance of the Bible or Bartlett's *Familiar Quotations*, it is all too easy to find some pseudoscriptual basis for whatever one really wants to do." Having cleared the brush, he then gives the key question that he asked himself before getting committed to a line of action. The question is not "Will I be criticized?" (After all, operating in the public sector, the answer to that question is frequently yes.) Rather, it is this: "If this action is held up to public scrutiny, will I still feel that it is what I should have done, and how I should have done it?"

Nailing Down the Main Points

1. Administrative responsibility is a collective term that covers those values people generally expect from government.

2. Responsiveness in organization, one such value, comes in various forms: unresponsive, usually responsive, highly responsive, and fully responsive.

The fourth type overcomes the "us and them" attitude by accepting its publics as voting members.

3. Another value associated with responsibility is flexibility, which simply means that administrators do not ignore individual gr ps, local concerns, or situational differences in formulating and implementing policy.

4. People also expect that government will perform competently, follow due process, remain accountable (not "faceless"), and, perhaps above all be honest.

5. Administrative responsibility is, therefore, an ideal—a castle in the sky. Not surprisingly, a number of pitfalls face any government in attaining it. First is the omnipresent possibility of collusion, for example, between an administrative agency and the group it is supposed to regulate. With massive law enforcement apparatuses, governments also run the risk of letting their zeal for consensus and public order become coercive. Or, zeal for the mission of the organization can transform the public information programs from their legitimate function of keeping the public informed into outright deception. More gently put, truth becomes distorted.

6. While the emergence of an amoral elite of experts does not seem imminent, the growth of professionalism raises four causes for concern: elite professions tend to dominate many agencies; they also dominate in matters of recruitment, selection, and advancement; they are becoming more specialized; and they can infringe upon the prerogatives of political leadership. Another concern for those interested in administrative responsibility is the ethnocentricism of some public administrators.

7. The measures that have been taken to avoid the pitfalls outlined under points 5 and 6 can be discussed within a framework of four categories of control: internal formal, internal informal, external formal, and external informal. No writer advocates exclusive reliance upon any one of these four, however.

8. Furthermore, even in combination, measures such as the following have distinct limitations in making the ideal of administrative responsibility a reality: executive, legislative, and judicial control; interest group representation; citizen participation; professional codes; representative bureaucracy; and public interest. The recent work in the field of moral philosophy has, however, sparked renewed interest in finding more effective measures. For example, work by John Rawls and Walter Kaufmann does suggest a couple of internal informal controls—justice-as-fairness and autonomous morality. The latter, while no more foolproof than the other measures, does at least seem workable.

Concepts for Review

accountability	external and internal controls
Administrative Procedures Act	flexibility
competence	institutionalized citizen participation
contractarianism	judicial review
due process	market segmentation
elitism	new integrity
ethnocentrism	new public administration

professional codes   responsibility
professionalism   responsiveness
public interest   stakeholder analysis
public relations   whistleblower
representative bureaucracy

Problems

1. "Loyalty is the virtue of a dog."—H. L. Mencken. Do you think loyalty to political executives is overrated in the United States? How far should loyalty extend? If you think it even possible, how would you rank that loyalty in comparison with the following: humanity, U.S. Constitution, public interest, political party, social class, religion, profession, union, and client?

2. President Franklin D. Roosevelt once said to an aide: "Tell that man to go see Dean Acheson to learn how a gentlemen resigns." In 1933, as undersecretary of the Treasury, Mr. Acheson was asked to do something he believed illegal. He left the government, but without public complaint, demonstrating his deference to the norm of team loyalty that qualified him to rejoin the Roosevelt administration eight years later as assistant secretary of state. Is this the way resignations should take place or should an individual either stay and fight or resign and fight? (See Weisband and Franck, 1975, for a full discussion of resignation in protest.)

3. Generally, the public accepts the right of business to publicize and advertise, even though the customer pays for it in the long run, but it often regards a similar expenditure of funds for government information as frivolous or a waste of the taxpayer's money. Would you conclude therefore that the public tends to apply a double standard? Why or why not?

4. Write a paper on the various proposals for a national databank.

5. The aim of the ombudsman, a Swedish idea, is to create a representative or agent of the legislation to protect citizens' rights against bureaucratic abuse. More precisely, the ombudsman is available to hear complaints of any citizen against erroneous, unfair, or even impolite action by government officials; and then, if necessary, investigate the complaint, publicize any abuse, and recommend corrective action. Research this idea further and then report on whether the United States should have the ombudsman.

6. "The ethical behavior of public servants . . . is higher than in most sectors of American society, but it can never rise much above the standard of its environment. It is rather difficult to build and maintain integrity in the administrative agencies of government when legislators and private interests connive to commit far greater damage to the general welfare than any bureaucrat has ever been accused of. As long as millionaires can get by without paying income taxes, as long as depletion allowances can help to create a culturally shabby 'nouveau riche' in the oil states, as long as factories can get away with shoddy or unsafe products and pollute our streams and our air with impurity—as long as these big thefts within the public weal are permitted, I cannot get too excited about the relatively

minor graft that may occasionally crop up in the bowels of the bureaucracy" (Stahl, 1971). Do you agree or disagree? Discuss.

7. Toward the end of the 18th century Edmund Burke said: "Constitute government how you please, infinitely the greater part of it must depend upon the exercise of the powers which are left at large to the prudence and uprightness of minister of state." Which ideas expressed in this chapter do you think Burke would be most comfortable with? the least?

8. Select one of the following works to discuss in class in terms of the ethical or value questions it raises for public administration:

> Anouilh, *Antigone.*
> Anouilh, *Becket.*
> Arden, *Left Handed Liberty.*
> Arrighi, *An Ordinary Man.*
> Austen, *Mansfield Park.*
> Bolt, *A Man for All Seasons.*
> Boyer, *Don Juan in Hell.*
> Brecht, *Galileo.*
> Camus, *Caligula.*
> Ibsen, *A Doll's House.*
> Ibsen, *Enemy of the People.*
> Kippardt, *In the Matter of J. Robert Oppenheimer.*
> MacLeish, *J. B.*
> Melville, *Billy Budd.*
> Shaw, *Mrs. Warren's Profession.*
> Stone and Edwards, *1776.*
> Vidal, *The Best Man.*

9. "In governing boards (of regents, trustees, or directors), in regulatory commissions, in regular government departments, or in corporate executive suites, there must always be provision for talking out in private the most controversial issues, for compromise and facesaving and graceful backing down. If all boards were required by law to have all their meetings in public, that would just increase the frequency of lunches and dinners among their members, as they negotiate in informal caucus the positions they are going to take in the formal meetings" (Cleveland, 1972:119). Do you agree with this statement? If yes, what are its implications for "sunshine laws" (discussed in Chapter 2)?

10. How effective do you think Kaufmann's ideal of autonomous morality would be in alleviating the four quandaries of democratic morality discussed earlier in the chapter (namely: coercion, collusion, distortion, and elitism)?

11. Should public officials ever lie? (Hint: Read S. Bok's *Lying.*)

12. Suggest a more ethical approach to the treatment of experimental "subjects" than the one you read about on pp. 141-143.

13. How do you explain the expanded role of the courts discussed in this chapter?

14. Prominent scientists have proposed the establishment of a science court for resolving technical disputes over questions of fact so as to provide a

basis for policy decisions. Prepare a report on the pros and cons of this proposal. (Back isues of *Science* should prove especially helpful.)

15. Explain the following statement: Citizen participation is one more way of posing the classical issues of political philosophy, namely, who should make, and at what level of government, what kinds of decisions, for how large a social unit.

16. How far should one go in embellishing his or her resumé. In 1985, Governor Cuomo of New York discovered that his newly appointed Commissioner of Commerce had credentials at variance with the facts. John C. Michaelson, 33 years old, had claimed to have been "a financial adviser to the Vatican" and a "partner" and a "principal" in a New York investment banking concern. Fact: Michaelson had been a low-ranking associate in a London-based investment banking firm that was doing work for the Vatican. Fact: He was not a partner but one of 30 vice presidents. Michaelson told reporters he had attended Oxford University on a scholarship. Fact: Oxford said he was not a scholarship student. Michaelson told reporters that he came from a poor family. Fact: His father was a lawyer who owned a textile mill. Discuss this incident from Governor Cuomo's standpoint and then from Michaelson's standpoint.

17. Explain how you would use ethical analysis to decide the proper action in each of the 12 incidents listed on p. 148.

Case 4.1
Controlling Biomedical Technology

The Asilomar Conference

In February 1975, many of the leading biologists in the United States gathered under a vaulted roof in the church of the Asilomar Conference Center a few miles north of Monterey, California, The purpose of the historic meeting was to discuss whether the evolving methods of recombinant DNA technology might lead to hazards for the general population.

The conference, arranged through the National Academy of Sciences, was a historic coming of age for molecular biology. At the time, the field was still mainly an academic pursuit with few practical applications for society. DNA was an acronym familiar only to scientists and a few precocious children; few non-specialists knew it as the hereditary material of our cells, the stuff that encodes information for living systems.

In recombinant DNA research, scientists develop organisms that may have never existed before. DNA, or deoxyriboneuclic acid, is the principal substance of genes, the units of heredity that govern how an organism behaves. In nature, DNA recombines within cells of the same or closely related species. In the laboratory, gene splicers chemically snip portions of the long DNA molecules and place them in another organism, usually a simple one such as a bacterium or yeast. The new host then behaves as if the instructions it received were part of its own genetic code, and passes them on to its offspring.

In this manner, bacteria can be turned into miniature "factories" producing valuable drugs, hormones, or proteins that are difficult to acquire from the human or animal cells that produce them naturally. In theory, although no one has done so yet, the same techniques could be used to transfer desirable traits from one human to another, or from one plant or animal species to another.

Asilomar helped lay the groundwork for this line of research. At the same time, both scientists and members of the general public were concened that genetic engineering might lead inadvertently to uncontrollable organisms that would threaten the public safety. Scientists at the conference therefore took the unusual but responsible step of agreeing to follow the advice of an expert watchdog committee before undertaking new kinds of experiments.

Being advisory rather than regulatory, this Recombinant DNA Advisory Committee (RAC) within the National Institutes of Health proved able in the ensuing years to maintain research at a vigorous pace while protecting the public safety. (RAC's guidelines were published in the *Federal Register*, July 7, 1976.) The committee was flexible and thoughtful, and partly as a result of its activities, most fears about genetic engineering threatening the public safety have been stilled.

The Benefits

The scientists at Asilomar had an inkling of the staggering developments that were about to occur. And, in the decade that has followed, techniques for manipulating genetic material went from rudimentary but promising to sophisticated and routine. Biologists today conduct experiments that would have been literally inconceivable in 1975.

It is not an exaggeration to say that *all* of biological research has been revolutionized. Molecular biology has emerged from the ivory tower; industry has developed around it and medicine is being transformed. Scientists now use genetic engineering techniques to study diseases, increase food production, and modernize industries. More than $2.5 billion has been invested since 1975 by companies dedicated to pioneering new medicines and products from biotechnology.

Among the most recent developments and forecasts, are these:

- A hormone that triggers growth in humans will allow thousands of children in the United States with growth disorders to develop normally, and may also help in the treatment of burns, bone fractures, and diseases of the aged.
- Genetically engineered human insulin and a vaccine for hoof-and-mouth disease (a costly scourge of livestock in developing nations) are already on the market, and vaccines against hepatitis, malaria, rabies, and venereal disease are being tested.
- Scientists believe that eventually they will develop food crops that can grow in salty soils, resist insects without the help of pesticides, and even provide their own essential nutrients for growth.
- On cattle and dairy ranches, all-female herds nurtured from handpicked embryos will reach the size of elephants and produce more milk and calves, while genetically altered steers will grow to full maturity in only six months.
- Special enzymes will turn solid waste into useful sugars and alcohol. Other lab-inspired microbes may separate valuable metals from ore and extract and purify oil from depleted wells. Eventually, as much as half of all industrial chemical stocks will be made biologically.

In the distant future, an "organic computer" may be developed if scientists can modify proteins from bacteria to create living "biochips" that will perform a calculation in about a millionth the time of today's best computer chips.

Predictions are that the payoff from these advances will be enormous, providing billions in profits and employment for tens of thousands. Some investment analysts believe that overall biotechnology will provide the spark to reestablish the United States as the undisputed world leader in technology and manufacturing.

By the year 2000, biotechnology will encompass a $23 billion market in medicine alone, according to an estimate by the Arthur D. Little Inc. consulting firm. In agriculture, other experts say, world sales could range from $50 billion to $100 billion by the end of the century.

But What If Something Goes Wrong?

In *The White Plague*, a novel by Frank Herbert, a biologist becomes insane after his wife and children are killed by a terrorist's bomb. Working alone in his basement laboratory, he produces a substance that seeks out and kills female embryos. The substance cannot be contained and becomes a global threat.

The story is fiction, but the issue it presents is among those related to biotechnology that haunt many scientists and government officials, who wonder if current safeguards are adequate to ensure public safety.

Fears of a runaway epidemic have subsided since they were raised at the Asilomar Conference over a decade ago. But equally difficult questions of morality, environmental hazards, and even the integrity of human heredity have been raised in recent years. Do we do violence to nature if new genes are implanted into experimental or domestic animals? Will engineered bacteria designed to prevent ice formation on crops permanently supplant natural organisms in the environment? Is the future of our own species imperiled by gene therapies?

David Baltimore, a recipient of the 1975 Nobel Prize in physiology and medicine, raises these concerns.

- "Scientists will soon discover many subtle genetic factors in the makeup of human beings, and those discoveries will challenge the basic concepts of equality on which our society is based. . . .

  "The ability to take apart very complex genetic characteristics such as intelligence is a long way off, so I'm not worried about genetic discrimination along those lines. But I am worried about discrimination because of an individual's propensity to get a specific tumor. Industry is already trying to get a genetic profile of workers in order to put those with one profile in this situation and those with a different profile in that setting."
- "How about the use of growth hormones in [people other than pituitary dwarfs] who want it for 'cosmetic' reasons and to increase proficiency in sports?"
- "We're learning a tremendous amount about hormones that affect brain function—mood, sleep, waking, anxiety, depression. Today, we abuse crude drugs that affect these elements of our personality. But what happens when we have drugs that will be much more specific and with fewer side effects? Will we find ourselves an increasingly drug-dependent, drug-using society?"

Is the profit motive inconsistent with medical matters? In 1983, a Virginia physician announced that he had formed a new organization, International Kidney

Exchange, to buy healthy kidneys from human beings and sell them to patients seeking kidney transplants.

The ethical questions raised by the for-profit sale of human organs are quite new. Somewhat similar questions were raised earlier with respect to surrogate motherhood. In this procedure, the husband donates sperm to fertilize the egg of a woman who is not his wife. This surrogate mother carries the resulting embryo to term for a fee (usually at least $10,000).

If we have succeeded in keeping our freedom in the age of television, snooping devices, and computers—and if we have thus far avoided nuclear wars and disasters (no one died at Three Mile Island)—then perhaps we can preserve our freedom and our safety during this biological revolution. But that will require that we properly identify the problems, keep in mind what matters most in life, and design an effective institutional arrangement to ensure the preservation of these fundamental rights.

Case Questions

1. What are the moral issues raised in the case—both expressed and implied? What should public policy be with respect to these issues? Why?
2. Who should be involved in science policymaking? In what forum would it be best for them to be heard?
3. Companies want to know the best way to protect proprietary interests in bioengineering processes and products. Is it better for a business to patent organisms or processes, or attempt to keep them secret?
4. Government regulations for research have been relaxed because research to date has proceeded without an accident. But some lawyers warn that business is underestimating the potential hazards associated with some bioengineered products, hazards that may only become apparent decades after these products have been introduced. What should public policy be?

Case References

Ronald Wetzel, "Applications of Recombinant DNA Technology," *American Scientist*, November–December 1980; Peter Singer, "Technology and Procreation: How Far Should We Go?" *Technology Review*, February 1985; John Diebold, *Making the Future Work* (New York: Simon & Schuster, 1984); "Special Report: Spawning New Forms of Life," *U.S. News & World Report*, March 16, 1983; Barnaby J. Feder, "Gene-Splicing: Legal Pitfalls," *New York Times*, December 1, 1981. David Baltimore, "Still No Such Thing as Playing God," *Houston Chronicle*, February 21, 1985.

Case 4.2
Eldridge's Complaint

The warm May sun shined friendly on Norton, Virginia, a small coal-mining town in the southwestern corner of the state. George Eldridge noticed a kindly western wind beginning to blow down from the mountains as he journeyed out to his mailbox. Even with his arthritis and diabetes, he felt pretty good.

At least until he saw the legal-sized envelope with the Social Security Administration (SSA) logo. His name had been typed—this was no form letter announcing something innocuous like a ZIP code change. He immediately riped it open and began to read, all the way to the last line: "unless additional evidence is submitted which shows that you are still unable to work because of your impairment."

Eldridge had had problems with the SSA before, beginning five years earlier, in 1967, when he first applied for complete disability benefits. After his application was rejected, he requested a hearing before a hearing examiner—now called an Administrative Law Judge (ALJ)— and received a favorable ruling. Then, in 1969, after reviewing his case but without seeing him or performing any medical tests, the state agency administering the disability program for SSA decided to terminate Eldridge's benefits.

Upon learning this, Eldridge requested that the agency reconsider his case. Feeling that the SSA decision-making process had been unfair and arbitrary, he also decided to challenge SSA on constitutional grounds. Specifically, Eldridge's attorney would argue that it was a violation of due process of law (protected by the Fifth Amendment) for the Secretary of HEW, David Mathews, who was responsible for SSA, to terminate a disability recipient's benefits without first affording that person an oral hearing. In other words, administrators should not be able to make decisions that will severely jeopardize a citizen's liberty or property without holding a hearing.

In March 1971, Eldridge finally got his hearing. The ALJ ordered payments resumed; accordingly, the district court declared the constitutional case moot.

Eldridge remembered these past battles all too well. Now, it looked as though he and his attorney would have to fight them again.

Eldridge could have chosen again to battle his way through reconsideration, hearing, and SSA Appeals Council (a process known as "exhaustion of administrative remedies") to get to the district court. There, a judge would have reviewed the record to see if there was substantial evidence to support SSA's decision (a process known as the "substantial evidence rule"). But Eldridge and his attorney, Donald Earls, were willing to concede that the agency had abided by all statutes and regulations. The crux of their argument was to be that those regulations were themselves unconstitutional. Therefore, they took the issue directly to court.

On April 9, 1973, a Federal District Judge held that the government must provide a pretermination hearing for those receiving disability benefits under Title II of the Social Security Act, just as the Supreme Court had required a hearing for those receiving benefits under Title IV, Aid to Familes with Dependent Children (*Goldberg* v. *Kelly*). The government had argued that a decision in favor of Eldridge would result in an intolerable financial and administrative burden, but the judge concluded that procedural due process does not exist to minimize costs and maximize efficiency.

The government promptly appealed this decision to the U.S. Circuit Court of Appeals and lost. The government then appealed to the Supreme Court.

On October 6, 1975, the Supreme Court heard oral arguments from Eldridge's attorney and Solicitor General Robert H. Bork. The fact that the solicitor general himself would make the argument was an indication of how important the case was to the government.

Essentially, there were three parts to Bork's argument:

- Existing procedures are fair; Eldridge just lacked the patience to use the available alternatives.
- Because the statute does not require proof of indigence, disability recipients are not as needy as welfare recipients.
- The interests of the government in avoiding excessive administrative costs outweigh Eldridge's interest in continued receipt of benefits. Moreover, a pretermination hearing requirement would pose costs that the government cannot at this time afford.

Bork elaborated on the last point as follows:

> We are, in effect, dealing with a cost benefit judgment; and so viewed the question becomes really how many? The decision of this case will have a heavy impact upon the decision of how many decisional processes of government must be conformed to a judicial model rather than to an administrative model. I think that is important and clearly there has to be a stopping point somewhere to the imposition of judicial models upon governmental decision making because it is very expensive; and in some circumstances, which I would contend this is one, adds little or nothing to the alternative procedures provided. . . .
>
> It would be nice to say, I suppose, that the system must be perfect. Nobody must ever be terminated, no matter how temporarily, but indeed I don't think any legal process, any chemical process, or any industrial process ever can afford to remove the last bit of impurities in that process. It gets extraordinarily expensive. Indeed, it begins to defeat the ends of the process. I can put an approximate dollar value on both sides of this due process equation. [The total figure he calculated for increased costs to government was $25 million per year.]

As Bork returned to his seat, Eldridge's attorney, Donald Earls, rose to make his argument:

- Eldridge had already been completely through the administrative process twice. Both times he had lost on the paper review but prevailed in the hearing. In one case, 18 months had elapsed between the termination decision and the hearing.
- Welfare was not a viable option to support him while he exhausted his administrative remedies, since welfare benefits (1) may require more stringent standards than qualification for disability, and (2) begin only after a lengthy investigation.
- Eldridge had as much entitlement to an opportunity for an evidentiary hearing concerning his termination of disability benefits as a welfare recipient concerning his or her welfare check. In each of the following instances, case law mandates a prior hearing: a wage earner concerning his or her paycheck, a parolee concerning his or her freedom, a prison inmate concerning his or her good-time credits, a consumer concerning his or her old stove, an uninsured motorist concerning his or her license, an elderly person concerning his or her medicare benefits, a student concerning his or her suspension from school.

Earls attacked Bork's contention that a claimant would not suffer because of lost benefits: "I feel in the George Eldridge case, where Mr. Eldridge was required to sleep in one bed with five children, lost his home that he had worked all his life for [first] as a laborer on the railroad and then as a soda distributor, driving a truck and carrying cases of soda: there certainly he lost everything which could not be recouped. . . . This is what happened in the George Eldridge case, and this is what happens in many of the cases."

Case Questions

1. If you were on the Supreme Court, how would you decide? Support your decision.
2. What is the public interest in this case?

Case References

Mathews v. *Eldridge*, 424 U.S. 319 (1976); Phillip J. Cooper, "*Mathews* v. *Eldridge*: The Anatomy of an Administrative Law Case," *Public Law and Public Administration*, (Palo Alto, Calif.: Mayfield, 1983), pp. 355–401.

Case 4.3
Relocating a State School

The division of corrections in a midwestern state has decided that the state boys' school is grossly inadequate and a dangerous firetrap. After some struggle, the state legislature has appropriated $6 million for a new reformatory.

The Division wishes to build it in a state forest. Such a location would provide attractive surroundings, isolation from cities, and constructive work for the boys.

Unfortunately, conservation groups issue vehement protests and threaten court action to block the move. They also start a public campaign to force the governor and the State Corrections board to reverse the decision. Meanwhile, the community in which the present reformatory is located organizes a committee to keep it there. The new reformatory appears to be in deep trouble.

Case Question

As a public relations director for the welfare department, what are your recommendations?

Case Reference

Based on Scott M. Cutlip and Allen H. Center, *Effective Public Relations* (Englewood Cliffs, N.J.: Prentice-Hall, 1982), p. 521.

PART II

Program Management

5

Planning

Introduction

Planning is the keystone of the arch of program management, and government success is often synonymous with planning success. Quite properly, then, Part II of this book on managing the public sector begins with planning.

As will be explained shortly, planning covers a far wider spectrum of meanings that can be encompassed in this chapter. Indeed, many of the things said in Chapter 2 about policymaking apply to planning, which we interpret in this chapter quite broadly: reasoning about how an organization will get where it wants to go.

The essence of planning is to see opportunities and threats in the future and to exploit or combat them by decisions taken in the present. It is therefore hardly an overstatement to say that planning, as defined here, shapes the whole field of public administration. It determines the limits of government responsibility, the allocation of resources and distribution of costs, the division of labor, and the extent of public controls. Nor is it an overstatement to say that the magnitude of current problems—such as pollution of air and water, exploitation of natural resources, and decline in the quality of urban life—are related to our inability to plan effectively.

If planning is an important area of public administration, it is also a relatively neglected one. Recent attempts to remedy this neglect of planning in the literature of public administration have yielded almost as much confusion as progress. For this reason, we begin our discussion by attempting to clarify what we mean, and what we do not mean, by planning. Then, we shall examine a formal model of the planning process. The importance of this model should be underscored: It sets a framework for organizing our thinking about the planning process and foreshadows the chapters that follow.

One final and crucial point: If, and only if, we keep the themes of the last three chapters firmly in mind can we hope to develop a balanced view of American public administration. I therefore warmly encourage the reader to test continually the crisp and, at times, cooly logical ideas suggested by the formal model against the messy and seemingly irrational forces of politics, intergovernmental relations, and values. The perennial question, in short, must be this: Given the environment of administration, how well will this or that management concept work? Worlds of certainty do not lie ahead.

Critical Definitions

In order that no doubt will be left in the reader's mind, it would be helpful to both scholars and practitioners of planning if a common vocabulary, accepted by all, were available. Such however is not the case. So, from the start, we find ourselves in a position uncomfortably close to that of Humpty Dumpty in *Through the Looking-Glass.* There, it will be recalled, Humpty defines *glory* as "a nice knock-down argument." To Alice's reasonable objections, he says scornfully, "when *I* use a word, it means just what I choose it to mean. . . . The question is which is to be the master. . . ."

Actually, our situation is not quite that bad. In the first place, while Humpty is merely being capricious, we can give solid reasons for defining planning a certain way. And, second, the definitions offered below—unlike Humpty's unique definition of *glory*—are supported by an increasing number of scholars.

A Variety of Meanings

Before offering a "common vocabulary," it might be useful to consider a few of the alternative ways of viewing planning.

Land-Use Planning.   To some, its meaning is virtually synonymous with *city planning* and thus stands for little more than development of *land-use plans.* These plans are concerned primarily with physical location and design: They include rules and regulations for subdivisions, building codes, and *zoning laws* (the principal tool for enforcing use of private property as prescribed by the municipality).

But not all planning at the local level has so narrow a focus. A *comprehensive plan*, for example, is an official document adopted by a local government as a guide to decision making about the physical development of the community for the next 20 to 30 years. *Comprehensive* means that the plan encompasses all geographic parts of the community and all functional elements that bear on physical development. According to Alan Black (1968:350), three technical elements

These drawings of San Francisco show that a tall building at the top of a hill (left) allows for an unobstructed view down the street and beyond, while a tall building on the slope severely restricts the view from above. In 1984, the city approved one of the toughest plans ever put together for an American downtown area. It strictly limits the height of new buildings and dictates more tapered, graceful designs for them. (Source: Department of City Planning, San Francisco. *The Urban Design Plan*, 1971, p. 82.)

are commonly included in comprehensive plans: the private use of land, community facilities, and circulation (i.e., transportation). "Comprehensive plans may cover other subjects, such as utilities, civic design, and special uses of land unique to the locality. Usually there is background information on the population, economy, existing land use, assumptions, and community goals."

In the last few years, many cities and states (Florida, for example) that once thought the population explosion the next best thing to sunshine have embarked on a "grow slow" campaign to protect their way of life. A study by the Council of Environmental Quality's Task Force on Land Use and Urban Growth identified this new mood in the nation. Increasingly, citizens are asking what urban growth will add to the quality of their lives. They are measuring new development proposals by the extent to which environmental criteria are satisfied—by what new housing or business will generate in terms of additional traffic, pollution of air and water, erosion, and scenic disturbance. In sum, comprehensive planning has become a logical vehicle to achieve agreement on growth management. Its scope, moreover, is much broader than earlier planning attempts, since it considers the social and economic ramifications of development in addition to the traditional physical factors.

Development Planning.   But not everyone wants to curb growth. In particular, the governments of the developing nations of Asia, Africa, and Latin America attempt to set out the chief measures they need to take in order to raise national output per person. This is *development* *planning.* The typical plan will include most of the following: a survey of current economic conditions and the current social situation, an evaluation of the preceding plan, a statement of objectives, estimates of growth, suggested measures to raise growth rate, and a program of government expenditures.

National Planning. When a government attempts to influence what kinds of goods and services will be produced, and in what amounts, it is engaged in *national planning.* The mere mention of the concept causes the pulse rate of most American business executives to rise. The reason is that they associate national planning with the coercive methods of socialist countries like the Soviet Union. But, as the Japanese and French governments have demonstrated, national planning can be indirect and noncoercive. For example, by providing information and incentives, government can encourage business investment to shift from "sunset industries" (like automobiles, steel, and textiles) to "sunrise industries" (like electronics, energy conversion, and chemicals). This is what recent talk about the reindustrialization of America is about. (Chapter 12 will treat this topic in more depth.)

Thus, national planning should not be confused with *fiscal planning* (which will be discussed in Chapter 9). The former attempts to influence industry (directly or indirectly), while the latter attempts to influence economic conditions. Nor should national planning be confused with attempts by the National Security Council and the Domestic Council to plan in broad areas of public concern like defense and welfare. When the national government is engaged in this kind of planning, it is engaged in an activity not unlike that of a large corporation. This version of planning we shall refer to as *managerial planning.*

Managerial Planning. Since the thrust of this book is toward the integration—not the fragmentation—of thought, this interpretation of planning will be emphasized. Thus, planning will be treated as a general process, recognizable in a great number of human situations. The definition of planning that opened this chapter reflects this more general approach. *Planning is reasoning about how an organization will get where it wants to go. Its essence is to see opportunities and threats in the future and to exploit or combat them by decisions taken in the present.*

To really grasp the dynamics of this process, it is of course necessary to understand its components. What, for example, is a *plan?* How does a plan differ from a *policy?* From a *program?*

Policy, Plans, Programs

For our purposes, a policy is a statement of goals and of the relative importance attached to each goal. It is translated into a *plan* by specifying the objectives to be attained. A proposed set of specific actions intended to implement a plan is called a *program.*

A simple example will perhaps clarify these terse terminological stipulations (see Helmer, 1968: 14-16). Assume that the mayor of a city has among his or her goals an increase in the physical safety of the city's inhabitants and improvements in housing conditions. The mayor might then announce a policy that these goals, in the order stated, are to have priority over all other goals. A plan to implement this policy might specify the objectives of *(a)* reducing the rate of crimes of violence in the city as well as the death rate from traffic accidents by 25 percent, and *(b)* providing an additional 10,000 housing units. A program would spell out in detail the action to be taken to achieve these objectives; for example, increasing the police force by 1,000 and providing city-backed, long-term loans to construction firms.

Figure 5-1 provides a more detailed example of this approach. At the

---

Figure 5-1
Objectives for the Fiscal Year, Charlotte, North Carolina:
Law Enforcement Administration

Provide leadership and management of all human and fiscal resources allocated to the police department so as to elicit high morale and interteam cooperation, enhance community relations, and deliver high quality, effective, law enforcement services. Responsibilities include administration, planning and research, personnel, inspection and internal investigations, and the training bureau.

1. Institute an active minority recruitment program so that their representation in the police force as ordered by the U.S. District Court will be accomplished at an early date. During FY 75 fill patrolmen vacancies at an average rate of over 40 percent with minorities, and sergeant vacancies at an average rate of over 30 percent with minorities. Investigate the possibility of filling at least one higher rank position with a minority member by arranging a one- to two-year intergovernmental transfer with a metropolitan city.

2. Investigate and report to city manager results within three weeks for 75 percent (and eight weeks for 100 percent) of all complaints concerning alleged police misconduct or misuse of force.

3. Report on findings within one week for 85 percent (and four weeks for 100 percent) of all accidents involving police equipment.

4. Promote an atmosphere of community safety and security through increased citizen involvement in police efforts and establish measurements that will indicate the degree of success attained.

5. Report monthly progress on implementation of the LEAA-funded program to reduce robberies, and on available results or indications found.

6. Increase the cost-effectiveness of the police department by reduction or elimination of less productive activities and simplification of procedures so as to reduce the operating budget by 2 percent in FY 75.

7. Increase in-service training hours by 3 percent to improve performance in areas such as those where a high incidence of officer injuries is occurring or where clearances/apprehensions can be improved.

Source: Budget and Evaluation Office, Charlotte, N.C., *Objectives FY 75.*

top of the exhibit, the city of Charlotte, North Carolina, stated its goals in the area of law enforcement. Note how general these are. But below are listed seven rather specific objectives to attain these goals. What specific actions would you recommend for each objective?

The crucial difference between the terms *policy, plan,* and *program* is level of generality. More specifically, an increasing number of writers suggest that the term *policy* should be reserved for statements of intention and direction of a relatively high order. Harold Lasswell (1951:5–8) puts it succinctly: "The word *policy* is commonly used to designate the *most* important choices made either in organized or in private life." The emphasis, then, is not upon the topical issues of the moment but upon the fundamental problems of society.

As we shall see below, these terminological stipulations are more than mere academic hairsplitting; they help to make better policy. Possibly, Confucius had something like this in mind when he said that because actions follow words, he would, if ruler of the world, fix the meaning of words.

The Formal Planning Model

To provide a meaningful and systematic framework for understanding the planning process, the now familiar and well-established model of the rational planning process is presented. According to this model, a planner is acting rationally if he or she undertakes the following five interrelated steps:

1. Identify the problem or problems to be solved and the opportunities to be seized upon.
2. Design alternative solutions or courses of action (i.e., policies, plans, and programs) to solve the problems, or seize upon the opportunities and forecast the consequences and effectiveness of each alternative.
3. Compare and evaluate the alternatives with each other and with the forecasted consequences of unplanned development, and choose the alternative whose probable consequences would be preferable.
4. Develop a plan of action for implementing the alternative selected, including budgets, project schedules, regulatory measures, and the like.
5. Maintain the plan on a current basis through feedback and review of information.

Although these steps are treated separately, and in linear sequence, in actual practice they represent a cyclic process. Evaluation procedures, for example, enter into the process at the outset in the identification of problems and opportunities; they also influence the design

Figure 5-2
Basic Planning Model

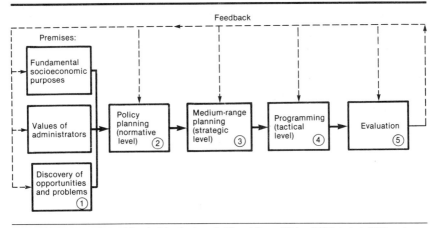

Source: This is a composite model, embodying the theoretical formulations of Steiner (1969), Jantsch (1969), and Ozbekan (1965), as well as the author's own work in forecasting and systemic planning.

of alternative solutions. Likewise, the problems of implementation enter into the design stages as constraints that must be taken into account. For this reason, it is probably preferable to present the model not as a list of steps but as a dynamic and iterative process. In this model, shown in Figure 5-2, the five steps have been rearranged in the form of a dynamic model and are indicated by the circled numbers.

Premises

At the left of the model are three underlying foundations of any government planning effort. The first, fundamental organizational socioeconomic purposes, refers to those underlying ends that society expects of its governmental institutions. Basically, this means that society demands that governments utilize the resources at their disposal to satisfy the wants of society. It is important for administrators to keep in mind this underlying reason for the existence of government. It explains why, as governments become larger and society becomes more complex, the things society wants from government become more numerous and sometimes contradictory.

The second fundamental set of foundations for planning are the values the top administrators hold—for example: conservation of resources, efficiency, beauty, equity, pluralism, individuality, and participation. Included here too would be the values of the elected officials, both executive (e.g., president, governor, and mayor) and legislative (e.g., Congress, legislature, and council). In fact, in the earlier stages of the planning process, where policy decisions are made, the influence of this group—especially through legislation—is usually decisive. Needless to say, their values do not always coincide with those of the administrator.

We now come to the final foundation of any government planning effort. A cardinal purpose of planning is to discover future opportunities and make plans to exploit them. Likewise, basic to planning is the detection of obstructions or problems that must be removed from the road ahead. The most effective plans are those that exploit opportunities and remove obstacles on the basis of an objective and systematic survey of the future. There is, in short, an enormous payoff to the skilled probing of the future and to relating the results of that probing to an unbiased study of an agency's strengths, weaknesses, and purpose. Today's administrators are not alone in their efforts to forecast; the formal study of the future has, in fact, become an industry. In the United States, a burgeoning network of future-oriented research institutes stretches from the Stanford Research Institute on the West Coast to the Hudson Institute on the East—and the Rand Corporation has branches on both. Further, Congress, by establishing a Technology Assessment Board in 1972, evidenced concern with the future. How might these studies be used?

If a city is planning for orderly community development, then the regular forecasting of change becomes vital. What should such a forecast include? At least such factors as number of people, number of school children, number and types of new residential and other buildings, and number and location of automobiles. Whenever possible, the forecast should include changes in the characteristics of the population, of land use, of the economic conditions, and of transportation patterns.

The essence of planning is to make *present* decisions with the knowledge of their future consequences. Hence, planning requires knowledge of the future. What do we have to do today if we want to be in a particular place in the future?

Our third premise of planning implies, however, more than good forecasts. The effective planner must also be able to discern clearly and accurately what the problem is. As the French novelist Georges Bernanas once wrote, the worst, the most corrupting, of lies are problems poorly stated. What is the problem facing the United States in Central America—the spread of communism, social and economic injustice, or a little of both? How one defines a problem is of crucial importance. In the 1960s, Washington planners defined the war in Vietnam as a "classic revolutionary war." Accordingly, President Kennedy reacted to that definition with the doctrine of counterinsurgency. But with hindsight it is clear that this approach was wrong. The guerrillas in South Vietnam did *not* achieve decisive results on their own; there was no popular uprising. They merely served to harass and distract both the

United States and South Vietnam so that North Vietnam regular forces could win in conventional battles (Summers, 1982).

During the 1960s, the problems of poverty were construed largely in terms of inadequate performance by the individual or group. Accordingly, the solution was a services strategy, that is, the provision of specific services that would change the modes of behavior that were presumed to be at the root of poverty. In time it became apparent that the cost-benefit ratios of service programs were, at the very least, depressing. An alternative way to look at the problem of poverty was in terms of a lack of money. This view was surely supported by social research: The one seemingly fixed correlation in the literature was that well-being rises with income. It was this new view of the poverty problem that led in 1969 to the development of the Family Assistance Plan (or guaranteed income). More recently, George Gilder, in his *Wealth and Poverty* (1981), has defined poverty in terms of expectation. Thus, the daughter of a Pasadena pediatrician attending Berkeley is not poor in quite the same way that a black teenager standing on a Newark street corner is—although both might wear the same tattered clothes and live in substandard housing.

But attention to the definition of problems must not replace attention to the discovery of opportunities. Actually, by consistently directing performance toward opportunity rather than toward problems, the administrator will tend to foster high morale. In contrast, the problem-focused organization is an organization on the defensive; it feels that it has performed well if things do not get worse. In short, administrators who want to create and maintain the spirit of achievement in their agencies stress opportunity.

Policy Planning

The next major structural element in Figure 5-2 is policy planning. *Policy planning* is the process of determining goals and their priorities. It is at this point in the planning process that the influence of political leadership is especially important.

According to journalist David Halberstam 1969:370-71), during the Vietnam War the highest level of American policymakers refused to accept the necessity for making decisions at this level. They tried to delay such decisions and thus buy a little more time. These policymakers "were above all functional, operational, *tactical* men, not really intellectuals, and tactical men think in terms of options, while intellectuals less so; intellectuals might think in terms of the sweep of history and might believe that 12 months would make little difference in Vietnam."

To no small extent, it was precisely this failure to distinguish properly between policy and program that undermined much of the extraordinary effort at social improvement in the 1960s. Daniel P.

Daniel Moynihan, who served in the subcabinets of Presidents Kennedy and Johnson and in the cabinet of Nixon, argues that too much American policy is defined in terms of program. In the picture above, Ambassador Moynihan prepares to argue in the United Nations. In late 1976, Professor Moynihan was elected senator from New York. (United Press International)

Moynihan (1973:272–73), who served in the subcabinets of Presidents Kennedy and Johnson and in the cabinet of President Nixon, argues that one of the more important things about the structure of American government is that too much public policy is defined in terms of *program* rather than true *policy.*

> In simpler times a simple pragmatic approach was an efficient way to go about the public business. The problem comes . . . when society becomes ambitious and begins to seek to bring about significant changes in the operation of complex systems such as society itself.

The problem with the program approach is that it deals only with a part of the system; policy, on the other hand, seeks to respond to the system in its entirety. Moynihan continues:

> The idea of policy is not new. We have for long been accustomed to the idea of foreign policy, including defense policy. Since 1946 Congress has mandated an employment and income policy more or less explicitly based on a "general theory" of the endlessly intricate interconnections of such matters. Yet our ways of behavior resist this: only great crises, great dangers, seem to evoke the effort. Or have seemed able to do so in the past. I believe, however, that a learning process of sorts has been going on. Increasingly the idea of systemwide policies commends itself to persons of responsibility in public affairs as an approach both desirable and necessary.

Apparently, President Carter learned little from the lesson of the 1960s, or was unable to act on principles Moynihan deduced from it. In any event, he came to the presidency with no agenda. He did not see the presidency as a chance to put any program into effect but rather as a job to be performed skillfully. Rather than *tell* his energy secretary, in broad outline, what energy policy he wanted developed, he *asked* the secretary for a policy.

Carter's economic policy pleased neither conservatives nor liberals. Consider these zig-zags: During his campaign, Carter endorsed standby wage and price control authority; between election and inauguration, he became an opponent. A week after inauguration, he declared the economy stagnant and proposed a package of stimulative spending increases and tax cuts; less than three months later, he abandoned the cornerstones of the package and, citing inflation as the principal economic menace, proposed the first of four antiinflation programs. A year later, he again asked for a major tax cut, only to have to again delay it and scale it back in response to inflationary pressures. In 1978, he offered his second and third antiinflation programs. But after a week of adverse reaction, the administration turned to the Federal Reserve for a sharp increase in interest rates as a rescue. In 1979, Carter began the decontrol of crude oil prices, having failed two years earlier to win approval of a tax that would have continued those price controls.

"Each time a policy was developed, the policy was too weak for the problems that appeared," Barry P. Bosworth, Carter's director of the Council on Wage and Price Stability and now a Brookings Institution economist said. "We had no overall framework of what are the things we stand for and what are our priorities" (*New York Times*, March 23, 1980).

This vacillation was only exceeded by Carter's handling of the Iran crisis. Rather than develop and adhere to a consistent policy on Iran's shah, the administration said the United States would not let the deposed Iranian leader in, then it would, then it would not let him stay, then it promised that if he left he could come back, then it did not want him back, then finally it did not want him to leave Panama. As Hugh Sidey wrote: "There is almost no precedent for such a ludicrous sequence executed in the name of serious statecraft. It is a kind of madness—not policy, or the exercise of conscience, or principle, or honor, or good sense, or anything but the evidence of a superpower lost and hesitant in the darkness" (*Houston Post*, March 31, 1980).

By way of contrast, let us consider the clear goals of the Apollo mission. Write Sayles and Chandler (1971:21):

> While both purposes and plans need to have a great deal of flexibility to allow for changes in sentiment, new information, and unforeseen problems and opportunities, objectives need to be relatively fixed and highly specific. They become the emotional symbols, the universally visible target that attracts and holds political support. They can also become the catalyst that mobilizes resources and encourages whole new technologies by capturing the imagination, the commitment, and the dedication of both those who will support the program and those who will actually do the work.

Medium-Range Planning

The best policy is only a policy—that is, good intentions—unless it is transformed into action. Medium-range planning is an important step in that direction. At this stage in the planning process, detailed, coordinated, and comprehensive plans are made for an agency to deploy the resources necessary to attain the goals laid down in the policy-planning stage. We are concerned, in particular, with two aspects of this stage: (1) the design of alternatives, and (2) the analysis of each alternative in terms of its consequences.

Design of Alternatives.   Let us return for a moment to the issue of poverty. It can be said that in the last three years of the Johnson administration there was fairly wide agreement that the existing welfare system constituted a major problem. Further, there was even considerable consensus on the goals of the welfare problem: to raise incomes of the poor; to narrow disparities among states in benefit levels; to reduce inequities in treatment of different kinds of poor people; to increase incentives to work; to remove incentives to break up families. But on the question of how to achieve these goals—that is, what the objectives should be—polarization was the rule.

According to Alice M. Rivlin (1971:19 ff), who served as assistant secretary for planning and evaluation during the Johnson administration, at least three alternative strategies on how to attain these goals were available and each had its spokespeople both within and outside the administration. One of these approaches was to improve the existing welfare system by a series of amendments to make it more uniform and more nearly adequate. Another was put forth by the advocates of a negative income tax. And the third was family or children allowance.

It would be a serious mistake to jump to the easy conclusion that the existence of such widely divergent alternatives is a bad thing. Consider the 1964 planning group headed by William Bundy. This group also presented President Johnson with a set of three alternatives—but these concerned the Vietnam War. The first alternative was light bombing with more reprisals and more use of covert operations. The second was very heavy massive bombing, including the Phuc Yen airfield at Hanoi and cutting the rail links with China. And the third was a moderate solution—a slow squeeze, which allowed the United States to put increasing pressure on Hanoi while "keeping the hostage alive" but still permitting it to pull back if it wished. What was significant about these proposals of course was that all three included bombing; there was, in other words, really no political option at all.

What lesson is to be derived from these two cases? Simply this: Effective planning calls for a multiplicity of inputs. To achieve this multiplicity, the planner must studiously avoid becoming the captive of any one group of advisers or experts. To emphasize this point, we might cite one more example—this time from the Kennedy administration.

Shortly after the Bay of Pigs disaster, a number of members of the Kennedy circle became increasingly uneasy with the decision-making processes of the administration. Arthur Goldberg, the new secretary of labor, finally asked the president why he had not consulted more widely, why he had taken such a narrow spectrum of advice, much of it so predictable. Kennedy said that he meant no offense, that even though Goldberg was a good man, he *was* in labor, not in foreign policy.

"You're wrong," Goldberg replied, "you're making the mistake of compartmentalizing your cabinet." The secretary then went on to point out—much to the president's surprise—that the two men in the cabinet who should have been consulted were Orville Freeman, the secretary of argiculture, and himself. Freeman had been a marine, made amphibious landings, and knew how tough such landings can be; and Goldberg had been in OSS during World War II and had run guerilla operations (Halberstam, 1969:90).

Analysis of the Consequences of Alternatives.   After an adequate list of alternatives is developed, the next step is to consider their consequences. In this respect, the case of the Family Assistance Plan (FAP) is again instructive. In the first place, thanks to the development in early 1969 of a simulation model (discussed in the next chapter), it was possible to actually test and cost out the various versions of FAP. The use of this technique, probably without precedence in the development of major social legislation in the opinion of Moynihan, did much to discipline and inform debate.

In the second place, the case of FAP is instructive because it involved the use of experimentation. Hence, those wanting to know the consequences of the various versions of FAP merely had to examine the preliminary results from carefully designed negative income tax experiments in New Jersey, Iowa, and North Carolina.

The case of FAP involved the use of yet a third procedure to scrutinize the consequence of the alternatives: congressional hearings. While not as modern as computer simulation and social experimentation, it is, all in all, just as effective. In fact, it was this process more than the other two that proved most effective in exposing the undesirable consequences of FAP.

In 1979, a series of case studies by the Advisory Commission on Intergovernmental Relations (ACIR) revealed that much of the growth of the federal government in recent years had been accidental. Simply put, many of the larger and more controversial federal programs were adopted *without much consideration of their long-range significance.* For this reason, the ACIR concluded, "the construction of the contemporary leviathan state must be judged in part to be simply a mistake." Consider this pair of examples.

In 1977, an apparently minor amendment was voted by Congress into the Small Business Administration's Disaster Loan Program, making farmers as well as businessmen eligible for benefits. The program was budgeted at $20 million, but within several months applications from farmers came to $1.4 billion.

When Congress enacted disability insurance in 1956, sponsors estimated that costs by 1980 would be $860 million for one million workers. But the costs surpassed that figure in the 1960s. From 1970 to 1978, costs quadrupled to about $13 billion and for 1980 there were 5.4 million beneficiaries on the rolls, more than five times the original estimate.

Not surprisingly, techniques to scrutinize consequences were certainly atrophied if not totally absent, in planning the war in Vietnam.

In early March 1965, a pessimistic Emmitt John Hughes, a former White House aide under Eisenhower, went to see McGeorge Bundy. What, Hughes asked, if the North Vietnamese retaliate by matching the American air escalation with their own ground escalation. Hughes would long remember the answer and the cool smile. "Just suppose it happens," Hughes persisted. Bundy answered, "We can't assume what we don't believe." (Halberstam, 1969:640)

These three anecdotes bring to mind an aphorism by the German philosopher Nietzsche: "A very popular error: having the courage of one's convictions; rather it is a matter of having the courage for an *attack* on one's convictions!!!" Good philosophy, good administration.

Programming

The planning process began, it will be recalled, on a lofty plane, where goals are set and policy established. That stage then merged into a consideration of alternatives and their consequences. Now we arrive at the point where these alternatives must be divided into specific targets that need to be met and actions that need to be taken in order that the objectives are attained. At this point in the process, money must be set aside or budgeted for these programs and actions.

A program is thus a governmental action initiated in order to secure objectives whose attainment is by no means certain without human effort. The degree to which the predicted consequences take place we call *successful implementation*. To put it inelegantly, implementation is the nuts and bolts of the planning process. (Programming or implementation is similar to what private sector managers call *control*).

Consider policies with the objective of improving environmental quality. A variety of specific actions are available to give effect to environmental policies. These approaches to policy objectives fall into four general sets (Caldwell, 1972). In brief:

1. Self-executory: for example, the pricing of pollution and other forms of environmental degradation through taxes, licenses, and rebates.

2. Self-helping: for example, establishment of environmental rights which may be enforced through judicial action.
3. Technological: for instance, specifications regarding applications of technology; assistance for development of ameliorating technological innovations.
4. Administrative: for instance, air and water quality standards; controls over emissions, land use, water disposal, and other environment-affecting behaviors.

What, then, should those at the top do? Perhaps the most important rule to follow is: Do not divorce programming or implementation from policy. Later we shall see that this rule is more than a homily. Chapter 7, which is concerned largely with implementation, focuses on a number of specific steps that the planner can take to tie policy and implementation together. Among such steps, we shall consider the role of incentives, penalties, and rewards; the reduction of the length and unpredictability of necessary decision sequences; and the creation of an effective communication system. Chapter 8 stresses the need for careful attention—early in the planning process—to the organizational structure for executing a program.

Evaluation

The last stage in our basic model is evaluation. It is axiomatic that effective planning requires periodic review to ensure not only that the plans are being carried out in the prescribed manner but also that they are achieving the expected results—an axiom of administration not always honored.

This task, in turn, requires that the output of public services be measured. A new and important area of social research, evaluation techniques, is discussed in Chapter 7 along with implementation.

The feedback loop, or information loop, plays a decisive part in the operation of the formal planning model. Feedback allows the policymaker to make adjustments in the policy according to how well or poorly it has been working and according to changes in the environment. The 1972 National Water Pollution Abatement Program provides a good illustration of feedback. The original goal called for universally clean water by 1985. By 1979, with $28 billion in federal money committed, it was rather apparent that the program needed technical, financial, and administrative adjustments. The federal government estimated that to make all the country's waterways "fishable and swimable" by 1985 would require at least $106 billion more. Communities, which had supported the goal of clean water, were aghast when their sewer rates tripled and they learned they faced further hikes. Once they realized how onerous the obligations were, they began asking elected officials to set more realistic goals and to look at the cost-effectiveness (Chapter 6) of current expenditures.

There are two kinds of feedback loops. Positive feedback loops contain the dynamics for change in a system (growth, for example). Negative feedback loops represent control and stability, the re-establishment of equilibriums.

What happens when planning takes place without feedback? For one thing, organizations continue to perform outdated tasks. A notable example is the Rural Electrification Administration, begun in 1935 to provide electricity to rural America. Today, 99 percent of rural homes have electricity, but the REA is still around and is getting bigger. A less well-known example that illustrates the positive results of paying attention to feedback can be found among certain religious organizations. The success of the evangelical churches (relative to mainline churches) may well be based less on their conservatism than on their willingness to face up to the fact that in today's overinstitutionalized society the first job of the minister is no longer to run a social agency— the job that made the American Protestant church so effective in the early years of the century. Today the priority may be to "minister" to the spiritual needs of the individual.

But by and large, few public sector organizations attempt to think through the changed circumstances in which they operate. Most believe that all that is required is to run harder (in the same direction) and to spend more money on the same program.

Reconciling the Formal Model with the Realities of Planning

The formal planning model (Figure 5–2) severely underemphasizes the role of politics, human behavior, and other qualitative and subjective factors in policy planning. This section will try to present a more accurate model of how planning unfolds in the real world of public administration. This model, which we shall call *logical incrementalism*, preserves the strengths and purges the weaknesses of the formal model. In this sense, it is more a refinement of than an alternative to the formal model. That being the case, let us begin by summarizing the strengths and weaknesses of the formal model before we try to define logical incrementalism.

Strengths and Weaknesses of the Formal Planning Model

If not followed too rigorously, the formal model can help public administrators avoid several serious mistakes.

The first thing the formal model alerts the administrators to is the need to translate lofty goals into concrete actions. To speak always of goals is to ensure that nothing will be accomplished.

The second thing the formal model helps guarantee is that priorities will be set and adhered to. Without concentration on priorities, efforts will be diluted over several objectives and squandered in areas where the payoff is low. Congressional investigations, for example, made it clear that outside critics were right when they complained that J.Edgar Hoover, former FBI director, had squandered bureau resources on penny-ante cases involving stolen cars and bank robberies. These made for impressive charts at budget hearings but had little real impact on crime. A General Accounting Office study that was commissioned by an oversight committee headed by Representative Don Edwards, Democrat of California who is a former FBI agent, showed that much of the bureau's domestic surveillance had been of questionable value.

The third thing the formal model can do is remind the administrator that structure follows strategy, that is, designing an effective organization should occur *after* goals have been set. Not all organizational structures are equally well suited to accomplishing a particular goal.

Fourth and equally important, the formal model alerts the administrator to the ever-present need to analyze, experiment, or evaluate to see what works before launching a program on a grand scale.

Fifth, the formal model highlights the vital and continuing role of feedback in the planning process. Only if the organization continues to learn through feedback can its performance improve and can it know when to abandon programs and activities that are no longer producing results.

Sixth, the formal model reminds administrators that they must periodically scan their environments for new threats and opportunities. Which is to say, formal planning systems force operating administrators to extend their time horizons and see their work in a larger, dynamic framework. Henry Kissinger (1979) puts it well: "The analysis of where one is overwhelms the consideration of where one should be going. Serving the machine becomes a more absorbing occupation than defining the purpose."

Seventh, to the extent that they require rigorous communications about goals, alternatives, and resource allocations, formal models help create a network of information that probably would not have otherwise been present in the agency.

But against these strengths we must weigh several weaknesses. The formal model suggests that executives should announce explicit goals. Yet research suggests that effective executives often proceed quite differently. Why? Quinn (1980:65–96) suggests the following reasons:

Goal announcements centralize and freeze the organization by telling subordinates that certain issues and alternatives are closed.

Explicitly stated goals provide focal points against which an otherwise fragmented *opposition* can organize. This is what often happens when a town reveals its land use plan. It also explains why President Reagan kept his specific budget cuts as fuzzy as possible for as long as possible in 1981.

Once top administrators announce their goals those goals are difficult to change; the administrators' egos and those of the people in supporting programs become identified with them. To change the goal is to admit to error. Thus, government plunges ahead with obsolete military, energy, and social programs.

As Figure 5-3 suggests, a few goals at least should be specific, though they should be generated with care. Why so much care? "Effective strategic goals do more than provide a basis for direction setting and maintaining freedom, morale, and timely problem sensing in an enterprise. The benefits of effective goal setting are greatest when people throughout the organization genuinely internalize goals and make them their own" (Quinn, 1980:81).

Figure 5-3
How Specific Should Goals Be?

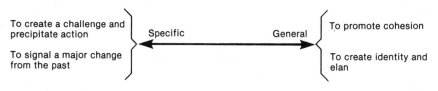

Source: Based on Quinn (1980:72-81).

A second weakness of the formal model is that it is based on a most dubious assumption—namely, that the planner can peer clearly and deeply into the future. In reality, a host of unforeseen problems and events can sweep down upon the set of new directions an agency might develop. While many frustrated Americans might wish for a more specific, cohesive energy policy, logic dictates that massive resource commitments be made as late as possible consistent with the information available. To begin "to go solar" today means that the United States must begin to build a solar industry at least on the scale of the automobile industry. But there are so many social, political, economic, and technological unknowns hiding between here and the year 2001 that logic dictates a more incremental, step-by-step approach.*

A third shortcoming of our formal model is that it fails to account for the politics within and outside the organization. In fact, one could argue that some planning decisions are the result of various bargaining

---

* For example, people might begin to seriously practice conservation, which would make massive solar investment less necessary. Or they might decide that acres and acres of solar collectors are an eyesore, which would make tomorrow's solar industry as besieged as today's nuclear. Political upheavals overseas might cut off the U.S. supply of raw materials needed to make photovoltaic cells. Even more likely are technological breakthroughs like fusion energy and hydrogen fuel (from water) that could make solar energy economically less attractive.

games among the political leadership. While this was not quite the thesis of Chapter 2, it was suggested that politics and administration cannot easily be separated. Or, it could be argued that some planning decisions are the result of regular patterns of behavior. Faced with a problem, the administrator focuses on certain concepts—the strengths, the standard operating procedures, and the fixed routines or "drills" of the agency—to formulate a strategy. (Graham T. Allison, 1971, has found both models—government politics and organizational process—useful in explaining the Cuban Missile Crises of October 1962.)

The fourth and final weakness in the rational model is not easily defined. Crudely put, the rational model discounts the role of subjective and qualitative factors in the policy-planning process. Its step-by-step view of the planning process is hard to reconcile with the experienced observations of flesh and blood administrators (see box, "Planning: The Theory and Reality").

A New Synthesis: Logical Incrementalism

The challenge to students of public administration is, therefore, easy enough to state: How can you build on the strengths of the formal model without including its weaknesses? James Brian Quinn, a professor of management at Dartmouth College, has suggested a possible solution. It is a synthesis of various behavioral, power-dynamic, and formal analytical approaches that more closely approximates the policy-planning process in major organizations (see Figure 5–4). Because the process does not result solely from power-political interplays, it is not what Charles E. Lindblom (1959, 1963) and others have called "muddling through" or "disjointed incrementalism." Because it does not explore all alternatives and factors, nor try to treat them quantitatively, it is not the formal model. Quinn (1980:58) explains:

> The most effective strategies of major enterprises tend to emerge step by step from an iterative process in which the organization probes the future, experiments, and learns from a series of partial (incremental) commitments rather than through global formulations of total strategies. Good managers are aware of this process, and they consciously intervene in it. They use it to improve the information available for decisions and to build the psychological identification essential to successful strategies. The process is both logical and incremental. Such logical incrementalism is not *muddling,* as most people understand that word. Properly managed, it is a conscious, purposeful, proactive, executive practice. Logical incrementalism honors and utilizes the global analyses inherent in formal strategy formulation models. It also embraces the central tenets of the political or power-behavioral approaches to such decision making. But it does not become subservient to any one model. Instead each approach becomes simply a component in a logical process that improves the quality of available information, establishes critical elements of political power and credibility,

Planning: The Theory and Reality

The Theory

(Continental Illinois National Bank and Trust Company of Chicago)

1. Identify the problem or problems to be solved and the opportunities to be seized upon.
2. Design alternative solutions or courses of action (i.e., policies, plans, and programs) to solve the problems or seize upon the opportunities and forecast the consequences and effectiveness of each alternative.
3. Compare and evaluate the alternatives with each other and with the forecasted consequences of unplanned development, and choose the alternative whose probable consequences would be preferable.
4. Develop a plan of action for implementing the alternative selected, including budgets, project schedules, regulatory measures, and the like.
5. Maintain the plan on a current basis through feedback and review of information.

creates needed participation and psychological commitment, and thus enhances both the quality of strategic decisions and the likelihood of their successful implementation.

In sum, a kind of logical incrementalism usually dominates policy planning in the real world of public administration. The process is,

The Reality

(Continental Illinois National Bank and Trust Company of Chicago)

I [the president of a company] start conversations with a number of knowledgeable people. . . . I collect articles and talk to people about how things get done in Washington in this particular field. I collect data from any reasonable source. I begin wide-ranging discussions with people inside and outside the corporation. From these a pattern eventually emerges. It's like fitting together a jigsaw puzzle. At first the vague outline of an approach appears like the sail of a ship in a puzzle. Then suddenly the rest of the puzzle becomes quite clear. You wonder why you didn't see it all along. And once it's crystallized, it's not difficult to explain to others. (Quoted in Quinn, 1980: 35)

* * * * *

How does one manage such a process? Typically you start with general concerns, vaguely felt. Next you roll an issue around in your mind till you think you have a conclusion that makes sense for the company. You then go out and sort of post the idea without being too wedded to its details. You than start hearing the arguments pro and con, and some very good refinements of the idea usually emerge. Then you pull the idea in and put some resources together to study it so it can be put forward as more of a formal presentation. You wait for "stimuli occurrences" or "crises," and launch pieces of the idea to help in these situations. But they lead toward your ultimate aim. You know where you want to get. You'd like to get there in six months. But it may take three years, or you may not get there. And when you do get there, you don't know whether it was originally your own idea—or somebody else had reached the same conclusion before you and just got you on board for it. You never know. The president would follow the same basic process, but he could drive it much faster than an executive lower in the organization. (Quoted in Quinn, 1980:102)

according to Quinn, "purposeful, politically astute, and effective." Like the formal model it begins with needs that may only be vaguely sensed at first. But, the managers who follow the logical incremental model usually do not jump next to an articulation of specific goals; rather, they will steadily build within the organization, support for and

Figure 5–4
The "Logical Incremental" Planning Model

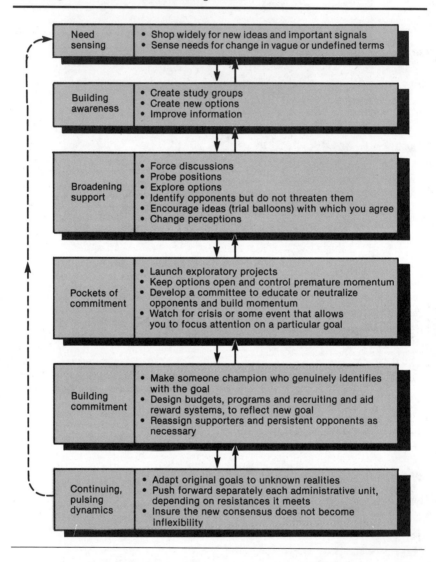

Need sensing	• Shop widely for new ideas and important signals • Sense needs for change in vague or undefined terms
Building awareness	• Create study groups • Create new options • Improve information
Broadening support	• Force discussions • Probe positions • Explore options • Identify opponents but do not threaten them • Encourage ideas (trial balloons) with which you agree • Change perceptions
Pockets of commitment	• Launch exploratory projects • Keep options open and control premature momentum • Develop a committee to educate or neutralize opponents and build momentum • Watch for crisis or some event that allows you to focus attention on a particular goal
Building commitment	• Make someone champion who genuinely identifies with the goal • Design budgets, programs and recruiting and aid reward systems, to reflect new goal • Reassign supporters and persistent opponents as necessary
Continuing, pulsing dynamics	• Adapt original goals to unknown realities • Push forward separately each administrative unit, depending on resistances it meets • Insure the new consensus does not become inflexibility

eventually commitment to new goals. Some common steps in this process and relevant management techniques are set forth in Figure 5–4.

Forecasting—A Critical Planning Ingredient

To plan is to make assumptions about the future. Unfortunately, the assumptions are usually made semiconsciously, but if articulated, they would sound something like this: "Tomorrow will be like today, only more so."

The error of this mindset can be seen clearly in the planning of Miami's Metrorail. Six months after the first 11 miles of elevated track were opened, average daily ridership was a paltry 9,500—about 10 percent of what had been expected. Why was the patronage estimate so far off the mark? The main reason is that the planners assumed that the costs of operating an automobile—gasoline, oil, parking fees, and maintenance—would increase severalfold between 1975 and 1985. As car costs rose, the planners believed, more people would switch to public transportation. When this forecast was made, tensions were high, between the United States and the Middle East and the United States was experiencing gas shortages and sharp price increases. Tomorrow, transit planners assumed, would bring more of the same. But tomorrow was different, and by 1985 the public transit system's deficits were climbing rapidly.

What was the bottom line in this story? Miami's elevated rapid transit system cost the federal government over $700 million but attracted only 10 percent as many riders as projected. It would have been cheaper to give each new rider $100,000!

What Is a Forecast?

Erich Jantsch (1967:15) provides us with this definition of a forecast: a probabilistic statement, on a relatively high confidence level, about the future. A prediction, in contrast, is a nonprobabilistic statement (X will occur). Jantsch also distinguishes between two types of forecasts. *Exploratory forecast* starts from today's knowledge and attempts to say what is likely to occur in the future. *Normative forecast*, however, starts in the future, assessing goals, needs, desires, and so forth. They then work backward to the present, attempting to spell out what should be done to attain, at some time in the future, the desired goal.

So much for definitions. How does this relate to the task of the administrator? In brief, forecasting provides a means of discovering and articulating the more important opportunities and problems in the future. Further, it provides a systematic method for estimating the trajectory likely to be produced by contemplated or existing governmental programs.

The number of forecasting methods available is vast. Below we discuss only four of the more basic methods: expert forecasting, trend extrapolation, leading indicators, and impact assessment.

Expert Forecasting

The expert forecast is the oldest and the most intuitive of the methods. Here, if one wants to know what is likely or unlikely to happen, one simply goes to the expert. The science fiction writer

Arthur C. Clarke documents the limitations to this approach by citing numerous failures by experts.

Lord Rutherford, for example, was certainly an expert on the atom—more than any other scientist he helped to lay bare its internal structure. But, as Clarke (1963:14) notes:

> Rutherford frequently made fun of those sensation mongers who predicted that we would one day be able to harness the energy locked up in matter. Yet, only five years after his death in 1937, the first chain reaction was started in Chicago. What Rutherford, for all his wonderful insight, had failed to take into account was that a nuclear reaction might be discovered that would release more energy than that required to start it.
>
> . . . The example of Lord Rutherford demonstrates that it is not the man who knows most about a subject, and is the acknowledged master of his field, who can give the most reliable pointers to its future. Too great a burden of knowledge can clog the wheels of imagination; I have tried to embody this fact of observation in *Clarke's law*, which may be formulated as follows: When a distinguished but elderly scientist states that something is possible, he is almost certainly right. When he states that something is impossible, he is very probably wrong.

To help overcome such limitations in forecasting by individual experts, consensus methods were developed. By far, the best known of these is the *Delphi technique*. Generally, a Delphi exercise asks a group of experts on a certain subject—economics, medicine, automation, population, education, and so forth—to state *anonymously* when a future event might occur. Their answers, with their reasons, are summarized and fed back to the entire group for a second round. This process may be repeated several times with the hope that eventually there will be a narrowing of the initial spread of opinions.

Trend Extrapolation

If one buys the assumption that trends established in recent history will continue, then *trend extrapolation* might be used. A parameter—for example, U.S. population, maximum aircraft speed, or even the world record in the mile run (see Figure 5–5)—is plotted on a graph against time. The analyst then extends the curve either by an "eyeball" extension or by a quantitative curve-fitting method. Table 5–1 shows the results this method gives when applied to track records.

As I see it, the biggest limitation to this method is the assumption that past trends hold, that we *know* what the curve is. Say that an analyst has the plot of historical data shown in Figure 5–6. How does this person know whether A or B is the proper extension? The first curve, represented by A, shows an exponential increase with no flattening in the time-range considered. For our purposes, we may think of an exponential growth curve as one that shows a constant *rate* of change; that is, the increase in December was greater than in November which, in turn, was greater than the increase in October,

Figure 5-5
Progress in the Mile Run

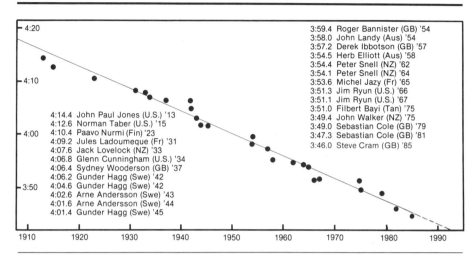

Source: Hopkins and Edwards (1976:45) (updated).

and so on. This characteristic is exhibited by a number of parameters (e.g., maximum transport aircraft speed and energy conversion efficiency in illumination technology) at least until certain limits are hit (e.g., Concorde and the gallium arsenide diode).

But not all trends are exponential. And when one ignores the possibility of an S-shaped curve, such as represented by B, ludicrous forecasts can sometimes result.

For example, the growth in the number of scientists between 1850 and 1950 was very steep and probably followed roughly the path of the

Table 5-1
Extrapolating World Records in Track

		Projections	
Distance	Present Record	1976	2000
100m	9.9	9.8	9.5
400m	43.9	43.7	42.1
800m	1:43.7	1:42.1	1:40.4
1,500m	3:32.2	3:30.6	3:20.8
5,000m	13:13.0	13:09.0	12:20.0
10,000m	27:30.8	27:10.0	25:17.0
Marathon	2:08:33	2:06:30	1:55:00

Insufficient data available on 200m and hurdle events to make calculations.

Source: Hopkins and Edwards (1976:44).

Figure 5-6
Trend Extrapolation Dilemmas

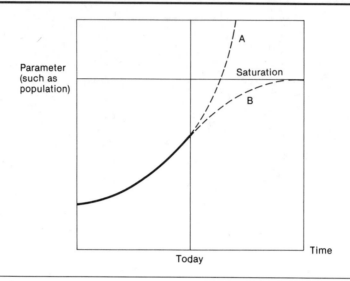

solid line in Figure 5-6. Someone who ignored the possibility of satura-
tion might be lead to the mind-boggling conclusion that, by the end of
the century, all the Earth's inhabitants over the age of six would be
holding doctorates in science. One also should be open to the possibility of certain external events or breakthroughs. In London in the
latter part of the 19th century, with the horse as the principle means of
rapid intracity transportation, the accumulation of manure in the
streets was cause for no little concern. Naive extrapolation, ignoring
the possibility of the technological breakthrough such as the automobile, would have forecasted a city buried in 30 years.

Leading Indicators

One of the more fascinating methods is Graham T. M. Molitor's
(1975:204–10) schema of forecasting public policy change through
leading indicators. Basically, Molitor suggests that by monitoring
events, intellectual elites, literature, organizations, and political jurisdictions, the policy analyst can develop a better idea of what to expect
in the future. The premise upon which this method builds goes something like this. Issues of public policy are almost always the result of
unusual events that give rise to abuse or excess so extreme that public
action eventually is required. Between the occurrence of the first
isolated event and the creation of public policy, Molitor thinks a fairly
consistent pattern of behavior unfolds. The analyst's job, then, is one
of monitoring this pattern as it unfolds. For example, we know that
intellectual elites, who analyze and articulate social problems, tend to

emerge around issues. Similarly, the victimized express their feelings and thus become powerful symbols for change. "By monitoring these . . . vanguards, whose ideas ultimately are diffused widely, early indications of change can be forecasted" (Molitor, 1975:206).

Meanwhile, the sequence by which different types of literature build up and provide a permanent written analysis and wider publicity of the new ideas and concepts follows a rough pattern. The sequence, which might cover over 100 years, could go like this. At first, the early warnings about emerging problems appear in the more visionary classes of literature. (For example, it would appear that the poet Blake was one of the first to recognize the arrival of the Industrial Revolution and its social implications.) Then, the idea is rendered into specifics in monographs and speeches in specialized journals. Next, these phases: corroboration of details; institutional responses through journals for the cause; consideration in the mass media; and politicization of the issue in government reports and a diffusion of the idea among opinion leaders.

For a cause to be translated into public policy requires, however, more than advocates and articles—it requires organizational support. "Growth of institutional backing for a cause—whether measured by number of organizations, persons involved, or resources committed— follows exponential increases which tend to force serious consideration of the issue by public policymakers" (Molitor, 1975:209).

Ultimately, political officials become involved. Certain leading political jurisdictions invariably are among the first to implement new policy solutions. These early innovators and experimenters show the way to others; then, after the idea is proven, other jurisdictions emulate.

Generally speaking, there are five states where most social invention occurs. The other 45 states usually follow. California is the key indicator state with Florida a close second. The other three trendsetting states are Washington, Colorado, and Connecticut (Naisbitt, 1980).

Impact Assessment

Inherent in all planning is the problem of unexpected consequences. The more profound and longer-term the program, the greater the possibility of horrendous side effects, yet people tend to ignore the potential dangers from the secondary effects of benevolent enterprises and good intentions. Can our late 20th- century public administrators overcome such a tendency? I think that a method is already in place that can help them look ahead more realistically. The general name for this method is *impact assessment*, though it takes a variety of forms.

The first of these is the *Environmental Impact Statement*. EIS is a document prepared either by a governmental agency or private concern that outlines how a proposed action (e.g., construction of a new dam or highway) might affect the quality of the human environment. The requirement for EISs began with the passage of the National Environmental Policy Act (NEPA) of 1969. Section 102 (2) (c) of the act sets forth the EIS requirement. The significance of this requirement was not initially apparent to most government agencies or to private industry. Today, the number and variety of EISs required at all levels of government are enormous.

A basic framework for an EIS might be something like the following: (1) describe present conditions; (2) describe proposed action (e.g., new highway or housing project); (3) describe probable impacts of each alternative to soil conditions, wildlife, climate, existing pollution, transportation congestion, aesthetics, and so forth; (4) identify the alternative chosen; (5) describe probable impacts of proposed action in detail; and (6) describe techniques to be used to minimize harm.

Similar to the writing of an EIS is *technology assessment*. Joseph T. Coates (1971:225) defines technology assessment as "the systematic study of the effects on society that may occur when a technology is introduced, extended, or modified, with a special emphasis on the impacts that are unintended, indirect, and delayed." Technology assessment became firmly established as a decision-making tool in 1972 when Congress created the Office of Technology Assessment. Figure 5–7 shows the seven major steps in technology assessment.

Either directly or indirectly, technological advance brings certain risks. One need look no further than the headlines of the press for evidence. Surely government has some responsibility to look for the side effects of new technology.

Let me give just one example. By 1980, evidence had begun to pile up that conserving energy can damage your health. More exactly, energy-efficient buildings can be dangerous because they not only prevent warmed (or cooled) air from escaping but also pollutants. According to one World Health Organization expert, indoor pollution is already doing more damage to human health than the outdoor pollution that regulatory authorities are fighting against throughout the industrialized world (*New Scientist*, May 24, 1980).

To see how this can be, consider the case of builders who install double insulation, triple-glazed windows, polyurethane caulking, and other advanced conservation measures to produce a house that uses only one third to one half as much energy as a conventional one. To their horror, they discover they have also produced one dangerous to inhabit—with very high levels of humidity, odors, pollutants, and even an accumulation of radioactive radon gas. The effect of swapping ventilation for energy conservation is a buildup in the house of pollutants from furniture polish, deodorants, hair sprays, and carpet adhesives. In less than an hour, a gas stove in the kitchen can produce levels of carbon monoxide that exceed standards for the outside. High humidity makes matters worse. In areas where sulphur emissions from

Figure 5-7
Seven Major Steps in Making a Technology Assessment

Step 1	DEFINE THE ASSESSMENT TASK Discuss relevant issues and any major problems. Establish scope (breadth and depth) of inquiry. Develop project ground rules.
Step 2	DESCRIBE RELEVANT TECHNOLOGIES Describe major technology being assessed. Describe other technologies supporting the major technology. Describe technologies competitive to the major and supporting technologies.
Step 3	DEVELOP STATE-OF-SOCIETY ASSUMPTIONS Identify and describe major nontechnological factors influencing the application of the relevant technologies.
Step 4	IDENTIFY IMPACT AREAS Ascertain those societal characteristics that will be most influenced by the application of the assessed technology.
Step 5	MAKE PRELIMINARY IMPACT ANALYSIS Trace and integrate the process by which the assessed technology makes its societal influence felt.
Step 6	IDENTIFY POSSIBLE ACTION OPTIONS Develop and analyze various programs for obtaining maximum pub- lic advantage from the assessed technologies.
Step 7	COMPLETE IMPACT ANALYSIS Analyze the degree to which each action option would alter the specific societal impacts of the assessed technology discussed in Step 5.

Source: Mitre Corporation, 1971.

coal combustion are high, the result can be indoor "acid rain" as the sulphur combines with oxygen to form sulphate. The sulphate then deposits to eat away at furniture—and lung tissue.

Safety equipment and emission-control technology on the automobile can even kill you. Lester B. Lave, a senior fellow at the Brookings Institution, estimates that reducing the size of automobiles increases fatalities by 1,400 a year and significantly increases serious injuries (*Science,* May 22, 1981).

What can public administrators do about risks? They must begin by recognizing that to head off undesirable side effects, a good tactic is prudence. Instead of proceeding full speed with any new technology, they can wait a bit, mull over any distant warnings, and approach risk in an incremental, experimental, trial-and-error way, and thus improve, reinvent, or redesign processes and devices. To succeed at risk management, the government bureaucracy will need unbiased feedback that is direct, immediate, and continuing on both the effects of new technology and the effects of government action. Finally, it needs to use technology assessment more extensively to attempt to see in advance the unintended, unexpected consequences of current actions. Otherwise, the bureaucracy will find itself experiencing even more technological blunders such as toxic seepage from chemical dumps.

Of course, good forecasts do not ensure good plans. Nor do good plans ensure organizational success. Plans merely set the stage for action. The action, in turn, will only be as good as the ability of the members of the organization to make decisions in a sound and timely manner and to implement plans in a coordinated manner.

Nailing Down the Main Points

1. The essence of planning is to see future opportunities *and* threats and to exploit or combat them by decisions taken in the present. More rigorously defined, a *policy* is a statement of goals and of the relative importance attached to each goal. It can be translated into a plan by specifying the objectives to be attained. A proposed set of specific actions intended to implement a plan is called a *program*.

2. The rational planning process goes thus: *(a)* Identify the problems to be solved; *(b)* Design alternative courses of action to solve the problem and forecast the consequences of each alternative; *(c)* Compare and evaluate the alternatives and choose the one whose probable consequences would be preferable; *(d)* Design a plan of action for implementing the preferred alternative, and *(e)* Keep the plan current through feedback and review.

3. Policy planning, the process of determining goals and their priorities, is often ignored in American government. Too much public policy is defined in terms of program; as such, it seeks to deal only with parts of the system. The influence of political leadership is perhaps greatest at this early stage in the planning process.

4. In the medium-range planning stage, policy begins to be converted into action. Here, in particular, we are concerned with the design of alternatives and the evaluation of each in terms of its consequences. Common errors in this stage: failure to consider enough alternatives and reluctance to question rigorously every alternative (and the assumptions upon which it is founded).

5. Implementation and evaluation are the final two stages in the planning process. They will be discussed more fully in Chapter 8.

6. The model of logical incrementalism can help us to remember the important role that politics, human behavior, and subjective factors play in policy planning. Unlike predictions, which attempt to make absolute statements about what *will* happen, forecasts offer probabilistic statements about what *may* happen. In recent years, the number of forecasting techniques has grown quite rapidly, but most are related to six of the more basic methods: expert forecasting, consensus methods, trend extrapolation, leading indicators, and impact assessment. Properly used, these methods can provide us with a somewhat less murky glimpse of the future of public administration.

Concepts for Review

city planning	logical incrementalism
comprehensive plan	medium-range planning
Delphi technique	planning premises
development planning	policy, plan, and program
Environmental Impact Statement	policy planning
expert forecastaing	programming; implementation, evaluation
exploratory and normative forcasts	ratoinal planning model
fiscal policymaking	trend extrapolation
forecasts, predictions	zoning laws
goals, objectives, and actions	
impact assessment	
land-use plans	

Problems

1. Public officials at all levels of government are frequently criticized for shortsighted decisions. Elected officials may be accused of looking forward only as far as the next election and of placing narrow, parochial interests above the general welfare. To what extent is such criticism justified? Do you see any solution?

2. The anecdote about Kennedy and Goldberg in this chapter illustrates the need for a chief executive to consult widely before making important decisions. Discuss the problems that might arise if this approach to decision making is pushed too far.

3. Planning, like other good things, has its limitations. One authority on planning lists among the more important shortcomings the following:

    a. Environmental events cannot always be controlled.
    b. Internal resistance can be encountered.
    c. Planning is expensive.
    d. Planning is ineffective during sudden crises.

    What might an agency do to overcome these shortcomings? Can you think of other limitations on planning?

4. Unlike several European countries, the United States does not have a full-fledged national planning body. Nonetheless, a number of institutions

such as the Council of Economic Advisors, do have important planning functions. What other institutions would you say contribute to planning at the national level? Should the United States have a central planning body?

5. The Environmental Protection Agency routinely disseminates air and water pollution abatement requirements that virtually dictate state and local land use in many situations; this activity reflects a national awareness that in a complex industrial society many sorts of public regulation and planning are inescapable. It also poses a national dilemma. On the one hand, the federal government can tamper with a 200-year-old national tradition of land use being determined primarily by private initiative. On the other, it can do nothing. The second option allows communities all over the country, beset by growth troubles, to adopt growth plans. (In 1971, for example, Boulder, Colorado, called for a population limitation.) Do you think local governments can effectively influence growth and development? Since the national population is to increase by at least 50 million people in the next 25 years, is growth control really just a fancy term for exclusionary policies? Will attempts to manage growth have a negative impact on the local economy?

6. Using back issues of local newspapers, survey the planning process in one urban area for one particular policy problem (e.g., mass transportation). Pay particular attention to when the need was first perceived, who the participants were, what the "leverage points" were, and where the sources of funds were. (The term *leverage points* refers to those participants who, at various times in the entire process, exhibited exceptional power or influence over the course of events.)

7. In his *Doomsday Syndrome*, John Maddox argues that forecasts, designed to influence public planners, are often so exaggerated and simplified that their effect is the very opposite of what their authors desire. Far from alerting planners to important problems, the doomsday syndrome may so condition them to disaster that it undermines the capacity of the human race to survive. Discuss.

8. Strategic planning, as discussed in this chapter, implies a comprehensive, systematic scanning of the external environment of an organization. With the basic mission of the organization in mind, administrators try to identify which parts of the environment are relevant for further study. List two to four questions that a college or university might want to consider under each of the following headings:

    a. Economic.
    b. Demographic.
    c. Sociocultural.
    d. Political and regulatory.
    e. Technological.

9. Explain the following quote from Friedrich Von Hayek's *The Road to Serfdom* (1944) with the use of specific examples:

    The dispute between the modern planners and their opponents is . . . not a dispute on whether we ought to employ foresight and systematic thinking in planning our common affairs. It is a dispute about what is the best way of so doing. The question is whether for this purpose it is better that the holder of coercive power should confine himself in general to creating conditions under which the knowledge and initiative of individuals are given the best scope so that they can plan most successfully; or whether a rational utilization of our resources requires central direction and organization of all our activities according to some consciously constructed "blueprint."

Case 5.1
What Is the Purpose of the Peace Corps?

For as long as Karen Williams could remember, she had been interested in the agricultural problems in developing countries.* She had worked as a Peace Corps volunteer in Ecuador after graduating from college and, upon returning to the United States in 1974, she had immediately begun graduate studies in agronomy. Within 13 years, she had become the first and only woman in the United States to be dean of a major school of agriculture. Late in 1988, the 41st president asked Williams if she would return to the Peace Corps—this time as its director.

With little hesitation, she accepted. In the few short weeks before she assumed her new position, Williams thought long and hard about the corps and its somewhat turbulent history.

Structure and Mandate

The Peace Corps was established by the Peace Corps Act of 1961 and was made an independent agency by Title VI of the International Security and Development Cooperation Act of 1981. Today it consists of a Washington, D.C., headquarters, 3 recruitment service centers that support 15 area officers, and overseas operations in more than 62 countries (see Exhibit 1). The Peace Corps' presence in foreign countries fluctuates as programs are either added or withdrawn.

The Corps' mandate reads: "to promote world peace and friendship, to help the peoples of other countries in meeting their needs for trained manpower, to help promote a better understanding of the American people on the part of the peoples served, and to promote a better understanding of other peoples on the part of the American people." In 1977, the Peace Corps Act was amended to emphasize the agency's commitment to programming geared to meeting the basic needs of those living in the poorest areas of those countries in which it operated.

To fulfill the agency's mandate, men and women of all ages and walks of life were trained for a 9-to-14-week period in the appropriate local language, the technical skills necessary for their particular job, and the cross-cultural skills needed to adjust to a society with traditions and attitudes different from their own. Volunteers served for a period of two years, living among the people with whom they worked. They were expected to become a part of the community and to demonstrate, through their voluntary service, that people can be an important impetus for change.

* Karen Williams is a fictitious person. All others in the case are real.

Exhibit 1
Peace Corps

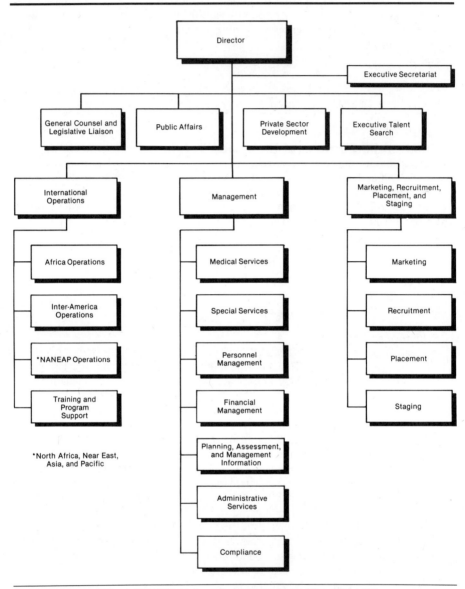

Source: *U.S. Government Manual, 1984/85* (Washington, D.C.: Government Printing Office, 1984), p. 854.

A Brief History
When originally conceived, the Peace Corps was supposed to be a humanistic program that sought to transcend politics and nationalism. Although the agency eagerly accepted volunteers such as physicians and agronomists, its membership

consisted largely of unskilled college graduates. At its peak in 1966, the Peace Corps had 15,556 volunteers and a $114 million budget.

President Richard Nixon began to change things in 1969. He felt the corps had been misdirected and overextended. Nixon saw the agency not as a people to people program but as a vehicle for teaching technical skills to developing nations. Consequently, more narrowly skilled volunteers, such as mechanics and engineers, began to replace the predominantly nontechnical "BA generalists." The training period was cut from 16 weeks to 7 weeks. In 1971, Nixon incorporated the Peace Corps into ACTION, an umbrella agency created to encompass all federal volunteer efforts. With the corps' visibility sharply reduced, the number of volunteers in the field dropped to under 7,000 in 1972.

Although the Third World was looking for more technically skilled people, the Nixon volunteers were less adaptable and had a harder time learning new languages than had the BA generalists. The Peace Corps was becoming a kind of small-scale version of the Agency for International Development. (AID's economic assistance programs were designed to help people of developing countries friendly to the United States enhance their human and economic resources, increase their productive capacities, improve the quality of their lives, and generally promote economic and political stability.)

Unlike Nixon, President Carter believed that aid to developing nations should take the form of fulfilling basic human needs. Sam Brown, appointed by Carter to head ACTION in 1977, shared this belief. Thus, his focus was to redirect the agency toward helping the "poorest of the poor," and to reinvigorate the training programs. But Brown also thought that the corps suffered from "cultural imperialism." He claimed that "the missionary zeal that gave us the Peace Corps was not far from the zeal that gave us the Vietnam War." He believed the corps had no business teaching English in countries with a high degree of illiteracy in their own language. The agency turned into a battleground for Brown's supporters and detractors.

When Richard Celeste took over as Peace Corps director in 1979, he commissioned a country by country review to settle the dispute. Completed in November 1980, the report showed massive support for the corps' education program.

Under President Reagan and his new director, Loret Ruppe, the Peace Corps assumed more of a business orientation. Ruppe claimed that this approach better met the needs of the volunteers *and* the developing nations and that it was largely a survival response to changing Third World philosophies and conservative domestic tides. Moreover, it corresponded to Reagan's emphasis on voluntarism, self-help, and private enterprise, to renewed interest by international agencies in the "trickle-up" effects of small-business development, and to a growing wave of requests for this type of help. As Ruppe once explained: "Income generation is the number one priority in the developing world. Many host countries say they need better business skills." The Reagan administration shift was formalized in the fall of 1982 with the addition of "competitive enterprise development" to agriculture, health, fishery, and other programs.

An auxiliary effort within the Reagan Peace Corps was the Peace Corps Partnership Program. This program provided opportunities for elementary, junior, and senior high schools, civic groups, and neighborhood and youth organizations within the United States to meet a specific need of an overseas community through financial sponsorship of the construction of a school, clinic, or community facility recommended by a Peace Corps volunteer; corporate and foundation support was also encouraged via matching contributions and pledges. Cross-cultural exchange was a major element in Partnership projects.

The Peace Corps also served as the sponsor for United States citizens who served in the United Nations volunteer program. Reagan removed the Peace Corps and its $100 million budget from the ACTION umbrella, hoping to revive its identity and mission.

But what was that mission? Or, more to the point, what should it be? As she prepared to lead the 5,000 volunteers into the 1990s, Karen Williams still was not sure.

Case Questions
1. How should Williams go about setting her priorities?
2. Assume that Williams has a 45-minute first meeting with the new president. What should her talking points be?
3. What other conceptual tasks does Williams face?

Case References
U.S. Government Manual, 1984/85 (Washington, D.C.: Government Printing Office, 1984); Michael A. Lerner, "Peace Corps Imperiled," *New Republic,* November 25, 1981; *New York Times,* January 15, 1985, January 23, 1985; Al Santoli, "Is the Peace Corps Obsolete?" *Parade Magazine, March 27, 1983; The Wall Street Journal,* February 15, 1985.

6

Decision Making

Introduction

Decision making means selecting from various alternatives, one course of action. As such, it cannot be divorced from the planning process described in the preceding chapter. Herbert Simon (1957:1) said that the "task of 'deciding' pervades the entire administrative organization quite as much as does the task of 'doing'—indeed, it is integrally tied up with the latter."

There are at least four steps in decision making.

1. Identifying the problem (or opportunity).
2. Gathering facts.
3. Making the decision.
4. Communicating and implementing the decision.

We shall explore the first three of these steps in this chapter, leaving the fourth step for the next chapter.

Identifying the Problem (or Opportunity)

First, decision makers should establish what kind of problem exists. More specifically, they need to ask if the problem is *generic* or *unique*?

Most of the problems that an administrator faces are generic, that is, they are part of a pattern of problems stemming from one underlying cause (see Figure 6-1). Since this underlying cause is seldom obvious, the tendency of the administrator is to view the problem as a unique, isolated event and to treat it as such. Thus, administrators often find

Figure 6-1

Generic and Unique Problems, or Why Effective Administrators Make Few Decisions

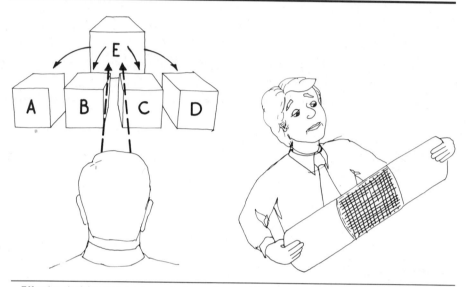

Effective decision makers know that very few problems or events are unique. Most are manifestations of underlying problems. Therefore, before attempting a quick-fix on problems A,B,C, or D, they will try to find the basic problem E. Once E is solved, A,B,C,D, and any future problems stemming from E are eliminated. Thus effective decision makers make few decisions.

Is this not what a good physician does? If a patient complains, on separate visits, of increased thirst, itching, hunger, weight loss, weakness, and nausea, the physician does not simply try to remedy each on an ad hoc basis but rather asks, what might this problem be a symptom of?

In contrast, many administrators are forever engaged in "quick fixes" and cosmetic solutions.

themselves treating symptoms rather than establishing rules or principles that remove the root cause. This is why many administrators make more decisions than they really need to.

Good administrators avoid cosmetic solutions. But the temptation to treat symptoms can be strong, particularly in an age of technology. Consider the concept of the *technology fix*. The concept was defined by Dr. Alvin M. Weinberg (1966) as an innovation devised for the purpose of correcting a social defect. Admittedly, the device has its advantages sometimes; for example, drugs taken orally to prevent unwanted conception as a measure of population control. But not always. Stronger locks, higher (perhaps electrified) fences, and more powerful police weapons can, for example, reduce the *symptoms* of crime without affecting the real causes.

But let us return to the distinction between generic and unique problems and ask, What does the decision maker do about truly unique problems? Peter Drucker (1966) maintains that even events that seem completely isolated turn out to be, upon closer examination, the first manifestations of a new generic problem. Surely this was true of the free speech movement at Berkeley, the 1965 power failure in the whole northeastern North America, and the thalidomide tragedy. These three "isolated" events were actually bellwethers—to the campus turmoil of the late 1960s, the energy squeeze of the early 1970s, and the increased concern over assessing new biomedical technologies of the 1970s and 1980s.

Such events call not for quick fixes but for bold solutions. Drucker (1966:166) argues that a major failure of the Kennedy administration was its tendency to treat generic problems as unique. In the name of pragmatism, its members refused to develop rules and principles and insisted on treating everything "on its own merits."

Gathering Facts

Framing a Decision

With the problem accurately defined, the administrator then turns to framing the response. Here careful attention should be given to what I shall term the upper and lower limits of the decision.

Upper limits refers to the ever-present limitations that determine how far the administrator can go. Sorensen (1963:22–42), in his lectures on decision making in the White House, notes five.

1. The limits of permissibility (Is it legal? Will others accept it?).
2. The limits of available resources.
3. The limits of available time.
4. The limits of previous commitments.
5. The limits of available information.

Though Sorenson's list is self-explanatory, his fifth point merits emphasis simply because administrators rely so much on past experiences in making decisions. The experienced administrator believes, often without realizing it, that past mistakes and accomplishments are an almost infallible guide in decision-making situations. Hardly, Sorenson seems to be saying. Rather, administrators must try to visualize the world as a whole and as a total system in which their own personal experiences are a very small and inadequate sample. A major corrective to this generalizing from personal experience is statistical analysis. Modern statistics is based on the concept of probability; it deals with the problem of making a probability judgment about a characteristic of the population (e.g., income) on the basis of information derived from a small sample of that population. Statistical analysis has come to play an increasingly important role among sophisticated administrators.

Lower limits refers to what at least must occur for the problem to be solved. For example, Germany knew at the outbreak of World War I that it could win if and only if two minimum conditions were met. Germany would (Condition I) put up weak resistance against Russia thus allowing it to (Condition II) concentrate forces for a knockout blow to France. But as Russia began to penetrate deeper and deeper into East Prussia, the German general staff decided to pull forces from the Western front. Condition II was therefore not met and the chance for victory was lost (Drucker, 1966:132).

Chester I. Barnard (1938:202–5) introduced an idea quite similar to that of lower limits. He calls it the *limiting (strategic) factor* in decision making. It is the factor "whose control, in the right form, at the right place and time, will establish a new system or set of conditions which meets the purpose. Thus, if we wish to increase the yield of grain in a certain field, and we analyze the soil, it may appear that the soil lacks potash; potash may be said to be the strategic (or limiting) factor." If an administrator can discover the strategic factor—can exercise control at the right times, in the right place, right amount, and right form—then the decision becomes not only simpler (for other factors tend to work themselves out) but also more economical.

Schematically, we can think of every possible solution to a problem as being represented by a point in the box below. Solutions in the top third, however, must be ruled out because they violate the upper limits of a decision. Solutions in the bottom third must also be ruled out because they fail to satisfy the lower limits of a successful decision. While this schematic does not directly provide a solution, it does drastically reduce the numbers of possible solutions an administrator might have to consider.

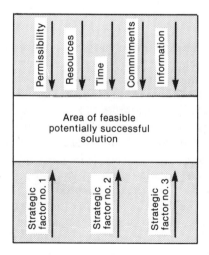

Consulting People

Even kings and queens consulted. Queen Elizabeth did not defeat the Spanish in 1588 by reading *Teach Thyself to Thrash Armadas.* No, she consulted underlings.

It is also generally a good idea to consult those who will be most affected by the decision, checking your facts with theirs and, above all, *listening* to what they have to say (more about this in the next chapter). The Great Pipeline Fracas of 1982 is a splendid example of what can happen when public executives forget to do this kind of consulting. The problem started a few years ago when four of America's closest allies—three of them NATO colleagues—arranged for a massive international project with the Soviet Union, a project that was to have been of considerable economic benefit to all parties. The project called for the use of large high-technology components designed and developed by American firms but manufactured by European subsidiaries of those firms, the companies with which the Soviet Union had signed the contracts. Enter Ronald Reagan. Sizing up the situation in a flash, he said "No way—until the Soviets lift martial law in Poland!"

At first blush, Reagan's seemed a perfectly reasonable position. The project was unquestionably beneficial to the Soviets (the acquisition of

Ever-present limitations determine how far decision making in the White House can go. One of John F. Kennedy's top advisers noted five: permissibility, available resources, available time, previous commitments, and available information (see text). (*Paris Match/* Carone)

badly needed Western currency), and why should America lend a hand to that? The pipeline decision would also be greeted enthusiastically by Polish-Americans. The trouble was that the pipeline decision had not been bounced off the other actors, and it was of considerable importance to their economies. They had been working on it for a long time; their governments were behind it; scores of companies and subcontractors and scores of thousands of jobs were involved.

Several weeks and many angry allies later, President Reagan lifted his sanctions against the pipeline. His move had been quietly and persistently pursued by George Shultz, secretary of state. Shultz had been on record for some time as believing that these kinds of sanctions not only would not work but also were counterproductive because they created problems with allies. However, Shultz announced his full support of the sanctions—and then quietly began what can only be called an end run. An associate explains: "He would go around town and just talk about it," the associate says. "He'd ask: 'Are we getting what we want? How do we get what we really want? Are we hurting our allies? Do the sanctions have effects we didn't foresee when they were imposed? Can we develop a broader strategy against the Soviets that won't harm our allies?'"(*Houston Chronicle,* November 14, 1985).

That was in August. By mid-September, administration officials began suggesting publicly that there might be alternatives to sanctions. By the end of October, the State Department quietly began discussions with key European allies on a new strategy, which led to Reagan's lifting of sanctions on November 13.

Shultz has made consulting with people into an art form. Leslie H. Gelb, a reporter for the *New York Times,* gives this profile:

> For as long as anyone can remember, the Secretary of State's conference room has contained a long mahogany table in two sections, embraced by two dozen or more chairs, with more chairs stacked arm to arm along the wall. Sometime after George P. Shultz's arrival in the building, the furniture was rearranged.
>
> Now the conference table is shorter and it is surrounded by only 10 chairs, with a few easy chairs on the periphery.
>
> The rearrangement was a signal from the new Secretary that things would be more intimate, more informal and personal than in times past. It was the mark of a man who pays a great deal of attention to dealing with people, a man who has a special way of exercising power.
>
> The Shultz approach seems to be, as aides quote it: "Let's get comfortable, talk things over, get everyone's ideas, see what the facts show, see if there isn't some commonsense approach to this problem that we can all feel comfortable with." (*New York Times,* September 7, 1982)

Making the Decision: Five Analytical Techniques

After gathering facts and suggestions, the decision maker should be ready to begin assessing the various alternatives. In this section, we shall consider five *analytical* techniques that can help the administrator in this critical task.

1. Cost-benefit analysis.
2. Multiobjective models.
3. Decision analysis.
4. Systems analysis.
5. Operations research.

The word *analytical* has been emphasized above in order to stress the fact that in this section we are examining one particular style of thinking. The analytical method is founded on formal logic; it seeks to break situations down into their component parts and to define problems by isolating them, thus making them more manageable. There are, however, other ways of looking at the world. The last section of this chapter will consider them, pointing out the strengths and weaknesses of each.

Cost-Benefit Analysis

In an era of scarcity, interest in weighing cost against benefits rises. Today, the federal government must do more than assess the benefits of goals such as a cleaner environment, safer products, healthier working conditions, and better mass transit—it must also weigh the cost and other side effects of such action.

The methodology for these kinds of assessments has been around at least since 1936. That was the year that cost-benefit analysis became a requirement with the Flood Control Act, which established the policy that "the federal government should improve or participate in the improvement of navigable water . . . for flood-control purposes if the benefits to whomsoever they may accrue are in excess of the estimated costs. . . ."

Most cost-benefit analysis involves familiarity with certain common elements: the measurement of costs and benefits, the discount factors and decision rules. The paragraphs below examine each of these elements.

Measurement of Costs and Benefits. Assume that the Corp of Engineers is about to dig a ditch. Maybe the project is more in the nature of an irrigation system—but I want to keep things simple. To capture all effects, the analyst must proceed systematically breaking down costs and benefits into major categories.

These categories are shown in Table 6–1 with examples. *Real benefits* are the benefits derived by the final consumer of the public project and, as such, represent an addition to the community's total welfare. They must, however, be balanced against the *real costs* of resources withdrawn from other uses.

Pecuniary benefits and *costs* "come about due to changes in relative prices which occur as the economy adjusts itself to the provision of the

Table 6-1
Major Categories of Costs and Benefits for Irrigation Project

Category	Costs	Benefits
Real		
Direct		
Tangible	Costs of pipes	Increased farm output
Intangible	Loss of wilderness	Beautification of area
Indirect		
Tangible	Diversion of water	Reduced soil erosion
Intangible	Destruction of wildlife	Preservation of rural society
Pecuniary		Relative improvement in position of farm equipment industry

Source: Musgrave and Musgrave (1973:142).

public service. As a result, gains accrue to some individuals but are offset by losses which accrue to others. They do not reflect gains to society as a whole" (Musgrave & Musgrave, 1973:141). For example, say that earnings of roadside restaurants increase because of a highway project. Such gains do not reflect a net gain to society, since they are offset by costs to others (i.e., restaurants and grocery stores elsewhere). Consequently, in cost-benefit analysis, we can ignore these benefits.

Real benefits and costs can be either direct or indirect. Direct benefits and costs are those closely related to the main project objective. *Indirect benefits and costs*—sometimes called "externalitics" or "spillovers"—are more in the nature of by-products. Admittedly the line between direct and indirect can be fuzzy, requiring a judgment call by the analyst.

The term *tangible* is applied to benefits and costs that we can measure in dollars; those we cannot—for example, gain in world prestige from moon-shot projects—are referred to as *intangible.*

The following items illustrate some of the problems in and techniques for measuring costs and benefits.

A frequent indirect cost in government programs is compliance costs, or simply red tape. For example, a new federal law designed to safeguard employee pension rights can cause small firms to terminate their plans because of paperwork requirements.

It is difficult to measure benefits with rigor. Consider the benefits from pollution control. The Council on Environment Quality says that dangers from air pollution are the least known but reports that the annual toll from air pollution, health, vegetation, materials, and property values was $16 billion. The figures used in reading this estimate were called "crude approximations." If these are crude approximations, then what would you call estimates for, say, aesthetic costs and human discomfort?

Not all cost-benefit studies reveal benefits exceeding costs. A study prepared for the Office of Science and Technology on the benefits and costs of pollution control devices added to autos to comply with federal laws revealed that estimated costs of emission controls exceeded savings from the resulting abatement of pollution caused by auto emissions.

Distributional Impacts of Public Programs.   In addition to trying to measure costs and benefits, some thought should be given in cost-benefit analysis to the distribution of the costs and benefits resulting from a public program (Bonnen, 1969:425–26).
For benefits:

1. What is the purpose or objective of the public program or legislation, part of which is the question. Who should benefit?
2. Who actually benefits? What groups? It is sometimes not easy to identify beneficiary groups clearly.
3. How much are the total benefits of the program? Placing a value on the benefits of many programs is also not an easy analytical proposition.
4. What is the distribution of program benefits among beneficiaries?
5. What is the current distribution of incomes and assets or other relevant dimensions of welfare among *(a)* actual beneficiaries and *(b)* intended or potential beneficiaries?

"Sure it's unfair to the little guy. . .
He's the easiest one to be unfair with.".
(From The Wall Street Journal, with permission of Cartoon Features Syndicate.)

For cost:

6. Who should pay the program costs? Sometimes the nature of the program contains strong implications as to whom the burden should be given; at other times, this is almost an unanswerable question.
7. Who actually does pay the cost of the program? Identification of the burdened groups should consider not only the tax structure, but direct price and income effects and the indirect effects of major factor and product substitution caused by the program.
8. What are the total program costs? Many times this includes, as it does in Question 7, economic and social costs not reflected in federal budget expenditures but market and nonmarket costs generated through the operation of the program itself. Thus, these are not simple questions.
9. How are program costs distributed among the burdened groups?
10. What is the current distribution of incomes and assets among *(a)* the actual burdened groups, and *(b)* the intended or potential burdened groups.

Discount Factor.   Most public projects and programs take place over time. How the analysis treats this time element is the subject of this subsection.

Again let us keep it simple. Think of time being divided into years and of future benefits and costs accruing in specific years. Table 6–2 shows, in column B, the dollar benefits over an interval of eight years: Since two years are required for construction, no benefits accrue until

---

Table 6-2
Hypothetical Cost-Benefit Study *(Dollars in Millions)*

Year (A)	Benefits* (B)	Costs* (C)	Net Benefits (D)	Discount Factor ($i = 10\%$) (E)	Present Value of Net Benefits (F)
1.	$ 0	$ 4	−4	.909	$ −3.6
2.	0	4	−4	.826	−3.3
3.	1	1	0	.751	0
4.	2	1	1	.683	.7
5.	3	1	2	.621	1.2
6.	4	1	3	.564	1.7
7.	4	1	3	.513	1.1
8.	4	1	3	.467	1.4
Total	$18	$14	4		$ −.8

* Generally, in cost-benefit computations, only the *direct* costs and benefits are used. The overall study should, however, include a discussion of indirect costs and benefits.

Optimism fills the air when voters are asked to approve construction or enlargement of a lavish public stadium for their communities. New Orleans' Superdome would make Houston's Astrodome "as obsolete as the Roman Colesseum." But soon reality sets in. The costs of remodeling Yankee Stadium (above) escalated from $24 million to $240 million. Because local taxpayers are obligated for such costs, one wonders whether stiffer user fees (see p. 356) might not be fairer. What *indirect and intangible costs* do you think might be involved in such projects? (New York Convention and Visitors Bureau)

the third year. Column C shows the costs, which are initially high but then level off. Column D simply shows the net benefits (benefits minus costs) for each year.

But is the one million dollar net benefit occurring in the fourth year really worth one million dollars in present dollars? No, these future proceeds must be adjusted to allow for the fact that future benefits are less valuable than present ones. The reason is that today's one million could be invested and certainly return more than one million to the investor four years later. Cost must be adjusted in a like manner. We call making these adjustments—that is, reducing future dollars to be comparable to today's dollars—*discounting*.

To find the value of a dollar in any future year, one need only multiply by a discount factor. The formula is

$$\text{Discount Factor} = \frac{1}{(1 + i)^t}$$

where i is the interest rate and t is the number of years. Equipped with this formula (or, more likely, a table of discount factors for different rates and years), we return to the question posed a moment ago: How much is $1 million four years from today worth today? Assuming a modest interest rate of 10 percent, we first calculate the discount factors and then multiply the $1 million benefit by it. Thus,

$$\text{Present value} = \frac{1}{(1 + .10)^4} \times \$1,000,000 = 0.683 \times \$1,000,000$$
$$= \$683,000$$

Column E, Table 6–2, gives the discount factors for the first eight years of the project. Now we can adjust the net benefits in column D to reflect their present values and show them in column F. If we sum column F, we shall see that by the eighth year the project's costs outweigh its benefits. Clearly, we should not proceed with the project. If we changed the discount rate to 5 percent, however, benefits would outweigh costs by $1.3 million—such is the power of a few percentage points in cost-benefit analysis.

Parenthetically, I cannot help but wonder how many college football players who sign half-million dollar professional contracts *to be paid over a five-year period* understand discounting. What is the present value of their income for the fifth year if the discount rate is 15 percent? (Answer on next page)*

Cost-Effectiveness Analysis. One technique closely associated with CBA is cost-effectiveness analysis. This technique attempts to answer the question: How much output do I get for a given expenditure? The advantage of cost-effectiveness analysis is that output or benefits need not be expressed in dollars.

Robert N. Grosse (1969:1197–1223) provides us with a clear example of how cost-effectiveness analysis might be used to determine the preferred mix of disease-control programs. Assume that we can determine as in the following table the number of lives saved by different expenditures on disease A and disease B:

	Expenditures	Lives Saved (Cumulative)
Disease A	$ 500,000	360
	1,000,000	465
Disease B	$ 500,000	200
	1,000,000	270

Writes Robert N. Grosse: "If we only knew the effect of spending $1 million, we might opt for a program where all our money was spent on controlling disease A. Similarly, if we only knew the effects of programs of half million dollars, we would probably prefer A, as we'd save 360 rather than only 200 lives. But if we knew the results for expenditures of both half a million and $1 million dollars in each program, we would quickly see that spending half our money in each program was better than putting it all in one assuming we have $1 million available."

The Concept of Opportunity Cost. Related to the above discussion of cost-benefit analysis is an even broader notion about cost. Unlike the man in the street, the administrator looks beyond the actual cash payments in evaluating the costs of public programs and projects. He realizes that some of the most important costs attributable to doing one thing rather than another stem from the foregone opportunities that have to be sacrificed in doing the one thing.

What is the opportunity cost of taking a course in public administration? In addition to registration fee, one must consider the implicit cost of the highest foregone alternative to the individual. This alternative might be income from a job, or it might be other available opportunities: playing tennis, taking another course, swimming, and so forth. This alternative cost economists term *opportunity cost*. Since public administrators must operate in a world of continual and eternal scarcity, it is a useful concept—indeed, it pervades the field.

Multiobjective Models

One limitation of CBA is that it accounts for only one objective, usually an aggregate of all accrued benefits in dollar terms. For that reason, the decision maker might want to either replace or supplement it with a newer technique that emphasizes multiple objectives.

Consider a project typical of the ones that spawned CBA: a waste treatment plant. Assuming four sites are under consideration, experts can be asked to rank them on an ordinal scale by five criteria:

Criteria 1: Effect of project on local transportation (from most positive to most negative):
   Project D.
   Project B.
   Project C.
   Project A.

Criteria 2: Effect on land-use planning:
   Project B.
   Project D.
   Project C.
   Project A.

Criteria 3: Effect on neighborhood:
   Project B.
   Project D.
   Project A.
   Project C.

* Answer: $49,700—or not much more than even a college professor earns.

Criteria 4: Effect on community economy:
> Project D.
> Project A.
> Project C.
> Project B.

Criteria 5: Effect on tax base:
> Project B.
> Project D.
> Project A.
> Project C.

The experts can also be asked to rank the projects on an interval scale ranging, say, from −100 (maximum negative effect) to +100 (maximum positive effect). For the first criteria, the results might look like this:

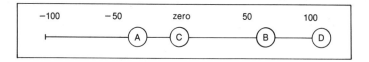

We have said nothing about the relative importance of each criteria. Therefore, decision makers may and probably should assign relative weights to each of the criteria. To see how this process works, consider a second example. How much weight would you accord to each of the following four criteria in judging a university faculty member?

Teaching effectiveness	?
Professional accomplishment	?
Community service	?
Compatibility with students and faculty	?
	1.00

Note that the sum of your relative weights must be 1.00.

Assume that one university weighted the criteria this way: teaching effectiveness (.40); professional accomplishment (.30); service (.15); and compatibility (.15). Professor Zarkov, who is on the faculty there, has these raw scores: teaching effectiveness (70), professional accomplishment (100), community service (80), and compatibility (60). Zarkov's weighted score would be computed thus:

$$70 \, (.40) + 100 \, (.30) + 80 \, (.15) + 60 \, (.15) = 79.$$

The preceding two examples have been highly simplified. In a real application, each criteria would need to be broken down into subfactors and then weight would need to be assigned to each subfactor. For instance, professional accomplishment in the second example might be broken down into research, consulting, publications, and professional activities.

If the multiobjective model seems tedious, then the reader is invited to consider other methods of making selections. . . .

"Since there are no women or children on board, Mr. Aaron here has suggested that we go in alphabetical order." (The Saturday Evening Post, May–June 1982, p. 48. Reprinted with permission from The Saturday Evening Post Society, a division of BFL & MS, Inc. © 1982.)

Decision Analysis

Suppose a general faces the following situation. According to the general's aides, unless he leads his soldiers to safety, all 600 will die. There are two escape routes. If he takes the first, 200 soldiers will be saved, if he takes the second, there is a one third chance that 600 soldiers will be saved and a two thirds chance that none will be saved. Which route should he take? Please pause to consider the question before reading any further.

Because most people reason that it is better to save those lives that can be saved than to gamble when the odds favor even higher losses, they will suggest that the general take the first route.

But suppose instead that the general's aides tell him that *these* are his two alternatives: If he takes the first route, 400 soldiers will die, if he takes the second, there is a one third chance that no soldiers will die and a two thirds chance that 600 soldiers will die. What is your recommendation now?

In this situation, most people will urge the general to take the second route, reasoning that the first involves certain death of 400 soldiers while with the second there is at least a one third chance that no one will die. What makes this recommendation surprising is that— although both situations are identical—it does not make sense in light of the first recommendation. The only difference between the two situations is that, in the first, the general's aides state the problem in terms of lives saved; in the second, they state it in terms of lives lost (example based on Kahneman & Tversky, 1979).

The point of this exercise is to show you that human reasoning is not always as reliable as we might wish to think. Even when we try to be coldly logical, we give quite different answers to the same problem if it is posed in a slightly different way.

Decision analysis is a technique that can help avoid such mental pitfalls by better structuring complex problems. In this approach, the decision is not viewed as isolated because today's decision depends upon the ones we shall make tomorrow. Thus, the decision problem is examined in terms of a tree of decisions. The tree uses decision forks and chance forks to indicate the interrelationships of choice and possible events.

A typical decision problem that would benefit from this approach is the case of a community threatened with a landslide sometime during the next year, before reforestation is completed (adopted from Public Policy Program, 1972). The basic decision is whether to build a retaining wall. In Figure 6–2, this decision is represented by the small square at the far left. Emanating from the square are two forks—the upper one representing the decision to build; the lower one, the decision not to build.

Figure 6–2
A Decision Tree

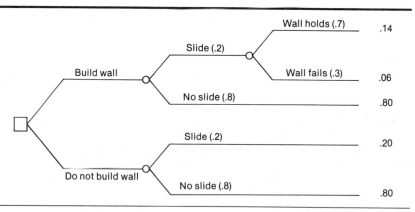

Regardless of the decision, however, the landslide could occur. This possibility is indicated slightly to the right of the decision square by the two chance nodes. Emanating from each node are two forks—the upper ones representing the actual occurrence of a slide. Based on expert judgment or historical records, a probability is assigned that a slide will occur. In this case the slide probability is 1 in 5 or simply .2.

Since retaining walls do not always hold, we must indicate the possibility of failure by yet another chance node even farther to the right. The probability of failure is estimated to be .3.

At the extreme right of Figure 6–2, we have calculated the probabilities of every possible outcome. Once we combine this information with certain costs figures, we are on the way to knowing whether to build. Basically, we need two costs figures. First, if a landslide occurs, we estimate that the only damages will be to property, valued at $3 million, since population can evacuate. Second, constructing a retaining wall will cost $200,000.

What is the cost of the decision to build? In addition to the outright cost of $200,000, we must figure the benefit from avoiding property damage. This would be $0.14 \times$ $3 million or $420,000. The net benefit of the decision to build is, therefore, $420,000 minus $200,000 or $220,000.

Systems Analysis

Systems analysis is not easily defined. In fact, it has been compared to the geological phenomenon known as "Roxbury puddingstone" in both history and construction. "This formation, located in a suburb of Boston, Massachusetts, resulted from glacial movement, which over the miles and the centuries dragged with it, accumulated, and then incorporated a vast heterogeny of types of rock, all set in a matrix and solidified in an agglomerate mass. Many fragments still retain their original identity and character; some have undergone metamorphosis in varying degrees. In like manner, the systems approach is kind of mosaic, made up of bits and pieces of ideas, theories, and methodology from a number of disciplines" (Hoos, 1972:27). Discernable among these disciplines are engineering, sociology, biology, philosophy, psychology, and economics.

Very broadly, the systems analysis approach forces us to look at problems as systems, that is, assemblies of interdependent components. While this may sound commonsensical—even trite—it is often ignored. Consider this classic example from Barry Commoner's *The Closing Circle* (1971:180).

A basic problem in sewage treatment is that, when organic sewage is dumped into a river or lake, it generates an inordinate demand for oxygen. But oxygen is needed as well for the bacteria of decay, which use the oxygen-converting organic matter to break down inorganic products. "As a result, this practice of dumping has commonly depleted the oxygen supply of surface waters, killing off the bacteria of decay and thereby halting the aquatic cycle of self-purification." Enter the sanitation engineer. His solution is simply to domesticate the decay bacteria in a treatment plant, artificially supplying them with sufficient oxygen to accommodate the entering organic material. Thus, what is released from the treatment plant is largely inorganic residues. "Since these have no oxygen demands, the problem, as stated, has been solved."

Unfortunately, the sanitation engineer did not recognize that he was dealing with a system, and that system includes nature's rivers and streams. The treated sewage is now rich in the inorganic residues of decay—carbon dioxide, nitrate, and phosphate—that support the growth of algae. "Now heavily fertilized, the algae bloom furiously, soon die, releasing organic matter, which generates the oxygen demand that sewage technology had removed."

In order to better appreciate the specifics of the systems approach, we shall break the methodology into four basic steps: problem formulation, modeling, analysis and optimization, and implementation.

Problem Formulation.   Problem formulation is perhaps the most difficult step, sometimes requiring three fourths of the total effort. This step includes the detailed description of the task, and identification of important variables and their relationships. Consider, for example, an investigation into some observed and perceived difficulties in an urban transportation system. In the systems approach, one begins by deciding whether the prime objective is better service, lower cost, less pollution, or something else. One must also decide what data are necessary: passenger miles by mode of transportation; passenger miles by sex, age, race, and income; passenger miles by time and place; and so forth. Finally, one must identify key decision makers in the urban area and their motivations.

Modeling.   The scene changes in the next step: One goes from the real world of the problem to the abstract world of the modeler. The modeler's task is probably more artistic than rigorous, more creative than systematic. He or she must strike a balance between including all relevant aspects of reality and keeping that model simply enough so that it is in line with existing theoretical loads, computation time, and data availability. Ultimately, of course, the test of a model's quality is how effective it is in helping to solve the original problem. Figure 6–3 shows a model for a criminal justice system.

To the uninitiated, a frequent cause of puzzlement is how models such as the one shown in Figure 6–3 can be "quantified." In other words, how can the analyst convert something as physical, as real as police and courts, into something as abstract as a set of mathematical relationships? While the equations relating the different components in Figure 6–3 probably present a level of sophistication far beyond the scope of this text, the idea behind representing a physical system mathematically involves no chicanery.

Take, for example, a simple inventory system. What would be some important variables in such a system? Among them would probably be:

$$C_O = \text{The cost of ordering per unit.}$$

Figure 6-3
Model of Criminal Justice System

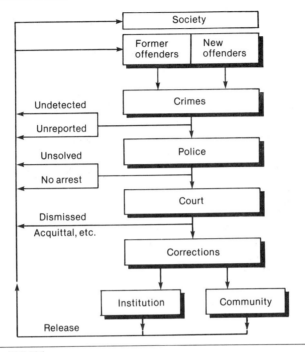

Source: Lapatra (1973:154).

C_H = The cost of holding per unit per time period.
D = The quantity of units used each time period.

A useful model, incorporating these variables, would be:

$$Q = \text{most economical quantity to order} = \sqrt{\frac{2C_O D}{C_H}}$$

Analysis and Optimization. During the analysis and optimization step, the model is studied to find the best strategy for resolving the problem given. Two options might be mentioned: (1) computer simulation, and (2) sensitivity analysis.

Simulation models allow users to replicate to a great extent the actual dispatch and patrol operations of most urban police departments. Incidents are generated throughout the city and distributed randomly in time and space according to observed statistical patterns. Each incident has an associated priority number, the lower numbers designating the more important incidents. For instance, a priority 1 incident would be an officer in trouble, a felony in progress, or a seriously injured person; a priority 4 incident could be an open fire hydrant, a lockout, or a parking violation. As each incident becomes

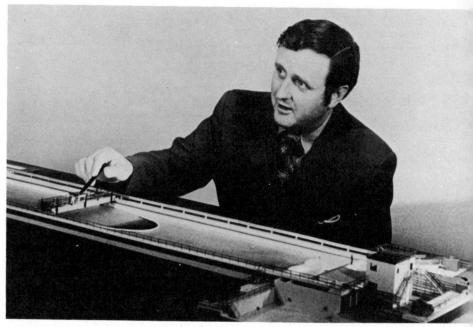

Simulation of models does not always take place on computers. Nor need it always involve sophisticated mathematics. The Federal Environmental Protection Agency, for example, has designed a tank to find better ways to handle oil spills. The principle involved is no different than the one used in the text with criminal justice: Much time and money can be saved by first testing various alternatives on a model rather than in the real world. (Environmental Protection Agency)

known, an attempt is made to assign (dispatch) a patrol unit to the scene. In attempting this assignment, the computer is programmed to duplicate as closely as possible the decision-making logic of an actual police dispatcher. In certain cases, this assignment cannot be performed because the congestion level of the accumulated incidents is too high; then, the incident report (which might in actuality be a complaint ticket) joins a queue of waiting reports. The queue is depleted as incidents are assigned to available patrol units. This simulation model is designed to study the patrol deployment strategy and the dispatch and reassignment policy.

The model tabulates several important measures of operational effectiveness. These include statistics on dispatcher queue length, patrol travel times, amount of preventive patrol, workloads of individual patrol units, amount of intersector dispatches, and others.

In sum, simulation provides a tool to assist in answering a wide range of allocation questions. Police administrators should find simulation models valuable for the following purposes:

They facilitate detailed investigations of operations throughout the city (or part of the city).

They provide a consistent framework for estimating the value of
new technologies.

They serve as training tools to increase awareness of the system
interactions and consequences resulting from everyday policy
decisions.

They suggest new criteria for monitoring and evaluating actual
operating systems.

Perhaps the most ambitious application of simulation is the previously mentioned model by Dennis Meadows that treats the entire world as an interdependent unit (read: system). When the model was simulated, the computer projected that the level of world pollution would eventually skyrocket and population would plummet; following this catastrophe, however, the quality of life would rise rapidly, reaching previously unknown heights (see Figure 6-4).

This simulation is useful for two reasons. First it shows how changes in one variable influence other variables; it captures nicely—and far better than the human mind can—the interrelation of things. Second, the Meadows simulation shows the limitations of simulation. Simulations are no better than the assumptions upon which they are built. Meadows seems to think that technological innovation will cease and that people are *not* influenced by the laws of supply and demand. Hence, the sharp dip in quality of life around the year 2060.

Figure 6-4
A Global Simulation

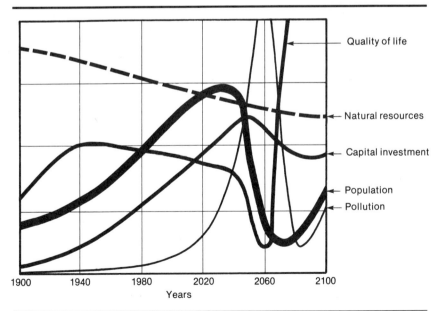

Source: Adapted from Meadows et al., 1972.

One of the advantages of simulation derives from the *counterintuitive* nature of public systems. To call these systems counterintuitive is to say that they do not react in ways we think they should. The reason intuition provides so little guidance in understanding a system's behavior is that the human brain cannot grasp the totality of relationships among all the variables. Thus, common sense tells us that wider highways reduce congestion, but as urban planners have learned, the reverse is often the case.

Not necessarily requiring the assistance of a computer, *sensitivity analysis* is another option that is available in analyzing the model to find the best strategy for solving the original problem. A sensitivity analysis process consists of making very small changes in the model to show the extent to which results may be importantly altered because of change in one or a few factors. To see how sensitivity analysis might work, let us reexamine Figure 6–3. Assume that the mayor calls for a large reduction in the total operating expenses. Since one does not want to reduce the strength of the police force (the patrol on the line), one looks elsewhere for "fat." Assume, therefore, that the typing pool in the probation division is reduced. As a result, the typing of presentence reports of convicted defendants waiting to be sentenced is delayed. Defendants now must spend even more time in jails, and the system's overall operating costs reach a new high.

Let us try a different tack: Discontinue night courts. But closing these courts add substantial costs to the police, who will have to house, feed, and guard defendants awaiting court action. Another suggestion might be to reduce the number of judges or prosecutors by 8 percent and the police by 3 percent. What results do you see from such a course of action? Do you see any effects on a city's tax base that might result from cuts in the area of criminal justice?

Implementation. In this subsection, we have discussed the systems approach in terms of four steps, giving particular emphasis to the first three. The last step, implementation refers to the procedure by which the results determined from the model are translated as a set of actions to the real world. The four steps, however, seldom occur in perfect sequence; indeed, the systems approach is highly iterative. As such, it might easily move through a sequence of steps such as the following: formulating the problem, selecting objectives, designing alternatives, collecting data, building models, weighting cost against effectiveness, testing for sensitivity, questioning assumptions, reexamining objectives, looking at new alternatives, reformulating the problem, selecting different or modified objectives, and so on (Quade, 1966:10).

Operations Research (OR)

Preceding the arrival of the systems approach in the decision-making centers of government was the use of operations research. The formal inception of operations research may, in fact, be traced to World War II. Faced with acute shortages of men and material and working against the clock, the military turned for assistance to the scientific and engineering community for help in resolving some knotty operations problems. These problems concerned, for example, the most effective setting of the time fuse of a bomb dropped from an aircraft onto a submarine; the optimal formation of bombers as a function of a target shape; the best bomber-fighter combination to achieve maximum security and still accomplish the mission; the measurement of the effectiveness of arming merchant ships against enemy aircraft; and the optimal location of radar stations. And, due to the revolution that began when electronic computers became commercially available as well as the increased demand for greater productivity on a large part of American industry, the use of operations research had by the early 1950s spread to industry.

While operations research (or *management science* as it is increasingly referred to) and the systems approach share many characteristics—for example, use of interdisciplinary teams, modeling, and sophisticated mathematics—they are not the same. The scope of the former is narrower. It tends to be concerned with problems that can be represented by mathematical models that can be optimized. For example, a typical operations research problem would determine (subject to certain constraints) the optimal (i.e., the very best) location in terms of service for a new fire station or a new bus route in a city. Operations research tends, we might say, to be concerned with problems in the small. Indeed, it was because the World War II teams studied small operational problems that the original (English) name was *operational research*; it was only later modified to operations research—with typical American lack of concern for syntax.

The systems approach, on the other hand, is concerned with problems of greater complexity and abstraction (hence: less emphasis on calculation). Actually, OR is one of the most important inputs to the systems approach. Thus, the relationship between the systems approach and OR is much like that between strategy and tactics.

Of all the quantitative techniques that OR emphasizes, *linear programming* is one of the most widely used. Accordingly, we conclude our discussion of OR by considering linear programming.

Linear programming is a mathematical technique for deriving the optimal solutions to linear relationships. Any problem concerned with maximizing or minimizing some economic quality (e.g., cost) subject to a set of constraints (e.g., human resources, materials, and capital) is a linear programming problem. In general, the technique has been used with enormous success to solve a variety of administrative problems in areas such as the following:

Determining a product mix that meets certain established specifications at minimum cost. Examples are found in establishing the lowest cost for meeting the standard requirements of adult nutrition. In 1973, one could live on about $95 per year. (But what a product mix this implies: kidneys, cabbage, beans, buckwheat flour, and not much else!)

Determining optimum product lines and production processes. Examples are found in those situations where capacity limitations exist and decisions must be made as to optimal production of scarce resources.

Determining optimum transportation routes. For example, a railroad must move a number of freight cars about and wishes to do it at the lowest cost. If there were 3 origins, 10 distributions, and 100 cars to distribute, then the total number of feasible solutions would be in the millions.

Writes Spencer (1971:277):

> Although linear programming has been applied primarily to industrial situations, there have been widespread applications of it by governmental agencies. For example, the military services have employed elaborate programming techniques to achieve optimum allocations of men and materials. Various bridge, highway, and airport administrative agencies (e.g., the Port of New York Authority) have made major utilization of specialized programming methods to find optimal solutions to such problems as stacking aircraft over airports, queuing ships at docks, and easing the congestion of vehicles at toll booths of tunnels and bridges.

The appendix to this chapter develops more fully some of the ideas behind linear programming.

The Perry Mason Syndrome, or Why You Need to Understand Analytical Techniques Even if You Do Not Use Them

In recent years, public administrators and their bright young staffs have displayed two disturbing tendencies in their decision making. First, they have tried to run the government by pouring over the data presented to them from various components in their agency and then subjecting a few experts or senior officials of those components to skeptical questioning. I call this the Perry Mason Syndrome. It is based on the fallacious idea that a smart administrator, like a smart lawyer, simply asks the right questions and thereby extracts the truth from the people with the data.

In practice, this approach seldom works. The questioner is helplessly dependent on the official for his or her information. As Henry Kissinger once pointed out, the decision memoranda that lower-level officials hand up tend to contain three alternatives—two ridiculous ones and their preferred one (which is usually listed second). Effective questioners, therefore, ensure that they have independent, firsthand knowledge against which to test alternatives. They are also keenly aware of the First Law of Expert Advise: Don't ask the barber whether you need a haircut. Finally, while they may not have a specialist's understanding of the techniques described earlier in this chapter, effective questioners know that a conceptual understanding is important. Such an understanding helps them ask the right questions about the expert's assumptions, methods, and results.

Making the Decision: Alternatives to the Analytical Approach

Late in 1983, ABC broadcasted on four consecutive nights *The Crisis Game*, a docudrama featuring 10 former high government officials acting the unscripted parts of the president and his National Security Council (see photo). Their task was to cope with an imaginary U.S.-Soviet crisis set in 1985. Ayatollah Khomeini had died and a civil war had erupted in Iran. The Soviet Union was rapidly moving battalions across Iran's border to join local communist forces.

The value of this docudrama was that it depicted as never before how presidents and their advisers make decisions. It unfolded spontaneously, and impressed many former insiders as being very like the real process. The discussions were often rambling and desultory—in short, quite different from the neat clear-cut techniques considered in the last section. There was stiltedness and pontification by the secretary of defense and showboating by senior advisers. There were also flashes of anger, knowledge tinted by political bias, impatience, and

For their *Crisis Game,* ABC cast Former Secretary of State and presidential candidate Edmund Muskie (not shown) as president. Former defense secretary, Clark Clifford (left) played Secretary of State, while James Schlesinger (center) had his old title of Defense Secretary again. (© 1985 American Broadcasting Companies, Inc.)

even occasional confusion. *The Crisis Game* demonstrated that, for better or worse, decision making is a very human affair involving far more than objective analysis.

As suggested in the introduction to the preceding section, and now in *The Crisis Game,* analysis is not the only approach to decision making. The reality is that administrative decision making is based on the epistemology men and women employ in their search for the truth. By *epistemology,* I mean the thinking and reasoning processes by which truth is reached and understood.

Broadly speaking, there are at least four other epistemological systems besides the analytical that are relevant to managerial decision making (see C. W. Churchman, 1968, 1971). For simplicity, we can refer to them as styles of thinking or approaches to decision making. The four other approaches are:

1. *Empirical,* which builds decisions on the basis of a broad survey of many facts. The Delphi method, discussed in Chapter 5, the statistical exhibits in Case 7.2, and the examples of bureaucratic malfunctions in Chapter 8 are good illustrations of this approach.
2. *Kantian,* named for the German philosopher Immanuel Kant (1724–1804), which says that neither rational models nor facts alone can lead to the truth; one must have a conceptual framework to make sense of and connect the data one gets through the senses.
3. *Pragmatic,* which says that decisions must be made in accordance with their effects; decisions are not to be judged by theoretical elegance, empirical rigor, or holistic frameworks but by whether they effect a desired result.
4. *Dialectical,* which strives for creative solutions through combining (synthesizing) two or more different ideas into a fresh and useful idea.

It would be beyond the scope of the book to develop these four ideas any further. Thus, it is sufficient to note that *(a)* each approach has its strengths and weaknesses, and *(b)* most executives use more than one approach in their day-to-day decision making. Because we have emphasized the analytical approach in this chapter and pointed out its usefulness, we shall conclude by considering some of its weaknesses. In so doing, I hope to suggest why decision makers need to be aware of—and indeed cultivate—other decision-making skills.

We shall begin by considering some specific criticisms of systems analysis and then turn to some more general reflections by one of the foremost intellects in the field of public administration.

Systems Analysis or Systems Paralysis?   Systems analysis begins, it will be recalled, with problem definition. Significantly, one of the most distinguished practitioners of the systems approach, Charles

Hitch (1960:11) maintains that Rand had never undertaken a major system study where satisfactory objectives could be defined. Where attempts were made, objectivity proved elusive. For example, in a classic systems study on water resources (McKean 1963), the goals read as follows: *Adequate* pollution control; *reasonable* irrigation development; *proper* erosion control and sediment reduction; *suitable* flood control; *optimum* contribution in alleviating the impact of drought; *full* development of the basin's resources for recreational programs. Where did these goals come from? What do the italicized words mean?

Gathering information is also a part of the first step. Writes Ida R. Hoos (1973:162–63):

> Dear to the hearts of technically oriented analysts is the information-gathering and processing state. In fact, so [agreeable] is the occupation with data that many systems designs, purported to deal with pressing social problems, never progress beyond that point. Displaying the ingestive propensities of a snake, the information system swallows up all the resources allocated to a given project and diverts attention from its larger purpose.

To buttress her point, Hoos cites the activity of the Bay Area Transportation Study Commission (BATSC), which was instructed to prepare a master regional transportation plan. In the end, the experts "listed as their accomplishments a total of 10 million pieces of information, converted to 1.5 million punch cards, which were recorded on 1,100 reels of magnetic tape, which require one and one-half hours of IBM 7094 time to reprocess."

In sum, too many analysts apparently think that, if only enough factual research is done, then somehow a valid generalization will automatically emerge. But such is not the case. What do frequently emerge are some very expensive price tags ($3 million in the case of BATSC).

Perhaps the first pitfall to note about the second step, modeling, is that the analyst structures the problem; that is to say, the analyst inevitably must view the problem through his or her own eyes and determine what the relevant variables are. Assuming one wants to wage war against poverty, how does one go about establishing the poverty level? What does one base the calculations on? The U.S. Department of Agriculture's Economy Food Plan?

The system itself must also be determined. But how inclusive should it be? Clearly, Barry Commoner's sanitation engineer was not inclusive enough. Conceivably, the criminal justice system in Figure 6–3 was not inclusive enough. (It had no way of indicating the economic effects of crime rate; e.g., reduced tax base as residents move away from city due to increase in crime.) Hoos (1973:161) puts the issue concisely: "Systems experts have made a great show of addressing totality but have actually dealt with shreads and patches."

The third step in the systems approach is analysis and optimization.

Here the analyst runs the risk of becoming locked into attaining the originally stated objectives of the study. This is no paradox, for a good systems study should be *heuristic*; that is, a method to help discover. Obviously, what we need to discover cannot be known in advance. A famous study of the location of military bases conducted by Albert Wohlstetter and his associates at Rand illustrates this nicely (see Wohlstetter in Quade 1964:125–26).

In 1951, the air force asked Rand to help them select locations for new airbases to be built overseas in the 1956 to 1961 period. Wohlstetter's approach was not to try to answer the straightforward request (where should the bases go?) but to examine the assumptions inherent in the question itself. After a year and a half of analysis, he and his staff concluded that adding such bases was too risky, since aircraft positioned overseas closer to the Soviet Union were too vulnerable to surprise attack on the ground. They further concluded that overseas bases were more costly, less of a deterrent, and more of a problem for U.S. foreign policy than an alternative. The alternative was to build more bases in the United States and supplement them with small overseas installations for refueling.

A final pitfall in the systems approach is to let the method supplant the problem. In other words, some experts tend to begin with the question: What problems are available for my techniques? The proper initial question is, of course: What is the problem?

Such experts are not unlike the drunk the police officer finds late at night under a streetlight. When asked what he is doing, the drunk replies that he is looking for his keys.

"Where did you loose the keys?" the officer asks.

"In the alley."

"Then why are you looking for them here?"

"Because," replies the drunk, "this is where the light is."

In spite of such failures as a description of decision making, systems analysis provides a useful framework for categorizing and diagnosing the nature of the departures of actual decisions from the requirements of rationality. In this sense, it provides a benchmark.

Limits to Rationality.   Although the rational view has dominated this chapter, the fact is that rationality is a necessary but not sufficient condition from an effective decision. In public administration, situations can emerge quite rapidly, available time and information can be quite limited, and the problem can be complex or ambiguous. Given this set of circumstances, public managers must depend as much on intuition, spontaneity, and faith as on analytical techniques.

In awarding the Nobel Price to Herbert A. Simon in 1978, the Swedish Academy of Sciences singled out his work in "the decision-making process within organizations." Simon had challenged one of the very bases of the rational method—the idea that individuals always maximize their satisfaction. More fully stated, the idea is that

Herbert A. Simon's Nobel Prize in economics was given for work on decision making. (Harry Coughanour, *Pittsburgh Post-Gazette*)

individuals have complete and consistent systems of preferences that allow them to choose among alternatives; that they are always completely aware of what these alternatives are; and that there are no limits on the complexity of computations they can perform to determine which alternatives are best. That, Simon thinks, is an extravagant definition of rationality.

In the last few decades, in its extension to administrative decision making, this body of theory (on rational decision making) has reached a state of refinement that possesses considerable academic interest but "little discernable relationship to the actual or possible behavior of the flesh-and-blood human." Fortunately, Simon has gone beyond merely saying that the emperor has no clothes. After he established the limits of rationality, Simon proposed another theory. This theory suggests that organizations rarely maximize because the cost of attaining all the information necessary is too high and anticipation of future conditions is too difficult. Public administrators—as opposed to the rational decision maker of the textbook—search until they find solutions to their problems that keep them out of unacceptable difficulties. Simon calls their process *satisficing.*

In short, no single technique or approach is sufficient to yield a solution to an administrative problem worthy of the human potential to understand.

Nailing Down the Main Points

1. Decision making means selecting from various alternatives one course of action. It prevades the entire administrative organization and planning process.

2. Decision making consists of at least four steps: identifying the problem, gathering the facts, making the decision, and communicating and implementing the decision.

3. Recognizing the kind of problem that exists (generic or unique) can significantly improve the quality of decision making.

4. Decision makers should consult other people and consider the upper and lower limits of the decision.

5. In recent years, as the costs of government became a greater concern to the taxpayer as well as to political leadership, cost-benefit analysis grew in popularity. Now, virtually all costly governmental programs are subjected to some type of cost-benefit analysis.

   This analysis does basically three things. First, it attempts to measure *all* the costs and benefits from a program. Second, since most programs or projects take place over extended periods of time, the flow of future costs and benefits must be converted into their present values. We call making these adjustments *discounting*. Finally, we must decide by one of several decision rules whether the benefits justify the cost.

6. The multiobjective model provides a way of ranking various alternatives according to weighted criteria or objectives. Decision analysis provides a way of choosing courses of action within acceptable limits of risk.

7. The systems approach, or systems analysis, forces us to look at problems as systems, that is, assemblies of interdependent components. The four basic steps in this approach are *(a)* policy formulation, *(b)* modeling, *(c)* analysis and optimization, and *(d)* implementation.

   During the analysis and optimization step, the model is studied to find the best strategy for resolving the problem. Among the options available here are computer simulation and sensitivity analysis.

8. While operations research (OR), or management science, shares many characteristics with the systems approach, it is not quite the same thing. The scope of OR is narrower; its nature, more mathematical. Of all the techniques that OR emphasizes, linear programming is one of the most widely used.

9. The analytical approach is only one style of thinking that decision makers use. Others include the empirical, Kantian, pragmatic, and dialectic (synthesis). Each approach, including the analytical approach, has certain strengths and weaknesses.

Concepts for Review

Cost-effectiveness analysis
Counterintuitive nature of public systems
decision analysis
decision making
decision rules for cost-benefit analysis
direct and indirect costs and benefits, spillovers, and externalities
discounting
four basic steps in systems approach
generic and unique problems
incremental approach
limiting (strategic) factor in decision making
linear programming
multiobjective model
operations research

opportunity cost
real and pecuniary costs and benefits, tangible and intangible costs and benefits
satisficing
sensitivity analysis

simulation
styles of thinking
systems approach
technology fix
upper and lower limits of decisions

Problems

1. "Decision making is the primary task of the administrator." Discuss.

2. Suppose you were to build a model that would forecast the nationwide demand for nurses 20 years from now. As a start, one must make assumptions about population growth and effects of new drugs. What else? Do you think the list of variables is endless?

3. Are defense and domestic spending really transferable as the concept of opportunity cost may suggest? In other words, do you see any fallacy in comparing a new navy destroyer to so many new hospitals or new schools? What other factors might make a dollar-for-dollar comparison difficult?

4. In October 1985, the Reagan Administration ordered U.S. warplanes to force down an Egyptian jet carrying four hijackers of the Achille Lauro cruise ship. The mission was a success in that the Egyptian jet landed at an Italian air base and the four hijackers had to go on trial in Italy. What were the limiting (strategic) factors in the decision? What were the upper limits? Show how these concepts might apply in other crisis situations.

5. A disgruntled group member once defined a camel as a horse put together by a committee. Group decisions are often frustrating and inadequate, but there can be real strength in group problem solving. Jay Hall ("Decision," *Psychology Today*, November 1971, 51 ff.) provides some thoughtful suggestions on how. Read this article and then conduct his experiment, "Lost on the Moon," to see how effective his methods are.

6. As the head of a city housing agency, you must decide whether to submit either plan A or B (but not both) to the mayor who, in turn, must submit it to the city council. You estimate that there is a 90 percent chance that the mayor would accept A but only a 50 percent chance the council would accept. The council likes B, indeed, you are certain they would accept it—if, that is, it ever got past the mayor (only 3-to-1 odds of this happening). You prefer A and evaluate its utility at 1.00. In fact, because you think it the most socially desirable, even if the mayor accepts and has it rejected by the council, you would assign a utility of 0.40 to these consequences. Of course, if the reject came first from your boss, the mayor, the utility would be somewhat less, say, 0.20. However, Plan B, if accepted by the city council, has a utility of 0.80 to you. But the worst situation is to have it rejected; there would be no utility in such a case. What should you do?

7. Conduct a systems analysis of your community. This may sound like an overwhelming job. Nevertheless, if you read the proposals Robert K. Lamb makes in "Suggestions for a Study of Your Hometown," *Human*

Organization, Summer 1952, you will find ways and means for shortcutting and sampling.

8. Care must be taken in systems analysis to ensure that the measures of effectiveness are appropriate. A classic example of how incorrect measures can throw off the analysis concerns the installation of antiaircraft guns on merchant vessels in World War II. While these guns made the crews feel safer, data on equipped and nonequipped ships showed that only 4 percent of attacking planes were shot down. Because the guns were expensive and needed elsewhere, their removal was proposed. Was the percentage of planes shot down the correct effectiveness measure of the guns? If not, then what was? (see Morse & Kimball, 1951: 52–53).

9. Use multiobjective criteria to help you decide among four models of automobiles. Using a form similar to the one on page 214, establish criteria and weight it. The final step in your analysis should be to divide the relevance number by the cost of the automobile; this will give you four benefit-to-cost ratios to compare.

10. Give several examples of recent nonincremental decisions in American government.

11. Gotham City has to dispose of 22,000 tons of refuse daily, an amount increasing by 4 percent a year. Currently, it has eight incinerators that have a usable capacity of 6,000 tons a day; residue and nonincinerated refuse must go to sanitary landfills that will be exhausted within five years. Four superincinerators, with a capacity of 20,000 tons a day have been proposed. Unfortunately, they are quite expensive: $1 billion to build and $50 million a year to operate. Moreover, they would add substantially to hazardous air pollution by emitting thousands of tons of soot particulates a year. Outline and discuss an analytic model that could help the mayor of Gotham City decide what to do. What additional information would you need? What are the upper and lower limits of the decision? Is the decision simply one of whether to build the superincinerators or are alternatives available?

12. The town of Broken Arrow needs a fire department and you must make recommendations concerning its size and structure. What would be a good rule of thumb for the number of fire engines? (The fire chief of Gotham City suggested that the number of fire engines should be proportional to the number of buildings.) Regarding structure, you have two basic alternatives: *(a)* one central department, or *(b)* several decentralized stations. Discuss how you decide between *(a)* and *(b)*.

13. Write a paper comparing the decision-making styles of two or more recent presidents. Which is most effective? Why?

14. "Experience is not only an expensive basis for decision making but also a dangerous one." Discuss.

15. What are the shortcomings in using "lives saved" as a measure of benefit?

16. Use the concept of opportunity cost to explain why lawyers and housewives are more likely than medical doctors to get involved in politics.

17. Given the following data, how would you spend $1 million? What idea is expressed in this exercise?

Disease A		Disease B	
Expenditures	**Lives Saved**	**Expenditures**	**Lives Saved**
$ 100,000	100	$ 100,000	50
200,000	180	200,000	50
300,000	250	300,000	135
400,000	310	400,000	170
500,000	360	500,000	200
600,000	400	600,000	225
700,000	430	700,000	240
800,000	450	800,000	255
900,000	460	900,000	265
1,000,000	465	1,000,000	270

18. Assume you are supervising the work of 12 engineers. Their formal training and work experiences are similar, permitting you to use them interchangeably on projects. Yesterday your manager informed you that a request had been received from an overseas office for four engineers to go abroad on extended loan for a period of six to eight months. For a number of reasons, the manager and you agreed that this request should be met from the group.

    The overseas assignment is in what is generally regarded in the agency as an undesirable location.

    How should this decision be made—authority, consultation, or group? (Hint: See Victor H. Vroom and Phillip Yetton, *Leadership and Decision Making*, 1973.)

Case 6.1
The Structure of a Government Decision

When William D. Ruckelshaus became head of the Environmental Protection Agency in 1983 (see Case 1.1), he immediately faced several tough decisions. But none was tougher than the question of what to do about acid rain. Within about three months, the president expected him to have a recommendation to present to OMB.

The Problem
Each year the eastern half of North America is drenched with rain turned acid by waste gases (see Exhibit 1). Some of the acid arises locally but much comes from coal-fired power plants in the Ohio Valley. The power-plants giant smokestacks, located in the valley since passage of the Clean Air Act of 1970, blow sulphur and nitrogen oxides into winds that carry the gases eastward, converting them into sulfuric and nitric acids that wash down in rain.

So far, the chemical and biological resilience of soils and lakes has enabled them to absorb the poison with little visible harm. But as the reserve for neutralizing the acid diminishes, the first signs of widespread damage are beginning to appear.

Exhibit 1
Precipitation Acidity—Annual Average pH for 1980

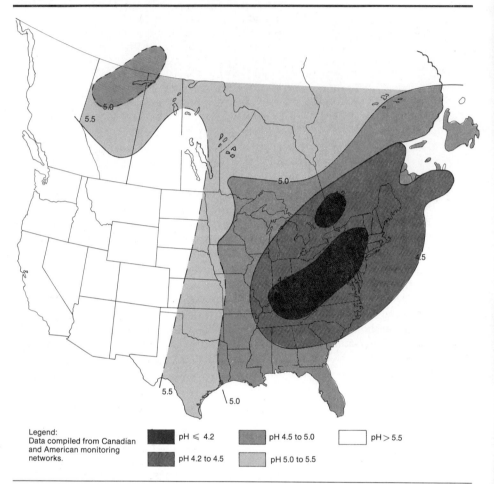

Legend:
Data compiled from Canadian and American monitoring networks.

pH ≤ 4.2	pH 4.5 to 5.0	pH > 5.5
pH 4.2 to 4.5	pH 5.0 to 5.5	

Source: Office of Technology Assessment, *Acid Rain and Transported Air Pollutants* (Washington, D.C.: Government Printing Office, June 1984), p. 6.

Utilities, resistant to the heavy costs of emission control, long disputed almost every link in the argument used by ecologists, which placed the acid rain problem on their doorstep. Backed by the administration, the utilities urged more study to pinpoint cause and effect. They contended that even if power plants paid to reduce emissions, there would be no guarantee of a corresponding reduction in acid rain. In a survey released just before Ruckelshaus was confirmed by the Senate, the Edison Electric Institute forecasted that electricity rates could rise as much as 50 percent if emissions-control legislation were passed.

At roughly the same time, a major turning point in this vexing debate was reached. Two major studies were completed, one by the National Academy of

Sciences, another for the president's science adviser. Between them they established the scientific framework within which Ruckelshaus and others would have to address the acid rain problem.

The academy's major finding was that—contrary to the utilities' contention—a direct relation holds between the amount of waste gas released and the amount of acid rain or gas deposited. This means that the more the Ohio coal plants cut back, the less acid will fall on New York and New England. Thus, control measures would buy something tangible.

The high-level review for the president's adviser confirmed the academy's finding—that acid rain is to blame for major changes in the biology of lakes and for increasing damage to forests. The review also concluded that even without further acid rain, it could take decades for the ecosystems to recover. But its summary stated: "The overall scientific understanding of the various aspects of acidic precipitation is quite incomplete at the present time and will continue to have major uncertainties well into the future."

Options

Three basic approaches to acid deposition and other air pollutants have been put forward.

1. Mandating emission reductions to further control the sources of transported pollutants. Legislated emission reductions could require modest reductions to keep emission at—or somewhat below—current levels. A previous academy committee concluded that cutting sulfur dioxide by half, or by some 10 million tons a year, would bring acid rain beneath the threshold at which biological systems are damaged. Utilities could approach that target by washing coal before it is burned. They could also switch to low-sulfur coal, particularly in spring when snow melt places an extra acid burden on lakes and streams. But washing and switching would not be enough. Some utilities would also need to install scrubbers, costly equipment that efficiently removes sulfur from emissions. Another potential technology, not yet proven, would be to burn limestone along with the coal.
2. Liming lakes and streams to mitigate some of the effects of acid deposition.
3. Modifying the current research program to provide more timely guidance to Congress.

Case Questions

1. Ruckelshaus has to think the options through seriously—but what is it he has to think through? What decision is he being asked to make?
2. Where could the decision-making techniques discussed in this chapter help Ruckelshaus the most?

Case References

Office of Technology Assessment, *Acid Rain and Transported Air Pollutants* (Washington, D.C.: U.S. Government Printing Office, June 1984); General Accounting Office, *An Analysis of Issues Concerning "Acid Rain"* RCED-85-13 (Washington, D.C.: Government Printing Office, December 11, 1984).

Appendix to Chapter 6
Linear Programming

Linear programming refers to several related mathematical techniques that are used to allocate limited resources among competing demands in an optimal way. Linear programming is the most popular of the approaches falling under the general heading of mathematical optimization techniques; dynamic programming and nonlinear programming are two other widely used (but generally more complicated) forms of mathematical optimization techniques.

The linear programming problems entails an optimizing process in which nonnegative values for a set of decision variables $X_1 X_2 \ldots X_n$ are selected so as to maximize (or minimize) an objective function in the form:

Maximize (minimize)
$$Z = C_1 X_1 + C_2 X_2 + \ldots + C_n X_n$$

subject to resource constraints in the form:

$$A_{11}X_1 + A_{12}X_2 + \ldots + A_{1n}X_n \leq B_1$$
$$A_{21}X_1 + A_{22}X_2 + \ldots + A_{2n}X_n \leq B_2$$
.
.
.
$$A_{m1}X_1 + A_{m2}X_2 + \ldots + A_{mn}X_n \leq B_m$$

where C_j, A_{ij}, and B_i are given constants.

Depending upon the problem, the constraints may also be stated with equal signs (=) or greater-than-or-equal-to signs ($\geq$).

For linear programming to be applicable, the following conditions must exist.

The objective function and each constraint equation must be linear. This excludes exponents and implies proportionality; for example, if it takes three people to produce one unit, it takes six people to produce two.

The constants must be known and assumed to be deterministic. In other words, the probability associated with the occurrence of any C_j, A_{ij}, and B_i value is presumed to be 1.0.

The decision variables must be divisible; that is, a feasible solution would permit half a unit of X_1, a quarter unit of X_2, and so on, to be produced. This obviously would eliminate such situations as scheduling air flights, since sending up half an airplane is not possible.

Though limited in application to problems involving two-decision variables (or three variables for three-dimensional graphing), graphical linear programming provides a quick insight into the nature of linear programming and illustrates what takes place in the general simplex method, which can be used to solve any type of linear programming problem but will not be described here.

The steps involved in the graphical method can best be understood in the context of sample problems. First let us consider the case of Spartan Cut-Rate Hospital (SCRH), which only offers two foods in its cafeteria. Each serving of stew costs 8 cents to make and each serving of mixed vegetables 4 cents. A serving of stew provides 8 grams of protein and 4 units of vitamin B_1. A serving of mixed vegetables provides 3 grams of protein and 7 units of vitamin B_1. Assume that patients must have a minimum of 24 grams of protein per day and 28 units of vitamin B_1.

If SCRH wishes to minimize costs, how many servings of stew and how many servings of mixed vegetables should they provide each patient each day?

1. *Formulate the problem in mathematical terms.* If X equals the number of servings of stew and Y

equals the number of servings of mixed vegetables, the objective function and constraints equation may be stated as follows.

$$\text{Minimize } Z = 8X + 4Y \text{ (costs)}$$

subject to

$$8X + 3Y \leq 24 \text{ (protein)}$$
$$4X + 7Y \leq 28 \text{ (vitamin } B_1)$$
$$X, Y \leq 0 \text{ (nonnegativity requirements)}$$

2. *Plot constraint equations.* This is easily done by letting one variable equal zero and solving for the axis intercept of the other. For the protein constraint equation, then, when $X = 0$, $Y = 8$, and when $Y = 0$, $X = 3$. For the vitamin B_1 constraint equation, when $X = 0$, $Y = 4$, and when $Y = 0$, $X = 7$. These points are graphed in Figure 6–1A.

3. *Determine the area of feasibility.* The direction of inequality signs in each constraint equation determines the area wherein a feasible solution will be found. In this case all inequalities are of the more-than-or-equal-to variety, which means that any combination of products to the left of any constraint line on the graph would not satisfy the requirements. The region of feasible solutions is shaded on the graph.

4. *Plot the objective function.* The objective function may be plotted by assuming some arbitrary total cost figure and then solving for the axis coordinates, as was done for the constraint equations.

For example, from the dashed line on the graph we can determine all possible combinations of stew and mixed vegetables that will cost 24 cents by picking a point on the line and reading the number of each product that can be made at that point. The combination yielding 24 cents at point A would be two servings of stew and two servings of mixed vegetable. This can be verified by substituting 2 and 2 in the objective function:

$$8(2) + 4(2) = 24 \text{ cents}$$

5. *Find the optimum point.* It can be shown mathematically that the optimum combination of decision variables will always be found at an extreme (corner point) of the feasible region. In Figure 6–1A, there is only

---

Figure 6–1A
Graph of Diet Problem

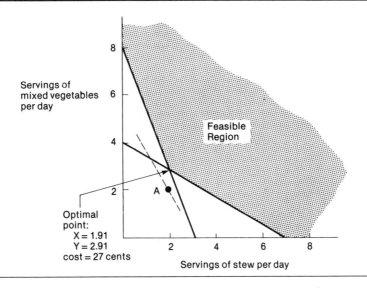

Servings of mixed vegetables per day

Feasible Region

Optimal point:
X = 1.91
Y = 2.91
cost = 27 cents

Servings of stew per day

Figure 6-2A
Graph of Range Management Problem

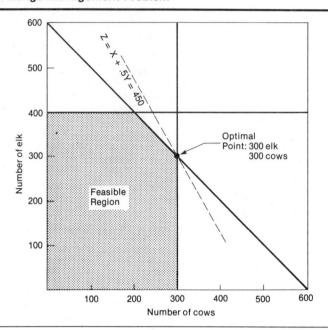

one corner point, and we can conclude that it must be the optimum by either of two approaches.

The first approach is to find the values of the corner solution algebraically. This entails simultaneously solving the equations of the pair of intersecting lines and substituting the quantities of the resultant variable in the objective function. For example, the calculations for the intersection of $8X + 3Y = 24$ and $4X + 7Y = 28$ would be as follows.

Substituting $Y = 28 - 4X/7$ in $8X + 3Y = 24$ gives $8X + 3(28 - 4X/7) = 24$. Multiplying both sides of that equation by 7, gives $7(8X) + 3(28 - 4X) = 7(24)$, or $X = 21/11 = 1.91$. Substituting $X = 1.91$ in the other equation, we get:

$$4(1.91) + 7Y = 28$$
$$Y = 2.91$$

Substituting $Y = 2.91$ and $X = 1.91$

in the objective function, we get:

$$Cost = 8(1.91) + 4(2.91) = 27 \text{ cents}$$

The second and generally preferred approach entails using the objective function line directly to find the optimum point. The procedure involves simply drawing a straight line parallel to any arbitrarily selected initial cost line so that it passes through the point closer to the origin of the graph. (In maximization problems, the objective would be to draw the line through the point farthest from the origin.)

The second linear programming example is typical of the one faced by the U.S. Forest Service ranger districts (problem based on Gile, 1974). The problem is to determine an optimum mix of the number of cattle and elk on the same range to maximize the animal units produced. On a given unit of land, a cow requires twice the land that an elk requires. If

X stands for the number of cows and Y for the number of elk, the objective function is:

Maximize $Z = X + .5Y$

The constraints in the problem depend on available range and differing feeding habits. There is only enough land to support 400 elk or 300 cows and certainly no more than a total of 600 animals. Therefore, our constraint equations are:

$$X \leq 300$$
$$Y \leq 400$$
$$X + Y \leq 600$$

Figure 6–2A presents the graphic solution.

7

Implementation and Evaluation

Introduction

Half the business of thinking is knowing what one is after in the first place. Before we launch into the last chapter of Part II, it might help to try to cut through the great mass of incidental and, sometimes perhaps, obscuring details presented in the last six chapters in order to lay bear the structure of program management.

The key is Figure 5–2, which showed policy planning as a dynamic process. Good program management begins with careful attention to goals and to the objectives for attaining goals. Careful attention to objectives, in turn, means considering alternative strategies for the attainment of each objective. In particular, the policy planner wants to ask what the likely effects of each alternative will be.

Decision making pervades the entire process of program management. Based on the assumption that today's administrator should be acquainted with the tools and techniques of rational decision making, most of Chapter 6 was devoted to exploring this approach to decision making.

The story does not end here, however. Two vitally important, exceedingly difficult, and frequently exciting steps remain—implementation and evaluation. Again, let us be crystal clear about what we are after. First, we want to know the potential problems the administrator faces when attempting to implement a program; then, too, we want to know the strategies available for overcoming such problems. Second, regarding evaluation, we need to know what it is and how it works. But this will not be easy, for few areas in the field of public administration are more neglected than evaluation.

The combination of two major subjects within one chapter can be, I think, justified to the extent they are closely related. Indeed, without decent evaluation, the administrator has little way of knowing how well implementation is going. A former secretary of HEW put it well: "Evaluation is a necessary foundation for effective implementation and judicious modification of our existing programs. At this point, evaluation is probably more important than the addition of new laws to an already extensive list of educational statutes. . . . Evaluation will provide the information we require to strengthen weak programs, fully support effective programs, and drop those which simply are not fulfilling the objectives intended by the Congress when the programs were originally enacted" (Robert H. Finch quoted in Wholey et al. 1970:19).

Because we are dealing with two major subjects, I have split the chapter into parts A and B.

Part A will begin by clarifying what implementation is and why it is a vital concern of the administrator. Then a number of techniques are discussed that, in combination, should improve the chances of success in program implementation.

In Part B, we shall begin by posing the same question about evaluation that we did about implementation—namely, why is it so important to the public administrator? The remainder of Part B examines evaluation as an aid to better decision making.

The chapter concludes with a discussion of how computers can contribute to planning, implementation, and evaluation.

A. Implementation

Understanding the Process

We shall let implementation mean just what the dictionary says it means: to carry out, accomplish, fulfill, produce, complete. But what is it that is being implemented? A policy, yes; but more exactly, that part of a policy that we defined in Chapter 5 as a program.

The distinction between policy and program is an important one when speaking of implementation. The great difficulty in government today is not so much determining what appear to be reasonable policies on paper as it is "finding the means for converting these policies into viable field operations" (Williams, 1975:453). In short, we have more good solutions (i.e., policies) than appropriate actions (i.e., programs).

We may view the implementation process from a variety of perspectives. Because the process entails so much bargaining and maneuvering, the political perspective sketched in Chapter 2 can be quite useful in understanding it. Because the process often involves intergovernmental relations, the discussion of grants found in Chapter 3 is also useful. Indeed, it is the division of authority among governments in the American federal system that explains more than anything else the failure of certain programs. Finally, because implementation occurs in all organizations—public and private—the management perspective adopted in the last six chapters is also relevant.

But there are two other relevant perspectives on implementation not analyzed elsewhere in the book: implementation as the complexity of joint action and implementation as a system of games.

Complexity of Joint Action

Pressman and Wildavsky (1973) note among the major difficulties in implementing new social programs or program modifications two in particular: multiplicity of participants and multiplicity of perspectives. These two seismic forces converge to delay—and, in many instances, stifle—administrative efforts to secure the joint action required in program implementation. The following discussion draws on an analysis by Pressman and Wildavsky of the Economic Development Administration's (EDA) efforts in Oakland.

On the face of things, the effort in 1966 to help the black unemployed of Oakland, California, began brilliantly. There were dedicated and powerful officials in Washington who were concerned that, if the city did not receive meaningful help quickly, it might be torn apart by riots. The officials were able to get a multimillion-dollar congressional appropriation to finance a program to provide jobs, while also enlisting Oakland businesspeople and governmental officials in the effort. And many of the usual bureaucratic barriers to action were struck down. It would be hard to think of a more propitious beginning for a government program—yet by 1969, the program was essentially a failure. Not very much money had been spent and the number of new jobs obtained for the hard-core unemployed was ridiculously small. Why?

One answer is that governmental programs, even when designed to be carried out in a direct and simple manner, eventually come to involve a large number of governmental and nongovernmental organizations and individuals. In the case of Economic Development Administration's employment effort in Oakland, the authors (1973:94) admit to oversimplifying the situation by restricting the participants to only the EDA, the rest of the federal government, and the city of Oakland, each with their constituent elements. The EDA consisted of the initial task force, EDA operating departments in Washington, the agency's leadership, the regional office in Seattle, and the field office in Oakland. Other federal government agencies that became involved included the General Accounting Office; the Department of Health, Education and Welfare; the Department of Labor; and the navy. Participants in Oakland were the mayor, city administrators, the Port of

Oakland, World Airways, and several of the city's black leaders, conservative groups, and tenants of the Port of Oakland.

Some of these participants (such as the Departments of Labor and Health, Education, and Welfare) became involved because they possessed jurisdictional authority over important parts of the project; others (like the navy) entered the process when they felt their interest being impinged on; and still others (such as black people in Oakland) were intentionally brought into the program by the EDA in order to build local support for the projects.

Pressman and Wildavsky found that each participating group had a distinctive perspective and therefore a different sense of urgency—although they still agreed on the ends of policy (developing jobs for unemployed minorities) and the means of achieving it (creating jobs through grants for public works). But different perspectives make or break a program. Several reasons why participants can agree on the ends of a program and still oppose (or merely fail to facilitate) the means for effecting those ends might be given (Pressman and Wildavsky, 1973:99–102):

1. Direct incompatibility with other commitments. Thus, HEW came to view one of EDA's training proposals as competing for scarce funds with one of their own training institutions in the area.

2. No direct incompatibility but a preference for other programs. Many EDA employees viewed rural areas and small towns—not urban areas—as the proper focus of the agency.

3. Simultaneous commitments to other projects. The Port of Oakland's architect/engineer delayed his work on plans for the marine terminal because his staff was busy on other port projects.*

4. Dependence on others who lack a sense of urgency.

5. Differences of opinion on leadership and the proper organizational role.

6. Legal and procedural differences. Discussing the frustrations of the early days of public works program implementation, an EDA task force member remarked that "There were all sorts of technical things that had to be decided. The job issue came later. There were a number of questions about EDA policy—how you process these things, how much meddling EDA would do. . . . In September, October, and November of 1966, there was hostility between the EDA and the port on construction

---

* This reason also probably helps explain why law enforcement agencies have not regulated obscenity more strictly, despite the 1973 U.S. Supreme Court's ruling that they could. As Manhattan's district attorney put it, "We've got more serious cases than we can handle already. When we have got more homicides, more rapes, and more assaults, prosecuting prostitution or pornography has to be low in priority" (*New York Times*, November 2, 1975).

issues." For example, regarding the quality of landfill, at every point, the port and EDA had their own engineering opinions.

A System of Games

Eugene Bardach (1977) uses the metaphor of "games" to analyze the implementation process. He argues that the game framework illuminates the process by directing our attention onto the players, their stakes, their strategies and tactics, their resources, the rules of play (which stipulate the conditions for winning), the rules of fair play, the nature of communication among the players, and the degree of uncertainty surrounding the outcome.

Using the game metaphor, Bardach offers an insightful definition of implementation: a process of assembling the elements required to produce a particular programmatic outcome and the playing out of a number of loosely interrelated games whereby these elements are withheld from or delivered to the program assembly process on particular terms. The list below identifies some of the most common implementation games.

The management game—The view that a constellation of troubles inherent in the process of implementation in a democratic society "can be solved by designing better management tools and procedures and by giving more power to institutions specializing in management, like the personnel department or the auditor's office."

Tokenism—The "attempt to appear to be contributing to a program element publicly while privately conceding only a small ('token') contribution."

Massive resistance—A means of obstructing program implementation by withholding critical program elements or by overwhelming the capacity of the administrative agency to enforce punishment for noncompliance. "Civil rights and antiwar demonstrators both in the streets and on college campuses showed very clearly, for a time, the great potential of large-scale noncompliance. Police forces could jail, and deans could expel, only so many people at a time."

Easy money—A game played by parties in the private sector who wish to make off with government money in exchange for program elements of too little value. (Around Washington, consultants are called the Beltway Bandits, because many of them have offices along I-495, a highway that loops downtown.)

Budget—As we will see in Chapter 9, heads of bureaus tend to be budget maximizers. "As part of their budget game, moving money somehow, somewhere, and fast, even at the price of programmatic objectives, is the characteristic strategy of virtually every governmental agency that channels grants to other levels of government or to nonprofit institutions."

Funding—Bureaus that receive grants try "to rescue not only money but flexibility in regard to its use."

Up for grabs—Often the mandate for a program will identify a lead agency and provide a modest budget but fail to clearly prescribe what other element might be involved and for what expected purpose. "In this confused situation, the few unambiguously mandated elements are up for grabs by a number of potential clientele groups to be converted into political resources."

Piling on—As onlookers see a program moving successfully in its intended direction, "some see it as a new political resource, an opportunity to throw their own goals and objectives onto the heap". The net effect of a large number of additional objectives added to the program is that the program may triple.

Keeping the peace—Quite a few programs originate with the desire to eliminate real or imagined evil. When activists or zealots run these programs, a backlash can form among other political interests.

Tenacity—This game can be played by anyone; all it requires is the ability and will to stymie the progress of a program until one's own terms are satisfied. While no one player may want to kill the program, the net effect of many actors playing tenacity may be just that.

Territory—All bureaucratic organizations struggle to ensure that some other organization is not given a program element that is perceived to be in "their" jurisdiction.

Not our problem—While bureaus may try to expand their territories, "this drive normally evaporates as soon as the bureau recognizes that the program will impose a heavy work load or that it will take the bureau into an area of controversy."

Toward More Effective Implementation

Start Thinking about It Early

The most important lesson to be learned from the preceding discussion is that implementation needs more careful attention during the policy development. That is to say, when the broad objective of policy is being set, efforts should be made to keep the number of participants and decision points small. Policy statements should contain action commitments and answer several distinct questions: What action has to be taken? Who is to take it? Do these people have the capacity to do it?

Given the psychological makeup of policymakers, however, this lesson might not be an easy one to put into practice. Write Pressman and Wildavsky (1973:136–37): "The view from the top is exhilarating. Divorced from problems of implementation, federal bureau heads . . . think great thoughts together. But they have trouble imagining the sequence of events that will bring their ideas to fruition. Other men, they believe, will tread the path once they have so brightly lit the way. Few officials down below where the action is feel able to ask whether there is more than a rhetorical connection between the word and the deed."

One good antidote for this psychological tendency to discount what could go wrong in the future is *scenario writing*. This method, Bardach (1977:254) writes,

> simply involves an imaginative construction of future sequences of actions→consequent conditions→actions→consequent conditions. It is inventing a plausible story about "what will happen if . . ." or, more precisely, inventing several such stories. Telling these stories to oneself and one's professional peers helps to illuminate some of the implementation paths that the designer does not want taken. He or she is then in a position to redesign some features of the system of implementation games that permit him or her and his or her colleagues to tell stories with happier endings. Trial and error through successive interactions produce better and better endings.

Perhaps Paul Bryant, the late University of Alabama football coach, said it even better: "It's the little-bitty, teeny-tiny things that beat you."

In addition to paying closer attention to implementation during policymaking, there are other ways of improving the effectiveness of

The most successful coach in the history of college football (323 victories), Paul Bryant, used to gesture from the sidelines with rolled-up sheets of paper that contained his carefully constructed game plan as well as a scribbled reminder not to forget "the itty-bitty, teeny-tiny things" that lose football games. Bryant would rehearse problems that might arise in a game over and over. In the language of management theory, we would call this not watching out for the itty-bitty things but contingency planning or scenario writing. (University of Alabama).

implementation. One is to pay as much attention to the creation of organizational machinery for *executing* a program as for launching one. Again, Pressman and Wildavsky (1973:145-46):

> EDA leaders took great pains to design the best organization they could think of for approving applications, committing funds, and negotiating initial agreements. But in most of the projects they did not spend as much time *ensuring that the initial commitment would be followed up* by the agency; in fact, the EDA itself seemed to lose its own intense interest in the program after 1966. Although those who design programs might not generally enjoy the less exciting work of directing their implementation, a realization of the extent to which policy depends on implementation could lead such people to alter their own time perspectives and *stay around for the technical details of executing a program.* [Emphasis added.]

Scheduling Models

Scheduling models, another implementation technique, facilitate the coordination of activities of an enterprise and help achieve a better utilization of resources. These models are useful for a wide range of activities, from a seemingly trivial task of scheduling a field office tour for a high-ranking official to a very complex job of scheduling activities in the space program. While a wide variety of such scheduling models are in use, we shall mention only three: Gantt chart, Critical Path Method (CPM), and Program Evaluation Review Technique (PERT).

In 1917, Henry L. Gantt developed the bar chart. Essentially, the bar chart describes progress by comparing work done against planned objectives. Figure 7-1 shows the application of the basic Gantt charting technique to a generalized project.

The Gantt chart might be redesigned as a CPM chart. This would have several advantages. First, because bars are replaced by a network

Figure 7-1
Gantt Bar Chart

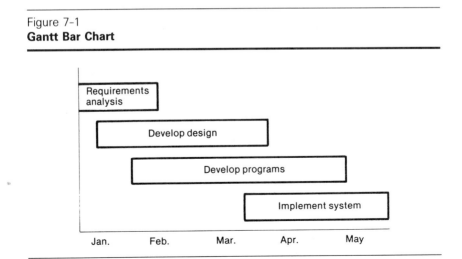

of flow plan, the network shows how the events and activities are related. In CPM and PERT charts, events (e.g., "start testing") are often shown as circles. Activities are the time-consuming elements of the program and are used to connect the various events; they are shown as arrows. Thus, the CPM chart reflects all significant program accomplishments and better approximates the complexity of the program.

Since most events depend on one or more prior events, the charts show the interrelationship of events leading to the accomplishment of the ultimate objective. Within the project is a *critical path*, that is, the longest possible time span along the system flow plan. To determine the critical path, events are organized in sequence. The starting point for plotting the critical paths is the final event in the total network. From the final event, related events are placed sequentially backwards, until the starting point is reached. Next, all the expected elapsed times (t_e) are summed throughout the network paths to determine the total expected elapsed time for every path of the network. The completion date of the project is dependent on the path that takes the longest time. Because this path has the highest total elapsed time, it is called the critical path. (In Figure 7–2 the critical path is indicated by heavy arrows.)

Knowing the critical path can be very useful to the decision maker. If an activity is on the critical path, any slippage or delay for the activity will delay the completion of the entire project. Conversely, slippage in an activity not on the critical path will not normally affect

Figure 7–2
PERT Network

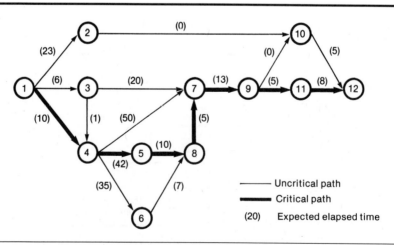

Source: Adapted from U.S. Air Force Systems Command (1963:11–18).

the project deadline since the difference between the lengths of time along the critical path and the noncritical paths is slack.

To determine the elapsed time between events, one must make estimates. When the decision makers have had some experience with the various activities in the project, they can use estimates based on this experience. This approach might be fine for public works projects such as street construction and repair, but when confronted with a nonregular project—for example, the Space Shuttle—estimation would be more difficult. In such cases, decision makers need a more systematic approach to estimation. PERT provides it.

With PERT, the expected elapsed time between events is based on three possible completion assumptions: optimistic completion time *(O)*, most likely completion time *(M)*, and pessimistic completion time *(P)*. Based on these three time estimates, a simple formula can be derived that will give an estimation of how long the activity will take. Assuming $O = 6$ weeks, $M = 8$ weeks, and $P = 16$ weeks, the expected elapsed time can be computed using the formula:

$$\frac{O + 4M + P}{6} = t_e = \frac{6 + 32 + 16}{6} = 9$$

The estimation is then used in the flow diagram.

While PERT has obvious strengths—it forces careful planning, permits experimentation, encourages participation in the planning process, permits effective control, and so on—it is not without its limitations. Recent evidence points to decreased use by NASA and its contractors. Many capable administrators insist that one cannot wait for a problem to make itself known through such schedule control techniques: Anticipating trouble requires closer observation.

Sapololsky (1972: chapter 4) suggests that PERT might have a political rather than management function. In his account of the development of the Polaris submarine (where PERT and a dozen other management techniques originated), he writes:

> Whenever there was a question on Polaris's development status or the like, program officials always had a colored chart, a slide, or a computer printout which would demonstrate the effectiveness of the management team. Actually, this strategy might well be labeled the "Slight of Hand Strategy" since few of these management techniques were ever used to manage the Polaris development. The use of PERT in the program, for example, was strongly opposed by those technical officers who were in charge of the development effort and there never was a complete application of the technique in the program, but the illusion of PERT's use was carefully cultivated. During most critical stages of the Polaris development when PERT's role was minimal, the program held hundreds of briefings and prepared thousands of booklets describing how PERT was guiding the missile's progress. The message was that no one need be concerned about the quality of the

Saturn Program Control with a control chart in background. Do you think it is for "evaluation and review" or for show? (National Aeronautics and Space Administration)

program's development decisions as the program itself was the pioneer in perfecting management systems for complex projects. And since enough people who could influence policy believed this to be the case, the program was able to gain the independence and flexibility it needed to deal effectively with the missile's technological uncertainties.

Expediters, Incentives, and Participation

Another way is to use an "expediter." At the rational level of government, it appears that OMB's Program Coordination Division—composed of a program implementation branch and a field coordination branch—fills this role. The Ash Council, which recommended the establishment of OMB, viewed the division as means by which the "president could demonstrate that things can work, that there is an expediter who can jump into the breach, representing the president's office and get something done."

But, in the final analysis, administrators must be their own expediters, which is a way of saying that they must *follow-up* (see box.)

Governments have, of course, a wide range of mechanisms for encouraging proper behavior among those involved in a program. (Proper behavior simply means behavior that leads to attainment of the program's objectives.) These mechanisms range from political techniques such as persuading (discussed in the second chapter) to former mechanisms such as those shown in Table 7-1. As indicated, the formal mechanisms are not without drawbacks when applied to an area of policy such as pollution control.

In addition to fully recognizing these drawbacks summarized in Table 7-1, the administrator should strive to build *incentives* into the

Table 7-1
Alternative Governmental Mechanisms for Pollution Control

Mechanism	Example	Difficulties
1. Prohibition	Full treatment of effluents and sewage required of all businesses and municipalities.	An optimal solution to pollution does not require full treatment, only "right amount," since the natural biological processes in lakes and streams give them a certain capability of cleansing themselves.
2. Directive	Government determines the *extent* to which municipalities bordering Lake Erie treat sewage.	It is very difficult to determine just what percentage of organic matter and phosphorous to remove. And even if a standard could be set, it must be translated into directives for each of the entities that emit pollutants.
3. Taxes and subsidies	Tax polluters give subsidies to businesses that hire hard-core unemployed.	Immense information requirements are necessary for the implementation of these schemes. Government must know the effect of pollution and unemployment so that a tax or subsidy could result in just the right amount of waste discharge or hiring.
4. Regulation	Require that all new cars be equipped with devices designed to reduce the level of pollutants in the exhaust.	Regulation, to be effective, must be accompanied by the practice of periodically inspecting all cars. Expensive. Inflexible.
5. Payment	Federal subsidy for capital costs of improving regional sewage facilities.	Crude: Does not easily provide proper coordination for all the relevant units in the system. Limited to problems where capital costs—rather than, say, operating expenses—are the block to improvement of the situation.
6. Action	Where the fish population of a lake is endangered by overfishing, the government continually stocks the lake.	Limited applicability.

Source: Adapted from Otto A. Davis and Morton I. Kamien (1969:67–86).

program. Perhaps the most notorious examples of ignoring the incentive question are to be found in social benefit programs. As a 1973 Joint Economic Committee report (cited in *New York Times*, July 8, 1973) put it, the combined benefits to recipients of New York City's welfare, medicaid, and eight other programs "can make it extraordinarily unprofitable to work."

But the problem of incentives applies to the administrator as well as the recipient. The Small Business Administration is a case in point. Writes former federal Budget Director Charles L. Schultze (1969:208, 213) "Measures have not been developed which can be used to judge the performance of various regional loan offices in terms of overall program objectives. Defaulted loans, on the other hand, are easily identified, and a significant default rate is sure to invite congressional questions. Loan officials, therefore, tend to avoid risky loans. As a consequence, far from meeting their original objectives, the programs end up, in many cases, simply in making loans of commercial quality at less than commercial rates." Schultze also points to how federal reimbursement formulas contribute to hospital inefficiency: "Essentially each hospital is reimbursed by the federal government for the 'reasonable costs' of delivering services to patients under medicare and medicaid programs. Payment is matched to the individual costs of each hospital. There are virtually no incentives for efficiency. Any savings from more efficient operations result in lower federal payments; any increased costs are fully passed on. To the extent that larger staffs bring prestige and promotion, there are positive incentives for inefficiency."

Yet another way of improving implementation, *participative decision making*, we turn neither to Washington nor Oakland but to Japan. When faced with policy decision, the top management in a Japanese organization refers it to a committee of "appropriate people." The decision-making process now becomes, to an American at least, excruciatingly slow, but finally a consensus is reached. What makes the resulting policy a good one is that the people who must participate in the implementation phase have participated in the policymaking phase; they are already presold. Moreover, this process "makes it clear where in the organization a certain answer to a question will be welcomed and when it will be resisted. Therefore, there is plenty of time to work on persuading the dissenters, or making small concessions to them which will win them over without destroying the integrity of the decision" (Drucker, 1973:470).

Communication

"If the oldest complaint is nobody asked us," Churchill once observed, "the next oldest is nobody ever told us." Churchill, who knew a thing or two about implementation, is suggesting that we carefully consider communication.

The sheer mass of communication that occurs during the implementation of a program is overwhelming. In an attempt to determine the time spent in communicating, one investigator (cited in Koontz & O'Donnell, 1974:336) reported that 232 technical employees of a research organization spent 61 percent of their eight-hour workday in this activity, 5 percent in speaking and listening, 16 percent in writing, and 10 percent in reading.

In the public sector, this problem is compounded by the fact that the public is often closely involved in program implementation. But, as the final example shows, the problem is not insoluable. Massachusetts' controversial bottle bill became law on January 17, 1983, amid turmoil created by uncertainty as to whether the law would be implemented on that date. State agencies were deluged with calls about the law. As a result, a statewide toll-free telephone hot line was installed.

The hot line quickly became not only an educational tool but also the critical link between the public and state officials, and the statewide focal point for questions and complaints about the law (*PA Times*, March 1, 1984).

Written and oral messages have their advantages and disadvantages. Written messages, for example, can be retained as permanent references to work from and guide action during implementation. Additionally, they have the advantage of providing a legal record, although, over time, the retention of voluminous written communications can be very expensive. As a general rule, memos should be used as seldom as possible and then only to remind, clarify, or confirm.

Of paramount importance in the use of the written message are clarity and simplicity. To ensure that messages leaving his headquarters met this dual standard. Napoleon, it is said, kept on his staff an exceptionally ungifted captain. The officer's responsibility was to read all outgoing messages; if he was able to understand them, then presumably no officer in the Grande Armée would have any difficulty. While it is unlikely that any agency head today could get such a position authorized, one can at least try to keep the reader in mind when drafting a memorandum.

But even then, the reader may still be uncertain as to the writer's fine meaning. Tone and nuance are not easily put into words. Accordingly, in certain instances, oral communication is preferable.

The biggest advantage of oral over written communication, at least during implementation, is that it is two-way. When the speaker's message creates ambiguity, the listener can ask follow-up questions (such as: "As I understand it, you mean so and so?"). At the same time the supervisor has the opportunity to *receive* as well as impart information.

One final point, closely related to oral communication: The importance of on-site inspections by top management during implementa-

The Gentle Art of Follow-Up

Carl Officer (second from right), the mayor of East St. Louis, Illinois, does not spend Monday through Friday in his office jotting memos and greeting visitors. Rather, he plays troubleshooter—inspecting buildings, seeing that fire crews are at their stations on time, and jumping into city police cars unannounced to ride along on the graveyard shift. (City of East St. Louis, Illinois)

Writing a sharp note in the margin of a memo will hardly ensure that something will or will not be done. Administrators must constantly check to see if their orders are being carried out.

Follow-up is hard but necessary work. As an aide to Franklin Roosevelt wrote (quoted in Edward, 1980:155):

Half of a president's suggestions, which theoretically carry the weight of orders, can be safely forgotten by a cabinet member. And if the president asks about a suggestion a second time, he can be told that it is being investigated. If he asks a third time a wise cabinet officer will give him at least part of what he suggests. But only occasionally, except about the most important matters, do presidents ever get around to asking three times.

If follow-up is necessary for the chief executive, surrounded by a huge and competent staff, then it must be even more critical at less exalted levels of administration.

Grove's Principle of Didactic Management

The following excerpt from *High Output Management* (1983) by Andrew S. Grove, president of Intel Corporation, one of the premier high-technology companies, addresses an issue often ignored in discussions of communications.

> What is the role of the supervisor in a one-on-one? He should facilitate the subordinate's expression of what's going on and what's bothering him. The supervisor is there to learn and to coach. Peter Drucker sums up the supervisor's job here very nicely: "The good time users among managers do not talk to their subordinates about their problems but they know how to make the subordinates talk about theirs."
>
> How is this done? By applying Grove's Principle of Didactic Management, *"Ask one more question!"* When the supervisor thinks the subordinate has said all he wants to about a subject, he should ask another question. he should try to keep the flow of thoughts coming by prompting the subordinate with queries until *both* feel satisfied that they have gotten to the bottom of a problem.

Source: Grove (1983:75–76).

tion of a program is hard to overemphasize. If we suffer from armchair generals, then surely we can suffer too from armchair administrators. (Recall the example of Mayor Officer on p. 254.) People in top positions tend to forget Gray's Law of Bilateral Asymmetry in Networks: "Information flows efficiently through organizations, except that bad news encounters high impedance in flowing upward" (quoted in Dickinson, 1978:74).

During face-to-face encounters, the listener must resist the tendency to evaluate communication prematurely. According to Rogers and Roethlisberger (1952), those who would communicate should be listened to in noncommittal, unprejudiced fashion and thus be encouraged to state their full position before response is generated. Halberstam (1969:305–6) reports that this dictum was repeatedly ignored during the American involvement in Vietnam. For example, during his on-site visit, McNamara tended to look for the war

> to fit his criteria, his definitions. He went to Danang in 1965 to check on the marine progress there. A marine colonel in I Corps had a sand table showing the terrain and patiently gave the briefing: friendly situation, enemy situation, main problem. McNamara watched it, not really taking it in, his hands folded, frowning a little, finally interrupting. "Now, let me see," McNamara said, "if I have it right, this is your situation," and then he spouted his own version, all in numbers and statistics. The colonel, who was very bright, read him immediately like a man breaking a code, and without changing stride, went on with the briefing, simply switching his terms, quantifying everything, giving everything in numbers and percent-

ages, percentages up, percentages down, so blatant a performance that it was like a satire. Jack Raymond of the *New York Times* began to laugh and had to leave the tent. Later that day Raymond went up to McNamara and commented on how tough the situation was in Danang, but McNamara wasn't interested in the Vietcong, he wanted to talk about the colonel, he liked him, that colonel had caught his eye. "That colonel is one of the finest officers I've met," he said.

Management by Objectives

A final way by which the implementation might be made more effective is with the use of a highly touted management system called management by objectives (MBO). According to McConkey (1975), MBO has four features that make it especially well suited for contributing to program implementation. First, those accountable for directing the organization determine what they want to achieve during a particular period; that is, they establish overall objectives and priorities. Second, all key management people are encouraged to contribute their maximum efforts to attaining these overall objectives. Third, the planned achievement of all key management people is coordinated to promote greater total results for the organization as a whole. Fourth, a control mechanism is established to monitor progress compared to objectives and feed the results back to higher levels.

The system has been applied successfully in a variety of organizations. Among the nonprofit-type organizations are hospitals, schools, police departments, nursing homes, defense departments, municipal governments, and federal agencies. Instrumental in bringing the system to 21 departments and agencies of the federal government in April 1973 was OMB Director Roy Ash. Now, as supervisors of the system, the OMB bosses have an excuse to drop in regularly on cabinet secretaries and other agencies to find out how well the work is being done.

Stripped of its business school jargon, the system works as follows (Brady 1973):

1. The annual MBO cycle begins when the department formulates its budget. Program managers are urged to accompany each request for funds with a list of measurable, specific, results-oriented objectives. Secretaries (or city managers) then compare these initial proposals with what they want the department to accomplish during the coming year. During this stage, they work closely with the agency heads.

   Here is a typical dialogue between former HEW Secretary, Elliot L. Richardson and an agency head as they formulated an objective (quoted in Brady, 1973).

   Agency head: One of our agency's most important initiatives this year will be to focus our efforts in the area of alcoholism and to treat an additional 10,000 alcoholics. Given last year's funding of 41 alcoholic treatment centers and the direction of other resources at the state and local level, we feel that this is an achievable objective.

Secretary: Are these 41 centers operating independently or are they linked to other service organizations in their communities? In other words are we treating the whole problem of alcoholism, including its employment, mental health, and welfare aspects, or are we just treating the symptoms of alcoholism?

Agency head: A program requirement for getting funds is that the services involved must be linked in an integrated fashion with these other resources.

Secretary: I am not interested in just looking at the number of alcoholics that are treated. Our goal ought to be the actual rehabilitation of these patients. Do you have data to enable you to restate the objective in terms of that goal?

Agency head: As a matter of fact, Mr. Secretary, we have developed a management information and evaluation system in which each grantee will be providing quarterly data on the number of alcoholics treated, as well as on the number of alcoholics who are actually rehabilitated.

Secretary: How do you define *rehabilitated?*

Agency head: If they are gainfully employed one year after treatment, we regard them as being rehabilitated.

Secretary: Please revise this objective, then, to enable us to track progress on how effective these programs really are in treating the disease of alcoholism and in rehabilitating alcoholics.

2. The staff of the secretary draws up the department's budget and forwards it to the president for action.

3. The secretary then prepares for his agency heads and regional managers a list of the priorities determined during the budget preparation. In light of these priorities, the executives review and alter as necessary their preliminary objectives. Typically, they will select 8 to 10 objectives that represent the most important results expected of their programs. Just prior to the start of the fiscal year, they submit these objectives—along with milestones that must be reached (e.g., expand OEO projects to increase capacity by 25,000 patients by September) and resources that must be expended for their accomplishment—to the secretary.

4. The office of the secretary and his staff workers in each agency monitor progress in meeting the objectives. The success of the entire MBO system depends largely on the bimonthly management conferences attended by principal staff aids. Here managers seek advice or assistance in meeting their objectives. Prior to the conference, managers must submit an evaluation of the status of each objective.

Gobbledygook, or Why Use One Word if 10 Suffice?

There is an old army axiom that should be carved on the desk of every public administrator: An order that can be misunderstood will be misunderstood. A desperate measure, defacing government policy, but how else can the administrator be forced to write in a clear straightforward manner?

Rather than struggle with that question, let us turn to a more answerable one: Why do administrators engage in gobbledygook?

One reason, I think, is to avoid unpleasantness. We do not fire incompetent employees; we "select them out" or "nonretain them." (Note too the use of the collective pronoun we.) Nor do we ever, ever cut the budget; we make "advance downward adjustments." Unions do not strike; they engage in a "job action." Prisons are "correctional facilities."

The military, despite all its axioms, is a goldmine of euphemisms. An aggressive first strike becomes "preemptive counterattack"; retreat, "tactical redeployment"; bombing, "limited duration protective reaction strike"; riot control, "confrontation management."

Meanwhile, in the more pacific corridors of our civilian bureaucracies, the ability to read between the lines is as vital for survival as a combat emplacement evacuator (i.e., shovel) is for a soldier. Here is a primer (from the *Empire State Dispatch,* reprinted in the *Wharton Magazine*):

It's in the process: We forgot about it until now.

We'll look into it: Meanwhile you may forget it, too.

Take this up at our next meeting: That will give you time to forget.

Project: A word that makes a minor job seem major.

Under consideration: Never heard about it until now.

Under active consideration: We're trying to locate the correspondence.

We're making a survey: We need more time to think up an answer.

Let's get together on this: You're probably as mixed up as I am.

Note and initial: Let's spread the responsibility.

Forwarded for your consideration: You hold the bag for a while.

Another reason for gobbledygook is the desire to dress up petty thoughts and make them sound impressive. Since the 1960s, the most popular way of doing this is to use computer jargon. It is really quite easy to do: "Based on integral subsystem considerations, a large portion of the interface coordination communication effects a significant implementation of the preliminary qualification limit."

The preceding four steps centered on the relationship between a secretary and agency heads. With only minor modifications, the system could, and should, be spread throughout the hierarchy. In other words, for MBO to work properly, managers at all levels should have objectives and milestones.

MBO delivers many benefits to the managers: a greater voice in determining his or her job, agreement on what is expected and appraisal based on results (not busyness or personality), better management of time by focusing on the priorities, and fewer surprises through continual monitoring (McConkey, 1975:chapter 9).

But the road to developing an effective MBO system is not without pitfalls. Given the increasing popularity of MBO, some organizations might be tempted to adopt the system without really understanding it. Or, organizations can overlook the fact that MBO takes time (three-to-five years) before it can reach an effective level of operation. As should have been apparent from the dialogue between Richardson and the agency head, setting good, measurable objectives is no easy task. Finally, MBO can be dealt a lethal blow by omitting periodic reviews (such as the previously mentioned management conference) or failing to reward managers who achieve high performance levels.

In summing up the first half of this chapter, I am reminded of a cartoon that appeared in *The Wall Street Journal* a few years ago. A baby bird, ready to dive from the edge of the nest, asks its mother, "Any instructions, or shall I just wing it?" What marvelous commentary on the typical approach to teaching implementation in many management courses. Of course, most public administrators know that winging it sometimes is unavoidable, that they have to learn from their own mistakes. But at the same time, the implementation process can be made a little smoother by paying attention to the concepts and techniques outlined above.

Implementation is closely connected to evaluation, the subject to which we now turn. Indeed, I can think of no two subjects in the field of public administration more closely related. Until a program has been properly implemented, administrators cannot reasonably evaluate it. Unless we have information on implementation, we do not know how to interpret results of evaluation studies. A program may have failed because the original design was poor *or* because the design was never implemented. Therefore, information on implementation is critical for making sense of evaluative studies (see Edwards, 1980:8–9).

B. Evaluation

Why Evaluation?

Program evaluation is the systematic examination of a program to provide information on the full range of its short- and long-term effects on citizens. Put simply, it asks: Is this program delivering?

The answer to that question should be of considerable interest to the administrator. Writes Carol H. Weiss (1972:16–17):

> Evaluation can be asked to investigate the extent of program success so that decisions such as these can be made: (1) to continue or discontinue the program; (2) to improve its practices and procedures; (3) to add or drop specific program strategies and techniques; (4) to institute similar programs

elsewhere; (5) to allocate resources among competing programs; and (6) to accept or reject a program approach.

Evaluation thus forces decision makers to take a closer look at their programs. While this seems only fitting and proper, it is not a popular notion; the practice of evaluation remains very much the neglected stepchild of program administration.

> The political appointees find they can score more points with the public by proposing new ways to do things rather than finding what went wrong in the past. Bureaucrats have a vested interest in protecting their empires and will not welcome meddlesome reviews by outsiders. Interest groups only reinforce these bureaucratic tendencies. The only one who really cares is the taxpayer, but until the problem is forcefully brought to his attention, he is blissfully ignorant of program performance. Even if the taxpayer were better informed, he is not organized to do anything about it. (Malek, 1978:212–13)

Barry Bozeman and Jane Massey (1982) of Syracuse University report widespread disappointment with the results of policy evaluation. Given the fact that the federal government alone spends around $2 billion a year on "social research and development" and that the resource base for the public sector is declining, attention should be given to the sources of dissatisfaction. Bozeman and Massey summarize some of the more commonly cited problems: political naivete (what is economically rational may not be politically rational); methodological difficulties; differences in evaluators', clients', and managers' needs; pretentious scientism (i.e., claiming more precision and control than has been achieved); inadequacy of data bases and cost of data; separation of evaluation and implementation; and ignoring qualitative factors. In sum, "policy evaluation is sometimes a good investment, but it is rarely a safe one." That is why both administrators and evaluators need to keep this list of problems in mind.

Decision making, as we noted in Chapters 5 and 6, pervades the policy-planning process. Similarly, evaluation affects all stages in that process. For this reason, the feedback loop in Figure 5–2 connects with the policy-planning process at several points.

This section builds on these ideas. Here we consider the effect of evaluation on decision makers at two levels: *(a)* policymakers, concerned with legislative changes and budget levels; and *(b)* program managers, concerned more with implementation.

Evaluation for Policymakers

Three major types of evaluation are of interest to policymakers: national program impact evaluation, demonstration projects, and field experiments.

National Program Impact Evaluation. Programs for disadvantaged preschool children that attempt to overcome the handicaps of poverty began about 20 years ago. Head Start, the largest of them, began in 1965.

Some early reports on the programs—particularly an evaluation of Head Start, done in 1969 by the Westinghouse Learning Corporation and Ohio State University—concluded that the preschool intervention did little to improve the academic performance of disadvantaged children. But such early evaluations could follow the progress of the children for only a few years.

By the early 1980s, it was possible to ascertain how children who were in the programs in the 1960s were doing as teenagers and young adults. Two longitudinal studies (i.e., measured over a certain period of time) found that the preschool programs were beneficial.

One report is *Young Children Grow Up* by Lawrence J. Schweinhart and David P. Weikart. The project started in 1962 among preschool children at an elementary school in Ypsilanti, Michigan. The 123 children included in the study were black and from low-income families. Over a period of four years, 58 of the children attended (for either one or two years) a preschool program that emphasized active learning, problem solving, motivation, and communication. The remaining 65 children received no special attention.

Tracing these children in recent years, Schweinhart and Weikart found several differences between the two groups. By age 15 the children who had attended the preschool program scored 8 percent higher than the children of the control group on tests of reading, mathematics, and language. The preschool students required and received fewer years of special education as they progressed through school. Preliminary data indicate they were completing high school at a higher rate and are showing more interest in attending college. They also have better employment records and lower rates of arrest than the members of the control group.

A 1979 cost-benefit analysis (see Chapter 6) done by Schweinhart and Weikart found that two years of preschool education for one child cost $5,984, whereas the benefits have a value of $14,819. These benefits include the reduced need for special education, an increase in the projected earnings of the students, and the value of the mother's time as a wage earner when the child attended the preschool program.

The second report, *Head Start: A Successful Experiment*, is by Bernard Brown and Edith H. Grotberg of the U.S. Department of Health and Human Services. They found that Head Start, which enrolled some 430,000 children in 1979, provided not only education but also assistance in health and nutrition. Parents were encouraged to participate, and social services were made available to the family. Brown and Grotberg summarize the conclusions of more than 700 studies of Head Start published between 1969 and 1977: "Head Start has brought about a quiet revolution in children's institutions. . . . Early childhood programs are now accepted and functioning. The acceptance can be seen

One major type of evaluation of interest to policymakers is national program impact evaluation. Two major reports issued in the early 1980s measured the long-term impact of preschool training and concluded that such preparation *does* provide a head start. Thanks in part to such analysis, Head Start escaped the deep cuts the Reagan administration made in the fiscal year 1982 budget. (*Wisconsin State Journal*)

not only in support for Head Start but also in the phenomenal rise in nursery schools, preschool programs in the public schools, and quality day care for middle-class children. It is evidenced in the large numbers of books, records, toys, and television programs for preschool children."

In 1981, the most thorough study of private schools ever sponsored by the federal government was completed by James S. Coleman, a University of Chicago sociologist. Using data collected by the National Opinion Research Center, Coleman looked at 58,728 students in 1,016 public and private high schools. Controlling for family backgrounds, he concluded that private-school students perform better academically than those in public schools.

Demonstration Projects. The philosophy of the demonstration project is quite simple: Before we launch a program nationwide, let us try it in a few selected cities or regions.

A good, straightforward example of evaluation by a demonstration project is the Police Fleet Plan. According to this plan, police are allowed to take their police cars home with them for their private use in off-duty hours—thus putting a lot more police cars on the city streets. A city that had some interest in the possibility of adopting the Police Fleet Plan might try it first in a few precincts before adopting it citywide. (The evaluation results were quite positive in the Urban Institute's study of the Indianapolis Police Fleet Plan: auto thefts went down, auto accidents went down, outdoor crime, purse snatching, and robbery went down.)

Field Experiment. One of the best ways to evaluate is to use a randomized, controlled field trial. This means, first, that individuals or groups are selected to be included in the new program entirely by chance and, second, that the program is observed under actual operating conditions ("in the field"). Finally, the results obtained from the participating individuals or groups are compared with results from a similar randomly selected *control group.*

Unlike program impact evaluations, which tend to be retrospective, the demonstration project and field trial may be introduced into public programs either before a major operating program is started or simultaneously with a major operating program. But the principal difference between the field trial and the demonstration project is that in the field trial those responsible for the evaluation exercise have control over input variables (e.g., purpose, staffing, clients, length of service, location, size of program, auspices, and management) and carefully measure outputs to determine the extent to which the project reaches its objectives. In short, the conditions are a little closer to those of the laboratory. An outstanding example of a field experiment is the Office of Economic Opportunity's negative income tax experiment (see Case 7.2).

Evaluation for Program Managers

Evaluative research is also useful to program managers at federal, state, or local levels who have responsibility for operating programs. According to Wholey (1972:365), "The primary evaluation payoff (in terms of decisions actually influenced) may be in evaluation that is done in enough detail to get at the effects of operational changes within operating programs. Many program managers really want to know what works best under what conditions." Wholey (1972:365–66) cites two examples of evaluation systems designed to help program managers.

> In 1971 the District of Columbia Sanitation Department, in conjunction with the Urban Institute, developed a monitoring system for solid waste collection activities. Inspectors, armed with reference photographs and a tape recorder, drove along city streets and alleys rating the cleanliness of the block (by comparison with reference photograph). Writes Wholey: "This system . . . produces data on the *outputs* of services not simply inputs or estimates of outputs. One can imagine this system being used to assess the results of operational changes in sanitation department activities or to justify budget requests." In sum, the system helps the managers determine if particular additional inputs (e.g., increased services) do in fact produce differences in outputs (e.g., moving a neighborhood's streets and alleys from an average rating of four to a rating of two).
>
> Public school personnel are rarely provided with data relevant to decision making. The Urban Institute, therefore, attempted to

develop a system for estimating the relative effectiveness of different public schools in Atlanta. In this project, schools were classified by the economic level of the students and by the amount of pupil turnover. The institute tested the notion that information on the relative effectiveness of schools running comparable student populations could be useful to the superintendent and staff.

How to Evaluate

In the preceding section, we noted several types of evaluation. To set down a general procedure for carrying out each type is not easy. Perhaps the best approach to such a formulation is to say that evaluation research follows, ideally, a procedure reminiscent of the classical research experiment: (1) find out the goals of the program; (2) translate the goals into measurable indicators of goal achievement; (3) collect data on the indicators for those who have been exposed to the program and for those who have not (i.e., the control group); (4) compare the data on program participants and controls in terms of goal criteria; and, if necessary, (4) terminate or modify the program.

Find Goals

There are three points to keep in mind about goals. First, programs are likely to have multiple goals: To evaluate only one is to evaluate partially. A program to reduce air pollution, for example, might be concerned with the reduction of several types of air pollution at several sources. For purposes of evaluation, the sweeping goal of "reduce air pollution" might be broken into components, represented by this matrix (adapted from Cook & Scioli, 1972):

	B_1	B_2	B_3	B_4	B_5
A_1					
A_2					
A_3					
A_4					
A_5					

where the As represent pollution types (*viz.*, carbon monoxide, sulfur oxides, hydrocarbons, nitrogen oxides, and particles) and the Bs, pollution sources (*viz.*, automobiles, industry, electric power plants, space heating, and refuse disposal). Thus, rather than consider air pollution in terms of one composite figure, the evaluator considers it in terms of several separate measures.

Second, many areas of public policy lack standards (or benchmarks) by which a goal can be established. The Schlitz Brewing Company may have as its goal for next year to increase sales more than Coors increases its sales. But how does the public decision maker know the proper goals for reduction of poverty and illiteracy in the year ahead?

Third, programs do not only move toward official goals. They accomplish other things, sometimes in addition to and sometimes instead of, as Weiss puts it (1972a:25). For example, programs that may increase the supply of workers in a particular occupation (intended consequence) may result in the exertion of downward pressures on the wages of existing workers in the occupation (unintended consequence). A good evaluator tries to look at all possible effects of program activity.

Translate Goals into Measurable Indicators

Program goals tend to be ambiguous, hazy. Consider this one for an urban transportation program: "To provide access to community services, facilities, and employment in a safe, quick, comfortable, and convenient manner for all segments of the community without causing harmful side effects." How would you translate these goals into measurable indicators of achievement?

Winnie and Hatry (in Hatry et al., 1973:27) suggest the following criteria:

For accessibility and convenience: (1) percentage of residents not within *x* distance of public transit service and more than one hour from key destinations; and (2) citizen perception of travel convenience.

For travel time: (3) time required to travel between key origin and destination points; and (4) congestion—duration and severity of delay.

For comfort: (5) road surface quality ("bumpiness") index; and (6) citizen perception of travel comfort.

For safety: (7) rate of transportation-related deaths, injuries, and incidents or property damage; and (8) number of transportation crime incidents.

For minimum cost to users: (9) costs per trip.

For maintenance of environmental quality: (10) noise level along transportation corridors and number of persons at risk; and (11) air pollution attributable to transportation sources and number of persons at risk.

For general public satisfaction: (12) citizen perception of adequacy of transportation services.

For monetary costs: (13) program costs.

Some experts distinguish different classes of program effects. *Output* is the service rendered—for example, number of children finishing a Head Start program. *Outcome* is the effect in more subtle terms—for example, reading levels and study habits. Finally, *impacts* are the long-term effects on society—for example, a literate population.

For another interesting example of how to measure impacts we might turn to the work in the area of *social indicators*. In a seminal work on this subject, Professor Raymond A. Bauer (1966:1) described social indicators operationally as "statistics, statistical series, and all other forms of evidence that enable us to assess where we stand and are going with respect to our values and goals."

The social indicator movement has developed concurrently with evaluation research. And, given the dearth of respectable evaluation studies, some have argued for social indicators as a substitute for experimental evaluations. In my opinion, this substitution would be unfortunate because social indicators cannot tell why a program succeeds or fails. Yet the *why* is often as important as the *how well*.

Suppose we wanted to measure the quality of life in 18 cities. The most desirable rating is numbered 1 and the least favorable is 18. The social indications are described as follows:

Unemployment: in percentage of labor force out of work.

Poverty: in percentage of households with cash incomes under $3,000 a year.

Income: in terms of money income per person, adjusted for cost-of-living differences.

Housing: in costs for a moderate-income family of four, using 75 percent renters, 75 percent homeowners.

Health: based on deaths of infants under one year of age per 1,000 live births.

Mental health: in terms of the rate of reported suicides per 100,000 population.

Public order: in terms of rate of reported robberies per 100,000 population.

Racial equality: comparing white and nonwhite unemployment rates.

Community concern: measured by individual contributions to United Fund charitable appeals.

Citizen participation: in terms of percentage of voting-age population that cast votes in presidential elections.

Educational attainment: measured by median school years completed by persons 25 years old or older.

Transportation: in terms of costs for a moderate-income family of four.

Air quality: measuring concentration of suspended particulates.

Social disintegration: in terms of estimated narcotics addiction rates per 10,000 population.

Collect Data

Data for evaluation research can come from a variety of sources and research techniques. To name but a few: interviews, questionnaires, observation, ratings, institutional records, government statistics, diary records, physical evidence, clinical examinations, financial records, and documents (e.g., minutes of broad meetings, newspaper accounts of policy actions, and transcripts of trials.)

Data must be collected not only for those who participated in the program but also for those who did not; the latter is termed the *control group*. Figure 7–3 shows the measurable effect (vocabulary scores) of a program (course work in Latin) on the control group in comparison to the program participants.

Figure 7-3

Quasi-Experimental Analysis for the Effect of Specific Course Work, Including Control Series Design

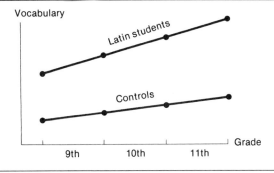

Source: Adapted from Donald T. Campbell in Weiss (1972b:206).

Compare Data

The classic design for evaluation is the experimental model that uses experimental and control groups. Out of the target population, units (e.g., people, precincts, or cities) are randomly chosen to be in either the group that gets the program or the control group. Measures are taken of the relevant criterion variable (e.g., vocabulary scores) before the program starts and after it ends. Differences are computed, and the program is deemed a success if the experimental group has improved more than the control (Weiss 1972b:60–61). Or, in terms of the model below, the program is a success if $(b - a)$ is greater than $(d - c)$.

	Before	**After**
Experimental	a	b
Control	c	d

The model is deceptively simple. How can the evaluator always ensure that nothing else caused the change but the program? For example, a few years ago, Washington, D.C., reported a drop in the crime rate. But to attribute this solely to the effects of one program would be exceedingly difficult. Writes Hatry (et al. 1973:66–67): "During the period, several major program actions occurred, including: major increases in the number of policemen, buildup of a large drug addict treatment program, and the extensive new street lighting in some portions of the city. In addition, some believe that various social conditions had changed in the city. . . . Some of these effects could be partially isolated, e.g., street-lighting effects presumably would occur in some areas and not others, but others would be extremely difficult, if not impossible, to extract."

The model simplifies in yet another way. Since experiments are only for a limited period of time, they may fail to allow for the clinical fluctuation of time series data (see Figure 7–4).

Regardless of the specific approach taken to evaluation, two final points need to be kept in mind; the first point applies mainly to the evaluator, the second applies more to the administrator to whom, presumably, the findings of evaluation studies go.

1. Evaluation, to be useful must be viewed as a tool of management. Ideally, evaluators and the administrator cooperate. When the policy decisions about program design are to be made, the evaluator should ask the manager to specify the objectives of the program. The evaluator also determines the administrator's set of assumptions about what is believed to happen when money is spent and the intervention is made—tests cannot be designed for people who are unable to state their assumptions. Finally, the evaluator determines what kind of data would cause the administrator to act (i.e., make adjustments in the management of the program) and the kinds of action the administrator has the authority and willingness to implement (see Horst et al., 1974:300–8).

2. Evaluation should not be a "go or no-go" proposition, with one test determining whether a major social program is to be launched; rather, evaluation should be built into the new program, its strengths and weaknesses being examined while it goes forward. Since most programs that work well usually produce only relatively small gains in their early stages, the "go or no-go" approach might force the admin-

Figure 7–4
Connecticut Traffic Fatalities

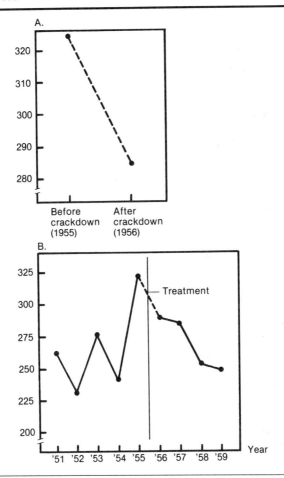

A.

320	● (Before crackdown 1955)
310	
300	
290	
280	● (After crackdown 1956)

Before
crackdown
(1955)

After
crackdown
(1956)

B.

Treatment

Year
'51 '52 '53 '54 '55 '56 '57 '58 '59

Source: Donald T. Campbell in Weiss (1973a:194–95).

istrator into a box where nothing is tried until we know it will work. Most social progress comes not in large leaps but in small changes continued through time. These small changes, eventually, can lead to large ones. To state that society's root problems are to be solved, especially in a massively successful way and in a short period of time, is just not a realistic objective for evaluation (Mosteller, Light, & Gilbert, cited in Olten, 1975).

The Ordeal of Termination

The major deficiency in most discussions of evaluation is not hard to pinpoint. Such discussions tend to overlook the question of what to do when the findings are purely negative. After all, the whole justification for evaluative studies is to discover programs that are not working and then either to fix them or to stop them.

But termination of a governmental activity does not follow automatically from a study's conclusion. According to Herbert Kaufman (1976) only 27 organizations in the federal government were terminated in a 50-year period ending in 1973, while the number of organizations increased from 175 to 394. While it is legitimate for an organization to resist premature evaluation, this resistance can lead to abuse of the sort Martin Anderson (1964) describes in *The Federal Bulldozer:* "Some say that it is too early to judge the federal urban renewal program; they say, 'The program is only 15 years old. . . .' This line of argument holds that government programs should not be judged unless they are finished or unless they are proceeding as planned. . . . To postpone evaluation is simply to advocate implicitly the continuance of a program without knowing why."

Of course, not all agencies are terminated as a result of an evaluative study. Sometimes the problem that the agency was established to address is resolved. In the case of the Civil Aeronautics Board (CAB), which died on December 31, 1984 (age: 46), the cause was legislative. The closing of the CAB was mandated in the airline deregulation enacted in 1978. But termination is still an exceptional event in federal government. Attempts to kill the Department of Education and the Small Business Administration turned out to be harder than their would-be pallbearers in the Reagan administration imagined—and unsuccessful.

Assuming one has the courage to actually try to eliminate a program that comes up over and over with failing marks in its evaluations, how does the would-be terminator proceed?

Robert D. Behn (in Levine, 1980) offers several hints. First, do *not* float a trial balloon (i.e., testing public reaction to a proposal by having another person suggest it, thereby avoiding embarrassment to the author if reaction is strongly negative). Such action will give the opposition time to mobilize. Second, enlarge the policy's constituency. To close the Massachusetts public training schools, the Department of Youth Services' commissioner "recruited a number of liberal interest groups that were upset with the treatment of juveniles at the institutions. This new constituency broadened the scope of the conflict." Third, focus attention on the policy's harm to *particular* groups and individuals. Fourth, preclude compromise; this puts the supporters of the policy on the defensive. "A stand-up fight ensues, and the terminator has a chance for a clean knockout."

Fifth, recruit an outsider as terminator. "The most obvious example of an outsider as administrator/terminator is Howard J. Phillips, who in January 1973 became acting director of the U.S. Office of Economic Opportunity (OEO) for the sole purpose of dismantling that agency.

Phillips fired existing personnel and hired a complete staff of other outsiders as fellow administrator/terminators." Conceivably, President Reagan could eventually try a similar approach with the Department of Education. Sixth, accept short-term cost increases, since terminating a policy often costs more in the short run than continuing it. Seventh, buy off the beneficiaries. Attempting to mollify those opposed to termination is one source of the short-term increases in costs. Eighth, advocate not "termination," with all its strong negative connotations, but "adoption," with the connotation of something new and better. "Consequently, the termination of policy A may best be realized through the adoption of policy B, when the selection of B necessitates the elimination of A."

Finally, terminate only what is necessary. "The distinction between a policy and the agency that administers it is important. Is the policy to be terminated because it is too expensive? The policy can be terminated and the agency maintained, or the agency can be terminated and the policy transferred to another department. To concentrate their energies, terminators must understand precisely what is their target."

The Role of Computers in Program Planning, Implementation, and Evaluation

The Information Gap

"The government is run horribly." This jarring criticism came from the chairman of the president's Private Sector Survey on Cost Control (PPSSCC), J. Peter Grace. The details can be found in 47 hefty blue-bound reports that the PPSSCC presented to President Reagan early in 1984. The Grace Commission, as it is more commonly called, claimed that if its 2,500 recommendations were adopted, the federal government could save $424 billion in just three years. Unfortunately, most of the savings involved more than running the government better. As a joint study by the U.S. Congressional Budget Office and General Accounting Office (1984) pointed out, these savings would require significant changes in current laws and policies (e.g., laws setting wages on government-sponsored projects).

But many of the recommendations were in the area of management operations. In particular, Grace was surprised by the way in which government used, and failed to use, computers.

The federal government is the world's single largest user of data processing systems. It operates more than 17,000 computers, maintained by more than a quarter of a million workers. More than 75 percent of the federal white-collar work force is involved in the processing of information. From mailing social security payments to processing tax returns, vast amounts of data must be efficiently and effectively handled. Today, there is absolutely no operation of the

J. Peter Grace, chairman and chief executive officer of W. R. Grace & Co., with the 23,000 pages of cost-cutting recommendations, at a 1984 press conference. (Courtesy W. R. Grace & Co.)

federal government—administrative, scientific, or military—that does not require effective and efficient computer hardware and software.

The government is spending billions of dollars trying to modernize its computers, but its efforts are often hampered by procurement policies and bureaucratic inertia. "Many government offices seem unwilling or unprepared to take advantage of the opportunities provided by the new technology," Jack Brooks, chairman of the House Government Operation Committee, contends (*The Wall Street Journal*, February 13, 1985). As a result:

- The Treasury loses interest on millions of dollars because there is not any integrated system to track the government's idle cash.
- The early-1960s computer that serves the Maritime Administration is so old that additional software cannot be used for fear of causing total system failure.
- The Social Security Administration's plan to eliminate waste by tracking earnings of beneficiaries and eliminating erroneous benefits is three years behind schedule.
- Today, the main information unit of the Immigration and Naturalization Service, which is responsible for tracking aliens, is an 8½-by-11-inch manila file folder.
- The federal government operates 332 different accounting systems and more than 100 payroll systems. This means that government managers confront a growing "information gap" caused by incompatible records.

According to J. Peter Grace, if the federal government reformed its information processing so that it had the right kind of data systematically entered on up-to-date, compatible computers that were running common software applications, this would go a long way toward reducing the federal "information gap," which the PPSSCC survey estimated costs the government $78.6 billion over three years. Even in an organization that spends $83 million an hour—as the federal government does—such a saving would be significant.

The Information Technology Package

To understand the use of computers in program planning, implementation, and evaluation, we should *not* focus exclusively on the technology—that is, the *hardware* (which includes the computer mainframes, storage devices, communication linkages, and user input and output equipment); and the *software* (which refers to programs that actually carry out specific computerized tasks such as billing). The effectiveness of computers in government depends on several interrelated components forming, so to speak, a "package." (I am indebted to John Leslie King [1982] for this metaphor.)

What else might we find in our information technology package? First, there are the organizational and managerial approaches to the development and use of computers. The federal government was not always as backward in the use of computers as the earlier examples might suggest. During the early 1960s, the U.S. government was actually the leader in state-of-the-art computer hardware and software. But through the late 1960s and 1970s, the government fell well behind because it failed to acquire common centralized computer systems, and because the very procedure for buying such systems is complicated and slow.

Another component in the information technology package is the infrastructure. More explicitly, there are certain external requirements for building and operating effective information technology systems within any organization. Private computer manufacturers, vendors, and software houses are obviously important, but so too are computer education, research, and professional organizations (which allow professionals to get together and discuss what is new). The fact that not a single major public administration program offers a strong concentration in computing and data processing cannot help but have an adverse effect on the use of computers in government (King, 1982:33).

Whether the government can solve the problem the Grace Commission decries will depend less on the availability of good, cheap technology than it will on knowledgeable personnel, the fourth component in our package. According to Richard May, the senior enforcement counsel at the EPA, a computer system designed to keep track of thousands of legal cases and enforcement actions gathered dust for its first few years because nobody knew how to use it *(The Wall Street*

(December 16, 1982. Reproduced by permission of Universal Press Syndicate. © 1982 by G. B. Trudeau.)

Journal, February 13, 1985). Until government employees become better acquainted with the computer and more computer personnel are hired, situations like this will remain too common.

And therein lies a challenge to the administrator. As one professional city manager recently put it:

> In the near term, a major challenge facing virtually every local government employer is the need to expand employee computer literacy at all levels of the organization. This specifically includes first-line employees who, ultimately, are in the best position to know how to improve the productivity of their jobs. (Griesemer, 1985:58)

To identify possible applications, however, employees and employer must have some awareness of the nature and capabilities of computers.

The Technology

Not so long ago, the only choice a public administrator had in computers was a huge expensive mainframe computer or a much less powerful minicomputer that was still beyond the financial reach of many smaller cities and government agencies. Today, the distinctions between the two have blurred considerably, as much smaller computers, so-called minis and superminis (minis to which extra components have been added), are challenging the mainframes in word length, speed, and memory capacity. A complete system in the supermini class can cost more than $700,000, but this is still far less than a mainframe ($1.75 million and up). Other minis, of course, are well within the price range of smaller agencies ($100,000 to $350,000 or so).

Even smaller than minicomputers are the personal and portable computers (or microcomputers) now being sold for between $1,000 and $25,000. Although many of these are sold as home computers—suitable for keeping track of the family finances, storing telephone numbers, and even playing video games—it has been estimated that more than half the "home" computers that have been bought in recent years actually end up in the store or office.

Beyond computer hardware, the software is critical. Software is the programming that tells computers exactly what to do. Below are seven ways in which computers can make government operations faster and cheaper.

Accounting.   One of the earliest uses of computers was for such routine but essential tasks as utility billing, accounting, personal records management, vehicle maintenance, parts inventory, and taxation. In recent years, cities have used microcomputers costing as little as $10,000 to monitor the use of water and electric loads, saving over $60,000 a year (Voss & Eikmeier, 1984:61).

Word Processing.   If anyone in an organization spends more than two hours per day at a typewriter, word processing would pay for itself in less than a year. For example, Craig Fuller, an assistant to President Reagan, uses his IBM Displaywriter to send memos to his staff, write briefing materials for the president, relay routine presidential decisions to the cabinet, and compose his own speeches. When President Reagan decides to cancel a cabinet meeting, Fuller sits down at his White House computer terminal, pushes a few buttons, taps his message onto the screen, and electronically sends it across town to cabinet members. To keep abreast of what cabinet members are saying publicly, Fuller programs their names into his computer, and any news service stories in which they are mentioned automatically pop into his "electronic mailbox" (*Houston Chronicle*, February 19, 1984).

Spreadsheet.   This software allows program, financial, budget, accounting, and audit analysts to do a number of things in short periods of time. Spreadsheet programs designed for microcomputers can quickly analyze and display results of changes in a matrix. A budget analyst, for instance, can ask "what if" $2 million is taken away from one program and put somewhere else, and see the effects.

Data Bases.   Like electronic spreadsheeting, data bases will be invaluable to some organizations, marginally useful to some, and useless to others.

For some, the data bases automatically created by the accounting or inventory programs may be all they need; for others, a simple mailing list program will suffice. Because a large segment of public administration deals with lists, names, and numbers, a data base program is probably ideally suited to handle this type of work easily. With such a program, lists can be sorted in nearly any fashion, items can be individually summarized, and analysis can be easily performed. Examples of this type of work include schedule of assessments for water or paving districts, voter registration, public safety records such as fire and ambulance calls, accident reports, lists of invested funds, annual budgets, library records, license plate registrations, and others (Voss & Eikmeier, 1984:60).

But if the management of information and its instant retrieval is important to an organization, or it deals with information that must be intricately cross-referenced, then a data base program is a must. For example, New Haven, Connecticut, uses a supermicrocomputer to produce a detailed profile of any one of the city's 25,000 houses and properties. Detailed census tract information was added, along with information on private businesses. New Haven can now produce instant profiles of the housing and economic status of any neighborhood, block, business, or house. Faced with a backlog of vacant buildings, New Haven has already used its supermicro to analyze each vacant structure, match potential buyers with houses, and track the rehabilitation process step by step (Peirce, 1984).

After long hesitancy, police departments are now using data bases to obtain leads and help them spot crime trends. For New York City police, one potential source of investigative leads in sex crimes, robberies, and certain grand larcenies is the department's eight-month-old Computer Assisted Robbery System (CARS). Investigators can ask the computer to search its files for suspects or crimes by matching body marks, nicknames, headgear, footwear, names, times, days, locations, modus operandi, and physical deformities (including odor). The system paid off when police arrested a robber who typically used a silver pistol and followed his female victims into their buildings. After his arrest, a CARS search was performed that turned up 21 other robberies matching that M.O. (Method of Operation). Victims in 18 of those cases identified the man as the culprit, creating an ironclad case against him (*The Wall Street Journal*, November 18, 1984).

Graphics.   Again, the usefulness of this software depends on the needs of the organization. If a pie chart or bar graph might help in understanding a problem or communicating how things are going, then graphics software is valuable.

Recently, project management techniques like Gantt charts (discussed on page 247) have come to minicomputers and even personal computers. Many programs go beyond the ability to schedule tasks; they help manage the resource requirements and costs of one or more projects (see photo).

Networking.   This software will prove important to many governmental organizations; it enables one computer to talk to another. If you only have one personal computer, there is no need to network. But, like telephones, personal computers tend to multiply in small offices. As soon as there is more than one computer, the advantages of networking becomes obvious.

The U.S. Department of Transportation (DOT) has been a pioneer among agencies using networking. Emphasizing the use of micros and portables in its field offices, especially for auditing, DOT has netted $40 million in fines for bid rigging on federally financed transportation projects (*High Technology*, January 1984). But, for the most part, the government's computers cannot talk to each other; most are incompatible. For instance, the Grace Commission discovered that the New York regional office of the Department of Health and Human Services alone uses 10 different brands of incompatible computers. This kind of needless incompatibility offers an open invitation to abuse and to the defrauding of government programs.

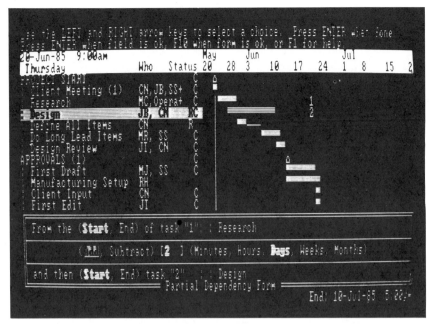

Breakthrough Software's Project Manager, like most project management packages, produces Gantt charts that indicate what tasks must occur when. It also graphs the level of specific resources required each day and juxtaposes this information with the relevant Gantt chart tasks. Compare this screen shot to Figure 7-1. (Courtesy Breakthrough Software)

Management Information Systems. Information networks can become quite complex within an organization, especially when each administrator deals directly with his or her own source—as well as every other administrator. As the organization grows and more people become involved, the information network becomes increasingly difficult to maintain.

At this point top management might consider the design and installation of a management information system (MIS). The new MIS allows for greater efficiency by reducing the complexity of the information networks. It also allows for specific information-processing needs to be identified, standardized, and scheduled as a matter of routine. In sum, a good MIS provides information useful to administrators in fulfilling their planning, decision making, implementation, and evaluation responsibilities; it gets the right information to the right people on a timely and cost-efficient basis.

Four Fallacies about Computers

Fallacy 1: The More Data the Better. One of the major findings of the Grace Commission was that the critical deficiency under which many public administrators operate is the lack of relevant information. But, in accepting that conclusion, we should not be blind to an opposite but equally valid deficiency—namely, an overabundance of irrelevant information—which does not curb the inclination of many administrators to ask for more and more information.

Russell Ackoff (1967), professor of systems science at the Wharton School of the University of Pennsylvania, offers one explanation for this phenomenon.

> For managers to know what information they need, they must be aware of each type of decision they should make (as well as do) and they must have an adequate model of each. These conditions are seldom satisfied. Most managers have some conception of at least some of the types of decisions they must make. Their conceptions, however, are likely to be deficient in a very critical way, a way that follows from an important principle of scientific economy: the less we understand a phenomenon, the more variables we require to explain it. Hence, the manager who does not understand the phenomenon he controls plays it "safe" and, with respect to information, wants "everything." The MIS designer, who has even less understanding of the relevant phenomenon than the manager, tries to provide even more of everything. He thereby increases what is already an overload of irrelevant information.

"Feeding time . . ." (From *The Wall Street Journal*, with permission of Cartoon Features Syndicate.)

Fallacy 2: Computers Radically Change Organizations. This myth comes in two versions: the optimistic and the pessimistic. Advocates of the optimistic version say that networking allows a decentralized alternative to rigid hierarchical structures. This is good, they believe, because these bureaucracies have failed to solve the problem of rigidity. (This theme will be explored in some depth in the next chapter.)

The pessimists see quite the opposite. According to them, giant computers allow governments and large corporations to intrude more on the lives of citizens and employees; computers may hold the potential for decentralization, but the reality is that they will be used to centralize power in the hands of a few executives.

Who is correct? Kenneth L. Kraemer and James N. Danziger (1984), both of the University of California, Irvine, carefully examined the effect of computers on the organizational environment of workers in U.S. municipal governments. They found that "substantial majorities of employees . . . report that computing has had no noticeable effect on supervision of their work or on their capacity to influence others." The second broad generalization is that the main effects of computing on work life are largely job enhancing. Over half of the managers surveyed (N = 498) felt that computing had raised their sense of accomplishment about their jobs.

Fallacy 3: A Computer System Cuts Costs.   Maybe. A computer system represents an expensive, high-technology capital investment, and such investments often promise high savings only for high risks. For instance, some estimate that county and city governments alone are spending about $1 billion a year on computer systems. At a minimum, such investments demand thoughtful and continuing attention from administrators. (See the caption to the photograph of Mayor Dianne Feinstein of San Francisco.)

There are several reasons why computers do not always live up to their promise. As suggested earlier, computers can motivate government employees to accumulate a lot of unnecessary data; and as we shall see in a moment, these systems do not always generate better information for making decisions. Danziger (1977) gives two good reasons why computers often fail to generate personnel savings. "Staff reductions are the exception on most of the more complex tasks which have been computerized. . . . [And] data coding and entry often involve more staff time per transaction than did the manual system." Furthermore, in the political areas of government, there is a reluctance to eliminate jobs that might be affected by automation, and other jobs are protected by civil service.

Fallacy 4: A Computer System Successfully Applied to a Problem Guarantees Improvement.   Richard L. Van Horn (1982), formerly head of management systems for Rand Corporation and now provost at University of Houston-University Park, makes the following point:

> A computerized inventory system with poor ordering rules will reorder the wrong quantities of the wrong parts faster and more consistently than its manual counterpart. The computer's outstanding attributes of speed, large memory, consistency, and the ability to follow complex logical instructions are of value *only to the extent that they are applied within a good management process.* Computers are a complement to, not a substitute for, careful management. [Emphasis added.]

Van Horn also issues a warning against "computational fundamentalism:"

> Computer users must remember that precision is not accuracy. Without question, computers operate with great precision. They can perform long and complex processing of instruction, text, and numbers without

Do computers cut costs? Mayor Dianne Feinstein of San Francisco says that she has "always been suspicious of the golden glow of technology." In 1983, she tightened considerably the city's computer buying policies. Now, the city buys from 4 suppliers rather than 44, thus ensuring compatibility.

In July 1985, she took a much more dramatic step by freezing expenditures for new computers and forming a committee of senior city managers to see how much computers actually raise productivity. She wanted to know, in short, how much computers are really worth. "If we're saving millions of dollars, I want to be able to keep the libraries open longer, have better park maintenance, or put more police on the street." (*Business Week,* June 24, 1985)

introducing any new errors. As a result, computer output neatly printed on display screen or paper is often treated like pages from Holy Writ. This computational fundamentalism is, as many managers have found through costly experience, a dangerous assumption.

Thus, we come back to Herbert Simon's point, noted in the last chapter: Human judgment and intuition are still required elements in any complex unstructured situation. Information needs of organizations are much broader than what the computer alone can supply. This is particularly true with respect to planning. Computers can help government do things right—as J. Peter Grace and all taxpayers want—but they can never ensure that it will do the right things.

This chapter takes us past the midpoint of Part II, "The Management of Governmental Programs." In Part III, we shall see that *program* management cannot be thought of as divorced from the management of fiscal and human resources. But these processes are not only tied together conceptually. As might be expected, they unfold in the same place—the organization.

Nailing Down the Main Points

1. With the organizational structure decided upon, the process of carrying out, accomplishing, or fulfilling the objectives of a program can begin. In short, we say implementation can begin. In the public sector, however, this task can be exceedingly difficult. Chances are the participants are heterogeneous and many. Chances are their perspectives on and priorities for a given program or project vary.

2. Given these difficulties, it becomes especially important to consider implementation at the start of the planning process—and that means during the policy planning stage (see Figure 5–2). Additionally, certain management techniques can increase the probability of success. Among these are scheduling models, expediters, incentives, good communication, and management by objectives.

3. Scheduling models facilitate the coordination of the activities of an enterprise. Among the leading types are Gantt chart, Critical Path Method (CPM), and Program Evaluation Review Technique (PERT). Regarding PERT, some authorities have suggested that it might be as much window dressing as a real control technique.

4. Program evaluation is the systematic examination of activities to provide information on the full range of the program's short- and long-term effects. Based on this information, the decision maker can know whether to continue the program, to modify its procedures, or to expand its application. In short, evaluation forces managers to take closer looks at their programs. While evaluative activity today remains a much underdeveloped activity, it is at least receiving increasing attention.

5. Three major types of evaluation in particular concern policymakers: national program impact evaluation, demonstration projects, and field experiments (using a control group). It appears that the second and third types of evaluation have the best chance of influencing policymakers. The principal difference between the field trial and the demonstration project is that in the former those responsible for evaluation exercise greater control; conditions, in other words, are closer to those of a laboratory. One advantage of the field trial is accuracy: It measures what it is supposed to.

   But evaluative research is useful to middle-level program managers as well as the policymakers at the top. Wholey thinks, in fact, that the primary evaluation, payoff—in terms of decision actually influenced—is evaluation that is done in enough detail to get at the effects of operational changes within operating programs. Performance auditing can also be quite important at this level.

6. One of the best approaches to carry out an evaluation is reminiscent of the classical research experiment: *(a)* Find out the goals of the program; *(b)* Translate the goals into measurable indicators of goal achievement; *(c)* Collect data on the indicators for those who have been exposed to the program and for the control group; and *(d)* Compare the data on the program participants and controls in terms of goal criteria.

7. Evaluators must remember that, above all, evaluation is a mangement tool. At the same time, managers need to remember that evaluation should not be a "go or no-go" proposition, with one test determining whether a major social program is to be launched; rather, evaluation should be built into the new program, examining its strengths and its weaknesses while it goes forward.

8. Although the federal government pioneered the use of computers, the Grace Commission found that by the mid-1980s government was facing a severe "information gap."

9. Computers can help administrators in a remarkably wide range of tasks, but they are no panacea for poor management.

Concepts for Review

analysis and evaluation	management information systems
complexity of joint action	(MIS)
control group	management by objectives
CPM, PERT	the metaphor of "games"
critical path	national program impact evaluation
data bases	networking
demonstration projects	performance auditing
expediter	premature evaluation of communi-
field experiments	cation
Gantt chart	scenario writing
implementation	scheduling models
incentives in public policy	social indicators
the information gap	spreadsheet
information technology package	steps in an evaluation
Japanese decision making	word processing

Problems

1. Crucial to the success of an MBO system is the writing of objectives. The objectives should tell *what* (the end result), *when* (a target date or period), and *who* (who is accountable for the objectives). Further, objectives should meet several criteria: cover only priority matters; be specific (no weasel words like *reasonable* or *highest*); be realistic yet set a level of

difficulty that stretches the manager; and be supportive of the objectives of other departments (McConkey, 1975:52–59). Now, in light of this criteria, develop several objectives for a specific administrative position (e.g., director, division of criminal investigation; executive director of mental health center; and training director).

2. What weaknesses can you find in each of the measures of quality of life on pp. 266–267? Can you think of better measures? How would you weigh each aspect to get an overall figure for the quality of a city?

3. Discuss the advantages and disadvantages of setting up a new agency to carry out a program.

4. The objectives of a city's recreation program are these: "To provide all citizens, to the extent practicable, with a variety of leisure opportunities that are accessible, safe, physically attractive, and enjoyable. They should contribute to the mental and physical health of the community, to its economic and social well-being and permit outlets that will help decrease incidents of antisocial behavior such as crime and delinquency." Establish some measurable evaluation criteria for these objectives.

5. Prepare a paper on recent evaluative research on the U.S. criminal justice system. You may want a narrower topic: "Does punishment cut down on crime?" "Do work-release programs boost a convict's chance of getting a job?" etc.

6. "Paradoxically, field offices often complain that they receive too many communications at the same time that they complain that they are insufficiently informed on new developments. The attempt of the central office to supervise closely the operations in the field often results in a steady flow of procedural regulations, instructions, bulletins, and what-not to the field offices. If too much of this material is trivial, detailed, or unadapted to local problems—and the field office will often feel that it is—it may remain unread, undigested, and ineffective. This problem is not one of geographical separation alone, but applies generally to organization communications." (Simon, Smithburg, and Thompson 1950) Do you agree? Can you think of instances where this has occurred? What concrete steps could the central office take to overcome this problem?

7. Can you think of possible external variables that could destroy the validity of a Police Fleet Plan demonstration project?

8. Translate the following examples of bureaucratese into plain English. Use no more than seven words for each. (Answers printed upside down at bottom of page.) The first example is an actual National Park Service regulation; the second is provided by John O. Morris, a Huntford lawyer.)

   a. "No person shall prune, cut, carry away, pull up, dig, fell, bore, chop, saw, chip, pick, move, sever, climb, molest, take, break, deface, destroy, set fire to, burn, scorch, carve, paint, mark, or in any manner interfere with, tamper, mutilate, misuse, disturb, or damage any tree, shrub, plant, grass, flower, or any part thereof, nor shall any person permit any chemical, whether solid, fluid or gaseous, to seep, drip, drain, or be emptied, sprayed, dusted on, injected upon, about or into any tree, shrub, plant, grass, flower."

   b. "We respectfully petition, request, and entreat that due and adequate provision be made, this day and the date hereinafter subscribed, for the satisfying of these petitioners' nutritional requirements and for the organizing of such methods of allocation and distribution as may be deemed necessary and proper to assure the reception by and for said petitioners of such quantities of baked cereal products as shall, in the judgment of the aforesaid petitioners, constitute a sufficient supply thereof."

9. Social researchers say that when the results of the experiment accurately reflect the effect the program had on the participants, the study has *internal validity*. When the results of the experiment can be generalized to a broader population, they say it has *external validity*. How do you think field trails, national program impacts evaluation, and demonstration projects compare in terms of these two types of validity?

10. Find the critical path in the following network. (Hint: Begin by working backward, assigning cumulative numbers to each mode. You do not need to test all possible paths. Follow this principle: If the optimal path from X to F passes through Y, and if the optimal path from T to F passes through X, then the optimal path from T to F passes through Y.)

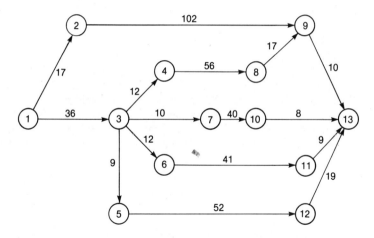

11. Your spouse has decided that you will build a patio and barbecue grill during your vacation. Since your annual vacation starts next week, you must have a plan in order to complete the patio on time. And because your spouse wants an enclosed patio, you will have to hire some help. Listed below are the activities and events involved. Prepare a PERT network for the patio project, including any additional events and activities you deem necessary to portray your plan adequately.

Events	Activities
Spouse's approval of design	
Building permit applied for	Apply for building permit
Building materials ordered	Order building materials
Ground leveled	Level ground

Answers: Do not hurt the plants, and give us this day our daily bread.

Events	Activities
Help hired	Hire help
Concrete forms laid out	Lay out concrete forms
Structure fabricated	Fabricate structure
Building inspection approved	Receive building permit
Lighting installed	Install lighting
Concrete work finished	Finish concrete
Project completed	Receive materials
Materials received	Pay help
Help paid	Order concrete
Ready-mix concrete ordered	Build barbecue
Barbecue completed	Paint
Painting completed	Building inspection
Building permit received	Receive concrete

12. Here is another translation exercise. Find respectable substitutes for this jargon that often clutters up writing and conversation in the administrative world.

ball park	optimize
bottom line	at this point in time
gameplan	due to the fact that
interface	parameter

Two of these terms, *optimize* and *parameter,* are correct under certain circumstances. What are they?

13. "The benefits of supermicros will be many. But the price may be life in an electronic goldfish bowl." Discuss.

14. "I am a great believer, if you have a meeting, in knowing where you want to come out before you start the meeting." Discuss.

15. Why may results (as in MBO) not always be an adequate basis for management control?

Case 7.1
Communicating and Implementing the Inchon Decision

Preliminaries

When the Korean War began in 1950, Douglas MacArthur—the most brilliant and among the most flamboyant American generals of the 20th century—was soon selected to command United Nations forces there. Only five days after North Korea began the war by invading South Korea, MacArthur seized on a concept for winning the war. Afterward he would write in his *Reminiscences:* "I was now ready for the last great stroke to bring my plan to fruition . . . a turning movement deep into the flank and rear of the enemy that would sever his supply lines and encircle all his forces south of Seoul." (See Exhibit 1.)

Upon returning to his headquarters in Tokyo on July 4, 1950, he ordered his staff to prepare plans for such an operation. Six days later they had developed Operation Blueheart, which called for a landing on July 22. The plan was, however, absurd; it did not allow sufficient time for preparation, and MacArthur did not have enough troops.

Exhibit 1
The North Korean Invasion—June 25, 1950

The North Korean invasion on June 25, 1950, headed by seven infantry divisions and a tank brigade, spilled across the 38th parallel and shattered the beach that had existed. The four poorly equipped South Korean divisions could offer little opposition. Seoul, the South Korean capital, fell in three days and the Allied forces retreated to the Pusan perimeter (shaded area). The United Nations Command offensive of September 1950 was the dramatic counterstroke devised by MacArthur. The crux of the operation was the landing at Inchon (arrow). The successful landing turned the tide of the war.

So MacArthur was forced to abandon Blueheart but not the idea. He turned his energies toward getting the troops he would need—no small task. As J. Lawton Collins, the army chief of staff told him: "General, you are going to have to win the war out there with the troops available to you in Japan and Korea." MacArthur replied: "Joe, you are going to have to change your mind."

Among his first steps was to get the marines on board. In explaining his bold idea of a landing at Inchon, he held out to General Lemuel C. Shepherd, Jr., commander of the Fleet Marine Force, Pacific, the opportunity for the marines to grab a significant role in the Korean War and then induce Shepherd himself to request from the Joint Chiefs of Staff (JCS) that more marines be sent from the United States.

The navy also had to be won over. During a visit to MacArthur in July, General Collins had spoken privately to Admiral James Doyle, the naval commander. He found the admiral unenthusiastic about the Inchon invasion. When Collins asked him about landing in an area with 35-foot tides, Doyle replied, "It will be extremely difficult . . . but it can be done." Collins had been in the military long enough to recognize a hedge when he heard one. Doyle was, in effect, saying: "The plan is foolhardy, but I'm not going to argue it with MacArthur. If ordered, I'll undertake it.''

Before returning to Washington, Collins met once more with MacArthur. Although Collins remained skeptical about an Inchon landing, he felt a marine division could be sent. This implied promise was good enough for now, MacArthur thought; when he got the marines under his control, he would deal with the Pentagon's worries about Inchon.

During the last part of July, MacArthur continued to send message after message explaining his reasons for wanting an amphibious assault. He also had the opportunity to argue this case directly to a White House emissary, effectively bypassing the JCS. Truman had sent adviser W. Averell Harriman to Tokyo to protest MacArthur's public statements in support of Chiang Kai-shek. Ironically, MacArthur was able to turn Harriman's remonstration into a successful opportunity to lobby for his Inchon plan.

On July 23, he cabled the JCS that plans for the operation, now renamed "Chromite," were ready. Two days later, he received word that he would get his cutting edge: The marines would be sent.

"A Masterful Exposition"

Yet the JCS remained wary. In August, having received little additional information from MacArthur about Operation Chromite, then the Chairman of the JCS Omar Bradley sent General Collins along with chief of naval operations, Admiral Forrest Sherman, across the Pacific—perhaps as much to dissuade as discuss.

Collins, Sherman, MacArthur, and various staff personnel met in Tokyo at 5:30 on the afternoon of August 23 in a paneled six-floor conference room in the Dai Ichi Building; it was the most impressive assemblage of military leadership since the war had begun.

It was not hard to see why the JCS and others were having second thoughts. MacArthur had chosen the unlikeliest harbor on the peninsula: Inchon, on the Yellow Sea, 150 miles north of Pusan, had no beaches, only piers and seawalls. The attack would have to be launched in the heart of the city. The waters approaching the harbor could easily be mined; currents there ran as high as eight knots. In any one of a hundred turns, a sunken or disabled ship could block the little bay. Worst of all were the tides, among the highest in the world. The only dates when the surf would be high enough to accommodate amphibious ships and landing craft in 1950 were September 15, September 27, and October 11. September 15 was best, but high tide then crested first at dawn, too early for awkward troop transports to maneuver beforehand in the narrow passage, and again a half hour after sundown, too late for a daylight attack. Therefore, as many marines as possible would have to be put ashore during the 2 hours of the first flood tide; 12 hours would pass before the second flood tide would permit reinforcement. As one naval officer said afterward: "We drew up a list of every natural and geographic handicap—and Inchon had 'em all. . . . Make up a list of amphibious 'don'ts' and you have an exact description of the Inchon operation."

Not surprisingly, every flag and general officer in Tokyo—including General Walker whose Eighth Army would be freed from the Pusan Perimeter (see Exhibit 1) by a successful drive against the North Koreans—tried to talk MacArthur out of the operation. Even MacArthur's own staff was unconvinced, but he turned a deaf ear to all.

For 80 minutes these objections were heard in the conference room that Wednesday afternoon in Tokyo. MacArthur sat silently, impassively, puffing on his pipe. When everyone finished, he remained silent a few more moments, possibly for dramatic effect: MacArthur enjoyed the suspense. He wrote later. "I waited a moment or so to collect my thoughts. I could feel the tension rising in the room. [General] Almond shifted uneasily in his chair. If ever a silence was pregnant, this one was. I could almost hear my father's voice telling me as he had so many years before, 'Doug, councils of war breed timidity and defeatism.' "

Then he spoke for 45 minutes without notes, quietly at first, then gradually "building up emphasis with consummate skill." Collins commented later: "Even discounting the obvious dramatics, this was a masterful exposition of the argument for the daring risk he was determined to take."

MacArthur began by telling them that "the very arguments you have made as to the impracticabilities involved" confirmed his faith in the plan, "for the enemy commander will reason that no one would be so brash as to make such an attempt." Surprise, he said, "is the most vital element for success in war." Suddenly he was reminding them of a lesson they had all learned in grammar school: the surprise British raid on Quebec in 1759, when a small force scaled supposedly impossible heights and caught the French totally unprepared.

The amphibious landing, he said, "is the most powerful tool we have." To employ it properly, "we must strike hard and deep." Inchon's hurdles were real, "but they are not insuperable." And he had another history lesson that they may not have learned: In 1894 and 1904, the Japanese had landed at Inchon and seized all Korea. He said: "My confidence in the navy is complete, and in fact I seem to have more confidence in the navy than the navy has in itself." Looking at Sherman, he said: "The navy has never let me down in the past, and it will not let me down this time." As to a Kunsan landing, farther south, he believed it would be ineffective. "It would be an attempted envelopment," and therefore futile. "Better no flank movement than one such as this. The only result would be a hookup with Walker's troops. . . . This would simply be sending more troops to help Walker 'hang on,' and hanging on is not good enough. . . . The enemy will merely roll back on his lines of supply and communication." Kunsan, the "only alternative" to Inchon, would be "the continuation of the savage sacrifice we are making at Pusan, with no hope of relief in sight."

He paused dramatically. Then: "Are you content to let our troops stay in that bloody perimeter like beef cattle in the slaughterhouse? Who will take the responsibility for such a tragedy? Certainly, I will not."

By pouncing on Inchon and then Seoul, he said, he would "cut the enemy's supply line and seal off the entire southern peninsula. . . . By seizing Seoul I would completely paralyze the enemy's supply system—coming and going. This in turn will paralyze the fighting power of the troops that now face Walker."

If he was wrong about the landing, "I will be there personally and will immediately withdraw our forces." Doyle, stirred, spoke up: "No, General, we don't know how to do that. Once we start ashore we'll keep going." MacArthur had reached them. When another man pointed out that enemy batteries could command the dead-end channel, Sherman, intractable till then, sniffed and said, "I wouldn't hesitate to take a ship in there." MacArthur snapped back: "Spoken like a Farragut!" He concluded in a hushed voice: "I can almost hear the ticking of the second hand of destiny. We must act now or we will die. . . . Inchon will succeed. And it will save 100,000 lives."

General Douglas MacArthur congratulates General Oliver P. Smith, commanding general of the First Marine Division, for the successful Inchon invasion. (Signal Corps photo/Sgt. Herbert Nutter)

The following Monday, four days later, the Supreme Commander of Allied Powers received approval from Washington for Operation Chromite.

The "Promptitude to Act"

MacArthur had little doubt about his ability to move his men rapidly, to display, in Churchill's words," that intense clarity of view and promptitude to act which are the qualities of great commanders." Two days after the cable from Washington, MacArthur's staff had issued bulk operation plans; none were sent, however, to the JCS.

In fact, the JCS were kept in the dark regarding the details until the last minute. MacArthur did send a young lieutenant colonel to Washington, who managed to arrive the night before the landing and briefed the JCS only six hours before it took place.

Early on the morning of September 15, the invasion armada, a total of 19 ships, approached their target under cover of darkness. MacArthur, age 70, came onto the flag bridge of the *McKinley* to watch the bombardment. As usual he wore his battered, salt-stained garrison cap.

The last bombs hit at 6:20 A.M.; four minutes later seven landing craft touched shore. At 6:55 A.M., Sergeant Alvin E. Smith tied an American flag on a shell-torn tree on the crest of Radio Hill. MacArthur, binoculars focused on the island, nodded approval. He told Admiral Doyle, "Say to the fleet, 'The navy and marines have never shone more brightly than this morning.' " He arose. "That's it," he said, "let's get a cup of coffee."

Epilogue
At the end of D-day all objectives had been taken, with 20 men killed, 1 missing, and 174 wounded. The surprise had been total. By the end of D + 1, the First and Fifth Marines had linked up and advanced to secure and establish a perimeter six miles inland from the landing sites. MacArthur's bold stroke paid off fully when Seoul was captured on September 22, and the demoralized remnants of the North Korean army fell backward after the Inchon landing forces linked up with the Eighth Army four days later.

Case Questions
1. What are the main lessons in this case about communicating and implementing a decision?
2. What do you think of the way in which MacArthur failed to keep the JCS informed?

Case References
Douglas MacArthur, *Reminiscences* (New York: McGraw-Hill, 1964); Joseph C. Goulden, *Korea: The Untold Story* (New York: McGraw-Hill, 1982); William Manchester, *American Caesar* (New York: Dell, 1978).

Case 7.2
American Social Policy, 1965–1985: Losing Ground?

Unintended Consequences of Government Programs
After 20 years and hundreds of billions of dollars spent on attempting to banish poverty in the United States, most scholars are not quite sure what to make of the effort. But Charles Murray, a senior fellow at the Manhattan Institute for Policy Research, is not one of them. In his book *Losing Ground,* Murray argues that the assessment of this problem should not be so murky.

Why is it, he asks, that poverty declined impressively from 1950 until 1968, only to begin growing and finally to stall while the greatest expenditure in U.S. history was being funneled toward the disadvantaged? (See Exhibit 1.) Why has the number of people living in "latent poverty"—those actually in need or those who would be in need without government assistance—risen almost steadily since shortly after Great Society programs began in earnest? (See Exhibit 2.) For years, latent poverty had declined. Why did the participation of young black males in the labor force (that is, those who had jobs or were looking for them) begin to fall sharply just when job-training programs began to expand?

Exhibit 1
The Poverty/Spending Paradox

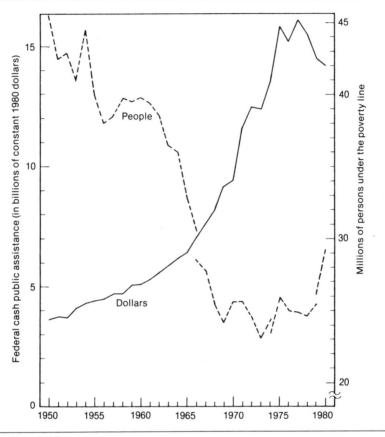

Source: Murray (1984:57)

The Labor department spent little on job training during the 1950s. From 1962 through 1980, however, nearly 33 million people enrolled in some kind of job-training program. Yet the performance of the very groups most targeted steadily worsened. Finally—to cite just one more of Murray's queries—why did the birthrate among unmarried teenagers rise during a period when the birthrates of virtually every other category of women, white and black, married and single, declined? Although the sexual revolution affected almost everyone, only single teenagers went counter to the general fertility trend, with one well-known result being the feminization of poverty. (In 1980, more than half of 5.3 million poor families were headed by women with no husband in the home, versus less than one quarter in 1959. In 1980, female-headed families accounted for more than half of the 11 million children living in poverty, versus less than 25 percent two decades earlier.)

Exhibit 2
Two Views of Poverty, 1950–1980

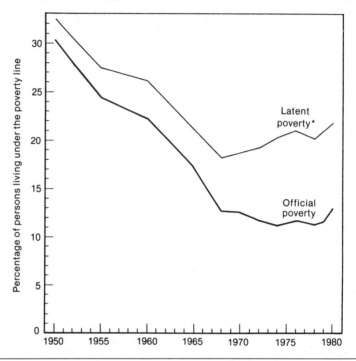

* *Latent poverty* is a term that applies to everyone who would be poor without government help. In 1964, when the War on Poverty began, almost all emphasis was on eliminating poverty in this more fundamental sense. In other words, the goal was to eliminate altogether the need for "a dole." The "official poverty" measure has nothing to do with people's ability to make a living for themselves.

Source: Murray (1984:65)

Murray gives a disturbing answer to these puzzling questions. He maintains that government programs, which changed incentives and thus behavior, are themselves the explanation. More specifically, Murray argues that these programs made it less likely that energetic talented men and women living in poverty would work their way out because the short-term benefits of doing so had diminished. Antipoverty programs even altered people's decisions about when and under what circumstances to bear children. In part, this phenomenon simply had to do with money, Murray thinks. Government programs narrowed the gap between the minimum wage and nonworking income, and in some states, the gap occasionally vanished. Moreover, the psychic rewards for escaping poverty also contracted as the notion took hold that society's flaws, and not individual behavior, explained everyone's plight.

Murray reminds us that historically the only path out of poverty has been long tedious hours of usually unpleasant, hard-to-get work; that is the way immigrants today still succeed. Contrary to conventional wisdom, education is not the normal ticket to prosperity for those at the lowest social levels. And, because the effort requires an unremitting commitment, it is not easily begun if short-term options make life tolerable.

The Social Scientists and the Great Experiment

What most clearly helps to establish these cause-effect relationships, Murray argues, is an ambitious attempt to evaluate the effect a guaranteed income would have on people's work effort. Briefly defined, a negative income tax provides payments to individuals whose income falls below a certain "floor," thereby guaranteeing, in effect, a minimum income.

The Office of Economic Opportunity's (OEO) vehicle for providing the proof took the form of the most ambitious social science experiment in American history. Known as the Negative Income Tax (NIT) experiment, it began in 1968, ultimately used 8,700 people as subjects, and lasted for 10 years.

The federally financed NIT experiment was launched at sites in New Jersey and Pennsylvania, then extended to Iowa, North Carolina, Indiana, Washington, and Colorado. At each site, a sample of low-income individuals was selected by researchers and was randomly split into two groups: the experimental group and the control group. Members of the experimental group were told that for a specified number of years (usually three) they would have a floor put under their incomes, whether they worked or not. The benefits to participants were varied in order to test their reactions to the gradations of generosity of the guaranteed income. Members of the control group received no benefits.

During the next decade, the results dribbled in. Finally, by the end of the 1970s, the social scientists had enough information to begin drawing some conclusions.

The key question was whether the NIT would reduce work effort among the poor. The answer was yes, and the reduction was substantial. In Seattle and Denver, for example, the NIT trimmed "desired hours of work" by 9 percent for husbands and by 20 percent for wives. ("Desired hours of work" was measured by actual employment after factoring involuntary work reductions, such as layoffs, out of the calculation.) Young males who were not yet heads of families— "nonheads" in the jargon—were especially affected. They were at a critical age in their lives—about to assume the responsibilities of marriage and just establishing themselves in the labor force. If they were going to escape from poverty, now was the time to start. The NIT had a disastrous impact on the number of hours they worked weekly—down 43 percent for those who remained nonheads throughout the experiment, down 33 percent for those who married. The NIT also produced a striking increase in the duration of unemployment after a participant in the experiment lost his or her job.

What about the impact of welfare on the family? Looking again at the Seattle and Denver experiments, the marriage dissolution rate was 36 percent higher for whites who received NIT payments than for those who did not and 42 percent higher for blacks. Interestingly, no such effect was observed among participants in Indiana because in that state couples were under the impression that they would lose their NIT payments if they split up.

Criticisms of Murray's Thesis

Murray naturally has many critics. They make the following points.

- Progress stopped in the 1970s because the economy began to slow. Things would have been worse without the poverty programs.
- Overall progress seemed to stop because of the growing number of old

people in the population. But progress really did not stop; blacks kept gaining.

- Progress did not really stop. The poverty measure is misleading because it is based on gross cash income. If one considers the dollar value of "in-kind" assistance (food stamps, medicaid, housing benefits), one gets a different picture.
- It would have been worse without the War on Poverty.

Case Questions

1. Assume Murray has just briefed you. What questions might you ask or criticisms might you make about Exhibit 1?
2. What biases, if any, do you see in the NIT experiment? Do you see any ethical problems in the experiment?
3. How would you test the objections Murray's critics raise? What data would you want, and what would you do with it?
4. Must final judgments in social science often rest on faith?

Case References

Charles Murray, *Losing Ground: American Social Policy, 1950–80* (New York: Basic Books, 1984); Martin Anderson, *Welfare* (Stanford, Calif.: Hoover Institution, 1978); Robert H. Haverman, *A Decade of Federal Antipoverty Programs* (New York: Academic Press, 1977); Blanche Bernstein, *Politics of Welfare* (Boston: Abt Books, 1982); John F. Schwarz, *America's Hidden Success: A Reassessment of Twenty Years of Public Policy* (New York: W. W. Norton, 1983.)

8

Organizing

Introduction

Planning, decision making, implementing, and evaluating, the subjects of the three preceding chapters, cannot be separated from *organizing*. If people are to work together effectively in implementing plans, making decisions, and controlling operations they need to know the part they are to play in the total endeavor and how their roles relate to each other. To design and maintain these systems of roles is basically the managerial function of organization.

This definition is a good one. While many management theorists give loose and woolly definitions, we shall simply try to look at the organization as the "practicing manager" does. Organizing thus becomes the grouping of activities necessary to attain objectives, the assignment of each grouping to a manager with authority to supervise it, and the provision for horizontal and vertical coordination in the agency structure (Koontz & O'Donnell, 1974).

We should keep continually in mind, however, that in this chapter we deal only with the formal structure of organization. How the people who fill the roles in these structures actually behave is the subject of Chapters 10 and 11.

The chapter begins with a survey of the various ways in which groups can organize themselves to attain some objective. Particular emphasis will be placed on how governments are organized and what problems follow from that type of organization. The chapter concludes by giving some thought to the design of organizations.

How does our key—namely, looking at organization the way a

manager must—differ from the more conventional, more theoretical ones usually encountered in introductory texts? Probably the most obvious difference is simply in appearance, for the latter can often look quite Byzantine—with concepts such as closed model, open model, and model synthesis taking the place of the longitudinal basilicas, circular domes, and large vaults. All in all, a bewildering experience the first time through. But conventional approaches involve more fundamental problems, and we may as well make them explicit lest we too succumb.

First, conventional approaches to organization tend to ignore environments such as politics. They start from the bogus assumption that managers can simply collect and weigh facts and probabilities, make an optimal decision, and see that it is carried out. Yet in large scale governmental projects, such a clear sequence of action is seldom possible because of their extended duration, the many technical and social unknowns, the continual discovery of new facts, and constantly changing pressures. Given these messy realities, what the manager needs is not an abstract model of other organizations to copy but rather an analytical discussion of the ways to design administrative systems that allow recommitment, reassessment, and redirection.

Second, conventional approaches are unlikely to cover the newer kinds of organizational forms one finds in government and business today. What is sorely needed is a more balanced discussion that covers not only the traditional organizational concepts but also the newer forms of organizations.

Third, conventional approaches separate the study of organization from the study of policy planning, even though the two are really quite inseparable. Organization should not be made an end in itself. If anything, the reverse is true: organization should *follow* policy. Otherwise our "practicing manager" might find himself in the same situation Halberstam (1969:635) discovered in the Vietnam War: "It was as if someone had ordered the greatest house in the world, using the finest architect, the best stonemason in the world, marble shipped from Italy, choicest redwood for the walls, the best interior decorator, but had by mistake overlooked one little thing: the site chosen was in a bog."

Five Types of Organizations

To the preceding list of shortcomings, we might add a fourth: Conventional treatments of organization ignore the considerable variety in organizational forms—old as well as new.

Some time ago, Kenneth Boulding developed a fascinating hierarchy of systems concepts ranging from the simple atom to imponderables beyond the galaxies. Gerald J. Skibbins (1974) took this powerful organizing concept, narrowed the focus considerably, and constructed a comprehensive list of systems of which humans are components. They range from the system most often used in history ("leader/follower cluster") to the system Skibbins sees next in the evolution of organizations ("the organic organization").

Which brings us to an interesting paradox: To know the future we must know the past; that is, to grasp adequately the significance of the newer organizational forms referred to in point two above, we must have some grasp of organizational evolution itself. Figure 8-1, which presents a simplified version of Skibbins's list, is a means to that end.

The Leader/Follower Organization

We can begin with the most natural of human relationships, that between leader and followers. The relationship is, however, not as simple as it might appear at first blush.

The leader's authority, for instance, can seldom be satisfied with obedience based merely upon the grounds of common sense or respect. Rather, as the great German sociologist Max Weber (Gerth & Mills, 1946:51-55, 246 ff.) was to note, authority seeks to arouse something else (love, fear, even awe) in the followers. This line of inquiry led

Max Weber (University of Heidelberg Museum)

Figure 8-1
The Seven Organizational Concepts

	Image	Structure	Examples	Life span	Ability to adapt technology and systems advances	Ability to alter own organizational structure
Leader/follower cluster 	Human	Leader at center, followers at periphery	Leader/tribe model, Napoleon's army, Hitler's Germany, Mao's China, Chiang's Taiwan, most R & D groups, performing arts companies, the military squad	5.5 million B.C. to today	Low	Almost none
Mosaic 	Social interdependence	Loosely connected assembly of subsystems	Holy Roman Empire, United Nations, NATO, SEATO, European Common Market, urban communities, voluntary associations, IGY, ILO, tribal nations, HMO groups, law partnerships, colleges	9000 B.C. to today	Low	Low
Pyramid 	Geometric	Hierarchy	U.S. Government departments (HSH, Agriculture, etc.), unions, utilities, banks, transportation companies, public education system, religions, foundations, public corporations such as N.J. Turnpike Authority, military establishments, organized churches, courts of law, political parties, governments in general, most small and middle sized businesses	2600 B.C. to today	Low	Fair
Conglomerates 	Geometric (cluster of pyramids)	Assembly of hierarchies united at summits	The 1900 trusts in the United States, modern LTV, Litton Industries, Sperry Rand, Gulf & Western, ITT, the Pentagon	A.D. 1000 to today	Moderate	Fair
Organic 	Biological growth with man as the model	Network	Possibly IBM, Xerox, NASA, Texas Instruments, Volvo, Battelle, and CSIRO (Australia); and unknown forms yet to be developed	A.D. 1950 to 3050 (est.)	High with unusual potential	Highest with capacities for complete metamorphosis

Source: Adapted by permission of the publisher from G. Skibbins, Organizational Revolution, end paper © 1975 by AMACOM, a division of American Management Association.

Weber to the conclusion that there are three types of legitimate authority: legal, traditional, and charismatic.

Legal authority we associate with constitutional governments; traditional authority with kings and parents. But it is charismatic authority that is most relevant to the leader/follower cluster. It is based on the members' abandonment of themselves to an individual distinguished by holiness, heroism, or exemplariness. The word itself, *charisma*, from the Greek means literally "gift of grace." All charismatic authority implies wholehearted devotion to the person of the leader who feels called to carry out a mission. Examples of this special type of leader/follower relationship would be Hitler's Germany and the guru/novitiate in arcane religions. Needless to say, the bonds are very firm.

The strengths of this relationship are also its weaknesses. Too often a leader is unwilling to adapt to new challenges. One reason for this low capacity for adaptation is that change could affect the leader's absolute power.

The British historian Arnold J. Toynbee (1946: vol. 1, 307 ff.) suggests another reason—the *nemesis of creativity*. According to Toynbee, it is most uncommon for the creative responses to two or more successive challenges in the history of a group to be achieved by the same individual. Indeed, the party that has distinguished itself in dealing with one challenge—probably an act that brought it to power—is apt to fail conspicuously in attempting to deal with the next. The failures here seem to derive from an overconfidence acquired after the leader's first triumphs ("idolization of an ephemeral self").

Mosaic Organization

The key problem with the mosaic organization is precisely this tenuousness between parts. Skibbins writes:

> As the name implies, the mosaic form involves the putting together of separate, distinct pieces, glued only at the edges, to form some pattern. The parts of mosaic organizations tend to be relatively autonomous and loosely connected for a few particular purposes. (1974, 60–61)

As Robert Hutchins is reported to have said of one mosaic organization, the University of Chicago, the only thing that held it together was its heating system. Figure 8–1 gives other examples of this kind of organization.

Pyramidal Organization

The pyramid is a geometric figure and it symbolizes the structure of the hierarchy. Interaction within a pyramid conforms to the hierarchical structure of the organization and emphasizes superior/subordinate relationships. The concept of hierarchy was defined on page 46.

A closely related concept is that of *bureaucracy*. Most of us have a general idea of what a bureaucracy is and I have admittedly taken the liberty of using the term in earlier chapters without providing a formal definition. But now I must. Once again, our surest guide is Max Weber (Gerth & Mills, 1946:196–98), who in the early part of this century, spelled out in considerable detail the features of the bureaucratic structure. In simplified terms those features are (a) a division of labor based on functional specialization; (b) a well-defined hierarchy of authority; (c) a system of rules covering the rights and duties of employment; (d) a system of procedures for dealing with work situations; (e) impersonality of interpersonal relations; and (f) promotion and selection based on technical competence.

The role of Weber and his bureaucratic model in relation to the pyramidal organizations, however, must be clarified in two respects. In the first place, the bureaucratic model was not a description of reality but an *ideal type*; that is, what organizations to varying degrees approximate. Some organizations are more bureaucratic than others, but none are perfect examples of bureaucracy. Second, Weber really represents a separate thread in the intellectual development of the pyramidal concept. His ultimate interest was bureaucracy in its political and social context; those that followed largely ignored not only this link to the social structure but also the historical context of bureaucracy.

A far more important thread in the intellectual development of the pyramidal concept begins with the American engineer Frederick W. Taylor (1856–1915) and the scientific management movement (see Chapter 1) and ends with Luther Gulick and Lyndall Urwick and the administrative management movement. The thrust of both movements, and this is where they diverge from Weber, was to discover principles that would enable the manager to build up and administer an organization in the most efficient manner. Below we discuss four of the more important of these principles.

Division of Labor. Without a doubt, the cornerstone of the four principles is the *division of labor* into specialized tasks. But how does the administrator do it? Begin by determining the necessary activities for the accomplishment of overall organization objectives. Then, divide these activities on a logical basis into departments that perform the specialized functions. In this way, the organization structure itself becomes the primary means for achieving the technical and economic advantages of specialization and division of labor.

But the procedure is hardly as simple as it sounds, for there are many ways by which the administrator can divide and place in separate departments the functions of the organization. The most common, of course, is by objectives. For example, the Department of Health and Human Services organizes in Washington along health and welfare lines; similarly, NASA subdivides into the Office of Manned Space Flight and the Office of Space Science and Applications.

Adam Smith began his classic study of economics, *Wealth of Nations* (1976/1776) with a discussion of specialization in pin making. Eight men, each performing a single task, could turn out far more pins than eight men each performing all required series of tasks.

Such divisions by use or objective, we might note parenthetically, can present problems. For example, the interrelationship among components often turns out to be much more complicated than would appear at first. Increasingly, the interfaces become blurred as technology progresses. In nuclear power plants, for instance, one finds no neat dividing lines among the functions of fueling, heating, and power generation.

Another criterion the manager might use in making these structural decisions is geographic. In other words, administrative authority is distributed not by function but by area. In the national government, only the Department of State, the Tennessee Valley Authority, and, to a lesser degree, the Department of the Interior have followed this criterion. In other departments and agencies, division by geography appears in modified form. In the case of HHS, referred to a moment ago, it could be added that the secretary also has regional representatives who try to shepherd into one flock the regional commissioner of social security, the regional Public Health Service offices, and the others.

Other bases for division of labor include process and client. Process-type departments have at their roots either a particular technology, a particular type of equipment, or both. Technology, as used here, refers not only to hardware technology (such as welding in a transportation maintenance work center) but also to software technology (such as accounting or operations research). Obvious examples of client-based agencies include the Bureau of Indian Affairs and Veterans Administration.

Hierarchy.   The second principle of administrative management is hierarchy. It is based on the *scalar principle*, which states that authority and responsibility should flow in a direct line vertically from the highest level of the organization to the lowest level. This flow is commonly referred to as the chain of command. In such an arrangement, a cardinal sin would be to fail to go through channels in trying to get an important message to the top.

Hierarchical components in the Environmental Protection Agency are evident in the organization chart shown in Exhibit 1, p. 24. As the accompanying box suggests, some leaders who blithely ignore this principle might be courting disaster.

Span of Control.   Closely related to the principles of division of labor and hierarchy is the *span of control*. This principle concerns the number of subordinates a superior can efficiently supervise. Traditional theory advocates a narrow span to enable the executive to provide adequate integration of all the activities of subordinates. According to James W. Fesler (1949:51), most federal agencies, apparently mindful of the span of control principle, have kept their principal subnational areas to less than 20. Yet until July 1979, President Carter had no chief of staff which meant that 200 individuals, commissions, departments, agencies, and other groups reported directly to him. (Referring again to Case 1.1, what is the span of control of the EPA administrators?)

Line and Staff.   The last principle we shall consider is *line and staff*. The simplest way to understand it is probably by military

The scalar principle at work. In the Reagan administration, decisions are made through a pyramid-shaped hierarchy. On the organization chart, the president's name is in the top box. In the second row of boxes are the names of cabinet officers, senior White House officials, and the vice president. In the third row are lesser White House aides and sub-cabinet officers (e.g., deputy and assistant secretaries).

Not since Eisenhower has a president integrated the cabinet and White House policymakers into a single chain of command. Advice flows to the president through the structure, and authority to perform flows to subordinates along the same lines. The full cabinet meets at least once a week to advise the president on broad policy of interest to all departments.

The danger of the system is that the president may become too aloof to govern effectively. The strength is that it adjusts better to the realities of the modern presidency. What are those realities? The job has become too large and complex for any single individual to deal with effectively—no matter how impressive his capacity for detail or for going without sleep. (The White House)

Who Is in Charge Here? or Why Unity of Command Really Does Matter

The concept of unity of command is simple. Over four decades ago, it was stated with beautiful simplicity in a federal publication this way:

> Everyone in an organization should know who's who. Everyone should know where he fits into the organizational pattern. He should know his superiors and his proper relation to them—not so he will know when and where to kowtow, but so he will know to whom he may go for advice and counsel, to whom he must look for supervision, and to whom he may turn if necessary to find access to still higher authority. Sometimes an organization in which lines of authority are hopelessly confused rationalizes by explaining that clear-cut lines are unnecessary because everyone is so cooperative: it is just "one big, happy family." But men cannot do their best, floating aimlessly about in a sea of ill-defined "cooperation." Good intentions or mere cooperation is not enough. To be effective, cooperation must be directed. It must follow some pattern or plan. (Hendrickson, 1940)

For all its simplicity, the principle apparently could not be grasped by the American planners of the Iranian rescue mission in 1980. Colonel Charles Beckwith, commander of the mission, said "It wasn't my responsibility."

How can anything not be the responsibility of the commander? The fact is that no one on the mission was in charge. A marine colonel was in charge of the helicopters. An air force colonel was in charge of the transport planes. A navy officer was in charge of the fighter cover. And Beckwith was in charge of the commandos. But nobody had overall responsibility on the scene.

Three short years later, in the days immediately after a terrorist truck-bombs attack in Lebanon killed 240 Marines, the man most identified with the United States mission was the

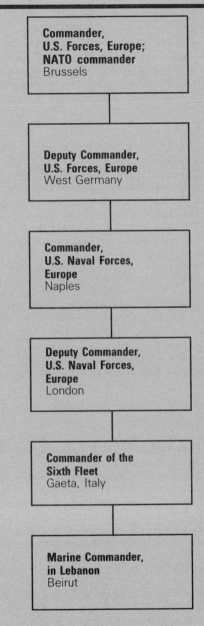

commandant of the Marine Corps, General Paul X. Kelley. But the officers actually responsible for supervising the marines were the admirals and generals in the U.S. European Command (p. 303). Under the organization of the military services, the marine commandant has authority over the recruiting, training, and equipping of marines, but the troops are under the operational control of theater commanders.

According to members of Congress and military officers, the Beirut bombing raised questions about the performance and organization of this chain of command. For example:

- Senior levels of a chain of command should provide guidance and sufficient resources to those at the bottom of the chain. Given the many known terrorist activities in the Beirut area, the chain of command should have sent in, along with the marines, some experts to help them handle the specialized kind of information they were getting on terrorism. That they did not was a colossal oversight.
- Senior levels of a chain of command should evaluate developing problems. Yet the chain of command for the marines in Beirut had neither the ability nor the will. It

was staffed with naval officers who had little or no knowledge of static land defense and counterterrorist tactics; the commander of the Sixth Fleet never went ashore to even look at security.

- Finally, the senior level of a chain of command should try to adjust the mission of lower levels to suit changing conditions. But, as the *New York Times* explained (December 11, 1983), that is not quite what happened in Lebanon. When the marines went into Beirut in September 1982, senior American military officers expected them to stay for no more than several months. As time passed and the initial welcome the marines received started to cool, the senior commanders did not change the deployment or seek revisions in the marines' restrictive rules of engagement, several officers said. According to military experts and historians, when the feasibility and safety of a military mission become questionable, it is considered the duty of officers, particularly those at senior levels, to study possible alternatives and, in extreme cases, to go back to policymakers to seek modifications in the mission.

analogy. Soldiers with weapons stand in the line, carrying out a military organization's essential functions; meanwhile, usually somewhere behind the front lines, stands (or sits) staff to investigate, to research, and to advise the commanding officer. Only through the commanding officer can the staff influence line decisions. What are staff positions in Figure 8–2?

As any organization—military or otherwise—becomes more complex, managers begin to need advice. Staffs aid managers in many ways. As Anthony Downs (1967:154) points out, a large staff can function as "a control mechanism 'external' to the line hierarchy, promote changes in opposition to the line's inertia, and act as a scapegoat

Figure 8–2
Line and Functional Authority

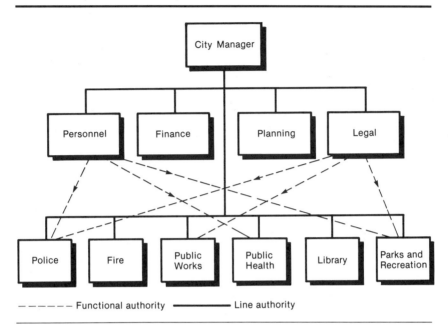

– – – – – – Functional authority ————— Line authority

deflecting hostility from its boss." The innovative advantage of a staff
Appears to result from (a) the technical orientation of its members,
who are younger and better educated; and (b) the incentive structure of
the staff, which is to help the top administrator improve the line's performance.

The importance of understanding the line-staff concept cannot be
overemphasized. Superior and subordinate alike must know whether
they are acting in a staff or line capacity. Lack of clarity on this point
often causes friction. And here, the notion of *functional authority* can
help. Functional authority is "the right that an individual or department has delegated to it over specified processes, practices, policies, or
other matters relating to activities undertaken by personnel in departments other than its own" (Koontz & O'Donnell, 1974:175). Thus, in
Figure 8–2, the functional authority of the personnel director might
cover and only cover giving competitive examinations and conducting
in-service training programs.

The Pathology of the Pyramid

Above we looked at the four principles of management—specialization, hierarchy, span of control, and line-staff—that characterize the
pyramidal organization. Now we need to reexamine the principles

Line and staff principle not at work. The tendency of the White House national security adviser, (a staff position) to become a highly visible policy advocate has handicapped secretaries of state (a line position). In the Carter administration the prominence of National Security Adviser Zbigniew Brzezinski alongside Secretary of State Cyrus R. Vance gave the impression at home and abroad of a fragmented foreign policy. Indeed, line-staff conflict eventually became so sharp that Vance decided to resign.

History repeated itself in 1982 as Reagan's first Secretary of State, Alexander Haig (center) accused National Security Adviser William Clark (left) of conducting a second foreign policy that was "bound to produce confusion." Some experts think that if the president's national security adviser spent less time trying to influence decision and more time serving as a neutral manager of the policymaking process, there would be less disarray. Rather than be a formulator and implementor of policy, advisers should present the chief executive with options and make sure that everybody gets a fair hearing. (Michael Evans/The White House)

through a more critical lens. Despite this essentially critical approach, our intent is not to debunk. Rather, we want to point out a *few* important shortcomings in the pyramidal form of organization.

It also should be kept in mind that, despite its flaws, the pyramidal form of organization, and its attendant principles, have often served the needs of government well. As a former top administrator of NASA noted, the systematization of these principles resulted in a body of doctrine, which, for all its publicized faults, still provided the building blocks from which parts of a large-scale endeavor could be constructed. The rub, of course, comes when one tries to apply this traditional doctrine too rigorously in large complex undertakings so indicative of all levels of government today.

Division of Labor and Problems of Coordination.   Litterer (1973: 370–71) notes at least three drawbacks to the division of labor by function. First, a high degree of specialization may tend to make the occupants of these subunits more concerned with their specialty than with the organization's goals. Selznick (in March & Simon, 1958:40–44) refers to this phenomenon as the "internalization of subgoals." Second, because of their interest in their specialty, people may find it increasingly difficult to communicate with other organizational members. Coordination suffers, though its need has increased because of specialization. Third, "in many instances people who have risen through several levels of the organization within a functional specialty have advanced within a very unique professional environment and, consequently, may be poorly equipped eventually to assume overall organization responsibilities. Hence, a company may have a very difficult time in finding presidents and key vice presidents within its own ranks."

Sayles and Chandler (1971:15) offer a fourth criticism of specialization: It conflicts with the interdisciplinary efforts required—almost by definition—in large mission or problem-oriented programs.

> The biologist is asked to conceive of the impact of a hard vacuum on genetics and to work with aerospace engineers on joint endeavors. The project manager is asked to move for six months to a distant location to be closer to a critical development team and to shift both his organizational identity and his family's home every several years. Specialists are asked to give up their specialties in favor of joining multidisciplinary teams and to learn from those whom they would normally ignore or consider beneath their dignity.

Hitler's master builder, Albert Speer (1970), adds a fifth criticism of specialization—one that surely has some points of reference with Chapter 4. In his memoirs, Speer notes that the ordinary party member was taught that grand policy was much too complex for him to judge. Consequently, one was never called upon to take personal responsibility. Indeed, the whole structure of the system was aimed at preventing conflicts of conscience from even arising. The result was the total sterility of all conversations and discussions among these like-minded persons. Further, the Reich's leaders explicitly demanded that everyone restrict his or her responsibility to their own field. "Everyone kept to his own group—architects, physicians, jurists, technicians, soldiers, or farmers. The professional organizations to which everyone had to belong were called chambers (Physicians Chamber, Art Chamber), and this term aptly described the way people were immured in isolated, closed-off areas of life. The longer Hitler's system lasted, the more people's minds moved within such isolated chambers."

Hierarchy and Rigidity. "I used to be in the government service," Dostoevsky tells us in *Notes from the Underground.* "I was a spiteful official. I was rude and took pleasure in being so. I did not take bribes, you see, so I was bound to find recompense in that, at least. When petitioners used to come for information to the table at which I sat, I used to grind my teeth at them, and felt intense enjoyment when I succeeded in making anybody unhappy. I almost always did succeed. For the most part they were all timid people—of course, they were petitioners." How do we account for this perennial difficulty that clients seem to experience with bureaucracies? One of America's foremost sociologists, Robert K. Merton (in March & Simon, 1958), in a marvelous, though involved, analysis of bureaucracy traces it to, among other things, that fearful symmetry, hierarchy.

His analysis begins with a demand for control made by the top administrators: more specifically, they are concerned with increasing the reliability of behavior within the organization. The techniques used to secure reliability draw upon what we earlier called the "machine model." Standard operating procedures (SOP) are instituted and control consists largely in checking to ensure that these procedures are followed.

Three consequences follow. First, the amount of personalized relationships is reduced. Second, the participants internalize the rules of the organization; in fact, rules originally devised to achieve organizational goals assume a positive value *independent* of the goals. Third, the categories used in decision making become restricted to a relatively small number. For example, when a specific problem arises, the bureaucrat tends to say that this problem is essentially a certain type of problem. And since the type has been encountered before, one knows exactly how to handle it. Never mind nuances. In this way, an increase in the use of SOPs—i.e., standard operating procedures—decreases the search for alternatives.

These three consequences combine to make the behavior of members of the organization highly predictable. Which is a nice way of saying that the result is an increase in the *rigidity of behavior* of participants.

In addition to satisfying the original demand for reliability, one of the major consequences of rigid behavior is increased difficulty with clients of the organization and with achievement of client satisfaction. Yet client satisfaction is a near-universal organizational goal.

Let us continue our critique of hierarchy by turning to the subject of how decisions are made. Surely, the principle of hierarchy is unequivocal on how decisions are to be made: Authority and responsibility for decision making flow in a direct line—follow a chain of command—vertically from the highest appropriate level to the lowest. Needless to say, this procedure can be very time consuming in an organization with many levels of supervision. Moreover, analysis by Willard Zangwill (in Sayles & Chandler, 1971:174) of the large procurement decisions at NASA suggests that the principle is routinely violated in more advanced organizations. One of the organizational mechanisms that NASA uses is an ad hoc Source Evaluation Board composed of a small team of informed *middle-level* people. After an extensive assessment of the potential competency and efficiency of the

One instance of bureaucratic pathology is the tendency for individuals (often well-meaning) to lose sight of the underlying purpose of the job at hand. The purpose of a university library, for example, is to facilitate the reading of books. Yet, for some librarians, a good library is one with every book on the shelf. In James Jones's novel *From Here to Eternity*, American soldiers are under surprise attack by Japanese planes at Pearl Harbor. The hero, Sergeant Warden, rushes to the arsenal for weapons only to find the door barred by another sergeant loudly proclaiming (over the din of exploding Japanese bombs) that he cannot pass out live ammunition without a written request signed by an officer.

Ken Kesey's *One Flew over the Cuckoo's Nest* provides another illustration of how, in bureaucracies, means have a way of displacing the ends they are designed to serve. Although the mission of a mental hospital is to make the sick well, the Big Nurse (portrayed by Louise Fletcher) places so much emphasis on scheduled routines that she will not allow the patients to see the World Series. What makes this refusal so shocking is that the protagonist, Randolf Patrick McMurphy (portrayed by Jack Nicholson) has gotten the patients—some catatonic and incontinent—to organize and vote for the change in schedule. The Big Nurse announces that the vote—which is actually the beginning of a cure—does not count and retreats behind her glassed-in nurse's station. (I am indebted to Howard E. McCurdy for these examples.)

industrial firms competing for a given contract, the board presents its findings to a panel consisting of the *top-level* executives of the agency. The SEB process capitalizes upon an interesting division of labor between the top administrators and middle-level board members. The board members, having spent several months on the topic, are intimately knowledgeable about the specific procurement and understand in detail its cost, technical, and management aspects. Top-management people, on the other hand, have a broader view of the entire agency, of the strengths and weaknesses of corporate management, and of the political-economic climate. But where exactly the locus of the decision is no one can say with certainty.

Span of Control and the Deformation of Management.   The principle that a manager can only supervise a very small number of people can lead to what Peter Drucker (1973:412) has termed the "deformation of management." What really matters in determining the span of control is not how many people report to the manager but how many people *who have to work with each other* report to the manager. For example, the secretary of energy, who has reporting to him a number of top administrators, each concerned with a major function, should indeed keep the number of direct subordinates to a fairly low number—between 8 and 12 is probably the limit. Why? Because these subordinates must work closely with each other. Consider how the secretary attempts to exploit solar energy as a potential solution to the energy squeeze. Solar research is assigned to the Office of Research; solar technology to the Office of the Assistant Secretary for Technology; implementation to the Office of the Assistant Secretary for Conservation and Solar Applications; and the Solar Energy Institute conducts and funds activities in all facets of solar energy. Clearly, the heads of these units have to work closely and frequently with each other. Accordingly, a small span of control is called for since the problems of coordination are greater than, say, a police sergeant, who supervises several patrols. Each patrol is discrete and relatively autonomous, since there is usually little need for interaction between them; hence, a broader span of control is possible.

A second shortcoming of span of control should be apparent from Figure 2–2. The span of control concept assumes that a manager's main relationship is downward, but this direction, as we saw, is only part of the picture. The upward relationship to overhead authority is at least equal in importance to the downward relationship to the subordinates. Likewise, lateral relations with cognate agencies and interest groups are also important. What is needed, then, is to replace the concept of the span of control with a more relevant concept: the span of managerial relationships. The span of control, in short, is a terribly limited concept in public sector management.

Line Staff and the Tooth-to-Tail Ratio.   The line-staff concept, likewise, needs rethinking. To state the problem more sharply: What is one to do about the ever-increasing size of staff functions in comparison to line functions? How, in short, can an administrator improve the tooth-to-tail ratio?

Rather than seek solutions, let us first seek an explanation of why staff functions seem, inexorably, to grow. Probably the most famous, and certainly the most witty, explanation comes from C. Northcote Parkinson.

Professor Parkinson (1957) notes, accurately but with mock scholarship, that the number of ships and men in the British Navy decreased by 68 percent and 32 percent between 1914 and 1928. Meanwhile, the number of officials in the admiralty *increased* 78 percent. He also notes, for the same period, that the dockworkers increased only 10 percent, while the dockyard officials and clerks increased 40 percent. More recently, Parkinson detected the law at work in sunny California. The Transbay Bridge between San Francisco and Oakland originally had a staff of 12 to keep it repainted. Over the years, the staff grew to 77, even though in the meantime they acquired labor-saving machinery.

Parkinson attributes this kind of growth not to increased work but to the dynamics of staff operations. To begin with, officials tend to multiply subordinates. Thus, if a civil servant—call him A—thinks he is overworked, he will have B and C appointed under him. This act increases his importance and precludes any colleague from taking over some of his work. In time, Parkinson suggests, B will find himself overworked; when A allows him subordinates D and E, he must likewise allow C the same numbers; hence, F and G. (One might wonder why *two* subordinates are necessary in each case. One subordinate would result in a division of work with the original supervisor and, to that extent, the subordinate might assume almost equal status.)

Seven officials are now doing what one did before. How can this be? Parkinson offers another "proposition": Officials make work for each other. For example, an incoming document arrives or comes to D, who decides it really falls within the province of E. A draft reply is then prepared to E and placed before B, who amends it drastically before consulting C, who asks F to deal with it. But F goes on leave at this point, handing the file over to G, who drafts an amendment that is signed by C and returned to B, who revises his draft accordingly and lays the new version before A.

Now, what does A do? This person is beset by many problems created by the new subordinates (e.g., promotions, leaves, domestic problems, raises, transfers, and office affairs). Mr. A could, of course, simply sign it unread. Parkinson (1957:20) thinks not:

A is a conscientious man beset as he is with problems created by his colleagues for themselves and for him—created by the mere fact of these officials' existence—he is not the man to shirk his duty. He reads through the draft with care, deletes the fussy paragraphs by B and G, and restores things back to the form preferred in the first instance by the able (if quarrelsome) E. He corrects the English—none of these young men can write grammatically—and finally produces the same reply he would have written if officials B and G had never been born. Far more people have taken longer to produce the same result. No one has been idle. All have done their best. And it is late in the evening before A finally quits his office and begins the return journey home. The last of the office lights are being turned off in the gathering dusk that marks the end of another day's administrative toil. Among the last to leave, A reflects with bowed shoulders and a wry smile that late hours, like gray hairs, are among the penalties of success.

Before you dismiss Parkinson's little story as mere whimsy, let me suggest you read the memo on the next page* (Figure 8–3).

The Bennis Critique

The preceding discussion revealed some of the shortcomings of the pyramidal or bureaucratic form of organization—a form, we must reemphasize, quite characteristic of the public sector today. Yet our critique was limited to four principles, and this hardly does justice to the breadth of the problem. To appreciate better the range of criticisms consider the following sample (see Bennis, 1966):

- Bureaucracy does not adequately allow for personal growth and the development of mature personalities.
- Its systems of control and authority are hopelessly outdated.
- It does not possess adequate means for resolving differences and conflicts between the ranks, and most particularly, between functional groups.
- The full human resources of bureaucracy are not being utilized due to mistrust, fear of reprisals, and so on.
- It cannot assimilate the influx of new, complex technology.

But the major problem with bureaucracy in the last quarter of the 20th century is probably none of the above. Rather, suggests Warren Bennis, it is the lack of adaptability inherent in the pyramidal struc-

---

* In recent years, several American economists have attempted a more rigorous examination of why bureaucracy continues to grow and grow. These scholars start from the assumption that politicians and bureaucrats behave like consumers and business executives. This assumption allows them to apply conventional economic analysis to the behavior and decisions of actors in the public sector. This field of economics is, accordingly, called public choice.

Among the most famous contributors to the field are Anthony Downs (1967), William Niskanen (1971), and Gordon Tullock (1965; 1971). According to Downs, the central problem is that government bureaucracy is not subject to disciplines like those that operate in the private sector. In the public sector, there is little competition and consumer choice to constrain the self-interest of bureaucrats. Because growth is in the self-interest of the bureaucrat (among other things, growth improves chances for promotion), bureaucracies grow far in excess of what the public wants or efficiency justifies. Public bureaucracies, these economists argue, are like private sector monopolies—except that they seek bigger budgets rather than bigger profits.

Figure 8-3

```
UNITED STATES GOVERNMENT        DEPARTMENT OF HEALTH, EDUCATION, AND WELFARE
                                          REGION IV — ATLANTA
Memorandum


TO    : Title IX team (Unit II)           DATE: November 18, 1977

FROM  : Carroll D. Payne                  REFER TO:
        Coordinator, Title IX team

SUBJECT: Routing of completed drafts of Title IX reports and letters.


        The above drafts come to me first for review and I then give them to
        Mr. Gregory for typing. The typist returns them to Mr. Gregory for
        his record of typing completions. Mr. Gregory will return the typed
        copies to the originator to review for typing corrections and/or
        sign off. The originator, after corrections and sign off, will route
        the typed report or letter to me for sign off and routing to Mr. Clements.
        Copies of mailed letters come back through Mr. Gregory for recording.
```

Source: *The Washington Monthly,* January, 1978.

ture of authority. While this form of organization may have been suitable for the undifferentiated and stable environment of the Industrial Revolution (when Weber wrote), its value in a rapidly changing, social, economic, and technological environment becomes highly questionable.

Why have we dealt a such length with pyramidal (or bureaucratic) organization? Simply because it is most representative of the way in which government at all levels is organized today. Now we must return to Skibbins's classification of organizations.

Conglomerate Organization

To conglomerate anything means to bring together, to work into a ball various disparate materials. However, Skibbins (1974:68) argues that in conglomerate corporations it is more likely that the organizations being clustered together are, as a rule, all pyramids. Authority over the entire structure is marked by a core management that prevails roughly over the authority structures of the pyramids, and "thus gradually erodes their spirit and drive."

Interestingly, in addition to the well-known commercial conglomerates of today (e.g., ITT, LTV, and Litton), Skibbins includes here the Pentagon. An unorthodox view but probably correct. In 1949, the army, navy, and air force—all pyramids, to be sure—were put under a single executive department, the present Department of Defense

(DOD). The Defense Reorganization Act of 1958 entrusted still greater authority to the secretary. Specifically, it gave him power to transfer, abolish, or reassign defense functions and to assign new weapons systems among the various services and a new director of Defense Research and Engineering. Beginning with Robert McNamara in 1961, centralization of control under the secretary of defense has proceeded energetically. (For a closer look at the organizational structure of DOD, see Case 8.2.)

In a sense, this idea is only a variation of an old theme, namely, *delegation of authority*. In other words, to the extent that authority is not delegated, it is centralized. Absolute centralization in one person is conceivable only in the leader/follower cluster discussed earlier; consequently, for most government organizations, we can safely say that some decentralization is inevitable. On the other hand, if *all* authority were delegated, the position of manager would cease to exist. Indeed, we could hardly say an organization still existed. As Ulysses put it in *Troilus and Cressida*:

> Oh, when rank is shaked
> Which is the ladder to all high designs,
> The enterprise is sick! How could communities,
> Degrees in schools and brotherhoods in cities,
> Peaceful commerce from divided shores . . .
> Privilege of age, crowns, sceptors, laurels
> But by rank, stand in authentic place?
> Take but rank away, untune that string,
> And hark, what discord follows! Each
>   thing meets
> In utter conflict.

Fortunately, centralization and decentralization (or delegation), like "hot" and "cold," are tendencies—not absolutes. But our concern is not, strictly speaking, with the general concept of decentralization but rather the idea of federal decentralization; that is, an organization based on decentralized operating authority *and* centralized policy control. Though quite characteristic of today's conglomerate-type organization, federal decentralization was first worked out by Pierre S. Du Pont in 1920 in the reorganization of the family-owned Du Pont Company. Shortly thereafter, General Motors, under the direction of Alfred P. Sloan, put into effect a far more polished version, which became the prototype of decentralization.

Drucker (1973: chapter 46) holds that this organizational philosophy has several important advantages.

> Both operating and innovative work can be done by decentralized units of the organization. Meanwhile, top management is free for top management tasks—especially policy control. In Drucker's

words: "There must be a kind of supremacy clause reserving to central management the decisions that affect the business as a whole and its long-range future welfare, and allowing central management to override in the common interest, local ambitions and pride."

It is easy for the autonomous subunits to understand their own missions as well as the missions of the total organization.

It focuses the vision and efforts of managers on performance and results; thus, it encourages manager development.

Organic Organization

"It is provocative to learn that of all systems man can distinguish around him, the most advanced and complex are of a biological nature. Nature is far ahead of our comprehension in its ability to construct systems" (Skibbins, 1974:69). With this mildly startling observation, we begin consideration of the fifth type of organization.

What characteristics of an organism could possibly be relevant to human organization? Consider these connections:

A loose network but a unified whole. As a result, individual parts tend to flower in this lively, growing environment that considers some of their needs.

Relative freedom of communication flow in many directions, especially from the environment that nurtures it.

Death. In contrast, the pyramidal form of organization seems to lack the biological notion of death. The consequences of this lack are seen most clearly in what, one hopes, is an extreme case. The Italian bureaucracy, as late as 1973, contained agencies to grant loans to persons who suffered damages in the 1906 eruption of Mount Vesuvius; to take care of war orphans, although the youngest of them must now be 28 years old; and to administer pensions for veterans of the Battle of Adewa, Ethiopia, in 1896.

If the analogy between organisms and organization seems somewhat fanciful, perhaps as if taken out of *Lord of the Rings*, then consider the analogy upon which most of today's organizations are based, the machine. While the machine analogy is perhaps most visible in the writing of Taylor and the scientific management school, it still remains the bedrock assumption upon which the pyramidal organization rests. Waldo (1948:173–74) described this view well: "People and organization parts are regarded more or less as though they were the interchangeable parts of modern machinery."

Some advocates of the organic model of organization go much further than simply rejecting this machine model. They argue that the ultimate model for organizations should be human beings rather than just any organism. But why? The crucial component that humans possess is their minds. But the concept of mind implies much: perfectibility, changeability, analysis, learning, and goal seeking. Writes Skibbins (1974:71; see also Deutsch, 1963): "An organization built with the idea of man as its model would possess a many-sensed awareness of the realities of existence and of life which more rigid forms could never achieve. In such an organization we could blend human minds with an organization consciousness and work together to achieve goals hitherto thought impossible. Within such a symbiotic relationship, NASA took us to the moon. Tomorrow, such organization will take us to the stars as well." Table 8–1 summarizes some of the key differences between mechanistic and organic organizations.

To conclude this survey of organizational evolution—which stretched from primitive leader/follower clusters to futuristic self-directing models reaching for the stars—two points are in order. First, the survey should make the manager more sensitive to the rich variety of organizations as well as the capabilities and limitations of each form. Second, it should provide us with some basis for deciding where our inquiry into organization structure should go next. Based on the foregoing survey, it appears that the organizational forms calling the loudest for more detailed study are the pyramidal—because it is most characteristic of government today—and the organic (human) type—because it is, apparently, the most attractive alternative to the former.

Table 8–1

Characteristics of Mechanistic and Organic Organizations

Mechanistic		Organic
High; many and sharp differentiations	SPECIALIZATION	Low; no hard boundaries, relatively few different jobs
High; methods spelled out	STANDARDIZATION	Low; individuals decide own methods
Means	ORIENTATION OF MEMBERS	Goals
By superior	CONFLICT RESOLUTION	Interaction
Hierarchical based on implied contractual relation	PATTERN OF AUTHORITY CONTROL AND COMMUNICATION	Wide net based upon common commitment
At top of organization	LOCUS OF SUPERIOR COMPETENCE	Wherever there is skill and competence
Vertical	INTERACTION	Lateral
Directions, orders	COMMUNICATION CONTENT	Advice, information
To organization	LOYALTY	To project and group
From organizational position	PRESTIGE	From personal contribution

Source: Litterer (1973:339).

Organizations of the Future: Three Forerunners

Organizations, like people, are hard to classify. Nevertheless, I have tried to catalogue below some of the organizational types that seem to be emerging and that are consistent with the broad characteristics of the organic organization.

The Systems Structure

The systems concept is much more widely discussed than understood. For purposes of this discussion, a *system* remains what it was in Chapter 7, namely, an assemblage of interrelated parts (components) forming a complex whole. Increasingly, that definition applies to modern organizations.

The systems structure is, therefore, the opposite of the bureaucratic one. The latter has neatly defined areas of specialization, and communication occurs through the hierarchy. In contrast, the systems structure presumes that interaction at all levels supports the total system. The systems structure deemphasizes the parochial goals of the subunits but emphasizes total system performance. In much the same way, all the cells and organs in a healthy human body sacrifice their own needs to ensure the survival of the entire system.

The Systems Development Corporation, the Strategic Air Command, and Lockheed have used this concept to redesign major phases of organization. But probably no organization has pushed the systems approach further than NASA. For, in essence, NASA has built a team out of a wide variety of different units (contractors, subcontractors, universities, research laboratories, government offices, and so on) and ensured that all these components work toward a common goal. NASA itself serves as a kind of mind or consciousness for the entire operation, attempting to integrate the functional units in a way that contributes to overall goals. NASA continually demanded systemwide performance and "used a large battery of techniques to attain it—data banks, [accounting systems], endless performance review meetings, and so on. It gave constant attention to the integration of widely separated efforts. It also nurtured an in-house capability that enabled it to know more about the total effort than any of the contracting parties" (Sayles & Chandler, 1971:319).

But the systems structure is not without problems. It requires a truly astonishing amount of communication. Key NASA executives, for example, spend something like two thirds of their time in meetings, often dealing with matters only remotely related to their own tasks. It requires that each management unit take responsibility far beyond its own assignment. It requires exceptionally clear objectives (e.g., land a man on the moon)—and this is just the rock that can sink a systems structure as it sallies forth to confront the less technical problems of society. The reason is that solving problems such as pollution, health, and urban development must occur in a highly politicized environment and with far less consensus on objectives.

In any event, the record still remains clear on at least one point. NASA's system structure proves unequivocally that large, complex systems, both human and technical, can be managed.

Task Force

Not long ago U.S. Customs Service agents seized a fishing boat returning to Miami from the Bahamas. The "fishermen" seemed unusual: one wore a Pierre Cardin pullover and the other a Sassoon jacket. Under a concealed floor the agents found 1,000 pounds of marijuana. The agents were part of the South Florida Task Force—a group that had all the characteristics of a second type of organization that seems increasingly common in government.

What are its characteristics? It is formed on an ad hoc or project basis. (As Bennis would say, it is "temporary.") It is problem oriented. It is interdisciplinary. It is a team. Thus the South Florida Task Force was made up of elements from not only the Customs Service (drawn

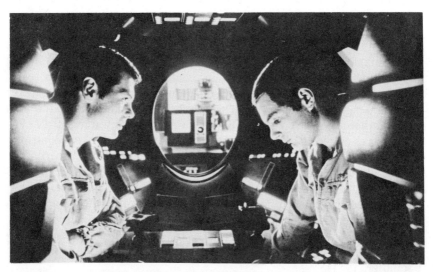

The organic model of organization is based on principles fundamentally different than the pyramid model. In Arthur C. Clarke's *2001*, which Stanley Kubrick made into a film, the two astronauts alternated command of the spaceship—clearly violating the principle of hierarchy. Today, fast-growing, high-technology companies are also violating it. Their central management concern is how to stay flexible and nimble in a rapidly changing environment and how to avoid sluggishness as they grow. Intel Corporation has a three-person executive office. One chief executive spends nearly half his time on outside matters (e.g., speaking to the financial and scientific community and government policymakers). A second chief executive does the long-range thinking, and the third runs the company on a day-to-day basis. (From the MGM release, *2001: A Space Odyssey*, © 1968 Metro-Goldwyn-Mayer Inc.)

from cities across the country) but also the army, navy, air force, coast guard, FBI, and Drug Enforcement Agency.

When should an administrator turn to the task force device? While there are no simple rules of thumb, here are three guidelines (Stewart, 1969: 291–302):

First, it might be useful when faced with a one-time undertaking that is (a) definable in terms of a single, specific end result, and (b) requires more people, dollars, and organizational units than any other infrequent undertaking in the organizations experience. In short, (b) says that the undertaking would overwhelm any single office or division.

Second, the problem being undertaken is unfamiliar and complex. Thus many new mayors and most recent presidents call upon task forces, rather than the existing bureaucracy, early in their administrations to generate policy initiatives.

Third, the unit of government must decide it has a stake in the outcome of the undertaking. In other words, would failure to resolve the problem—through, say, "benign neglect"—entail serious penalties for the unit?

Having opted for the task force device the administrator should be aware of the special sources of trouble associated with this organizational form. Many task force leaders find that their working relationships with other agency heads have not been clearly defined by the top-level political executives. Though political executives can seldom give the leader as much guidance and support as he or she might wish, they can easily jeopardize the task force's success by lack of awareness, ill-advised intervention, or personal whim. Further, there are innumerable possibilities for interagency conflict. Finally, the severe penalties of delay in resolving the problem often compel the task force leaders to base their decisions on relatively few data, analyzed in haste.

These problems, however, are hardly insurmountable. Moreover, as long as administrators must face unfamiliar and complex problems, it seems safe to say that the task force form of organization will be a part of public administration for some time to come.

Matrix Organization

A kind of compromise between the task force and the pyramidal form of organization is the matrix organization. It gets its name from the fact that a number of project (team) managers exert planning, scheduling, and cost control over people who have been assigned to their projects, while other managers exert more traditional line control (e.g., technical direction, training, and compensation) over the same people. Thus, two administrators share responsibility for the subordinate. The subordinate, in turn, must please two supervisors.

A simple matrix arrangement is shown in Figure 8-4. The program manager is essentially a "contractor" who "hires" personnel from the

Figure 8-4
Matrix Organization

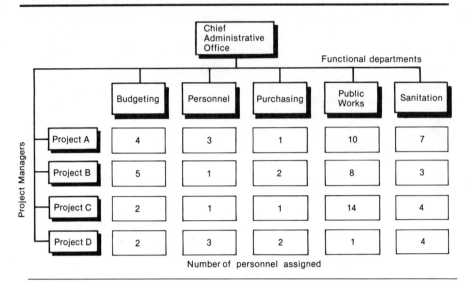

	Budgeting	Personnel	Purchasing	Public Works	Sanitation
Project A	4	3	1	10	7
Project B	5	1	2	8	3
Project C	2	1	1	14	4
Project D	2	3	2	1	4

Chief Administrative Office

Functional departments

Project Managers

Number of personnel assigned

line organization. The project manager is assigned the number of personnel with the essential qualifications from the functional departments for the duration of the project.

Again, the question arises, when should this particular form of organization be used? Let us approach the answer from the opposite direction. A matrix organization should *not* be used when the work performed by an agency is applied to standardized services with high volumes (e.g., waste disposal). But it can be used effectively when the work performed is for specific, narrowly defined projects (e.g., antitrust cases). As specific projects end, they can be deleted from the organization, for the matrix organization is a fluid organization. A general rule then would be this: When an organization has a large number of specialists—and coordination is therefore difficult—the matrix organization might be a solution.

But project groups have their problems. They tend, for example, to narrow the training experience of personnel. Technical personnel, who are often shifted back and forth among projects, can feel isolated and rootless. Finally, with personnel constantly shifting from one project to another, an organization can find it difficult to build up a source of accumulated wisdom, such as is possible in functional departments.

Thomas J. Peters and Robert H. Waterman, Jr., in their influential *In Search of Excellence*, report that none of the companies they identified as excellent spoke of having formal matrix structures, except for project management companies like Boeing.

But in a company like Boeing, where many of the matrix ideas originated, something very different is meant by matrix management. People operate in a binary way: they are either a part of a project team and responsible to that team for getting some task accomplished (almost all the time), or they are part of a technical discipline, in which they spend some time making sure their technical department is keeping up with the state of the art. When they are on a project, there is no day-in, day-out confusion about whether they are really responsible to the project or not. They are. (1982:307)

The key to making organizations like Boeing and NASA work, Peters and Waterman say, is to make sure that one dimension (e.g. geography or function) has "crystal-clear primacy."

The answer is . . . simplicity of form. Underpinning most of the excellent companies we find a fairly stable, unchanging form—perhaps the product division—that provides the essential touchstone which everybody understands, and from which the complexities of day-to-day life can be approached. Clarity on values is also an important part of the underlying touchstone of stability and simplicity as well.

Beyond the simplicity around one underlying form, we find the excellent companies quite flexible in responding to fast-changing conditions in the environment. . . . Because of their typically unifying organization theme, they can make better use of small divisions or other small units. They can reorganize more flexibly, frequently, and fluidly. (1982:308)

The Process of Organizational Design

The Organization Chart: A Few Cautionary Remarks

Despite the importance of organizational design, most administrators approach it rather informally—indeed, one might almost say the approach amounts to little more than drawing boxes on a page. Eventually, a new organization chart appears, which the administrator can more or less defend.

Organization charts are by no means useless in designing and understanding organizations. The organization chart of most agencies shows—indeed is designed to show—at least two things: the division of work into components, and who is (supposed to be) whose supervisor. Moreover, it implicitly shows several others things: the nature of the work performed by each component; the grouping of components on a functional, regional, or service basis; and the levels of management in terms of successive layers of superiors and subordinates.

Nevertheless, what the chart does not show is often the most interesting part—at least to someone interested in organization design (Stieglitz, 1969:372–76). In the first place, the chart by itself cannot tell us much about the degree of responsibility and authority exercised by positions on the same management level. Two persons on the same management level may have vastly different degrees of authority. In a word, the chart cannot show the degree of decentralization.

Second, attempting to determine line and staff positions from an organization chart is an arduous academic chore. In some agencies, charting methods are used to attempt to make this distinction. For example, the so-called staff units are charted on one horizontal plane, line units on another. Other agencies use skinny lines to connect staff but robust ones to connect line units. To try to interpret these differences in terms of line-staff responsibilities, authorities, and relationships is as difficult as reading the degree of decentralization from the chart.

Third, some people view the linear distance from the chief executive officer as a measure of status or importance. But this interpretation may or may not be correct. It has the same limitations as trying to infer relative importance from size of office, files, parking lot space, and so forth.

Fourth, while the chart shows some major lines of communication, it does not show all. It is axiomatic that every organization is an intricate network of communication; if it were not, then nothing would get done.

Closely related to the preceding limitations to the organization chart is a fifth one. The chart fails to show the *informal organization*, that is, "those aspects of the structure which, while not prescribed by formal authority, supplement or modify the formal structure" (Gross, 1968:238). The formal organization, therefore, encompasses all the relationships and channels of communication that people are expected to develop and use in order to meet organizational and often, personal objectives. "It is informal," writes Harold Stieglitz (1969:375–76), "only in the sense that nobody has found it necessary to inundate the organization with memorabilia that fully spell out its workings."

In sum, we would do well to heed former Secretary of State Acheson's (1959) advice that "organization or reorganization in government can often be a trap for the unwary. The relationships involved in the division of labor and responsibility are far more subtle and complex than the little boxes which the graph drawers put on paper with their perpendicular and horizontal connecting lines." In an effort to follow Acheson, and avoid the organization chart pitfall, a process for thinking through a new organizational structure will be given in skeletal form. This process should facilitate the complex task of separating those things that must be taken into account so far as structure is concerned from those that have less bearing on organizational performance.

Three Critical Steps

In designing an organization, Peter Drucker (1973: chapters 42–44) suggests that we consider at least three questions: (1) What should the units be? (2) What units should join together, and what units should be kept apart? (3) Where do decisions belong? (The discussion that follows builds around these questions and draws largely on Drucker, 1973: chapters 42–44.)

The analysis suggested by each question should always be kept as simple and brief as possible. In a small agency or office, it can often be done in a matter of hours and on a few pieces of paper. But in a very large and complex enterprise (e.g., Department of Transportation and the executive branch of the state of New Jersey), the job may well require months of study.

In either case, organization design begins not with a consideration of the principles of organization but with a review of the organization's goals. In fact, one could even define organization as the ideal concrete reflection of an agency's goals. A review of goals enables us to begin to determine what are the *key activities*. That is, in what area is excellence required to attain the agency's goals? Conversely, in what areas would lack of performance endanger the results, if not the survival, of the enterprise? Finally, what are the values that are truly important to us?

What Should the Units Be?   This line of inquiry puts us in a better position to answer the question, What should the units be? Clearly, key activities require organizational representation.

Roughly, *all* activities in an organization fall into one of four categories. First, are *top-management activities*. These, according to Drucker, include maintaining external relations, thinking through the mission of the agency, making decisions during major crises, and

Born in Vienna in 1909, Peter F. Drucker was educated as a lawyer. Today, he is probably the world's best-known management consultant. According to Drucker, organizational design must follow organizational purpose. In other words, we cannot properly design an organization until we are clear on its goals. (Irwin Gooden)

building the human organization. Second, are *results-producing activities*. These contribute most directly to the performance of the entire enterprise. While results-producing activities are not hard to discover in the private sector (just look for those directly producing revenue), they are less obvious in the public sector. (Turn ahead to Table 12–1), which offers some examples of the output of these activities for local governments.) Third are *results-contributing* or *staff activities*, for example, advising, teaching, legal research, and training. Fourth are the *hygiene and housekeeping activities*, which range from the medical department to the people who clean the floor.

What Should Their Relationship Be? Why go through this exercise in classification? The answer Drucker (1973:534–35) gives is that "Activities that differ in contribution have to be treated differently. Contribution determines ranking and placement." By suggesting a few tentative propositions, perhaps we can begin to see how this classification can help us better answer the question, what units should join together?

1. Results-producing activities should never be subordinate to nonresults-producing activities.
2. Support activities should never be mixed up with results-producing activities. Halberstam reports, for example, that General Harkins, when commander of Military Assistance in Vietnam, kept his intelligence-gathering activity in the same shop as his operations. Not surprisingly, intelligence reports were edited down by the operations people; rather than reflect what was happening in the field, Harkins's shop reflected Washington's hopes. The split of the Atomic Energy Commission into the Energy Research and Development Administration (ERDA) and the Nuclear Regulatory Commission might be viewed, on the other hand, as an effort to follow this proposition. Until this split, the AEC, in effect, combined rather closely a result-producing activity (the development of nuclear energy) with a support activity (the monitoring of safety standards). Today, ERDA activities are part of the Energy department.
3. Top-management activities are incompatible with other activities. The emergence in recent decades of a "presidential establishment" provides, I think, proof. Robert C. Wood (quoted in Otten, 1973), former secretary of housing and urban development for Lyndon Johnson and now political scientist at Massachusetts Institute of Technology, argues that a huge White House staff increasingly became involved in day-to-day decisions, spending less and less time on broad, long-range policy issues (the latter activity is of course what we have termed *top-management activity*). Observes Wood: "Confusion is created

when men try to do too much at the top . . . a curious inversion occurs. Operational matters flow to the top, as central staffs become engrossed in subduing outlaying bureaucracies, and policymaking emerges at the bottom."

4. Advisory staffs should be few, lean, and nonoperational. Further, advisory work should not be a career; that is, it is work to which a manager or career professional should be exposed in the course of his growth but not work that a person should do for long.

5. Hygiene and housekeeping activities should be kept separate from other work or else they will not get done. In a hospital where these activities are technically under the upper levels of management, they tend to be neglected. No "respectable" manager in a hospital wants to have anything to do with them. As a result, they are left unmanaged; and this means they are done badly and expensively. But what can be done? One solution is to farm out these activities to somebody whose business is to provide these hotel services. The federal government's General Services Administration is an excellent example of this proposition's application. Drucker (1973:540) again: "For the senior soil scientist in the Department of Agriculture, managing the automotive fleet for his unit is a chore for which he has neither interest nor respect. Yet there obviously is a good deal of money at stake. . . . For the General Services Administration the administration of the government automotive fleet is its business and can be organized as such."

Where Do Decisions Belong? If we can successfully answer this question, we achieve two things. We gain a better idea of where the structural units (discussed above) belong, and we reduce the risk that, in the new organization, decision will have to go looking for a home.

The crux of the issue is *delegation of authority*; that is, the determination of the proper level at which a decision should be made. Are any guidelines available? Robert Townsend, a business-executive-turned-writer, gives a forceful (but grossly oversimplified) one: "All decisions should be made as low as possible. The charge of the Light Brigade was ordered by an officer who wasn't there looking at the territory." We shall proceed to essentially the same conclusion, only more circumspectly.

To begin, it seems safe to say that the level of a decision will depend on the nature of the decision. Specifically, the more a decision is characterized by these three factors, the higher the level at which it must be made:

Futurity; that is, how long into the future the decision commits the organization.

Impact; that is, how many other functions in an organization it affects.

Rarity; that is, how distinct the event is.

Now, with some appreciation of the factors that *limit* how low in an organization a decision can be made, we might rephrase Townsend's position as follows: (1) a decision should be made as close to the scene of action as possible, yet (2) high enough to insure that all activities affected are fully considered. "The first rule tells us how far down it *can* be made. The second how far down it can be made, as well as which managers must share in the decision and which must be informed. The two together tell us where certain activities should be placed. Managers should be high enough to have the authority needed to make the typical decisions pertaining to their work, and low enough to have detailed knowledge and the first-hand experience" (Drucker, 1973:345).

This rule explains why—contrary to traditional organization theory—functions are not bundles of related skills. If we followed the logic, we would probably, as the Office of Economic Opportunity once did, put the evaluation function into the Office of Research, Plans, Programs, and Evaluation, because it already had responsibility for analysis related to program planning. But the Urban Institute (Wholey et al., 1973) found in a 1968 study that, when evaluation is formally assigned to a "planning and evaluation" unit that has many program-planning and development responsibilities, "evaluation is never done or is done very poorly" (Wholey et al., 1973:69). Accordingly, the institute recommended that the evaluation function be based on differences in the types of decisions made at different levels of an organization.

Design Criteria

Upon completion of the design process one should then reexamine the final product in terms of three standards: clarity, simplicity, and adaptability.

Clarity. "The failure to clarify relationships probably more than any other mistake, accounts for friction, politics, and inefficiencies" (Koontz & O'Donnell, 1974:221). In other words, the members of an organization need a clear understanding of the authority and the responsibility for action; people in an organization need to understand their assignments as well as those of their co-workers.

But how does the administrator achieve this? One widely used vehicle is, of course, the organization chart. Despite the limitations noted earlier, the chart can, by mapping lines of decision-making authority, *sometimes* show inconsistencies and complexities and, thereby, lead to their correction. On the other hand, the administrator who believes that team spirit can be engendered by not clearly spelling out relationships is opening a Pandora's box of organizational ills: politics, intrigue, frustration, lack of coordination, duplication of effort, vague policy, and uncertain decision making. A second vehicle, to be discussed in greater detail in Chapter 13, is the position description. "A good managerial position informs the incumbent and others about what he is supposed to do and helps determine what authority must be delegated in order to carry out the job" (Koontz & O'Donnell, 1974:228–29).

Simplicity. "Simplify, simplify, simplify." This might well be the plaint of a modern administrator, as it was of the author of *Walden*. Most overorganization results from failure to realize that an organization is merely a framework for the efficient performance of people.

Narrow spans of control and numerous levels of supervision are two signs that this criterion is probably being ignored. They were not being ignored, however, by Truman when he vetoed an early proposal by scientists for a National Science Foundation. He took particular exception to the provisions insulating the director from the president by two layers of part-time boards and warned that "if the principles of this bill were extended throughout the government, the result would be utter chaos" (quoted in Seidman, 1980:22).

Other signs of overorganization include excessive procedures ("red tape"), too many committees and meetings, and unnecessary line assistants. The last-named item comes in for especially harsh criticism by Townsend, who once remarked that the only people who thoroughly enjoy being assistants-to are vampires. "The assistant-to recommends itself to the weak or lazy manager as a crutch. It helps him where he shouldn't and can't be helped—head-to-head contact with his people" (Townsend, 1970:23). No mercy for the executive assistant to the principal deputy assistant secretary of defense of program analysis!

Adaptability.   As noted toward the end of the previous chapter, one of the most obvious traits of postbureaucratic organizations is greater flexibility, greater adaptability. "Internal redesign," reports Alvin Toffler (1970:117–18) "has become a byword in Washington. When John Gardner became secretary of HEW, a top-to-bottom reorganization shook that department. Agencies, bureaus, and offices were realigned at a rate that left veteran employees in a state of mental exhaustion. During the height of this reshuffling, one official . . . used to leave a note behind for her husband each morning she left for work. The note consisted of her telephone number for that *day*. So rapid were the changes that she could not keep a telephone number long enough for it to be listed in the departmental directory."

Let us now turn from the technical issues of organizational design to the political issues the process involves. As a kind of bridge between the two issues, I would like to pose the question, Can reorganization be carried too far? The answer is, I think, yes. And a word has even been coined for this chronic affliction—*organizitis*. The following section attempts to put the phenomenon in perspective.

The Politics of Reorganization

Rationale

Some (not all) attempts at reorganization are in reality efforts to escape rethinking the principles of sound management outlined above. At the first sign of trouble, the cry goes out for reorganization. As might be expected, the times when this kind of surgery is needed are limited.

Perhaps the most obvious occasion for reorganization is growth. Thompson (cited in Litterer, 1973:656–57) colorfully illustrates this by pointing out that, if the giant in *Jack the Giant Killer* were to exist many times larger than normal man, he could not have the same form as man. In other words, if the giant were to have the same proportions as normal man but were a hundred times larger in size, his bone structure would be entirely inadequate. Biological design must conform to the square-cube law that says: If a giant were a thousand times the size of man, his volume would increase ($10 \times 10 \times 10$) and so roughly would his weight. But his area would increase only 10×10; hence, the cross-sectional area of his bones would increase at a far lower rate than the weight that they had to support. So, when the giant attempts to stand, his legbone breaks. In short, the *form* of man is inadequate for a larger being. The square-cube law explains why larger beings walk on four legs like the elephant or float in the ocean like the whale. And the law seems to hold for organizations: Larger organizations require different forms than the smaller ones.

Frederich C. Mosher (1967:494–97) notes five additional conditions that warrant reorganization: (1) changes in social needs that must be mirrored in organizational structure and responsibility; (2) a changing philosophy on the role of government in policy development and group regulation; (3) new management techniques, equipment, and technology that would modernize an agency's work processes; (4) increasing qualifications of personnel for policy analysis and administrative oversight, which can trigger administrative reorganization to utilize the rising talent of such individuals; and (5) the obsolescence of low-ranking organizations in the light of fundamental policy changes instigated within upper hierarchical echelons.

Realities

Assuming then that there are only select instances in which reorganization is called for, what can we say about its effectiveness; that is, does it increase economy and efficiency? At the national level, at least, its track record is poor: Of the 86 reorganization plans transmitted to the Congress between 1949 and 1969, only three were supported by precise dollar estimates of savings. No evidence exists that reorganization has ever had much effect on economy and efficiency (see also Seidman, 1980; Meier, 1980).

These observations lead us to a second perspective by which to view reorganization process. No reorganization can be politically neutral. In one way or another, it must reflect certain political values and interests. The following examples, I think, support this position.

Reorganization can be used to exclude billions in expenditures from the budget and centralize the chief executive's control over the executive branch. In 1971, President Nixon proposed to Congress legislation that would reorganize the domestic executive departments and a number of independent agencies into four new major purpose departments—Human Resources, Natural Resources, Community Development, and Economic Affairs. As it turned out, his effort was unsuccessful. But should this abortive effort be viewed purely in terms of economy and efficiency? From a political perspective, it would appear that it was, as well, an attempt to abolish many of the programs and agencies that had become symbols of President Johnson's Great Society.

Reorganization can also provide a means for dumping an unwanted official. This purpose certainly seems behind Secretary Rusk's plan to abolish the State Department's Bureau of Security and Consular Affairs, a brainchild of Senator Joseph McCarthy. This ploy, which was not successful, would have allowed Secretary Rusk to shift the director to another post.

Reorganization can be used to bypass troublesome committee or subcommittee chairmen. The transfer in 1961 of civil defense activities from the Office of Civil and Defense Mobilization to the secretary of defense was expected to remove the shelter program from the jurisdiction of an unfriendly appropriations subcommittee chairman.

Reorganization may be necessary to save a program with little political support. "The frequent reorganization and renaming of the foreign aid agency," writes Seidman (1980:26), "reflect efforts to bolster congressional support . . . rather than to . . . improve management."

And let us not forget the forcefield of politics (see Figure 2–2) that showed, among other things, that each agency had external clients. These clients can provide an agency threatened with reorganization support, especially when the clients perceive that the reorganization is not in their best interest. Quite clearly, teachers and their unions perceived President Carter's creation of a new Department of Education as increasing their access to and influence on the president.

These examples provide yet another example of the intrusion of politics into administration—an intrusion that makes public administration among the most exciting and difficult of professions. But politics is not the only challenge for administrators seeking to cope with the problems of a community. As we are about to see, there is still the need to manage well human and fiscal resources within the organization.

Nailing Down the Main Points

1. Organization follows policy. In other words, not until we have decided where we want to go, can we know the part people are to play in the total endeavor and how their roles relate to each other.

2. Roughly speaking, people have organized themselves throughout history in one of five ways: leader/follower cluster, mosaic, pyramid, conglomerate, and organic. The pyramid especially concerns us, since so many public organizations follow this pattern.

3. Closely related to the pyramidal organization is the concept of bureaucracy, which Max Weber defined in these terms *(a)* a division of labor based on functional specialization, *(b)* a well-defined hierarchy of authority, *(c)* a system of rules, *(d)* a system of procedures, *(e)* impersonality of interpersonal relations, and *(f)* promotion and selection based on technical competence.

4. Also closely associated with the pyramidal organization is the administrative management movement, which sought to discover the "principles" of organization. Among these principles were: *(a)* division of labor, *(b)* hierarchy, *(c)* span of control, and *(d)* line and staff. In certain situations, these principles can be destructive to an organization's mission.

5. Quite unlike the mechanistic pyramidal model of organization is the organic model—less rigid (hence, more flexible), more democratic, less authoritative, more project oriented, and more adaptive.

6. To not a few observers, the organic organization, because it adapts so well to a rapidly changing environment, might be termed the organization of the future. In fact, at least three forerunners are already visible: the systems structure, task force, and matrix organization.

7. Intelligent organizational design requires more than moving boxes around on an organizational chart; it demands careful attention to four related questions: *(a)* What should the units be? *(b)* What units should join together, and what units should be kept apart? *(c)* What is the appropriate placement and relationship of different units? *(d)* Where do decisions belong?

8. Upon completion of the three-step design process, the results can be reexamined in terms of three standards, which form a kind of design criteria: clarity, simplicity, and adaptability (or flexibility).

9. Reorganization is radical surgery and should be undertaken only when truly warranted. No reorganization can be politically neutral.

Concepts for Review

bureaucracy

design criteria

division of labor, departmentation

five types of organization

functional authority

key activities

legal, traditional, and charismatic authority

limitations to the organizational chart

line and staff

matrix organization

organizational design

organizing

the process of organizational design

scalar principle, hierarchy

span of control

systems structure

task force

Problems

1. Two traditional bases for organizing work are by functional units or by product/service units. Which of the following units are examples of the former and which are examples of the latter?

   Criminal justice systems   Space shuttle development
   Pathology lab   Surgical patient care
   Telecommunications   Operations research
   Stagehands   Probation department
   MPA degree program   Opera production

2. What are the advantages and disadvantages of using charts to illustrate organization structure?

3. It has been alleged that one of the reasons that the sophistication of organization in government lags behind that of business is due to the lack of competition. Do you agree? If you agree, how might a small dose of competition be introduced?

4. Do you think the presidency is overloaded? Discuss in terms of span of control. What modifications might be made?

5. How might the following institutions look if they were restructured along the lines of the futuristic organizations discussed at the end of the chapter: garbage collection service, library, drug treatment clinic, state highway patrol, and university?

6. To make the staff work better, it is suggested that the manager "make" the line listen to the staff and keep the staff informed. The staff, in turn, should strive to make sure its recommendations are as clear and complete as possible. What are some specific ways in which these abstract goals might be realized?

7. How can the line-staff concept be viewed as a compromise between hierarchy and division of labor?

8. "In the modern world," wrote Bertrand Russell in *Authority and the Individual*, "and still more, so far as can be guessed, in the world of the near future, important achievement is and will be almost impossible to an individual if he cannot dominate some vast organization." Do you agree or disagree? Why?

9. Analyze some recent decision by a public executive in terms of the three traits of a decision that determine where it should be made (i.e., futurity, impact, and rarity). Was it made in the right place?

10. Some management theorists say build the organization around people. Quite clearly, this approach was not taken in Chapter 8. What weaknesses do you see in their approach? What do the most successful football coaches do?

11. Apply the design criteria (clarity, simplicity, and adaptability) to some organization with which you are familiar.

12. Develop some general guidelines for the reorganization of an agency: How would you deal with outside interest groups? What sequence of steps should be followed in implementing the change? How would you minimize personal disruption?

13. Answer the three questions below for a university, a prison, a welfare office, and a church:
    a. Where is excellence required to attain the agency's goals?
    b. In what areas would lack of performance endanger the results?
    c. What are the values that are truly important to us?
    Remember, you will need first to establish goals for each. Do you think you have made the key activities the central, load-carrying elements in your organizational structure? Have the organization's values been organizationally anchored?

14. What do you think the drawbacks are to allowing advisory (staff) work to be a career?

15. Given a choice should you delegate activities that are familiar to you or those that are not?

Case 8.1
Senator Judson Blair's Office

Judson Blair is a newly elected U.S. senator from a southern state. He is in the process of putting together an office staff and defining its organization. Based on his experience in state government (he had been governor of his home state), familiarity with Washington, D.C., and a conversation with his predecessor, Senator Blair understands that the duties of his office will include:

1. Vote on bills on the Senate floor (which only the senator personally can do). These average about five to six a day when the Senate is in session (approximately 10 months a year). Votes are spread out but generally in the afternoon and early evening. The senator must go to the Senate floor for each vote, a trip of about seven minutes each way.

2. Monitor all legislative debate in the Senate and read all proposed bills.

3. Draft proposed legislation (mainly amendments; most bills as a whole come from committees).

4. Attend and vote at committee meetings. Anyone can listen to most committee deliberations and hearings, but only the senator member can ask questions, participate in the debate, and vote. Senator Blair expects to be assigned to four

committees which generally meet in the morning (but committees' chairpersons do not coordinate scheduling meetings so conflicts are frequent).
5. Respond to constituent mail. This tends to fall into three categories: *(a)* mail commenting on how senator votes or expressing criticism or support for his positions; *(b)* requests for assistance on a wide variety of personal matters ranging from social security benefits, stationing of a child in the military service, to job requests; and *(c)* local governments seeking assistance in dealing with some department of the executive branch of the federal government. Based on the experience of the other senators from similar states, category *(a)* should run about 2,000 letters per week; category *(b)*, 500 letters per week; and *(c)* 10 per week.
6. Respond to personal, political, and all other mail (approximately 100 letters per week).
7. Receive telephone calls and visitors to the office. These include constituents visiting Washington, D.C., and wanting to say hello to their senator and lobbyists wanting to argue for or against proposed legislation. Senator Blair expects about 100 visitors per week.
8. Attend various functions in Washington and the home state as political and social demands arise. Most senators feel this is necessary in order to return favors and keep in touch with home state conditions. Blair expects to return to his home state approximately three times a month when Congress is in session and to spend four weeks a year there when not in session.

The Senate offers little guidance on dealing with these duties although there are certain traditional positions across all 100 offices. The title and position of administrative assistant is universal as is that of the principal aide to the senator and general staff administrator. A position of executive, personal, or appointments secretary is also extremely common as is that of press representative, assistant or secretary. A distinction between professional and nonprofessional staff is common to all officers. Professional staff usually consist of young (under age 35) college graduates many with masters or law degrees, who are variously termed *legislative assistants, legislative aides,* or *staff assistants.* The nonprofessionals are frequently categorized as support staff and include position titles like secretary, support aide, staff aide, typist, and file clerk. Most of them are young college graduates; a few part-timers are current undergraduates, graduate, or law students.

Most offices also have a position called caseworker which is usually seen as a nonprofessional except in a few offices where casework (response to requests for assistance) is assigned to professional staff. About one half of the senators have their caseworkers located in offices in the home state because they feel these people should be close to constituents. This also saves room in the Washington offices which are very crowded. The other senators have the caseworkers located in their Washington office because they are easier to supervise and most of their work involves telephone contacts with executive branch officials located in Washington. Exhibit 1 gives the organization chart for one senator's office that is fairly typical. Exhibit 2 summarizes the self-described duties of these personnel.

Senator Blair is both idealistic and pragmatic. He wants to respond to constituents and reflect their views in his voting if they are consistent with his personal views (or not *too* inconsistent), but he also desires to be reelected. The importance of his constituents to him is reflected in his belief that *all* letters should receive replies even if they are just handwritten diatribes against him. And he

Exhibit 1
Organizational Chart for Comparable Senator's Office

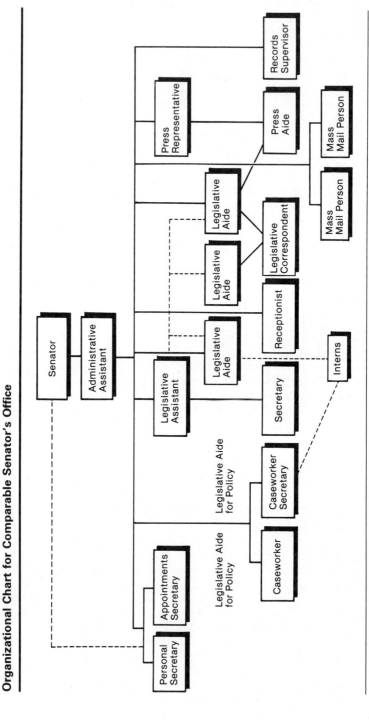

Exhibit 2
Summary of Self-Described Job Duties by Personnel in a Comparable Senator's Office

A. Activities and responsibilities of personal secretary and appointments secretary.
   1. Personal secretary.
      a. Takes personal dictation.
      b. Handles office accounts, personal checking account, political account, and charitable account.
      c. Prepares tax information for accountants.
      d. Performs personal errands for senator.
   2. Appointments secretary.
      a. Answers telephone; takes messages.
      b. Schedules appointments; coordinates office appointments, speeches, and staff.
      c. Makes travel arrangements.
      d. Takes and transcribes dictation; types.
      e. Files.
B. Legislative assistant and legislative aides.
   1. Legislative assistant.
      a. Has general responsibility for all legislative action.
      b. Has specific responsibility for matters arising from several committees.
      c. Writes speeches and floor statements in specific areas.
      d. Reviews all floor statements prepared by other legislative staff.
      e. Handles constituent mail in specific area.
      f. Reviews policy-establishing constituent responses prepared by other legislative staff.
      g. Oversees Senate floor activities to make sure the senator is prepared for floor action by appropriate staff member.
      h. Oversees keeping of records of senator's legislative activity.
   2. Legislative aide 1.
      a. Takes care of all legislation in energy, civil service, and post office.
      b. Supervises mass mailings with interns.
      c. Coordinates intern program.
      d. Performs administrative duties.
   3. Legislative aide 2.
      a. Follows and initiates legislation in Committees on Human Resources and Finance.
      b. Writes speeches in specific area.
      c. Answers constituent mail in specific area.
      d. Oversees agency in specific area.
   4. Legislative aide 3.
      a. Covers Committees in Commerce, Judiciary, Armed Services, Banking, Housing, Urban Affairs and related matters.
      b. Drafts speeches, position papers, and statements in specific areas.
      c. Drafts legislation in specific areas.
      d. Advises senator on bills reaching Senate floor from committees.
      e. Works out approaches to some of the more complex cases arising in home state.
      f. Drafts responses to legislative mail in specific areas.
      g. Assists constituents with federal agency problems.
C. Caseworkers.
   1. Caseworker 1.
      a. Receives, researches, writes, and types answers to constituent inquiries in specific areas.
      b. Liaisons with federal agencies, state, and local officials.
      c. Counsels constituents on problems.
      d. Performs administrative duties.
   2. Caseworker/secretary 2.

Exhibit 2 *(continued)*

a. Receives, answers, and types responses to inquiries from constituents.
b. Does casework for constituents.
c. Assists legislative aide in supervising interns.
d. Helps elsewhere in office when needed.
e. Takes dictation from administrative aide or legislative aide when needed.
f. Takes over reception desk when receptionist is away.

D. Support staff.
1. Receptionist.
   a. Opens, reads, sorts, and delivers mail.
   b. Answers telephone; takes messages; transfers calls.
   c. Places phone calls for senator.
   d. Handles walk-in constituent requests for information.
   e. Answers some constituent mail.
   f. Meets and greets all incoming people.
   g. Orders office supplies for Washington and home state offices.
2. Secretary to legislative assistant.
   a. Researches, drafts, and types constituent correspondence.
   b. Catalogs *Congressional Record* activities.
   c. Handles Interior Committee for office.
   d. Works on special legislative projects.
   e. Catalogs senator's voting record and voting record scores.
   f. Files legislative records.

3. Press aide (press representative position was vacant).
   a. Writes and processes press releases.
   b. Clips and files news items referring to senator.
   c. Handles legislation and correspondence with regard to Agriculture and Forestry Committees.
   d. Assists legislative aides in their specific areas including doing casework.
   e. Does typing for legislative aides.
   f. Makes up speech scheduling.
   g. Handles press inquiries.
   h. Writes some statements for media.
   i. Lays out and types newsletter.
   j. Produces triweekly TV show for two senators.
4. Legislative correspondent.
   a. Has secretarial responsibility for two legislative aides.
   b. Drafts, types constituent mail in specific areas of people for whom s/he works.
   c. Acts as backup receptionist.
   d. Answers phone; welcomes visitors; makes appointments.
5. Records supervisor.
   a. Classifies all mail done in office.
   b. Sets up files for home staters and controls.
   c. Handles all calls and questions with respect to files.
   d. Sets up home state files and control.
   e. Sets up subject files and control.

would like replies back to the writer in a week. He deems it essential that all letters have precisely the correct degree of formality in salutations and closing. That is, if the letter is from someone who knows him personally, he wants the response letter to be headed "Dear (first name)" and signed either "Jud Blair" or "Jud" depending on how close they are. More formal letters should be more conventionally addressed "Dear Mr. (last name)" and signed "Judson Blair." This

Exhibit 3
Plan of Office Rooms

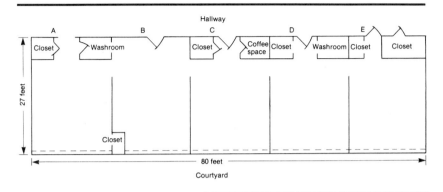

consistent differentiation is very important to maintain political relationships and the image of friendship or approachability.

As a junior senator he realizes that his direct influence as committee member and legislator will be limited unless his legislative initiatives are extremely well researched and drafted.

Blair has been assigned office space in the Dirksen Senate Office Building. It consists of five rooms as indicated in Exhibit 3. He also is allowed a room across the street in an old apartment house the Senate has taken over. Most senators put their part-time mail openers and handlers there. For additional Washington space he would have to pay out of his personal funds (as far as he knows, only two senators do this—space in the home state in various federal buildings is free and virtually unlimited). His budget will allow him to hire from 15 to 25 people depending on the relative salaries and proportions of professionals and support staff. Blair has already promised positions to four of his long-term state government staff. They have been approximately equals in terms of past duties, status, and friendship. They include: Sylvia Conrath, his personal secretary; Frank Wilson, former state budget director; Samuel Jamison, former state legislative liaison; and Anthony Kingsley, his former state transportation department head and primary political manager. Blair has not yet told them what positions or duties they will have in his Senate Office.

Case Questions
1. What are some possible strategies for Senator Blair in developing an organization chart for his office?
2. What are the criteria for selection?
3. Propose an organization chart defining the duties of each position.
4. Propose an office layout locating the various people in the space. What guided your assignments?

Case Reference
Ross A. Webber, *Management: Basic Elements of Managing Organizations* (Homewood, Ill.: Richard D. Irwin, 1979), pp. 430–38.

Case 8.2
Restructuring the Pentagon

The Department of Defense (DOD) is the biggest executive department, employing more civilians than all the other departments combined. Although DOD is not a business and its test of efficiency cannot be the same as that used for a *Fortune* 500 company, many Americans might wonder how it can justify purchasing a $7,000 coffeepot. Does the $300 billion a year the United States spends on defense buy all the security it should? Some analysts, who are willing to accept an occasional $100 widget, question the effectiveness of the defense establishment's organizational structure.

Background
A mixture of agreement and compromise resulted in the National Security Act of 1947 and the current U.S. military structure. Definitive discussion of the background of the act is beyond the scope of this case, but a few key elements in that reorganization decision were:

- The desire of President Truman to replace the separate Departments of War and Navy with a single organization, the Department of Defense.
- The determination of the Army Air Corps to gain autonomy.
- The determination of both the army and the navy to remain autonomous, with the army willing to be rid of its factional Air Corps but the navy unready to release control of naval aviation.
- The belief that strategic bombing would be decisive in the next war.
- The president's desire to strengthen his control of the armed forces as components of the federal government.
- A widespread recognition that the structure of the armed forces had to take into account the strategy and fighting organizations needed in the field.

What emerged was a centrally organized Department of Defense containing three separate service branches, each assigned a distinct mission. Arguably, the structure fit the security environment of 1947. Since then, however, enough problems have emerged to question this structure. The march of events and the onrush of new military technology over the past 35 years have resulted in an unanticipated evolution and overlapping of the missions assigned to the individual armed services in 1947.

Current Organizational Structure
This giant organization can best be understood if it is broken down into four major parts: the Office of the Secretary of Defense (OSD), the Joint Chiefs of Staff (JCS), the military departments, and the field commands (see Exhibit 1).

The Office of the Secretary of Defense (OSD). The Department of Defense is under the secretary of defense. The secretary is responsible for exercising the president's authority over DOD. Specifically, the secretary fulfills three main roles:

- *Manager,* controlling the department's resources and directing the activities of the subunits.
- *Deputy commander in chief,* controlling the actions of U.S. military forces in crises.
- *Adviser,* advising the president on national security policy.

Exhibit 1
Organization Model of DOD

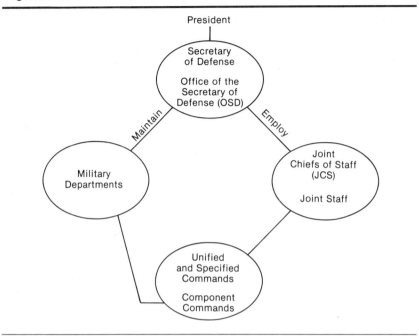

To help him in fulfilling these three roles, the secretary has a staff of about 1,700 people (1,250 civilian, 450 military).

The Joint Chiefs of Staff (JCS).   By law, the Joint Chiefs of Staff are composed of five military officers: The Chief of Staff of the Army, the Chief of Naval Operations (CNO), the Commandant of the Marine Corps, the Chief of Staff of the Air Force, and a chairman. The latter is a member of one of the armed services, but during his tenure on the JCS he has no service responsibilities.

All of the Joint Chiefs are appointed for a fixed nonrenewable term of four years. The chairman is appointed for a two-year term, and, except in wartime, can only be reappointed once. His term is not fixed and he serves at the pleasure of the president.

The JCS perform four functions. First, they *advise* the president and secretary of defense primarily through the National Security Council. Second, they *prepare* plans that provide guidance for the development of the defense budget, industrial mobilization plans, research and development programs, and contingency plans of the field commanders. Third, they *review* and *comment* upon the plans and programs of the separate services and field commanders. Fourth, the chiefs *assist* the president and the secretary of defense in carrying out their command responsibilities. Powerful though the JCS chairman may be, he and his JCS colleagues do not exercise operational control over the field commands. Without secretary of defense authority, they cannot move a ship, a squadron, or battalion.

By law, the Joint Staff cannot exceed 400 military officers, and is composed of equal numbers of officers from the army, navy, and air force. The Marine Corps is allotted 20 percent of the navy complement.

The Military Departments.   Within the Department of Defense there are three military departments separately organized and administered: army, navy, and air force. These organizations, however, are departments in name only. The secretaries of these departments do not have cabinet level status nor are they responsible directly to the president or Congress. For all practical purposes, the army, navy, and air force are agencies or bureaus within the Department of Defense.

The primary function of the Departments of the Army, Navy, and Air Force is to recruit, train, and equip forces for the unified and specified commands. These departments have no control over military operations. The chain of command goes from the president through the secretary of defense and the JCS to the field commands.

Field Commands.   The operational forces of DOD are under the control of either unified or specified commands. A unified command is composed of forces of two or more services, while a specified command is normally composed of forces from only one service.

At the present, there are six unified commands and three specified commands. Commands tend to be associated with particular geographic areas—the European command, discussed on pp. 303–304, is a case in point. The three specified commands, composed primarily of air force personnel, tend to be associated with functions, for example, the Military Airlift Command.

The Defense Reorganization Act of 1958 placed unified and specified commands directly under the control of the secretary of defense. Prior to that time, unified commands were subject to the authority of the military departments and service chiefs.

Each unified command consisted of a headquarters with an integrated staff composed of personnel from each of the services with units assigned to the command. The forces or components (e.g., the 3rd Infantry Division in Würzburg) assigned to a command are not integrated, however. They are organized as service components.

Organizational Politics

The U.S. military system has been criticized in a succession of studies. Opponents have said the lack of strong central discipline in the Pentagon has allowed service fiefs to flourish, leading to duplication of weapon systems, neglect of such unglamorous needs as ammunition, and poor training for joint operations.

Exhibit 2 indicates that the two dominating organizations in the Department of Defense are the central management (the secretary of OSD) and the services. As a result, the relationship between secretary/OSD and the services is the anvil on which the major decisions concerning both maintaining and employing functions are hammered out in DOD. As the exhibit suggests, the service secretaries have relatively little influence.

Military advice, the principal function of the Joint Chiefs of Staff, is flawed by the inability of the chiefs, also imbued with individual service responsibilities, to address a broad range of contentious issues as a corporate body. The JCS act as a forum for arriving at united service positions through negotiations in which each service seeks to maximize its position.

By this reading, the JCS fail to fulfill their purpose. In the first place, the JCS bargaining approach produces military advice fundamentally different from what was intended by the authors of the National Security Act—and, more important, of less value to the president and secretary of defense. The framers of the act sought an organization to produce military advice derived from the deliberations of

Exhibit 2
Model of DOD—as Portrayed by Its Critics

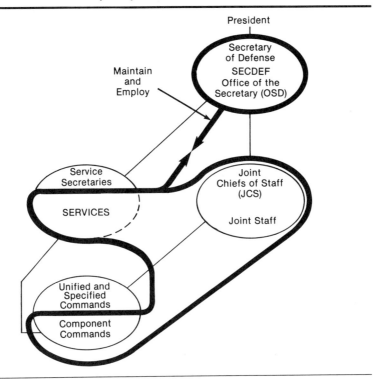

a corporate body of the highest military leaders considering issues from a national perspective detached from, but cognizant of, service interests. Furthermore, because bargaining is unable to produce compromises acceptable to the services in areas of contention, the JCS evades a broad range of issues crucial to defense policy. These issues include the allocation of resources; basic strategy; roles and missions of the services; and the functions, responsibilities, and geographical assignments of unified and specified commands.

Exhibit 2 also suggests that the commanders in chief of the unified and specified commands (CINCs), who would actually direct the fighting of a war, have neither the influence nor formal links with higher authority commensurate with their responsibilities. In crucial decisions determining the composition and war-fighting capability of theater forces, subordinate component commanders and, by extension, the services, overshadow the CINCs. No central authority exists to analyze the preparedness of each unified theater force and then relate this assessment to resource allocation decisions. Instead, readiness evaluations are controlled by the services themselves and linked to their own budget proposals.

Finally, the CINCs' chain of command from and to the secretary of defense is rendered potentially indecisive by its routing through the Joint Chiefs of Staff, a committee, as opposed to a single military official acting as the secretary of defense's agent in supervising the CINCs.

General Wallace H. Nutting, commander of the United States Readiness Command in charge of troops and aircraft based in the United States, thinks that the current system depends inordinately on cooperation and good will among the services in order to function. Another unified commander, Admiral William J. Crowe, Jr., head of Pacific Command, suggests that if a commander tried creative or unusual tactics, subordinates may dispute his judgment through service channels.

Strategy and Structure

The upshot of this arrangement is that military input into decision making, whether through service secretaries, the JCS, Joint Staff, CINCs, or components, is predominantly service oriented. On a broad range of contentious issues, military advice from a national perspective is unavailable to civilian decision makers who are forced to provide this perspective themselves, whether or not they are qualified to do so.

The navy, for example, seeks a 600-ship fleet without a strategic rationale. Some critics argue that the high priority given the navy, particularly the funds committed to build two new "supercarriers," makes little sense from a strategic standpoint. The marines are devoted to amphibious forces of dubious value for today's warfare. For the pilot-dominated air force, it is manned aircraft that count—and badly needed conventional (i.e., nonnuclear) missiles go unbuilt. As for the army, it insists on retaining its role in preparing ballistic missile defenses— a role better suited to the air force.

Each separate service pays for a variety of forces, many of which overlap with those of other services. The totality is largely unplanned and uncoordinated, and it corresponds to no coherent strategy.

Case Questions

1. What does this case reveal about the relationship of organizational structure to other management processes discussed in Part II; namely, planning, decision making, implementing, and evaluating?
2. Two men who do not think the Pentagon needs restructuring are Caspar Weinberger, secretary of defense, and John F. Lehman, Jr., secretary of navy. Weinberger says it is the people in the boxes and not the boxes that count. How would you respond? Why do you think Lehman thinks the overall organization of DOD sound?
3. Without being too specific, what broad strategies are available to a president interested in reorganizing DOD? What fundamental problems should he try to correct?

Case References

Archie D. Barrett, *Reappraising Defense Organization* (Washington, D.C.: National Defense University Press, 1983); Edward N. Luttwak, *The Pentagon and the Art of War* (New York: Simon & Schuster, 1984); Bill Keller, "Military Leaders Reject Plans to Overhaul U.S. Combat Forces," *New York Times,* April 8, 1985; *U.S. Government Manual 1984/85;* John L. Byron, *Reorganization of U.S. Armed Forces,* (Washington, D.C.: National Defense University Press, 1983).

PART III

Resources Management

9

Public Financial Administration

Introduction

Public financial administration encompasses a wide range of activities vital to the operation of any government, including the process of revenue generation and all portions of the budget cycle.

The subject of the first half of this chapter is public finance. By *public finance* we mean the package of problems and issues that involve the use of tax, borrowing, and expenditure measures for public purposes. Sometimes it is asserted by students of public administration that public finance is a dull subject—perhaps best left to experts in accounting and bookkeepers with green eyeshades. But this claim goes soft on detailed investigation.

Many of the most significant political questions of the day are questions of public finance. Is the problem of poverty best approached through a guaranteed income? What is the proper balance between defense spending and domestic spending? How is unemployment reduced without increasing inflation? What effect do taxes have on economic growth? What is the best way to finance education and other local services? Are tax loopholes just? Do the benefits from pollution control measures exceed their costs? The preceding series of questions serves not only to expand our definition of public finance but also to preview the kinds of issues with which we shall be grappling in this chapter.

While I do not intend to neglect financial administration at the local level, it is perhaps best that we begin our discussion at the top. In particular, we shall note the three major objectives of federal government spending and taxing and try to sort out the differences between supply-side and demand-side economics.

Since many administrators at all levels of government become involved in the issue of how to tax, this chapter will focus next on revenues. We shall be interested in understanding the full implications of each possible source of revenue.

Governments tax in order to spend. Not surprisingly, a major portion of this chapter focuses on how governments spend. Modern budgeting concerns primarily the commitment of funds to the various programs and projects decided upon in the strategic plan (see Chapter 5). It also concerns the expected sources of funds from which those expenditures are to be met. In earlier years, as we shall see in this chapter, budgeting typically had as a basic function the custody of funds, that is, making sure they were spent honestly. The increasing complexity of government operations, and scarcity of financial resources have dictated a vast increase in responsibility for budgeting. The direction of cost-control programs and the measurement of results have fallen increasingly to the budgeting function. In short, budgeting is now directly related to the mission of an agency.

Functions of Federal Fiscal Policy

In 1651, the English philosopher Thomas Hobbes maintained that the sole reason for the institution of government is to provide security: *Salus populi suprema lex* ("The safety of the people is the supreme law"). While such a statement has a certain aphoristic resonance, it seriously misrepresents the economic role of modern government.

In this section we examine one important part of that economic role, *fiscal policy*. Thus our concerns center on government spending, tax rates, and, consequently, the size of budget surplus or deficit; other aspects of economic policy—regulation of competition, the operation of public corporations, and changes in the supply and cost of money by the federal reserve system (i.e., *monetary policy*)—are kept very much in the background.

The effects of federal tax and spending measures on the economy are varied, but we can distinguish at least three broad functions:

1. Allocation: the provision of various government goods and services to society.
2. Distribution: adjustments to the distribution of income and wealth in society.
3. Stabilization: efforts of the government to use fiscal and monetary policy to get rid of inflation, unemployment, or both, and to maintain an appropriate rate of economic growth.

The Allocation Function

Resource Scarcity and What to Do about It. Let me begin with an idea that is, I hope, easy to accept. At any given moment, the productive resources—land, labor, and capital—available to a society are limited.

However, the total human wants in a society are another matter. It is rather unlikely that any Gallup poll will discover that everyone has everything he or she wants. How then does a society resolve this conflict between wants and resources?

The setup is called an *economic system*, and it comes in a variety of types. At one extreme is the command system in which the government makes all major decisions regarding what goods and services will be produced and who will get them. At the other extreme is the market system in which these decisions are determined by the supply and demand among many firms and individuals casting their "dollar votes" in the marketplace. All advanced industrial societies (which include the Soviet Union as well as the United States) contain an admixture of both command and market systems.

But public finance in the United States is not about socialism versus capitalism. Rather it concerns *how* allocation will occur within a market-oriented economic system. What are the justifications for government intervention into the market? What are the alternative techniques for intervening? Let us take these two questions in order.

The Case for Intervention. Beyond supplying law and order, why should government meddle in the operations of a free market? The short answer is that free markets often reveal certain imperfections. A more thoughtful analysis would require us to note at least three such imperfections.

1. Certain firms in any industry can become so large relative to the competition that they are no longer subject to any pressure to keep their output up and prices down. The extreme situation is when there is only one firm, a *monopoly*. Monopoly is not necessarily bad. Think of the inefficiencies that would result if there were dozens of utility companies serving one city. Each company would have to have its own lines, cables, meters, and so on. In such cases, the prudent thing to do seems to be to allow the monopoly but to have some public body control it.

2. Markets do not take account of wider social impacts of certain business operations—for example, contamination of water, congestion, or depletion of resources. These impacts are often referred to as negative *externalities*. Thus, many firms in a free market sell products at a price that does not include the full costs of production. These costs are fobbed off on society as a whole.

3. Markets are stacked in favor of *private goods* (e.g., food, autos, cigarettes, hair sprays, and socks) and against *public goods* (e.g., public television, public beaches, clean streets, and clean air). Perhaps no one stated imbalance with more verve than John Kenneth Galbraith (1958:199–200) in his influential *The Affluent Society.*

> The family which takes its mauve and cerise, air-conditioned power-steered, and power-braked automobile out for a tour passes through cities that are badly paved, made hideous by litter, blighted buildings, billboards, and posts for wires that should long since have been put underground. They pass on into a countryside that has been rendered largely invisible by commercial art. They picnic on exquisitely packaged food from a portable icebox by a polluted stream and go on to spend the night at a park which is a menace to public health and morals. Just before dozing off on an air mattress, beneath a nylon tent, amid the stench of decaying refuse, they may reflect indeed, is this the American genius?

Techniques of Public Sector Intervention.   The list below shows some of the major alternative techniques that government can use to influence resource allocation. These range from those that are applied directly and completely to those where the public sector's influence is extremely indirect and incomplete.

Nationalization—the public sector finances and produces the good or service.

Subsidies and market-based incentives—the public sector provides outright monetary payment, low-interest loans, or tax preferences (loopholes) to private enterprise.

Direct regulation—the public sector sets the price that can be charged, determines certain performance and safety standards the product must meet, or screens personnel practices within the company.

Taxes, penalties, or fees—the public sector discourages the production or consumption of certain products.

Licenses—the public sector restricts the entry to certain professions or industries.

Public-private ownership—the public sector may share ownership and control of a firm or industry.

Distribution Function

Critics of the market system argue that, if left alone, it would produce an income distribution that is socially undesirable. In particular, it appears that a pure market system would provide inadequate income to the very young, the very old, the sick, and the disabled.

Several techniques of income redistribution are available. Musgrave and Musgrave argue that the tax-transfer schemes—such as social security and unemployment benefits—are the preferable devices. But redistribution may also be affected by implementation of *progressive taxation;* that is, a policy whereby the fraction of income paid increases as income rises. Finally, redistribution may be implemented by the government directly financing public services, such as public housing, that are available only to low-income groups.

Those with a conservative economic philosophy look with alarm on the rise in *transfer payments;* that is, direct payments to individuals with no goods and services provided to the government in return. These payments have been increasing at the rate of nearly 9 percent a year. Furthermore, transfer payments would in the not-too-distant year make up 80 percent of all federal dollars spent, compared to 20 percent in 1950.

According to the Bureau of the Census, almost half of all households in the nation—47 percent to be precise—were receiving some kind of check from the federal government during the first quarter of 1984. Among the millions who benefited directly from federal spending programs under the fiscal 1986 budget were:

People collecting social security	37,333,000
People helped under medicare	30,800,000
Medicaid beneficiaries	22,517,000
People receiving food stamps	20,120,000
Beneficiaries of Aid to Families with Dependent Children	10,696,000
Families in subsidized housing	4,159,000
Veterans or survivors collecting pensions or compensation	3,949,000
Aged, blind, disabled receiving aid	3,754,000
Government workers	2,800,000
Military personnel	2,200,000
Civil service retirees	2,004,000
Military retirees	1,493,000
Railroad-retirement beneficiaries	942,000
Disabled coal miners	377,000

If the bureau's survey were truly encompassing, so that it covered all kinds of federal subsidies for individuals (e.g., farm price supports, college student loans, and GI Bill), it would probably reveal that two thirds of American households benefit in some direct fashion from federal programs.

Stabilization Function

The three components of the stabilization function are (1) price stability, (2) full employment, and (3) economic growth.

1. When the total demand of people, business, and government exceeds the capacity of the nation's total resources to supply them—when too many dollars are chasing too few goods—we have *price instability or inflation.* Since the mid-1960s, this condition has been common in the United States.

2. In the opposite case, where the quantity supplied exceeds the quantity demanded, the result is a surplus and businesses will be forced to use less labor. This, of course, leads to increased *unemployment*. But unemployment also results from other factors: lack of education or skills, job discrimination, pay scales set above the productive value of some member of the labor force, and urban decay.

3. Today, *economic growth* has become an uncertain concept. Some advocate zero growth; others, the substitution of quality of life for economic growth as the proper goal. Others think growth essential to combating unemployment.

Now that we have some idea of what is meant by stabilization we can ask how fiscal policy attempts to achieve it.

Assumptions behind Fiscal Policy

We will begin with John Maynard Keynes's prescription for national economic ills, which for convenience we shall call *demand-side economics*. Then we shall consider the alleged weaknesses of demand-side economics. We shall conclude our discussion of fiscal policy by exploring a somewhat different way of looking at how the American economy works. This new view (which is really not that new) we shall call *supply-side economics*.

The Traditional View

Lord Keynes (1883–1946) was a British economist who came onto the American scene during the 1930s. To combat depression, Keynes suggested that government actively stimulate demand levels. In other words, when growth is slow and unemployment high, government should reduce taxes to stimulate purchasing and production. Government expenditures produce similar effects, so during periods of economic decline, governments should increase their expenditures, thereby stimulating production.

Note that Keynes's prescription has two sides. In inflationary periods, when the economy is growing too rapidly and employment is high, government should *increase* taxes to lessen the dollars available for purchasing. And cuts in governmental expenditures, which reduce demand, also help slow inflation.

Until the 1930s, American government had rejected these ideas. For the government to spend more than it received—to engage in deficit spending—would, it was feared, wreck the economy. But after World War II, Keynesian manipulation of the spending level to stabilize the economy became widely accepted. This acceptance was institutionalized in the passage of the Full Employment Act of 1946, which created the Council of Economic Advisors and authorized the president to deliver an annual economic report to Congress. The Economic Report of the President recommends actions to achieve high levels of employment.

In recent years, with the economy suffering from both unemployment and inflation, these recommendations require considerable economic artistry and sorting out of values. Some economists even began to wonder whether the United States was in a new economic ball game. Certainly a number of factors, which Keynesian theory did not fully account for, seemed to have a decisive effect on economic performance. First was the increasingly interdependent global economy. Second was the large role the government bureaucracy played in the modern economy. Third was the possible exhaustibility of certain natural resources. Fourth was the effect that consumer expectations have in shaping or even thwarting the economic policies of government. For example, if consumers are convinced in their own minds that more inflation is ahead, they will act accordingly—no matter what economic program the president might set forth. Fifth were the pricing decisions of large manufacturing companies, which seemed to depend at times on the funds needed to finance future growth rather than on demand. Sixth was the role the technological advances play in the growth and productivity of industry. Seventh was the combination of unemployment and inflation. In the past, there seemed to be a trade-off between the two; that is, high inflation brought low unemployment and low inflation brought high unemployment. In the 1970s, this relationship all but disappeared, and a combination of high unemployment and high inflation seemed to be the norm.*

The Supply-Side View

A somewhat different view of how the economy works began to emerge very rapidly in the late 1970s and became a cornerstone of economic policy in the early 1980s. The new prescription was that economic policy should concentrate directly on increasing the *supply* of goods and services. To do this government should provide tax cuts to stimulate harder work and investment in new plants, new equipment, and more research. Government should also try to cut regulations that unnecessarily burden business.

The idea is not new. Adam Smith explained supply-side theory as follows in his classic *Wealth of Nations* (1776:V:2): "A tax may . . . take out of the pockets of the people a great deal more than it brings into the public treasury. . . . [I]t may obstruct the industry of the people, and discourage them from applying to certain branches of business which might give maintenance . . . to great multitudes.

---

* Many economists refer to this combination as *stagflation.* Here I must side with John Kenneth Galbraith, who will not use the term because, "One has to draw a line. There are some additions to the English language that are too wretched."

While it obliges the people to pay, it may thus diminish, or perhaps destroy, some of the funds which might enable them to do so." But will people react to tax cuts (or tax increases) as supply siders and Adam Smith thinks? That is, will people invest more and work harder?

Assessment of Reagan Fiscal Policy

When Ronald Reagan was elected in 1980, prices were rising 12 percent a year. Employment and labor productivity (output per hour of labor) stood still. The dollar was at a new low, interest rates at new highs. Four years later, "Reaganomics" had altered the economic landscape. Throughout 1984, the GNP was 6.8 percent higher than in 1983—the largest increase since 1951. And inflation was up only 3.7 percent—the smallest increase since 1967. Today, there are millions of new jobs in a growing private sector. (In 10 years, all of Europe has not come close to generating the 6 million jobs the U.S. economy produced in 18 months.) No matter what history ultimately decides about Reagan's massive budget and tax cutting policies, there will be little dispute that Ronald Reagan proved a successful salesman of free-market economics.

Nevertheless, we cannot dismiss the effects of other inflation-reducing factors. Clearly the money supply, which was the responsibility of Paul Volker and the Federal Reserve Board, had a decisive effect on inflation reduction. Also helping in the fight against inflation were moderate wage demands by union workers, a fall in energy prices, and increased productivity by management.

The only economic failure of the Reagan administration was its inability to cut spending. The first budget proposal in 1981 called for inflation-adjusted federal spending to drop 5.6 percent from fiscal year 1981 to fiscal year 1984—but it went *up* by 9.4 percent. Forecasts show spending at 24 percent of GNP—1.2 percentage points higher than the rate Reagan inherited. In retrospect, it appears the president should have pushed harder for spending cuts during his first year. In fact, Reagan never asked Congress for all the cuts the administration assumed in its first budget projections.

To increase spending without raising taxes led, as many economists predicted, to high deficits. One school of supply-side economics held that you could have it both ways. That is, the tax cuts would be so stimulative that total revenues would increase even if the tax rate remained the same. But the economic pie (or GNP) just did not grow quite that fast; hence, a $200-billion plus deficit in 1985.

Meeting the Costs of Government

The subject of this section is taxes. And the problem it presents to the administrator and legislator, as the French Finance Minister J. B. Colbert once said, resembles the problem of plucking a goose: how to get the largest amount of feathers with the fewest squawks.

Thinking about Deficits

Frequently, we hear that deficits are a national calamity. Tom Wicker of the *New York Times* describes the "budget hysteria" this way: "Not since Confederate General Jubal A. Early threatened to capture Washington in 1864—maybe not even since the British burned the Capitol in 1814—has there been such hysteria along the Potomac. If the federal budget deficit is not cut drastically, everyone from President Reagan on down seems to be saying, the skies—maybe even the Republic—will fall" (February 5, 1985).

Deficits are a serious matter, requiring serious thought, but we must not overstate their adverse consequences for the economy. Consider the following points.

Point one is that when government runs a deficit, it is putting more money into citizens' hands than it is taking away in taxes. Neither supply siders nor Keynesians think this will cause a *recession*, that is, zero or negative growth for two consecutive quarters. But how about high inflation and high interest rates? Are these not connected somehow to high deficits?

Which brings us to *points two and three*. High deficits need not be inflationary, provided the Federal Reserve Board does not permit the money supply to grow too quickly, nor need they cause interest rates to rise. Throughout the early and mid-1980s, as deficits rose, interest rates and inflation fell.

Point four is that current deficits should be kept in perspective. At roughly 5 percent to 6 percent of GNP,

the deficit is not overwhelming. Private corporate debt is far larger. And, as we saw in Chapter 3, states and local governments are running surpluses. If unemployment were reduced from 7.4 percent to 5.4 percent, the deficit would be cut by $58 billion.

If deficits are not necessarily going to cause a financial crisis, why the worry? The damage occurs in the long term and comes in two forms. The first problem is the sharp rise in the cost of servicing the national debt. Since that debt is expanding by about $200 billion a year, the cost of financing it rises by about $20 billion a year (at an interest rate of 10 percent), a cost that then threatens to push the *next* year's deficit still higher. Without strong economic growth, reductions in spending, or higher taxes, deficits automatically grow larger by the amount of each year's additional interest outlays in a self-propelling spiral.

The other problem is that deficits raise the value of the dollar and reshuffle the growth of jobs and output away from industries that compete in international markets and toward services and other trade-protected sectors. These *short-run effects* have been widely noted, but our real concern should be with the likelihood of their creating a *long-term* competitive disadvantage for American businesses. Fortunately, ownership of debt securities by foreign countries has declined from 24.8 percent in 1976 to 16.3 percent in 1983. The rest of the debt, "we owe to ourselves."

Figure 9-1

Total Revenue by Major Financial Sectors for the Federal Government and for State and Local Governments

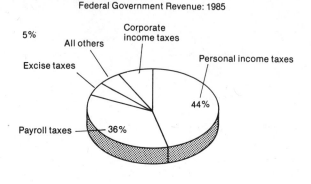

Federal Government Revenue: 1985

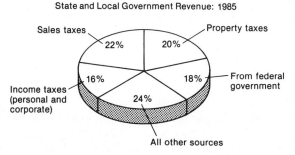

State and Local Government Revenue: 1985

Source: U.S. Office of Management and Budget, *The Budget of the United States* (Washington, D.C.: Government Printing Office, 1985); and U.S. Bureau of the Census, *Statistical Abstract, 1985* (Washington, D.C.: Government Printing Office, 1985), p. 270.

Tax Structures

Figure 9-1 summarizes not only the size of the revenues generated by the federal, state, and local governments in the United States but also the distribution of sources at both levels. Before considering the individual merits of these sources, let us note three pragmatic concepts with which a financial manager in the public sector should be acquainted when developing a tax system: tax equity, tax efficiency, and tax overlapping. (The following discussion of these three concepts draws on Slinger, Sharp, & Sandmeyer, 1975.)

Tax Equity.   A fair tax would be, first, one that treated equally people in equal economic circumstances. A tax distribution that adheres to this principle provides for what is technically known as *horizontal equity*.

A fair tax should also treat unequals unequally; this principle is called *vertical equity*. What is its justification? First, that taxes should be distributed among taxpayers in relation to their ability to pay. For example, those with higher incomes should pay a higher proportion of their income in taxes. If they do, then the tax is progressive. However, some American conservatives have advocated an income tax that takes the *same* proportion of taxes at each income level. For example, everyone pays 30 percent of their income in taxes, regardless of what the income might be; this kind of tax we call, for obvious reasons, *proportional.* A *regressive tax* means that the ratio of tax payments to income *declines* as income rises: The more you earn, the less you pay proportionally. An excellent example of this kind of tax is a sales tax on food. Consider a family of four with an annual income of $10,000. Assuming they spend $4,000 on food and that the sales tax on it is 5 percent, they are paying a $200 per year tax on food, or 2 percent of their annual income. Now contrast this hypothetical family with a professional couple (no children) making $60,000 a year. They eat well, spending $4,000 a year. But what percentage of their income goes to taxes on food? Obviously far less than our family of four. Of these three kinds of taxes, therefore, we generally say that the ability-to-pay principle is most closely associated with *progressive taxation.*

The second justification for the concept of tax equity is the "benefit received principle." In a sense, the principle attempts to apply a free-market approach to the distribution of taxes. Direct charges or *user fees* for government goods force individuals to reveal their willingness to pay for these goods. Noting that it costs $1.3 billion a year to run the U.S. Coast Guard, President Reagan in 1981 proposed that American boat and yacht owners pay a user fee for the services they receive. While this principle faces many practical limitations at national level (how do you apply it to a social good such as national defense?), local governments are able to apply it to many services—parking, recreation, garbage collection, libraries, utilities, and so on. Yet, even at the local level, there are limitations to the application of this principle. Many benefits, such as fire and police, accrue collectively and are difficult to measure. Or, sometimes the objectives of government are in direct opposition to the principle, public assistance being a case in point. "In spite of these limitations, in those cases where it is possible to measure individual benefits with reasonable accuracy and where the purpose of the government service is not to redistribute income, many economists hold that taxes should be selected in such a fashion that they can be defended by reference to the benefit received principle. Such procedure, it is held, is more likely to result in an equitable and efficient distribution of taxes" (Slinger, Sharp, & Sandmeyer, 1975:44).

Tax Efficiency.   Another useful concept in developing a tax system is *tax efficiency.* This concept involves basically two things: economic efficiency and administrative efficiency. Economic efficiency concerns the effect the tax has on the private sector; that is, does it disturb the relative prices of private goods, the pattern of consumption and saving, and the pattern of leisure? Ideally, all these effects would be minimal.

Administrative efficiency concerns how easy the tax is to collect. In some cities, for example, it is necessary for city agents to raid those businesses that have been remiss in paying the selected sales tax. The city of Boston made news a few years ago with its aggressive efforts to get delinquent payments. The efforts featured unveiling photographic blowups of prominent citizens who owed taxes, publishing past-due tax rolls, and locking doors of businesses that had not paid their taxes.

The costs of compliance to the taxpayer should not be overlooked. From the standpoint of efficiency, a flat rate national income tax would appear superior to a progressive tax with multitudinous loopholes and exemptions.

Tax Overlapping. The concepts of *tax overlapping* and *tax coordination* are not difficult. In a federal system like that of the United States, two or more levels of government frequently use the same tax base. In New York City, for example, all three levels tax personal income. At the same time, in a relatively mobile society like that of the United States, it is not uncommon for businesses and individuals to carry out economic activities that make them liable to taxes in many different taxing jurisdictions at the same level of government, for example, in different cities.

While total elimination of these types of overlap is probably impossible, the administrator, if concerned with economic efficiency and taxpayer inequities, cannot ignore them. It is therefore necessary to try to coordinate taxing efforts at one level of government with those at the other two. Fortunately, each level tends to rely mainly on one type of tax.

Coordination between jurisdictions at the same levels can also be important. For example, different tax rates on cigarettes sometimes result in wholesale smuggling of cigarettes across state lines.

Sources of Revenue

Knowledge of these three concepts—tax equity, tax efficiency, and tax overlapping—can help an administrator and legislator appreciate the advantages and disadvantages of selecting different sources of taxes. But they must also know the characteristics of each source (see Table 9–1).

Taxes are not the only source of revenue. Actually, nontax revenue of cities in recent years increased in relative importance, reaching close to one half the general revenue of cities by the end of the 1960s. In general, municipal nontax revenue is composed of user charges and state and federal aid. Since the latter was discussed in Chapter 3, we limit our remarks below to user charges.

The use of the price system offers significant advantages in terms of both resource allocation and equity. As William Vickrey (in Mushkin, 1972) notes, if prices are closely related to costs, there are "substantial possibilities for better utilization of resources, reduced levels of

Table 9-1
Comparison of Revenue Sources

Type	Pro	Con
1. Personal income tax	1. Ease of collection (withheld) 2. Progressive 3. Stable source of revenue	1. Unpopular with public 2. Difficult to collect if not withheld 3. Tends to be borne more by middle-income groups due to law loopholes for higher-income groups 4. Reduces monetary rewards of greater effort and risk taking
2. Corporate income tax	1. Ease of collection 2. Popular with general public 3. Progressive 4. Tends to redistribute wealth	1. Depresses rate of return on invested capital 2. Is displaced to consumers of corporate products or services 3. Reduces capital available for reinvestment 4. Double taxation—shareholder's dividends are taxed after corporation is taxed
3. Property tax	1. Very stable source of revenue 2. Revenue increases as value of property and improvements increase 3. Constantly expanding tax base	1. Difficult to collect delinquent amounts except by foreclosure 2. Are very regressive at low-income level 3. Resources and needs are unequally distributed through society (e.g., some communities) have high public needs but little taxable property 4. Difficult to assess property
4. Estate, inheritance, and gift tax	1. Progressive 2. Burden not easily displaced 3. Tends to redistribute wealth and create equality of opportunity among new generation	1. Difficult to collect 2. Unpopular with general public 3. Tends to reduce large family fortunes that might be used for capital investments 4. Double taxation from federal and state levels
5. Sales tax	1. Ease of collection 2. Relatively stable source of revenue 3. Less visible—paid pennies at a time 4. Reaches nonresidents	1. Regressive 2. Difficult to enforce
6. User charges	1. Efficient 2. Improved equity from direct pricing 3. Registers public demand for a service	1. Most government services do not fit requirement for finance by price (e.g., fire protection) 2. Some beneficiaries (e.g., poor) ought not pay

charges on the average, and improved service, all of which are inherent in pricing policies that are imaginatively concerned in terms of economic efficiency." A few examples should serve to make concrete Vickrey's remark.

Imposition of user charges can prevent excessive wasteful use of electric power or water within an urban area.

Imposition of a price charge can ration facilities among users. A park or outdoor concert has a limited capacity; excessive demand, therefore, can bring demand into line with supply.

Imposition of fees and charges can help control activities that damage air and landscape or cause pollution or congestion. This is the rationale for what some think are excessive taxes on downtown parking lots. User charges also have advantages in terms of equity. Due and Friedlaender (1973:100) put the case in a nutshell: "Except where special circumstances dictate otherwise, usual standards of equity dictate that persons pay for what they get."

Who Pays?

Let us conclude this survey of taxes and other revenues with a particularly difficult question: Who ultimately pays a particular tax? The question is not as easily disposed of as might be imagined. Taxes placed on a producer or a retailer may be shifted forward, in the form of lower wages, rents, interests, and profits. Hence, one cannot assume that a person, who the law *says* a tax is levied on, will end up paying the tax.

Table 9-2
Who Bears the Tax Burden?

	Percentage of Income	
Taxable Income	Required to Be Paid by Tax Law	Paid in Actual Taxes after Using Loopholes
$ 3,000	—%	—%
5,000	11	3.5
10,000	14	8.2
15,000	16	10.5
25,000	25	14.3
50,500	38	22.7
100,000	45	32.4
250,000	50	42.6
1 million	50	48.1

Note: Table does not show the effects of transfer payments and state and local taxes on net income. Rates are for married couple filing jointly in 1985.

A collateral problem concerns how progressive or regressive our *overall* tax and expenditure system actually is. Personal income tax is a function of the definition of income, allowable deductions, personal exemptions, and tax rates. Given the numerous exclusions and deductions, the income tax base in the United States is "eroded." Table 9-2 shows the practical effect of erosion.

How Government Spends

Expenditure Structure

Figure 9-2 summarizes not only the size of federal and statewide expenditures in fiscal year 1984 but also the composition of expenditures at each level. Over the last two decades, the most important change in the federal expenditures has been the rapid decline in the share of defense expenditures, notwithstanding the inclusions of large sums for the Vietnam War. The decline in the relative importance of defense was almost exactly matched by the increasing share of budget

Figure 9-2

Expenditure by Major Financial Sectors for the Federal Government and for State and Local Governments

Federal Expenditures: 1984

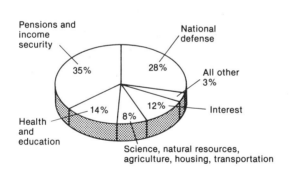

State and Local Expenditures: 1984

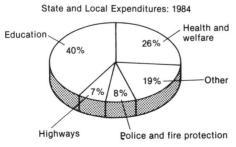

Source: U.S. Bureau of Economic Analysis, *Survey of Current Business,* July 1984.

allocated to transfer payments. In the 1960s, this use could be attributed to Great Society programs in education, manpower, social services, and health; in the 1970s, to income security and public assistance. In 1981, President Reagan boldly set out to reverse this trend.

What can we say about the size and composition of state and local expenditures in recent years? Cities and states are spending more and more money with every passing year. The percentage of local government expenditures as a proportion of the gross national product crept up from 7.5 percent in the late 1950s to about 10 percent in the early 1970s. But, by the mid-1970s, these increases slowed or even disappeared. Payroll costs continue to be the most rapidly rising expenditure.

Tax Expenditures

These two words seem contradictory, I admit. Yet, the term *tax expenditure* provides a concise way of drawing attention to the many tax subsidy provisions in the present federal income tax. Our discussion of expenditure structure would be incomplete without noting this increasingly popular approach to national problems. Let us begin with a few examples of these loopholes:

National defense: The supplements to salaries of military personnel, including provision of quarters and meals on military bases and quarters allowances for military families, and virtually all salary payments and reenlistment bonuses to military personnel serving in combat zones, are excluded from tax.

Agriculture: Farmers, including corporations engaged in agriculture, may deduct certain costs as current expenses even though these expenditures were for inventories on hand at the end of the year or capital improvements.

Community and regional development: Taxpayers may, under certain conditions, select to compute depreciation on rehabilitation expenditures for low- and moderate-income rental housing over a five-year period.

Education, training, employment, and social services: Taxpayers may elect to amortize over a five-year period expenditures incurred in acquiring, constructing, reconstructing, or rehabilitating child-care or on-the-job training facilities. Recipients of scholarships and fellowships may exclude such amounts from taxable income, subject to certain limitations.

Health: Payments by employers for health insurance premiums and other medical expenses are deducted as business expenses by employers and excluded from income by employees.

Income security: Most forms of government transfer payments to individuals, such as social security and unemployment benefits, are excluded from taxable income.

Parkinson's Law of Triviality

Finance committee considering a multimillion-dollar nuclear reactor.

People who understand high finance are of two kinds: those who have vast fortunes of their own and those who have nothing at all. To the actual millionaire a million dollars is something real and comprehensible. To the applied mathematician and the lecturer in economics (assuming both to be practically starving) a million dollars is at least as real as a thousand, they having never possessed either sum. But the world is full of people who fall between these two categories, knowing nothing of millions but well accustomed to think in thousands, and it is of these that finance committees are mostly comprised. The result is a phenomenon that has often been observed but never yet investigated. It might be termed the Law of Triviality. Briefly stated, it means that the time spent on any item of the agenda will be in inverse proportion to the sum involved.

Finance committee considering refreshments supplied at meeting of joint welfare committee.

Source: Parkinson (1957:39–40).

According to Professor Stanley S. Surrey of Harvard Law School, these tax preferences really should be viewed as subsidy payments to preferred taxpayers. Such subsidies include efforts to assist particular industries, business activities, or financial transactions and to encourage nonbusiness activities considered socially useful, such as contributions to charity. For fiscal year 1980, these items totaled over $170 billion. By 1984, the cost of tax breaks was about $270 billion.

During hearings before the Joint Economic Committee, Surrey (1973:83) cut to the heart of the problem created by tax expenditures:

> It can generally be said that less critical analysis is paid to these tax subsidies than to almost any direct expenditure program one can mention. The tax subsidies tumble into the law without supporting studies, being propelled instead by clichés, debating points, and scraps of data and tables that are passed off as serious evidence. A tax system that is so vulnerable to this injection of extraneous, costly, and ill-considered expenditure programs is in a precarious state from the standpoint of the basic tax goals of providing adequate revenues and maintaining tax equity. It is therefore imperative that the process and substance of these tax subsidies be reexamined.

The Changing Role of the Budget

Budgeting is a common practice to the extent that everybody—households, corporations, clubs, agencies, and so on—must anticipate income and expenses. Historically, the word *budget* referred to a leather bag in which England's chancellor of the exchequer carried the statement of the government's needs and resources to Parliament. In time, however, the budget came to refer to the papers within the bag rather than to the bag itself.

Today, budgets are not carried in bags but are bound in volumes that, for at least the major units of government, contain an extensive array of data in standardized formats. The massiveness and complexity of major budgets are generally so intimidating that one wonders if those responsible have purposefully made budget-reading unappetizing. In any case, public administrators must be able to understand the development and functioning of budgets if they are to perform effectively.

The generally accepted purposes of budgeting are, according to Allen Schick (1966), control, management, and planning. *Control* he identifies as legislative concern for tight control over executive expenditures. The most prevalent means of exerting this type of expenditure control has been to appropriate by object of expenditure—for example, felt tip pens, half-ton trucks, salaries, and no-lead gasoline. Financial audits then are used to ensure that money has in fact been spent for the items authorized for purchase. This focuses information for budgetary decision making upon the things government buys, such as personnel, travel, and supplies, rather than upon the accomplishments of governmental activities. In other words, responsibility is achieved by controlling the input side.

The *management* orientation emphasizes the efficiency with which ongoing activities were conducted. Emphasis is placed upon holding administrators accountable for the efficiency of their activities through such methods as work performance measurement (e.g., how many forms typed do we get for X dollars spent).

Finally, *planning* is reflected in the budget message for fiscal 1968: "A federal budget lays out a two-part plan of action: It proposes particular programs, military and civilian, designed to promote national security, international cooperation, and domestic progress. It proposes total expenditures and revenues designed to help maintain stable economic prosperity and growth." Here we see an obvious emphasis on programs and the relationship between revenues and expenditures to accomplish objectives.

The overall development just outlined should be viewed, however, not in terms of three separate phases but in terms of accretion. Thus, the function of the budget today is really a combination of all three purposes.

Line-Item Budgeting

The first image that generally comes to mind with the utterance of the word *budget* is a list of items and their associated costs. Indeed, a *line-item budget* used for projection and control of expenses remains at the heart of the budgeting process. The line-item budget is designed to keep spending within the limits set by the legislative body. Cost categories are established for the recording of all expenditures, and backup bookkeeping systems contain sufficient detail to ensure that all disbursements (i.e., expenditures) are made in accordance with the law. The makers and keepers of line-item budgets rely on accounting skills—the ability to keep track of revenues and expenses in a systematic way. They focus on answering the question: "How was the money spent?" While tabulations of line-item costs are still fundamental to any budgeting process, the concept of budgeting has generally been extended beyond the strict definition of expenditure control.

Performance Budgeting

Oscar Wilde once defined a cynic as "a man who knows the price of everything and the value of nothing. "Perhaps, then, President Franklin Roosevelt was trying to battle cynicism in government when his second administration introduced the concept of performance budgeting. In 1939, the Bureau of the Budget was transferred from the Treasury Department to the newly formed Executive Office of the President with the directive to "keep the president informed of the progress of activities by agencies of the government with respect to work proposed, work actually initiated, and work completed." The idea was that the work programs of the several agencies could be coordinated and that the monies appropriated by the Congress could be expended in the most economical manner possible. The bureau would prevent overlapping and duplication of effort.

Thus began the search at the federal level for an answer to the question that, over 40 years later, still haunts government at all levels: Is the public getting its money's worth? As the end result of line-item budgeting, government should be able to tell the public that an agency spent, say, $19,872,403.91, with so much going to salaries and wages and fringe benefits, so much spent on various materials and supplies, and so much paid out under each of numerous contracts. But with performance budgeting, government should be able to tell the public how much public service was delivered for this $19,872,403.91. If the agency is a city sanitation department, performance measures could be given to show how many tons of trash were collected; the cost per ton and the cost per pickup; and comparative unit costs to indicate efficiency of the department against previous years, comparable departments in other cities, and comparable services provided by private sanitation companies.

The development of valid performance measures for public agencies ranges from the difficult to the impossible. Unique problems are encountered in each field of public endeavor at each level of government. Currently, most government budgets include an aspect of performance budgeting, often in the form of a narrative describing the accomplishments and work in progress of the agency or department. But objective, quantitative evaluations of governmental units—evaluations that attempt to answer the question, "Is the public getting its money's worth?"—are rarely done either within the budgetary process or outside of it.

As noted in Chapter 1, a basic difference between business and government concerns the way they are paid. The former are paid for satisfying customers; the latter, out of a budget allocation. "Being paid out of a budget allocation changes what is meant by performance. Results . . . mean a larger budget. Performance is the ability to maintain or increase one's budget. Results . . . that is . . . achievement toward goals and objectives, are, in effect, secondary." Hence efficiency becomes sin. "The importance of a budget-based institution is measured essentially by the size of its budget and the size of its staff. To achieve results with a smaller budget or a smaller staff is, therefore, not performance" (Drucker, 1975:141–47).

Can anything be done? Consider how hypothetical university President Albert James might conduct his annual planning session. Due to a mandate from the governor, he announces that the total budget for all units under his direction will be reduced by 10 percent from the previous year's level.

Further, James gives the following ground rules to his vice presidents: (1) emphasis is to be placed on increased productivity; (2) standards of quality are to be maintained; (3) budgetary allocations, both in total and by individual units are fixed; and (4) final budgets are due on September 1.

Each of the vice presidents submits his or her budget when the deadline falls. Not surprisingly, it reflects exactly what the president had called for; he is ebullient in commending his staff for their planning expertise.

Is anything wrong in this approach? Certainly, on the surface at least, the president's desire to cut old programs is not wrong. But what is questionable is his approach. First, this approach precludes real participation by the managers; he deliberately refuses to establish any competition among his managers for the available capital. In contrast, the Department of Defense has five committee members on a resource allocation committee each of whom heads units competing for the same resources.

Second, the inefficient as well as the efficient are rewarded (or penalized) with equal severity. The most efficient unit is cut by precisely the same percentage as the least efficient—namely 10 percent.

Third, the president puts the budget at the wrong end of the planning process; he should consider his priorities first, and then make cost allowances.

The lesson is this. Top administrators, as well as members of Congress, can cut programs, but they need, as far as possible, to establish competition *within* the organizational units for the resources.

Program Budgeting

Without ever having really mastered performance budgeting, the federal government proceeded to develop an even broader view of budgeting in the early 1960s. Robert McNamara, as secretary of defense in the Kennedy administration, introduced the Planning-Programming-Budgeting System (PPBS) into the Defense Department. Where line-item budgeting is limited to *accountability* and performance budgeting extends only to the realm of *efficiency*, program budgeting attempts to stretch the process into issues of *allocation* among various competing agencies and programs. It was not as if funding allocation had never before taken place—legislative bodies had historically performed this function based on inputs from constituents and from affected agencies. What the proponents of program budgeting hoped to accomplish was the injection of greater rationality into the process, by first planning *goals* and *objectives*, then developing *programs* to achieve these goals, and finally budgeting for projects within each program.

In 1965, President Johnson began requiring other federal agencies to implement PPBS. But nondefense agencies found their domains far less quantifiable; goals and objectives did not easily translate into programs and projects. Meanwhile, some state governments switched to program budgeting but did not find the system workable. Many state and local governments, after a review of the system, decided to keep what they had. While much of the terminology of program budgeting remains at the federal level, the program-budgeting process is more honored in the breach than the observance.

Zero-Based Budgeting

Much of the decision making in the budgetary process is incremental, that is, involving minimal increases or decreases from last year's budget. Not so with zero-based budgeting—a recent variation of PPBS. Here the basic objectives of a program are examined by taking an if-we-are-to-start-all-over-again look; that is to say, each program is challenged for its very existence each budget cycle. In 1962, at the same time the Defense Department was developing and refining PPBS, the U.S. Department of Agriculture engaged in a zero-based budget experiment. In 1971, Georgia (under Jimmy Carter) and in 1977 the United States (also under Carter) attempted to use it.

Zero-based budgeting (ZBB) involves three basic steps. First, all current and proposed programs must be described and analyzed in documents called decision packages. These documents are designed to help top management evaluate the programs in terms of purpose, consequences, measures of performance, alternatives, and costs and benefits. Next, the program packages are ranked through cost-benefit analysis (see Chapter 6). Finally, resources are allocated in accordance with this ranking.

Now that at least 20 states along with the national government have tried incorporating ZBB into their budgeting procedures, we should be able to draw some conclusions about the effectiveness of this technique.

In general, ZBB does not substantially reduce state or federal expenditure growth. This should not be surprising. Many programs in a state's budget (e.g., statutory entitlements, federal grant policies, and court rulings) are excluded from ZBB guidelines. Similarly, a large part of the federal budget is uncontrollable in the short run. Budgeters are wasting their time if they try to apply the techniques to entitlement programs like social security. The chances for ZBB to reduce budgetary growth for cities appear brighter, however. The reason is that the majority of city budgets are mostly salary expenses—which are relatively controllable (see Draper & Pitsvada, 1981).

In general, ZBB does not appear to aid in the identification of program initiatives and improvements. While a number of state officials say that the technique facilitates the elimination of unproductive programs, few report substantial reductions in these programs (*P.A. Times*, March 1, 1980).

On the positive side, ZBB does force top managers to pay more attention to everyday operations, because they must rank specific expenditure items. But it is too burdensome and detailed for normal budgeting purposes. In any event, good managers should be well acquainted with the programs in their organizations. ZBB can be useful as a resource allocation device to flag programs needing particularly close attention. The remaining activities can be budgeted for on an incremental fashion or, as is done in the province of Ontario in Canada, through the use of the following format (Herzlinger, 1979:67):

Last Year's Budget	Changes Caused by Change in			This Year's Budget
	Quantity	Quality	Inflation	

To summarize the discussion thus far, Figure 9–3 suggests how one government bureau might arrange the same budgetary information in four different ways: line-item, program, performance, and zero based.

Capital Budgeting

Should the federal government have a capital budget like state and local governments, foreign governments, and corporations? Some economists say yes; others disagree.

A capital budget separates long-term investments in buildings, bridges, roads, vehicles, computers, and the like from current operating expenses. Although the federal government separates budget items by categories (such as defense, energy, and income security programs), it combines all capital and operating expenses; therefore, the construction of a new dam is treated the same way as, for example, a purchase of potatoes for the White House kitchen.

Cities manage their resources differently. They have an operating budget intended for day-to-day expenses (such as payment of salaries), and financed through revenues. But they also have a capital budget intended for changes in the physical plant of the city (such as new schools and mass transit systems). It is financed through borrowing. Although important relationships exist between the two types of budgets, there are special characteristics of capital projects that justify their separation from operating expenses. The following characteristics of capital projects have contributed to the segregation (Moak & Hillhouse, 1975:98–99):

Because of their life span, capital projects have a long-range effect upon the community; therefore, they need to be planned within a long-range (five or six years) perspective.

Figure 9-3
Four Ways to Prepare a Budget *(Dollars in Thousands)*

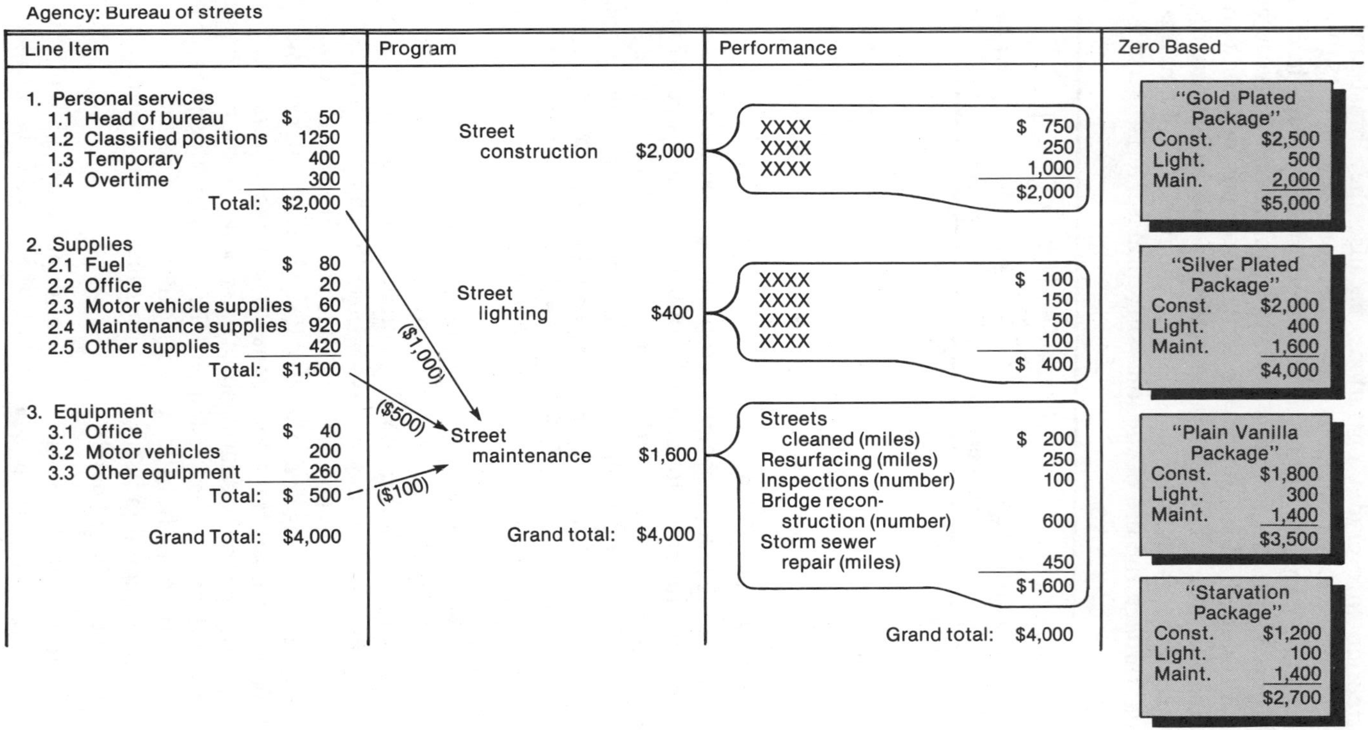

Agency: Bureau of streets

Line Item	Program	Performance	Zero Based
1. Personal services			
1.1 Head of bureau $ 50			
1.2 Classified positions 1250			
1.3 Temporary 400			
1.4 Overtime 300			
Total: $2,000			
2. Supplies			
2.1 Fuel $ 80			
2.2 Office 20			
2.3 Motor vehicle supplies 60			
2.4 Maintenance supplies 920			
2.5 Other supplies 420			
Total: $1,500			
3. Equipment			
3.1 Office $ 40			
3.2 Motor vehicles 200			
3.3 Other equipment 260			
Total: $ 500			
Grand Total: $4,000			

Arrows: ($1,000), ($500), ($100)

Program

Street construction	$2,000
Street lighting	$400
Street maintenance	$1,600
Grand total:	$4,000

Performance

Street construction $2,000
XXXX $ 750
XXXX 250
XXXX 1,000
$2,000

Street lighting $400
XXXX $ 100
XXXX 150
XXXX 50
XXXX 100
$ 400

Street maintenance $1,600
Streets cleaned (miles) $ 200
Resurfacing (miles) 250
Inspections (number) 100
Bridge reconstruction (number) 600
Storm sewer repair (miles) 450
$1,600

Grand total: $4,000

Zero Based

"Gold Plated Package"
Const. $2,500
Light. 500
Main. 2,000
$5,000

"Silver Plated Package"
Const. $2,000
Light. 400
Maint. 1,600
$4,000

"Plain Vanilla Package"
Const. $1,800
Light. 300
Maint. 1,400
$3,500

"Starvation Package"
Const. $1,200
Light. 100
Maint. 1,400
$2,700

Since capital projects affect land use, traffic circulation, the density of population, and the future physical look of the municipality, they require a special expertise, namely, that of the architect-city planner. When applying the principle of a division of labor, the programming of capital improvements has been assigned to those especially equipped to do the job.

Many current operating decisions are subject to reversal, in whole or in part, at the end of (or even during) the current budget. New York City's budget is changed about 5,000 times during its July 1 to June 30 lifetime, as funds are shifted about through "budget modifications." In contrast, capital decisions are irreversible for an extended period; mistakes last longer and are apt to be more costly.

The ability to postpone more capital projects (usually much more easily than current services) means that, without a separate budget, important capital expenditures would often be neglected by cities.

Some opponents, however, are concerned that a capital budget for the federal government would serve as an excuse for more, not less, deficit spending by inviting more spending on public-works' projects. They fear that a capital account could open the United States to what some call "the New York City syndrome," making it all too easy to disguise unbudgeted operating expenses as long-term capital outlays.

Other opponents are concerned about the *negative* impact a capital budget could have on social welfare programs. Because it is far easier to value such tangible assets as roads and public buildings, the argument goes, a capital budget would make it increasingly difficult to justify spending to feed the hungry or to send a young person to college on a government loan.

Finally, there is a fear that trying to run the United States by business standards could blur the role the federal government plays in stabilizing the economy. The overall fiscal policy ought to be related to the needs of the economy as a whole; for example, it may sometimes be appropriate for the government to run a deficit during a recession.

But any accounting system is open to abuse, especially when, like the U.S. budget, it serves as a political document. A more businesslike budget would be neither a panacea for past ills nor a threat to the nation's fiscal priorities. The key reason for changing the way the budget is drawn would be to improve the information it offers about the country's true financial condition.

The Future of Public Budgeting

The question remains: Why do more sophisticated techniques like PPBS and ZBB keep ebbing? Or, to put the same question differently, why does the traditional budget continue to last? The short answer, as

Aaron Wildavsky (1978:508) has put it, is that the traditional budget has the "virtue of its defects." It makes calculations easy because it is not comprehensive. History provides a stronger base on which to make current budgetary decisions than the future makes. The future is the more logical base, of course. But because it is largely unknowable, it offers a weaker base. The traditional budget allows one to change the objectives of a program without attacking the entire policy or agency. Its year-by-year budgeting, while not too good for long-range planning, does allow for adjustment, accountability, and price changes. In sum, Wildavsky writes, "Traditional budgeting lasts . . . because it is simpler, easier, more controllable, more flexible than modern alternatives."

Perhaps it is asking too much of the budgeting process to attempt to answer (as PPBS and zero-based budgeting do) the question, "Why is a government program needed?" But beyond this issue of feasibility, critics see yet another. Should budgeters be devising an ersatz decision-making process of their own or should they really be implementing the decision of the political leadership? To adequately address that question, requires, first, some familiarity with the phases of the budgetary cycle, and, second, an appreciation of the attendant politics. The next two sections, which deal respectively with the federal and local budgetary cycles, attempt to provide both.

The Federal Budget Cycle

The connection between governmental plans, the focus of Chapter 5 and the budget, the subject at hand, is strong. Strictly speaking, a plan is really no more than a statement of purpose, a piece of paper, a mere shadow. Not until it appears in the budget does it take on life, begin to matter. In this sense, the budget animates a plan.

And more. Because the budget must reveal how funds are allocated among many and varied programs, it provides us with probably the most clear-cut way of determining national priorities.

Remember the concept of opportunity cost introduced in Chapter 6? This concept can help us see more clearly what we mean by choice of priorities. Opportunity cost represents the implicit cost of the highest foregone alternative to an individual or group; in short, it is the true cost of choosing one alternative over another. The president each year is confronted with a multiplicity of such choices. He soon learns that spending in one area is viewed by certain groups as money not spent in their areas of special interest.

As President Reagan learned when trying to sell his cuts in the 1982 budget, there is no universally acceptable fair way to cut a budget. Speaking of his plan to cut all mass transit operation subsidies by 1985, he tried to explain his approach with a rhetorical question: Is it fair to ask people in Omaha and Des Moines to get the people in Chicago and New York to work on time? New Yorkers and Chicagoans found that philosophy hard to buy since they help the farmers of Omaha and Des Moines with water projects and agricultural subsidies. Nevertheless, the reordering of priorities was not hard to see. What words could never convey, the shift in 1982 from welfare to defense was easy enough to see in figures: The $55 million in the Pentagon budget for military bands went untouched while funds for children with learning disabilities were cut 25 percent.

Space programs come in for similar questioning—not only by groups of urban activists but also groups of certain scientists. A case in point is the American Miscellaneous Society, a group, which despite its whimsical title, is composed of quite serious oceanographers and other less space-oriented scientists. Their slogan: "The ocean's bottom is at least as important as the moon's behind."

Keeping these ideas in mind, we now turn to the four overlapping phases of the budget process: (1) executive formulation and transmittal; (2) congressional authorization and appropriation; (3) budget execution and control; and (4) review and audit.

Executive Formulation and Transmittal (Phase I)

The president's transmittal of his budget proposals to the Congress early in January climaxes many months of planning and analysis throughout the executive branch. Formulation of the budget for fiscal year 1985, for example, began in the spring of 1983 (see Figure 9-4).

Figure 9-4
Major Steps in the Budget Process

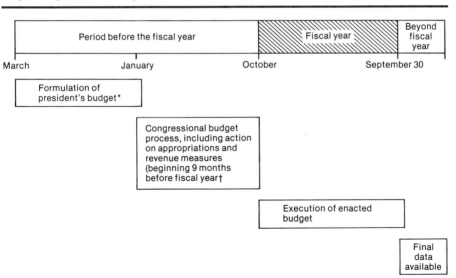

* The President's budget is transmitted to the Congress within 15 days after the Congress convenes.

† If appropriation action is not completed by September 30, the Congress enacts temporary appropriations (i.e., a continuing resolution).

This is the way it works. In the spring, agency programs are evaluated, policy issues are identified, and budgetary projections are made, giving attention both to important modifications and innovations in programs and to alternative long-range program plans. In early June, preliminary plans are presented to the president for his consideration. At about the same time, the president receives projections of estimated receipts, prepared by the Treasury Department, and projections of the economic outlook, prepared jointly by the Council of Economic Advisors, the Office of Management and Budget, and the Treasury Department.

Following a review of both sets of projections—that is, of expenditures and receipts—the president establishes general budget and fiscal policy guidelines for the fiscal year that will begin about 15 months later. Tentative policy determinations and planning *ceilings* are then given to the agencies as guidelines for the preparation of their final budget requests during the summer.

Agency budget requests are reviewed *in detail* by the Office of Management and Budget throughout the fall and are presented, along with OMB recommendations, to the president for decision. Overall fiscal policy issues—relating to total budget receipts and outlays—are again examined. The actual budget data from the most recently completed fiscal year provide an essential reference base in this review and decision process.

The president hardly has a free hand in allocating resources. In fact, OMB classified about 74 percent of the 1984 budget as "relatively uncontrollable"; that is, as impossible to cut through appropriation bills. Thus, the only way this part of the budget could have been reduced was if Congress had passed other kinds of legislation cutting these programs. Table 9–3 shows the kinds of budgetary items that fall into this category. Note also the steep rise since 1970 in the percentage of the budget that is uncontrollable.

For purposes of analysis, we can put the various uncontrollable items on a continuum, running from those most beyond the reach of congressional action to those easiest to control (see Havemann, 1975). Legal commitments made by the government in previous years—such as interest on the national debt—are naturally uncontrollable. Next along the continuum might come payments to meet contracts for weapons systems, spacecraft, highways, and sewers. In sharp contrast to these contracts are programs that guarantee individuals that they will receive benefits if they meet certain qualifications (e.g., old age and poverty). To reduce the costs of these programs, Congress need only change the laws authorizing them—which is hardly a way to win votes.

Yet, it is clear that these uncontrollable programs require fundamental change. For example, in 1972 the formulas used to compute social security benefits were modified in an attempt to make incomes keep pace automatically with the cost of living. Now benefit payments

Table 9-3
"Uncontrollables" in the Federal Budget (All Figures in Billions of Dollars)

Outlays	1970	1984 Estimated
Total Outlays	**$195.7**	**853.8**
Relatively Uncontrollable Outlays	**$121.8**	**632.7**
Percent of total outlays	62.2	74.1
Open-ended programs and fixed costs	79.8	479.1
Payments for individuals	60.1	363.9
Social security and railroad retirement	30.7	180.2
Federal employees' retirement and insurance[1]	8.7	49.4
Unemployment assistance	3.1	19.1
Medical care	9.4	83.8
Assistance to students[1]	1.0	4.6
Public assistance and related programs	6.4	20.3
All other relatively uncontrollable payments for individuals[1]	.9	3.0
Net interest	14.4	108.2
General revenue sharing	(x)	4.6
Farm price supports[2]	3.8	6.7
Other	1.6	−4.2
Prior-year contracts and obligations[3]	41.9	153.6
National defense	24.1	83.1
Civilian programs	17.8	70.5
Relatively Controllable Outlays	**76.3**	**229.9**
National defense	51.6	137.6
Civilian programs	24.7	92.3

X Not applicable.

[1] Includes items previously classified in the veterans' benefits grouping.

[2] Prices from Commodity Credit Corporation.

[3] Excludes prior year contracts and obligations for items under open-ended programs and fixed costs.

Source: U.S. Office of Management and Budget, *The Budget of the United States Government*, annual; and unpublished document, "Federal Government Finances," February 1984 edition.

for those not working are rising faster than wages and some months even faster than inflation. After the turn of the century, a beneficiary's pensions could exceed his or her other preretirement wages. Moreover, the systems's financing problems will then be intensified by the increasing proportion of aged in the population.

Congressional Authorization and Appropriation (Phase II)

The Budget Act of 1974. For decades, the president's budget was the only comprehensive statement of priorities and revenue and spending recommendations. But in 1974 Congress, seeking a greater role in managing the government, passed the *Congressional Budget and Impounding Control Act*, which requires it to adopt an annual budget.

Working Profile: David Stockman

On August 1, 1985, Reagan's outspoken and brilliant Director of the Office of Management and Budget (OMB), David Stockman, resigned to become a managing director with an investment firm.

Stockman was one of the principal designers of the budget and tax cuts that Reagan proposed upon taking office in 1981. As the leading administration spokesman for economic policy, Stockman, then 34 years old, was credited with putting together the biggest package of domestic cuts ever voted by Congress and engineering the first major swing in federal budget policy since President Franklin Roosevelt began expanding domestic programs 50 years earlier.

During his tenure, Stockman talked candidly about flaws in Reagan's economic policies. He once confessed: "None of us really understands what's going on with all of these numbers."

David Stockman, The White House. (Wide World Photos)

The Budget Act attempted to control impoundment—the refusal of the executive branch to spend money appropriated by Congress—and required Congress to adopt a resolution that sets a floor under revenue and a ceiling on spending. The resolution also includes categories of spending limits for 13 major federal functions such as the military, agriculture, and transportation.

The law is also intended to force Congress, after it completes work on the separate appropriations and authorizations it customarily enacts each year, to fit them into an overall framework by passing a second resolution setting final, binding targets.

The Budget Act sets up a timetable for Congress to make its major fiscal decisions. All measures are to be in place by the beginning of the government's budget year, October 1, but these deadlines are often not met.

As the first step in the budget process, the president is required to submit his budget 15 days after Congress convenes in January. For the next several weeks, both House and Senate Budget Committees conduct hearings to examine the president's estimates and projections.

On March 15 the Joint Economic Committee and the Joint Committee on Internal Revenue Taxation submit their recommendations to the budget committees.

On April 15 the Budget Committees are scheduled to report the first budget resolution, which sets overall goals for tax and spending broken down among major budget categories. Congress is supposed to complete action on the first budget resolution by May 15, but it has often been adopted later in the session.

On the basis of the guidelines set in the first budget resolution, Congress is supposed to approve the individual authorization and appropriation bills. The second budget resolution, due September 15, establishes firm ceilings on spending categories. But Congress has found the budget debate so contentious and time-consuming that it has been writing into the first budget solution language that automatically readopts it as the second.

On September 25 Congress is scheduled to complete action on the reconciliation bill and by October 1 to complete action of all 13 appropriation bills.

How Well Has the Budget Act Worked?   In recent years Congress has found it impossible to pass all the appropriation bills before the start of the fiscal year. So it has resorted to a device known as a continuing resolution, which authorizes money for departments and agencies that have not received their regular appropriations. More and more, the continuing resolutions have become omnibus appropriations bills, wrapping several measures into one package and in principle conforming to the spending levels set in the overall budget resolutions. But perhaps the most damaging criticism that can be made of the Budget Act is not that members of Congress have failed to follow procedures but that the act itself has failed to control rising federal deficits.

Such concerns led Senators Gramm, Rudman, and Hollings to introduce in 1985 a bill to "mandate" a scheduled reduction of the federal deficit, in $36 billion dollar decrements, to zero by 1991. The most striking feature of the plan is that which would authorize the president, when Congress exceeds its own limits, to cut spending "across the board" (social security excepted). Thus Congress would cancel, at one stroke, the Budget Act of 1974, which had attempted to prevent presidents from *not* spending (i.e., impounding) money it had authorized. In short, the plan would give the president extraordinary budgetary discretion. It became law in December 1985.

Whatever the effects of this law are, it marks another fascinating episode in the story of Congress' effort to achieve fiscal self-discipline. Yet such an assessment might be too harsh. As Alice M. Rivlin, the first director of the *Congressional Budget Office* (an analytical staff set up by the act itself), has correctly observed: "We want more government than we can pay for, and no process can help solve that problem."

One final observation regarding the first and second phases of the budget process needs underscoring. To be effective in the budgetary process, the administrator should understand the various strategies that are available (see box).

Budget Execution and Control (Phase III)

Once approved—whether by salesmanship, analysis, or a little of both—the budget eventually is passed and becomes the financial basis for the operations of the agency during the fiscal year.

Under the law, most budget authority and other budgetary resources are made available to the executive branch through an apportionment system. Under authority delegated by the president, the Director of the Office of Management and Budget apportions (distributes) appropriations and other budgetary resources to each agency by time periods (usually quarterly) or by activities. *Obligations* may not be incurred in excess of the amount apportioned.

Obligations refer to the amount of orders placed, contracts awarded, services rendered, or other commitments made by an agency during a given period. Sometime during this period, payment will have to be made, probably by check.

The objective of the apportionment system is to assure the effective and orderly use of available authority and to reduce the need for requesting additional or supplemental authority.

What happens if an agency has funds not obligated by the end of the year? The general view among all bureaucrats—whether they are providing services to Eskimos in the frozen tundra of Alaska or pursuing drug traffic in the Florida Keys—is that the cash turns into pumpkins on September 30. At the very least, they had better have a good story for Congress, OMB, and even their bosses if they expect the same level of funding the following year.

The result of this view is the bureaucratic phenomenon of the year-end spending spree. Fourth quarter obligations of the federal government tend to run about 30 percent higher than those obligated in the second quarter (U.S. General Accounting Office, 1980).

Review and Audit (Phase IV)

This step is the final one in the budget process. The individual agencies are responsible for assuring—through their own review and control systems—that the obligations they incur and the resulting *outlays* are in accordance with the provisions of the authorizing and appropriating legislation, as well as other laws and regulations relating to the obligation and expenditure of funds. (Outlays are the values of checks issued, interest accrued on the public debt, or other payments made, *minus* all refunds and reimbursements to the government.) The Office of Management and Budget reviews program and financial reports and keeps abreast of agency programs in attainment of program

The Politics of Budgeting

Aaron Wildavsky (1964), in a master-piece of analysis, inventories several strategies that have been used by agencies when defending their budgetary requests before Congress. The strategies might just as well be used by federal, state, and local agencies when presenting their initial request before the central budget office.

Find, serve, expand, and use a clientele. As noted in Chapter 2, interest groups can be a valuable, indirect vehicle for the furtherance of agencys' aims.

Inform the public of the good the agency does and, in some instances, create a climate of opinion that will influence Congress. Thus, one administrator replies to a student who requested a summer job: "Because of our inadequate funds at this critical time many students, like yourself, who would otherwise receive the professional training that this work provides, will be deprived of that opportunity. . . . Only prompt action by Congress in increasing these funds can make the success of our mission possible."

Before the hearing, visit members of Congress or invite them to the agency. Sargent Shriver, when head of Peace Corps, called on at least 450 of the then 537 members in their offices.

At the hearings, display candor, supportive analysis (e.g., cost-benefit studies), and mastery of detail. To ensure mastery of details, rehearsals in the agency are frequently held to uncover weak spots in the administrator's defense of his or her budget.

Guard against cuts in old programs. When the NIH wants to start, say, a new dental research program, it has been known to begin by cutting one or all of the more popular institutes (e.g., heart, cancer, and mental health). Presumably, these cuts will generate citizen complaints. Complaints, in turn, lead Congress not only to restore the funds but also to approve the whole package, which includes the dental research program.

Add new programs. Every effort is made in the agency to make new programs appear old, or temporary, or insignificant ("the wedge or the camel's nose"), or relevant (related to defense, energy, and so on).

Try salesmanship. It is no secret that on more than one occasion, legislators have been irritated by the use of "Peter Rabbit" presentations with graphs, brochures, flashy pictures, and warnings of cures. Salesmanship, notes Wildavsky, runs the gambit from cops-and-robbers appeal—for example, agents of our Narcotics Bureau engaged in a 45-minute gun battle with Mexican smugglers—to the agony sessions at the NIH hearings. The effect on a legislator of these drama-ridden hearings—including vivid descriptions of disease—is revealed by one representative (cited in Wildavsky, 1964:120): "A week ago, Mr. Chairman, after this hearing about cancer, I went home and checked all the little skin flecks and felt for bumps and bruises. And then more recently I lay awake listening to my heart after hearing the heart-trouble talk. I listened to see if it went too fast or if it was too weak or if it was irregular or whether it was pumping too hard. . . . And here I am listening to all this mental health talk . . . and I wonder what I am going to dream about tonight."

objectives. In addition, the comptroller general, as agent of the Congress, regularly audits, examines, and evaluates government programs. His findings and recommendations for corrective action are made to the Congress, to the Office of Management and Budget, and to the agencies concerned.

Why audit? One audit, conducted by the Defense Department in May 1984, found that more than half the spare parts the department purchased were "unreasonably" priced. The auditors estimated that the Pentagon was probably paying about 13 percent more than it showed. With a $22-billion space parts budget, that amounts to a tidy sum (Bernstein, 1984). According to the General Accounting Office, lax auditing resulted in the Medicaid program spending $500 million to over $1 billion unnecessarily (*New York Times*, February 12, 1985). Much of the fraud occurs in programs designed to provide services, training, and aid to the disadvantaged. But it is not the recipients of the services who are doing most of the cheating but those relatively well-to-do individuals who contract with government to provide their services. They include a former employee of the Department of Transportation who embezzled some $856,000 by putting his name on checks intended for an Atlanta subway. They include the officials of a health plan in California who persuaded some people to sign enrollment forms by telling them that it was a petition to impeach the then governor, Ronald Reagan. And they include the case of the dentist who extracted healthy teeth from poor children so that he could collect fees from a Medicaid dental plan. "It was just awful," said Joel W. Collins, the assistant United States attorney who prosecuted that case. He said the dentist had been found to have billed the government for thousands of dollars worth of work not actually performed as well as for work that was not required. "There was one girl about 13 years old who only had about three teeth left in her mouth," Collins said. "Looking at her just broke your heart" (Marro, 1978). Why audit, indeed!

State and Local Budgeting

While the federal budget process might appear mind boggling, with its extended cycle, series of deadline dates, multiyear outlook, and intermittent congressional involvement, state, local, and institutional budgeting is relatively simple to comprehend. It will be even easier if, at the outset, we clear away some features that are peculiar to certain governments, leaving a common-core budgeting process to describe. (With certain modifications, much that follows applies equally to service institutions such as universities and hospitals.)

Most states place budgeting responsibility solely with the executive, but some establish a budget commission that has legislative representation. In one state, Arkansas, budgeting is entirely a legislative function. Virtually all local budgets are prepared by the executive, although this distinction is blurred under the commission form of municipal government.

The federal budget cycle, as we saw, begins in October. But this is not the case with most other jurisdictions in the United States. Many local governments have fiscal years beginning in January. All state governments (except Alabama, Michigan, New York, and Texas) start their fiscal years in July. The fiscal year in Alabama and Michigan coincides with the federal fiscal year, but New York has an April start and Texas a September start.

One can sense quite different priorities for spending among the various U.S. cities. Minneapolis, for example, spends significant sums on snow removal (as could be expected), and also, perhaps not as predictably, has a relatively large traditional commitment to the park board. Houston, on the other hand, must spend considerable amounts on storm drainage due to its low topography, but it spends nothing on municipal zoning because, uniquely among large U.S. cities, it does not have a zoning code.

Leaving aside peculiarities in budget responsibility and reporting cycles, the state and local budgeting process can be readily conceptualized. The nine-step process shown in Figure 9-5 on the following page summarizes the public sector budgeting effort.

All the steps described in Figure 9-5 require record keeping. *Accounting* is the system of recording, classifying, and reporting financial transactions in an orderly way.

The oldest type of accounting is cash accounting. Receipt transactions are recorded at the time funds are received, and disbursements are recorded when checks are issued. Other types of accounting are accrual and cost. *Accrual accounting* records expenditures when an obligation is incurred (as you record a check when written, not when your bank actually makes payment) and records revenues when earned (for example, when taxes are due, not when the taxpayer actually pays). *Cost accounting* concentrates on reporting the cost of providing goods and services (for example, how much did it cost to repair 1 mile of city streets last year?)

While there are many similarities between government accounting and business accounting one difference is worth noting. In business accounting all the available resources are, in effect, in one cookie jar. But, in a public sector organization, the resources may be accounted for in several separate cookie jars, each of which is called a *fund*. Each fund has its own set of accounts, and each fund is therefore a separate entity, almost as if it were a separate business. The purpose of this device is to ensure that the organization uses the resources made available to each fund only for the purpose designated by that fund. And that is why a university president may not use the scholarship fund to expand the faculty club.

Figure 9-5
State and Local Budget Process

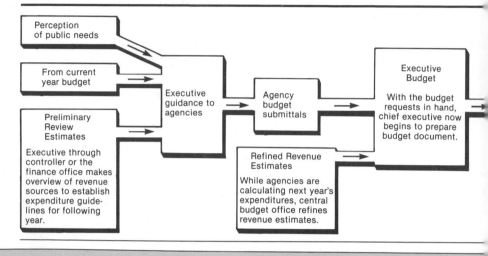

Perception of public needs should begin any governmental budgeting process. Public perceptions are almost always felt, at least implicitly, through election results or annual surveys. If the government's job is to maximize public benefits using available resources, then public needs and priorities must be the starting point for budgeting.

Next, **preliminary estimates** are made for each category of revenue (tax proceeds, fees and user charges, and intergovernmental transfers). The resultant gross revenue projection is compared against the **current year budget** level to see what kind of growth in public services can be sustained.

With a perception of public needs and preliminary revenue estimates, the public executive is prepared to offer **guidance** to **executive agencies** in its budget preparation. Usually, this guidance is incremental—a certain percentage of change in expenditure from the previous year is specified. Sometimes, the executive may require an agency to prepare a zero-based budget, providing justification for both existing and new elements of the program.

Four basic categories of expenditure in **agency budget submittals** must be forecasted: personnel, materials, service contracts, and direct client payments. Of these, personnel is the most important.

The Central Budget Office must prepare **refined revenue estimates** for those revenues that come directly to the government's general fund. Not all revenues, however, are under the purview of the central office. User charges, which derive from the performance of a public service (e.g., transit fares, university tuition, and public hospital payments), are generally budgeted by the agency responsible for the service.

The purpose of the **executive budget** is to present to the legislative body a comprehensive picture of proposed operations for the budget year, expressed both verbally and statistically. The term *budget document* refers either to a single document or—as in the case of larger local governments and states—to several documents. Regardless of its size, the important elements of the budget document generally include the following: the budget message of the chief executive officer

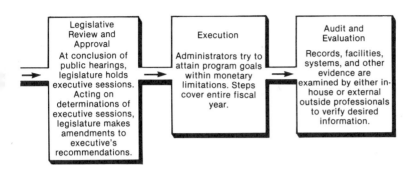

Legislative Review and Approval	Execution	Audit and Evaluation
At conclusion of public hearings, legislature holds executive sessions. Acting on determinations of executive sessions, legislature makes amendments to executive's recommendations.	Administrators try to attain program goals within monetary limitations. Steps cover entire fiscal year.	Records, facilities, systems, and other evidence are examined by either in-house or external outside professionals to verify desired information.

(which sets forth in broad outline the aims of the proposed budget); the official estimate of revenue; a summary of the proposed expenditures for the budget year; and detailed expenditure estimates (which present and justify overall expenditure needs in terms of perceived requirements).

The budget is now ready for presentation for **legislative review and approval** and, through the mass media, to the people. In local governments, initial consideration of the budget by the legislative body ordinarily takes place in public session. Heads of departments and agencies are invited to defend their requests for funds, and the finance officer is asked to explain the revenue measures called for to balance the budget. At this time, citizens are offered an opportunity to present their views on any aspect of the budget that interests them.

Some cities and states provide for the possibility of executive veto and legislative reconsideration of the budget as adopted. The veto comes in several varieties: the entire budget, an entire item, and reduction of an item.

In government organizations and in some other nonprofit organizations, there are actually two budgets. One, which may be referred to as the *legislative budget,* is essentially a request for funds. Most of the media reports about government budgets relate to the legislative budget, and many textbook descriptions of government budgeting focus exclusively on this budget. The second budget, the *management budget,* is especially important during the **execution** phase of the process. It is prepared after the legislature has decided on the amount of funds to be provided. This budget corresponds to the budget prepared in a profit-oriented company; specifically, it is a plan showing the amount of spending that each responsibility center is authorized to undertake.

Audits and evaluations take different forms. *Financial audits* determine whether funds were spent legally and whether financial records are complete and reliable. *Management* or *operations audits* focus on efficiency of operations. *Program audits* examine the extent to which desired results are being achieved. *Performance audits* assess the total operations of an agency. Sunset reviews (see p. 47–48) provide one opportunity for such an audit.

Nailing Down the Main Points

1. Public finance concerns the package of problems and issues that involve the use of tax, borrowing, and expenditure measures for public purpose.

2. The three functions of federal fiscal policy are allocation, distribution, and stabilization. The first function essentially refers to the federal government's efforts to overcome the inherent tendency of a market system to ignore public goals in favor of private goods. The second function refers to the government's efforts to provide adquate income to the very young, the very old, the sick, the disabled, and otherwise disadvantaged. While several techniques of income distribution are available, many experts maintain that tax-transfer schemes are the preferable devices. Since 1970 these payments have grown quite rapidly. The third function, stabilization, contains three components: price stability, full employment, and economic growth.

3. Expansionary fiscal policy can cure recession, but it normally creates a cost in terms of higher inflation. This dilemma has led to a great deal of interest in "supply-side" tax cuts designed to stimulate aggregate supply. If successful, these tax cuts can expand the economy and reduce inflation at the same time. But critics point out three problems of supply-side tax cuts: they also stimulate demand, they make income distribution more unequal, and large tax cuts lead to large budget deficits.

4. Three important concepts that a financial manager ought to keep in mind when developing a tax structure are tax equity, tax efficiency, and tax overlapping. A fair or equitable tax would: (a) treat equally people in equal economic circumstances, and (b) treat unequally people in unequal economic circumstances. Tax equity further implies that, when feasible, people will be charged according to benefit received.

   Tax efficiency means that the tax will neither disturb the public sector too much nor prove difficult to collect. Last, tax overlapping refers to the coordination of taxing effort by various levels of government.

5. Among the leading sources of revenue for governments are personal income tax; corporate income tax; property tax; estate, inheritance, and gift tax; and sales tax.

6. Personal income tax, the leading source of federal revenue, is a function of the definition of income, allowable deductions, exemptions, and tax rates. Given the numerous exclusions and deductions, the income tax in the United States is "eroded" at upper levels. In a sense, these exclusions and deductions are examples of a larger phenomenon: tax expenditures. Some experts and government analysts think these tax preferences really should be viewed as subsidy *payments* to preferred taxpayers.

7. The generally accepted purposes of budgeting are control, management, and planning. Significantly, emphasis on each purpose has shifted over the years, but today the function of the budget is really a combination of all three.

8. Associated with each purpose or function are certain specific types of budgets. For example; line-item and performance budgeting go with the control and management functions; planning-programming and zero-

based budgeting, with the planning function. A capital budget is a plan for investment in capital assets (e.g., buildings and bridges) separate from current or operating expenditures.

9. The federal budget cycle, which was changed considerably by the Congressional Budget Act of 1974, consists of four phases: *(a)* executive formulation, *(b)* congressional authorization and appropriation, *(c)* budget execution and control, and *(d)* review and audit. The Congressional Budget Act of 1974, which established the Congressional Budget Office to serve both houses and a committee on the budget in each house, substantially changes *(b)*. In the past the president would send his budget to Congress each January and then Congress would pass a series of bills authorizing various programs and appropriating the money to pay for them. But these bills were enacted on a *piecemeal* basis. Under the new act, however, overall targets are set on income and expenditures (in broad categories); how one spending bill relates to another is emphasized. The new Congressional Budget Office, meanwhile, helps analyze the president's budget and suggests alternatives.

10. State, local, and institutional budget processes vary considerably. Nevertheless, we can generally characterize such budgeting as a nine-step process: *(a)* perception of public needs, *(b)* preliminary revenue estimates, *(c)* executive guidance to agencies, *(d)* agency budget submittals, *(e)* refined revenue estimates, *(f)* executive budget, *(g)* legislative review, *(h)* execution of budget, and *(i)* audit and evaluation.

11. The first step in execution of state, local, and institutional budgets is the allocation of elements of the appropriation. The most common and systematic scheme by which money is allocated is a numerical one in which a number is assigned to every fund; each fund, in turn, is divided into accounts. The next step in the execution of the budget is to allot the money for a specified period of time.

    Accounting plays a major role in both these steps. Indeed, no organization—public or private—can function effectively without a good accounting system. Why? Because expenditures must be kept within the approved budget totals; because what has been paid must be available to legislative audit; and because accounting systems (such as cost and accrual) serve as excellent management tools.

Concepts for Review

accounting
budgeting
capital budgeting
Congressional Budget and Impoundment Control Act of 1974
cost accounting, accrual accounting
deficits
demand-side economics (Keynesian)
economic growth
economic system

externalities
fiscal policy, monetary policy
fiscal year
four phases of federal budget cycle
functions of federal fiscal policy
funds
horizontal and vertical equity
impounding
justifications for regulation
  (market failures)

legislative budget
line-item budget
management budget
monopoly
obligations
outlays
performance budget
political strategies in the budget
    process
price instability or inflation
private and public goods
program budgeting
progressive and regressive taxation

public finance
purposes of budgeting
sources of revenue
state/local budget process
supply-side economics (Reaganomics)
tax efficiency
tax equity
tax expenditure
tax overlapping, tax coordination
transfer payments
"uncontrollables" in federal budget
user fees
zero-based budgeting

Problems

1. The following two statements illustrate what principle discussed in this chapter?

    "The average cost of tax collection is 4.4 percent of the local income tax revenue in Pennsylvlania local governments."

    "With the progress of industrial society and the development of a pecuniary economy, there followed a successive shift in emphasis to income rather than property as an index of ability to pay. Today, wealth is reflected in the person's income—earned and unearned—not real property," (*Public Administration Times*, November 1, 1980).

2. Plot the data in Table 9–2 on a graph with taxable income as the horizontal axis. What conclusions do you draw?

3. One of the most critical issues in public finance is how to distribute the goods of our system more equally without undermining the efficiency of the system. The problem, essentially, is to continue efficiency with greater equality—even at some cost to efficiency. To crystalize the issue, Arthur M. Okun (1975), who was chairman of the Council of Economic Advisors under President Lyndon B. Johnson, invites us to participate in what he calls "the leaky-bucket experiment." Suppose that you could transfer $4,000 from each of the 5 percent of families at the top of the income distribution to the 20 percent of families at the bottom. Each family at the bottom would then get $1,000. But there's a hitch—the bucket in which you transfer this income leaks. Some of the money carried from the rich to the poor will leak out of the bucket and never reach the poor—as a result of a loss of efficiency. Some, like John Rawls (see Chapter 4), would give a clear, crisp answer: Make the switch to increase equality, unless an unequal distribution of income would definitely be to everyone's advantage. Equality should have priority. But others, like Milton Friedman, give an equally clear, crisp, and opposite answer: Efficiency should have priority. What if 10 percent—$100—leaked out so that each poor family got only $900? Would you still make the switch? What if $500 leaked out? What if $999?

4. One response to revenue-raising limitations being placed on local govern-

ment is to delete exemptions. For example: "Welfare and charitable groups enjoying property tax exemption include a diverse group of organizations such as the YMCA, fraternal clubs, chambers of commerce, labor unions, the American Legion, Masonic Lodges, orphanages, humane societies, hospitals, and retirement and nursing homes" (Florestano, 1981:124). Which exemptions would you delete? How would you justify it?

5. "Some students of the federal system argue that our budgetary procedures should be so adjusted as to free large and complex endeavors from the uncertainties and vagaries of the annual authorization-appropriation process. They say that once a major undertaking like the space program or an urban renewal program is underway, too much is at stake to risk a loss in momentum or serious change in direction every 12 months." Do you agree? James Webb (1969:110–101), who made the statement, continues: "On the other hand, considering the great concentration of resources and power that the large-scale endeavor represents and the far-reaching consequences that would follow from absences, there must be effective means to protect the interest of society." Do you still agree with the original statement?

6. There are two ways to cut a budget. One is a general cut, a 5 percent or even 1 percent cut across the board. With some justification, this approach is called using the meat ax. But at least it avoids the drawback of the second way to cut the budget, proposing specific cuts. When specific cuts in particular programs are proposed, strong objections are raised by special interests.

   In reducing expenditures, Alan Reynolds (1978) recommends examining every program to see whether there are effective ways of accomplishing its intended results. Using a current copy of the *Budget of the United States* (or your state or university budget available in the library) and following Reynolds' five basic rules below, see how many cuts you can come up with. For each program cut, assess in relative merits, suggest alternative ways of accomplishing it, and outline a strategy for handling opposition. Here are Reynolds' rules:

   1. Eliminate or reduce subsidies.
   2. Eliminate unnecessary aid to state and local government.
   3. Eliminate "temporary programs" that no longer serve their purpose.
   4. Eliminate unnecessary educational programs.
   5. Eliminate programs that are dubious in their purposes or effects.

7. An interesting ethical question arises when the rules under which an agency is forced to operate are such that effective and efficient operations are inhibited. Should managers get the job done and cover up the fact that in order to do the job they had to break rules, or should they use the existence of the rule as an excuse for not getting the job done? Managers, with different temperaments answer this question in different ways. For example, in a certain state the legislature has set maximum rates at which part-time psychiatrists can be employed by state mental health

institutions. These rates are about one half the going rate for psychiatrists, so at these rates few psychiatrists would work for the state. Administrators therefore hire psychiatrists for half a day and pay them for a full day. This is the only way they can hire psychiatrists. On balance, have they done wrong? (Anthony & Herzlinger, 1980:446).

8. Political considerations prevade budgeting as well as all phases of program management. Anthony and Herzlinger (1980:344) suggest a variety of ploys used in the budget game. Within each of the following two categories, match the ploy (left column) with the appropriate example (right column).

Ploys for New Program

1. Foot in the door: Sell a modest program initially; conceal its real magnitude until after it has gotten underway and has built a constituency.

2. Hidden ball: Conceal the nature of a politically unattractive program by hiding it within an attractive program.

3. Divide and conquer: Seek approval of a budget request from more than one supervisor.

4. Distraction: Base a specific request on the premise that an overall program has been approved when this is not in fact the case. (Difficult, but not impossible, to use successfully.)

5. Shell game: Use statistics to mislead supervisors as to the true state of affairs.

Examples

a. A state decided to build a highway, reckoning the cost as low since the federal government would reimburse it for 95 percent of the cost. The state overlooked the fact that maintenance of the highway would be 100 percent a state cost.

b. At a legislative committee, a university presented arguments as to why some buildings should be replaced with a new set of buildings in order to implement an "approved plan" for doubling the capacity of a certain professional school. The argument was that newer buildings would be more useful and efficient than the existing buildings. The merits were discussed in terms of the return on investment arising from the greater efficiency of the new buildings. This discussion went on for some time until a committee member asked who had approved the plan for expansion of the school in the first place. It turned out that the expansion had never been approved; approval of the new buildings would have de facto approved the expansion.

c. It is alleged that the supervisor was late in transmitting budget instructions, or that the instructions were not clear, and that this accounts for inadequacies in the justifications furnished.

d. Some years ago it was difficult to get air force funds for general-purpose buildings but easy to get funds for intercontinental missiles, so there was included in the budget for the missile program an amount to provide for construction of a new office building. Initially this building was used by a contractor in the missile program, but eventually it became a general-purpose air force office building.

e. The City Planning Commission in New York City was so organized that each member was supposed to be responsible for certain specified areas. The distinctions were not clear, however, so budgetees would deal with more than one supervisor, hoping that one of them would react favorably.

6. It's free: Argue that someone else will pay for the project so the organization might as well approve it.

f. In the early 1960s the National Institutes of Health were unable to obtain approval for the construction of new buildings but were able to build "annexes." It is said that building 12A (the annex) is at least double the size of building 12.

7. You're to blame: Imply that the supervisor is at fault and that defects in the budget submission therefore should be overlooked.

g. In a certain state the legislature was sold on a program to educate handicapped children in regular schools, rather than in the special schools they currently used. The costs were said to be transportation costs and a few additional teachers. Within five years, the definition of "handicapped" had been greatly broadened, and the resources devoted to the program were four times the amount originally estimated.

8. If we don't, someone else will: Appeal to people's innate desire to be at least as good as the competition.

h. The budgetee was head of the Model Cities program for a certain city. He wanted available funds to be used primarily for health and education programs but knew that his superiors were more interested in "economic" programs (new businesses and housing). The budgetee emphasized to the mayor and interested groups that over half the funds ($2,350,000 out of $4,365,000) was intended for economic purposes. The catch was that the source of "other" funds was not known, and there were no firm plans for obtaining such funds.

9. Call it a rose: Use misleading, but appealing, labels.

i. A university budgetee argued that a proposed new program was breaking new ground, was important to the national interest, and that if her university didn't initiate it, some other university would start it, obtain funds from the appropriate government agency, and thus make it more difficult for her university to start the program later on.

Ploys for Maintaining or Increasing Ongoing Programs

Examples

1. Show of strength: Arrange demonstrations in support of the request; occasionally threaten violence, work stoppages, or other unpleasant consequences if the request is not approved.

a. This well-known ploy derives its name from an incident in which Robert McNamara was involved when he was with the Ford Motor Company. In a period of stringency, all division heads were asked to make a special effort to cut costs. Most responded with genuine belt tightening; however, one division manager, with $100 million sales, reported that the only cost reduction opportunity he had found was to eliminate the gold watches that were customarily given to employees upon their retirement with 30 or more years of satisfactory service.

2. Razzle-dazzle: Support the request with voluminous data, but arranged in such a way that their significance is not clear. The data need not be valid.

b. The budget guidelines requested a "complete justification" of requested additions to inventory. The motor vehicle repair shop of a state did not submit its budget on time. At the last minute, it submitted an itemized list of parts to be ordered, based on a newly installed system of calculating economic order quantities. It argued that its tardiness was a consequence of getting the bugs out of the new system (which was installed at the controller's instigation), but that it was generally agreed that the economic order quantity formula was the best way of justifying the amount of parts to be purchased.

3. Delayed buck: Submit the data late, arguing that the budget guidelines required so much detailed calculation that the job could not be done on time.

c. In the summer of 1966 when the Community Development Agency of New York City was trying to decide which 50 of the 500 summer programs would be funded for the full year, a director of one of these programs got the entire staff of about 150 people to come down to the central office to sit in. The director had told the staff that for no apparent reason the city had not forwarded the last reimbursement, and therefore the payroll could not be met. On leaving the central office, the director dropped the hint that the sit-in might recur if his program was not extended.

4. Make a study: The budget guidelines contain a statement that a certain program is to be curtailed or discontinued. The budgetee responds that the proposed action should not be taken until its consequences have been studied thoroughly.

d. In 1975 the General Accounting Office made a report demonstrating that the navy's patrol hydrofoil missile ships were not cost effective. On April 6, 1977, the secretary of defense announced that this program was being discontinued at a savings of $300 million. On August 16, 1977, however, the navy awarded a contract for these ships. Someone had made an end run around the secretary of defense and had convinced the Congress that the ships were needed.

5. Gold watch: When asked in general terms to cut the budget, propose specific actions that do more harm than good.

e. When Mayor Abraham Beame was asked in 1975 by the federal government to reduce spending in New York City in order to avoid bankruptcy, he responded by dismissing 7,000 police officers and firefighters and closing 26 firehouses. Many people believe he did this to inflame public opinion against budget cuts. It did have this effect, and the order was reversed.

6. Arouse client antagonism: When a budget cut is ordered, cut a popular program, hoping to divert attention away from lower priority areas where cuts are indeed feasible. (This is a variation of the gold watch ploy.)

7. End run: Go outside normal channels to obtain reversal of a decision.

f. A public works department submitted a 20-page list of repairs to municipal buildings that were said to be vitally needed, couched in highly technical language. This was actually a "wish list," prepared without a detailed analysis.

g. Well before the budget period, the program analysis staff of a city completed a study that concluded that one fire station should be closed. It was sent to the public safety department for comment. No comment was forthcoming until almost the completion of the budget process. At that time, the head of public safety said that he thought the report contained errors and that further study was necessary before any action was taken.

Case 9.1
Formulating the Reagan Tax Plan

At a White House meeting on the administration's new tax plan earlier [in May 1985], Vice President George Bush—opposing a proposal to curtail tax breaks for oil and gas drillers—pointed across the table at President Reagan.

"This man and I," the vice president, a former Texas oilman, declared, "campaigned on a platform of keeping the energy industry strong." But White House Chief of Staff Donald Regan argued that oil and gas tax breaks should be reduced because the administration tax plan ought to treat all industries equally.

President Reagan, troubled by the dilemma, muttered: "Oh, Lord." He eventually decided the issue in Mr. Bush's favor.

Another debate that shaped the tax plan took place in the book-lined office of Bob Packwood, the chairman of the Senate Finance Committee. At one meeting, the Oregon Republican warned Treasury Secretary James Baker that the administration's plan must back off from earlier proposals to tax company-paid employee benefits, such as health insurance. "I'll kill the bill if I have to," Senator Packwood vowed.

Kirkland's Suggestion

Later, the senator advanced a compromise privately suggested to him by Lane Kirkland, the president of the AFL–CIO and an outspoken defender of tax-free fringe benefits. The compromise would tax only a small amount of employer-paid health insurance premiums. "We're going to give you what you want," Deputy Treasury Secretary Richard Darman told Senator Packwood.

The two episodes illustrate how the president's tax plan was crafted through compromise and concession. Over the past six months, the administration steadily retreated from the bolder tax-overhaul program advanced by the Treasury [in November 1984]. Traditional Republican constituencies—industry and investors, in particular—prevailed in case after case.

Yet White House and Treasury officials fought the temptation to yield on many other fronts, despite many pleas from lobbyists and corporate chiefs. They knew that for tax revision to succeed, their plan must have strong "populist" appeal. Thus they weeded and pruned the thicket of preferences in the tax code to pay for a steep reduction in tax rates, and they produced a package that—incredibly, for a conservative administration—would raise corporate income taxes substantially while lowering the bite on individuals. (See exhibits.) Strong lobbying even backfired in one instance: An insurance-industry TV ad campaign angered Treasury officials, who decided to tax the buildup in the value of new life insurance policies.

Much Uncertainty

The outlook is full of uncertainty. By making concessions to interest groups ranging from oil drillers to charities, the administration probably has enhanced the chances for congressional approval of a major tax bill. But the compromises have made the plan less sweeping and have invited still more concessions to interest groups, as congressional hearings begin today. By producing a hybrid rather than a more pristine tax-revision package, the White House has given Democrats more room to construct an alternative.

Interviews with administration officials, congressional sources, and lobbyists who participated in many of the crucial decisions and closed-door meetings show how billions of dollars in tax benefits were battled over to shape President Reagan's tax plan. Among the broad themes characterizing this six-month exercise are the following:

- Mr. Baker's Treasury and Mr. Regan's White House staff clashed often. Mr. Regan maintained a substantial pride of authorship in his own plan, dubbed "Treasury I" and drafted last year while he was treasury secretary. It was Mr. Regan, a former Wall Street leader, who urged the president to lower the top capital-gains tax rate to 17.5 percent from the current 20 percent; ironically, his initial Treasury plan would have taxed gains at higher, ordinary-income rates.

- Though the administration was trying to make its plan politically palatable, it ignored the advice of its chief congressional ally, Chairman Dan Rostenkowski of the House Ways and Means Committee. The Illinois Democrat exhorted Mr. Baker not to give in to the oil and gas interests of the secretary's native Texas. "Jim, that's going to be pretty much the measure of your mettle," the lawmaker warned him, but Mr. Baker decided to keep some oil breaks anyway. At the same time, the administration gained a promise of noninterference from Senator Packwood by placating him on fringe benefits. That promise was a sizable concession from a lawmaker who had once declared that he liked the current tax code "the way it is."

- Congressional authors of competing tax-overhaul plans were caught in surprising crosscurrents. [In December 1984], Mr. Regan, still Treasury secretary, invited New Jersey Senator Bill Bradley, coauthor of a Democratic tax plan, for lunch at his Florida retreat and convinced him of the administration's commitment to broad tax "reform." While wooing Senator Bradley, who since then has frequently discussed the plan with the administration, the White House has been less responsive to Representative Jack Kemp, the coauthor of a GOP plan. The New York Republican campaigned in vain—one time before the president—to lower the top individual tax rate even further than the administration's 35 percent.

- After all of its concessions to interest groups and lawmakers, the administration realized earlier this month that its purportedly "revenue-neutral" plan, over the next five years, would generate about $80 billion less for the government than would current law. The hastily arranged solution was to propose taxing the corporate "windfalls" that would result from companies continuing to enjoy generous writeoffs on existing plant and equipment while their tax rates fall to 33 percent from the current maximum of 46 percent. Smokestack industries have already begun attacking the plan as burdensome. Congressional leaders worry that the Reagan plan would reduce revenues despite the new windfall provision.

In his Feb. 6 [1985] State of the Union address, Mr. Reagan had promised that his plan would raise the same amount of revenue as does the existing system, while cutting the top individual rate at least to 35 percent—the rate proposed in Treasury I—and "significantly" increasing the personal exemption from the present $1,040. A higher exemption would remove many poor people from the tax rolls, a move considered necessary to win Democratic support. The president's promises would mean an annual revenue loss of about $100 billion, which would be made up partly by increasing taxes on corporations.

When Messrs. Baker and Darman took over at Treasury, they started to look for ways to make the November tax blueprint politically salable, yet economically sound. Each Saturday the secretary met with about 9 or 10 top departmental officials to go over sections of the tax code for four to six hours at a stretch. The meetings were informal, with Secretary Baker often appearing in corduroys and cowboy boots and chewing Red Man tobacco. But sometimes the meetings grew tense as the politically savvy Messrs. Baker and Darman battled with the Treasury's professional tax staff.

One of the first decisions Mr. Baker made was to stand firm on the decision to end the deductibility of state and local taxes. Then he took aim at some revenue-losing provisions in Treasury I to help finance some of the more costly concessions that he knew the administration would have to make. He decided to cut back a proposal that would have allowed corporations to deduct tens of billions of dollars in dividend payments and to drop a costly, complex proposal to index interest income and payments to inflation. Much of the revenue saved through these moves was used to pay for a far more generous corporate depreciation system than the original Treasury plan had envisioned.

A prolonged struggle broke out over how to tax capital gains. Business lobbyists led by John Albertine, the president of the American Business Conference, attacked the Treasury I proposal as harmful to risky ventures. Over lunch March 4 [1985] at the Hay-Adams Hotel, Mr. Darman told Mr. Albertine that he was sympathetic. According to Mr. Albertine, "Darman said, 'I think American business is too risk averse, and the last thing we want to do is bias the tax code even more in that direction.'"

Mr. Darman wanted to address the problem by creating a special preference for start-up companies, a proposal that business groups disliked. Eventually, the department decided to keep the exclusion of capital gains at a level that would maintain the top rate very close to the current 20 percent for stocks, bonds, and certain other assets. Later, Mr. Regan persuaded the president to drop the rate to 17.5 percent.

Briefing the President
Starting in late April, Secretary Baker, Mr. Darman and Assistant Secretary Ronald Pearlman began briefing the president on their plan. They presented two

options—a 34 percent top rate for individuals with a $1,900 exemption, or a 35 percent top rate with a $2,000 exemption. Mr. Regan strongly urged the president to retain the 15 percent, 25 percent, 35 percent rate structure and the $2,000 exemption of Treasury I; the figures were "symmetric," he said. The president made a couple of changes, including a veto of Mr. Baker's proposal to allow a deduction for charitable contributions only above 1 percent of income. "I thought we were trying to encourage the private sector to do things so that government won't have to," Mr. Reagan said.

In Congress, Secretary Baker set out to woo key lawmakers, particularly Representative Rostenkowski. At first, the chairman was willing to prepare a tax bill jointly with the White House. But in a series of breakfast meetings, the Reagan-wary Democrats on his Ways and Means panel nixed the idea; they wanted the president to take full responsibility for his package.

At each of the closed-door breakfasts of the Ways and Means Democrats, the chairman emphasized that "everything is on the table" for repeal in the cause of rate reduction, including, at least for discussion, the sacrosanct deduction for mortgage interest. Representative Rostenkowski took this hard-line view into his long series of private meetings with Mr. Baker. The street kid from an ethnic Chicago neighborhood and the Texas aristocrat somehow had "good chemistry," according to a Rostenkowski aide, and they had frank, good-humored and some-times salty discussions. At one meeting, Representative Rostenkowski dismissed Mr. Baker's suggestion that decisions weren't yet final by saying, "Who do you think you're doing business with, a cub?"

Need for Compromise

Representative Rostenkowski told Mr. Baker he wanted a "tough" White House bill, and he warned that the congressional process is slow and compromise inevitable, Mr. Baker disagreed. "He felt that with the president's backing, it [the White House bill] could move very quickly," a Rostenkowski aide says. "He felt it could be kept together and still feels that way."

In the Senate, Chairman Packwood, a vocal opponent of tax revision, quietly campaigned to protect the sole area of tax law that really concerned him—tax-free employer-paid fringe benefits. The plan that the White House eventually bought—to tax a small amount of health insurance premiums would partly satisfy its need for revenues and the AFL-CIO's desire to protect generous benefits won for its members. Union aides, who officially want no taxation of fringe benefits, acknowl-edge that Senator Packwood and Mr. Kirkland discussed "options."

In contrast, Representative Rostenkowski and AFL-CIO Chief Kirkland held a highly contentious meeting over the fringe-benefit issue. Representative Ros-tenkowski told the labor boss: "You're not going to get me to wink. . . . I'm going to come to that table with clean hands." Soon thereafter, hordes of union lob-byists ascended to Capitol Hill and, for the first time, workers were organized to lobby in Representative Rostenkowski's own district.

The administration initially had hopes of corralling the support of the four congressional authors of tax-overhaul plans—dubbed "the four horsemen." The shirtsleeves meeting in Florida between Senator Bradley and Mr. Regan helped cement the senator's belief that he should aid the administration, but he never negotiated away his own plan. In fact, Senator Bradley repeatedly urged fellow Democrats to become players, once making a special trip to Chicago to talk to Representative Rostenkowski after Treasury I was unveiled.

Representative Kemp, a rival of Vice President Bush for the 1988 GOP presidential nomination, was intent on getting individual tax rates lower than the Treasury proposed. But his idea, after intense study, was rebuffed as too beneficial to the wealthy. A well-briefed president debated the issue with Representative Kemp in an 11th hour White House meeting requested by the congressman.

Other lawmakers possessed varying degrees of interest—and grounding—in the details of the plan. In a meeting over a plate of cheese in the basement of Secretary Baker's home, Senator Robert Kasten of Wisconsin, a coauthor of a GOP tax plan, said of a fringe-benefit mechanism called a cafeteria plan, "We can't tax those lunches." (He says he meant the comment as a joke.)

In mid-May, Mr. Baker came to the White House with some bad news: The plan, with a $2,000 exemption, would lose revenue in the 1986 to 1999 period; it would be necessary to start the exemption lower, say at $1,500, for a few years. Then the Treasury chief dropped another bomb: A Treasury foul up had led to a huge overestimate of the 1990 revenue figures.

Mr. Regan and other White House aides, who felt the $2,000 exemption provided the GOP with a great political advantage, were upset. "So, we have to give up the $2,000 exemption because of this mistake you made?" the chief of staff demanded. Mr. Baker bridled. No, he replied, the Treasury would propose the corporate "windfall" tax, which would regain most of the lost revenue. But the plan was still short of revenue because it allowed an immediate drop in rates while tax breaks were being phased out slowly. At a later meeting, some provisions were tightened up and the $2,000 exemption was fully restored.

The final decision concerned the controversial oil and gas issue. Mr. Baker had suggested scaling back many of the Treasury I proposals that would have eliminated two big oil-tax breaks, although he tried to score some political points by treating big oil companies less favorably than small ones. Vice President Bush argued on national security grounds for an even fuller retreat from Treasury I. U.S. oil production is down, Mr. Bush observed; the administration could catch oil millionaires with a minimum tax, he said, "but don't decimate the industry." Mr. Regan countered that oil drilling is off because of falling world oil prices.

The president was won over by the national-security argument, officials say. But some acknowledge another consideration: 22 Republican senators are up for reelection in 1986—many in energy-producing states—and ever since the release of Treasury I, angry oilmen have been mailing back the "Eagle pins" they earned for big contributions to the GOP.

That point once came up around the cabinet table, a top official recalls. "Someone said, 'You know, there are four compelling economic reasons why tax preferences should be retained for the oil industry.' And we all said, 'What are they?' And he said, 'Texas, Oklahoma, Louisiana, and Arkansas.' "

Exhibit 1
Changing Tax Plans: Who Pays *(Shares of Revenue, 1990 Estimates—in Percent)*

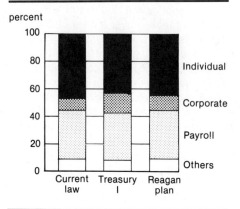

Source: U.S. Treasury Department.

Exhibit 2
Changing Sources of Tax Revenue *(Historical Shares of Revenue—in Percent)*

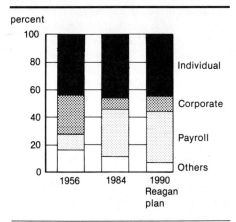

Source: U.S. Treasury Department.

Exhibit 3
Shifting Burden

Income Group	Percent of Total Income Taxes Paid	
	Current Law	**Proposal**
Less than $10,000	.5%	.3%
$10,000–15,000	1.8	1.5
$15,000–20,000	3.3	3.0
$20,000–$30,000	10.3	10.1
$30,000–50,000	24.3	24.4
$50,000–100,000	32.7	33.7
$100,000–200,000	12.3	12.7
$200,000 and over	14.8	14.3

Note: The Reagan plan would cut individual taxes by a net of $22.1 billion. But
Americans at some income levels would pay more.
Source: U.S. Treasury Department.

Exhibit 5
Tax Rates in U.S., Other Major Industrial Countries (1985 *Tax Laws*)

	Reagan Plan	U.S. Current Law	West Germany	Japan	Britain
Individual tax rates	3 brackets, from 15% through first $29,000 to 35% above $70,000	14 brackets, from 11% at $3,401 to 50% above $169,020	11 brackets, from 12.7% through first $3,225 to 56% above $41,945; fewer deductions	15 brackets, from 10.5% through first $1,988 to 70% above $318,091—plus fewer deductions, heavy prefecture taxes	6 brackets, from 30% through first $19,327 to 60% above $47,815; fewer deductions
Income for 50% bracket	No one pays 50% rate	$169,020	$22,580	$59,642	$37,650
Corporate tax rates	Sliding scale to 33% $100,000 income	Sliding scale to 46% $100,000 income	56% for firms with unlimited tax liability; others 36%	42% on most income, but 32% on income distributed as dividends	Flat 40% going to 35% next spring
Capital gains (individuals)	Maximum 17.5% rate for non-depreciable assets	Maximum 20% rate; 40% included in income	Exempt, except for short-term "speculative" profits	Taxed as ordinary income; securities sales exempt	30% on net gains over $7,028
Mortgage interest	Fully deductible for primary residence; limits for second homes	Fully deductible	Not deductible	Not deductible	May deduct interest on first $37,650 of first home

Sources: Coopers & Lybrand, U.S. Treasury.

Exhibit 6
Tax Overhaul: How Various Plans Compare *(1986 Tax Year)*

	Reagan Plan	**Current Law**
Individual tax rates	3 rates: 15, 25, 35%	14 rates from 11% to 50%
Personal exemption	$2,000	$1,080
Mortgage interest	Principal residence deductible	Fully deductible for all mortgages
Other interest	$5,000 plus amount equal to investment income	$10,000 plus amount equal to investment income
Employer-provided health insurance	Taxed up to first $10/month for single; $25 for family	Not taxed
Charitable contribution	Deductible, but only on itemized returns	Fully deductible
State and local taxes	No deduction	Fully deductible
Capital gains	50% excluded for 17.5% top rate, but fewer items covered	60% excluded for 20% top rate
Corporate tax rates	33% top rate, graduated rates up to $75,000	46%; graduated rates up to $100,000
Depreciation	Somewhat accelerated, but less generous than current law	Accelerated

Case Questions

1. Does the Reagan plan have an appropriate balance between sources of tax revenue (Exhibit 2)?
2. Is Reagan concerned with vertical or horizontal equity?
3. To what extent do the criteria used by the participants in this case match those described in the chapter? What are the differences? What might cause those differences?
4. Who are the winners and losers in the plan?
5. Based on this case, what generalizations about the formulation of public policy would you make? (You may wish to review Chapter 2.)

Case References

Paul Blustein and Jeffrey H. Birnbaum, "President's Tax Plan Took Shape in Months of Talks, Compromises," *The Wall Street Journal,* May 30, 1985; President's Tax Reform Plan (Washington, D.C.: Treasury Department, May 28, 1985).

10

Organizational Behavior

Introduction

This chapter is animated by a single question: How does the administrator motivate people within an organization to be more productive?

People are an important part of every organization's resources, although budgets and financial plans do not recognize them as such. The task of stimulating creativity and productivity in the public sector is one of the great managerial challenges of our age, a task that is complicated by the significant changes that have been occurring in the value systems and attitudes toward work. Few government agencies have adequately adjusted their systems of managing and motivating to accommodate these changes. Nor have they adjusted their systems of promoting and paying people, as we shall see in the next chapter.

The first section of this chapter explains the way in which the behavioral sciences have increased our understanding of how a manager can motivate. Modern approaches to management recognize that the prescriptions of the behavioral sciences do not apply universally in every situation; instead, these approaches realize the need for administrators to know what will work best in any given situation. Modern management theories try to balance the rational/economic assumptions of the classical school—Taylor (Chapter 1), Fayol (Chapter 1), Weber (Chapter 8), and others—with the social/self-actualization assumptions of the behavioral school. Instead of assuming one or the other, or assuming everyone has the same needs, personalities, and attitudes around work, the modern approach assumes *contingency*. Unfortunately, there is no "one best way" to manage; it depends on the situation. The chief objective of this chapter, then, is to show when and under what circumstances various assumptions and their associated management guidelines hold.

In this chapter, I have deviated from the standard academic practice of focusing exclusively on employee behavior in organizations. It is my experience that effective administrators know how to manage themselves as well as others. Arguably, self-management is a prerequisite to the management of others. If there is chaos within oneself, how can there be order in the organization one manages? Therefore, in the last section of this chapter, I shall focus on the subject of self-management.

Behavioral Approaches to Management

What is meant by the output of administrators? Not the number of memos they write, phone calls they answer, meetings they attend, or deals they cut. In a fundamental sense, their output is the output of the people over whom they have influence. Management, we must never forget, is a *team* activity.

Administrators have two principal ways to elicit better performance from people: motivation (the subject of this chapter) and training (a topic for consideration in the next). In his research on motivation, the eminent American psychologist and philosopher William James found that employees can maintain their jobs—that is, avoid being fired—by working at only 20 percent to 30 percent of their ability. But, if highly motivated, employees will work at 80 percent to 90 percent of their ability. The simple equations below illustrate the difference these two factors can make for a hypothetical individual (let us call him Stakhanov) with a natural ability level of, say, 100.

First assume the employee has a supervisor who neither motivates nor trains Stakhanov.

$$\text{Performance} = 100 \times .20 \times 1.00 = 20$$

Now assume he has a supervisor who does motivate and train:

$$\text{Performance} = 100 \times .80 \times 1.50 = 120$$

While we probably cannot measure motivation as precisely as our example suggests, we have learned a few things about it in the last 60 or so years. The story itself is fascinating. It begins in the 1920s, when the Harvard Business School, under the supervision of Elton Mayo (1933), conducted a series of experiments in the Hawthorne, Illinois, plant of Western Electric.

Hawthorne Studies

An Experiment—and a Puzzle. In 1924, Western Electric efficiency experts designed a research program to study the effects of illumination on productivity. The assumption was that increased illumination would result in higher output. Two groups of employees were selected: a test group, which worked under varying degrees of light, and a control group, which worked under normal plant illumination. As expected, when lighting increased, the output of the test group went up. But something else happened—and it was entirely unexpected: The output of the control group also went up.

At this point, Western Electric turned for help to Mayo and his associates. Mayo's researchers then began to implement a variety of changes, behavioral as well as physical. Rest periods were scheduled. Work hours were altered. Hot snacks were served. But no matter what was done to the workers, output continued to soar.

Baffled by the results, the researchers took a radical step: They restored the original conditions. This change was expected to have a tremendous negative psychological impact and most certainly reduce output. But output jumped to an all-time high. Why? The answer was fairly simple, but the implications were catastrophic, bringing an almost precise reversal of the whole line of management thought and practice since the Industrial Revolution. In a nutshell, what the Harvard team found—after further investigation, including interviews with over 20,000 employees from every department in the company— was this: The workers' productivity went up because the attention lavished upon them by the experimenters made them feel that they were important to the company. No longer did they view themselves as isolated individuals. Now they were participating members of a congenial cohesive work group.

The general lesson was patent. The significant factor affecting organizational productivity was not the physical conditions or monetary rewards derived from work but the interpersonal relationships developed on the job. Mayo found that when informal groups felt that their own goals were in opposition to those of management and their control over their job or environment was slight, productivity remained low.

In a word, the new goal for management, the golden key, seemed to be *morale*. To maintain a high level of output, the administrator had only to develop ways to satisfy the worker, to make him or her feel good about his or her work, boss, and organization. Dr. Feelgood had replaced the grim efficiency expert.

Behavioral science was making progress. The discovery of the informal group—and, in a larger sense, the humanity of the worker—was, as we said, a real breakthrough in management thought. But the same cannot be said for the concept of morale. As subsequent research began to show, morale was no panacea. Given happy employees, it by no means follows with iron logic that they will feel an urge to work harder and harder. So, disillusionment set in and the scientists began to look for a new tack to improving the effectiveness of organizations.

The Hawthorne Effect Revisited. One of the seminal ideas in contemporary social science is the phenomenon of the "Hawthorne effect"; that is, the tendency of humans to alter their behavior when they are under study by social scientists and thereby jeopardize the accuracy of the study. Using the statistical methods available to them at the time, the Hawthorne researchers found only a small correlation between physical and material factors and output. They concluded that unquantifiable "human relations" accounted for changes in output.

Recent research by Parsons (1978) and Franke and Kaul (1978) has apparently invalidated much of the Hawthorne study.

Parsons finds hard evidence that the workers at Western Electric's Hawthorne plant were systematically receiving information feedback, that is, knowledge of results about their output rates. Workers also received a differential monetary award; the faster they worked, the more money they got. The combination of information feedback and differential monetary rewards—not changing environmental conditions—seem to offer the best explanation for the gradually increasing productivity at the Hawthorne plant.

The research of Franke and Kaul is even more surprising. It virtually reverses the original findings of the Hawthorne study. Reanalyzing the raw data using more sophisticated statistical techniques and computers, Franke and Kaul found a significant correlation between output and "managerial discipline." The firing of two workers during the course of the experiments explains most of the changes in output. "Human relations" do partially govern output—not in the sense of "humane treatment" but rather in the sense of simple discipline. Franke and Kaul also concur with Parson that the group pay incentive was of some value in raising output.

Perhaps the main lesson to be drawn from this story is that social science researchers must avoid enthusiastically embracing something scientifically unproven just because it is congenial with their own values.

Maslow's Hierarchy of Needs

The next scene in our story opens with a question, much as the Hawthorne affair did. Money, presumably, was a great incentive to work hard, but when people were asked what was most important to them in their jobs, money often took third, fourth, or even fifth place. Factors like "full appreciation for work done," "feeling in on things," "sympathetic understanding of personal problems," and "job security" ranked higher. Why?

Speaking broadly, we might say that human motives or needs form a more complicated pattern than one is likely to suppose. In the early 1950s, U.S. psychologist Abraham Maslow (1954) did much to describe

Abraham Maslow (1908–1970). Abraham H. Maslow, who died in 1970, was one of the foremost spokespersons of humanistic psychology. In order to pursue the truth of things, to discover a way of experiencing the highest levels of human awareness, and to research the best social conditions in which people might bring themselves to a "full humanness," he found he could not separate the empirical methods of science from the aesthetics of philosophical inquiry. "Experiencing is only the beginning of knowledge," he said, "necessary, but not sufficient." He introduced the hierarchy of needs, which included self-actualization. In 1965, he described in *Eupsychian Management* the interrelations between psychological theory and an enlightened modern management. (Source: The Bettmann Archive Inc.) (Photography by William Carter)

this pattern by suggesting the existence of a hierarchy of needs. According to Maslow, the behavior of an individual at a particular moment is usually determined by his or her strongest need. If this is so, then it would seem useful for administrators to have some understanding about the needs that are commonly most important to people. Maslow notes five (see Figure 10-1).

1. Physiological.   In his formulation, the physiological needs (e.g., food, clothing, and shelter) are at the bottom of the hierarchy. The satisfaction of these needs is usually associated in our society with money. But as these basic needs begin to be fulfilled, other levels of needs become important and motivate and dominate the behavior of the individual.

2. Security.   Above physiological needs, Maslow places the need for safety or security. As with other motives, security can be either above the surface and apparent to the individual or largely subconscious and not easily identified. The second form can be developed during early childhood through identification with security-minded parents who are willing to accept whatever fate comes along.

Do you want a job that offers a challenge to imagination and ingenuity and that penalizes failure? Or, do you find real satisfaction in the precision, order, and system of a clearly laid out job? (Remember Sinclair Lewis's Babbit, for whom "a sensational event was changing from the brown suit to the gray the conents of his pockets.") How you answer these questions is a good indication of how important the security motive is to you. Some organizations, it has been suggested

Figure 10-1
Maslow's Hierarchy of Needs

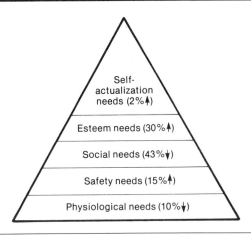

Note: Several years ago, a group of researchers at the Stanford Research Institute asked what percentage of the U.S. population was living on each of the five levels in 1965 and what percentage would be living on each level in 1990. The numbers indicate the 1965 percentages; the arrows indicate whether these should increase or decrease by 1990.

(Gellerman, 1963), tend to overemphasize the security motive by providing elaborate fringe benefit programs; for example, medical insurance and retirement plans. While this emphasis can make employees more predictable, it cannot necessarily make them more productive. And if creativity is necessary in their jobs—which is often the case in the public sector where a high percentage of employees are knowledge workers—overemphasis on security can actually thwart creativity.

3. Social.   Once physiological and safety needs are fairly well satisfied, social needs become dominant. Considerable sophistication is required to deal effectively with these needs.

In the first place, the administrator needs to recognize that the social needs of decision makers in the organization can lead to *groupthink*. This mode of thinking is regularly encountered in studies of group dynamics when concurrence-seeking becomes so dominant that it tends to override realistic appraisal of alternative courses of action. And no level of decision making is immune to this strain of social conformity.

An important symptom of groupthink is pressure. "Victims of groupthink apply direct pressure to the individual who momentarily expresses doubts about any of the group's shared illusions or who questions the validity of the arguments supporting a policy alternative favored by the minority. This gambit reinforces the concurrence-seeking norm that loyal members are expected to maintain" (Janis, 1971).

James C. Thompson, Jr., a historian who spent five years as an observing participant in both the State Department and the White House, reports that whenever a member of President Johnson's ingroup began to express doubts about Vietnam, the group exerted subtle social pressure to "domesticate" him. The dissenter was made to feel at home provided he did not voice his doubts to outsiders and kept his criticism within the bounds of acceptable deviation. Thompson tells us when one such "domesticated dissenter," Bill Moyers, arrived at a meeting, the president greeted him with, "Well, here comes Mr. Stop-the-Bombing" (cited in Janis, 1971:218).

One behavioral scientist concludes, after pouring over hundreds of relevant documents, that social need is the only explanation of why groupthink continues to occur in the corridors of power. Writes Irving L. Janis (1971): "My belief is that we can best understand the various symptoms of groupthink as a mental effort among group members to maintain . . . emotional equanimity by providing social support to each other."

A second thing that the administrator needs to recognize about social needs concerns not the corridors of power but the informal work group. Administrators are often suspicious of informal groups that develop in organizations because of the potential power these groups have to lower productivity. But why are such work-restricting groups formed? Studies show that they sometimes form as a reaction to the insignificance and impotence that workers tend to feel when they have no control over their working environment. In fact, the situation is made worse when, at the same time, workers are closely supervised but have no clear channels of communication with the top (see Schachter, 1959). In this type of environment, work restriction becomes a means to preserve the identification of individuals within the group. Yet, informal groups *can* be an asset to administration.

But how? To answer that question we might first note a cardinal insight of recent studies on informal groups: An inherent conflict exists between the social needs of the individual and the requirements of the organization. Social psychologists draw a useful distinction here: The social needs of the individual are called *primary needs* and the requirements of the organization *secondary needs*. One need not spend much time in public organizations to find out that the vocabulary of bureaucracy abounds with avowals of secondary needs at the expense of primary ones. Consider: "Nothing personal, *but*." "I'm sorry to have to do this, *but*."

In contrast, the effective administrator not only tries to avoid this officious approach but also *tries to integrate primary and secondary relationships*. But how does one go about this integration? The successful administrator, according to Katz and Kahn (1966:325–56) "mediates and tempers the organizational requirements to the needs of persons." But this mediating is done in ways that are not damaging but actually enhancing to the organization. Further, the administrator "promotes group loyalty and personal ties. He demonstrates care for persons as persons." In trying to influence the people in the organization, the administrator seldom relies on formal powers, such as those found in rules and regulations, but on (a) *referent power*—influence based upon liking or identification with another person; or (b) *expert power*—influence based upon the expertise of the administrator that is relevant to the task.

Write Katz and Kahn (1966:325–66):

> He encourages the development of positive identification with the organization and creates among his peers and subordinates a degree of personal commitment and identification. He does these things by developing a relationship with others in the organization in which he introduces what might be termed primary variations on the secondary requirements of organization. Within limits he adapts his own interpersonal style to the needs of other persons. In so doing, he generates among members of his group a resultant strength of motivation for the achievement of group and organizational goals which more than compensate for occasional bureaucratic irregularities. The secondary role requirements remain the dominant figure in his behavior, but they appear on a background of, and are embellished by, an attention to primary interpersonal consideration.

4. Esteem.   Assuming then that the individual social needs are met within the organization, a fourth need comes into prominence: esteem. Failure to understand this need often lies behind the administrator's complaint: "We've given our people everything—good salary, pleasant working conditions, even affection—and yet some are still dissatisfied." In other words, it is precisely because employees have had the three basic needs sufficiently satisfied that a fourth need emerges. And, like social needs, it can cause organizational problems unless the administrator finds ways of satisfying it.

While the need for esteem appears in a variety of forms, we shall discuss only two—recognition and prestige. But with each form, the message for the public administrator remains the same: Do things to make employees feel important.

William James (1952:189) gave an especially gripping explanation of the importance of recognition:

> We are not only gregarious animals, liking to be in sight of our fellows, but we have an innate propensity to get ourselves noticed, and noticed favorably, by our kind. No more fiendish punishment could be devised, were such a thing physically possible, than that one should be turned loose in society and remain absolutely unnoticed by all the members thereof. If no one turned round when we spoke, or minded what we did, but if every person we met . . . acted as if we were nonexisting things, a kind of rage and impotent dispair would be a relief; for these would make us feel that, however bad might be our plight, we had not sunk to such a depth as to be unworthy of attention at all.

The need for esteem and prestige is fourth on Maslow's hierarchy. The French government distributes a be-wildering array of awards each year, which the model displays. According to one sardonic French saying, half the riders in the Paris metro wear the Legion of Honor, while the other half have applied for it. Apparently, Maslow's hierarchy applies crossnationally. (Picherie—*Paris Match*)

In an organizational setting, what this means is that people look for support from their supervisors. Studies show, for example, a strong relationship between an administrator's supportiveness and the self-esteem of his subordinates (see Bowers, 1964). Further, studies by members of the Institute for Social Research at the University of Michigan have shown that supervisors who exert pressure for produc-tion *but do not support their people* end up with a low production organization.

Despite the importance of recognition, most contemporary organi-zations are deficient in it. This is evident, says Harry Levinson (1968:183) of Harvard's Business School, in the repetitive response to a simple question. "If one asks people in almost any organization, 'How do you know how well you are doing?' 90 percent of them are likely to respond, 'If I do something wrong, I'll hear about it.'" According to Levinson, what people are really saying is that they do not feel suffi-cient support from their supervisors.

The power to gain ascendency over the minds of men and women, and to command their admiration for distinguished performance is prestige. To be sure, some tend to seek only the material symbols of status. Salary, to the extent it carries social value, can certainly be included here as well as under physical needs. Michael Korda's book *Power!* would hardly merit our attention except that its very popularity evidences how widespread (one might say even pathological) the need for people to have their importance clarified has become. In a chapter entitled "Symbols of Power," Korda offers detailed advice on how shoes, typewriters, telephones, office furniture, briefcases, and clocks can all increase status. Sample: "A full calendar is proof of power, and for this reason, the most powerful people prefer small calendars, which are easily filled up, and which give the impression of frenetic activity, particularly if one's writing is fairly large. One of the best power symbols is a desk diary that shows the whole week at a glance, with every available square inch of space filled in or crossed out. It provides visible evidence that one is busy—too busy to see someone who is anxious to discuss a complaint or a burdensome request." The author even suggests, if necessary, filling the diary up with entries such as "gray suit at cleaners" or "Betsy's birthday." "The effect from a distance is awe inspiring" (Korda, 1975:208).

5. Self-Actualization.   According to Gellerman (1963), the need for prestige is more or less self-limiting. Once people have gained the level they think they deserve, the strength of this need declines. Prestige now becomes a matter more of maintenance than of further advancement. At this point, too, we witness the emergence of Maslow's fifth and final need: self-actualization.

What exactly is self-actualization? In *The Farther Reaches of Human Nature*, a book light-years removed from Korda's, Maslow (1971:43) provides us an answer.

> Self-actualizing people are, without one single exception, involved in a cause outside their own skin, in something outside of themselves. They are devoted, working at something, something which is very precious to them—some calling or vocation in the old sense, the priestly sense. They are working at something which fate has called them to somehow and which they work at and which they love, so that the work-joy dichotomy in them disappears.

Admittedly, this explanation lacks the rigor indicative of good social and behavioral science; and there is no gainsaying the fact that the concept of self-actualization is difficult to pin down. But we must try. (I harbor the belief that the great undiscussed paradox in management literature is that in discussions of Maslow's hierarchy of needs the most underdeveloped part, self-actualization, is the most important.)

An especially well-researched motive, closely related to self-actualization, is the urge to achieve. By considering this phenomenon, perhaps we can better understand self-actualization.

Adapting a simple example from David McClelland (1961) can help us distinguish the achievement motivated person from the social motivated and esteem motivated. Given the task of building a boat, the achievement motivated person would obtain gratification from the making of the boat. This intense interest in the work is, of course, quite consistent with the above quote from Maslow. The socially motivated person would have fun in playing with others and with the boat but would be less concerned about its seaworthiness. Finally, the esteem-oriented person would be concerned with the specific role he or she had in the project, and the rewards of success.

Achievement motivated persons set moderately difficult but potentially surmountable goals for themselves; they prefer situations where they can obtain tangible information about their performance; and they habitually think about how to do things better. Maslow relates an anecdote about Brahms that illustrates the last point. Somebody had been fiddling around at the piano and was idly playing notes and chords and, in the middle of playing, left the piano. Brahms had to get up and finish the progression. He then said, "We cannot let that chord go unresolved forever."

From the various achievement studies, we have learned that this motive can be taught and developed in people. But how? Levinson (1968:243) provides these guidelines: The administrator "should make demands on people, expect them to achieve reasonable goals, and even some that border on the unreasonable. He should respect their capacity to chart their own course toward those goals if they are adequately protected and supported, acknowledge what they have to contribute toward reaching collective goals, and, following Diogenes's dictum, 'Stand out of their light.'"

After Maslow

To summarize: Maslow contended that human needs could be classified on five levels, each succeeding need becoming more pressing as the more primitive ones were satisfied. In ascending order these are physical needs, safety needs, social needs, esteem needs, and self-actualization needs. To my mind, this theory was a significant contribution, for Maslow was saying—with far more precision than any of his predecessors—that different people require different treatment by management (in the vernacular: different strokes for different folks). And more: that the same person may over time require different treatment and that management should never expect a cessation of complaints but only different ones.

This humanistic orientation remains a major influence on how we think about human behavior in organizations. We shall find some implicit criticism of it later in this chapter when we examine con-

"Of course, my door is always open, Adams! But it's for fresh air—not complaints."

Self-Actualization in Critical Perspective

Maslow would describe himself as an existential psychologist, and this is reflected in the title of one of his most important books, *Toward a Psychology of Being*. Over the last few decades, a worldwide existential psychology movement has developed. One of the leading members of this movement is Viktor E. Frankl (1984), who was confined in a Nazi concentration camp during World War II. The experience gave him deep insight into human nature under pressure. Since all living is a form of pressure, Frankl has extended these insights to apply to what we call ordinary life.

Being human is being always directed, and pointing, to something or someone other than oneself: to a meaning to fulfill or another human being to encounter, a cause to serve or a person to love. Only to the extent that someone is living out this self-transcendence of human existence, is he truly human or does he become his true self. He becomes so, *not by concerning himself with his self's actualization*, but by forgetting himself and giving himself, overlooking himself and focusing outward. . . . What is called self-actualization is, and must remain, the unintended effect of self-transcendence; it is ruinous and self-defeating to make it the target of intention. And what is true of self-actualization also holds for identity and happiness. It is the very "pursuit of happiness" that obviates happiness. [Emphasis added.]

tingency approaches to management (see also problem 18 on p. 233 and the box above). But, for now, let us pick up the trail and see how Maslow's work influenced the theories of Douglas McGregor and Chris Argyris.

Douglas McGregor: Theory X and Theory Y

Douglas McGregor was heavily influenced by both the Hawthorne studies and Maslow's work. His classic book *The Human Side of Enterprise* advanced the thesis that managers can benefit greatly by giving more attention to the social and self-actualizing needs of people at work. McGregor felt that managers must shift their view of human nature from a perspective he called *Theory X* to one called *Theory Y*. These are important terms in the vocabulary of management.

According to McGregor, managers of the Theory X model view their subordinates as by nature

- Disliking work.
- Lacking ambition.
- Irresponsible.
- Resistant to change.
- Preferring to be led than to lead.

Theory Y, by contrast, involves an alternative set of assumptions. A manager operating under a Theory Y perspective views subordinates as naturally

- Willing to work.
- Willing to accept responsibility.
- Capable of self-direction and self-control.
- Capable of creativity.

Theory Y is not just Theory X's opposite (although that is what many observers conclude). McGregor did not intend that the two sets of assumptions be forced into the hard versus soft mold. Rather, he meant Theory Y to be an integrative set of assumptions. As McGregor (1960:49) notes in describing the paradoxical qualities of Theory Y:

> The central principle of Theory Y is that of integration; the creation of conditions such that the members of the organization can achieve their own goals best by directing their goals toward the success of the enterprise. . . . The concept of integration and self-control (also) carries the implication that the organization will be more effective in achieving its economic objectives if adjustments are made in significant ways to the needs and goals of its members.

Chris Argyris: Personality and Organization

Argyris argues that the management principles discussed in Chapter 9 are in conflict with the view of human nature advanced by Maslow and McGregor. For example, the principle of specialization assumes people will behave more efficiently as tasks become specialized . . . but specialization inhibits self-actualization. The principle of chain of command assumes efficiency is increased by a clear-cut hierarchy in which the top controls the bottom . . . but hierarchy creates dependent, passive, and subordinate workers with little control over their work environments. Span of control assumes efficiency will increase when a supervisor's responsibility is limited to seven employees . . . but span of control also creates dependent, passive, and subordinate workers with little control over their work environments.

Argyris predicts that when people suffer incongruence between their mature personalities and management practices, they will be prone to absenteeism, turnover, aggression toward higher levels of authority, apathy, alienation, and a focus on compensation as the ever-increasing trade-off for their unhappiness. His advice to administrators, in turn, is to accommodate the mature personality by (1) *expanding job requirements* to include *more task variety and responsibility* and (2) adjusting supervisory styles to include *more participation*. In sum, Argyris suggests that managers who respond to "mature" personalities will achieve productivity. Psychological success, Argyris says, requires that individuals define their own goals.

In light of the remarkable productivity gains in Japanese companies that practice techniques like job design and participation, there is more reason than ever to believe Argyris. And because he just might be right, we had better take a closer look at these techniques.

Three Ideas for Achieving Greater Worker Productivity

Job Design

In an era of intensive specialization, the tendency is often to make position description very narrow. Narrowness may result in greater expertise; it may also result in more boredom. Fortunately, through careful job design, employee apathy and alienation can be avoided. But the question is: How?

A good place to start looking for an answer is in the work of Frederick Herzberg, another behavioral scientist, and his ground-breaking *The Motivation to Work* (1959). Figure 10–2 shows the results of Herzberg and his associates' empirical investigation of motivation. Essentially, they found five factors that determined job satisfaction: achievement, recognition, work itself, responsibility, and advancement. In addition, they found five factors that were associated with job dissatisfaction: company policy and administration, supervision, salary, interpersonal relations, and working conditions. Significantly, the satisfying factors were all related to job content.

These findings are most suggestive. They tell us that jobs should be designed to be challenging and provide ample opportunity for worker recognition. They tell us that employees should be given as much discretion as possible. They tell us that employees should be able to

Figure 10–2
Comparison of Satisfiers and Dissatisfiers

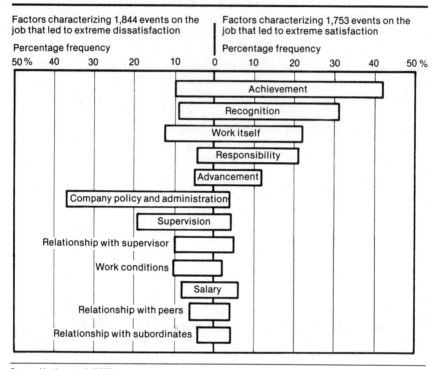

Factors characterizing 1,844 events on the job that led to extreme dissatisfaction

Factors characterizing 1,753 events on the job that led to extreme satisfaction

Percentage frequency

Percentage frequency

| 50% | 40 | 30 | 20 | 10 | 0 | 10 | 20 | 30 | 40 | 50% |

Achievement
Recognition
Work itself
Responsibility
Advancement
Company policy and administration
Supervision
Relationship with supervisor
Work conditions
Salary
Relationship with peers
Relationship with subordinates

Source: Herzberg et al. (1959).

diversify activities, which is not the same thing as merely taking on more work. And finally they tell us that employees should be able to witness some of the result of their output.

How well does job enrichment work? According to Roy W. Walters (1972):

> The best proof of any theory is the hard, fast results which occur when the theory becomes practice. Job enrichment efforts in a number of cases over the last few years have produced excellent results, both for the companies and for the individual workers. In one organization, job enrichment saved $300,000 for the company by increasing production per employee. This was done by expanding job responsibilities and by reducing verification of the work. In another organization, the savings were $100,000, realized through increased production and reduction in the number of employees. In still another company, quality of output improved 35 percent.

One further point. Effective job design does not apply solely to workers. Drucker (1966:78–92) offers these guidelines for designing executive and professional jobs:

Do not start out with the assumption that jobs are created by nature or God. Know they have been designed by highly fallible men. Therefore, guard against the "impossible" job, the job that simply is not for normal human beings. "Any job that has defeated two or three men in succession, even though each had performed well in his previous assignment, must be assumed unfit for human beings." Examples of such "undoable," people-killer jobs include the presidency of a large university and the ambassadorship of a major power.

Make each job demanding and big. "It should have challenge to bring out whatever strength a man may have. It should have scope so that any strength that is relevant to the task can produce significant results." Surveys of physicians in the Army Medical Corps, chemists in the research lab, nurses in the hospital produce the same results: "The ones who are enthusiastic and who, in turn, have results to show for their work, are the ones whose abilities are being challenged and used."

By way of conclusion, I cannot help but note the fact that many of the nation's largest and most successful corporations—AT&T, Texas Instruments, General Foods, Monsanto, Polaroid, and so forth—have long had vigorous job-design programs. The public sector, some charge, has been guilty of trailing far behind. In this area, however, the consequences are especially costly. Albert Camus put it accurately and briefly when he wrote: "Without work all life goes rotten; but when work is soulless, life stifles and dies."

Participative Management

Warren Bennis, who was mentioned in Chapter 8 during our discussion of future organizations, argues that democracy in an organizational context is inevitable. In Bennis's view, the nature of work in the future in both the public and private sectors will be increasingly scientific and technological. Today, we are already aware that this type of work leads to a more free-form, democratic organization. A chain of command inhibits the quick and crosscutting flow of information required in scientific-technological enterprises.

Certain social forces are also pushing organizations toward a more democratic form. Workers today, public and private, are less docile; they are less likely to passively accept the edicts of management and more likely to want to have their say in decisions that affect them. In the decades ahead, few concerns of public personnel management will be more critical than participatory management.

Basically, there are two approaches to participative management. The first, which we shall discuss here, is to establish a formal mechanism; the other, which we shall address a little later, is for administrators to make participation an integral part of their leadership style.

Employee participation can take many forms. (Drawing
by Whitney Darrow Jr.: 1972. *The New Yorker Magazine Inc.*)

A formal plan allows workers to participate through joint union-
management or worker-management committees that encourage, collect, and pass on suggestions for improving productivity. In most cases,
there is some explicit scheme for sharing between workers and management the fruits of increased productivity. Thus, the formal approach does not rely exclusively upon the same hierarchical channel
for downward instructions and allocation of individual rewards and
penalties *and* for upward communication of ideas and influence. (Since
1933, TVA has been a pioneer in this approach to employee participation. In the U.S. Forest Service, headquarters personnel regularly poll
field officers for opinions on major decisions, and constructive dissent
is encouraged.

The idea of involving workers in addressing their organization's
mission as a group, with the purpose of talking about how to do the job
better in terms of both output and self-realization, is contagious. When
the state of North Carolina, for example, found itself in a period of
declining fiscal resources, it turned to its employees to devise ways to
do more with less. How was it possible to do this in the typically
bureaucratic structure that characterizes most governmental bodies?

A special governor's commission on government productivity, together with the management of Wake County, North Carolina, called
on the Productivity Research and Extension Program (PREP) of North
Carolina State University to work with them in developing *quality
circles* in the public sector. A quality circle is a group of employees
who meet periodically to discuss problems regarding quality, output,
and similar issues. PREP set up a curriculum built around 12 hours of
workshop discussions, which started with 185 volunteers (out of a
total work force of 1,200 employees), followed by significant out-of-

class activity. The participants became the core of employee quality circles that would search out and try to solve problems. The discussion leaders became the "captains" of their teams.

From an examination of the work of some 39 productivity circles, the American Institute of Industrial Engineers estimated that there were savings of about $151,000 in the first year—approximately $1,000 per employee. "At the close of the project, PREP concluded that government employees at all levels, given the proper vehicle through which to communicate their ideas, can contribute a wealth of knowledge to improve the productivity of their departments" (*World of Work Report*, September 1981, p. 65).

While the quality circle is no panacea, it does represent a growing trend toward employee participation in the decisions of the workplace. It denotes the respect for the worker—the willingness to ask for the employee's opinion—that Maslow, McGregor, and Argyris have so strongly urged.

The Theory Z Organization

Ideas like participative management and quality circles are encompassed by a larger idea—Theory Z. This idea, as expounded by William Ouchi (1981), represents an attempt to integrate common management practices in the United States and Japan into one middleground framework. The Z organization is based on concepts such as long-term employment (which fosters more commitment by employees to the organization's long-range goals); participatory and consensus decision making; individual responsibility for performance yet a recognition that everyone is interdependent; slow evaluation and promotion; rotation of managers (which prevents extreme specialization); and informal controls (for example, the use of mentors to help younger managers see how they are doing.)

Perhaps Theory Z is a somewhat awkward way of saying that teamwork still matters. To create a team requires more than patching the workplace with hybrid innovations, a quality circle here, and a matrix reorganization there. Such single shot measures do not make up for the shortcomings of rigid organizational structures and shortsighted management practices. Teams are built not on techniques but trust and involvement. When employees and supervisors trust each other, organizational flexibility and information flow are enhanced enormously. When everyone believes that their participation counts, when employees look for ways to complement rather than compete with each other, output goes up.

Keeping Things in Balance

George Homans has also been a pioneer in the application of behavioral science to problems of the workplace. We should not forget, he reminds us, that old-fashioned authority has its advantages. Even in much-admired Japanese organizations, as the more thoughtful students of Japanese culture point out, deference to authority is profoundly important.

Homans asks participation zealots (my term, not his) what happens when people do not have the time to participate. As he explained in an interview (in Dowling 1974:125):

> There are extraordinary limits on possibilities of participation because of the time people have available. If you participate all the time in decisions on what you're going to do, obviously nothing is done. That's driving it to the extreme. When you're talking about reforming an industrial system, you have to talk about something that can be operated across the board. With much attention, very skilled people, and small groups, reform always can be successful in some sense. But then people jump from this to something that's going to operate across the board and reform the whole industrial system. They forget the Homan principle that no society, no governmental system, or no industrial system can work successfully if it depends on extraordinary abilities on the part of the people who run it. It has to be operable by ordinary damn fools like me. And that's what bothers me about Chris Argyris, for instance, toward whom I'm very sympathetic in some ways. I don't think the system he has in mind can be operated by ordinary damn fools.

The number of scholars who have tried to answer the question of what motivates employees is quite staggering. Thus far in this chapter, you have been introduced to only a tiny fraction.

While these scholars put their theories and findings in different bottles, the contents are pretty much the same. I do not think that many of them could argue with or greatly add to the following statement by Fritz J. Roethlisberger, one of the pioneers in the study of human behavior and an early chronicler of the Hawthorne studies:

> People at work are not so different from people in other aspects of life. They are not entirely creatures of logic. They have feelings. They like to feel important and to have their work recognized as important. Although they are interested in the size of their pay envelopes, this is not the matter of their first concern Sometimes they are more interested in having their pay reflect accurately the relative social importance to them of the different jobs they do. Sometimes even still more important to them than maintenance of socially accepted wage differentials is the way their superiors treat them.
>
> They like to work in an atmosphere of approval. They like to be praised rather than blamed. They do not like to have to admit their mistakes—at least, not publicly. They like to know what is expected of them and where they stand in relation to their boss's expectations. They like to have some warning of the changes that may affect them.
>
> They like to feel independent in their relations to their supervisors. They like to be able to express their feelings to them without being misunderstood. They like to be listened to and have their feelings and points of view taken into account. They like to be consulted about and participate in

the actions that will personally affect them. In short, employees, like most people, want to be treated as belonging to and being an integral part of some group. (Quoted in McNair, 1957)

Contingency Approaches to Management

The student of history may wonder what all this behavioral theory has to do with the great leaders of yesterday. What would Charles De-Gaulle or Abraham Lincoln—to name but two—make of it? Such questions cannot be dismissed lightly because behind them is a recognition that the prescriptions of the behavioral school might not apply universally in every situation. Indeed, current approaches recognize a need for managers *to know what will work best in any given situation.*

Would DeGaulle's imperious manner have been as effective in another culture? Would there be a Confederate States of America today if Lincoln had practiced a more participative style of leadership after the Battle of Fredericksburg?

Instead of assuming that everyone has similar needs, personalities, or orientations toward work, the modern approaches build from a base of *contingency.* In other words, modern theorists want to know under what conditions their management guidelines will hold.

But before offering a more formal statement of contingency theory, I want to focus on a much older but closely related concept.

The Concept of Leadership

Behavioral scientists, as well as thoughtful executives (public and private), have become more sensitive to the problem of leadership, though for somewhat different reasons. First, they have begun to express concern within recent years that more than a few of the motivational theories and techniques were manipulative. The danger no longer was that organizational life would come to resemble totalitarian *1984* but that it would resemble technocratic *Brave New World.* Thus, they argued, management should stop looking upon employees as merely a problem to be solved and start thinking about the leadership of people.

Scientists and managers have had a second revelation. Leadership can provide the influential increment over and above the level of motivation normally expected when many routine needs have been met. In other words, when the administrator thinks in terms of *leadership*—in contrast to establishing a pleasant work environment, giving generous recognition, and so on—he or she may be able to more fully realize the potential of a group.

Leadership can be spoken about in at least two ways. The first is sweeping. It conjures up visions of an indefatigable Washington crossing the Delaware, and echoes of the message that went out to the fleet in 1939 when Churchill was reappointed to his old post in charge of the Admirality: "Winston is back." The French critic Henri Peyre (*Time,* July 15, 1974) defined it lucidly:

> A broad ideal proposed by the culture of a country, instilled into the young through the schools, but also through the family, the intellectual atmosphere, the literature, the history, the ethical teaching of that country. Will power, sensitivity to the age, clear thinking rather than profound thinking, the ability to experience the emotions of a group and to voice their aspirations, joined with control over those emotions in oneself, a sense of the dramatic . . . are among the ingredients of the power to lead men.

In this section, however, we are concerned more with a second meaning of leadership. While its definition is less sweeping than the first, its presence in administration is more pervasive. Leadership, in this second sense, we define as the process of influencing the activities of a group in efforts toward goal attainment in a given situation. The key elements in this definition are *leader, followers,* and *situation.* Leadership, then, is a function of three variables. Symbolically,

$$L = f(l,f,s).$$

For convenience, we term this approach to the study of leadership the contingency approach. But that is not the only way to think about leadership.

Can Leadership Traits Be Identified?

In the past (especially from 1930 to 1950), the most common approach to the study of leadership focused on traits; it sought to determine what makes the successful leader from the leader's own personal characteristics. These inherent characteristics—such as intelligence, maturity, drive, friendliness—were felt to be transferable from one situation to another. The list of traits grew and grew, but no clear-cut results appeared. Finally, Eugene E. Jennings (1961) did for trait approach to leadership what Glenden Schubert did for the concept of public interest (see Chapter 4)—conduct a careful and extensive review of the literature. Jennings concluded, "Fifty years of study have failed to produce one personality trait or set of qualities that can be used to discriminate leaders and nonleaders."

Jennings or no Jennings, the quest for traits—and *the* traits continues. Richard E. Boyatzis (1982) and the staff of McBer and Company in Boston studied over 2,000 managers in 41 different management jobs. He found 10 skills relating to managerial effectiveness that stood out.

1. Concern with impact (i.e., a concern with symbols of power that have an impact on others).
2. Diagnostic use of concepts (i.e., a way of thinking that recognizes patterns in situations through the use of concepts).

With apologies to Eugene E. Jennings, who concludes that 50 years of study have failed to produce any set of qualities that can be used to discriminate leaders, here is Jefferson's assessment of Washington: "His mind was great and powerful, without being of the very first order. . . . Perhaps the strongest feature in his character was prudence, never acting until every circumstance, every consideration was maturely weighed; refraining when he saw a doubt, but, when once decided going through with his purpose whatever obstacles opposed. His integrity was most pure, the justice the most inflexible I have ever known. . . . He was indeed, in every sense of the word, a wise, a good and a great man." Unlike the French model who appeared earlier in the chapter, the general wears no medals. How might Maslow explain their absence? (Courtesy of the Pennsylvania Academy of Fine Arts)

3. Efficiency orientation (i.e., a concern with doing something better).
4. Proactivity (i.e., a predisposition toward taking action to accomplish something).
5. Conceptualization (i.e., ability to see and identify patterns as concepts when given an assortment of information).
6. Self-confidence (i.e., decisiveness or presence).
7. Use of oral presentations (i.e., effective communication).
8. Managing group process (i.e., stimulating others to work together effectively in group settings).
9. Use of socialized power (i.e., using forms of influence to build alliances, networks, coalitions, or teams).
10. Perceptual objectivity (i.e., ability to be relatively objective; not limited by biases, prejudices, or perspectives).

The model above focuses on middle-level managers. Management knowledge is not stressed because Boyatzis found that such knowledge represents threshold competency, and that the successful managers selected were already well grounded.

Harry Levinson (1980) suggests 20 "dimensions of personality" that those responsible for selecting leaders can use to evaluate their behavior. As might be expected Levinson's and Boyatzis' lists overlap—but a forced comparison of the two reveals the absence of the following items on Boyatzis' list:

1. Tolerance for ambiguity (i.e., can stand confusion until things become clear).
2. Achievement (i.e., is oriented toward organization's success rather than personal aggrandizement).
3. Maturity (i.e., has good relationships with authority figures).
4. Sense of humor (i.e., does not take self too seriously).
5. Vision (i.e., is clear about progression of his or her own life and career, as well as where the organization should go.
6. Perseverance (i.e., is able to stick to a task and see it through regardless of the difficulties encountered).
7. Personal organization (i.e., has good sense of time).
8. Integrity (i.e., has a well-established value system, which has been tested in various ways in the past).
9. Social responsibility (i.e., appreciates the importance of assuming leadership in the larger community).

A different approach to evaluating traits that enhance executive success was used by Korn/Ferry International and a group of UCLA graduate students (cited in Stone, 1981). The study covered 1,708 senior managers in *Fortune* 500 companies. The respondents were questioned on the traits they thought enhanced their success and the following picture emerged.

Concern for results (73.7 percent)
Integrity (66.3 percent)
Desire for responsibility (57.8 percent)
Concern for people (49.2 percent)
Creativity (44.7 percent)
Ambition (38.1 percent)
Aggressiveness (36.2 percent)
Loyalty (23.4 percent)
Exceptional intelligence (19.5 percent)
Social adaptability (16.4 percent)
Appearance (14.8 percent)

Using the Contingency Approach

The contingency approach has an important practical advantage over the trait approach. By emphasizing behavior and the environment, more encouragement is given to the possibility of training individuals. In other words, people can increase their effectiveness in leadership through training in adapting their leadership style to the situation and the followers. Needless to say, this approach does require that the administrators be good enough diagnosticians to identify clues in an environment and flexible enough to vary their behavior.

Dorwin Cartwright (1962) claims that all group objectives fall into one of two categories: (1) the achievement of some group goal, or (2) the maintenance or strengthening of the group itself. The first, which we shall call *task behavior*, refers to "the leader's behavior in delineating the relationship between himself and members of the work group and in endeavoring to establish well-defined patterns of organization, channels of communication, and methods of procedure." When leaders assign group members to a particular task, ask group members to follow the rules, and let group members know what is expected of them, we can say that they are exhibiting task behavior.

The second dimension of leader behavior, which we shall call *relationship behavior*, refers to "behavior indicative of friendship, mutual trust, respect, and warmth in the relationship between the leader and the members of his staff." When the leader finds time to listen to group members, is willing to make changes, and is friendly and approachable, we can say that he or she is exhibiting relationship behavior.

Using only various combinations of these two kinds of behavior, we can plot on Figure 10-3 an infinite number of leadership styles.

Using various combinations of these two kinds of behavior, William Reddin (1970) develops four basic management styles:

- Quadrant I: Supporting style—This manager has less than average task orientation and more than average relationship orientation.

Figure 10-3
Leadership Styles

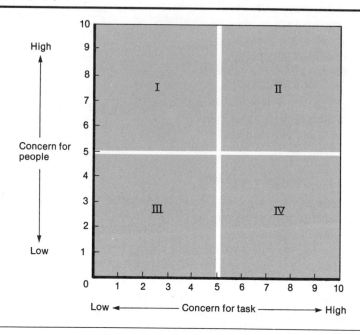

- Quadrant II: Coaching style—This manager has more than average task orientation and more than average relationship orientation.
- Quadrant III: Delegating—This manager has less than average task orientation and less than average relationship orientation.
- Quadrant IV: Directing style—This manager has more than average task orientation and less than average relationship orientation.

The crucial point about these four styles is this. *The effectiveness of managers depends on whether the style they use is appropriate for their situation.* More specifically, to know what is the appropriate style, managers must look to the culture or climate of their organization; to the nature of the work performed (auditing, street repairs, research and development, and so on); to the styles, expectations, and maturity of their superiors, subordinates, and co-workers. All these factors will help determine what style is effective and which styles are less so.

Because effectiveness results from having a style appropriate to the situation in which it is used, the same basic style can be perceived as being particularly effective or particularly ineffective. Stated differently, a style that works beautifully in one situation might cause a

Two Case Studies in Failing to Size Up the Situation

The untoward effects of failing to size up the situation—particularly the maturity level of subordinates—are well illustrated in the following two quotes.

> Normally, in basically crisis-oriented organizations like the military or the police, the most appropriate style tends to be high task, since under combat or riot conditions success often depends upon immediate response to orders. Time demands do not permit talking things over or explaining decisions. For success, behavior must be automatic. While a high task style may be effective for a combat officer, it is often ineffective in working with research and development personnel within the military. This was pointed out when line officers trained at West Point were sent to command outposts in the DEW line, which was part of an advanced-warning system. The scientific and technical personnel involved, living in close quarters in an Arctic region, did not respond favorably to the task-oriented behavior of these combat-trained officers. The level of education, research experience, and maturity of these people was such that they did not need their commanding officer to initiate a great deal of structure in their work. In fact, they tended to resent it. Other experiences with scientific and research oriented personnel indicate that many of these people desire, or need, a limited amount of socioemotional support. (Hersey & Blanchard, 1972: 138–39)

> There were seminars, meetings, and training sessions for staff in the various participating agencies, yet for the most part they had little or no impact on the lower operating levels, which in many cases had very different agendas. This was best expressed by Henry Timmy, a black instructor in one of the skill-training centers. Henry was over six feet, an ex-professional basketball player who grew up on the streets of Brooklyn and had what he liked to call a Ph.D. in streetology. We were having a drink one day at Suerkin's. "Schrank," he said, "it's easy for white people like you who sit on your ass in your comfortable downtown office to tell us who are out here on the ghetto streets that we ought to be democratic and participatory, but you know you don't know shit about this street world. If you're not tough out here, you know what? The people you is trying to help are gonna eat you up alive. Yeah, they'll strip your ass and eat you alive. So you just keep your nice ideas down there, and when I get a job down there in your nifty office, I'll try democracy out here. You know what? It ain't gonna work cause we ain't got nothing to be democratic with or about. We got nothing but poors to share. You want some, come join us. We got to keep discipline. That's the most important thing." I tried to answer because I did not want to accept Henry's cynicism, yet there was a part of me that was now beginning to say that he was right. Life in the ghetto becomes so infected with daily violence that it may be terribly naive to think that an open, participatory organizational model could survive there. (Schrank, 1978: 209–10)

lynch mob to form in another. What is the best management style? It all depends.

Consider the two lists at the top of page 425 (from Reddin, 1970:45). Each pair of terms could refer to identical behavior. When that behavior is exhibited in the appropriate situation, everyone nods their heads while muttering the words on the left. But when a manager exhibits the very same pattern of behavior in a different situation, people might shake their heads and mutter the words on the right.

Table 10-1
The Less Effective and More Effective Versions of the Four Basic Management Styles

Basic Style	When Used in the Appropriate Situation, Effective	When Used in the Inappropriate Situation, Ineffective
Coaching	An executive is a good motivating force who sets high standards, treats everyone somewhat differently, and prefers team management.	A compromiser is a poor decision maker, one who allows various pressures in the situation to influence him or her too much, and avoids or minimizes immediate pressures and problems rather than maximizing long-term production.
Delegating	A bureaucrat is primarily interested in rules and procedures for their own sake, wants to control the situation by their use, and is conscientious.	A deserter is uninvolved and passive or negative.
Directing	A benevolent autocrat knows what he or she wants and how to get it without creating resentment.	An autocrat has no confidence in others, is unpleasant, and is interested only in immediate task.
Supporting	A developer has implicit trust in people and is primarily concerned with developing them as individuals.	A missionary is primarily interested in harmony.

Source: Based on Reddin (1970).

warm-hearted	sentimental
flexible	weak-minded
dignified	pompous
firm	rigid
businesslike	brusque
conservative	reactionary
progressive	left-wing
sensitive	soft
dynamic	overbearing

Based on your own experience, can you think of examples of how a situation has determined the appropriateness of a person's actions?

By now, it should be clear that the effectiveness of an administrator depends to a large degree on his or her ability to size up a situation. To climb outside ourselves, so to speak, and see our situation and study our actions objectively is not easy. Many mechanisms make us insensitive to our situation.

For example, we tend to rationalize or kid ourselves. ("I didn't complete the job because other things came up." "I wasn't promoted because my boss is biased.") Second, we see in others what we do not want to see in ourselves. Freud called this tendency projection. So the slacker sees others as lazy; the selfish person complains that others do not share; the administrator with low concern for people complains no one seems to take an interest in him or her. To maintain projection, administrators must continue to distort reality. Third, we mistake symptoms for cause (this was discussed in Chapter 6). Fourth, we are consumed by a single value—all problems are human ones, all work must be satisfying, or all bigness is bad. Fifth, we may have a high stress level. This is likely to distort our perceptions and feelings about others. (Reddin, 1970:141–47)

Now we are in a position to summarize Reddin's theory very briefly. There are four basic styles that an administrator can adopt: supporting, coaching, delegating, and directing. Each of these styles can be either effective of ineffective—depending on the situation. Thus, there are really eight management styles: executives and compromisers; bureaucrats and deserters; benevolent autocrats and autocrats; and developers and missionaries (see Table 10–1).

Managing Your Most Important Resource

The literature of public administration gives much attention to motivating employees in order that they might achieve higher levels of performance. The literature also gives some attention to allocating monetary resources in an efficient, effective, and responsible manner.

But on the question of how the administrator should manage himself or herself, the literature is as silent as snow.

One of the keys to increasing one's present performance and developing one's future career is knowing how to best utilize one's time. Therefore, this section examines both short-term and long-term problems of time management. It will discuss short-run causes of time waste and methods for effective time utilization. It will also discuss a longer-term condition that can waste time. That condition is stress. Finally, it will discuss how public administrators can become architects of their own achievements, provided that they have a time perspective that allows for maturation and growth.

Managing Short-Term Time

Categorizing Time Usage. A number of management advisors recommend that their clients keep a log of how they spend their time. After a week or so, one can then draw a profile of how his or her time has been spent. Invariably, the exercise provides a mild shock. Most administrators find that they spend far more time on trivialities or, at least, peripheral activities than they imagined. Conversely, they spend far *less* time on the truly important activities—that is, on the activities that are *directly* related to the accomplishment of the organization's prime mission.

The effective administrators will therefore group their daily and weekly activities according to importance. Here is one possible categorization.

Important and urgent.
Important but not urgent.
Urgent but not important.
Busywork.
Wasted time.

Needless to say, these administrators try to work on the things that matter most.

Effective administrators, in fact, almost define a good year, week, or day in terms of the objectives they want to accomplish, and they allocate their time accordingly.

In doing this, they try to work on the most difficult or unpleasant tasks at the time of the day when they are freshest and most creative. For many people, this period is in the early morning. As Benjamin Franklin put it, "plough deep while sluggards sleep."

In allocating their time, effective administrators try to bear in mind the principle of concentration. This principle says that similar activities should be grouped together (e.g., make all your phone calls at the same time). It further says that progress on difficult tasks requires uninterrupted chunks of time.

How does a lower-level administrator avoid interruptions for one- or two-hour periods? Well, arriving early at the office is one way. While not ideal, it is probably better than carrying work home at night and on weekends. Spending the lunch hour in the office is another tactic that can be used on occasion. Arranging with the supervisor to work one afternoon a week at home is also a possibility. Perhaps the most basic tactic is simply to know how to handle interruptions. Phone calls can be screened. (For example: "Ms. Peterson is busy right now, but I can interrupt her if you wish.") If one does not have the luxury of a secretary or answering machine to do the screening, then one can at least minimize the length of the interruption. (For example, begin by cordially asking the caller, "What can I do for you?") Of course, administrators should also try to develop nonintrusive methods for dealing with others.

Closely linked to the principle of concentration is the so-called Pareto rule: Significant items in a group constitute a small part of the total group.* Schematically the rule looks like this.

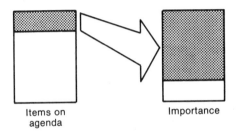

Items on
agenda

Importance

The rule tells us that on any list of items the "vital few," which are seldom more than 20 percent of the total number, can account for 80 percent of the total value or cost. The rule seems to apply (and do not ask me why) across a wide range of phenomena. Twenty percent of an agency's clients account for 80 percent of the agency work hours. Twenty percent of an agency's programs account for 80 percent of its revenue. Twenty percent of an agency's employees account for 80 percent of total sick time. Twenty percent of all callers account for 80 percent of total phone calls. Twenty percent of a political candidate's speaking engagements account for 80 percent of his or her public exposure.

Handling Correspondence and Meetings.   Incoming mail should be screened and sorted. Some can be thrown away unopened; second- and third-class mail dumped in a pouch for opening and reading when one's energy level is low; the rest should be opened and handled immediately. (A good rule is to handle each letter only once.) If possible, write

* Named after Vilfredo Pareto (1848–1923), the Italian economist and sociologist.

a reply on the letter itself, making a copy for your files and returning the original with your note at the bottom.

For administrators who must answer each letter every day two items are extremely valuable. One is a dictating machine. While a dictated message may lack some of the polish of a drafted reply, the time saved in most cases is well justified.

On longer letters, the administrator may want to jot down an outline to dictate from. Like the dictating machine, boilerplates or model letters are useful. For example, many agencies find that the vast majority of inquiries they receive fall into a dozen or so categories. Having a set of boilerplate letters handy can help the administrator avoid drafting new replies each time.

(From *The Wall Street Journal*, with permission of Cartoon Features Syndicate.)

Meetings are a necessary part of public administration. But, if allowed to grow unattended, they can spread like crabgrass and choke an agency. A good way to combat that danger is to write out the purpose of the meeting, what is to be accomplished, what each attendant might contribute, and whether other alternatives for communication are possible.

Joseph D. Cooper (1971:279–80) recommends the following list of legitimate reasons for calling a meeting:

1. The matter concerns some important change from existing practice. It should have an important bearing on operations or require *collective* judgments in reaching a position.

2. A variety of *interacting* knowledges, opinions, and judgments must be brought to bear, especially when new ideas, solutions, and approaches are needed.

3. Time is not available for the handling of the matter step-by-step, referral-by-referral, through ordinary administrative channels. The meeting is expected to bring all relevant interests together at the same time to permit a timely decision to be made.

4. An excuse is needed to take a matter out of ordinary administrative channels where it has languished.

5. The decisions reached are more likely to be carried out if those affected participate in making them.

6. The matter calls for judgment of a collective nature in an area in which the group called together has had prior experience, especially when intangibles are involved.

7. Action assignments on decisions to be reached must be clarified for the benefit of each participant to assure properly coordinated action.

8. The discussions have a training value for some participants in terms of subject matter or of opportunities to observe how people interact and reach judgments.

Before the meeting, the convenors should publish an agenda of the issues to be dealt with and distribute any relevant printed matter in advance. The meeting should be started on time, unless the convenor wants to punish those who came on time and reward those who came late. Group members will work more efficiently if the ending time is stated clearly at the outset. At the end of the meeting, the convenors should summarize what was covered and agreed to; then they should follow up with a memo.

Delegation.   While there are certain duties that should not be delegated, many can be; for example, fact-finding prior to a decision, representing you at meetings, and tasks that will help develop subordinates through exposure to new problems. Administrators should delegate anything another can do better, sooner, or cheaper—and reward subordinates for taking initiative.

Administrators must also learn to say no: They must avoid taking on so many extra tasks that they will become too bogged down to have time left for the truly important. Similarly, they must avoid letting certain subordinates bring them into the solution of a problem or the performance of a task that is quite properly the province of the subordinate. (In other words, do not let subordinates put the monkey on your back.)

The Habit of Work.   The work *habit* has a generally bad connotation. This is unfortunate, for it blinds us to the fact that there are good habits. Effective administrators develop the habit of making themselves work. Each time they take on an unpleasant task first, avoid detours, or decide a trifle quickly they are reinforcing good work habits. They learned through experience the Virgilian motto: "Things live by moving, and gain strength as they go."

Like world-class runners, effective administrators know that hitting one's stride is important. However, tempo and pace do not mean driving yourself beyond your capacities. To be sure, under the stress of external conditions, you may be compelled to overextend yourself. But it is doubtful that the result will be optimal performance. In any event it is certainly not a level of performance that can be maintained over a lifetime.

Managing Long-Term Conditions that Waste Time

Running a small city in the United States consists not only of attending Rotary luncheons and Boy Scout weiner roasts. In fact, a small town mayor or city manager faces many of the crises that their big city counterparts have—threatened nuclear disaster for the mayor of Harrisburg, Pennsylvania; an armed Ku Klux Klan on the rampage in Decatur, Alabama; and serious flooding in Meridian, Mississippi. So it is not surprising that when they attend the annual meeting of the U.S. Conference of Mayors, in addition to sharing wisdom on drafting municipal budgets and motivating employees, they also want to learn how to cope with stress.

What is Stress?   Technically speaking, stress is the body's response to any demand made on it. Psychologists call the demand the "stressor." A stressor can take many forms—dealing with red tape; negotiating with a union; meeting a project deadline; getting a promotion, a demotion, a transfer, a divorce; and so on.

These stressors affect the body's chemistry and its nervous and hormonal systems. If unchecked, the pressures can lead to some real time wastes such as heart attacks, high blood pressure, strokes, neuroses, depression, backaches, headaches, and ulcers. Stress and its related disorders probably cost government several million dollars a year by cutting productivity, ending careers early, causing absenteeism, and prompting alcohol and drug abuse. Of course, some jobs tend to be more stressful than others.

Recent research suggests that workers whose jobs involve high stress but little decision making are more subject to cardiovascular illness. Jobs to the right of the curve in Figure 10–4 are among the top 25 percent in risk. Machine-paced assembly line workers were from 70 percent to 200 percent more likely to develop heart disease than low-level managerial personnel.

Methods for Coping with Stress.   A number of techniques are available to break the pattern of tension. Each administrator must pick his or her own method or combination of methods.

Many experts think that transcendental meditation, a simplification of yoga, is the best technique with which to begin. One chooses a

Figure 10–4
Stress at Work

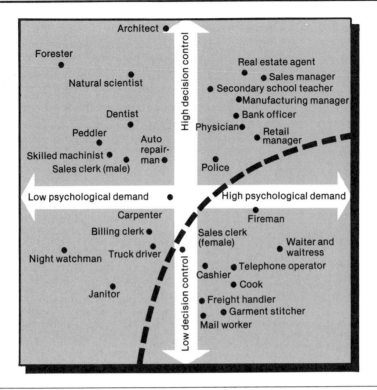

Source: Karasek et al. (1982).

target for concentration known as a mantra (usually a word) and meditates sitting in a relaxed position with eyes closed. This quietude allows the mind to rest and clear itself of fears and anxieties. According to Barrie Greiff, a psychiatrist on the staff of Harvard Business School, "The trick is to do TM consistently and learn to enjoy it" (quoted in *Business Week*, August 23, 1976).

Herbert Benson in his *Relaxation Response* (1975) suggests a variation of the TM technique that requires no formal instruction. According to Benson, a professor of medicine at Harvard, one can use "a word, a sound, a prayer, or an object as a focal point for concentration" to evoke a quieting effect.

One of the newer routes is biofeedback. This technique attempts to enhance an individual's voluntary control over significant bodily functions with the aid of an electronic instrument. Biofeedback has been reported effective in the treatment of migraine.

Finally, physical exercise—from walking to marathon running—can provide some release from tension. Because the mind and body are interrelated, plain physical work affects the state of the mind as well as lowering the heart rate and blood pressure.

The preceding techniques all concentrate on increasing one's tolerance for stress. But one may also need to change the circumstances causing stress. Thus, if something at work does not work, fix it. Time management, such as discussed earlier in this section, can also help one gain inner control on the job. Focusing only on what one can do, doing one's best, and not worrying about the outcome (when it is too late to matter) can all help reduce stress. Of course, if none of these tactics work, the easiest thing to do is avoid the problem altogether: quit the job or go on vacation.

Whatever the technique employed, the objective is not to totally eliminate stress but to optimize it.

Medical research finds stress productive up to a certain point. This holds true not only for administrators but also for managers of all kinds. "It's important to me to be in a high-pressure environment," Thomas W. Landry, the Dallas Cowboys coach, says. When the pressure is off, "I'm already looking forward to the next time" (quoted in *Business Week*, April 30, 1979). Landry has flourished under the stress of professional football coaching for more than 20 years.

The lesson is clear: Each administrator needs to balance the value and the dangers of stress for himself or herself (see Figure 10-5).

Figure 10-5
Yerkes-Dodson Law

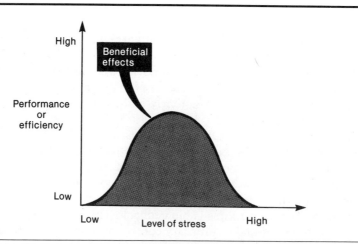

In 1908, Robert M. Yerkes and John D. Dodson demonstrated that as stress increases, so do efficiency and performance. But this relationship persists only to a certain level, then deleterious effects begin to appear (see Benson & Allen, 1980).

Transcending Time and Moving up the Career Ladder

Few people who spend any time in the world of administration hold the belief that promotion always goes to the best and the brightest. Other variables are also involved—especially a clear sense of where one wants to go, a capacity to learn from mistakes (while not worrying about them), and an ability to grow and broaden oneself intellectually.

Several brilliant professors were surprised to learn that a less talented colleague had been made assistant president of their university. The man was not especially gifted or even well liked, but he had a clear sense of where he wanted to go (namely, high in academic administration). Consequently he devoted much of his free time to work on committees chaired by the president, to observing and reading about how a university president's job was handled, and to helping the president whenever he could. In time, he became a sort of unofficial aid to the president. So when the board of trustees created the new position of assistant president, he was the obvious choice.

In addition to knowing where one wants to go, moving up the career ladder involves several other things.

Avoiding Obsolescence.   Elsewhere I have written about the accelerating obsolescence of a master's degree in business administration (see Starling, 1980:33–41). This point is equally valid for a degree in public administration. Some of what a student is taught today will not be taught five years from today. Throughout this century, and especially since World War II, the rate at which knowledge of administration becomes obsolete has increased. Thus, the pressure on today's student to stay current after leaving the university is greater than ever. In my estimation, an administrator that tries to operate only on the skills developed at school will cease to advance in about 12 years.

To combat this creeping obsolescence several strategies are available. One can read broadly as well as stay up with one's own specialty. One can seek new experiences and assignments within the organization. One can list his or her assumptions about the best way a certain task should be performed. And, of course, one should take advantage of the organization training programs (see Chapter 11).

Develop an Executive Attitude.   The best executives, public and private, all share certain characteristics: a strong desire for personal achievement; a respect for authority (which is just a way of saying that they are good followers); a decisiveness (which means they are not afraid to make decisions); courage of their convictions; an ability to view critically their own accomplishments; and maturity (which means they realize that the world was not put here solely for the purpose of making them happy).

To this list of characteristics others might be added: Throughout their careers, the best executives learn from their own supervisors. They do this by observation, but they also do it by asking questions,

Political Do's and Don'ts for Moving up the Career Ladder

Do	Don't
• Look at the downside of linking up with powerful factions.	• Assume your boss always has your best interests at heart.
• Let friends offer advice about political problems.	• Get involved in a showdown you are pretty sure to lose.
• Speak up to your boss if it means keeping peer respect.	• Try to imitate the social graces of a smooth rival.
• Discern what your boss wants in return for a raise or promotion.	• Accept blindly anyone's claim that he or she is the boss's friend.
• Establish your walkaway point—and stick to it.	• Talk about things you are not officially supposed to know.
• Admit your mistakes before the boss discovers them himself.	• Respond in kind to smear campaigns—they can backfire.
	• Be a corporate loner. You do need friends to get ahead.

Source: Bell (1984).

since most top managers are delighted and even flattered to talk about how they got where they are and how they operate. And the best executives are aware that, for better or worse, politics *does* matter. (See box insert on Do's and Don'ts.)

For women who enter the administrative world, this learning process is especially important. Because that world is still governed by the male lifestyle, career-oriented women need to learn the subliminal rules of the game. Margaret Henning and Anne Gardim (1977) offer some advice that amounts to learning to play the game the way men do:

Define your goals: analyze the costs and rewards of a management career. What do you really want 5, 10, 20 years from now? Set specific targets.

Acquire technical competence, but beware of overinvesting in a specialty: Be ready for a broader perspective.

Look for someone in a higher management position who will act as your mentor and coach. Expand your horizons and make yourself visible to other departments.

Be prepared to take risks and sometimes to fail, but stay on the lookout for opportunities to prove your managerial skills.

To summarize this chapter is a difficult but necessary task. When pressed to nail their subject down to its quintessence, some economists have been known to reply, "TINSTAAFL" (There is no such thing as a free lunch). Can students of organizational behavior do the same? I know of no instances. But I think if I were so pressed, and free to let my bias come into play, I would look to leadership as the key to motivation. Now, by leadership I do not necessarily mean the kind of star quality recorded in the mass media, though it certainly has a measure of greatness in it. And, while I cannot describe it in eight words, I can come close by quoting the sixth century B.C. Chinese philosopher Lao-tzu: "Of a good leader . . . When his work is done . . . They will all say, 'We did this ourselves.'"

Nailing Down the Main Points

1. Management is a team activity. The performance of an administrator is inextricably linked to the output of his or her employees.

2. Because of its profound influence on employee performance, motivation is a subject that no manager can afford to ignore. In this century, the behavioral sciences have helped to expand the manager's understanding of motivation. First, the Hawthorne studies revealed that organizational productivity was the result not only of physical condition or monetary rewards (as perhaps Frederick Taylor would have it) but also of interpersonal relationships developed on the job. In particular, the researchers found that when informal groups felt their own goals were in opposition to those of management and their control over their job or environment was slight, productivity remained low. In short, morale affects productivity.

3. In the early 1950s, Abraham Maslow suggested that human motives or needs formed a more complicated pattern than generally thought. Behavior of an individual is actually determined by his or her strongest need; that is, by the need in the following hierarchy that has not been, as yet, satisfied:

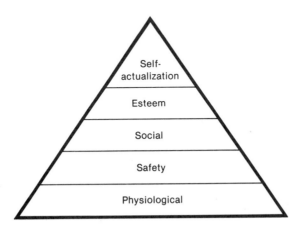

4. According to McGregor, Theory X managers believe that subordinates are uninspired workers who seek to avoid responsibility and work assignments. By contrast, Theory Y managers hold that all subordinates view work as rewarding, if given a chance by management. McGregor thought

that management's perception of subordinate behavior played a significant part in determining leadership style.

5. Argyris believes that many modern organizations keep their employees in a dependent state, thus preventing individuals from achieving their full potential.

6. The Theory Z approach to management attempts to overcome the problems cited by Argyris by involving workers. Ouchi argues that the adoption of Theory Z characteristics to U.S. organizations will not only improve worker satisfaction but also result in productivity increases.

7. In the past, a popular approach to the study of leadership was to list traits. Unfortunately, this approach leaves little room for considering such important variables as the maturity of the followers and the nature of the situation.

   Thus, the contingency approach to leadership tells us that the appropriate style will depend on the personality of the leader, the maturity of the followers, and the nature of the situation. A useful way of classifying leadership styles is in terms of the relative emphasis the leader places on tasks and on people.

8. Effective public administrators try to control the way in which they spend their time. Former Cabinet Secretary Joseph Califano had a poster on his office wall with a quotation from Thoreau that expresses this idea well: "It is not enough to be busy. ! . . The question is: what are we busy about?" Effective administrators know also that stress must be used in productive—not self-destructive—ways.

Concepts for Review

basic management styles	participative management
contingency approach	quality circle
group think	stress
Hawthorne studies	task behavior, relationship behavior
hierarchy of needs	Theory X
job design	Theory Y
job satisfiers and dissatisfiers	Theory Z
leadership	trait approach to leadership
morale	
motivating	
organizational development (see	
problem 9)	

Problems

1. "Most theories about human behavior in organizations say the same thing only with different language." Using only the ideas in this chapter, can you support this assertion?

2. Think of specific ways in which a supervisor could motivate through the prestige needs of employees. Are they meaningful?

3. In terms of Maslow's hierarchy, what motivates you? How would you determine what motivates employees?

4. John Gardner says that when people even in a democratic organization develop sacrosanct rights, the organization itself rigidifies. Indeed, the more democratic an organization is, the more the vested interests of its members will be reflected in its policies. Thus a democratic organization may be especially resistant to change. Do you agree with this analysis? Can you think of any examples that either prove or disprove it?

5. Though rarely discussed in the management literature, protection might be considered a part of good leadership. In other words, it is expected that those who have leadership power will be protective in varying ways. Discuss.

6. Katz and Kahn (1967:302) consider the essence of organizational leadership to be the "influential increment over and above mechanical compliance with the routine directives of the organization." Despite the fact that all supervisors at a given level in the hierarchy are created equally, they do not remain equal. Why? (In thinking through this question, the various sources of power noted at the end of Chapter 2 might prove useful.)

7. Read the following statements about Paul Bryant and then try to place his management style on Figure 10-3.

   What fascinates Bryant about winning football games is not diagramming plays or deciding when to kick a field goal or gamble for a first down, but the challenge of molding 95 very young men into a whole, making each man's vision of himself interdependent with those of his teammates. For all its excesses—and football has more than its share of faults—the sport can be, at its best, a social compact of a high order. Creating this bond is what Bear Bryant excels at (*Time*, September 29, 1979).

8. Write a report on quality circles in government.

9. In management literature, *organizational change* is defined as change involving some modification in the goals, structure, tasks, people, and technology that constitute the essence of the organization. *Organizational development* (OD) is defined as the application of behavioral science knowledge in a long-range effort to improve an organization's ability to cope with change in its external environment and increase its internal problem-solving capabilities.

   Discuss the relevance of Figure 5-4 to these two concepts. How does logical incrementalism help an administrator cope with potential sources of resistance to change such as fear of the unknown, need for security, no felt need to change, vested interests threatened, and contrasting interpretations?

10. A study shows that more than 50 percent of a city's bills are not being paid within 30 days, and some are not being paid within 18 months. As a consequence, most first-rate suppliers do not want to do business with the city. As city manager what do you tell your 10 department heads?

11. What, if anything, in this chapter might help to explain the following statement about the boxer Joe Frazier:

> It astounds Joe Frazier that anyone has to ask why he fights. "This is what I do. I am a fighter," he says. "It's my job. I'm just doing my job." Joe doesn't deny the attractiveness of money. "Who wants to work for nothing?" But there are things more important than money. "I don't need to be a star because I don't need to shine. But I do need to be a boxer because that's what I am. It's as simple as that." (Quoted in Grove, 1983:169)

12. For years the performance of a state's facilities maintenance group, which is responsible for keeping government buildings in the state capital clean and neat, was mediocre. No amount of pressure or inducement from the Secretary of State, who had ultimate responsibility, seemed to do any good. What recommendations would you make?

13. You receive a rush assignment late on Friday afternoon, requiring that certain difficult engineering drawings be completed as soon as possible. The only employee you feel can do this complex task is independent, outspoken, and adverse to overtime. How do you get this employee to do something above and beyond the explicit duties of the job?

14. Suppose that you have a boss that is a bully (likes to scream a lot), or incompetent, or unethical (tends to ask *you* to do nefarious things), or all of the above. What advice do you think the champions of Theory Y would give you? What advice do you think the champions of Theory X might offer?

Case 10.1
Sanitation Workers at the Gate

Centerville is a beautiful, peaceful, but rapidly growing town in the heart of the Sun Belt. One winter day, Roland Jackson, B.S. (psychology), M.P.A., an assistant city manager of a large midwestern town, decided he would answer an ad for a new city manager in Centerville. The city council liked him, and he liked what he saw of the town.

At 8:10 A.M. on his 10th day at the helm, his intercom bleeped. In hushed tones, his secretary said, "Mr. Jackson, there are five garbage collectors here demanding to see you. They seem angry."

Though Jackson had a crowded schedule that day and was six organizational levels removed from a sanitation worker, he told his secretary to send them in. He believed in an open-door policy.

Sanitation workers were the lowest paid and least skilled workers on the city's payroll. Their occupation, as most people know, involves hard, dirty work in all kinds of weather. The five, who were all black, wished to complain that their supervisor, who was white, always assigned them to the toughest routes and never allowed them to drive the truck. They wanted that changed, pronto.

Jackson was obviously in a tough position. The grievance had clear racial overtones and could escalate. Yet he did not want to undermine the authority of all those managers and supervisors that stood between him and the five angry men seated across from him. Nor could he afford to offend the union that purported to represent these workers. These workers had gone out of channels in more ways than one.

Case Question

You are Jackson. It is now 8:12 A.M. How do you play it?

Case 10.2
Fred the Great

Fred Pfeifer has planned a special meeting with Dan Rodriguez, director of the Bureau of Intelligence and Research. The bureau, which Dan heads, coordinates programs of intelligence, research, and analysis for the U.S. Department of State and other federal agencies. It also produces intelligence studies and current intelligence analyses essential to foreign policy determination and execution.

Dan seldom deals directly with Fred Pfeifer, who is two levels below him on the bureau's organization chart. Fred's immediate supervisor is Lloyd Briggs. In Fred's view, Lloyd fits the image of the State Department well: clubby, establishmentarian, all-white, all-male. Fred is convinced there still exists an "old-boy" network within the department, spawned in upper-crust universities and maintained in mahogany-paneled men's clubs along the East Coast.

Fred believes that Dan respects him. They are, after all, very much alike: hard-driving young men, endowed with quicksilver minds, and outside the "network."

What motivates Fred? Like other public administrators, he wants a good income and job security; but unlike some, he is motivated by work itself. Unless there is a challenge, a variety of problems, he gets too relaxed. He played football in high school and intramural sports in college; he likes to take risks and is fascinated by new techniques and methods.

Fred is also a highly paradoxical man: cooperative but competitive; detached and playful but compulsively driven to succeed; a team player who would be a superstar; a team leader but a rebel against bureaucracy; fair but contemptuous of "losers" (his term). He does not want to build an empire, but he does enjoy running things well. He was the driving force in getting a state-of-the-art decision support system installed in the bureau. As Lloyd once joked, "There are two kinds of people in my shop—first are those who do not understand that damn system, and then there is Fred Pfeifer."

Because of an exceptionally high score on the foreign service examination, Fred was pretty much able to choose his field of work. Thus, he avoided the consular career path; stamping foreigners' visas and listening to the complaints of distraught American travelers would have been a dispiriting grind for him. He likes to be where the action is, at the center.

Even a person as gifted as Fred imagines himself in an unreal, romantic fantasy. Ignoring the fact that he seldom leaves the comfortable surroundings of Washington, D.C., he once told a colleague that he is like "the cowboy entering a village alone on his horse. Without even a pistol—just armed with his machete of wit."

Although that quip got around the office and caused much laughter, Fred did not bother to take down the Clint Eastwood poster some wiseacre had hung on his office door.

Some of the people on his staff have trouble making sense of Fred's metaphors. He speaks of the "game plan," of making "the big play," "going to have to punt," and "trying an end around." His staff meetings have a locker-room atmosphere, where discussion of operations is punctuated with detached, mildly sadistic humor. As he once told Lloyd, "The superior has to keep the inferior in his place." He is neither bigoted nor hostile—just insensitive.

Today, as his meeting with Dan Rodriguez begins, Fred is the steely-eyed cowboy, playing for high stakes. As always his approach is direct.

"Dan, I've been here two years, and I think you know what I can do." He pauses momentarily, allowing for an obligatory nod. "Well, I've also had a chance to observe Lloyd closely. It is my considered opinion that he does nothing for the bureau. If this were the Bureau of Pinecones and Squirrels, or something like that, it wouldn't matter, but as you well know, we are involved here in deadly serious business. Lloyd is a likable loser and ought to go."

Not allowing Dan to respond, Fred reveals his plan. "I think it is time that the performers were recognized and the deadwood eliminated. I've always felt I must either move up the ladder or quit. I hope you agree."

Case Questions

1. What is the problem here?
2. What are Dan's options?
3. What course of action would you recommend Dan take?

Case 10.3
Diane Wilson and Steve Carmichael

Diane Wilson is an OEO clerk who processes grants to organizations for the poor. She speaks: "Life is a funny thing. We had this boss come in from Internal Revenue. He wanted to be very, very strict. He used to have meetings every Friday—about people comin' in late, people leavin' early, people abusin' lunch time. Everyone was used to this relaxed attitude. You kind of went overtime. No one bothered you. The old boss went along. You did your work.

"Every Friday, everyone would sit there and listen to this man. And we'd all go out and do the same thing again. Next Friday he'd have another meeting and he would tell us the same thing. (Laughs.) We'd all go out and do the same thing again. (Laughs.) He would try to talk to one and see what they'd say about the other. But we'd been working all together for quite a while. You know how the game is played. Tomorrow you might need a favor. So nobody would say anything. If he'd want to find out what time someone come in, who's gonna tell 'em? He'd want to find out where someone was, we'd always say, "They're at the Xerox." Just anywhere. He couldn't get through. Now, lo and behold! We can't find him anywhere. He's got into this nice, relaxed atmosphere. . . . (Laughs.) He leaves early, he takes long lunch hours. We've converted him. (Laughs.)

"We had another boss, he would walk around and he wouldn't want to see you idle at all. Sometimes you're gonna have a lag in your work, you're all caught up. This had gotten on his nerves. We got promotion and we weren't continually busy. Anytime they see black women idle, that irks 'em. I'm talkin' about black men as well as whites. . . .

"One day I'd gotten a call to go to his office and do some typing. He'd given me this handwritten script. I don't know to this day what all that stuff was. I asked him, 'Why was I picked for this job?' He said his secretary was out and he needs this done by noon. I said, 'I can't read this stuff.' He tells me he'll read it. I said, 'Okay, I'll write it out as you read it.' There's his hand going all over the script, busy. He doesn't know what he's readin', I could tell. I know why he's doing it. He just wants to see me busy.

"So we finished the first long sheet. He wants to continue. I said, No, I can only do one sheet at a time. I'll go over and type this up. So what I did, I would type a paragraph and wait five or ten minutes. I made sure I made all the mistakes I could. . . .

"I took him back this first sheet and, of course, I had left out a line or two. I told him it made me nervous to have this typed by a certain time, and I didn't have time to proofread it, 'but I'm ready for you to read the other sheet to me.' He started to proofread. I deliberately misspelled some words. Oh, I did it up beautifully. (Laughs.) He got the dictionary out and he looked up the words for me. I took it back and crossed out the words and squeezed the new ones in there. He started on the next sheet. I did the same thing all over again.

"I'm gonna see what he does if I don't finish it on time. Oh, it was imperative! I knew the world's not gonna change that quickly. It was nice outside. If it gets to be a problem, I'll go home. It's a beautiful day, the heck with it. So 12:30 comes and the work just looks awful. (Laughs.) I typed on all the lines, I continued it anywhere. One of the girls comes over, she says, 'You're goin' off the line.' I said, 'Oh, be quiet. I know what I'm doin'. (Laughs.) Just go away.' (Laughs.) I put the four sheets together. I never saw anything as horrible in my life. (Laughs.)

"I decided I'd write him a note. 'Dear Mr. Roberts: You've been so much help. You proofread, you look up words for your secretary. It must be marvelous working for you. I hope this has met with your approval. Please call on me again.' I never heard from him." (A long laugh.)

Steve Carmichael is a twenty-five year old project manager for the Neighborhood Youth Corps. "I doubt seriously if three years from now I'll be involved in public administration. One reason is each day I find myself more and more like unto the people I wanted to replace.

"I'll run into one administrator and try to institute a change and then I'll go to someone else and connive to get the change. Gradually your effectiveness wears down. Pretty soon you no longer identify as the bright guy with the ideas. You become the fly in the ointment. You're criticized by your superiors and subordinates. Not in a direct manner. Indirectly, by being ignored. They say I'm unrealistic.

"The most frustrating thing for me is to know that what I'm doing does not have a positive impact on others. I don't see this work as meaning anything. I now treat my job disdainfully. The status of my job is totally internal: Who's your friend? Can you walk into this person's office and call him by his first name? It carries very little status to strangers who don't understand the job. People within the agency don't understand it. (Laughs.)

"Success is to be in a position where I can make a decision. Now I have to wait around and see that what I say or do has any impact. I wonder how I'd function where people would say, 'There's hotshot. He knows what he's talking about.' And what I said became golden. I don't know if it would be satisfying for me. (Laughs.) That might be more frustrating than fighting for everything you want. Right now I feel very unimportant."

Source: Studs Terkel, *Working* (New York: Pantheon Books, 1972), pp. 448, 450, 458, 460–61.

Case Questions
1. What is the problem in this case?
2. How would you motivate Wilson and Carmichael?
3. Which techniques discussed in the chapter do you find most useful in answering the last question?

Case Reference
Studs Terkel, *Working* (New York: Pantheon Books, 1972).

11

Human Resources Management

Introduction

Regardless of the particular leadership style, the administrator can and should turn to others for help with certain people related activities. What kind of help might this be?

Some managerial concerns, which might require expert assistance, are basic. For example, the work to be performed in the organization must be broken down into jobs; each job in turn should have a clear description of the work it entails. At the same time, a plan must be developed to assure equal pay for equal work, that is, the compensation scale should be based on the skills required by the job. These two areas of concern, position classification and compensation, provide the basis for effective recruitment.

Recruitment, or staffing, is the process of matching individual skills and aptitudes with job specifications. It is another area of managerial concern in which help might be desirable. Too often administrators agonize over termination decisions when a wiser investment of time would have been in the selection decision. Closely associated with the staffing concern are the procedures used to recognize accomplishment and to take optimal advantage of individual abilities. In particular, the public executive frequently needs assistance in such critical areas as examination, performance evaluation, and promotion.

For help in the never-ending task of motivating employees, the administrator might turn to others for help with training and counseling. Similarly, in those difficult cases of individual suspension and dismissal, the prudent administrator might seek assistance.

The foregoing concerns—classification and compensation, staffing, training, and separation—are the traditional concerns of public personnel management (PPM). They form the core of this chapter.

But to these traditional concerns we must add a second layer, which can be called the "new concerns" of PPM. One of the better publicized of these concerns is organizational culture, that is, the shared values of an organization. Because some climates are more conducive to productivity than others, this idea is an important one.

Another layer to consider is the legal environment of PPM. Of particular importance are laws and court cases involving labor relations and affirmative action.

The Goals and Structure of Personnel Systems

The importance of the "people" factor in government cannot be overestimated. Today, more than one out of every six Americans works for a government either at the federal, state, or local level. And about one out of every eight in the total labor force is a state or local government employee. State and local employment has tripled to more than 12 million since 1955, while federal employment has risen modestly to 2.8 million from 2.4 million. Salary costs (not counting fringe benefits) come to almost half of every state and local dollar spent. Thus, the way federal, state, and local administrators recruit, select, and develop their employees will be crucial to the quality of government and the effective use of the tax dollars. If public administrators are to be held accountable for results, they must be provided with a personnel system that is comprehensive and conducive to a high level of performance.

The Aims of Public Personnel*

Over the years, the purpose of public service has become diffused by the growing size and complexity of government, the increased specialization of personnel functions, and the multiplicity of political goals associated with public employment. To refocus attention on the principal purpose of public service—providing effective, efficient, economical, and fair government—government personnel policy tries to emphasize the following five priorities.

Revitalizing the Merit Principle.   Public employees should be selected, assigned, promoted, and compensated on the basis of ability and performance. Yet, some state governments and numerous local governments have never formally adopted the merit principle. In many of those that have done so, the personnel systems have developed rigidities, such as overreliance on seniority, that impede the appropriate use of the most qualified people. Specialized personnel administra-

---

* The following discussion is in large part from the Committee for Economic Development (1978).

tion has at times been preoccupied with techniques that bear little relation to assuring that the best people are available for assignment. Collective bargaining has in many instances led management to agree to restriction on the basis of race, cultural background, sex, or other factors not related to the job, and has kept talented people from being hired and promoted.

Restoring the Authority of Managers to Manage. Mangers obviously need the authority and the resources to accomplish the objectives for which they are responsible and should then be held accountable for results. The maze of personnel restrictions sometimes prevents public administrators from doing their jobs or, at the very least, provides excuses for poor performance.

The style of management is not the issue here. As we saw in the last chapter, the effectiveness of various styles of approaches to management depends largely upon the nature of the operation and the people involved. Whatever approach is taken, however, someone should be clearly designated to be responsible for results, and that person should be given adequate authority to ensure that the skills and energies of employees are used effectively to accomplish those results.

Protecting the Rights of Employees. Employees need to be protected from political abuse and arbitrary bureaucratic action. Protection of individual rights and respect for individual interests in employment are independent goals worthy in their own right. Moreover, effective and efficient government is best provided by employees who are secure in the knowledge that they will be judged on the basis of how well they serve the public and that they will be treated with fairness and dignity.

Enhancing Personal Performance, Development, and Job Satisfaction. Public personnel policy should be geared to enhancing performance, encouraging the development of individual capabilities, and improving the quality of working life. Many employees who are otherwise highly motivated are frustrated by bureaucratic impediments, lack of clear objectives, or inadequate feedback on their performance. In other instances, deficiencies in supervision result in the waste of employee time and talent.

Matching Human Resources with Anticipated Needs. Human resources planning is the process of matching human resources with anticipated needs. For example, if a state highway department realized that four additional civil engineers would be required to implement an expanded construction program over the next year, the human resources planning would provide alternative ways of filling that need. Four civil engineers could be assigned from lower priority work being performed elsewhere. Four or five technicians, or mechanical engineers, could be trained in the specific skills needed for the task. Four civil engineers could be hired as new employees. Or the agency might choose some combination of these alternatives. The point is that the agency must take action *today* if it is to have a cost-effective and feasible solution to next year's requirement.

The point is worth emphasizing. As you know from Chapter 9, personnel costs generally account for the majority of an operating budget in a public-sector organization. Consequently, how human resources are used is perhaps the crucial variable in the never ending struggle to minimize costs.

The Structure of Public Personnel

Framing a satisfactory typology of personnel systems is, as Frederick C. Mosher (1968:135–175) correctly notes, a challenge. "American governments have displayed almost unlimited ingenuity in developing different kinds of arrangements for the employment of personal services, ranging from compulsion (selective service) to volunteers (Peace Corps, Vista, etc.) and without compensation (WOC), with a great variety of categories in between." Nevertheless, for purposes of description, analysis, and comparison, Mosher is able to classify the public service into four main types of personnel systems: political appointees, general civil service, career systems, and collective system.

Political Appointees.   Political appointees are those public officials appointed to an office without tenure who have policymaking powers and are outside the civil service system. When Reagan took office in 1981, he was allowed about 5,000 political appointments to top positions within the executive branch. These jobs ranged from cabinet officials to confidential secretaries. At the state and local level, civil service law and practice vary so widely that generalization is hazardous; but as Mosher (1968:166) notes: "It is safe to assume that most of the larger governments in industrialized areas have political executives in approximately parallel capacities and roles. Some have a great many more proportionately than the federal government; some have many fewer."

The General Civil Service.   In the federal government, the *general civil service* system is composed of white-collar personnel, mostly nonprofessional, who have tenure. Their employment is administered in keeping with traditional civil service practices.

That tradition is easily traced back to the 1870s, when the obvious abuses of the *spoils system* (i.e., the right of elected officials to reward their friends and supporters with government jobs) had produced demands for reform that could not be ignored. By 1883, the first civil service law, the *Pendleton Act*, passed. This legislation, also known as the Civil Service Reform Act, established the bipartisan Civil Service Commission to choose the federal employees from lists of those who had passed competitive examinations (the so-called merit system).

The examinations under the civil service system are practical rather than scholarly. Each available position is described in detail and the examinations are geared to the needs of each. After passing a written test, the candidate might take an oral examination if the job warrants it. If successful with both, the person's name is placed on an eligibility list, which is set up on the basis of examination scores. Federal law requires that the agency choose from among the top three to five scores on the list, without passing over veterans. In many merit systems there are further job requirements, such as height and weight requirements for police officers, high school or college graduation for particular occupations, and certifications or licenses for many civil service positions, such as those for the position of attorney or physician. Such requirements, however, must be clearly job related.

Merit systems can be organized in many ways. In many jurisdictions, a nonpartisan or bipartisan commission or board is charged with general program direction and appellate functions, leaving to a personnel director (appointed by the board or the chief executive) the responsibility for day-to-day program administration. In others, a personnel director reporting to the chief executive is responsible for general program direction, with a civil service commission or board serving in a watchdog, advisory, or appellate role (or all three).

Career Systems. Government jobs outside the civil service system are not necessarily appointive, for many agencies have developed their own *career systems*. These systems are composed of white-collar personnel, generally professionals and paraprofessions, who are tenured in the agency and occupation though not in the position. Their employment is administered as a progressive, preferably planned development. In such a system, repeated failure to attain promotion—being "passed over" too many times—can result in dismissal; hence, the expression "up or out."

The model of the career system is that of military officers. In fact, the military system has been copied in or adopted to a number of other federal activities—for example, the Foreign Service, the Public Health Service, the Federal Bureau of Investigation, the Central Intelligence Agency, and the Tennessee Valley Authority. In varying degrees, it has also been a model for state and local police systems and local fire departments.

Unlike the civil service system, a career system emphasizes the individual rather than the position. Thus, as Mosher points out, a "nonprofessional civil servant working in the Department of the Navy is most likely to respond, 'I work for the Navy Department'; an officer, 'I am an officer (or an admiral or captain) in the navy.'" Career systems possess several challenges to the manager. For example, members of a career personnel system, such as the naval officer above, must work with other personnel within the organization who lack comparable career status. Obviously, when personnel are working together on the same project but under two distinct employment systems, the possibility of friction is great.

The Collective System. The *collective system* is composed of blue-collar workers whose employment is governed primarily through bargaining between union or association and governmental jurisdiction.

One final word. Mosher sees the boundaries between these four personnel systems moving. For example, as labor organization accelerates among white-collar workers, general service and career systems begin to show characteristics of the collective system. On the other hand, as high-level occupational specialities develop standards, coalesce, and become recognized, the general service system looks more like a career system.

A Framework for Analysis

Figure 11–1 illustrates how the various aspects of human resources management fit together. People enter public service through one of the four personnel systems. These four appear at the top of the model as inputs to the model.

At a bare minimum, human resources management consists of the five functions shown in the middle box: staffing; classification/compensation; training/management development; advancement; and discipline/grievances. These five functions affect employees at many junctures in their careers. More pervasive in influence are the culture (or shared values) of the organization and the laws affecting personnel practice. A human resources management system that neglects the former misses an opportunity to enhance the productivity of employees, but one that neglects the latter risks protracted legal battles and adverse publicity.

Even Methuselahs must sooner or later depart the systems. As indicated at the bottom of the model, exit occurs in three ways: dismissal, retirement, or resignation.

Five Basic Functions of a Public Personnel System

Staffing

The term *staffing* refers to the process of recruiting, selecting, and advancing employees on the basis of their relative ability, knowledge, and skill.

Recruiting and Testing. Merit recruiting means more than just posting an examination announcement on a bulletin board. Every possible source of qualified candidates within the appropriate labor market must be reached in a positive way. A program of positive recruitment includes elements such as the following (U.S. Civil Service Commission, 1974):

Writing examination announcements in clear understandable language.

Figure 11-1
Framework for Analyzing Human Resources Management

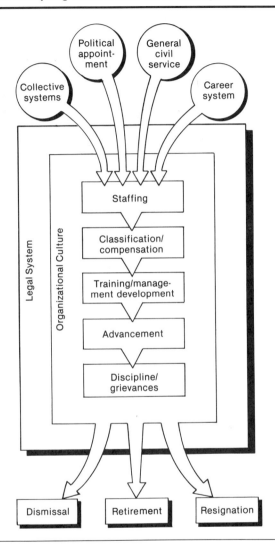

Advertising in publications that circulate to the various segments of
the population, and using other media such as radio and
television.

Establishing easily reachable job-information centers.

Visiting colleges, high schools, and community organizations.

Using mobile or storefront recruiting centers.

Developing continuing contacts with minority and women's
organizations.

Selection on the basis of "relative ability" presumes being able to draw distinctions among the qualifications of competing candidates fairly and objectively. Recent court decisions have made it clear that all selection tools must be valid and job related. In other words, performance on a test has to match performance on the job.

On March 8, 1971, the Supreme Court ruled in *Griggs* v. *Duke Power Co.* that psychological tests given to job applicants had to be job related. "What Congress has commanded," Chief Justice Warren Burger ruled, in what many lawyers consider one of his finest opinions, "is that any tests used must measure the person for the job and not the person in the abstract."

The particulars of the case vividly illustrate this point. Prior to the date the Civil Rights Act of 1964 went into effect, Duke Power Company openly discriminated against blacks. After July 2, 1965, any black employee could become a coal handler provided he had a high school diploma and passed the Wonderlic Personnel Test and the Bennett Mechanical Comprehension Test. Not surprisingly, the company's lawyers were hard pressed to prove what these two tests or a high school diploma had to do with measuring how well a person could shovel coal. The Supreme Court voted eight to zero that the screening devices were illegal. As we shall see in the next chapter, this greater emphasis on evaluating the relevance of entry requirements has led to a greater opening up of opportunity in the public service to all groups— and, in particular, minorities and women.

Employers have, of course, other methods besides written tests to evaluate candidates for initial employment or advancement: performance tests, panel interviews, ratings of relevant training, and experience, or any combination of these with other tests. For most jobs, a combination of job related testing devices, rather than any single one, provides a better measure of the knowledges, skills, and abilities needed for successful job performance.

David McClelland (1973) proposes testing for competence rather than intelligence. He attacked the circular reasoning that links psychological tests to our credential happy society. The basic problem with many proficiency measures for validating ability tests is that they depend heavily on the credentials—the habits, values, accent, interests, and so on—that people bring to the job and that makes them acceptable to management and to clients. Employers have a right to select people who have gone to the right schools because they do better on the job, but psychologists do not have a right to argue that it is the intelligence of these people that makes them more proficient in their · jobs.

McClelland is also interested in getting away from multiple-choice tests. A. N. Whitehead once wrote that these tests require only one level of mental activity beyond being awake: recognition. In any event, according to McClelland, sorting out the trivial from the absurd is hardly a good way for a person to prove his or her capabilities. Mc-Clelland therefore wants tests that measure, for example, capacity to learn.

Peter Koening (1974) tells about a screening program McClelland set up for the U.S. Information Agency that used the PONS (Profile of Nonverbal Sensitivity) Test. McClelland played short tape segments to job applicants and then asked them what emotion was being expressed. Presumably, this kind of sensitivity would be important to diplomats. The State Department, however, vetoed the program: "Too experimental." A more traditional graphite-pencil-on-standardized-form tester was called.

Ironically, in China, where the Mandarins first set up a civil service testing program around 2200 B.C., the job test no longer exists. Reports Koening (1974:102): "In 1949 Mao Tse-tung fundamentally rearranged the hierarchy of test developers, test publishers, test users, and test takers. Today in China, peers select peers for jobs."

Selection.   Once a competitive examination is completed, an employment list based on the examination results is established and the names of the highest ranking eligibles are *certified* to the appointing official for selection. According to merit concept, only a limited number of qualified eligibles should be certified. To do otherwise, such as certifying a whole list of eligibles, for example, would change the basis for hiring from competitive merit to a "pass-fail" system.

Personnel systems usually follow the *rule of three*, which permits the appointing official to choose among the top three individuals certified to him or her, without passing over veterans. Why have a rule of three? First is to overcome the objection that written tests cannot appraise personality factors adequately, that the examining process can produce individuals who may qualify intellectually but have serious personal problems. Second is to appease appointing officers by bringing them more into the process.

Significantly, the Hoover Commission recommended instead that applicants be grouped into several categories such as "outstanding," "well qualified," and "unqualified," and that appointing officials select individuals from the higher categories, moving down as each list was exhausted. Today, as the crucial issues in public administration become productivity and efficiency—not patronage, which the civil service system was designed to eliminate—these recommendations are more acceptable than ever.

An increasing number of critics claim that state and local civil service commissions—usually appointed by successive mayors or governors and removable only for cause—cannot easily be controlled by a single elected executive. Because elected officials have little control over the selection of their employees, they are obviously hampered in instituting the programs they were elected to carry out.

In short, critics maintain that civil service commissions are archaic and inflexible. Denver police officers, for example, are still required to have a minimum of four molar teeth, an apparent holdover of "bite the bullet" to remove the wax that bullets used to be encased in. And until only recently, Denver police regulations stipulated that Civil War veterans be given preference for job vacancies (Laing, 1975).

Regardless of the process by which candidates are certified, the managers eventually face the decision of selecting one individual to fill the vacancies. This decision is perhaps the heart of staffing. But what should the manager look for?

In a word, strength. Writes Drucker (1966:chapter 4):

> Whoever tries to place a man . . . in an organization to avoid weakness will end up at best with mediocrity. The idea that there are well-rounded people, people who have only strengths and no weaknesses . . . is a prescription for mediocrity . . . strong people always have strong weaknesses, too. Where there are peaks, there are valleys. And no one is strong in many areas. There is no such thing as a "good man." Good for what? is the question.

Drucker relates the familiar story of how Lincoln learned this lesson the hard way. Before Grant came a string of generals whose main qualifications were their lack of major weaknesses.

> In sharp contrast, Lee . . . had staffed from strength. Every one of Lee's generals, from Stonewall Jackson on, was a man of obvious and monumental weaknesses. Each of them had, however, one area of strength, and only this strength, that Lee utilized and made effective.
>
> One story about Lee captures especially well the meaning of making strength productive. After learning that one of his generals had, again, disregarded his orders, Lee, who normally controlled his temper, became furious. Finally, an aide asked, "Why not relieve him?" Lee turned in complete amazement, looked at the aide, and said, "What an absurd question—he performs."

Classification and Compensation

At all levels of government, the basis of the civil service is the *position classification system.* Simply stated, position classification involves identifying the duties and responsibilities of each position in an organization and then grouping the positions according to their similarities. A good system can help the administrator make better decisions regarding the relationship of duties and responsibilities to the other concerns of personnel administration. After all, a fair compensation plan does require an understanding of the duties and responsibilities of each position ("equal pay for equal work"); effective examination and recruiting do require knowledge of what the agency is examining and recruiting for; and determining the qualifications necessary for performing the job does require an understanding of what the job entails.

How *Not* to Staff a White House

All presidents like to surround themselves with trusted friends from their home state. But Carter, James Sundquist observed, seemed "to have carried home-state cronyism beyond the point of any other recent president. The result was an inner circle that, far from compensating for Carter's personal weaknesses, compounded them." His press secretary, Jody Powell, had served Carter in the same capacity as governor of Georgia. His principal political adviser, Hamilton Jordan, had been there too.

Sunquist writes:

At the beginning of his presidency, it is clear, Jimmy Carter did not recognize quite what was wrong. He saw the need as one not of management but of a management improvement project. So he launched a series of major undertakings to improve administration through new organizations and new techniques—government reorganization, civil service reform, zero-based budgeting, multiyear budgetary planning, and so forth. But at the critical time when the new administration was being put together, he paid no systematic attention to building managerial competence in the most direct and immediately effective way—by appointing to the key managerial positions in the executive branch persons whose capacity to administer large organizations had been tried and proven.

In bureaucratic organizations far less complex than the executive branch of the national government, the responsibilities of management are seen as too crucial and too difficult to be placed in the hands of amateurs. But in the United States government there is no such doctrine. The prevailing concept is what Alan Dean has called "neo-Jacksonianism"—the notion that in this democracy any citizen can do any public job. Anybody, chosen for whatever reason unrelated to management experience or talent, can run any government agency. (*Public Administration Review*, January/February 1979)

Staffing can be crucial to the success of any enterprise. That is why many sportswriters think that the personnel director of the Dallas Cowboys, Gil Brandt, is more crucial to that team's success than either the general manager, Tex Schramm, or the head coach, Tom Landry.

Most public administrators seem to recognize this better than the 39th president did. In 1977, I surveyed over 700 public administrators in all levels of government on what they considered to be the strategic factor that determined the success of their organization. The most frequently selected item out of a list of 45: "Get high quality top management" (Starling 1979:191). As Frederick E. Terman, former provost of Stanford University, reminds us, if you want a track team to win the high jump, you find one person who can jump 7 feet—not two who jump 5 feet.

Though position classification evolved as a convenient and useful tool, today the concept is frequently under attack. First, the procedures for classification can be a paperwork maze in which job incumbents have considerable influence, though they often view the process with trepidation. "For all practical purposes, the technicians evaluate the jobs in the government system, and the line or functional management must accept their judgments. Industry reverses the process. The line or functional managers—who certainly know the jobs best—evaluate the various positions and tell the technicians in personnel where they should be valued in the structure" (Patton, 1974a:34).

While evaluating the difficulty of duties may not cause too many problems, evaluating and comparing *responsibilities* often does. How many subordinates are supervised? How much time is spent in actual supervision? Who is supervised? How much innovation is expected? To attempt to weigh these factors objectively is no easy task.

Some attack position classification as being obsolete. Although it once provided a way of treating people equitably and eliminating spoils, position classification is not always relevant to activities performed by the more sophisticated organizations discussed in Chapter 8. In such organizations, the work situation becomes too collegial, too freeform for rigid position classifications. In such an organization, position classification (or rank-in-job approach) might be replaced with the *rank-in-person-approach*, which uses the abilities and experience of the individual as the basis for making various personnel decisions (e.g., setting of compensation). Examples of this kind of system include the military and college faculties. The rank-in-person concept, therefore, means that a person carries a rank regardless of the duties performed at a particular time.

Like position classification, compensation of public employees is a very important and often a very controversial part of public personnel administration. Based on our discussion of motivation in the preceding chapter, the importance to the employee of an adequate and equitable compensation schedule should be apparent. If the employee perceives that the plan is unfair, conflict is likely.

But how does one establish a good pay plan? The general rule is this: Pay according to differences in levels of duties and responsibilities.

The expert who has probably thought the most about this question is Elliott Jacques (1979) at England's Brunel University. At the heart of Jacques' findings is a concept that he calls the time frame of the individual. His research indicates that individuals vary radically in terms of the time periods they need to think out, organize, and work through. What makes this research relevant to compensation is his finding that there is a sort of natural structure to organizations engaged in work wherein most jobs can be classified according to the time frame required of the incumbent. Jacques thinks that the best organizations, in terms of morale and productivity, are those whose structure follows what might be called the natural hierarchy. That is, one-day time-frame workers report to a supervisor who can organize at least the next three months; that supervisor, in turn, follows the directions of a manager who can plan a year or longer; that manager reports to an executive with a two-year time frame; and so on.

The federal government pays it employees at salary levels that are generally comparable to those in the private sector. However, the government provides fringe benefits that are 76 percent higher than those in the private sector. Why is this the case? In the 1920s, it was felt that neither civil service nor military pay was competitive with salaries in private business. Rather than simply raise pay, Congress decided to push costs far into the future (where current taxpayers and voters would not notice them) by setting up an exceedingly generous pension system.

The federal government employs roughly 1.4 million men and women under its General Schedule (GS) in grades 1 through 15 (see Table 11-1). Another 1,000 civil servants are in grades 16 through 18; about 7,000 top executives are in the Senior Executive Service (SES) (more about the SES later); and 660,000 persons are in blue-collar jobs that are paid by the hour. Each of the 15 basic grades has 10 levels. Thus, the theory of comparability involves matching salaries in the federal government and in the private sector under 150 combinations of skill, experience, and demand. Finally, the government's GS salary scales operate uniformly throughout the nation, wherever a federal worker is employed.

Critics charge that GS pay scales are too low at the bottom, too low at the top, and generally too high in between.

Training and Management Development

How important is training? The consequences of a slipshod training program were dramatically revealed in the early 1970s by a series of raids by federal narcotics officers against innocent people. Threats and abusive language were common. Eventually, Justice Department officials were forced to admit that many narcotics agents had little enforcement experience and went to the agencies right out of college. Although the Bureau of Narcotics and Dangerous Drugs operated a national training institute for its agents—which provided eight weeks of training on searches, seizures, and constitutional rights—attendance was not required. Investigation revealed that quite a few of the officers involved in the mistaken raids had not taken the training.

Proper training can, of course, do much more than reduce the possibility of such indelicacies as midnight raids in the bedrooms of innocent citizens. In the first place, by providing employees with the opportunity to improve themselves, specific training and development programs help to reduce the number of dead-end jobs in an agency. Reducing such jobs, providing opportunity for advancement can, in many instances, increase motivation. Further, training programs can help to remedy a situation faced by many minority groups, namely, the difficulty of attaining a government position because of skill deficiencies.

Finally, training helps prepare employees for certain jobs that are unique to the public sector. As government continues to serve as the

Table 11-1
White-Collar Civilian Employment in the Federal Government, by Sex and Grade: 1970 to 1983

Grade[1]	Total (1,000)				Percent Female			
	1970	1975	1980	1983	1970	1975	1980	1983
General Schedule and equivalent pay system	1,259	1,428	1,473	1,484	40.3	42.1	45.1	46.5
Grades 1–6 ($8,676–$19,374)	521	585	561	541	72.2	71.6	74.1	74.6
Grades 7–10 ($16,559–$29,003)	302	344	357	360	33.4	38.4	46.3	48.8
Grades 11–12 ($24,508–$38,185)	264	297	335	362	9.5	13.5	19.3	24.2
Grades 13–15 ($34,930–$63,115)	164	196	217	220	3.0	5.1	8.2	10.3
Grades 16–18 ($56,945–$78,184)[2]	8	7	3	1	1.4	2.7	4.4	5.8

[1] Pay ranges shown for General Schedule grades are as of Oct. 1, 1982.

[2] Beginning 1980, change in number reflects shift of senior-level employees to Senior Executive Service.

Source: U.S. Office of Personnel Management, Occupations of Federal White-Collar and Blue-Collar Workers, biennial.

armature of technological progress as well as the champion of social progress, the number of these unique jobs will, very likely, increase.

For these reasons, then, managers should not prejudge training programs as time-consuming frills. On the contrary, they should look to their agency's employee development branch as a key ally in their own tasks of employee motivation and program management.

A manager should also be aware of the types of training programs available. The orientation program is perhaps the most elementary, but it is not unimportant. When well conceived, an orientation program can make employees more productive more quickly. On-the-job training (OJT) is a second type. Basically, an individual without all the needed skills or experience is hired and then learns the job from another employee.

For administrative, professional, and technical (APT) personnel, a wide variety of development programs are available, inside and outside the organization. For example: workshops and institutes (such as the Federal Executive Institute at Charlottesville, Virginia), professional conferences, university and college programs, management development programs, internships, and sabbaticals. The Intergovernmental Personnel Act of 1970 opened up federal in-service training programs to state and local employees and authorized grants to them. Similarly, the Labor Department's Public Service Careers Program and the Justice Department's Law Enforcement Assistance Administration also attempt to foster state and local programs. Since the development of in-service training programs at these levels has lagged behind that of the federal government, these trends are to be applauded.

Nor should *job rotation*—that is, transfer from unit to unit—be neglected as a method of providing for employee development. Herbert Kaufman (1960) furnishes an excellent example of how this type of

An aerial view of the Federal Executive Institute reveals the attractiveness of the setting.

training works. Transfers in the forest service, he found, do not wait for vacancies; rather, they are made every three or four years to acquaint employees with the various perspectives of duties of employees at all job levels and with a variety of specialities. According to the service, such a practice seeks "the development, adjustment, and broadening of personnel." The advantages of such a program for developing a pool from which top management can be drawn are obvious. Compare it to an agency that allows its top management to progress up the ranks within one functional specialty.

In general, the purpose of a management development program in the public sector is to extend the years of usefulness of those administrators who may be confronted with premature obsolescence and to prepare high potential mid-managers, whose past performance has been outstanding, for assuming higher managerial functions (Pomerleau, 1974). Because management development is a way of increasing the supply of managerial talent, it is at the heart of public personnel management today.

What criteria should an organization use in selecting relatively inexperienced managers in whom to invest its management development resources? The use of the *assessment center* method is one answer. This method involves multiple evaluation techniques (see Table 11–2) selected to bring out behavior related to the qualities identified by research as important to job success in the jobs for which the participants are under consideration. By observing, over a one- to three-day period, a participant's handling of the simulated problems and challenges of higher level jobs, assessors are able to get a feeling for a participant's ability before the promotion (Byham & Wettengal, 1974).

While the first recorded use of assessment procedures was by the German Army to help select officers during World War I, the first major use of it in the federal government was by the Internal Revenue Service in 1969. The last few years, however, have witnessed increasing application by government jurisdictions in the United States and Canada.

The current curriculum of the State Department's orientation course uses simulated situations and crises, such as trying to negotiate freedom for an American tourist jailed in the unfriendly land of Z (see photograph). The diplomats in training also attend seminars at centers where for two and a half days they simulate every aspect of an embassy's operation. Their instructors, all veteran Foreign Service officers, alternately praise and goad, pushing and stretching to get the maximum performance. James H. Morton, who runs some of the seminars, says: "The tougher and more realistic the training is back here in the States, the fewer surprises the new guys are going to run into overseas" (quoted in Ayres, 1983).

Table 11-2
Description of Exercises Used at the Assessment Center

Assigned Role Group Discussion

In this leaderless group discussion, participants, acting as a city council of a hypothetical city, must allocate a $1 million federal grant in the time allotted to make other judgments on the varying proposals offered. Each participant is assigned a point of view to sell to the other team members and is provided with a choice of projects to back and the opportunity to bargain and trade off projects for support.

Nonassigned Role Group Discussion

This exercise is a cooperative, leaderless group discussion in which four short case studies dealing with problems faced by executives working in state government agencies are presented to a group of six participants. The participants act as consultants who must make group recommendations on each of the problems. Assessors observe the participant's role in the group and the handling of the content of the discussion.

In-Basket Exercise

Problems that challenge middle- and upper-level executives in state government are simulated in the in-basket exercise. These include relationships with departmental superiors, subordinates and peers, representatives of other departments, representatives of executive and legislative branches, the public, and the news media. Taking over a new job, the participants must deal with memos, letters, policies, bills, and so on, found in the in-basket. After the in-basket has been completed, the participant is interviewed by an assessor concerning his or her handling of the various in-basket items.

Speech and Writing Exercises

Each participant is given a written, narrative description of a policy, event, situation, and so on, and three specific situational problems related to the narrative, each requiring a written response. The participant is also required to make a formal oral presentation, based upon the background narrative description, before a simulated news conference attended by the Capitol Press Corps and interested government officials and citizens (assessors).

Analysis Problem

The analysis problem is an individual analysis exercise. The participant is given a considerable amount of data regarding a state agency's field operations, which he or she must analyze and about which he or she must make a number of management recommendations. The exercise is designed to elicit behaviors related to various dimensions of managerial effectiveness. The primary area of behavior evaluated in this exercise is the ability to sift through data and find pertinent information to teach a logical and practical conclusion.

Paper and Pencil Tests

Three different commercially available, objectively scoreable tests are included in the assessment: a reading test used for self-development purposes, a reasoning ability test, and a personality test. The latter two are being used experimentally at present, and as with the reading test, are not made available during assessor discussions.

Source: Byham and Wettengal (1974). Reprinted by permission of the International Personnel Management Association, 1313 East 60th Street, Chicago, Illinois 60637.

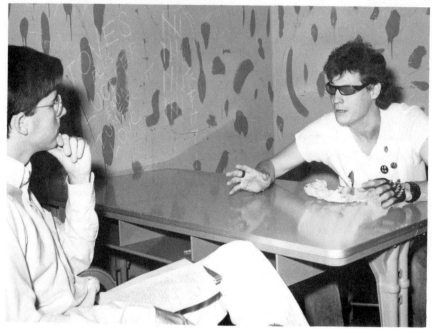

In a mock jail cell at the Foreign Service Institute, two trainees enact an embassy official counseling an American tourist imprisoned in the hostile country of Z. (U.S. State Department)

Advancement

Most jurisdictions provide that a new employee must serve a probation period for a limited time, usually six months. During this period, the manager should give him or her special attention in matters of instruction, indoctrination, and general adjustment to the job. In theory, probation is the last phase of the testing process, for at this time the individual may be discharged without the right of appeal and reinstatement. Unfortunately, very few dismissals occur during probation. Apparently, few managers have the fortitude to judge others when careers are at stake.

A career service must provide opportunity for advancement. But this does not preclude filling positions from outside as well as from within the service to keep an organization from becoming too inbred, or to obtain especially outstanding persons for positions above the entry level. To maintain an organization's vitality and competence, without harming employee morale, many jurisdictions provide for filling positions from within unless a better qualified person is available from outside. Using the same approach, some jurisdictions turn to the outside only when there is an insufficient number of well-qualified persons for consideration within the organization.

In state and local jurisdictions, a competitive promotional examination—covering general administation, psychology, personnel, and so on—is often required of employees. Supporters maintain that the open competitive promotion helps motivation and combats inertia. But most federal agencies have avoided competitive promotion by examination.

In addition to examination, performance ratings can take the form of measurement of output (such as in management by objectives system, discussed in Chapter 7), rating characteristics, or narratives. The checkoff or objective evaluation consists of rating employees on a scale concerning such qualities as writing ability, initiative, and promptness. The narrative approach allows managers to be more flexible in discussing the good and bad points of subordinates; but because they are difficult to compare and more time consuming, they are less popular than the objective form.

One criticism of performance appraisal as practiced in government might be cited. The process is periodic rather than continuous. But the manager should not wait until, say, the end of the year to tell an employee he or she is not performing. The good and bad aspects of performance should be discussed as they occur.

An excellent vehicle for the latter is the conventional interview. If an administrator is squeamish about expressing judgments regarding subordinates, then he or she should at least stay away from managing large nonroutine public programs. On this point James Webb (1969:166), former NASA administrator, deserves a careful hearing:

> As NASA administrator it became my practice to meet privately once each week with each of NASA's eight top executives for an hour of face-to-face, structured discussion that amplified and expanded the feedback process that had been continually going on between us. Inputs from all sources were brought into focus in these meetings, where no holds were barred. There were no intermediaries and no agreed ground rules. There were just two men, each charged with heavy responsibilities and vested with substantial powers, sitting face-to-face, probing each other's minds on problems, possible solutions, and how we and our other associates were doing our jobs. These were not staff meetings; we had staff meetings, too. The face-to-face evaluation and discussion meeting was a penetratingly personal confrontation on many matters that neither would have wanted to bring up in meetings with broader attendance.

Discipline and Grievances

Two of the more sensitive concerns of public personnel management are disciplining employees and listening to their complaints. Reprimands, suspensions, demotions, reassignments, and dismissals can obviously have an adverse effect on the career of an employee; accordingly, few managers enjoy situations that call for such forms of discipline. And yet, the public expects, quite rightly, efficient service from those paid by its taxes.

Nor do managers usually enjoy the complaints of subordinates. Even administrators who pride themselves on their open-door policy usually become unhappy when an employee begins to complain. The complaint seems to indicate that somehow they have failed to a degree as a manager. Whether an administrator finds discipline and grievances sensitive matters are not, he or she needs to keep several points in mind about each.

In disciplinary matters, the administrator should strive for improvement in employee performance. This improvement is only possible if disciplinary policy and standards of performance are clearly understood by all, and are impartially applied. Further, disciplinary actions should always be based on a careful assessment of the facts. Failure to do so can result in considerable embarrassment for the administrator if the employee decides to refute the charges and have the disciplinary action reviewed by an impartial body.

Discipline in an organization takes many forms, oral and written reprimands being the most common. And if the administrator can make it clear (a) that the objective of the reprimand is solely to correct employee actions, and (b) that mutual respect exists between the two, then these forms should work. Still, the administrator should not turn to them too readily. Is the employee's action sufficiently important to require a reprimand? If the answer is yes, then are more indirect, less formal approaches available? A well thought-out hint or joke might suffice for the moderately perceptive employee.

If reprimands continue to prove ineffective, then more severe forms of discipline need to be considered: suspension, demotion, reassignment, and dismissal. In such cases, the administrator will probably need to turn to the personnel office for assistance.

Suspension and demotion are less than satisfactory, except when an employee has demonstrated lack of ability in a particular position. Suspension often creates hostility. Demotion, or reassignment, by reducing motivation, can hamper agency performance, as the following interview by Terkel (1972:454) indicates:

> When management wants to get rid of you, they don't fire you. What they do is take your work away. That's what happened to me. They sent somebody down to go through my personnel file. "My God, what can we do with her?" They had a problem because I'm a high-grade employee. I'm grade 14. The regional director's a 17. One of the deputy directors told me, "You're going to be an economic development specialist." (Laughs.)
>
> I'm very discouraged about my job right now. I have nothing to do. For the last four or five weeks I haven't been doing any official work, because they really don't expect anything. They just want me to be quiet. What they've said it's a 60-day detail. I'm to come up with some kind of paper on economic development. It won't be very hard because there's little that can

Learning to Handle Grievances: Advice from the Experts

According to management consultants, the following simple points, if remembered, will help you to handle employees who have grievances or require discipline.

1. *Watch for signs of dissatisfaction and act before the problem becomes too serious.* Maintain open lines of communication and be accessible.
2. *Get all the facts.* Give the employee a chance to present his or her side fully. Try to see the employee's side.
3. *Remain calm and courteous.* Grievances and disciplinary matters can be very emotional experiences. Recognize this from the start and resolve to remain in control no matter how loud and angry the other party may be.
4. *Be positive not punitive.* Rather than treating employees harshly (e.g., making threats) and expecting them to "shape up," stress why certain rules must be enforced. Express confidence that the employee can improve.
5. *Be firm when necessary.* After every effort has been made to change an employee's behavior, discharge might be the only permanent solution.

be done. At the end of 60 days I'll present the paper. But because of the reorganization that's come up I'll probably never be asked about the paper.

Dismissal means being fired for cause; it does not refer to those employees who must leave government because of economic measures.

Public administrators, like their counterparts in industry, avoid dismissal as long as possible. And for good reason: The process is unpleasant and difficult—especially when the administrator has failed to document fully the case against the employee. Even when the dismissed employee has no right of appeal for reinstatement, the administrator may suddenly face strong external pressure from legislators, influential friends, and professional groups. Internally, he or she might face displeasure from other employees.

To guarantee fair play in personnel actions most agencies provide for appeals. What this statement does not convey is how grueling a hearing can be for the administrator. The employee's lawyer naturally tries to discredit the administrator's motives. At times, an observer might wonder if the administrator is on trail. Yet, much can be said in favor of the hearing procedure: It helps forward not only individual rights but also administrative responsibility.

In contrast to appeals, grievance procedures are designed more for hearing employee complaints about working conditions and other aspects of employment (e.g., job evaluation) and resolving them. While such procedures obviously benefit the employee, they also promote better management. Most administrators think they are fair, equitable, considerate, and sensitive to their employees. And perhaps they are, but the power and authority of their position can keep employee grievances from surfacing directly. Consequently, the effects of unresolved grievances begin to surface in other, more indirect ways such as higher turnover figures, reduced motivation, and more union organizing.

Grievance procedures are generally prescribed in civil service rules or regulations rather than in laws; but regardless of jurisdiction, for a grievance to work, certain elements are essential. First, the procedures should specify the steps to be followed by employees and supervisors to resolve differences. Established lines of authority should normally be followed—the immediate supervisor first and then up the line. Some jurisdictions provide a final avenue of review to an impartial panel when all else fails. Finally, employees filing grievances must be protected from reprisal.

Organizational Culture

Toward a Definition

As indicated in Figure 11-1 these five functions—staffing, classification/compensation, training/management development, advancement, and discipline/grievances—are embedded in something called organizational culture, which can have a powerful influence on performance.

Organizational culture can be defined as the predominant value system of an organization. When an organization's underlying values and beliefs are internalized by its members, several benefits ensue: The culture eases and economizes communications, facilitates organizational decision making and control, and may generate higher levels of cooperation and commitment. In short, organizational culture helps to overcome the centrifugal tendencies of a large bureaucracy by instilling in its members a sense of unity and common purpose.

This process can be encouraged through selection—people are hired because their personal values are already consistent with the organizational culture. It can also be encouraged through socialization—newcomers learn values and ways of behaving that are consistent with those of the organization. And, if you will recall the example from the first chapter of Peter Ueberroth and the Los Angeles Olympic Organizing Committee, organizational cultures can even operate in temporary organizations.

Two Case Studies in Organizational Culture

Two organizations in the public sector have been particularly successful in matching culture and goals: The U.S. Forest Service and the Marine Corps.

Herbert Kaufman describes how the Forest Service selects people "who fit." Weakly motivated people are advised to turn to other pursuits. "To a considerable extent, those who persisted were self-selected, a rather dedicated group prepared to accept whatever the profession had to offer" (1960:163). "Recruiting publicity tends to deter the impatiently ambitious, the seekers after the easy job and comfortable and stable life" (1960:164). Almost all the professional employees of the Forest Service were educated in forestry, which leads to widespread consensus on technical matters within the organization. "Appropriate behaviors, receptivity to agency directives are in this sense 'built into' them. Postentry training is designed to intensify in the rangers the capacity and willingness to adhere to the service's goals."

But the Forest Service also makes an effort to ensure an environment that promotes its members' identification with the well-being of the organization. For example, a policy of rapid transfer builds identification with the Forest Service as a whole. "Whenever a younger man severs his ties in a location to which he has just become adjusted and takes a new place, an experienced Forest Service officer—a mentor—is there to receive him, support him, guide him" (Kaufman, 1960:178). Promotion is relatively slow and, for senior-level positions, is always *from within* the Forest Service. This practice ensures that top administrators absorb many of the prevailing values, assumptions, and customary modes of operation.

(Used by permission of the
USDA Forest Service)

Identification is heightened by the use of symbols. The Forest Service insignia—the shield-shaped badge with the agency name and a tree emblazoned on it—is a familiar and respected one the country over. In Washington, the agency uses distinctive wooden plaques rather than the standard signs to identify its offices, while rustic signs bearing its emblem appear on almost all the properties it manages. Indeed, it has been said the adoption of the designation "Service"— now a fairly commonplace term, but a novelty when it was originally selected—instead of the more common "bureau" helped set it in a class by itself, accentuating its self-consciousness and corporate spirit.

These are all small things, but they do set the agency apart. Many public servants, asked who their employer is, are likely to name "the government," or perhaps their department. Forest officers will almost invariably respond, "the Forest Service." (Kaufman, 1960:185)

To understand why the Forest Service has placed such emphasis on developing a strong culture, we must understand the fundamental principle upon which it was founded, namely, that resource management begins and belongs on the ground. It follows then that the ranger district, and *not* headquarters in Washington, D.C., must be the backbone of the organization. But given that principle, how can one delegate great responsibility and authority to the men on the ground, pursue a unified policy direction, maintain high morale, and avoid any trace of scandal—all at the same time? So far, the only explanation the Forest Service has been able to come up with is to build and maintain a strong organizational culture.

Strong organizational cultures have strong traditions. Many of the Forest Service's values and beliefs can be traced back to the creed of Gifford Pinehot (the service's first chief), which was proclaimed in 1905.

The traditions of the Marine Corps go back much farther—to the battle honors it earned from its inception in 1775. Alan Ned Sabrosky (in Bonds, 1983:206) of the Center for Strategic and International Studies explains how the Marine Corps uses this tradition to strengthen its organizational culture and how the values of that culture manifest themselves.

> As with any military establishment, the U.S. Marine Corps has its own set of traditions, reflecting an institutional interpretation of the corps' past performance. In part, of course, such traditions are self-serving, highlighting only that which is worthy of emulation and ignoring or discarding anything that is not. Yet traditions cannot be dismissed lightly, especially in the case of a military institution. For such traditions not only influence the way in which the corps sees itself, and how others view the corps. They also shape the missions assigned to the corps, and the way in which it organizes itself for battle.
>
> Over the years, the Marine Corps has traditionally viewed itself as an elite force of infantry, highly disciplined and reliable (its motto is *Semper Fidelis*, or "Always Faithful"), which constituted the "cutting edge" of American diplomacy and power. The dictum that "every Marine was first and foremost a rifleman," while often only nominally accurate, reflected this perception. Even today, the fact that Marine ground combat formations are relatively large units with a high proportion of infantry is evidence of its continued significance.

To summarize, organizational cultures can have an important effect on the success of an organization. By codifying and symbolizing so that everyone can see "the way we do things here," organizational culture can have a positive influence on the behaviors and working environments of all employees. In organizations with strong cultures everyone knows and supports the organization's objectives; in those with weak cultures—perhaps the Peace Corps (Case 5.1) can serve as an example—no clear purpose exists. Thus, organizational culture complements not only human resources management but also the sense of mission, the process of strategy formulation discussed in Chapter 5.

Organizational culture is not, of course, without liabilities. Important shared beliefs and values can interfere with the needs of the organization, the people who work in it, or the public. To the extent that the content of an agency's culture leads its people to think and act in inappropriate ways, the culture will retard the attainment of positive results. Because cultures are not easily or quickly changed, this condition should not be dismissed lightly. In a rapidly changing environment, such inertia could be fatal.

The Legal Environment of Human Resources Management

The previously mentioned Pendleton Act is by no means the only law affecting public personnel management practices in the United States. Since the passage of that act in 1883, a number of important laws have come into being.

The Hatch Act

One of the oldest concerns in public personnel administration is that public employees should be removed from partisan politics. This notion was embodied in the Political Activities Act of 1939, commonly referred to as the Hatch Act. Over time, the act was broadened to cover state and local employees working on federally funded projects. Several states have enacted similar legislation.

The Hatch Act was provoked in 1939 by rampant corruption, by party pressures on jobholders. During the depression, some Works Progress Administration (WPA) officials used their positions to win votes for the Democratic party among the legion of WPA workers. Therefore, democratic Senator Carl Hatch of New Mexico introduced the bill to end such corrupt practices in national elections.

The Hatch Act today forbids bribery or intimidation of voters and limits political campaign activities among federal employees—no ringing door bells in someone's election campaign, running a political fund-raising operation, and so forth. Such activities on behalf of an incumbent legislator or a winning challenger would presumably magnify that civil servant's political influence and make Congress more beholden to him or her.

The Occupational Safety and Health Act (OSHA) of 1970

Contrary to popular opinion, dangers facing public sector employees can go well beyond dropping coffee cups on a toe or choking on a doughnut. As you can see in Figure 11–2 the risks to life and limb in

Figure 11-2
Dangerous Jobs *(Three-Year Injury Rates in Selected Public and Private Sector Jobs, 1974–1976)*

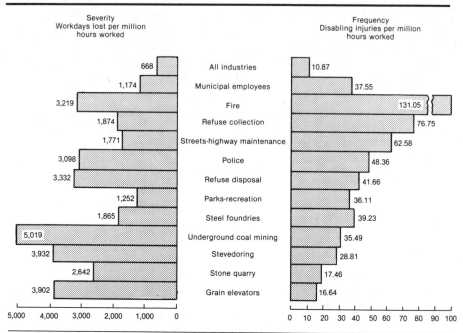

Severity Workdays lost per million hours worked		Frequency Disabling injuries per million hours worked
668	All industries	10.87
1,174	Municipal employees	37.55
3,219	Fire	131.05
1,874	Refuse collection	76.75
1,771	Streets-highway maintenance	62.58
3,098	Police	48.36
3,332	Refuse disposal	41.66
1,252	Parks-recreation	36.11
1,865	Steel foundries	39.23
5,019	Underground coal mining	35.49
3,932	Stevedoring	28.81
2,642	Stone quarry	17.46
3,902	Grain elevators	16.64

Source: National Safety Council, 1977.

the public sector can be every bit as high as in the private sector. On the average, working for the public is more than three times as dangerous as performing the average job in private industry.

According to a Labor Department study, injuries to federal workers are costing the government about $5 billion a year in direct costs and lost productivity (*Houston Post,* July 6, 1978). Unfortunately, no figures exist on what public employee injuries are costing state and local government, but those costs are likely in the billions as well.

OSHA requires that employers furnish to their employees "employment and a place of employment which are free from recognized hazards that are causing or are likely to cause death or serious physical harm." Federal and state OSHA auditors inspect government agencies on a random basis. As a result of reported violations, public managers are required to institute corrective measures and, in some cases, are held personally liable for punitive damages as well.

But city and state employees have no such federal protection. The Occupational Safety and Health Act of 1970 specifically excludes state and local workers from its provision. Twenty-four states have adopted

OSHA-like safeguards for public employees. But in the remaining 26 states, public workers have virtually none of the workplace safety protections that private sector workers have.

Civil Service Reform Act of 1978

Critics had long argued that personnel practices made it difficult for presidents to assemble teams of highly competent officials to implement new programs. To overcome this problem, President Jimmy Carter and the head of the Civil Service Commission, Alan K. Campbell, developed a package of reform proposals. After a major struggle in Congress and Carter's spending of large amounts of political capital, the reform bill passed in 1978.

Its major provisions were

- Creation of a Senior Executive Service (SES) of some 8,500 top civil servants who would be eligible for large cash bonuses for work performed, but also liable to transfer or demotion.
- A provision that raises for middle-level bureaucrats, other than those for cost-of-living increases, must be based strictly on merit rather than being virtually automatic, as had been the case.
- Legal recognition of the right of government employees to join unions and bargain collectively.

Jimmy Carter selected Alan K. Campbell (left), then dean of the Maxwell School of Public Administration, to oversee the implementation of the Civil Service Reform Act of 1978. Looking back on the reform, Campbell was forced to conclude: "The line between political appointees and career officials remains an obstacle to responsiveness, effective management, and intelligent policy formulation" (*Washington Post*, January 16, 1983). The second director of the Office of Personnel Management was Donald Devine (right) who generated controversy in the Senate by substantially cutting federal employment outside the Defense Department and reducing civil service pay and benefits. He cut his own OPM's staff and budget by one fourth. (U.S. Office of Personnel Management)

- Streamlininig of the appeals process for bureaucrats who are fired, so that firing for incompetence, if justified, can be more quickly expedited.
- Division of the Civil Service Commission into (1) an Office of Personnel Management (OPM) to manage the federal work force by setting pay scales and selection procedures, and (2) a Merit Systems Protection Board (MSPB) to hear appeals of employees charging mistreatment. Alan Campbell would become the first head of OPM (see photo).
- Prohibition of reprisals against whistle blowers, that is, employees who disclose evidence of gross mismanagement by the government (see p. 148).

Unfortunately, the act has had little significant impact on the federal agencies and workers it was supposed to help. And most social scientists agree that it has had little effect on equal employment practices, has not created the kind of corps of professional managers that was intended, and has been ignored by some agencies.

Laws at the Grassroots*

Throughout the era of New Federalism (see Chapter 3), Congress passed a number of laws that indirectly affected state and local government practices. For example, the Equal Employment Opportunity Act of 1972, the Fair Labor Standards Act of 1975, and the Federal Election Campaign Act of 1974 changed specific personnel practices in state and local governments. In a more direct fashion, the *Intergovernmental Personnel Act (IPA) of 1970* provided categorical grants to assist state and local governments that were willing to upgrade their personnel systems. Early in his administration, Reagan called for a reduction in the number of IPA grants; and later for elimination of IPA—presumably on the grounds that public personnel management in state and local government was not a federal concern.

In some ways, the Supreme Court is less restricted than Congress in its ability to influence state and local personnel management. Late in 1984, the Court overturned an earlier ruling, *National League of Cities* v. *Usury* (1976), which had held that the Constitution did not permit Congress to "directly replace the state's freedom to structure integral operations in areas of traditional government function." In the new ruling, *Garcia* v. *San Antonio Metropolitan Transit Authority*, the Court said that 13 million state and local government employees *are* subject to federal wage and hour standards.

Actually, the impetus for reform came at the local level before it did at the federal. In 1877, the New York Civil Service Reform Association was pushing hard for the elimination of patronage and the establish-

* Based on Committee on Economic Development (1978:42–44).

ment of merit principles for the public service in New York City, New York State, and the federal government. Similar organizations were soon formed in other cities, and in 1881, they merged to create the National Civil Service Reform League (the forerunner of the present National Civil Service League). It was this movement that formulated and lobbied for the passage of the Pendleton Act of 1883, which established the federal civil service system.

In 1883, New York State also passed a civil service law that applied to county and city as well as state employees. Massachusetts followed suit in 1884. Several big cities subsequently passed their own civil service laws.

In 1939, the federal government gave new impetus to the adoption of merit standards in state governments by requiring that state employees administering Social Security Board programs be covered by a merit system. In 1970, as we saw above, Congress passed the Intergovernmental Personnel Act, which has been instrumental in developing a broader perspective on public personnel management and encouraging experimentation with means of improving the public service at the state and local levels. Thirty-five states now have central personnel agencies employing merit standards generally in conformance with IPA principles.

The Legal Environment of Labor-Management Relations*

The language of labor relations—with such terms as steward, strike, and arbitration—is not particularly exotic. But when these terms are applied to employees in the public sector, misunderstandings arise. Are municipal employees, such as fire fighters and police officers, allowed to strike? How does the organization of public employees affect services such as garbage collection and highway repair? The purpose of this section is to answer questions that commonly arise about public-sector labor relations.

Legal Cornerstones

The Federal Level. In 1962, President John F. Kennedy issued *Executive Order 10988* granting federal civil service employees the right to bargain collectively. It requires agency administrators to deal with the employee organizations and to grant them official recognition for negotiation or consultation. For those organizations that had the support of the majority of the employees in the unit, Executive Order 10988 provided exclusive recognition and contract negotiating rights covering all employees in a bargaining unit. It also put certain limits on collective bargaining in the federal service. For example, salaries,

---

* This section draws heavily on the Committee on Economic Development (1978) and the Midwest Center for Public Sector Relations (1976).

The Squeeze on Public-Employee Unions

Once upon a time public employees were so docile a group that they scarcely seemed part of the American labor movement. Public-employee uprisings were few, and they met severe censure. The Boston police strike of 1919, which helped make then Massachusetts Governor Calvin Coolidge president, was stopped so effectively that 55 years passed before policemen dared strike in another large American city—Baltimore.

The first broadly based public workers' union, the American Federation of State, County, and Municipal Employees (AFSCME), was not formed until the mid-1930s. By the early 1960s, AFSCME and similar organizations formed the fastest-growing—virtually the *only* growing—segment of the trade-union movement.

U.S. Department of Labor figures show that the number of government workers—federal, state, and local—in national unions and employee associations rose steadily from 3.9 million in 1968 to 7 million by 1980. But by 1980, it appeared that membership was beginning to shrink for the first time since 1951. As Jerry Wurf, AFSCME's president says: "We'll have to organize like hell just to stay even" (quoted in *Business Week,* June 23, 1980).

With its growing power and escalating demands, AFSCME is finding growing hostility among taxpayers. In response, it has begun to do what big corporations do—namely, remind people through advertising that it performs useful services. The television advertisement below depicts the varied roles of government workers.

On your way to work tomorrow, look around you. There's a union out there called AFSCME . . .

. . . doing a lot of work you take for granted. For example, we pick up your trash . . .

We get your kids to school safely . . .

We keep your roads in good shape . . . We help take care of the sick and the troubled . . .

We keep up your parks and playgrounds . . . and we make sure your drinking water is pure.

We're AFSCME. American Federation of State, County and Municipal Employees . . . a union that represents public employees.

Hard-working, tax-paying people . . . working to make life better for you and your family.

AFSCME. The union that works for you.

wages, hours of work, and fringe benefits *cannot* be bargained, but tours of duty, lunch periods, sanitation, health services, vacation scheduling, training programs, and the like can.

The order that succeeded 10988 was Executive Order 11491. By establishing unfair labor practices for unions as well as management, this order brought the relationship between the federal government and unions more in line with the private sector relationships established under the National Labor Relations Act of 1935 (Wagner Act). For example, Executive Order 11491 provided for a Federal Labor Relations Council (FLRC) similar to the National Labor Relations Board (NLRB), which had monitored labor disputes in the private sector since 1935.

Both Executive Orders 10988 and 11491 clearly placed bargaining for wages *outside* the collective bargaining process. Nevertheless, in March 1970, about 200,000 postal employees left their jobs in a wage dispute. The federal government decided to bargain for the first time with unions representing public employees whose compensation was set by congressional statute. In August 1981, 13,000 air-traffic controllers staged the first national strike ever called by a union against the federal government. This time the federal government was not so complacent. President Reagan counterattacked with court orders, arrests, fines, and mass firings. At stake was the government's ability to make its own employees obey U.S. laws.

Reagan's tough stand against the Professional Air Traffic Controllers Organization (PATCO) had a profound effect on labor relations in a number of areas in the public sector. It greatly enhanced the ability of the Postal Service to obtain ratification of its agreement with two militant postal unions (representing 500,000 workers). And it reinforced the resolve of local and state officials to hold the line with their unions.

The previously mentioned Civil Service Reform Act of 1978 codified all provisions of the executive orders. Furthermore, Title IV of the act changed the FLRC, which unions had viewed as a management tool, into the independent Federal Labor Relations Authority (FLRA). Collective bargaining for federal employees now had a firm legal foundation.

State and Local Level. In the absence of federal guidance, the responsibility for establishing the framework for state-local labor relations has fallen to the state governments. When there has been no clear state guidance, that responsibility has fallen to local jurisdictions. In some cities, collective bargaining relationships originally developed by direct action of city or county councils, or by order of the elected executive, without state statutes. In jurisdictions that do not formally provide for collective bargaining, associations or unions representing employees often negotiate informally with management.

Proponents of federal legislation establishing collective bargaining for state and local governments argue that the states have lagged in their responsibility to assure equal treatment for public employees and

The Reagan administration's legal offensive in 1981 to put the Professional Air Traffic Controllers Organization (PATCO) permanently out of the business of representing federal employees opened a new chapter in American labor history. According to experts in labor law, attorneys for the government, and the controllers' union, never before has the government attempted to use the law to destroy a union so completely and irrevocably. John H. Fenton, a federal administrative law judge, recommended that the union's legal authority to represent federal employees be indefinitely suspended for its "open and flagrant" and repeated violation of laws barring strikes by federal employees. His recommendation was upheld by the three-member Federal Labor Relations Authority.

that the diversity among states in public labor relations is confusing and disruptive.

Although an argument can be made for federal legislation, leaving the authority to the states to determine the legal framework for state and local government labor relations in their jurisdictions has its advantages. The states are in a better position than the federal government to create and develop a structure that best accounts for the variable economic, organizational, and especially, political conditions that so importantly affect public-sector labor relations.

Of the more than 30 states with collective bargaining laws, only 22 now have what unions consider "full scope" or comprehensive statutes providing for negotiations on wages, hours, and conditions of employment. In the rest, unions are working to expand the scope of more limited laws that vary widely in coverage from state to state and to win adoption of statutes where there are none.

Duties and Restrictions. To generalize, labor laws impose several duties on public administrators:

- To bargain in "good faith." This means that the parties make an earnest effort and act meaningfully to help bring an agreement into being. For example, the parties should be willing to sit down at reasonable times and exchange nonconfidential information, views, and proposals on subjects that are within the scope of bargaining. Both sides should be represented by duly authorized spokespersons. When bargaining fails to bring agreement, differences should be justified with reasons. The parties must be ready to put into writing whatever agreement they arrive at. Most important, they must be willing to consider compromise solutions to their differences with an open mind, and to make an effort to find a mutually satisfactory basis for agreement.
- To work with an employee organization that is the exclusive representative of the employees in the bargaining unit.
- To bargain over wages, hours, and other terms and conditions of employment.
- To commit to writing the agreement that is reached on the subjects of negotiation—if the employee organization requests it.
- To abide by that agreement day by day in those departments and agencies covered by the agreement within a given jurisdiction.

The laws also impose several restrictions on public administrators:

- Interference, intentional or unintentional, with the employee's right to (1) organize or join organizations for collective bargaining purposes; (2) participate in collective bargaining through representatives; or (3) engage in other legal activities, alone or in a group, designed to affect the terms and conditions of employment, is prohibited.
- Interference in any way with the formation or administration of any employees' organization, or contribute financial or other support to that organization is prohibited.
- Discrimination, direct or indirect, for or against employees to discourage or encourage membership in any employees' organization is prohibited.

The Collective Bargaining Process

Figure 11–3 shows the normal sequence of events in establishing a collective bargaining relationship.

Organizing At this beginning stage, the employees try either to create an organization or to select one from those already existing outside organizations that want to represent them. These organizations will try to win the support of the employees by an organizing

Figure 11–3
The Collective Bargaining Process

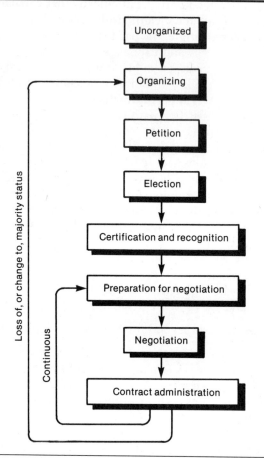

Source: U.S. Office of Personnel Management (1979:137).

campaign. They will use such techniques as distributing literature, soliciting membership, and holding discussion meetings.

Election Two fundamental issues must be resolved at this second stage: (1) The bargaining unit must be determined. This means it must be decided which employees in the political jurisdiction will be grouped together for collective bargaining purposes. (2) The bargaining agent must be named. In other words, it should be decided what organization, if any, will represent the employees within the *bargaining unit* for the purpose of labor relations activities.

Negotiation This is when the actual process of collective bargaining begins. The main intention of these negotiations is to reach an agree-

How to Avoid Grievances

A few pointers may help one manage more effectively and minimize employee grievances:

Be alert to the usual cause of grievances. Do not knowingly violate the contract. For example, distributing overtime unequally in violation of a contract provision is an open invitation to a grievance.

Keep workers informed regarding the quality of their work.

Correct minor irritations promptly.

Encourage constructive suggestions.

Keep promises.

Assign work impartially to employees with equal skill and ability.

Explain your orders unless they are obvious.

Be consistent unless there's an obvious reason for change.

Explain change, even when the change doesn't require negotiation.

Act as soon as possible on requests. Avoid showing favoritism.

If you must take corrective action, do not make it a public display.

In short, use common sense and assume that fair treatment will pay off in cooperation. When a dispute does arise, resolve it (if possible) before it becomes a formal grievance. Personnel or labor relations officers can help prevent an issue from escalating into a grievance.

ment between the public employer and the employee representative. The agreement should be one they both can "live with" concerning the job terms and conditions of those employees involved.

This step also includes impacts resolution or dispute settlement. Although it is not a true stage of labor relations, it is a situation that sometimes arises when the parties are unable to reach an agreement by themselves. An outside party intervenes to settle the impasse (see below). Types of dispute settlement vary, ranging from limited intervention to a type in which the outside neutral person imposes an agreement upon the parties.

Contract Administration This final stage is the very heart of labor relations because it involves putting the collective bargaining agreement into practice on a day-to-day basis. No matter how hard negotiators work to write a clear and understandable agreement, disputes inevitably arise about the true meaning of the written agreement and the intent of the parties when they agreed to particular provisions. These disagreements occur even among reasonable and well-intentioned people. They are handled through grievance procedures, a vital part of contract administration (see box). These procedures resemble impasse procedures because here again a neutral person is often called in to help resolve the dispute.

Impasse Procedures

An impasse is a condition during negotiations when either party feels that no further progress can be made toward reaching a settlement. If collective bargaining is to work, provisions must be made for the resolution of such conditions in a manner that recognizes the rights, legitimate interests, and power of both labor and management as the representative of the public. The most desirable way to resolve impasses is for both sides to reopen negotiations and bargain until they reach an agreement or to employ neutral third parties to help break the deadlock. If such efforts do not succeed, more formal steps are required. The responsibility for resolving, or facilitating the resolution of, impasses in collective bargaining should be given to a neutral agency that is professionally staffed, adequately compensated, and equipped with a range of procedures for settling, or facilitating the settlement of, public-sector labor disputes. Such responsibility might be given to the public-employee relations board or lodged in a separate agency committed exclusively to dispute resolution. Creation of a separate agency may enhance the perception of neutrality, although public-employee relations boards might accomplish the same purpose by establishing a separate division for providing mediators, fact finders, and arbitrators or lists of professionals experienced in public-sector dispute resolution.

The dispute-resolution procedures for which the agency should be equipped include the following:

Mediation A mediator is a neutral third party who attempts to conciliate disputes between labor and management but does not have the power to enforce a settlement.

Fact-finding A fact finder (or panel of fact finders) is a neutral third party who hears the cases presented by each side, often in a formal

"Another setback—the mediators just went out on strike." (From *The Wall Street Journal*, with permission of Cartoon Features Syndicate.)

proceeding, and generally makes specific recommendations for resolving the dispute. Fact-finding is typically the second step after mediation has failed.

Arbitration An arbitrator is a neutral third party who goes beyond fact-finding to decide in favor of one side or the other. In binding arbitration, the decision of the arbitrator is final. ("Interest arbitration" refers to resolution of impasses arising in bargaining; "grievance arbitration" refers to the settlement of disputes in interpretation of a contract that has already been executed.) In last-offer arbitration, the arbitrator must find in favor of the last offer (or separable items in the last offer) presented by each of the parties; this presumably encourages each side to bargain seriously and to be reasonable in their positions in the knowledge that an unreasonable offer will result in the adoption of the other side's proposal. Seventeen states now provide for arbitration of collective bargaining impasses. However, compulsory and binding arbitration is typically opposed by managers who fear that these mechanisms provide a third party who is unfamiliar with local conditions and unaccountable to local authority with the power to bind government to costly settlements. In 1978, Dayton, Ohio, voters rejected a proposal to submit future impasses in bargaining with fire fighters to arbitration even though the city had recently suffered a strike by fire fighters.

Preoccupation with the techniques of resolving bargaining impasses or other labor disputes should not divert attention from a more fundamental source of labor peace, that is, mutual respect between employees and management based on good day-to-day working relationships and concern for the legitimate interests of both sides. (Chapter 10 suggested points to consider in establishing such a relationship.) Nevertheless, building a tradition of harmonious employee relations depends upon the existence of fair and workable arrangements for resolving disputes.

Similarly, preoccupation with the issue of public-employee strikes should not divert attention from the task of establishing workable mechanisms for dispute resolution. However, achieving peaceful dispute resolution depends in part upon how the issue of strikes is handled.

Laws concerning Discrimination

Title VII: The Cornerstone

The key provision of the Civil Rights Act of 1964 is Title VII, Section 703(a) which states, in part:

It shall be an unlawful employment practice for an employer— (1) to fail or refuse to hire or to discharge any individual, or otherwise to discriminate against any individual with respect to his compensation, terms, conditions, or privileges of employment, because of such individual's race, color, religion, sex, or national origin; or

(2) to limit, segregate, or classify his employees or applicants for employment in any way which would deprive or tend to deprive any individual of employment opportunities or otherwise adversely affect his status as an employee, because of such individual's race, color, sex, or national origin.

The road to equal opportunity in America has been a tortuous, uphill one that eventually led to a great national consensus expressed legislatively in the Civil Rights Act of 1964. Its meaning was clear: No longer would there be any discrimination on the grounds of race, color, religion, or national origin in voting, public education, public accommodation, or employment. The 1964 act also provided, however, that:

(i) Nothing contained in this title shall be interpreted to require any employer . . . to grant preferential treatment to any individual or to any group because of the race, color, religion, sex, or national origin of such individual or group on account of an imbalance which may exist with respect to the total number or percentage of persons of any race, color, religion, sex, or national origin employed by any employer.

Thus, the emphasis of the 1964 act was on *equal opportunity* for the individual. Preferential treatment, including, it would appear, such devices as quotas, was not only not required, but expressly forbidden. In addition, discrimination was seen as an intentional, calculated act to exclude some people from work.

No sooner had the Civil Rights Act seemed to fulfill old promises at last than President Johnson was observing at his historic commencement address at Howard University in June 1965:

But freedom is not enough. You do not take a person who, for years, has been hobbled by chains and liberate him, bring him up to the starting line of a race and then say, "You are free to compete with all the others" and still justly believe that you have been completely fair.

Thus it is not enough just to open the gates of opportunity. All our citizens must have the ability to walk through those gates.

This is the next and the more profound stage of the battle for civil rights. We seek not just freedom but opportunity. We seek not just legal equality but human ability, not just equality as a right and a theory but equality as a fact and equality as a result.

The outgrowth of that promise for positive approaches is that *affirmative action* efforts have been developed at all levels of government. Affirmative action plans require employees to demonstrate good faith in their efforts to increase opportunities for *deprived groups*—a term inclusive of blacks, Chicanos, native Americans, Asian-Americans, and women. The Equal Employment Opportunity Commission (EEOC) is only one of many federal agencies administering the Civil Rights Act in general or the affirmative action programs in particular.

There are overlapping jurisdictions of the Labor Department; the Department of Health and Human Resources; Department of Education; the Justice Department; the EEOC; and the federal courts. When one federal agency approves or requires a given practice, this in no way protects an employer from being sued. Indeed, federal agencies have sued one another under this act.

Developing an Affirmative Action Plan

The line between quotas and goals is exceedingly thin. Yet, as I think the National Civil Service League's *Model Public Personnel Administration Law* illustrates, an effective affirmative action plan does not necessarily require quotas.

Consider the following two recommendations that can do much to help break down artificial barriers to minority group employment:

> Offer preferential treatment to disadvantaged persons and minority group members. This recommendation means that a jurisdiction will take affirmative action to remedy the results of past discrimination and increase its employment of minorities. Specifically, preferential treatment includes aggressive recruiting for minorities, selective certification for certain positions, and training programs to allow the disadvantaged to become fit for merit system jobs.
>
> Establish selection systems based on job related, culture-fair evaluations. The essential point is that we need not find coal shovelers who can scan Virgil correctly, but coal shovelers who are properly qualified for shoveling.

Likewise, the examination should not be culturally biased. An obvious example of cultural bias is an overly sophisticated English vocabulary on a written test for a Chicano. Similarly, individuals that have spent the majority of their lives in a low-income urban setting might find that some examinations favor a more middle-class suburban background.

The U.S. Equal Employment Opportunity Commission (1974) suggests these basic steps to develop an effective affirmative action program:

A. Issue a written equal employment policy and affirmative action commitment.
B. Appoint a top official with responsibility and authority to direct and implement your program.
   1. Specify responsibilities of program manager.
   2. Specify responsibilities and accountability of all managers and supervisors.
C. Publicize your policy and affirmative action commitment.
   1. Internally. To managers, supervisors, all employees, and unions.

2. Externally. To sources and potential sources of recruitment, potential minority and female applicants, to those with whom you do business, and to the community at large.

D. Survey present minority and female employment by department and job classification.
   1. Identify present areas and levels of employment.
   2. Identify areas of concentration and underutilization.
   3. Determine extent of underutilization.

E. Develop goals and timetables to improve utilization of minorities, males, and females in each area where underutilization has been identified.

F. Develop and implement specific programs to achieve goals. This is the heart of your program. Review your entire employment system to identify barriers to equal employment opportunity; make needed changes to increase employment and advancement opportunities of minorities and females. These areas need review and action:
   1. Recruitment. All personnel procedures.
   2. Selection process. Job requirements, job descriptions, standards and procedures, preemployment inquiries, application forms, interviewing.
   3. Upward mobility system. Assignments, job progressions, transfers, seniority, promotions, training.
   4. Wage and salary structure.
   5. Benefits and conditions of employment.
   6. Layoff, recall, termination, demotion, discharge, disciplinary action.
   7. Union contract provisions affecting above procedures.

G. Establish internal audit and reporting system to monitor and evaluate progress in each aspect of the program.

H. Develop supportive in-house and community programs.

Recent Developments

Thus far in this section, only one law has been discussed: the Civil Rights Act of 1964. While this focus keeps things simple, it is highly misleading. The cold fact is that the legal environment of public personnel management is an increasingly tangled skein of lawsuits, guidelines, and racial quotas (see Table 11–3).

Consider the case of one college president who not long ago wrote to lawyers at the Equal Employment Opportunity Commission that "Colby (College) is prepared, as we have always tried to do, to comply with the law of the land, but first it would be helpful to know what the law of the land is." The cause of Colby's befuddlement was the position the EEOC had taken on retirement plans, namely, that men and women employees of equal status should get the same monthly pension. But women live longer than men on the average; therefore, equal monthly benefits mean that contributions to pension funds would have to be higher for women than men. Enter a second federal agency: the Office of Federal Contract Compliance of the Department of Labor,

Table 11–3
Laws, Executive Orders, and Court Decisions on Discrimination

The Equal Pay Act of 1963. This amendment to the Fair Labor Standards Act (1938) prohibits employers from discriminating against employees on the basis of sex. The act requires "equal pay for equal work," defining as work "the performance of which demands equal skill, effort, and responsibility."

The Age Discrimination in Employment Act of 1967. This act prohibits employers from discriminating in employment practices on the basis of age, specifically employees aged 40 to 70. Amendments to the Fair Labor Standards Act (1974) extended its coverage to state and local government employees.

The Equal Employment Opportunity Act of 1972. This act amended certain provisions of the Civil Rights Act of 1964 (see pp. 000). The most significant change concerns Title VII exemptions. The term *person* was expanded to include governments, government agencies, and political subdivisions. These amendments also required state and local governments to develop their own affirmative action plans.

Title VI of the Vocational Rehabilitation Act of 1973. Section 503 of this act requires all federal contractors with government contracts over $2,500 to take affirmative action to hire and advance in employment qualified handicapped individuals—that is, those who, with reasonable accommodation, can perform the essential functions of the job.

Executive Order 11141. This 1965 order declares it to be the policy of the federal government that government contractors and subcontractors not discriminate in employment on the basis of age.

Executive Order 11246, as Amended. This 1965 order bans discrimination in employment on federal government contracts based on race, creed, color, national origin, or sex. The Philadelphia Plan was issued in 1969 under this order, which charges the secretary of labor with responsibility for administering the government's policy requiring equal employment opportunity in federal contracts and federally assisted construction work. The Philadelphia Plan is an equal opportunity compliance program that requires bidders on all federal and federally assisted construction projects exceeding $500,000 to submit affirmative action plans setting specific goals for the utilization of minority employees.

***Griggs et al.* v. *Duke Power Company* (1971).** This is perhaps the most significant Supreme Court decision concerning the validity of employment examinations. The court unanimously ruled that Title VII of the Civil Rights Act of 1964 "proscribes not only overt discrimination but also practices that are discriminatory in operation." Thus, if employment practices operating to exclude minorities "cannot be shown to be related to job performance, the practice is prohibited." The Griggs decision applied only to the private sector until the Equal Employment Opportunity Act of 1972 extended the provisions of Title VII of the Civil Rights Act of 1964 to cover public as well as private employees.

***Carter* v. *Gallagher* (1971).** A federal district court found that the Minneapolis Fire Department had all white employees because of hiring and practices that whether by design or not, discriminated against minority applicants. The court ordered an arrest question stricken from the applications, the minimum age lowered from 20 to 18, and the high school diploma requirement dropped. They also ordered a new exam designed and the development of a massive affirmative action plan.

***Franks* v. *Bowan Transportation Company* (1976).** Minority applicants denied jobs as drivers were awarded retroactive seniority, that is, seniority status retroactively awarded back to the date that a minority group member was proven to have been discriminatorily refused employment. The U.S. Supreme Court has interpreted the "make whole" provision of Title VII of the Civil Rights Act of 1964 to proven discriminatees; however, retroactive seniority cannot be awarded further back than 1964—the date of the act.

Table 11–3 *(concluded)*

***Washington* v. *Davis* (1976).** Verbal ability tests that discriminate against black police applicants are *not* unconstitutional. The Supreme Court held that although the due process clause of the Fifth Amendment prohibits the government from invidious discrimination, it does not follow that a law or other official act is unconstitutional solely because it has a racially disproportionate impact. The court ruled that, under the Constitution (as opposed to Title VII of the Civil Rights Act of 1964), there must be discriminatory purpose or intent—adverse impact alone is insufficient.

***Dothard* v. *Rawlinson* (1977).** The Supreme Court upheld an Alabama regulation that prohibits the employment of women as prison guards in "contact positions" (requiring continual close physical proximity to inmates) within the state's correctional facilities.

***Regents of the University of California* v. *Allan Bakke* (1978).** The Supreme Court upheld a white applicant's claim of reverse discrimination because he was denied admission to the University of California Medical School at Davis when 16 minority applicants, with lower test scores, were admitted. The court ruled that Bakke must be admitted to the Davis Medical School as soon as possible, *but* that the university had the right to take race into account in its admissions criteria.

***United Steelworkers of America* v. *Weber* (1979).** The Supreme Court cleared much of the murky air surrounding affirmative action programs on the job. The Court ruled five to two that hiring and promotion preference plans do *not* necessarily violate the Civil Rights Act of 1964. (Title VII of that act had forbidden discrimination in employment on the basis of race). Civil rights advocates called the ruling a triumph for affirmative action plans.

***Gunther* v. *County of Washington* (1981).** The Supreme Court ruled that women who are paid less than men may sue their employers for sex discrimination, even if the jobs of both are not identical. But the court failed to resolve the underlying volatile issue of "comparable worth." (That means that if a secretary or nurse contributes as much to an agency as a deputy director or janitor, their salaries should be equivalent.)

***Firefighters Local Union No. 1984* v. *Stotts* (1984).** The Supreme Court ruled that, without proof of actual discrimination, a last-hired, first-fired seniority system is permissible.

which says that monthly contributions for men and women should be equal. Whose definition of equality is to prevail?

Rather than pile anecdote on anecdote, let us focus on just two post-Title VII court cases.

***Firefighters* v. *Stotts* (1984).**   As we have already seen, after the Civil Rights Act of 1964, rapid progress toward equality under the law took place. It was only in the 1970s that a new goal, affirmative action, was introduced. But Ronald Reagan, who entered the White House in 1981, and Clarence Pendleton, Jr., the new chairman of the U.S. Civil Rights Commission, viewed this policy, especially the use of racial quotas, as a new form of discrimination; they wanted to return to the original policy of equal opportunity.

A major milestone in their efforts came in June 1984, when the Supreme Court, in a case involving the Memphis Fire Department, ruled that hiring quotas can only be used to benefit people who are victims of past discrimination. This decision sent shock waves through the civil rights lobby, which had been arguing that you do not have to show past discrimination, and could prove to be the beginning of the end for all court-ordered quotas where racial discrimination had not been proven.

Specifically, in *Firefighters Local Union No. 1984* v. *Stotts*, black firefighters brought a class-action suit demanding that they not suffer from budget cutbacks in the Memphis Fire Department. The Supreme Court ruled that without proof of actual discrimination, the Memphis last-hired, first-fired seniority system was permissible.

If the justices had stuck narrowly to the facts, the Stotts case would only mean that the Court stood by the priority of seniority over affirmative action. But Justice White's majority opinion went well beyond the call of explanatory duty. Returning to the first principles— the 1964 Civil Rights Act and its Title VII—Justice White wrote that the act was intended "to provide make-whole relief only to those who have been actual victims of illegal discrimination." Here, "mere membership in the disadvantaged class is insufficient to warrant a seniority award; each individual must prove that the discriminatory practice had an impact on him."

But the most important changes have been at the Equal Employment Opportunity Commission (EEOC), cornerstone of the government's campaign against job bias. EEOC Chairman Clarence Thomas has instructed his staff to restudy the guidelines issued jointly in 1978 by all federal agencies that enforce EEO laws. The 1978 guidelines say, for instance, that if the hiring rate from black applicants is at least 80 percent of the rate for white males, the company is assumed to be in compliance. Behind all this activity are three unifying themes:

- Suspicion of discrimination charges based on statistics rather than on evidence of bias against identified workers.
- Belief that remedies for past bias should be tailored more narrowly, to aid the particular persons injured by bias.
- Definitions of affirmative action that emphasize recruiting techniques and training programs geared to minority workers rather than specific minority hiring goals.

It is too soon to say whether affirmative action, which is alleged by many to require reverse discrimination, is on its last legs. Advocates of quotas certainly have not given up and the debate is likely to continue.

Comparable Worth: "Beyond Equal Pay for Equal Worth."   In recent years, there has been considerable controversy surrounding something called *comparable worth*, the term used by those who think that men and women performing nominally different jobs should receive equal pay if those jobs are of "comparable" value to the employer. The Equal Pay Act of 1963 required equal pay for equal work; for example, it was illegal to pay a male telephone operator more than a female telephone operator.

The issue of equal pay for comparable work, however, is vastly more complex. It arises because studies show that jobs traditionally held by women and demanding the same level of skills, responsibility, and effort tend to pay less than jobs traditionally held by men. This is a major reason why working women, despite equal pay laws, still earn only about 60 cents for every dollar earned by men. But there are a number of other reasons too, as the box that follows explains.

The crucial question is whether courts and the government have the right, or the practical ability, to calculate the relative worth of disparate jobs and then to mandate that wages be adjusted accordingly. Normally, pay levels are and should be determined by supply and demand in the job market. But women's wages have been depressed because the work they do, while truly comparable to that done by men for the same employer, is classified as something else. That condition gave rise to a legal theory of "comparable worth," a measure by which such discrimination might be rooted out.

The theory received its biggest boost in 1983 from federal Judge Jack Tanner, who concluded that the state of Washington had practiced illegal discrimination by segregating differently paid jobs by sex where sex was not a legitimate consideration *(American Federation of State, County, and Municipal Employees* v. *State of Washington)*. Female dental assistants, for example, were paid 20 percent less than predominantly male X-ray technicians; "barbers" were paid 5 percent more than "beauticians" by state institutions; and mostly male counselors

Two of the still-rare women park rangers at ruins in Mesa Verde National Park. As one female bureaucrat put it, "We've still got to deal with the resistance that comes from the 'strong man in uniform image.' " (Roger Neville Williams, *New York Times*)

Measuring the Change in Women's Economic Status

According to June O'Neill, the male-female "pay gap" is not quite as wide as is commonly assumed. Feminists have popularized the fact that the annual earnings of women who work full time average 60 percent of men's pay. But "full-time" workers include all those who work 35 or more hours weekly. Men put in more hours and more overtime than do women and are more likely to hold second jobs.

A better measure of the gap is hourly pay. By that standard, women earn 69 percent as much as men.

Women's career decisions, O'Neill argues, account for part of the remaining gap. A 1968 survey of women from age 20 to 24 revealed that 68 percent planned to be homemakers by the time they reached age 35. Yet a checkup 10 years later showed that 60 percent of these women were still working. "Early expectations," O'Neill writes, "influence courses chosen in school, early job experience, the extent of job search, and other activities that will have an impact on later earnings."

Many young women of the 1960s, in other words, never intended to become permanent members of the work force and therefore invested less in their future careers.

Childbearing, of course, affects women's careers. Women who leave their jobs to have children gain less work experience than do men. A 1977 survey of white jobholders from age 40 to 49 showed that the men had been working virtually without interruption since leaving school, while the women had held jobs in only about 60 percent of the years since graduation.

Family responsibilities also influence the kinds of jobs women take. "Amenities such as short hours, long vacations, flexible schedules, or a [convenient] location . . . are paid for through lower wages," O'Neill observes. And women tend to avoid jobs that pay extra for enduring harsh conditions, such as construction work.

O'Neill adjusted for most of these factors by statistical means in a 1983 study. Women earned 80 percent as much as males with equivalent schooling, work experience, and type of job.

Must the 20-point gap be explained entirely by sex discrimination? Not necessarily, O'Neill cautions. Unquantifiable differences, such as degree of job commitment or the "marketability" of one's education, may provide part of the explanation. On the other hand, some discrimination may have escaped measurement—for example, employers could be denying women on-the-job training.

In any event, O'Neill predicts, the pay gap will narrow "perceptibly" during the 1980s. Women are catching up to men in years of schooling and work experience. Younger women, in particular, seem to be ready to make the investments and personal sacrifices necessary to win high-paying jobs. In 1978, roughly 77 percent of the 25- to 29-year-old women interviewed for one study declared that they would still be working women, not homemakers, when they turned 35.

Source: "The Change in Women's Economic Status." (Paper presented before U.S. Congress, Joint Economic Committee, November 9, 1983).

at correctional institutions were paid 8 percent more than mostly female counselors at mental institutions.

In 1985, the 9th U.S. Circuit Court of Appeals reversed Judge Tanner's decision. The three-judge panel said federal laws banning sex discrimination in employment do not require an employer to provide equal pay for equal work even if the employer's own studies say that the jobs have the same value. The appeals court said that a wage gap does not indicate that the state intentionally discriminated against women. The 1964 Civil Rights Act "does not obligate [Washington State] to eliminate an economic inequality which it did not create." The decision was a devastating but not fatal blow to the supporters of comparable worth. Not surprisingly, they appealed the decision to the Supreme Court.

Obviously, making these adjustments would be quite expensive. If the Supreme Court upholds Judge Tanner's ruling, the state of Washington may have to pay over $400 million. According to Dan Glasner of the Philadelphia consulting firm Hay Associates (which has been producing job-evaluation systems for more than 40 years), raising the wage scales of jobs traditionally held by women to eliminate disparities in the earnings of men and women would cost some $320 billion in added annual wages and increase inflation by 10 percent (*Time*, February 6, 1984).

But can theory overcome the much less deliberate, socially rooted patterns of segregation? A generation ago, for example, because they were mostly barred from many occupational fields, women were far more likely than men to become teachers, nurses, or stenographers. The better remedy for that kind of segregation, some argue, is to keep expanding women's opportunities in other lines of work.

With reference to the lever, Archimedes said, "Give me but one firm spot on which to stand and I will move the earth." The art of public administration, similarly, lies in this capacity to select from many activities of seemingly comparable significance the one or two that provide the best *leverage* and then to push hard on them. As we saw in Part I, political management requires careful attention to time and place when seeking to influence the policymaking process. As we saw in Part II, program management requires identification of strategic factors in a decision-making situation.

Part III has discussed a number of high-leverage activities. The budget is, of course, crucial in determining where an organization goes and how to keep it on track. It is hard to think of anyone in the executive branch—besides presidents themselves—having had more influence in redirecting government than David Stockman, and certainly not anyone in his or her 30s. That Stockman had such influence was due in part to his ability; the main reason, however, was that he was director of the Office of Management and Budget.

Because management is a team activity, the performance of administrators must be judged, in the final analysis, by how effectively they enhance the performance of others. Three high-leverage activities discussed in Chapters 10 and 11 are particularly worth administrators' attention: motivating, training, and performance appraisal.

Nailing Down the Main Points

1. Frederick C. Mosher classifies personnel systems into four main types: *(a)* political appointees, *(b)* general civil service, *(c)* career systems, and *(d)* collective system.

2. The aims of public personnel are to revitalize the merit system, restore the authority of managers to manage, protect the rights of employees, and enhance personal performance, and match human resources with anticipated needs.

3. Public personnel management (or, more accurately, human resources development) can provide public administrators specialized help in managing people. The federal government has clearly recognized the importance of human resources through the passage of such legislation as the Intergovernmental Personnel Act and Civil Service Reform Act of 1978.

4. At all levels of government, the basis of the civil service is position classification; that is, identifying the duties and responsibilities of each position in an organization and then grouping the positions according to their similarities. Nevertheless, today the concept is frequently under attack. Like position classification, compensation is a very important and controversial part of public personnel administration. The general rule for establishing a good pay plan is to pay according to differences in levels of duties and responsibilities.

5. Staffing refers to the process of recruiting, selecting, and advancing employees on the basis of their relative ability, knowledge, and skill. Drucker says staff for strength.

6. In disciplinary matters, the administrator should strive for improvement in employee performance.

7. Organizational culture, the shared values of an organization, exercises a powerful influence on performance in the area of public personnel management.

8. One of the most visible concerns of public personnel management is labor relations. The growth in public sector employee unions really got underway in 1962 when President Kennedy signed Executive Order 10988, which guaranteed them recognition and bargaining rights.

9. The collective bargaining process provides systematic procedures for the resolution of management-labor conflict. It consists of four major steps: organizing, election, negotiation, and contract administration.

10. In 1965, President Johnson said that it is not enough just to open the gates of opportunity. "All our citizens must have the ability to walk through those gates." The outgrowth of that pronouncement was that affirmative

action efforts developed at all levels of government. Affirmative action plans require employers to demonstrate good faith in their efforts to increase employment opportunities for deprived groups in accordance with Title VII of the Civil Rights Act of 1964.

11. Recent Supreme Court rulings and Reagan Administration efforts have refocused antidiscrimination law on equal opportunity rather than affirmative action.

Concepts for Review

affirmative action plan
AFSCME
assessment center
bargaining unit
certification
Civil Rights Act of 1965
Civil Service Reform Act of 1978
the collective bargaining process
comparable worth
compensation
equal opportunity, affirmative action
Executive Order 10988
four types of public personnel systems
Griggs v. *Duke Power Co.*
Hatch Act
impasse procedures
Intergovernmental Personnel Act of 1970
job rotation

management development
merit system, merit recruiting
Merit Systems Protection Board
Occupational Safety and Health Act (OSHA) of 1970
Office of Personnel Management
OJT
organizational culture
Pendleton Act
performance appraisal
position classification
public personnel management
rank-in-person approach
reprimands, suspensions, demotions, reassignments, and dismissals
rule of three
Senior Executive Service
spoils system
staffing
Stotts Case
Title VII

Problems

1. Select a public-sector job and then decide from among the following what the examination used to determine the fitness and ability of the applicants should consist of: *(a)* a written test, *(b)* a performance test, *(c)* an evaluation of education and experience as shown on the application, *(d)* oral examination, *(e)* interview, *(f)* physical test, and *(g)* health examination. How would you weigh each part? Be prepared to defend your choices.

2. Should employees know each other's salaries? Discuss.

3. Write a paper on one of the following topics: *(a)* repeal of the Hatch Act, or *(b)* the British and American public personnel systems compared.

4. As noted in this chapter, some experts think that the most important reason some industries compensate executives well above the average is that quality of executive decisions is what makes profit in the business. What do you think? If you agree, does this mean public-sector pay scales need radical alteration?

5. Do you agree with Peter Drucker's statement on the primary importance of job skill in hiring (p. 452)? Can you think of any other traits that might be at least equally important?

6. "Thanks to machinery, air conditioning, and noise control, work has become much less nasty—only in the civil services, the police and fire departments, and the imagination of sociologists has work become more degrading and unpleasant in recent years" (Mayer, 1976:55). Discuss.

7. Take an administrative position in the public sector and, using Table 11–2, design your own assessment center exercise. Be prepared to defend your design.

8. Write a paper on the right to strike in the public sector.

9. The public sector is becoming increasingly co-ed, particularly at the higher administrative levels. This generates dilemmas for both men and women in an organization. Some are trivial, but others are quite serious affecting both careers and agency operations. Slowly, case by case, pragmatic solutions are evolving. In a sense, they constitute a series of do's and don'ts. The following series was suggested for corporate women and their male associates (*Business Week*, March 22, 1976). Which do you find appropriate? Inappropriate? What would you add?

For Men Executives	*For Women Executives*
Do:	Do:
Be as supportive or critical of a woman as of a man.	Plan your career and take risks.
Practice talking to her if you are self-conscious.	Stress your ambition. Ask "What can I do to get ahead?"
Let her open the door if she gets there first.	Speak at least once in every 10-minute meeting.
Tell your wife casually about a woman peer.	Take the chip off your shoulder.
Don't:	Don't:
Make a fuss when appointing the first women.	Say "I worked on . . ." when you wrote the entire report.
Tune her out at meetings.	Imitate male mannerisms—or do needlepoint at meetings.
Say "Good morning, gentlemen—and lady."	Hang on to the man who trained you.
Apologize for swearing.	Leap to serve coffee when someone suggests it's time for a break.

10. Identify some organization with which you are reasonably familiar. Then design a performance appraisal form for managers. (Hint: The three lists of leadership traits on pp. 418–421 might be a good place to start.) Would you weight the traits in order to determine a raw score? Why or why not?

11. Develop a set of questions that you would ask a job candidate. (Specify the position.) With one of your classmates playing the role of candidate, conduct your interview before the class. Have them critique your performance.

Case 11.1
Three Ways to Fire an Employee

The Carter Approach

It was July 17, 1979. Joseph A. Califano, Jr., secretary of Health, Education and Welfare (later Health and Human Services) and former assistant to President Johnson, left his office for lunch with Tip O'Neill, Speaker of the House. The rumor was out in Washington that President Carter was going to get rid of a couple of cabinet officers.

Just a few minutes later, Califano arrived at the Speaker's private office. Between bites of cold cuts, O'Neill said, "Well, hell, Joe, I can't believe Carter would ever get rid of you. You're the best damn cabinet officer he's got."

Later that afternoon, Hamilton Jordan, one of Carter's assistants, placed a conference call to all cabinet members. He read a statement about to be issued to the press: "The president had serious and lengthy discussions with his cabinet and senior White House staff about the priorities of his administration. He reviewed with them the progress of the past few years and the problems that remain. All members of the cabinet and senior staff have offered their resignations to the president during this period of evaluation. The president will review these offers carefully and expeditiously." Jordan added that Carter said he would be in touch with them individually.

Somewhat stunned, Califano put down the phone. He knew Jordan and other presidential staff wanted him out, but he felt his relationship with Carter was basically sound.

The next morning he had breakfast with his former law partner, Edward Bennett Williams. Sitting almost alone in the vast dining room of the Metropolitan Club, the two discussed the Jordan call. Leaning across the table, Williams told Califano that a firing would be the best thing that could happen to him. "Carter is through and it will give you a way out."

On the 19th, after receiving a late afternoon invitation, Califano met with Carter in the president's small study by the Oval Office. Carter sat behind a desk, perched slightly higher than Califano, who sat on a couch to the right against the wall. Califano recollects what happened next:

Carter [smiling nervously]: I have decided to accept your resignation.

Califano [automatically, as if rehearsed]: Mr. President, you are entitled to have the cabinet people you want. I will work for an orderly transition.

Carter: Your performance as a secretary has been outstanding. You have put that department in better shape than it has ever been in before. You've been the best secretary to HEW. The department has never been better managed. I have never said a bad word about you or your performance and I never will. If anyone does around here, I will fire him.

I intend to name Pat Harris secretary of HEW. I talked to her this morning and she wanted time to think about it. She told me she did not think she could do as good a job as you were doing, but I told her you have the department in good shape; she will be able to take over easily. [Smiling.] The problem is the friction with the White House staff. The same qualities and drive and managerial ability that make you such a superb secretary create problems with the White House staff. No one on the staff questions your performance as secretary. Stu [Eizenstat] and Fritz [Mondale] are very high on you. Stu will be particularly disappointed with my decision. But you and some members of the staff—particularly Ham [Hamilton Jordan], Jody [Powell], and Frank Moore—have not gotten along.

Califano [now a little stunned]: It's your decision, Mr. President.

Carter: We have a job to get the cabinet and the administration in shape for the 1980 election.

Carter offered Califano another job, ambassador to Italy. Califano declined, pointing out that the position was already filled. Carter then invited him to Camp David for the weekend to "play some tennis" and "talk to each other about the future." Califano, now beginning to hurt a little, asked the president what schedule he wanted to move on. It was agreed that there should be an announcement as soon as possible and an exchange of letters. They shook hands and Califano exited through the door and down the corridor.

The Koch Approach

By late July 1979, 20 months after having been elected mayor of New York, Ed Koch had decided that the city's government was top-heavy, that with seven deputies things were "falling through the cracks."

Herman Badillo, who had assumed the title of deputy mayor for policy at the start of 1979, had 24 people working for him many of whom Koch considered incompetent. Although the payroll for Badillo's office was nearly $1 million, Koch was not sure what he was getting from it. What was Badillo's output?

On Monday, July 30, 1979, Koch began a process that he compared to having an ulcer—worry, pain, piercing, and finally relief.

One of his first conversations was with Ronay Menschel. He asked her to give up her title of deputy mayor and take the title of executive administrator. He gave her all the organizational reasons for the change.

Menschel: Well, there is really no reason. I have done a good job.

Koch: No question about it, Ronay. You are one of the best. But we don't need seven deputy mayors. And if I can't recognize that and change your title, then I can't do it with any of them. That is why I am doing it first with my friends and then those with whom I don't have that personal relationship. I know you are going to have a problem with Richard [her husband, an early supporter of Koch]. But if Richard were in a comparable position—if he saw that his office at Goldman, Sachs was not being well run—he would do whatever it was that had to be done and personal relationships wouldn't have anything to do with it.

Menschel: Well, Richard always said that you don't care about personal relationships. He says it's one of your defects.

Koch: Well, I'm sorry if that's the way it comes over, but as I've said, government isn't for friends. It's not a sorority house here. I want my friends in government, but only if government needs them and they do the job. And you do it and you know it. But what you do isn't what a deputy mayor does. You don't need the staff.

Menschel: [weeping]: I will try. I'll see if it works.

Then Koch made a number of other changes, perhaps less difficult than Ronay, but difficult nonetheless. For example, Koch let his deputy mayor for finance go with these words:

Phil, this is very difficult, but I am going to end your position with the government. The reason is very simple: It hasn't worked. You are a guy with great ability. You are a guy who can take very complex concepts and explain them to someone like me in such a way that I can grasp those concepts. You are also a marvelous guy to have around. I like talking to you. But Phil, I asked you four months ago to take on the matter of our capital spending. You were to find a construction czar, and you haven't done it. You have procrastinated. I asked you to study the budgets of the deputy mayors to see where we could cut. And you procrastinated there. I asked you to form a revenue-enhancement committee. You got the committee, but they never met. You never called them together. What good are they if you don't use them? Phil, you didn't follow through.

Finally, on the morning of August 4, Koch had his meeting with Herman Badillo as reporters gathered outside his office.

Koch: Herman, it is bad. And I really think that the best way out of this is that I announce that you will be leaving by the end of the year along with the others. I have been trying to get you the HUD job. I have called Jack Watson and Rafshoon, Bob Strauss, and Hamilton Jordan on that.

Badillo *[almost cheerfully]:* Oh, you don't have to get me a job. I can get one for myself. If it works out, okay. Or I'll go back to private practice. It's okay.

Koch: Sure.

Badillo: I will say I am leaving at the end of the year, but I will probably leave before that.

Koch: I hope we are still friends.

Badillo: Oh, sure.

Koch: So we will make you a part of the announcement today.

Badillo: No. I will announce it myself.

Koch: Fine.

But things turned bad quickly. Within two days Badillo was saying that he was leaving because it was impossible to work with such a "cowardly" mayor. Koch, knowing the professional relationship was over, called him.

Koch: Herman, it is distressing to me the way you are attacking me.

Badillo: I have not been attacking you.

Koch: I view calling someone "cowardly" as a personal attack.

Badillo: Well. . .

Koch: And, by the way, it is ridiculous. What are you doing? You are going to need me.

Badillo: Well. . .

Koch: Okay, so what are your plans? When are you leaving?

Badillo: Well, I am having difficulty reaching the partners of the law firms that I am negotiating with. They are all on vacation until after Labor Day.

Koch: Look, the reporters are constantly asking me, as a result of your attacks upon me, "When is Herman leaving?" So I can tell them you will be gone at the end of September?

Badillo *[cryptically yet stoically]:* Yes, you can tell them that.

The next day Badillo did resign, effective the end of September.

The Reagan Approach

"Al," the president asked his Secretary of State, Alexander Haig, "What would you do if you were a general and one of your lower commanders went around you and acted alone?"

"I'd fire him, Mr. President," Haig replied.

"No, no. I didn't mean that. But this musn't happen again. We just can't have a situation where you send messages on your own that are a matter for my decision." Reagan was referring to instructions that Haig had sent to Special Ambassador to the Middle East Philip Habib—without the president's approval.

Haig tried to explain. He told Reagan that a cease-fire in Lebanon had been delayed, and loss of life needlessly continued as a result of the "petty maneuvering" by the White House staff. It was a situation that served neither Reagan nor the American people well. If the president "could not make the necessary changes to restore unity and coherence to his foreign policy, then it would be in the country's best interests to have another secretary." Haig suggested that the best time for his departure might be in five months, or after the midterm elections in November 1982, to minimize the political effect.

A few days later, William Clark, national security adviser, told Haig that the president wished to see him again. The lack of warmth, the troubled mood that had characterized Reagan's behavior during the last meeting was gone. Haig now detected a mixture of apprehension and almost fatherly concern. Conversation quickly returned to the subject of their last meeting.

"You know, Al, it's awfully hard for me to give you what you're asking for," Reagan said. Haig then handed the president some papers documenting instances in which the administration had appeared to be speaking inconsistently on foreign policy. Glancing at the papers, Reagan said, "I'm going to keep this, Al. This situation is very disturbing."

"If it can't be straightened out," Haig replied, "then surely you would be better served by another secretary of state." Reagan said nothing.

The following day, after a "working lunch" with the National Security Council, Haig was asked to step into the Oval Office. Reagan, standing behind an oaken shipboard desk made of the timbers from the old USS *Resolute*, spoke: "On that matter we discussed yesterday, Al, I have reached a decision."

The president then handed Haig an unsealed envelope. Haig opened it and read the single typed page it contained. "Dear Al," it began, "It is with the most profound regret that I accept your letter of resignation." The president, thought Haig, was accepting a letter of resignation that he (Haig) had not even submitted.

Case Questions

1. Examine each of these three episodes. What would you have done under similar circumstances?
2. How would you characterize these three episodes?
3. How and when should an executive fire an employee?

Case References

Joseph A. Califano, Jr., *Governing America* (New York: Simon & Schuster, 1981); Edward I. Koch, *Mayor* (New York: Warner Books, 1985); and Alexander Haig, *Caveat: Realism, Reagan, and Foreign Policy* (New York: Macmillan, 1984).

Case 11.2
Gardner City Police Department

In 1967 officers of the Gardner City Police Department became affiliated with the American Federation of State, County, and Municipal Employees (AFSCME). At this time, the middle-management ranks of the Gardner City Police Department, especially sergeants, lieutenants, and captains, decided not to be represented by the union.

At the beginning, the benefits AFSCME gained through the collective bargaining process were small and automatically given to middle management. AFSCME has now been in operation for six years, and during the last two years has won some very good fringe benefits and wage increases for its members.

In 1973 AFSCME invited middle management to join the union. The middle-management echelon of the police department was the only group in Gardner City not affiliated with a union. The fire department had been totally organized since the inception of the firemen's union. The police middle management met and discussed the offer to join AFSCME. They decided not to join since it would be detrimental to the mission of the officers. They also felt that their affiliation with a union would cast a shadow of doubt as to where their loyalty rested. This decision on the part of middle management left them without any representation in regard to benefits and wages.

Up until this time, the city manager, through the city council, had immediately passed on all union gains to middle management without a request from them.

One of the issues included in the 1971 contract was a 10-cent night-shift differential. This benefit, however, was not passed on to middle management.

In the 1975 negotiations, more new benefits were gained for union members. Middle management, once again, did not receive any of these new benefits. As a result of this action, middle management decided it was time to bring these inequities to the attention of the city manager. A formal letter (Exhibit 1) was drafted and sent to the city manager. All middle-management members of the Gardner City Police Department signed the letter. The city manager then wrote a reply (Exhibit 2) to their letter responding to their expressed inequities.

Exhibit 1
Letter to City Manager of Gardner City

February 14, 1975

Dear Sir:

We, the members of the supervisory and management echelon of the Gardner City Police Department, would like to take this opportunity, with all due respect, to voice our collective opinions regarding several inequities which we believe may devleop from the ranks which are not included in the bargaining unit.

We consider our echelon, supervision and management, as an extension or arm of the city manager and the chief of police, and as such our loyalty must and does

Exhibit 1 (*continued*)

in fact remain with these administrators. We have vividly demonstrated this loyalty in the past by voting against our inclusion in the bargaining unit representing the operational echelon of the department.

Recently, in what appeared to be a job action by members of the department bargaining unit, the responsibility for providing police protection fell on the shoulders of supervisory personnel whose loyalty was demonstrated by reporting for duty and performing all required services for the citizens of Gardner City. We feel that in order to prevent a conflict of interests and perpetuate the strong loyalty to the administration, we cannot and should not become affiliated with a bargaining unit. No man can serve two masters and be equally loyal to each.

However, self-preservation and self-esteem are two most intense behavioral drives possessed by man and to these ends we have composed this communication.

First and of long-standing concern to our numbers is the inequity which exists between bargaining-unit members and our ranks with respect to the night-shift differential. The night-shift differential has been in existence for several years and was not initially offered to nonunion employees nor has it ever been discussed with our numbers. Currently, only eight supervisors would be concerned with this pay differential, but it is an inequity to the supervisory ranks of the department.

The next area of concern to nonunion personnel was the apparent fact that the bargaining unit has obtained an additional $35 uniform allowance. No additional allowances were forthcoming to supervisors which was embarrassing and thought provoking. Embarrassing since it was apparent on that payday when two checks were received by union-employees and none by supervisors that "you guys don't rate,"—a somewhat grating statement heard by most supervisors upon reporting for pay.

Thought-provoking in that if initially we were not included in the night-shift differential then not included in the allocation of funds for additional uniform allowance, it is apparent that the future is not getting brighter for supervisors who are loyal nonunion members.

These inequities should not have accrued initially. To allow the initial oversight to carry over from year to year and to overlook the appropriation of funds to guarantee those additional benefits to supervisors is most detrimental to the morale of the supervisory echelon.

We respectfully request that the nonunion supervisors of the police department be placed on parity with other city employees and that this be standard for each subsequent contractual agreement. This would eliminate the annual apprehension and the requirement that we must communicate inequities on a yearly basis.

We request these aforementioned conditions be considered in the light of fairness, equality, and an opportunity to provide a prideful environment for supervisors who are not union-affiliated.

Respectfully,

Supervisors of the
Gardner City Police Department

Exhibit 2
Letter to Chief of Police of Gardner City

February 27, 1975

Dear Chief:

This is in reply to the letter dated February 14, 1975, signed by all sergeants, lieutenants, and captains, in which they set forth certain alleged inequities in the benefits offered to nonunion personnel.

I would point out that, with the exception of the chief and assistant chief, all other supervisors receive overtime pay at the rate of one and one-half times regular pay. This benefit is not extended to any other supervisor in Gardner.

In addition, I must remind you that last year the classification for chief and assistant chief was upgraded in order to compensate for the lack of time-and-one-half provision in these two positions.

In order for me to secure money to implement the requests contained in their letter, it will be necessary for me to request an additional appropriation from the city council. If you will provide me with the cost figures to cover the numerous requests made, I will present this to the city council.

Very truly yours,

City Manager

Case Questions
1. What is the problem?
2. How do you think middle management will respond to Exhibit 2?
3. Should the city council automatically pass on to middle management benefits that police officers gained through contract negotiations?
4. What problems can you foresee as a result of permitting supervisory personnel to be members of a police officer's union?

Case Reference
Prepared by Richard M. Ayers, FBI Academy, and Thomas L. Wheelen, College of Business Administration, University of South Florida, as the basis for class discussion. Copyight © 1975 by Thomas L. Wheelen and Richard M. Ayres.
Presented at a case workshop and distributed by Intercollegiate Case Clearing House, Soldiers Field, Boston, Massachusetts 02163. All rights reserved to the contributors. Printed in the U.S.A.

PART IV

Looking Ahead

12

Looking Ahead— Trends and Challenges

Introduction

The preceding 11 chapters dealt with three major themes—political management, program management, and resources management. These themes, I maintain, pretty much make up the study of public administration. But a final chapter on the future of American public administration is well justified. For the advice of the Greek historian Thucydides still holds: Those who must be thought the causes of events have reason to foresee them. So, in this concluding chapter, rather than luxuriate in grand summations, we shall be very much in the realm of the future. For that reason, Figure 12-1 replaces the old swivel chair of Figure 1-2 with an electronic desk (to be discussed in this chapter).

In this chapter we shall consider three trends that will likely have a decisive influence on the future course of American public administration—advances in electronics and telecommunication, the increasing interdependence of the globe, and shifts in the demography of the United States. In the last half of the chapter, we shall turn our attention to matters of more immediate concern: the problem of productivity, the search for more cooperative relations between business and communities, and the debate over industrial policy. We shall also examine new directions of thought in the increasingly active field of public administration. Even though this topic must always remain speculative, its study may reveal new insights into the skills and knowledge that the next generation of administrators must possess.

Figure 12-1
The Environment and Tasks of the Public Administrator

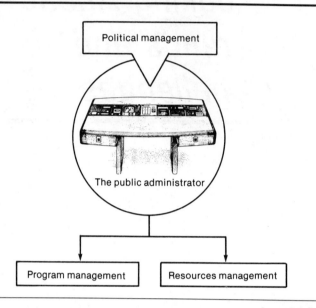

Advances in Electronics and Telecommunications

Samuel Finley Breese Morse in 1840 obtained a patent for the construction of a telegraph. With bulldog determination, he three years later managed to persuade a reluctant Congress to appropriate $30,000 to build a telegraph line from Baltimore to Washington, D.C. It was built in 1844, and it worked.

Today, we are on the threshold of a new development—namely, the consolidating of all telecommunication devices and the linking of them to computers. There is no good term to describe this revolution, so I hope to be forgiven for using the neologism, *compunications.* Formally stated, it is "the merging of telephone, computers, and television into a single yet differentiated system that allows for the transmission of data and interaction between persons or between computers through cables, microwave relays, or satellites" (Bell, 1979:21).

The Office of the Future

This is not the place to discuss the technical details of CPUs and RAMs (central processing units and random access memories) or of bandwidths and megabytes. The important point is that it is the *combination* of these technologies and their extraordinary performance characteristics that are having a major effect on public administration.

The futuristic vision of subdued antiseptic cubicles with video displays and a keyboard is rapidly converging with the reality. Already in quite a few government agencies one can find video and audio receivers; voice facsimile and keyboard transmitters; word processing equipment; and information storage boxes. Usually this new equipment sets alongside the traditional in-out boxes, bookshelves, liverwurst sandwiches, cluttered desks, the usual evergrowing "to be read" pile of papers and reports, urgent cables filed under inactive, and the now old-fashioned photocopies.

One of the chief characteristics of the office of the future is the absence of paper. Several benefits flow from this. First is the speed with which information can be communicated. A memo or report becomes available to others as soon as it is finished, without a secretary having to use precious time to hand-deliver it. Second, multiple copies (all originals) can be made and distributed instantly without walking to the photocopying room and waiting in line. Third, and perhaps equally important, the costly, bulky filing cabinets are no longer needed for this type of correspondence.

Implications

It would be wrong to think of the electronics revolution as affecting only clerks and typists. It affects executives too. Indeed, with the annual federal payroll for administrators and professionals running around $20 billion a year (or 50 percent higher than for clerical workers), this is where the greatest productivity gain will probably occur. A workstation should provide executives both text and data processing capabilities, quick access to information at the touch of a button, electronic mail, calendar management, electronic filing, and the ability to create graphics and to access a company's many data banks. Any executive workstation has to be simple to operate since most managers will be too busy to learn programming and complex operating procedures.

Better decisions, less travel, and fewer mail problems also result from another office trend: the increasing use of *teleconferencing* and facsimile transmission. Teleconferencing allows executives in different cities to communicate with each other by minicomputer, and facsimile transmission eliminates mail delays by sending pictures and other printed documents electronically, often by communications satellite. By eliminating much travel, teleconferencing will increase the time administrators can give to analysis and decision making. Televised transcontinental meetings are already a reality. The Metropolitan Regional Council, an organization of regional government representatives, operates a facility at its headquarters (in New York's World Trade Center) through which members can interface with the main office and with each other via television.

Because it is so large and so dispersed, the federal government is particularly well suited to capitalize on this technology. One of the hardest things for an executive in Washington to know is what is going on outside of Washington—in the shadowy substructure of the federal bureaucracy where thousands of field offices blanket the country in more than 22,000 locations.

What are the other ways in which the electronic revolution might change administrative practice?

Perhaps the most obvious advantage of the automated office is that it saves time. Experts estimate that most executives today spend between 18 percent and 30 percent of their time doing what might be termed less productive tasks—seeking people, scheduling, and so on. Access to data bases creates, as was seen in Chapter 6, the capability for executives to almost instantly call up historical data, budget information, and current operating information; to make modeling ("what-if") analyses; and to conveniently perform a variety of data manipulations without ever leaving the office.

Furthermore, there is little technical or economic reason why this capability could not be located in one's home to supplement or even replace the office. It is a workaholic's dream, and it can be addictive to administrators—to the point of letting their jobs overtake them.

Some heavy users of electronic messages have reported, along with the information overload, an increased incidence of emotional outbursts such as "where the hell is the assignment you owe me?" In the language of computer users this phenomenon is called "flaming." But whatever the name, it surely is not the kind of thing you want to see flash on the screen first thing in the morning. Students of office sociology believe such communication failures will become common in the future. Written messages cannot readily reflect irony or put the right emphasis in a sentence. The example above might have been well-intentioned humor between friends, though the receiver has no clue that this is the case. Of course, because computers do protect the sender from seeing the recipient, outright abrasive behavior may in fact increase. Perhaps the office of the future will require a new set of manners to avoid misunderstanding and misbehavior.

Finally, the public sector, because it draws so heavily on expert advice, is also well suited to employ *expert systems*. By programming the knowledge bases and problem-solving techniques of human experts, researchers in artificial intelligence have created computer systems that outperform experts. Expert systems are like neither the conventional programs for number-crunching computers nor even the management information systems discussed in Chapter 6. They are the first systems designed to help humans solve complex problems in a commonsense way, and they are being applied in the fields of oil exploration and geology, medicine, genetic engineering, finance, accounting, and air-traffic control.

Globalization

One More Time: The Concept of the Global Village

By now it is commonplace to speak of the global village. The electronics revolution and jet aircraft have made, for better or for worse, the remotest corners of the earth neighbors.

This change has brought new unprecedented pressures on the administration of national governments. Few issues today are purely domestic. And a growing number of critical issues are thoroughly international. Among the many areas that must be dealt with "globally" are population, pollution (including acid rain, the subject of Case 6.1); food, energy, and materials distribution; frequency spectrum allocation; global monetary system(s); management of the oceans, polar regions, moon, and space; terrorism; world health; and most important of all, peacekeeping.

To effectively deal with such issues requires cross-national and multiinstitutional approaches. Unfortunately, the field of public administration has hardly begun to recognize this gap in the literature, much less grope toward the new concepts and institutional forms that will be needed to fill it.

At a minimum, scholars and practitioners will need to develop better procedures for tracking and assessing early warning signals. They will need to develop techniques for dealing with the interests of several radically different governmental bureaucracies. They will need to develop perspectives that allow managers to span multiple cultures. They will need to organize structures that allow for rapid transformation, as environmental conditions shift unexpectedly.

A "New Comparative Administration"

Perhaps the answer to this challenge of the next decade appeared in the 1960s—at least in embryonic form. The years of the late 1960s, some would say, were the heyday of *comparative administration*. This subfield was an attempt to broaden public administration to other cultures and environments. Because it was an offshoot of American foreign aid programs that were concentrated in Third World countries, comparative administration focused largely on the problems of political and economic development. Whatever the focus, the comparative administration subfield never developed a conceptual framework that spelled out research priorities.

I believe the time is ripe for scholars and practitioners to begin work on a "New Comparative Administration." The focus would be on the problems not just of the nations of Asia, Africa, and Latin America but on *all* nations. Nor would the focus be on exclusively internal developmental problems. Rather, it would be on global problems like those listed above, which are now festering in the interstices between the 170-plus nations of the world.

It is equally important to be clear on what the focus is not. It is not a call for more studies of the problems. We are already up to our elbows in prestigious policy studies. It is a call for some systematic thought on how the recommendations of such studies can be made to work in the world the way it is. This, in turn, will require that attention be given to new cross-national institutional arrangements and cross-cultural management techniques.

Forging an "Urban Foreign Policy"

As domestic markets become saturated, mayors from mighty Los Angeles to Battle Creek, Michigan, are turning to the world market where they are trying to help firms in their cities land investments or trade deals. International trade represents jobs and tax revenues. The well-being of many urban economies through the rest of the 1980s may hinge as much on the success of their export development efforts as on their ability to fix potholes.

Only 10 percent of American companies are involved in exporting, notwithstanding surveys identifying 30,000 firms producing goods that are potentially competitive in international markets. So cities are turning their attention to the world marketplace. Some, like San Antonio, have set up their own foreign trade offices. Philadelphia has tried to establish a special export-trading company to buy goods from local firms and to take the risks involved in, and help manage the problems of, overseas selling. Mayor Ernest Morial of New Orleans has helped organize trading missions to Mexico, Central and Latin America, China, Japan, West Africa, and Europe. According to Morial, "There is no substitute for direct contact with foreign business and government officials to attract them to do business in your community" (*New York Times*, September 8, 1984).

Meanwhile, foreign investors are seeking safe havens and access to the U.S. market. Foreign assets in 1983 totaled $781 billion compared to $174.5 billion in 1973. Foreign investment now accounts for 5 percent of all U.S. jobs—up from 2 percent in 1975.

Demographic Change

Pig in a Python

Demographic changes have substantial effects on public administration. Fortunately, some of these changes can be anticipated fairly accurately. For example, we can estimate fairly accurately the number of people that will reach retirement age a few years hence. Other effects may be harder to predict, not least because demography is only one factor affecting change.

During the depression of the 1930s, relatively few children were born in the United States—fewer than 2.5 million in most years. After the Second World War, this country experienced a baby boom, which peaked in 1957 when 4.3 million children were born. Now, although there are many more women of prime childbearing age (the women born during the boom), their fertility is only half that of their mothers, and in recent years only about 3 million children have been born annually. Consequently, the baby-boom generation constitutes a huge "age lump" in our population—a demographic tidal wave. This demographic bulge will always remain undigested.

In 1970, half the U.S. population was age 27 or younger; by 1983, the median age had risen to 31. The trend is expected to continue as the early baby-boom generations head toward middle age. Assuming no further decline in fertility rates by the year 2040, half the population will be age 46 or older.

Implications

This tidal wave has many important consequences for American society—and for the budget, which includes many programs that serve specific age groups. Over the course of the life cycle, from youth to old age, people make different demands upon, and contributions to, society, the economy, and government. Children need support, education, and adult supervision. Young adults seek housing of their own and jobs—and it is from this age group that the armed services recruit. Middle-aged workers are at their peak earning, saving, and tax-paying years. The elderly need pension support and more health care than younger people generally require.

The magnitude of future social and institutional changes resulting from fluctuations in fertility will depend in part on future fertility— which is difficult to forecast. U.S. fertility rates have been declining since 1800 (with the one exception of the baby boom). Currently, the U.S. fertility rate is significantly below the replacement rate needed to maintain a constant population in the long run. Zero population growth requires that an average of about 2,100 children be born to each 1,000 women of childbearing age. In 1982, the rate was 1,815 per 1,000 women. Recent birthrates, if continued indefinitely, would imply an eventual decline of the U.S. population by about 17 percent per generation, in the absence of net immigration.

The Labor Force.   The most rapid rate of growth in the labor force since World War II is occurring now, as the "baby boomers" reach working age. Large influxes of young (and inexperienced) new workers into the labor force may increase the unemployment rate if there are not enough new jobs in the economy that meet the aspirations of young people in search of jobs. Productivity may decline due to the inexperience of the new workers. (Thus, the entry of the baby boom into the work force may help to account for the high unemployment and low productivity growth of the past decade.) Conversely, once the bulk of the baby-boom generation is employed, the average age and experience of the work force as a whole will begin to rise, which, in turn, may tend to *increase* productivity and *decrease* the unemployment rate.

As labor force growth slows in future years, and as the number of teenagers in the labor force begins to decline, labor markets may tighten, and it is possible that labor shortages will develop. If so, the federal investment in training, employment, and labor services will need to be reexamined. Possibly, there will need to be less emphasis on youth programs and public sector jobs, and more emphasis on retraining and retention of older workers, increasing the mobility of workers, and providing services (child care, transportation) to people who otherwise would have difficulty working.

Anticrime, Retirement, and Medical Programs. The national crime rate is generally affected by the number of people in the high-crime age group. Two thirds of arrests in 1975 were of people between the ages of 13 and 29. The absolute size of this high-crime age group reached a peak in 1980 and then began to decline. It is possible, though not certain, that the United States can literally grow out of its high-crime problem. Recent trends suggest leveling or declining crime rates despite demographic trends. However, demography may still be a factor in considering anticrime programs.

The elderly population in the United States has grown dramatically in the past century, not only in absolute terms but as a percentage of the total population. An increasing elderly population, rising life expectancy, the distinct trend toward declining average retirement ages, and the trend toward declining labor force participation by older people could combine to create a retirement and medical system funding problem in the 21st century. If present trends continue, civil service pension costs alone will reach $261 billion by 1998.

Total federal, state, and local taxes in recent years have amounted to about 33 percent of GNP—11 percent for social insurance programs, including medicare, and 22 percent for other purposes. If requirements for other purposes remain at 22 percent of GNP and if the ratio of the average retirement benefit to the average wage were to remain at current levels, the total tax burden 50 years hence would have to be close to 50 percent. There are alternatives to such high future tax rates, such as lower benefits and later retirement ages. But these are not easy choices. In addition, there would be major transition problems if the terms of retirement programs are to be modified significantly. This is because there are implicit or explicit understandings between government and private-sector employers and their workers concerning their retirement benefits. Ultimately, the issue will be how much of the resources produced in 2035 by the labor force employed at that time will be transferred to the retired generation.

The Productivity Challenge

Thus far in this chapter, we have dealt with three basic trends affecting all of society. Now we need to focus on issues that confront the public administrator directly. We shall begin—not unrelated to the trends—by considering *productivity*.

The Meaning of Productivity

Simply put, productivity is a measure of the efficiency with which resources (land, labor, capital) are converted into products or services. In other words:

$$\frac{\text{Output}}{\text{Input}} = \text{Productivity}$$

A productivity ratio could be expressed, therefore, as tons of garbage collected per hour.

Finding good measures for output is, in the public sector at least, a difficult task. Table 12–1 on p. 510 attempts to show a few of the measures that have been developed to measure the output of services in an urban government. Note carefully the two right-hand columns, which indicate the multitude of variables that must be taken into consideration when interpreting these measures.

Productivity, it should be stressed, is not effectiveness. The latter is not a ratio but an attempt to estimate the consequences of a particular program or output. Suppose, for example, that the goal of a particular governmental program is to reduce the damage by fires in a given area. To accomplish this goal, additional fire hydrants are installed. A productivity measure may indicate that the hydrants are being installed very efficiently, but this measure of hydrants installed to worker hours does not tell whether additional hydrants affect fire damage. This fact raises an important point: Governments must sharpen their goals and priorities if greater productivity is to progress. They must, in other words, keep asking "efficiency for what?" Otherwise, productivity becomes an end in itself, and we find ourselves doing more and more efficiently what should never have been done in the first place.

The Importance of Productivity

Despite the persistent rise in productivity levels—increasing sixfold in the past eight decades—the United States has in the last decade experienced a considerable slowing down of this rise. According to a 1979 study by the Joint Economic Committee, productivity increases in the federal government have lagged 25 percent behind those of the private sector. Since the rate of increase in the private sector was only 1.7 percent, that is like saying someone is slower than a turtle. With nearly 20 percent of working Americans employed by government,

Table 12–1

Illustrative Set of Output Measures, Qualitative Factors, and Local Condition Factors in Local Government

Selected Service Functions	Illustrative Output Measures	Illustrative Qualitative Factors that Should Be Considered in Interpreting Output	Illustrative Local Condition Factors that Should Be Considered in Interpreting Output
Solid waste collection	Tons of solid waste collected	Visual appearance of streets	Local weather conditions
Law enforcement (police)	Number of calls Number of crimes investigated	Response times Citizen feeling of security	Public attitude toward certain crimes
Law enforcement (courts)	Number of cases resolved	Delay time until resolution	Number and types of cases
Health and hospital	Number of patient days	Duration of treatment and "pleasantness" of care Accessibility of low income groups to care	Availability and price of health care Basic community health conditions
Water treatment	Gallons of water treated	Amount of impurities removed	Basic quality of water supply source
Recreation	Acres of recreational activities	Participation rates Crowdedness indexes	Amount of recreation provided by the private sector
Street maintenance	Square yards of repairs made	Smoothness/"bumpiness" of streets	Density of traffic
Fire control	Fire calls	Fire damage Injuries and lives lost	Type of construction
Primary and secondary education	Pupil days Number of pupils	Achievement test scores Dropout rates	Basic intelligence of pupils Number of pupils

Source: Based on Hatry (1972:779–80).

growth of output per worker hours in the public sector becomes, therefore, critical.

Without digressing into economic theory, it can be said that this decline in the rate of productivity growth, to no small degree, was responsible for the rapid rise in inflation experienced during the 1970s. Some authorities go further, calling productivity improvement the keystone to better environments and standards of living, and international competitiveness.

Productivity as a State of Mind

Productivity should not be the exclusive concern of presidential task forces, thickly carpeted productivity centers, and three-day conferences in Hawaii. Nor should productivity be the exclusive concern of little rooms in agency headquarters, whose occupants ("efficiency experts") make a nuisance of themselves to line administrators. Productivity should be a state of mind. Productivity should permeate the entire organization, from agency head to newest trainee. Productivity should be a matter of dedication and an area of general management concern. It is my opinion that the relative absence in the public sector of this state of mind explains better than anything else why that sector lags behind the private sector in productivity.

There are no shortcuts to productivity. The principal requirement is the proper state of mind—one that continues to search for improvements. Let me give a well-known example of this. While it is not drawn from the public sector, it does involve a service institution.

Fast-food restaurants like McDonalds and Burger King are, from a productivity standpoint, incredibly well-run operations. Everything is designed for efficiency and quality control. Yet the search for improvements in these operations is never ending. When customers drive up to the speaker to give their order, a device signals the attendants inside to come to their microphones and take the order. One day recently, a Burger King manager suddenly asked the question, Why not move the signaling device up a few feet so that the attendant can be in place by the time the customers are ready to give their orders? By cutting delay time during peak hours by just a few seconds for each customer, more hamburgers can be served, and, of course, more money earned.

Opportunities for improving efficiency in public-sector operations are almost infinite.

Costs of maintaining a municipally owned automobile fleet were analyzed and found to be 30 percent to 50 percent higher than the cost of leasing equivalent vehicles. This finding led to an experimental leasing program and measures designed to raise productivity in the city's maintenance shops, which were found to be responsible for part of the high costs.

A program of alerting police officers in advance of changes in scheduled court appearances helped to eliminate unnecessary appearances for arresting officers. (This program reported a potential annual savings in the time of arresting officers of 200 person years.)

A study of the lifetime costs of sanitation and fire trucks resulted in a policy of shorter-term replacement to reduce maintenance costs and the amount of time vehicles were out of service.

Barriers to Productivity

In what follows, we shall attempt to summarize the obstacles to public-sector productivity and the means to overcome them (based on National Commission on Productivity, 1973). To help frame the discussion, the obstacles are grouped into four categories: incentives, information, financial restrictions, and organizational constraints.

Productive Questions

The simplest, and often the most effective, method of finding opportunities for improving continuing operations is to ask questions. Never ask an organization to justify itself or you will be covered in facts and figures. The criterion, according to Amrom Katz of the Rand Corporation, should rather be, "What will happen if the outfit stops doing what it's doing?" The value of an organization is easier to determine this way (cited in Dickson, 1978:96-97). Procedures that have been accepted for a long time may turn out to have no sound reasons behind them.

Example No. 1
The following is the reminiscence of a member of the team from Ernst & Ernst, a consulting firm, that examined the operations of the Louisville, Kentucky, Police Court:

You remember one clerk, in particular, who was industriously banging away at a typewriter. You asked her what she was doing. She looked up briefly from her keyboard to explain that she was typing case dispositions. What happens to them when they're typed? you asked. Why, she answered, they go into the judge's order book. What's the book used for? you asked. She didn't know. So you went to her superior. Why is this done? you asked. You learned why. It's done because a city ordinance says it must be done. But nobody ever uses the book. The same information is available in other records that are easier to use.

Example No. 2
The following example is from New York City, which has undertaken a major effort to increase productivity.

In 1968, 38 percent of the garbage trucks were off the streets on the average. The city bought new trucks, but this "down-time" didn't change. So the city asked Andrew P. Kerr, a management consultant who now is the city's housing chief, to look into the problem.

The maintenance system, it seems, had a central repair shop for major over-

Source: Anthony and Herzlinger (1980:209-10).

Incentives. Government management systems generally penalize bad performance more than they reward good performance. Thus, there is more incentive to avoid egregious failure than to achieve success.

A similar incentive problem might be labeled misdirection by the budget. In contrast to business (other than monopolies), government agencies are typically paid out of a budget allocation. The budget allocation is not directly tied to their performance. Being paid out of a budget allocation changes the incentive system. Performance often becomes the ability to maintain or to increase one's budget. In such an atmosphere, the successful manager is seldom the individual who, at the end of the year, returns large sums of his allocation saved through productivity improvements.

Governments, therefore, need to take a more positive approach to incentives: explicit public recognition of good work, productivity bonuses, and bonuses tied to overall organizational success.

hauls, plus 76 local garages. "But because of union seniority," Mr. Kerr says, "the best mechanics wound up in the local garages doing simple jobs because they were near their homes." The solution: The central shop was replaced with district garages where the senior mechanics could work and still be close to home.

The percentage of trucks in disrepair began to fall. Then another problem came to the surface: Because of fear that any parts kept in district garages would be stolen, needed parts had to be ordered from a central warehouse; trucks were idled for days, waiting for parts.

It was decided that the fear of theft was essentially groundless, that the private demand for sanitation-truck parts was low. "Nobody steals sanitation-truck parts," Mr. Kerr says. "If they do, we can afford it more than we can afford not having trucks on the streets." The district garages were given their own parts. Downtime dropped to 18 percent.

Example No. 3

Another approach is to compare costs and, if feasible, output measures for similar operations. Such comparisons may identify activities that appear to be out of line, and thus lead to a more thorough examination of these activities. Such comparisons can be useful even though there are problems of achieving comparability, finding a "correct" relationship between cost and output in a discretionary cost situation, and danger in taking an outside average as a standard. For example, they often lead to the following interesting question: If other organizations get the job done for $X, why can't we? Good cost data for such comparisons exist on a national basis for only a few types of nonprofit organizations, principally hospitals and certain municipal functions. Nevertheless, it may be possible to find data for activities within a state, or it may be feasible to compare units performing similar functions within a single organization, as in the case of local housing offices.

How do productivity bonuses work? A good example is found in the solid waste collection area, where collectors are permitted to go home without losing wages as soon as they finish their collection routes. Another example is found in the law enforcement area, where police are given an extra day off for every 90 days of perfect attendance. Using this approach, Plainville, Connecticut, was able to reduce sick leave to an average of five days per person per year. How does the public administrator tie bonuses (e.g., promotions) to overall organization success? One method is to install a management-by-objectives system (discussed in Chapter 7).

Naturally, a large part of the responsibility for providing incentive belongs to the elected official, the politician. The realities of political survival, however, emphasize short-run results, and this factor militates against long-run efforts to achieve productivity improvement. Perhaps the day is not too far off when demonstrated productivity improvement will be the key to political success—after all, the mood of voters can shift suddenly.

Information.   Productivity does not necessarily require exotic new technology, but it does require the effective exploitation of existing technology and the timely dissemination of productivity improvement ideas. For example, when one city figures out a cheaper way to dispose of solid waste, every city ought to hear about it; or if letting police-officers take cars home reduces crime, every police department ought to know about it. Significantly, a study of productivity improvements by the Urban Institute recommended, among other things, a national clearinghouse for the transference of such information.

Financial Restrictions.   Financial restrictions in public management systems are a third obstacle to productivity improvement.

Funds are not always as available as they seem. Some are earmarked for a given purpose and cannot be transferred to clearly related alternative purposes. Thus, specifically committed highway funds cannot be transferred to a public transit system—even when the public might be better served by the latter.

Similarly, it is more efficient in the planning of long-range projects, which require heavy capital investment, if the public administrator can know what funds will be available over the life of the project. Trying to plan such projects on a year-to-year basis can prove quite costly.

Organizational Constraints.   Statutory and constitutional constraints obviously limit the public executive far more than his or her business counterpart in making desirable organizational readjustments. Moreover, many purely administrative positions in local government are elective offices and, as such, beyond the pale of the chief executive's jurisdiction. Political boundaries often clash, rather than coincide, with mutual economic interests. For example, rivers that provide economic and commercial unity to a region are frequently used as boundaries. The ideal solution in such situations would be consolidations or other joint arrangements to obtain what the economists call *economies of scale*, that is, savings that result from doing things on a larger scale than individual cities or towns. (A business example would perhaps serve best in clarifying this concept. An instance of economies of scale would be when an automobile manufacturer decides to make 100,000 rather than 500 of a new model and the cost per unit is thus reduced.)

Finally, as we saw in Chapter 3, there are many problems between governments: the federal government's fiscal restrictions and reporting requirements—plain old red tape in many instances—often impede state and local productivity efforts. The availability of federal multi-year funding is always in question. And the uncertainties of the federal appropriations process create scheduling problems in any given year.

*Effective Productivity Management Efforts Tend to Include
Seven Elements*

After examining the formal productivity management efforts at six companies and several state and local governments, reviewing the literature, and meeting with experts, the General Accounting Office (GAO) (1983:35–37) identified seven common elements in the effective productivity improvement efforts. These elements, which have been found in effective productivity efforts in both the public and private sectors, are considered applicable to the federal government. The elements, listed below, are broad and allow considerable latitude for designing specific programs.

1. *A manager serving as a focal point for productivity in the organization.* The focal point can be a single person operating alone or with a large staff. A permanent focal point appears needed to (1) institutionalize and highlight the productivity effort, (2) accumulate and disseminate information on productivity to managers and employees, and (3) provide top management with data on productivity performance.

2. *Top-level support and commitment.* This does not mean that the agency head or chief executive merely states that productivity is important. Rather, this element requires top managers to periodically review the productivity performance of the organization and the organization's managers and hold employees accountable for improved productivity. Clear, top-level support can develop and maintain the legitimacy and effectiveness of the entire productivity effort.

3. *Written productivity objectives and goals and an organization-wide productivity plan.* An organization must have clear goals and objectives to have an effective productivity effort. These goals can be broad, such as improving the entire organization's productivity by 10 percent in 5 years, or they can be detailed, such as assigning certain objectives to specific organizational components. The overall goals and objectives and the methods to achieve them should be brought together in a productivity plan. Although the type of plan most appropriate for an organization varies considerably, the plan itself is essential since it clarifies for all employees the organization's goals and objectives and what needs to be done to meet them.

4. *Productivity measures that are meaningful to the organization.* Productivity measurement is an essential element of an effective productivity improvement effort. Productivity measures need not be precise total-factor measures. Often, a series of measures that are easy to understand and calculate and that are meaningful to managers and employees are more useful. For

example, some companies use gross output over labor input measures; others use more detailed measures such as number of documents processed each hour.

5. *Use of the productivity plan and measurement system to hold managers accountable.* Productivity plans and measurement systems are of little value unless they are used. Accountability can be achieved by specifying expected productivity rates for various measured activities, comparing actual performance to expected, and using this information to assess managerial and organizational performance. As with measurement systems, there is no one best way. Each organization must develop its own appropriate productivity accountability system.

6. *Awareness of productivity's importance to the organization and involvement of employees in the improvement efforts.* Because productivity is a commonly misunderstood concept, management must initiate awareness compaigns and help employees recognize their importance to the productivity effort. Employees should also participate in company activities aimed at developing ideas on how to improve productivity.

7. *An ongoing activity to regularly identify productivity problems and opportunities for improvement throughout the organization.* This activity may be accomplished with productivity assessments or reviews performed by ad hoc task forces or a permanent staff. It should emphasize helping managers improve productivity by looking at their operations in a new light.

None of these elements is particularly innovative in itself. But their integration distinguishes systematic productivity improvement from other approaches and makes it a powerful technique for improving productivity and reducing costs.

Specific Strategies for Improving Productivity

One of the first steps toward a better understanding of a subject is classification. In this section, we shall try to categorize, in a preliminary sort of way, the growing body of information on how administrators have increased productivity in organizations. To improve productivity, an administrator might want to look to one or more of these seven categories.

1. Human resources management (in Chapters 10 and 11).
2. Client behavior.
3. Volunteers.
4. Technology.
5. Infrastructure (i.e., physical plant).
6. Incentives.
7. Privatization.

Client Behavior

The behavior of clients or consumers is of critical importance to a service organization bent on improving its productivity. Therefore, increasing productivity is a matter of changing client behavior and expectations, and enlisting client acceptance of that change for three basic reasons (Lovelock & Young, 1979).

First, service organizations typically involve the client in the delivery process. To mail a letter requires that you address, stamp, and deposit it.

Second, service organizations are typically labor intensive, with the service being part of the overall "product" being delivered. Sometimes though, clients can do some of the work themselves, replacing all or part of that work previously done by the agency employee. Now, at university cafeterias and similar restaurants, it is accepted behavior for people to clear their own tables. By placing trash at the curb in plastic bags, people cut the time and cost of trash pickup.

Third, a service organization's product tends to be time bound; that is, it cannot be stored. Thus, the opportunity to sell an empty seat on the 5:15 P.M. bus to downtown is lost once the city bus drives off. Because of the time-bound nature of service, public administrators place a heavy emphasis on avoiding both excessive demand and excess capacity. Consequently, the U.S. Postal Service has, through intensive advertising and promotional efforts, convinced many people to mail early during the Christmas season, and some school districts have begun to reschedule terms so that multimillion-dollar facilities are not boarded up three months a year.

Volunteers

Some argue that as government began to intervene in many corners of society the voluntary and cooperative spirit of Americans suffered. In any event, this much is increasingly clear: As government begins to retrench in the 1980s, public administrators will need to encourage volunteer work. Otherwise, certain services (e.g., child care, libraries, and alcohol rehabilitation) will no longer be provided at current levels.

Actually, polls tend to belie the notion that the spirit of voluntarism has dried up in America. George Gallup (1979) reported that a great untapped resource—a massive army of American citizens—is ready to work as unpaid volunteers to improve the quality of life in their cities and neighborhoods. Based on a nationwide survey conducted in November 1978, Gallup says that 7 out of every 10 adults living in urban America would be willing to work an average of nine hours per month, serving on committees, working on neighborhood uplift projects, or helping the elderly and the handicapped.

The survey findings reveal that 57 percent of urban residents—as many as 70 percent to 73 percent of college-educated, high-income

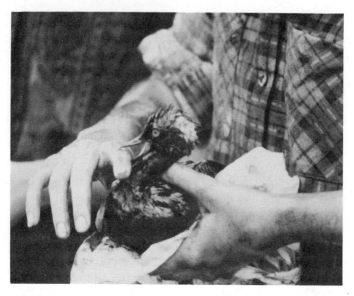

Cleaning oil-soaked bird. Volunteer work is no longer the special provi-
dence of upper middle-class ladies, no longer a kind of obligation of the
privileged. Today, it includes college students cleaning oil-soaked birds,
grandparents teaching preschool children, and minority women organizing crisis centers for destitute and battered women. (Al Satterwhite—
Camera 5)

residents—are ready to serve on city advisory committees without
pay. The matters that interest them most involve schools and education, the plight of senior citizens, parks, sports and recreational facilities, and developing programs for youth. Some 18 percent of those
polled were willing to work as teachers' aides or in neighborhood child-
care centers; 14 percent were willing to help pick up trash and litter; 23
percent to work with handicapped residents; and 15 percent to work in
neighborhood health centers.

In sum, it makes sense to use public funds to attract citizen resources on a regular, systematic basis. Work voluntarily done for the
good of others benefits not only the recipient but also the donor. As
Herman Melville wrote: "We cannot live for ourselves alone. Our lives
are connected by a thousand invisible threads, and along these sympathetic fibers, our actions run as causes and return to us as results."

Technology

Closely related to the preceding category is the development of new
or improved technology.

Unlike aggressive business firms, many governmental agencies are
reluctant to experiment with new techniques and procedures. Unfortunately, private firms doing business with government devote relatively

little time and money to research and development of new products for the public sector. (The notable exception is the widely applicable, aggressively marketed computer.) Yet examples such as better sanitation trucks, better police radios and relay systems show that ingenuity and interest can get results. In some cases, the demand will have to be created by state and local governments. They have to decide what they need, tell suppliers, and involve them aggressively, providing for experiment and installation.

Examples of how technology can make the public sector more productive are endless, though not well publicized. They range from a polymer that can reduce the friction of water through fire hoses (rapid water) to the linkage of computers with telecommunications devices. But public administrators should not be so dazzled by space-age technology that they fail to make better use of equipment at hand. More efficient repair, more preventive maintenance, better replacement policies, and equipment sharing can help squeeze more benefits out of costs previously incurred.

Infrastructure

Most people associate infrastructure with roads, bridges, and streets. A few "in the know" link it with water-supply and sewage-treatment systems, as well as with waterways, ports, railroads, and mass transit. Evidence that it is decaying is as close as the nearest pothole, detour sign, or broken bridge.

Already the decaying physical plant is costing dearly. In Houston, for example, city planners estimate that motorists pay a "traffic congestion tax" of $800 a year in time and gasoline wasted on the city's snarled expressways. U.S. Steel spends an extra $1 million a year detouring its trucks around a closed bridge in Pittsburgh. The Road Information Program (TRIP), a highway-industry group, estimates that the aggregate cost to the private sector of bad roads and bridges is $30 billion a year—for everything from broken axles to lost business. Even worse, the infrastructure crisis is exacting a heavy human toll. A recent Federal Highway Administration study found that spending an extra $4.3 billion to fix dilapidated bridges and roads could prevent 480,000 injuries and save 17,000 lives over 15 years.

There are many reasons for infrastructure decay. It is only natural that public works of all kinds deteriorate over time. After all, so do homes, driveways, and garbage disposals. This natural process reaches a crisis only if we do not have the wherewithal to repair or replace these items.

The problem is not, as some might think, a matter of money. Billions of dollars have been spent on public works in recent years. But they have not been spent productively. In 1983, the Congressional Budget Office (CBO) released a detailed study of the public-works infrastructure. The CBO determined that reducing the current bias toward investment in public facilities and emphasizing investments with clear national significance could improve the cost-effectiveness of federal spending. The report stated that "Federal costs to meet the nation's infrastructure needs could in fact be reduced to about $20 billion a year—$4 billion less than current (fiscal year 1983) spending."

In other words, although billions of dollars have been spent on public works in recent years, the vast bulk of expenditures has gone not to maintain old facilities but to build ambitious new pork-barrel projects, often determined more by politics than actual need. E. S. Savas, former assistant secretary for housing and urban development asks: "Have you ever seen a politician presiding over a ribbon-cutting for an old sewer line that was repaired?" (*Newsweek*, August 2, 1982).

Incentives

The quality of an employee's job performance must be related to the benefits he or she receives for doing that job. Indeed, without a properly functioning incentive system that actually rewards productivity, many of the previously noted strategies will fail.

In state and local governments, incentives for good performances and penalties for poor performance are all too rare. Bonus systems, where they exist, tend to be underfunded. Merit raises, where they exist, tend to be awarded almost across the board.

Most employees are bothered by this. In a recent Common Cause poll of state employees, 60 percent said they would be willing to trade some degree of their job security for an opportunity to obtain a higher salary or bonus for superior job performance. The same poll shows that two thirds of the employees believe that more productive employees should receive more pay than less productive workers in the same job class.

Thanks largely to the news media's tendency to seek out dramatic examples of misdeeds, public attention concentrates on negatives. There are too few mechanisms that acclaim productiveness in the public sector. This need not be. The National Governors Association and U.S. Conference of Mayors, for example, could make awards to outstanding administrators. And the media could publish stories of their accomplishments to provide not only additional recognition for the recipient but also models of administrative excellence for the classroom.

Privatization

Privatization is the idea of putting government activities into private hands to improve services, lower costs, or both. For many cities and the Reagan administration, privatization may be the wave of the future.

View from the Grassroots.   Many cities are finding that they can increase productivity by hiring profit-making companies to perform such functions as refuse collection, police and fire protection, paramedic services, sewage disposal, accounting, computer operation, and street maintenance. Milwaukee hired a private firm to pick up dead animals; Phoenix replaced the public defender's office with private lawyers; and Scottsdale, Arizona, saves $2 million a year by contracting for fire protection. One third of the refuse in Newark, New Jersey, is privately collected, saving the city $200,000 a year. Dallas closed its municipal late-night gasoline depots; now police cars and some fire vehicles use gas pumps at 7-Eleven Food Stores after midnight, saving $200,000 annually. A private firm operates the Orange County, California, computer center at an annual saving of $1.6 million. Butte, Montana, contracted for the private operation of its municipal hospital; annual savings are $600,000. Newton, Massachusetts, saves $500,000 a year through a contract with a firm that supplies the city with paramedical and ambulance service (*New York Times*, March 29, 1984). While about 99 percent of local governments now contract out some functions, full-time city employees still perform over 75 percent of all work.

Contracting by local governments can carry certain risks. In Albany, New York, charges of mismanagement, corruption, and political favoritism in the awarding of contracts resulted in a sharp reduction of that city's use of private contractors. In Southern San Francisco, when the city turned over many of its municipal chores to a private firm, residents complained about shoddy work, dozens of city employees were dismissed, staff heads resigned, and morale disintegrated. After nine months, the contract was terminated.

Finally, some charge that initial cost savings can be misleading. Jerry Wurf, past president of the American Federation of State, County, and Municipal Employees, says: "Generally, the savings and improved services turn out to be a very temporary situation. . . . The contractor tries to make it look good the first year; then the cost overruns begin to grow and the contracts are renegotiated and somebody's brother-in-law ends up making money" (Quoted in the *New York Times*, November 23, 1979). By that time, of course, the city has sold its equipment and finds it too costly to get back into business. But union arguments aside, cities appear to be turning increasingly to private contractors.

Reagan Administration Efforts. In Washington, the Reagan administration has made a concentrated effort to transfer a wide range of public assets and programs to private enterprise, and it estimates that the changes will save more than $200 million a year by 1989.

As a major part of its strategy, the administration has identified 11,000 commercial activities to be performed by private contractors when economically feasible. Some of these activities include health services, fire protection, geological surveys, industrial shops, landscaping, laundry and food services, data processing, and transportation. The administration has also intensified efforts to put entire programs in private hands, including such services as rail transportation, space satellites, correctional facilities, low-income housing, health care, and education.

In addition, the administration has experimented with a wide range of voucher programs that would enable recipients of federal services to turn directly to private providers for housing, health care, supplemental education, and health and unemployment insurance.

These initiatives have sparked criticism from liberals, who fear that the administration seeks to abdicate governmental responsibility; and from conservatives, who say government is still trying to do too much. Moreover, some members of Congress fear a loss of control over policy and personnel.

What Are the Advantages and Disadvantages of Contracting? Among the advantages, we might note, first, is greater efficiency. As indicated above, certain operations (e.g., trash collection) can be as much as three times more expensive when handled by government rather than by a private contractor. But this is not always the case.

In Chapter 2, we noted that bureaucracies tend at times to disturb legislative intent. Under the contract system, where performance specification can be written in fairly specific language, such distortion becomes less likely.

A third advantage of contracting is that it may reduce the opportunity for empire building within government. I do not wish to imply, however, that terminating a large-scale project can be done with the stroke of a pen; congressional pressure to keep lucrative projects going can be fierce.

A fourth advantage of contracting is that it would help free public administrators from routine details. As government begins to get out of the "doing," it becomes freer to concentrate its efforts on differentiating public needs from public wants; to sort out who can do what most effectively in society; to consider new approaches to long-standing problems; and to discover and disclose inconsistencies or overlapping among all its interacting parts. In short, government becomes better focused.

But contracting has its disadvantages. Perhaps the most obvious is that too-cozy relationships between business and government contracting personnel might develop. The possible result of such relationships is graft. And some observers, looking further ahead, see totalitarian tendencies resulting. Contracting officers and the contractors could simply begin to bypass both the legislative and executive branch, enrich themselves, and build a syndicate state, responsive to hardly anyone.

Another fairly obvious disadvantage is that, in certain areas of public policy, contracting seems inappropriate. Should, for example, Westinghouse be responsible for the education of third graders? The implications of a corporation-shaped curriculum for young minds are sobering.

Contracting can also be inappropriate for economic reasons. The managers of one housing project in Brooklyn recently hired four consulting companies to study the idea of using methane from an adjacent sewage plant to heat the apartments. Using a $1.2 million grant from the Department of Energy, the managers were told such a system could in fact be built—for as little as $600,000. When the study costs more than the project, we can safely say that the contract for the study was inappropriate.

Which leads us to a final disadvantage: How does the government control the quality (as opposed to cost) of public interest services? Lyle C. Fitch (1974:511) writes: "For goods and services which can be identified, weighed, and measured, or tested as to performance and use, tests concentrate on how well the product meets specifications." But, he continues, "Where the product is not easily measurable as to quality *or* quantity, the apparatus of control involves product inspections, investigations of complaints (as of faulty service), and monitoring of production processes. Internal controls are subject to various intramural pressures—for example, hostility of administrative agencies toward auditors. External controls are vulnerable to friendly relationships between representatives of contracting agencies and contractors' representatives, political pressure, and outright bribery. In this respect, contracting out has no clear advantages over government inhouse account production; in fact, the difficulties of quality control in many cases may be greater with private contractors."

Still, the contract system does not necessarily diminish the government's ability to incorporate political objectives such as small business preference, fair employment practices, labor regulation, and safety standards into their contracts.

Government contracting is an important aspect of public administration that has thus far not been as systematically investigated as other areas. How, for example, do contracting officials balance bureaucratic and elective politics with the frequently repeated goal of acquisition of the best goods and services at the lowest possible price? How should the Defense Department go about improving internal auditing to keep better track of where dollars are spent and to determine the validity of prices charged to the government? (Is it necessary to pay $9,606 for a 12-cent wrench?) What are the trade-offs between letting contractors through *competitive bidding* and letting them on a *sole-source basis*—in which the desired firm is found "uniquely qualified" and all competition is waived? As government contracting continues to be a major instrument for attaining public goals in the 1980s, perhaps these and scores of other critical questions will begin to get the attention they deserve.

Public-Private Partnership: A Challenge for Urban Communities

Given declining federal aid (Chapter 3) and flagging local resources, American communities will be compelled to develop new ways of encouraging growth and providing needed services. It follows then that a stronger partnership between business and government could provide the basis for revitalizing America's urban areas.

Evidence from the last decade demonstrates that communities that actively mobilize their resources—public and private—can deal effectively with difficult problems and create new growth opportunities.*

Redefining Urban Management

Local governments will need to define their role and manage their operations in new ways. To make full use of the private sector's potential, they will have to adopt an entrepreneurial approach that anticipates needs, seeks out opportunities, and encourages an effective coalition for public-private efforts. Increasingly, local governments will have to choose between the role of policymaker and that of service provider. Government should identify goals, set priorities among needs, and then determine the best way of meeting these goals—using

Reprinted with permission from *Minneapolis Star and Tribune.*

*The following discussion draws on the report of the Committee for Economic Development, 1982.

public means, private means, or a combination of both (see Eadie, 1983).

To strengthen their economies, local governments have several available options. First, public promotion campaigns can build a favorable image of a locality and thereby help attract new residents and businesses. For example, the "I Love New York" campaign spurred tourism in New York City.

Second, local government should make more use of its powers to assemble parcels of land with roads, sewage, and other services to attract new businesses.

Third, while regulatory and financial incentives can be used to encourage business development, caution should also be exercised. By the mid-1980s, many states and cities had involved themselves in bitter competition for wandering industries. The classic example of this "smokestack chasing" was when 25 states and 100 cities scrambled in 1985 to get General Motors to build its multibillion-dollar Saturn automobile plant in their area. While such big catches may look good, they are exceedingly rare. Moreover, research shows that it is small- and medium-sized firms, not big business, that are the greatest creators of jobs in the United States today.

And here is another fact overlooked by state and urban economic planners: Tax breaks (or "business climate") are not the only factor companies consider when deciding where to build. Actually, such factors as the attractiveness of location, capital availability, and presence of skilled labor play an equally, if not more important, role. Unless the planners have made investments in those areas, they will be in poor shape to capture any but the most basic (and low-paying) assembly plants.

Private-Sector Contributions

Businesses, business associations, and other organizations can make community benefit an integral part of operating, purchasing, and investment decisions. Private actions can promote neighborhood self-help organizations and offer support and expertise to local governments in efforts to raise revenues, improve management and productivity, and provide essential services at lower costs. More specifically, the Committee for Economic Development, a group of business and education leaders, recommends that the private sector consider doing the following:

- Develop a process for planning and coordinating their public/private-involvement decisions.
- Integrate management of the public-involvement function into the corporate structure by placing accountability for its success with a senior officer. Career advancement for middle and senior

managers should be based in part on effective community (public) involvement.

- Establish standards governing their corporate contributions and other community activities and periodically review their own performance against those standards.
- Hold branch operations responsible for effective community involvement in the communities where the branches are located.
- Analyze community impact when making decisions on corporate purchasing, siting, hiring, and investment.
- Loan employees, facilities, and technical expertise to local governments and community groups.
- Join with other businesses to create an expanded level of involvement for all businesses in a community and broaden the base of corporate support for community activities.

The private sector has a special role to play in community economic revitalization. Today, many companies are trying creative approaches to help improve local economies. The committee cites a number of private initiatives including:

- Development planning. In some cities, the private sector has commissioned broad-gauged studies of local economic needs and has formulated comprehensive plans to meet those needs. For example, the Minneapolis Downtown Council developed a plan for the downtown retail district that led to the acclaimed Nicollet Mall.
- Private development initiatives (such as Detroit's Renaissance Center). Such initiatives can be the result of the work of many private businesses and institutions, can create new jobs, and can encourage development of adjacent areas.
- Hiring and training of the hard to employ. Some firms, such as Chicago's Continental Illinois Bank, have had successful experiences with special programs that provide training and productive jobs to disadvantaged urban residents.
- Giving aid to the local economy by providing technical assistance to small growing firms and entrepreneurs, and by locating plants or branches in areas needing development.

Perhaps a word of caution should be entered here. The private sector needs to determine what it realistically can contribute. If it sets its goals too high, its performance will fail to match its expectations. The private sector cannot assume full responsibility for meeting needs that result from cutbacks in federal domestic programs.

Collaborative Efforts

A key goal for local government is to establish a positive climate for attracting and keeping local businesses. Public administrators ought to improve communication between business and government, respond quickly to the needs and problems of local business, and minimize paperwork and regulatory requirements.

Today, there is growing interest in public-private collaboration on economic development projects, particularly in larger cities where there are limits to independent initiatives in responding to complex urban economic development programs. The following are examples of collaborative economic partnerships:

- Inner Harbor, a large commercial redevelopment project in Baltimore, includes a world trade center, a new office, new residential units, a marina, aquarium, theater, college campus, and parkland, all financed through both private and public investment.

- Dallas's Reunion Development, a hotel, sports center, terminal building, and recreation area in downtown Dallas that created over 800 new jobs was financed through both publicly and privately generated funds.

- Wacker Siltronix's silicon-wafer manufacturing plant, when deciding to settle in Portland, Oregon, negotiated an unusual arrangement with the city to hire disadvantaged workers trained under a city-sponsored program.

If collaborative ventures are to be successful, both sectors need new skills and new levels of flexibility and adaptability. Local administrators need to provide the expertise necessary for evaluating potential joint projects and for negotiating contractual arrangements with private-sector participants. Business participants must develop the necessary skills for negotiating with local governments, recognizing that they cannot dictate the terms of cooperation.

The private sector can work with local governments to develop the most effective means of providing essential services. Besides contracting with the private sector to reduce costs, communities have the following two additional options for coping with public-service problems:

- Increase revenues. In addition to raising taxes, businesses can help government develop ways to improve property-tax administration, cut back special tax preferences, broaden the tax base, increase returns on municipal funds, and cooperate to secure funds from state and federal sources.

- Improve productivity. Private sector expertise can help raise public sector productivity. Pittsburgh's Committee for Progress in Allegheny County might be cited as a pioneering model for public-private efforts to streamline local government.

Public-sector private-sector partnerships at the local level are not a panacea. Thus, the federal government, even in its somewhat reduced capacity, will continue to have an important role in urban development. Furthermore, the federal government will also need to develop its own productive partnership with the private sector.

Public-Private Cooperation: A Challenge for America

Much has been written about declining American industries and whether the federal government should actively promote industrial rebuilding. (See, for example, Magazines & Reich, 1982; Etzioni, 1983; Bluestone & Harrison, 1982; Watchter & Watcher, 1981; Adams & Klein, 1983.) The debate was fueled by the 1982 recession, with its impact on many manufacturing industries, but basic concerns go far deeper. On the one side stand supporters of a new activist industrial policy who would have government intervene more in support of business activity. On the other side stand those who would prefer to use current policy tools to achieve economic goals, together with free-market advocates who argue that the government already interferes too much in the economy and that it could aid business more by doing less.*

The term *industrial policy* is so new to public administration that it has yet to acquire a specific meaning. In its broadest sense, industrial policy encompasses everything government does that affects business activity—from fiscal and monetary policy to Chrysler Corp. loan guarantees. But the term is not used to mean *any* policy affecting industry. Rather, it implies (1) a focus on long-term structural economic problems; and (2) an emphasis on industries or sectors of the economy.

In its narrowest sense, industrial policy may be thought of as applying primarily to the manufacturing sector. In this sense, industrial policy would be like other sectoral policies, such as those that apply to agriculture, financial institutions, transportation, and energy. A broader conception takes the view that important economic developments cannot be neatly confined to individual sectors. The development of the computer industry, for example, has involved nearly all economic sectors.

The Problem: The Changing Structure of the Private Sector

Industrial policy proposals draw their impetus from the problems associated with adjusting to the long-term trends in the U.S. economy, trends which may not be amenable to resolution through fiscal and monetary policy or through perfectly functioning private markets. These trends seem to be related to major structural changes that have been taking place in the U.S. economy: the maturation of basic indus-

---

*The discussion that follows is based largely on the Congressional Budget Office, 1983b.

In the Minneapolis-St. Paul area, a coalition of public and private interests have come together to create jobs. A prominent leader in this effort has been William Norris (above), chairman of Control Data. Under Norris, the computer firm has helped sponsor a torrent of projects with names like the Minnesota Cooperation Office and Minnesota Wellspring. Two years ago, the latter, whose varied membership includes both business and government officials, persuaded state lawmakers to give tax breaks to big companies that sell, license, or lease technology to small ones.

William Ouchi (1984) calls the Minneapolis approach to public-private teamwork a model for regaining America's competitive edge. "Minneapolis has done what many other American cities now hope to duplicate: it has succeeded at developing one new major industry after another, thus continuing to provide jobs, growth, and prosperity for its citizens." (Control Data)

tries; increased international competition in domestic as well as foreign markets; a rapid expansion of the labor force; and the lingering effects of the oil squeezes of the 1970s.

As industries mature, they tend to grow more slowly. This has been so for a number of U.S. manufacturing industries. In a healthy economy, new expanding industries can compensate for the long-term decline of older industries and lead to a new growth cycle. Data on compositional change in the economy, however, indicate that the rate at which new industries are replacing older ones seems to have slowed during the 1970s, accounting in part for the economy's relatively poor performance.

Increased international competition is one factor accelerating the maturation of older industries and inhibiting the development of new ones. Competition comes not only from the highly developed European and Japanese economies but from newly industrializing nations (e.g., South Korea). The diffusion of new technology abroad has become very rapid. The United States has thus lost much of its former predominance in world trade. Some U.S. industries have lost export markets and even part of their domestic markets to foreign competition, creating major adjustment problems.

The expansion of the labor force in the 1970s also brought a number of economic problems. Although employment grew rapidly, the number of people seeking employment grew even faster. This also contributed to the difficulty of conducting economic policy, since efforts to increase employment ran counter to measures aimed at reducing inflation. From this perspective, the huge employment growth of the 1970s must be considered a major accomplishment.

The oil squeezes of the 1970s had direct harmful effects on the U.S. economy, raising the inflation rate and cutting real incomes. They also helped foreign competitors capture large portions of certain U.S. domestic and international markets, particularly in automobile production, as Americans shifted to smaller cars that had been developed abroad. The resulting uncertainties, particularly reflected in high interest rates, have led businesses to focus increasingly on short-term goals, making them hesitant to undertake new expansion.

Current Federal Policies toward Industry

An industrial policy implies the formulation of goals for specific sectors or industries and coordinated efforts to achieve them. The United States does not have a unified industrial policy, although it has a potpourri of policies that affect industrial growth—often unintentionally. These include monetary and fiscal policies, credit subsidies, and specific features of tax laws, as well as policies in the areas of procurement, trade, research and development, economic adjustment, regional development, and competition.

Procurement. Federal procurement of major equipment, most of it for defense, is estimated at $58.2 billion in fiscal year 1983. These purchases take major shares of output in some industries, such as aircraft and shipbuilding, and affect many others as well. Other important outlays go to public works infrastructure, costing $24 billion a year.

Trade. Trade programs seek either to promote exports or to inhibit imports. Credit subsidies through the Export-Import Bank, and tax benefits from Domestic International Sales Corporations, provide most of the impetus to increase exports. Protection against import competition is provided by a variety of tariffs, quotas, and regulations.

Research and Development. The Congress has supported research through a variety of tax subsidies and funding programs and through building facilities and testing prototypes, particularly in defense and energy projects. Support for R&D is usually justified on the ground that private firms tend to underinvest in these activities. Federal support has played a major role in the development of the agriculture, aerospace, communications, nuclear energy, and computer industries.

Economic Adjustment. Some federal programs seek to ease the process of adjusting to change. The Reconstruction Finance Corporation, established during the Depression, was one such program. The Job Training Partnership Act of 1982 established new programs to assist displaced workers, while Trade Adjustment Assistance provides some adjustment benefit to workers displaced by import competition.

Regional Economic Assistance. Various federal programs encourage economic development in particular regions or among targeted populations. These programs are uncoordinated and highly politicized.

Competition. The Congress has taken action to regulate competition in several distinct areas through antitrust laws and laws aimed at destructive competitive practices. It has also intervened to ensure that business practices reflect the public interest as they affect the environment and health and safety. These policies define the rules of competition and represent the most basic form of industrial policy.

Alternative Industrial Policy Strategies

A myriad of proposals have been made to establish a consistent industrial policy. Among them three broad categories of alternatives can be discerned.

1. Leave the current policy framework intact. Rely instead on the standard instruments of fiscal and monetary policy to facilitate stable growth.
2. Reform current policies that relate to industrial growth.
3. Establish a new industrial policy institution. Three distinct, although not mutually exclusive, options for this are:
   a. An information/consensus-building agency.
   b. An executive-branch coordinating agency.
   c. A financial institution.

Staying with Current Policy Instruments. The current policy view of industrial problems is one of managing aggregate levels of investment, employment, and economic growth. It allows private markets to determine the composition of economic activity and to resolve industry-specific problems. Essentially, it relies on monetary and fiscal levers to guide the economy. (See Chapter 9.) There are also numerous programs (such as those mentioned above) that assist or retard specific forms of industrial development, whether purposefully or not. These measures constitute an implicit industrial policy in that they affect incentives to work, save, and invest.

Proponents of current policy argue that further government intervention is unlikely to be successful, and that current problems are not so different from those of the past that they cannot be addressed within the current policy framework. To the extent that there are new problems, they can be handled by existing agencies such as the Departments of Commerce and Labor and the Council of Economic Advisers. According to this point of view, many of the industrial problems now faced by the United States are short-term in nature and will abate as economic growth takes hold. Longer-term problems are best addressed by private markets and existing institutions. This approach would avoid new government intervention, the creation of new government agencies, and the further intrusion of politics into economic decision making.

Arguing against a reliance on current policies, it may be said that no matter how vigorous and sustained the economic recovery proves to be, many long-term structural problems may remain. Productivity growth, for example, seems unlikely to return to historic levels. Unemployment rates are projected to remain high for the foreseeable future. And the economy may undergo further structural changes to which free markets cannot adjust.

Moreover, many of today's problems are new, especially the level and scope of international competition. American companies, it is fair to say, must today compete with foreign companies heavily subsidized and protected (through non-tariff barriers) by their governments. It is also fair to say that *some* American firms are subsidized as well (generally the ones with the most political influence rather than trade and growth potential) and that American business managers have not been as internationally minded as their foreign counterparts.

Still, it can be argued that new policy tools are necessary to avoid the kind of economic dislocation—such as the shift from agriculture to manufacturing—associated with previous structural changes in the economy.

Reform Current Policy.   Those who would reform current policy feel it is necessary to make American industry more competitive internationally by freeing it from certain domestic restraints. This option views industrial problems as caused by marginal imperfections in current laws and institutional practices.

For example, some believe that U.S. firms are at a disadvantage when competing with foreign firms that are able to merge or form cartels. Moreover, some activities, in particular research and development, might be more efficiently carried out on a cooperative basis. This view calls for changes in the antitrust laws.

Efforts to reduce the burden of social regulation—such as consumer protection, environment, and job safety rules—are based on the belief that these regulations force industry to bear excessive compliance costs and that they hinder competitiveness. Other deregulatory proposals, such as repeal of certain banking regulations, are aimed at changing the rules of competition in order to channel more funds into long-term investment. As Table 12-2 indicates, the federal government has been moving in this direction since 1968.

Table 12-2
Milestones toward Deregulation

Year	Event
1968	The Supreme Court's Carterfone decision permits non-AT&T equipment to be connected to the AT&T system.
1969	The FCC gives MCI the right to hook its long-distance network into local phone systems.
1970	The Federal Reserve Board frees interest rates on bank deposits over $100,000 with maturities of less than six months.
1974	The Justice Department files antitrust suit against AT&T.
1975	The SEC orders brokers to cease fixing commissions on stock sales.
1976	Railroad Revitalization and Regulatory Act allowed railroads limits rate-setting autonomy; the first piece of deregulation legislation in the recent wave.
1977	Merrill Lynch offers the Cash Management Account, competing more closely with commercial banks.
1978	Airline Deregulation Act instructed the Civil Aeronautics Board (CAB) to place maximum reliance on competition in its regulation of passenger service; provided that the board's authority over domestic fares and mergers would end January 1, 1983, and that the CAB would be abolished January 1, 1985.
1979	The FCC allows AT&T to sell nonregulated services, such as data processing.
1980	The Federal Reserve Board allows banks to pay interest on checking accounts.
1980	Staggers Rail Act limits the Interstate Commerce Commission's (ICC) jurisdiction over rates to those markets where railroads exercise market dominance; introduces price competition.
1980	Motor Carrier Act allowed truckers to form subsidiaries and expand into additional regional markets; ended necessity of demonstrating public need; placed fewer restrictions on certain industry hauling practices; eased entry and introduced price competition.
1980	Depository Institutions Deregulation and Monetary Control Act allows mutual savings banks to make commercial, corporate, and business loans equal to 5 percent of their assets; allows payment of interest on demand deposits; removes interest rate ceilings.
1981	Sears, Roebuck & Co. becomes the first one-stop financial supermarket, offering insurance, banking, and brokerage services.
1982	Bus Deregulatory Reform Act allows companies to obtain operating authority without applying to the ICC in many circumstances.
1982	Thrift Institutions Restructuring Act authorizes savings and loans to make commercial loans equal to 10 percent of their assets; allows investments in nonresidential personal property and small-business investment companies.
1984	AT&T divests itself of its local phone companies.

Proposals to stimulate trade include greater funding for traditional export promotion programs as well as action to lower and stabilize the dollar's foreign exchange rate. Proposals to protect domestic industry from import competition include greater use of countervailing duties and passage of domestic content legislation for automobiles.

Programs have also been proposed to assist workers who are unemployed because of economic change. These programs include readjustment services to help dislocated workers find new jobs, wage subsidies to encourage employers to hire them, and additional income support to ease the difficulty of adjustment.

A strategy based on policy reform would have several potential advantages. Some would accrue from updating current policies to take account of economic changes that have made them out of date—for example, reforming antitrust laws and banking regulations that were developed under different economic conditions. At the very least, such reforms might lead to better competitive practices. Other advantages would include (1) effecting change with minimal budgetary costs (as through deregulation); (2) improving U.S. competitiveness in specific product areas through export promotion; and (3) avoiding further intrusion of the federal government into the marketplace.

Critics of this strategy call it an inadequate, piecemeal response to a complex set of problems. It would affect industrial policy concerns only indirectly, often more as a result of addressing other legitimate concerns such as deregulation. Moreover, some of the specific reforms might involve a cost to the general public by reducing competition and weakening consumer protection.

Establishing a New Institution The third approach to industrial policy calls for the development of new institutions. Proponents of this approach argue that present industrial problems are so new and qualitatively different from previous economic problems that they require new institutions and policies to address them. In addition, it is argued that worldwide industrial competition forces the United States to match the policy devices of other industrial countries with institutions of its own. This is the only one of the three approaches that qualifies as a true break from the past in creating a new, coordinated industrial policy.

An Information/Consensus-Building Agency The least obtrusive of the proposed new agencies would be set up outside the executive branch to gather and disseminate information on the problems of industry, to develop consensus among opinion leaders, and to guide action. It would have no program to enforce. Some have proposed using such an agency as a means of working out an incomes policy through consensus agreements on wages and prices. One version would give it the power to spend public funds to help industries modernize along agreed-upon lines. In general, this approach presupposes that part of the problem of industrial competitiveness is a lack of market information.

The information/consensus agency is the least risky of the proposed new institutions, because it would have no administrative power. It would not interfere with private decision making or efficient resource allocation. Rather, firms or groups might revise their intended actions as they saw fit on the basis of new information or after participating in consensus agreements.

To be successful, the agency would need to persuade a variety of competing interest groups to subscribe to a common understanding of the economy and to agree to the necessary policy measures. But its likelihood of success would be small, particularly if it had no financial assistance to offer and no ability to compel attention or action. The administrative costs of the agency might then exceed its social benefits. Comparable agencies in other industrialized nations have failed to accomplish much. Even where successful, as in Japan, the agency may have reduced adaptability to change because of the need for agreement before action.

A Coordinating Agency A second type of institution, a coordinating agency, would coordinate and rationalize executive-branch programs, marshaling the resources of the federal government to address industrial problems. It would view the industrial problem as due, in part, to inadequate, conflicting, and poorly focused federal industrial programs. The Reagan administration's proposed Department of International Trade and Industry (DITI) is one variation of such an agency.

Greater coordination of policy could lead to more effective assistance to industry. It could avoid inconsistencies between programs—for example, between free trade and economic adjustment policies. In addition, such an agency would provide a forum for discussion of problems and issues, and could inform the president about instances in which executive-branch programs and policies were working at cross-purposes.

On the other hand, a centralized agency for industrial policy might tend toward bureaucratic intervention into certain industries at the expense of the economy as a whole. Or it might add to the cumbersome nature of decision making without improving the quality of decisions. Examples of the bureaucratic failure of centralized foreign industrial policy agencies abound, such as France's efforts in computers and aerospace.

A Financial Institution Several major proposals would establish a financial institution that would in essence be a national industrial development bank, or several regional development banks. A national industrial development bank could target assistance to specific industries and offer financial aid to induce industrial change. Specific proposals vary in the powers and duties they would give the bank. Some would have it provide limited funds to industries in need of them, either to assist new industries or to revive declining ones, others would give the bank greater funding as well as other powers, such as guaranteeing prices for new products.

The advantages of such a financial institution would lie in its ability to address structural problems that are outside the reach of fiscal, monetary, and existing policy instruments. It would be justified to the extent that the financial market fails to meet the capital requirements of industry, particularly the needs of distressed firms or regions, or to provide capital for the reorganization of troubled industries.

The key question about such an institution is whether it would yield better overall economic performance than the unassisted marketplace. A new institution, reallocating financial resources, could create serious inefficiencies if it were to make poor decisions. A related risk is that it would further politicize the economic system by introducing an element of political negotiation into economic decisions. A large permanent institution would be likely to become a magnet for special-interest pleadings, and could provide an incentive for poorly managed firms to fail in such a way as to require bailing out. This risk may be small, however, if current policy is already seen as politicized by the numerous government involvements in the economy. A new institution might serve to make such involvement more consistent and straightforward if it replaced, but did not add to, some of the interventions under current policy.

Much would depend on whether the mission of the agency was defined as promoting growth industries ("sunrise industries") or as subsidizing the restructuring of declining industries ("sunset industries"). Some would argue that promoting growth industries could contribute to higher output, productivity, and employment. But given the apparent willingness of U.S. capital markets to provide funds, these industries may not need financial assistance. If the mission was to restructure mature industries, the case for the agency would be its ability to promote actions that individual enterprises cannot pursue on their own, such as coordinated capacity reductions or industrywide modernization. A federal financial institution could enforce the necessary sharing of the burden, as the government was able to do in the cases of the Chrysler Corporation in 1979 and New York City in 1975.

All of the options put forward carry economic or political costs that are not easy to assess in advance. A weakness of the industrial policy debate is that too much attention has been given to the competing proposals and not enough to defining the problems and the desired outcomes. As the Organization for Economic Cooperation and Development (1979) warned several years ago, the costs should be made as explicit as possible: "Careful attention should be paid to the cost to consumers of action which raises prices, to the cost to taxpayers, and to the effects of subsidized competition on employment elsewhere."

A Final Word

It would be hard to imagine the foregoing trends and challenges as having no effect on administrative behavior in the decades ahead. By

What kind of administrators will NASA's space station need in the 1990s? (Photo courtesy National Aeronautics and Space Administration)

way of conclusion—not only to this chapter but to the entire work—let me suggest four traits that may go a long way toward characterizing tomorrow's administrators, public or private.

First, they will need to be generalists. Only generalists can provide the kind of leadership necessary in large complex undertakings that have numerous direct as well as indirect—and often unintended—consequences for society. They must be not only politically astute but also able to grasp their staffs' analytical work.

Second, they will need to be low-keyed. And once more the reason is that large complex undertakings seem to necessitate it. As Harlan Cleveland (1972:81) put it: "Complexity of operation magnifies small errors and makes the whole system vulnerable. People who get too easily excited are likely to get in the way, and will be asked to simmer down regardless of rank." And this applies not only in the control room of a modern aircraft but also in the office of a city manager or a hospital administrator. Collegiate management—with an emphasis more on steering than on controlling—requires a low-key administrative style.

Third, tomorrow's administrator will tend less and less to see only one side of each issue. Consider the case of the Alaskan pipeline: What is the "proper" solution, the proper trade-off between ecology on the one hand and unemployment (due to energy shortages or high energy costs in industry) on the other? One thinks here of that ferocious

American journalist H. L. Mencken who once said that for every knotty problem, there is a solution: neat, simple, and wrong.

So, increasingly, tomorrow's administrators must become skilled in analyzing issues in terms of trade-offs and reconciling what now often seem irreconcilable conflicts between the interests of different groups.

Finally, they will accept the ever-increasing difficulty and challenge of managing the public sector. Maslow had something of this in mind when talking about the choice between being a hero or a worm. "So many choose wormhood. They have a hopelessness, a lack of regard for what one person can do, an adolescent disillusionment because the whole world doesn't change when one new law is passed. . . . It is this disillusionment that has so often taken the heart out of social reformers and men of good will generally, so that as they grow older they get tired and hopeless and glum and go into privatism instead of conscious social betterment."

And Maslow (1965) sees only one alternative for tomorrow's managers: they "must learn . . . to thrill with pride, to get excited, to have a strengthened feeling of self-esteem, to have a strong feeling of accomplishment when [just] one particular little reform or improvement takes place." But, alas, these are things books cannot teach.

Nailing Down the Main Points

1. Three trends seem especially important to the future of public administration in the United States. The first trend is the electronics revolution that has made the "office of the future" a reality. The second is an aging population. The third is the increasingly global dimension to public policy issues.

2. Simply put, productivity is a measure of efficiency with which resources are converted into products or services. Or:

$$\frac{\text{Output}}{\text{Input}} = \text{Productivity}$$

And with nearly 20 percent of working Americans employed by government the importance of the growth of productivity in the public sector can hardly be overemphasized.

Yet barriers to increasing productivity exist: (a) lack of incentives, (b) lack of information on how to increase it, (c) legal and political restrictions on how public monies may be spent, and (d) jurisdictional restrictions that sometimes make economies of scale impossible.

3. Despite these barriers, opportunities for improvement are largely untapped. For example, contracting to private firms can in some instances result in the same output at less cost; public funds can be used to attract citizen resources; or, citizens and business can be requested to do more on their own and the possibilities for improvements in specific areas of public service (e.g., law enforcement) are virtually limitless.

4. Collaborative efforts by business, government, and private organizations can include establishing joint development goals, joint venture development projects, cooperative efforts to train and find jobs for the hard-to-employ, and financing packages that include public and private funds. Collaborative efforts can also be used to coordinate neighborhood improvement efforts and improve service delivery. Local governments can assemble unused land for development, help business expand or remain in the area, establish incentives for business growth, modify zoning and tax laws, or devise creative means of reducing costs of community services.

Concepts for Review

barriers to productivity
client behavior
comparative administration
competitive bidding
contracting
deregulation
efficiency effectiveness
expert systems
globalization

industrial policy
infrastructure
"new comparative" administration
privatization
procurement
productivity
sole-source basis
teleconferencing
"urban foreign policy"

Problems

1. What trends were not mentioned in this chapter but might profoundly affect public administration?

2. Discuss how the three trends might "cross-impact" each other.

3. How far should a city go in attracting industry? What guidelines would you suggest to a mayor trying to effect economic development in a city?

4. Should the United States have an industrial policy? What risks, if any, do you see in some of alternatives that have been proposed?

5. At the national level does it seem likely that the debate over industrial policy will continue well into the 1980s? Specifically, should government help industry? If yes, then which industries and how? To what degree might an industrial policy politicize economic decision making? What would be the consequence if the policy failed?

6. In this chapter a number of governmental functions were noted that have been contracted to the private sector. What other possibilities can you think of? What problems can you see in this trend?

7. In the last decade or so national planning in Japan and France has received considerable attention from American observers. Prepare a paper that discusses the role of government in the planning process in either or both countries. What are the lessons you find for the United States?

8. "Schools of public administration generally do not train managers, focused as they are on the relatively abstract conceptualization of policy problems and only slightly concerned with the function of the executive. The merger of business schools and public administration schools would

be an excellent thing, right in step with the movement to synthesis. Clearly, the old distinctions between what is private and what is public have less and less meaning; in many areas they are merely artificial remnants of the old ideology, figments of the old notions of property, competition, and the limited state. The management problems of Consolidated Edison, the oil companies, General Electric, IBM, ITT, AT&T, savings and loan associations, and the like are as inseparably involved with public questions of community need as are those, let us say, of the TVA, COMSAT, the Port of New York Authority, and HUD. The management of garbage disposal, health systems, land use, and welfare is equally complex and in many ways quite similar to the management of the so-called private sector. There may be different measures of efficiency, different sources of capital, different allocations of profit, different problems of incentive, but these differences are closing and they do not detract from the overall similarities. Yet consolidation of the business school and the public administration school is hindered by traditional academic bureaucratization and deeply felt loyalties to old specializations. In consequence, both sets of schools are in danger of obsolescence" (Lodge, 1975:335–36). Discuss.

9. Review the four traits for tomorrow's manager noted at the end of the chapter. Which would you eliminate? Which traits need to be added?

10. How would you explain this paradox: the public mistrusts government, yet wants more.

11. Critique the productivity factors indicated in Table 12-1; that is, show how they could give an inaccurate picture of actual productivity.

12. Now that you have completed *Managing the Public Sector*, would you answer question number one on p. 22 any differently?

Bibliography

Acheson, D. 1959. Thoughts about thoughts in high places. *New York Times Magazine,* October 11.

Ackoff, R. L. 1967. Management misinformation systems. *Management Science,* December.

Adams, F. G., and Klein, L. R., (Eds.). 1983. *Industrial policies for growth and competitiveness.* Lexington, Mass.: Lexington Books.

Allison, G. 1971. *Essence of decision.* Boston: Little, Brown.

Anderson, J. E., 1975. *Public policymaking.* New York: Praeger.

Anthony, R. N., and Herzlinger, R. E. 1980. *Management control in nonprofit organizations.* Homewood, Ill: Richard D. Irwin.

Appleby, P. H. 1952. *Morality and administration in democratic government.* Baton Rouge: L.S.U. Press.

Atcheson, G., and Neubauer, M. 1975. Committees power bases for special interest. *Houston Post,* July 10.

Ayres, B. D. 1983. A new breed of diplomat. *New York Times Magazine,* September 11.

Bailey, S. K. 1966. *The office of education and the education act of 1965.* Syracuse: Inter-University Case Programs.

──────. 1968. Objectives of the theory of public administration. In *Theory and practice of public administration.* Philadelphia: American Academy of Political and Social Science.

Baker, R. J. S. 1972. *Administrative theory and public administration.* London: Hutchinson University Library.

Balz, D. J. 1975. Economic focus, how much is enough and for whom? *National Journal,* February 15.

Bardach, E. 1977. *The implementation game.* Cambridge, Mass.: MIT Press.

Barnard, C. I. 1938. *The function of the executive.* Cambridge, Mass.: Harvard University Press.

Bauer, R. A. (Ed.). 1966. *Social indicators.* Cambridge, Mass.: MIT Press.

Baumol, W. J. 1973. Interview. *Princeton Quarterly,* Winter.

Behn, R. D. 1978. Terminating public policies. *The Wall Street Journal,* October 16.

Bennis, W. 1966. *Changing organizations.* New York: McGraw-Hill.

Bennis, W., and Slater, P. E. 1968. *The temporary society.* New York: Harper & Row.

Benveniste, G. 1972. *The politics of expertise.* Berkeley, Calif.: The Glendessary Press.

Bell, D. 1979. Communications technology—for better or for worse. *Harvard Business Review,* May–June.

Bell, R. 1984. *You can win at office politics.* New York: Times Books.

Benson, H. 1975. *The relaxation response.* New York: Morrow.

Benson, H., and Allen, R. L. 1980. How much stress is too much? *Harvard Business Review,* September–October.

Beer, S. H. 1978. Federalism, nationalism, and democracy in America. *American Political Science Review,* March.

Berle, A. A. 1968. What GNP doesn't tell us. *Saturday Review,* August 31.

Berle, A. A., and Means, G. C. 1933. *The modern corporation and private property.* New York: Macmillan.

Berle, A. A., and Means. G. C. (Eds). 1969. *The modern corporation and private property.* New York: Harcourt Brace Jovanovich.

Bernstein, P. W. 1984. What's behind the spare parts follies. *Fortune,* October 29.

Black, A. 1968. The comprehensive plan. In W. I. Goodman and E. C. Freund (Eds.), *Principles and practices of urban planning.* Washington: CMA.

Blake, R. R., et al. 1964. Breakthrough in organization development. *Harvard Business Review,* November–December.

Blechman, B. M., Gramlich, E. M., and Hartman, R. W. 1975. *Setting national priorities: the 1976 budget.* Washington, D.C.: Brookings Institution.

Blodgett, J. 1972. Costing out pollution: the state of the art. *SPPSG Newsletter,* May.

Bluestone, B., and Harrison, B. 1982. *The De-industrialization of America.* New York: Basic Books.

Blumenthal, R. 1969. The bureaucracy: antipoverty and the community action program. In A. P. Sindler (Ed.). *American political institutions and public policy.* Boston: Little, Brown.

Bonds, R. 1983. *The U.S. war machine: An encyclopedia of American military equipment and strategy.* New York: Crown.

Bonnen, J. T. 1969. The absence of knowledge of distributional impacts. In Joint Economic Committee, *The analysis and evaluation of public expenditure.* Washington, D.C.: Government Printing Office.

Boss, R. W. 1976. Decision making: Theories and applications to the budgetary process. In R. T. Golembiewski, et al. (Eds.), *Public administration,* Chicago: Rand McNally.

Bowers, D. G. 1964. Self-esteem and supervision. *Personnel Administration,* July–August.

Bowman, D. M., and Fillerup, F. M. 1963. *Management: Organization and planning.* New York: McGraw-Hill.

Boyatzis, R. 1982. *The competent manager: A model of effective performance.* New York: John Wiley & Sons.

Boyer, W. W. 1964. *Bureaucracy on trial: Policy making by government agencies.* Indianapolis: Bobbs-Merrill.

Bozeman, B., and Massey, J. 1982. Investing in policy evaluation: Some guidelines for skeptical public managers. *Public Administration Review,* May/June.

Brady, R. 1973. MBO goes to work in the public sector. *Harvard Business Review,* March–April.

Bright, J. 1964. *Research, development and technological innovation.* Homewood, Ill.: Richard D. Irwin.

————. 1972. *A brief introduction to technology forecasting.* Austin, Tex.: Permaquid Press.

Broder, D. S. 1975. Governor Brown: An honest approach. *Washington Post,* May 31.

Burnham, D. 1974. A.E.C. files show effort to conceal safety perils. *New York Times,* November 10.

Burnham, J. 1942. *The managerial revolution.* New York: John Day.

Burns, J. M. 1974. Interview. *Meet the Press,* NBC, July 15.

Buskirk, R. H. 1976. *Handbook of managerial tactics.* Boston: Cahners Books, Inc.

Byham, W. C., and Wettengel, C. 1974. Assessment centers for supervisors and managers. *Public Personnel Management,* September–October.

Caldwell, L. K. 1972. Environmental quality as an administrative problem. In *The Annals.* Philadelphia: American Academy of Political and Social Science.

Carmichael, S. 1971. Black power and the third world. In K. T. Fenn and D. C. Hodges (Eds.), *Readings in U.S. imperialism.* New York: Herder & Herder.

Cartwright, D. (Eds.). 1962. *Group*

dynamics: Research and theory. Evanston, Ill.: Row & Peterson.

Centron, M. J., and Bartocha, B. (Eds.). 1973. *Technology assessment in a dynamic environment.* New York: Gordon & Breach, Science Publishers, Inc.

Cervantes, A. J. 1973. Memories of a businessman-mayor. *Business Week,* December 8.

Churchill, W. S. 1959. *Memoirs.* Boston: Houghton Mifflin.

Churchman, C. W. 1968. *Challenge to reason.* New York: McGraw-Hill.

_____. 1971. *The design of inquiring systems.* New York: Basic Books.

Christensen, C. M. 1983. 'Bureaucrat' need not be a dirty word. *The Wall Street Journal,* November 7.

Cleveland, F. 1973. The changing character of the public service and the administrator of the 1980s. *Public Administration Review,* July–August.

Cleveland, H. 1972. *The future executive.* New York: Harper & Row.

_____. 1975. How do you get everybody in on the act and still get some action? *Public Management,* June.

Coates, J. F. 1971. Technology assessment. *Futurist,* December.

_____. 1974. Some methods and techniques for comprehensive impact assessment. *Technology Forecasting and Social Change,* June.

Committee for Economic Development. 1978. *Improving management of the public work force.* Washington, D.C.: CED.

Committee for Economic Development. 1982. *Public-private partnership,* New York: CED.

Commoner, B. 1971. *The closing circle.* New York: Knopf.

Cook, T. J., and Scioli, F. P. 1972. A research strategy for analyzing the impact of public policy. *Administrative Science Quarterly,* September.

Cooper, J. D. 1971. *How to get more done in less time.* New York: Doubleday.

Coulam, R. F. 1975. The importance of the beginning: Defense doctrine and the development of the F-111 fighter-bomber. *Public Policy,* Winter.

Crespi, I. 1979. Modern marketing techniques: They could work in Washington, too. *Public Opinion,* June–July.

Danziger, J. N. 1977. Computers, local governments, and the litany of EDP *Public Administration Review* January/February.

Davis, O. A., and Kamien, M. I. 1969. Externalities, information, and alternative action. In Joint Economic Committee, *Analysis and evaluation expenditures.* Washington, D.C.: Government Printing Office.

Deutsch, K. 1963. *Nerves of government.* New York: Free Press.

Deshpande, R. 1979 Marketing management. In *Management principles for non-profit agencies and organizations.* New York: AMACOM.

Destler, I. M. 1980. A job that doesn't work. *Foreign Policy,* Spring.

Dickinson, P. 1978. *The official rules.* New York: Dell.

Dowling, W. 1978. *Effective management and the behavioral sciences.* New York: AMACOM.

Downs, A. 1967a. *Inside bureaucracy.* Boston: Little, Brown.

_____. 1967b. A realistic look at the final payoffs from urban data systems. *Public Administration Review,* September.

Drucker, P. 1973. *Management: tasks, responsibilities, practices.* New York: Harper & Row.

_____. 1966. *The effective executive.* New York: Harper & Row.

Due, J. F., and Friedlaender, A. F.

1973. *Government finance.* Homewood, Ill.: Richard D. Irwin.

Eadie, D. C. 1983. Putting a powerful tool to practical use: The application of strategic planning in the public sector. *Public Administration Review*, September–October.

Eddy, W. B. 1970. Beyond behavioralism? Organization development in public management. *Public Personnel Review*, July.

Edwards, G. C., II. 1980. *Implementary public policy.* Washington, D.C.: Congressional Quarterly Press.

Elazar, D. 1972. *American federalism.* New York: Crowell.

Ellul, J. 1964. *The technological society.* New York: Knopf.

Etzioni, A. 1973. The third sector and domestic missions. *Public Administration Review*, July–August.

————. 1983. *An immodest agenda: Rebuilding America before the twenty-first century.* New York: New Press, McGraw-Hill.

Fairlie, H. 1965. Johnson and the intellectuals. *Commentary*, October.

Farney, D. 1975. Is the nation ready to be baroodied? *The Wall Street Journal*, February 25.

Farrell, W. E. 1976. Decentralizations of control over use of U.S. funds. *New York Times*, March 8.

Fenno, R. 1966. *The power of the purse.* Boston: Little, Brown.

Fesler, J. W. 1949. *Area and administration.* Tuscaloosa: University of Alabama.

Finer, H. 1941. Administrative responsibility in democratic government. *Public Administration Review*, Summer.

Fitch, L. G. 1974. Increasing the role of the private sector in providing public services. In W. D. Hawley and D. Rogers (Eds.). *Improving the quality of urban manage-*

ment. Beverly Hills, Calif.: Sage Publications.

Flax, M. T., and Garn, H. A. 1973. *A study in comparative urban indicators: conditions in 18 large metropolitan areas.* Washington, D.C.: Urban Institute.

Fowles, A. M. 1974. Public information. In S. P. Powers, F. G. Brown, and D. S. Arnold (Eds.). *Developing the municipal organization.* Washington, D.C.: ICMA.

Florestano, P. S. 1981. Revenue-raising limitations on local government. *Public Administration Review*, 1981.

Franke, R. H., and Kaul, J. D. 1978. Hawthorne experiment—First statistical interpretation. *American Sociological Review.* October.

Frankl, V. 1984. *The unheard cry for meaning.* New York: Washington Square.

French, Jr., T. R. P., and Raven, B. H. 1962. The bases of social power. In D. Cartwright's *Group dynamics: research and theory.* New York: Harper & Row.

Friedman, M. 1969. Statement. In U.S. Congress, Joint Economic Committee, *Economic Analysis and the Efficiency of Government.* Hearings of the Subcommittee on Economy in Government, Part 3, September–October.

Fuerbringer, J. 1984. Warts and all, the budget Act is 10 years old. *New York Times*, July 13.

Galbraith, J. K. 1958. *The affluent society.* Boston: Houghton Mifflin.

————. 1967. *New industrial state.* Boston: Houghton Mifflin.

————. 1975. *Money: Whence it came, where it went.* Boston: Houghton Mifflin.

Gallup, G. 1979. The cities: Unsolved problems and unused talent. *The Antioch Review*, Spring.

Gardner, J. W. 1961. *Excellence: Can we be equal and excellent too!* New York: Harper & Row.

Gellhorn, W., and Byse, C. 1974. *Administrative law: Cases and comments.* Mineola, N.Y.: The Foundation Press.

Gellhorn, W., and Byse, C. 1974. *Administrative Law:* Mineola, N.Y.: Foundation Press.

Gellerman, S. W. 1963. *Motivation and productivity.* New York: American Management Association.

Gerth, H. H., and Mills, C. W. (Eds.). 1946. *From Max Weber: Essays in sociology.* New York; Oxford University Press.

Gieringer, D. H. 1985. The FDA's bad medicine. *Policy Review,* Winter.

Gilbert, C. E. 1959. The framework of administrative responsibility. *Journal of Politics,* May.

Gilder, G. 1981. *Wealth and poverty.* New York: Basic Books.

Giles, R. H. 1974. Wildlife operations research. In *Encyclopedia of Environmental science.* New York: McGraw-Hill.

Gilmore, T. S., and Duff, M. K. 1975. *Boom town growth management.* Boulder, Colo.: Westview.

Glazer, N. 1976. *Affirmative discrimination.* New York: Basic Books.

Ginzberg, E., and Vojta, G. J. 1981. The service economy in the U.S. economy. *Scientific American,* March.

Golembiewski, R. T. 1974. Public administration as a field: Four developmental phases. Georgia Political Science Association *Journal,* Spring.

Greenberg, D. S. 1967. *The politics of pure science.* New York; New American Library.

Grodzins, M., and Elazar, D. J. 1966. *The American system.* Chicago: Rand McNally.

Gross, B. M. 1968. *Organizations and their managing.* New York: Free Press.

———. 1970. Friendly facism: A model for America. *Social Policy,* November–December.

———. 1971. Planning in an era of social revolution. *Public Administration Review,* May–June.

Grosse, R. N. 1969. Problems of resource allocation in health. In U.S. Congress, Joint Economic Committee, *The analysis and evaluation of public expenditures.* Washington, D.C.: Government Printing office.

Gulick, L., and Urwick, L. (Eds.). 1937. *Papers on the science of administration.* New York: Augustus M. Kelley.

Gwertzman, B. 1983. The Shultz method *New York Times Magazine,* January 2.

Hahn, W. A. 1981. Technological change and the public work force. In *The changing character of the public work force,* U.S. Office of Personnel Management Document 134–59-7. Washington, D.C.: Government Printing Office.

Halberstam, D. 1969. *The best and the brightest.* Greenwich, Conn.: Fawcett Crest Books.

Hall, T. 1976. How cultures collide. *Psychology Today,* July.

Hatry, H. P. 1972. Issues in productivity measurement for local governments. *Public Administration Review,* November–December.

Hatry, H. P., and Fisk, D. M. 1971. *Improving productivity and productivity measurement in local governments.* Washington, D.C.: Urban Institute.

Hatry, H. P., Winnie, R. E., and Fisk, D. M. 1973. *Practical program evaluation for state and local government officials.* Washington, D.C.; Urban Institute.

Haveman, J. 1973. White House Report/OMB's 'management by objectives' produces goals of uneven quality. *National Journal,* August 18.

———. 1975a. Budget Report/ Ford, Congress seek handle on 'uncontrollable spending. *National Journal*, December 29.

———. 1975b Budget Report/first fiscal resolution. *National Journal*, May 24.

Heller, W. 1966. *New dimensions of political economy*. Cambridge, Mass.: Harvard University Press.

Helmer, O. 1968. *Report on the future of the future—state-of-the-union reports*. Report R-14. Middleton, Conn.: Institute for the Future.

Hemenway, G. D. 1973. *Developer's handbook—environmental impact statements*. Berkeley, Calif.: Associated Home Builders of the Greater Fast Bay, Inc.

Hendrickson, R. F. 1940. Organization. In U.S. Department of Agriculture, *Personnel Bulletin*, July.

Hennig, M., and Jardim, A. 1977. *Managerial woman*. New York: Anchor.

Herriot, R. A., and Herman, P. M. 1971. The taxes we pay. *The Conference Board Record*, May.

Hersey, P., and Blanchard, K. H. 1972. *Management of organizational behavior*. Englewood Cliffs, N.J.: Prentice-Hall.

Hess, S. 1984. *The government-press connection*. Washington, D.C.: Brookings Institution.

Hewlett, R., and Duncan, F. 1974. *Nuclear navy, 1946–1962*. Chicago: University of Chicago.

Herzberg, F., et al. 1959. *The motivation to work*. New York: John Wiley & Sons.

Herzlinger, R. E., and Sherman, H. D. 1980. Advantages of fund accounting in 'nonprofits'. *Harvard Business Review*. May–June.

Herzlinger, R. E. 1979. Managing the finances of nonprofit organization. *California Management Review*, Spring.

Hill, G. 1970. Pollutors sit on anti-pollution boards. *New York Times*, December 7.

Hitch, C. J., and McKean, R. N. 1960. *The economics of defense in the nuclear age*. Cambridge, Mass.: Harvard University Press.

Hitch, C. J. 1960. *On the choice of objectives in systems studies*. Santa Monica, Calif.: Rand.

Hoos, I. R. 1972. *Systems analysis in public policy: A critique*. Berkeley: University of California Press.

———. 1973. Systems technique for managing society: a critique. *Public Administration Review*, March–April.

Hopkins, B., and Edwards, D. 1976. Where does the time go? *Runner's World Magazine*, July.

Horwitch, M., and Prahalad, C. K., 1981. Managing multi-organizational enterprises. *Sloan Management Review*, Winter.

Horst, P., et al. 1974. Program management and the federal evaluator. *Public Administration Review*, July–August.

House, K. E. 1976. Energy agency spend much energy to insure a long life, foes say. *The Wall Street Journal*, March 9.

Howitt, H. M. 1984. *Managing federalism: Studies in intergovernmental relations*. Washington, D.C.: CQ Press.

Humphrey, H. H. 1975. Points of view/national economic planning. *New York Times*, December 21.

Huntington, S. P. 1952. The marasmus of the ICC: The commission, the railroads, and the public interest. *The Yale Law Journal*, April.

Hyatt, J. C. 1976. In the federal garden of Eden, Eve is taking more bites from the apple—but not getting half. *The Wall Street Journal*, February 24.

Ikle, F. C. 1964. *How nations negotiate*. New York: Harper & Row.

James W. 1952. *Principles of psy-*

chology. Chicago: Encyclopaedia Britannica.

Janis, I. L. 1971. Groupthink. *Psychology Today*, November.

Jantsch, E. 1967. *Technology forecasting in perspective*. Paris: OECD.

————. 1969. *Perspectives of planning*. Paris OECD.

Jaques, E. 1970. *Work, creativity, and social justice*. New York; International University Press.

Jacques, E. 1979. Taking time seriously in evaluating jobs. *Harvard Business Review*, September–October.

Jennings, E. E. 1961. The anatomy of leadership. *Management of Personnel Quarterly*, Autumn.

Johnson, S. K. 1975. It's action, but is it affirmative? *New York Times Magazine*, May 11.

Kahn, R. L., et al. 1975. Americans love their bureaucrats. *Psychology Today*, June.

Kahneman, D., and Tversky, A. 1979. Intuitive prediction: Biases and corrective procedures. *Management Science, 12.*

Karasek, R. A. et al. 1982. *Social Science Medicine*, March.

Karr, A. 1975. The 'wild man' of transportation. *The Wall Street Journal*, October 27.

Katz, D., and Kahn, R. L. 1966. *The social psychology of organizations*. New York: John Wiley & Sons.

Kaufman, H. 1960. *The forest ranger: a study of administrative behavior*. Baltimore: John Hopkins Press.

Kaufmann, W. 1973. *Without guilt and justice*. New York: Peter H. Wyden.

King, J. L. 1982. Local government use of information technology: The next decade. *Public Administration Review*, January–February.

Kissinger, H. 1979. *White House Years*. Boston: Little, Brown.

Klingner, D. E. 1980. *Dictionary of personnel management and labor relations*. Oak Park, Ill.: Moore.

Koch, Edward I. 1985. *Mayor: An autobiography*. New York: Warner Books.

Koening, P. 1974. They just changed the rules on how to get ahead. *Psychology Today*, June.

Koontz, H., and O'Donnell, C. 1974. *Essentials of management*. New York: McGraw-Hill.

Korda, M. 1975. Power! New York: Random House.

Kotler, P. 1975. *Marketing for nonprofit organization*. Englewood Cliffs, N.J.: Prentice-Hall.

Kotter, J. P. Power, dependence and effective management. *Harvard Business Review.* July–August.

Kotz, N. 1969. *Let them eat promises: The politics of hunger in America*. Englewood Cliffs, N.J.: Prentice-Hall.

Kraemer, K., and Danziger, J. N. 1984. Computers and control in the work environment. *Public Administration Review*, January–February.

Kranz, H. 1974. Are merit and equity compatible? *Public Administration Review*, September–October.

Krause, E. 1968. Functions of a bureaucratic ideology: Citizen participation. *Social Problems*, Fall.

Krauthammer, C. 1984. The moral equivalent of . . . *Time*, July 9.

LaBrecque, M. 1980. On making sounder judgements. *Psychology Today.* June.

Laing, J. R. 1975. Civil service setup: Born as a reform idea, now hit by reformers. *The Wall Street Journal*, December 22.

Lambright, W. H. 1967. *Shooting down the nuclear plane*. Indianapolis: Bobbs-Merrill.

————. 1976. *Governing science and technology*. New York: Oxford University Press.

Landau, M. 1962. The concept of decision making in the 'field' of public administration. In S. Mailick and E. H. Van Ness (Eds.), *Concepts and issues in administrative behavior.* Englewood Cliffs, N.J.: Prentice-Hall.

———. 1969. Redundancy, rationality, and the problem of duplication and overlap. *Public Administration Review*, July–August.

Langbein, L. 1980. *Discovering whether programs work: A guide to statistical methods for program evaluation.* Santa Monica, Calif.: Goodyear.

Lapatra, J. W. 1973. *Applying the systems approach to urban development.* Strousburg, Penn.: Dowden, Hutchinson, and Ross.

Large, A. J. 1975. Federal agencies fight bill to open meetings to screening by public. *The Wall Street Journal*, September 23.

Larson, R. 1973. Resource allocation in public safety services. In *Proceedings of the first symposium: Research applies to national needs.* Washington, D.C.: NSF.

Lasswell, H. 1951. The policy orientation. In H. Lasswell and D. Lerner (Eds.). *The policy science.* Stanford, Calif.: Stanford University Press.

Lesieur, F. G. 1958. *The scalon plan: a frontier in labor management cooperation.* New York: John Wiley & Sons.

Levinson, H. 1968. *The exceptional executive.* Cambridge, Mass.: Harvard University Press.

———. 1973. *The great jackass fallacy.* Cambridge, Mass.: Harvard paperback.

Levitan, S. A., and Warzburg, G. 1979. *Evaluating federal social programs: An uncertain act.* Kalamazoo, Mich.: Upjohn Institute for Employment Research.

Levitt, T. 1976. Management and the 'post industrial' society. *The Public Interest*, Summer.

Lewis, W. A. 1968. Development planning. In *The International encyclopedia of social sciences.* New York: Macmillan.

Likert, R. 1961. *New patterns of management.* New York: McGraw-Hill.

———. 1967. *The human organization: its management and value.* New York: McGraw-Hill.

Lile, S. E. 1976. Tax report. *The Wall Street Journal*, January 21.

Lindblom, C. E. 1959. The science of muddling through. *Public Administration Review*, Spring.

———. 1968. *The policy making process.* Englewood Cliffs, N.J.: Prentice-Hall.

Lindblom, C. E., and Braybrooke. 1963. *A strategy of decision.* New York: Free Press.

Lippmann, W. 1955. *The public philosophy.* Boston: Little, Brown.

Litterer, J. A. 1973. *The analysis of organization.* New York: John Wiley & Sons.

Long, N. 1949. Powers and administration. *Public Administration Review*, Autumn.

Lovelock, C. H., and Young, R. F. 1979. Look to consumer to increase productivity. *Harvard Business Review*, May–June.

Lower Merion Township. 1975. *Report*, Winter. Ardmore, Pa.

MacIntyre, A. 1984. *After virtue: A study in moral theory.* Notre Dame, Ind.: University of Notre Dame Press.

McClelland, D. 1961. *The achieving society.* Princeton, N.J.: D. Van Nostrand.

———. 1973. Testing for competence rather than for 'intelligence.' *The American Psychologist*, January.

McConkey, D. D. 1975. *MBO for nonprofit organizations.* New York: AMACOM.

McCurdy, H. E. 1978. Selecting and training public managers: Business skills versus public administration. *Public Administration Review*, November–December.

McGregor, D. 1960. *The human side of enterprise.* New York: McGraw-Hill.

McKean, R. H. 1963. *Efficiency in government through systems analysis.* New York: John Wiley & Sons.

McNair, M. P. 1957. What price human relations? *Harvard Business Review*, March–April.

Magaziner, I., and Reich, R. 1982. *Minding America's business.* New York: Harcourt Brace Jovanovich.

Malek, F. V. 1978. *Washington's hidden tragedy: The failure to make government work.* New York: Free Press.

March, J. G., and Simon, H. A. 1958. *Organizations.* New York: John Wiley & Sons.

Marini, F. (Ed.). 1971. *Towards a new public administration: the Minnowbrook perspective.* Scranton, Pa.: Chandler.

Maslow, A. H. 1954. *Motivation and personality.* New York: Harper & Row.

————. 1965. *Eupsychian management.* Homewood, Ill.: Richard D. Irwin.

————. 1971. *The farther reaches of human nature.* New York: Viking.

Marro, A. 1978, Fraud in federal aid may exceed $12 billion annually, experts say. *New York Times*, April 16.

Mayer, M. 1976. *Today and tomorrow in America.* New York: Harper & Row.

Meadows, D. L. et al. 1972. *The limits to growth.* New York: Universe Books.

Meier, K. J. 1980. Executive reorganization of government: Impact on employment and expenditures, *American Journal of Political Science*, August.

Mesarovic, M., and Pestal, E. 1974, *Mankind at the turning point: the second report of the club of Rome.* New York: E. P. Dutton.

Midwest Center for Labor Relations. 1976. *Questions and answers in public sector labor relations: A practitioner's guide.* Bloomington, Ind.

Milgram, S. 1974. *Obedience to authority: An experimental view.* New York: Harper & Row.

Mills, T. 1975. Human resources—why the new concern. *Harvard Business Review*, March–April.

Mintzberg, H. 1973. *The nature of managerial work.* New York: Harper & Row.

Mitre Corporation. 1971. *A technology assessment methodology.* Washington, D.C.: Office of Science and Technology.

Molitor, G. T. T. 1975. Schema for forecasting public policy change. In A. A. Spekke (Ed.), *The next 25 years.* Washington, D.C.: World Future Society.

Morrow, W. 1975. *Public administration: politics and the political system.* New York: Random House.

Morse, P. M., and Kimball, G. E. 1951. *Methods of operations research.* New York: John Wiley & Sons.

Mosher, F. C. (Ed.). 1967. *Governmental reorganization: cases and commentary.* Indianapolis: Bobbs-Merrill.

————. 1968. *Democracy and the public service.* New York: Oxford University Press.

Morse, P. M. 1967. *Operations research for public systems.* Cambridge Mass.: MIT Press.

Morstein, M. F. (Ed). 1959. *The elements of public administration.* Englewood Cliffs, N.J.: Prentice-Hall.

Moynihan, D. P. 1970. Policy vs. program in the 1970's. Reprinted with permission from *The Public Interest*, No. 20, Summer 1970. Copyright © 1970 by National Affairs, Inc.

————. 1973. *Coping: essays on the practice of government.* New York: Random House.

Muller, R. 1980. *Revitalizing America: Politics for prosperity.* New York: Simon & Schuster.

Musgrave, R. A., and Polinski, A. M. 1971. Revenue sharing: A critical view. *Harvard Journal Legislation,* January.

Musgrave, R. A., and Musgrave, P. B. 1973. *Public finance in theory and practice.* New York: McGraw-Hill.

Mushkin, S. (Ed.). 1972. *Public prices for public products.* Washington, D.C.: Urban Institute.

Muskie, E. 1975. Interview. *The Wall Street Journal,* March 6.

Nathan, R. P., and Doolittle, F. C. 1984. The untold story of Reagan's 'New Federalism'. *Public Interest,* Fall.

National Commission on Productivity. 1973. *Productivity in state and local government—the wingspread conference.* Washington, D.C.: Government Printing Office.

National Training and Development Service. 1975. *Urban management curriculum development projects.* Washington, D.C.: NTDS.

Niskanen Jr., W. A. 1971. *Bureaucracy and representative government.* Chicago: Aldine-Atherton.

Neustadt, R. D. 1960. *Presidential power.* New York: John Wiley & Sons.

Newland, C. A. 1972. Introduction, a symposium on productivity in government. *Public Administration Review,* November.

Nozick, R. 1974. *Anarchy, state, and utopia.* New York: Basic Books.

Okun, A. M. 1975. *Equality and efficiency.* Washington, D.C.: Brookings Institution.

Organization for Economic Cooperation and Development. 1979. *The case for positive adjustment policies.* Paris: OCED, June.

Otten, A. L. 1973. Bureaucracy in the White House. *The Wall Street Journal,* August 23.

————. 1975. Learning what works. *The Wall Street Journal,* April 17.

Ouchi, W. 1980. *Theory Z.* Reading, Mass.: Addison-Wesley Publishing.

Orth, M. 1984. Profile: Elizabeth Dole. *Vogue,* October.

Parkinson, C. N. 1957. *Parkinson's law and other studies in administration.* Boston: Houghton-Mifflin.

Parson, H. M. 1978. "What caused the Hawthorne effect?" *Administration & Society,* November.

Patton, A. 1974a. To reform the federal pay system. *Business Week,* March 9.

————. 1974b. Government's pay disincentive. *Business Week,* January 19.

————. 1974c. Fallacies in federal pay standards. *Business Week,* January 26.

————.1974d. The hidden costs of federal pensions. *Business Week,* April 27.

————. 1974e. The new look in civil services pay. *The Wall Street Journal,* November 21.

Pechman, J. A. 1971. *Federal tax policy.* New York: W. W. Norton.

Pechman, J. A., and Okner, B. A. 1974. *Who bears the tax burden?* Washington, D.C.: Brookings Institution.

Pierce, N. R. 1980. The state of American federalism. *National Civic Review,* January.

Perkins, J. 1985. A new role model for black officials. *The Wall Street Journal,* April 3.

Peter, L. J. 1967. The Peter principle, or the incompetent shall inherit the earth. *West Magazine,* April 16.

Peters, C. 1980. *How Washington really works.* Reading, Mass.: Addison-Wesley Publishing.

Peters, T., and Waterman, Jr., R. H. 1982. *In search of excellence.* New York: Harper & Row.

Petro, S. 1975. *Sovereignty and compulsory public sector bargaining.* Wake Forest, N.C.: Wake Forest Law Review Association.

Pierce, N. R. 1984. How much information is enough? *Houston Chronicle,* March 18.

Pious, R. M. 1979. *The American presidency.* New York: Basic Books.

Pomerleau, R. 1974. The state of management development in the federal service. *Public Personnel Management,* January-February.

Powers, S. P. 1974. Management concepts and organization models. In S. P. Powers, F. G. Brown, and D. S. Arnold (Eds.). *Developing the municipal organization.* Washington, D.C.: ICMA.

President's Private Sectory Survey on Cost Control. *A Report to the President.* 1984. Washington, D.C.: Government Printing Office, January.

Pressman, J. L., and Wildavsky, A. 1973. *Implementation.* Berkeley: University of California Press.

Price, D. K. 1965. *The scientific estate.* Cambridge, Mass.: Belknap Press.

Public Policy Program. 1972. *Teaching and research materials, public policy 210 problem sets.* Cambridge, Mass.: Kennedy School of Government.

Pyhrr, P. A. 1971. Zero-base budgeting. *Harvard Business Review.* May.

Quade, E. S. 1966. *System analysis techniques for planning-programming-budgeting.* Santa Monica, Calif.: Rand.

Quinn, J.B. 1980. *Strategies for Change: Logical Incrementalism.* Homewood, Ill.: Richard D. Irwin.

————. (Ed.). 1964. *Analysis of military decisions.* Chicago: Rand McNally.

Rawls, J. 1971. *A theory of justice.* Cambridge, Mass.: Belknap Press.

Reed, 1978. Bureaucracy: The Cleverest Lobby of Them All. *Washington Monthly.* April.

Reddin, W. J. 1970. *Managerial effectiveness.* New York: McGraw-Hill.

Remy, R., and Lawson, C. 1984. L. A. readies for administrative marathon. *PA Times,* February 1.

Rendon, A. 1971. *Chicano manifesto.* New York: Macmillan.

Richardson, E. 1973. The maze of social programs. *Washington Post,* January 21.

Riker, W. H. 1962. *The theory of political coalitions.* New Haven, Conn.: Yale University Press.

Rivlin, A. 1971. *Systematic thinking for social action.* Washington, D.C.: Brookings Institution.

————. 1975. Statement before the Joint Economic Committee, April 3.

Rogers, C. R., and Roethlisberger, F. J. 1952. Barriers and gateways to communications. *Harvard Business Review,* July–August.

Roos, N. P. 1975. Contrasting social experimentation with retrospective evaluation. *Public Policy,* Spring.

Roosa, R. V. 1976. Economic planning: a middle way. *New York Times,* February 8.

Roszak, T. 1973. *Where the wasteland ends.* Garden City, N.Y.: Anchor Books.

Rourke, F. E. 1972. *Bureaucratic power in national politics.* Boston: Little, Brown.

————. 1969. *Bureaucracy, politics and public policy.* Boston: Little, Brown.

Safire, W. 1978. *Safire's political dictionary.* New York: Random House.

Sapolsky, H. M. 1972. *The Polaris System Development:* Cambridge, Mass.: Harvard University Press.

Schrank, R. 1978. *Ten thousand working days.* Cambridge, Mass.: MIT Press.

Savas, E. S. 1971. Municipal monopoly. *Harper's Magazine,* December.

Sayles, L. R., and Chandler, M. K. 1971. *Managing large systems: organizations for the future.* New York: Harper & Row.

Sayles, L. R. 1979. *Leadership: What effective managers really do . . . and how they do it.* New York: McGraw-Hill.

Schachter, S. 1959. *The psychology of affiliation.* Stanford, Calif.: Stanford University Press.

Schlesinger, A. M. 1965. *A thousand days.* Boston: Houghton-Mifflin.

Schon, D. A. 1971. *Beyond the stable state.* New York: Random House.

Schorr, B. 1975. More federal workers take on a second job: Assailing government. *The Wall Street Journal,* June 16.

Schubert, G. 1962. Is there a public interest theory? In C. T. Friedrech (Ed.). *The public interest.* New York: Atherton Press.

Schultz, G. P. 1961. Strikes: The private stake and the public interest. In *Report of the president's task force on employee-management relations in the federal service.* Washington, D.C.: Government Printing Office.

Schultze, C. L. 1969. The role of incentives, penalties, and rewards in attaining effective policy. In The Joint Economic Committee, *Analysis and evaluation of public expenditures.* Washington, D.C.: Government Printing Office.

Siedman, H. 1980. *Politics, position, and power: the dynamics of federal organization.* New York: Oxford University Press.

Selznick, P. 1949. *TVA and the grass roots.* New York: Harper & Row.

Seyler, W. C. 1974. Interlocal relations: cooperation. *Annals,* November.

Shafer, R. G. 1975. Revenue-sharing versus raised tempers as law comes up for renewal. *The Wall Street Journal,* March 27.

————. 1976. More cities sign up a "man in Washington" to help them win grantsmanship game. *The Wall Street Journal,* January 15.

Shafritz, J. (Ed.). 1975. *A new world: readings on modern public personnel management.* Chicago: PMA.

Sharkansky, Ira. 1972. *Public Administration.* Chicago: Markham.

Sharkansky, I. 1969. *The politics of taxing and spending.* Indianapolis: Bobbs-Merrill.

Sherrill, R. 1974. *Why they call it politics.* New York: Harcourt Brace Jovanovich.

Schick, A. 1966. The road to PPB: the stages of budget reform. *Public Administration Review,* December.

Silk, L. 1975. Economics for the perplexed. *New York Times Magazine,* March 21.

Simon, H. A. 1957a. *Administrative behavior.* New York: Macmillan.

————. 1957b. *Models of man.* New York: John Wiley & Sons.

Skibbins, G. J. 1974. *Organizational evolution.* New York: AMACOM.

Slinger, B. F., Sharp, A. M., and Sandmeyer, R. L. 1975. Local government revenues. In J. R. Aronson and E. Schwartz (Eds.), *Management policies in local government finance.* Washington, D.C.: ICMA.

Sorensen, T. C. 1963. *Decision making in the White House.* New York: Columbia University Press.

————. 1965. *Kennedy.* New York: Harper & Row.

Speer, A. 1970. *Inside the third reich.* New York: Macmillan.

Spencer, M. H. 1971. Administrative science. In S. E. Seashore and R. J. McNeil (Eds.), *Management of the urban crisis.* New York: Free Press.

Stahl. O. G. 1971. Summary and prospects. In Public Personnel Association, *Personnel dialogue for the seventies,* Personnel Report 712, Chicago.

Starling, G. 1980. *The Changing Environment of Business.* Belmont, Calif.: Wadsworth.

Steiner, G. A. 1969. *Top management planning.* New York: Macmillan.

Sternberg, C. W. 1985. States under the spotlight: An intergovernmental view. *Public Administrative Review,* March–April.

Stewart, J. M. 1969 Making project management work. In D. I. Cleland and W. R. King (Eds.), *Systems, organization analysis, management.* New York: McGraw-Hill.

Stieglitz, H. 1969. What's not on the organizational chart. In D. I. Cleland and W. R. King (Eds.), *Systems, organization, analysis, management.* New York: McGraw-Hill.

Stone, D. C. 1981. Innovative organization require innovative managers. *Public Administration Review,* September–October.

Strafritz, J. M. 1980. *Dictionary of personnel management and labor relations.* Oak Park, Ill.: More.

Summers, H. 1982. *On strategy.* Novats, Calif.: Presidio Press.

Surrey, S. S. 1973. Tax expenditures and tax reform. In R. H. Haveman and R. D. Hamrin (Eds.), *The political economy of federal policy.* New York: Harper & Row.

Tanenhaus, J. 1960. Supreme Court attitudes toward federal administrative agencies. *The Journal of Politics,* August.

Tannenbaum, S. (Ed.). 1968. *Control in organizations.* New York: McGraw-Hill.

Terkel, S. 1972. *Working.* New York: Pantheon Books.

Thompson, F. 1976. Types of representative bureaucracy and their linkage. In R. T. Golembienski, et al (Eds.), *Public administration.* Chicago: Rand McNally.

Time. 1975. The truth about Hoover. *Time,* December 22.

Toffler, A. 1980. *The third wave.* New York: Bantam Books.

Tullock, G. 1965. *The politics of bureaucracy.* Washington, D.C.: Public Affairs Press.

_____. 1971. Public decisions or public goods. *Journal of Political Economy.*

Townsend, R. 1970. *Up the organization.* New York: Knopf.

Toynbee, A. J. 1946. *A study of history,* abridged ed. New York: Oxford.

U.S. Advisory Commission on Intergovernmental Relations. 1983. *Regulatory federalism: Policy, process, impact and reform.* Washington, D.C.: ACIR.

U.S. Air Force Systems Command. 1963. *PERT-time system description manual.* Washington, D.C.: Headquarters AFSC.

U.S. Bureau of Census. 1974. *Current population reports,* series P-25, No. 533. Washington, D.C.: Government Printing Office.

_____. 1975. *City government finances 1973-1974.* Washington, D.C.: Government printing Office.

_____. 1980. *Statistical Abstract of New York.* Washington, D.C.: Government Printing Office.

U.S. Civil Service Commission. 1976. *Upward mobility through job restructuring.* Washington, D.C.: Government Printing Office.

U.S. Congress, House. 1973. Representative Craig Homer's extension of remarks, *Congressional Record,* E 6500–1, October 15.

U.S. Congress, Joint Economic Committee. 1975. *Hearings on the economic impact of environment regulations.* Washington, D.C.: Government Printing Office.

U.S. Congressional Budget Office. 1983. *The industrial policy debate,* Washington, D.C.: Government Printing Office.

U.S. Congressional Budget Office and General Accounting Office. 1984. *Analysis of the Grace Commission's major proposals for cost control.* Washington, D.C.: Government Printing Office.

U.S. General Accounting Office. 1977. *Benefits from flexible work schedules.* Washington, D.C.: Government Printing Office.

————. 1979a. *The federal government needs a comprehensive program to curb its energy use.* Washington, D.C.: Government Printing Office.

————. 1979b. *Hatch Act reform.* Washington, D.C.: Government Printing Office.

————. 1979c. *Difficulties in Evaluating Public Affairs Government-Wide and at the Department of Health, Education and Welfare.* (LCD-79-405). 18 January.

————. 1980. *The alternative work schedules.* Washington, D.C.: Government Printing Office.

————. 1983. *Increased Use of Productivity Management Can Help Control Government Costs,* AFMD-84-11, Washington, D.C.: G.P.O., 10 November.

U.S. Office of Management and Budget. 1984. *Budget FY 1985.* Washington, D.C.: Government Printing Office.

Van Horn, R. L. 1982. Don't expect too much from your computer system. *The Wall Street Journal,* October 22.

Ventriss, C. 1985. Emerging perspectives on citizen participation. *Public Administration Review.* May/June.

Virtullo-Marting, J. 1979. Sin will find you out. *New York Review of Books,* May 17.

Voss, L. E., and Eikmeier, D. 1984. Microcomputers in local government. *Public Administration Review,* January–February.

Vroom, V. H., and Yetton, P. W. 1973. *Leadership and decision making.* Pittsburgh: University of Pittsburgh Press.

Wachter, M., and Wachter, S. (Eds.). 1981. *Toward a new U.S. industrial policy?* Philadelphia, Pa.: University of Pennsylvania Press.

Wald, E. 1973. Toward a paradigm of future public administration. *Public Administration Review.* July–August.

Waldo, D. 1948. *Administrative state.* New York: Ronald Press.

————. (Ed.). 1971. *Public administration in a time of turbulence.* Scranton, Pa.: Chandler.

Walters, R. W. 1972. Job enrichment isn't easy. *Personnel Administration Review,* September–October.

Weidenbaum, M. 1969a. *The modern public sector.* New York: Basic Books.

————. 1969b. Budget "uncontrollability" as an obstacle in improving the allocation of government resources. In Joint Economic Committee, *Analysis and evaluation of public expenditures.* Washington, D.C.: Government Printing Office.

Weinberg, A. M. 1966. Can technology replace social engineering? *Bulletin of the Atomic Scientists,* December.

Weisband, E. D., and Frank, T. M. 1975. *Resignation in protest.* New York: Grossman.

Weiss, C. H. 1972. *Evaluation research.* Englewood Cliffs, N.J.: Prentice-Hall.

————. (Ed.). 1972. *Evaluating ac-*

tion programs. Boston: Allyn &
Bacon.

Wildavsky, A. 1978. A budget for all
seasons? Why the traditional budget last. *Put Administration
Review*, November–December.

White, L. D. 1927. *The city manager.* Chicago: University of
Chicago Press.

Whitehead, A. N. 1929. *The aims of
education.* New York: Macmillan.

Wholey, J. S., et al. 1970. *Federal
evaluation policy.* Washington,
D.C.: Urban Institute.

_____. 1973. *Federal evaluation
policy.* Washington, D.C.: Urban
Institute.

Wildavsky, A. 1964. *The politics of
the budgetary process.* Boston:
Little, Brown.

Williams, W. 1975. Special issue on
implementation: Editor's comments. *Policy Analysis*, Summer.

Wilson, W. 1941. The study of administration. *Political Science
Quarterly*, December.

Wolfe, T. 1970. *Radical chic &
mau-mauing the flak catchers.*
New York: Farrar, Straus, and
Giroux.

Wood, R. 1981. Managing a school
system under court order. *The
Wall Street Journal*, March 30.

Zangwell, W. 1969. Top management and the selection of major
contractors at NASA. *California
Management Review*, Fall.

Zalenznik, A. 1966. *The human dilemmas of leadership.* New York:
Harper & Row.

Index *

A

Accountability, 123-24
Accounting, 379
  and computers, 275
Accrual basis of accounting, 379
Acid rain, 233-35
ACTION, 199
Adaptability, as criteria in organizational
  design, 327-28
Adjudication, 41
Administrative law judge, 41
Administrative management movement,
  300
Administrative Procedures Act (1946),
  39-40-41, 136
Administrative processes, 10-11, 10 n
Administrative responsibility
  accountability, 123
  coercion, 126-27
  collusion, 125-26
  competence, 119
  distortion, 127-30
  due process, 119-123
  elitism, 131-36
  ethical analysis, 145-52
  and external and internal controls,
    133-52
  flexibility, 117-19
  honesty, 124-25
  institutionalized citizen participation,
    139-41

Administrative responsibility—*Cont.*
  judicial control, 136-39
  professional codes, 141-43
  public interest, 144-45
  representative bureaucracy, 143-44
  responsiveness, 115-17
Advancement, 460-61
Affirmative action (AA), 480
  development of plan, 481-82
  legal background of, 479-81
Age Discrimination in Employment Act
  (1967), 486
Albany, New York, 132
Allocation function, of fiscal policy,
  347-48
**American Federation of State, County,
  and Municipal Employees**
  (AFSCME), 472
  AFSCME v. *State of Washington* (1983)
Analysis and evaluation: the
  effectiveness of a program can be
  assessed "before the fact" or "after
  the fact." The former activity is
  policy analysis, the latter is
  evaluation.
Analytical tools, 12
Appointees, political, 49-52, 446
Apollo mission, 175
Arbitration, 479
Argyris, Chris, 409-11
Arkansas, budgeting process in, 378
Army Corps of Engineers, 53, 207
Assessment center, 458-60

* Concepts for Review listed in **bold face.**

Atomic Energy Commission, 61, 324
Audit, 377–78, 381
Authority, 46
  charismatic, 299
  delegation of, 325
  legal, 299
  traditional, 299

B
Babbitt, Bruce, 93
Bardach, Eugene, 244
Bargaining, as policy-setting strategy, 63
Bargaining unit, 476
Barnard, Chester, 20
Bay Area Transportation Study Commission (BATSC), 227
Beckwith, Charles, 303
Behavioral sciences, and human behavior, 399–425
Benefits, real, pecuniary, tangible, and intangible, 207–8
Bennis, Warren, 312, 413
Biomedical technology, 156–59
Block grants, 83
Blough, Roger, 66
Brzezinski, Zbigniew, 306
Bryant, Paul, 246
Buckley, William F., Jr., 139
Budget; see Budgeting
Budgeting, 362
  capital, 367–69
  and changing role of budget, 362–67
  and federal budget cycle, 370–78
  future of public, 369–70
  line-item, 363
  performance, 363–65
  program, 365–66
  politics of, 377
  purposes of, 362–67
  by state and local government, 378–81
  zero-based, 366–67
Bundy, McGeorge, 178
Bundy, William, 176
Bureaucracy, clients, 52–53; see also Pyramidal organization
Burford, Anne McGill, 23, 26–27, 52
Burger King, 511
Business administration, differences in, from public administration, 14–18

C
Califano, Joseph, 492–93
Campbell, Alan K., 469
Capital budgeting, 367–69
Career ladder, moving up, 433–35

Career system of government employment, 447
Carter, Jimmy
  domestic program, 85
  firing an employee, 492–93
  and Peace Corp., 199
  versus Reagan, as politician, 34–35
  White House staff of, 453
Carter v. *Gallagher* (1971), 483
Categorical grants, 80
Certification, 451
Cervantes, A. J., 34, 56
Charisma, 299
Charlotte, North Carolina, 169
Chicano, 134
Churchill, Winston
  on communication, 252
  and leadership, 418
  on MacArthur, 289
  style, 68–69
Circular A-95, 85, 99–100
Citizen advisory committees, role of, in policymaking, 140–41
Citizen participation and administrative responsibility, 139–41
City planning, 166
Civil Rights Act (1964), 479–81, 488
Civil service, 446–47
Civil Service Commission, 469
Civil Service Reform Act (1978), 469–70
Clarity, as criteria in organizational design, 326–27
Clark, William, 306
Cleveland, Harlan, 139, 152, 537
Client behavior, as strategy for improving productivity, 517
Clients, of bureaucracy, 52–53
Clifford, Clark, 60, 225
Closing circle (Commoner), 217
Coalition
  art of building, 64
  as policy-setting strategy, 64
Coercion and administrative responsibility, 126–27
Coercive power, 58
Cognate agencies, role of, in setting policy, 53–54
Colbert, J. B., 352
Coleman, William T., Jr., 151–52
Collective bargaining, 475–77
  administration of contract, 477
  and determination of bargaining units, 476
  and impasse resolution, 478–79
  importance of negotiations, 476–77
  legal framework of, 471–75

Collective system of government employment, 448
Collusion, and administrative responsibility, 125–26
Commoner, Barry, 217, 227
Communication, role of, in implementation, 252–56
Community Action Program, 44
Compacts, 98
Comparative administration, 505–6
Comparable worth, 485–88
Compensation, in civil service, 453–56
Competence, and administrative responsibility, 119
Competition, as policy-setting strategy, 65–66
Competitive bidding, 523
Complexity of joint action, 242–44
Comprehensive plan, 166
Compromise, as policy-setting strategy, 63
Computers, role of, in planning, implementation, and evaluation
fallacies about, 277–81
government use, 271–73
software, 274–77
technology, 273–74
Conflict, as policy-setting strategy, 66–68
Congress
authority over agencies, 47–49
role of, in budget preparation, 373–76
role of, in setting policy, 47–49
Congressional Budget and Impoundment Control Act (1974), 373–75
Congressional Budget Office, 375
Congressional oversight, 70
Connection power, 58
Consumer satisfaction, evaluation of, 120
Contingency approach, 398, 417–25
Contracts, 522–23
Contractarianism, 149
Control group, 263, 267
Collidge, Calvin, 472
Cooperation, as policy-setting strategy, 63–65
Cooperative arrangements, 99
Cooperative federalism, 80
Co-optation, 65
Corporate income tax, 357
Cost accounting, 379
Cost-benefit analysis, 207–13
discount factor, 210–12
distribution of impacts, 209–10
measurement of costs and benefits, 207–9
and opportunity cost, 213

Cost-benefit analysis—*Cont.*
reasons for, 207
Cost-effectiveness analysis, 212–13
Costs, real, pecuniary, tangible, and intangible, 207–8
Council of Economic Advisors, 37
Council of governments, 79, 85
Counterintuitive nature of public systems, 222
Counties, 96
Creative federalism, 80–82
Creativity, nemesis of, 299
Crime Compact (1934), 98
Crime rate, effects of changes in, on public administration, 508
Crisis Game, 225–26
Criminal justice system, 218–19
Critical path, 248–49
Critical Path Method (CPM), 248

D
Dallas, Texas, 18, 521
Data base, 275–76
Decertification, of union, 494
Decision analysis, 215–17
Decision making, analytical approaches, 206–25
Decision rules in cost-benefit analysis: Assuming that benefits exceed costs, what one does next depends on decision rules. One rule would be to do the project if B > C. Another would require that the cost-benefit ration (B/C) exceed some number, say, 1.7.
Decision trees, 216
Decisions
lower limits, 204
framing, 203–4
upper limits, 203
Defense, Department of, 338–42
Deficits, 353
Delegation of authority, 314
Delphi technique, 188
Demand side economics, 350
Demographic changes, effects of, on public administration, 506–8
Demonstration projects and evaluation, 262
Demotion, 462
Denver, Colorado, 452
Departmentation; *see* Division of labor
Deprived groups, 480
Deregulation, 532–33
Design criteria, for organizations, 326–28
Developmental planning, 167–68
Dillon's rule, 91, 94

Direct and indirect cost and benefits, 208
Discipline, as concern of public person-
nel management, 461–64
Discount factor, in cost-benefit analysis,
210–12
Discounting; *see* Discount factor
Discrimination, laws concerning, 479–88
Dismissal, 462–63
Disraeli, Benjamin, 68
Distribution function, of fiscal policy,
348–49
Division of labor, 300–301, 306–7
Dole, Elizabeth, 2–3, 7
Dothard v. *Rawlinson* (1977), 484
Downs, Anthony, 144, 304
Drucker, Peter, 203, 323, 412, 452
Dual federalism, 79–80
Due process, and administrative respon-
sibility, 119–23

E
Economic Development Administration,
242
Economic growth, 350
Economic Opportunity Act (1964), 38, 44
Economic system, 347
Effectiveness, 15, 509
Efficiency, 15, 509
Ehrlichman, John, 60, 146
Eisenhower, Dwight D., 63
Electronics, advances in, 502–4
Elitism, 131–36
Energy Research and Development Ad-
ministration, 324
Enforcement, 43
Enterprise zones, 96–98
Environment need for knowledge on, 7, 9
*Environmental Impact Statements
(EIRs),* 191–92
Environmental Protection Agency,
23–30, 233–35
Epistomology, 226
Equal employment opportunity (EEO),
480
Equal Employment Opportunity Act
(1972), 483
Equal Employment Opportunity Com-
mission, 481–82, 485
Equal opportunity, 480
Equal Pay Act (1963), 483, 485
Escalation, as problem in conflict
situation, 67
Estate, inheritance, and gift tax, 357
Ethical analysis, 145–52

Ethics
definition of, 145
reasons for studying, 146–47
Ethnic representation, 143
Ethnocenticism, 134–36
Evaluation, 179–80, 241
for policymakers, 260–63
for program managers, 263–64
reasons for, 259–60
steps in, 264–69
Executive Order 10988, 471
Executive Order 11491, 473
Expediter, role of, in implementation,
250
Expenditure structure, 359–60
Expert forecasting, 187–88
Expert power, 59, 405
Expert systems, 504
Exploratory forecast, 187
External auditing, 285
External and internal controls, 133
Externalities, 208, 347
of administration actions, 62

F
Fact-finding, 478–79
Family Assistance Plan (FAP), 177
Fayol, Henri, 19
Federal Administrative Procedure Act
(1946), 41
Federal Bureau of Investigation (FBI),
61–62
Federal Drugs Administration, 126–27
Federal Executive Institute (FEI), 457
Federal government
budget cycle of, 370–78
relations of, with state, 90–91
Federal policies toward industry, 530–31
Federal Regional Council, 85
Federal regions, 85
Federal Register, 39–40
Federal Reserve Board, 48
Federal Surface Mine and Reclamation
Act (1977), 102
Federal Trade Commission (FTC), 126
Federalism, 78
comparison of, with intergovernmental
relations, 78–79
cooperative, 80
creative, 80–82
dual, 79–80
layer cake model of, 78
marble cake model of, 78
Feinstein, Dianne

Field experiments, and evaluation, 262–63

Fifth Amendment, 119

Firefighters v. *Stolts* (1984), 484–85

Fiscal planning, 168

Fiscal policy
allocation function of, 347–49
distribution function of, 348–49
functions of, 246
stabilization function of, 349–50
and supply side economics, 350–52

Fiscal policymaking; *see* Fiscal planning

Fiscal year, 371, 379

Fitzgerald, Ernest, 148

Flexibility, and administrative responsibility, 117–19

Flood Control Act (1936), 207

Follow-up, role of, in implementation, 250–253

Ford Foundation, 3, 16

Forecast, 187

Forecasting
defined, 186–87
expert, 187–88
impact assessment, 191–94
leading indicators, 190–91
trend extrapolation, 188–90

Forest Service, 465–66

Fourteenth Amendment, 119

Frankl, Victor, 409

Franks v. *Bowan Transportation Company* (1976), 483

Free enterprise zones, *see* Enterprise zones

Freedom of Information Act (1966), 47

Freeman, Orville, 177

Functional authority, 305

Fund accounting, 379

G

Galbraith, John Kenneth, 348

Gantt, Henry L., 247

Gantt chart, 247–48

Garcia, Robert, 97

Garcia v. *San Antonio Metropolitan Transit Authority* (1984), 470

Gardner, John, 327

Gateway special, 120

General Accounting Office (GAO), role of, in legislative control, 49

General civil service, 446–47

General revenue sharing, 83

General Services Administration, 52

Globalization, 505–6

Goals, 168–70

Gobbledegook, 256

Goldberg, Arthur, 177

Golden Fleece Award, 48

Grace Commission, 271–73

Gramm, Rudman, and Hollings deficit reduction bill, 375

Grants-in-aid, 80

Grantsmanship, 104–5

Graphics, computer, 276–77

Gray's law of bilateral asymmetry in networks, 255

Grievances, handling of, as concern of public personnel management, 461–64

Griggs et al, v. Duke Power Company, 450

Groupthink, 403

Grove, Andrew S., 255

Gulick, Luther, 19, 21, 300

Gunther v. *County of Washington,* 484

H

Haig, Alexander, 306, 495

Hall, Edward T., 134

Hardware, computer, 273

Hatch, Carl, 467

Hatch Act (1939), 467

Hawthorne studies, 399–400
revisited, 401

Head Start, 261–62

Health and Human Services, Department of, 301

Heinlein, Robert A., 11

Hepburn Act (1906), 43

Herzberg, Frederick, 411–12

Hierarchy, 46, 301–2, 307–10

Hierarchy of needs theory, and human behavior, 401–9

Hippocratic oath, 141

Hitch, Charles, 227

Homans, George, 415–16

Honesty, and administrative responsibility, 124–25

Hoos, Ida, 227

Hoover, J. Edgar, 61–62

Hoover Commission, 451. The first Commission on Organization of the Executive Branch was created by Congress in 1947 and named for its chairman, former President Herbert Hoover. Congress created a Second Hoover Commission in 1953. It recommended accrual accounting (see

Hoover Commission—*Cont.*
p. 379] rather than cash flow accounting for fiscal management and
that no more than a new upper-eche-
lon administrative class of about
3000 persons to be called the "senior
civil service." Although the latter
idea was not adopted at the time, it
was resurrected in 1978 and became
part of the Civil Service Act (see
p. 469-70). The two Hoover Commissions produced a total of 587 recommendations, over two-thirds of
which were adopted.
Horizontal equity, 354
Hughes, Emmitt John, 178
Human resources planning, 445-46

I
Impact assessment, 191-94
Impass procedures, 478-79
Implementation, 178-79, 240-41
complexity of joint action, 342-44
and management by objectives, 257-59
need for more effective, 245-59
role of communication, 252-56
role of follow-up, 253
as system of games, 244-45
Impoundment, of budgeted funds, 375
Incentives, 252
Income tax, personal, 357
Incremental approach: an approach to
decision making that starts with ex-
isting policies and then makes only
minimum departures from them.
Opposite of the rational approach
which searches widely for alternative
solutions to a problem.
Indirect benefits and costs, 208
Industrial policy, 528-36
Inflation, 349
Infrastructure, 519-20
Information gap, 271-72
Innovation, in intergovernmental system,
102-3
Inventory model, 218-19
Institutionalized citizen participation;
see Citizen participation and admin-
istrative responsibility
Interest groups, role of, in setting policy,
52-53
Intergovernmental lobby, 89, 91
Intergovernmental Personnel Act (IPA)
(1970), 457, 470

Intergovernmental relations, 78
administrative implications, 100-6
diversity, 103-4
model, 88-90
International City Managers Association,
89
Interstate Commerce Commission, 43,
57
Intervention of government in the economy, 347-48
techniques, 348
Iranian rescue mission, 303
Item veto: a line-item veto allows executive to reject any legislative spending
increase over what was recommended in original budget.

J
Jackson, Jesse, 146
James, William, 399, 405
Japanese decision making and implemen-
tation, 252
Job design, 332-37, 411-13
Job dissatisfiers, 412
Job rotation, 457
Job satisfaction, 445
Job satisfiers, 412
Johnson, Lyndon B., 80, 176
Judicial control, and administrative
responsibility, 136-39
Judicial review: the right of review by a
court for any person wronged by
actions or inactions of an agency; re-
quired by the Administrative
Procedures Act

K
Kant, Immanuel, 226
Kaufman, Herbert, 270, 457, 465-66
Kaufmann, Walter, 150-51
Kemp, Jack, 97
Kennedy, John F.
Profiles in Courage, 126
and State Department, 49
and U.S. Steel, 66
Key activities; *see* Organizational design
Keynes, John Maynard, 350-51
King, Martin Luther, 59
Koch, Ed
closing Sydenham Hospital, 72-76
and Coast Guard, 101
firing an employee, 493-94
and judicial control, 138
Korean War, 285-90

L
Labor force, effects of changes in, on
    public administration, 508
Labor laws, 475
Labor-management relations, 471
    bargaining process, 475-79
    legal framework, 471, 473-74
    legal obligations of, and public
        officials, 475
    and public-employee unions, 472
Laird, Melvin, 60-61
Land-use plans, 166-67
La Raza, 134
Law enforcement, 43
Layer cake federalism, 78
Leader/follower organization 297-99
Leadership
    of political administrator, 58-62
    quest for, and human behavior,
        417-21
    styles, 421-22
Leak, 55
Lee, Robert Earl, 452
Legitimate power, 59
Legislative budget: Although the text has
    refered to "the" budget as if there
    were only one, in government orga-
    nizations and in some other
    nonprofit organizations, there are ac-
    tually two budgets. One, which
    maybe referred to as the *legislative
    budget,* is essentially a request for
    funds. Most of the media reports
    about government budgets relate to
    the legislative budget, and many
    textbook descriptions of government
    budgeting focus exclusively on this
    budget. The second budget, which
    may be called the *management bud-
    get,* is prepared after the legislature
    has decided on the amount of funds
    to be provided. This budget corres-
    ponds to the budget prepared in a
    profit-oriented company. That is, it
    is a plan showing the amount of
    spending that each *responsibility
    center* is authorized to undertake.
Legislative clearance, 50-51
Lewis, Drew, 52, 130
Limiting factor *(strategic),* 204
Lincoln, Abraham, 417
Line and staff, 302-5, 310-12
Linear programming, 223, 236-39
Lippmann, Walter, 144

Local government
    relations of, with federal government,
        94-98
    relations of, with state government, 91,
        94
Lockheed Corporation, 4, 317
Logical incrementalism, 180, 183-86
Logrolling, as policy-setting strategy, 64
Lucas, William, 1-3, 7

M
MacArthur, Douglas, 285-90
McClelland, David, 408, 450-51
McDonalds, 511
McGregor, Douglas, 409-10
McNamara, Robert, 20, 60, 255
Madison, James, 115
Management by objectives (MBO),
    257-59
Management development programs,
    455-59
Management information systems (MIS),
    277
Management science, 19, 223
Management styles, 421-22
Managerial planning, 168
Managerial processes, 10-12
Marble cake federalism, 78
Marine Corps, 466
Market segmentation, 117, 119
Marketing mix, design of, for public
    sector organization, 120-22
Maslow, Abraham, 401-9, 538
Mathews v. *Eldridge* (1976), 159-62
Matrix organization, 319-21
Mayo, Elton, 399-400
Meadows, Dennis, 221
Media, role of, in setting policy, 54-55
Mediation, 478
Medium-range planning, 175-78
Merit principle, 444-45
Merit recruiting, 448-51
Merit Systems Protection Board (MSPB),
    470
Metaphor of "games," 244-45
Metternich, Prince Klemens, 66
Micromanagement, 50-51
Milgram, Stanley, 141
Milwaukee, 529
Mintzberg, Henry, 20
Modeling, 218-20
Monetary policy, 346
Monopoly, 347
Morale, 400

Mosher, Frederick C.
on personnel systems, 446–47
on professionalism, 47, 132
Motivation, 399
Moynihan, Daniel P., 174
Multiple objective models, in decision making, 213–15
Murray, Charles, 290–94

N
Naisbitt, John, 102–3
Nannyism, 126–27
Napolean I (Emperor, France), 254
National Aeronautics and Space Administration (NASA)
formulation of policy, 37
managerial processes of, 11
performance assessment, 461
resources, 57
systems structure, 317
National Association of Counties, 89
National Association of Schools of Public Affairs and Administration (NASPAA), 7
National Governors Association, 89
National Governors' Conference, 89
National Labor Relations Act (NLRA), 473
National League of Cities, 89
National League of Cities v. *Usery*, 470
National program impact evaluation, 260–62
National Science Foundation (NSF), 61
Negative income tax experiment, 293
Networking, with computers, 276
New comparative administration, 505–6
New federalism, 82–88
cities and, 94–96
New integrity, 150–51
New public administration, 145
New York Civil Service Reform Association, 470–71
Nietzsche, 178
Niskanen, William, 312 n
Nixon, Richard M., 82–85, 199
Normative forecast, 187
Norris, William, 529
Nuclear Regulatory Commission, 324

O
Oakland, California, 242–44
Objectives and actions, 168–70
Obligation power, 59
Obligations, 377

Occupational Safety and Health Act (OSHA) (1970), 467–69
Office of Economic Opportunity, 270, 293
Office of Management and Budget (OMB)
apportioning budget, 376
auditing, 376, 378
functions, 49–51
reviewing budget requests, 372
Office of Personnel Management (OPM), 470
On-the-job-training (OJT), 457
Operations research, 20, 222–25
Opportunity cost, 213
Optimization, 219–22
Organization chart, 321–22
Organization, types
conglomerate structure, 313–15
leader/follower structure, 297–99
matrix structure, 319–21
mosaic structure, 299
organic structure, 315–16
pyramidal structure, 299–313
Bennis critique, 312–13
division of labor, 300–1, 306–7
hierarchy, 301–2, 307–10
line and staff, 302–5, 310–12
span of control, 302, 310
systems structure, 317–18
task force structure, 318–19
Organizational behavior, 12, 398–99
Organizational culture, 464–67
Organizational design, 321–28
criteria of, 326–28
key activities, 323–24
critical steps in, 322–26
process of, 322–26
Organizational development, 437
Organizing, 295–330
defined, 295
Ouchi, William, 415, 529
Outlays: Payments, normally in the form of checks issued or cash disbursed, net of refunds, reimbursements, and offsetting collections. Outlays include interest accrued on the public debt.
Oversight, role of, in control of agencies, 70

P
Parkinson, C. Northcote, 311–12, 361
Participative management, 252
Patton, George, 59

Peace Corps, 197–200, 467

Pecuniary benefits and costs, 207

Pendleton Act (1883), 446

Performance appraisal, 483

Performance auditing: the assessment by an *independent* group of the performance of a government program or service to determine its success in efficiently achieving its explicit and implicit objectives. What distinguishes it from other kinds of program evaluation is that performance audits focus on the administrative processes of the agency rather than the results achieved. 381

Performance budgeting, 363–65

Perry Mason syndrome, 224–25

Personnel systems, goals and structure, 444–48

Persuasion, as policy-setting strategy, 63

Philadelphia plan, 584

Phoenix, 521

Plan, 168–70

Planning, 165–94

  city planning, 166

  development, 167–68

  formal model for, 170–83

  land-use, 166–67

  managerial, 168

  national, 168

  premises, 171–73

  reconciling formal model with realities, 180–86

Planning-programming-budgeting system (PPBS), 365–67

Planville, Connecticut, 513

Policy, 168–70

  definition of, 9, 36

  formulation of, 37–39

  implementation of, 39–44

  setting of

    role of client in, 52

    role of cognate agencies in, 53–54

    role of Congress in, 47–48

    role of media in, 54–55

    role of president in, 49

Policy analysis, 9–10

Policy implementation, 39–44

Policy formulation, 37–39

Policy planning, 173–75

Policymaking, 36–37

Political appointment, 49–52

Political competency, 55–68

Political culture, 103–4

Political force field, 44–47

Political management, 13

Political strategies, 63–68

Politics-administration debate, 34–35

Politics, in public administration, 35–70

Pollution, mechanisms for controlling, 251

Port of New York Authority, 98

POSCORB (planning, organizing, staffing, directing, coordinating, reporting, and budgeting), 19

Position classification system, 452

Poverty, War on, 290–94

Power, bases of, 58–59

Prediction, 187

Premature evaluation of communication, 255

Price instability, 349

Private good(s), 348

Privatization, 520–23

Problems

  generic, 201–2

  identification, 201–3

  unique, 201–2

Procurement: This is a general term for the purchase, or acquisition, of resources that an agency might need. The difference between procurement and contracting is that contracting describes a situation where a discrete and specialized task is designed, implemented, and administered by a non-government unit.

  barriers to, 511–14

  effective productivity management efforts, key elements, 515–16

  importance of, 509–10

  meaning of, 509

  as state of mind, 510–11

  strategies for improving, 516

    client behavior, 517

    privatization, 520–23

    incentives, 520

    infrastructure, 519–20

    privatization, 520–23

    technology, 518–19

    volunteers, 517–18

    worker, 411–17

Professional Air Traffic Controllers Organization (PATCO), 474

Professional codes, and administrative responsibility, 141–43

Professionalism, 57–58

Profiles in Courage (Kennedy), 126
Program, 168-70
Program budgeting, 365-66
Program cones, 89-90
**Program Evaluation Review Technique
(PERT),** 248-50
Program management defined, 13
Program operations, 43-44
Programming, 178-79
Progressive movement, 35
Progressive taxation, 349
Project grants, 81
Property tax, 357
Proportional tax, 355
Prospective rules, 39
Proxmire, William, 48
Public administration
compared to business administration,
15-18
defined, 1, 3
Public administrator
basic knowledge and skills of, 7-12
roles of, 5-7
Public choice economics, 312 n
Public finance, 345
Public good(s), 348
Public interest, and administrative re-
sponsibility, 144-45
Public personnel management (PPM),
443-44
aims of, 444-46
Public personnel systems, types, 446-48
Public-private cooperation, 528-36
Public-private partnership, 524-28
Public programs, distributional impacts,
209-10
Public relations, 127-30
Public sector
definition of, 4
interdependence with private sector, 18
size and importance of, 4
Pyramidal organization, 299-313

Q
Quality circle, 415
Quasi governmental institution(s), as part
of public sector, 3

R
Reddin, William, 421-25
Rand Corporation, 228
Rank-in-person-approach system, 454
Rational planning model; *see* Planning,
formal model for
Rationality, limits to, 228-29

Rawls, John, 149-50
Reagan, Ronald
and accountability, 123-24
and Alexander Haig, 306
and EPA, 25
firing an employee, 495
new federalism, 85-88
pipeline controversy of 1982, 205
proposes user fees for government
services, 355
Reagan Tax Plan, 389-97
Reaganomics, 352
Real benefits, 208
Reassignment, 462
Recruiting, 448-50
Referent power, 59, 405
*Regents of the University of California
v. Allan Bakke,* 484
Regional councils, 99
Regressive taxation, 355
Regulation, justifications for, 347-48
Relationship behavior, 421
Relative utility, in decision making,
213-15
Reorganization politics, 328-30
Reprimands, 462
Representative bureaucracy, and admin-
istrative responsibility, 143-44
Resource management, 13
Responsibility; *see* Administrative
responsibility
Responsiveness, 9-10
and administrative responsibility,
115-17
Retirement and medical programs for the
aged, public administration, 508
Revenue sharing, 82-85
Revenue sources, 356-59
Reverse discrimination, 485
Reward power, 59
Rivlin, Álice, 176
Roethlisberger, Fritz J., 416-17
Roosevelt, Franklin D., 80, 123
Rotation, as form of training, 457
Ruckelshaus, William, 23-30, 233-35
Rule making, 39-41
Rule of three, 451
Rural Electrification Administration
(REA), 180

S
Sales tax, 357
Satisficing, 229
Scalar principle, 301
Scenario writing, 246

Scheduling models, 247–50
Schlesinger, Arthur M., Jr., 49
Schlesinger, James, 60, 225
Schultze, Charles L., 252
Science Administry Committee, 57
Scientific management movement, 19
Securities and Exchange Commission
    (SEC), 18
Selection, 451–55
Self-actualization, 407–8
Self-management, 425–35
Senior Executive Service (SES), 469
Sensitivity analysis, 222
Servan-Schreiber, Jean Jacques, 11
Shriver, Sargent, 38
Shultz, George P., 20, 206
Simon, Herbert A., 228–29
Simplicity, as criteria in organizational
    design, 327
Simulation, 219–21
Situation ethics, 146–47
Small Business Administration (SBA),
    177–78
Snelling, Richard A., 93–94
Social indicators, 266
Software, computer, 273
Solar Energy Institute, 310
Sole-source basis, 523
Span of control, 302, 310
Special districts, state relations with, 96
Special revenue sharing, 83
Spillovers, 208
Spoils system, 446
Spreadsheet, 275
Stabilization function, of fiscal policy,
    349–50
Staffing, in civil service, 446–52
Stagflation, 351 n
Stakeholder analysis, 149
Standard Metropolitan Statistical Area
    (SMSA), 105–6
Standard operating procedures (SOP), 308
Stare decisis, rule of, 41
State, Department of, 458
State government
    interlocal relations, 99–100
    interstate relations, 98–99
    relations of, with federal government,
        77–100
    relations with local governments and
        special districts, 91, 94–98
Statutes at Large, 39
Stevenson, Adlai, 1
Stockman, David, 58, 374, 488
Strategic Air Command, 317

Strategic Arms Limitation Treaty, 148
Strategic factor, 213
Stolts Case, 484–85
Stress, 430–32
Styles of thinking, 226
Subsystem or triple alliance, phe-
    nomenon of, 56
Sullivan, David, 148
Sunset laws, 47
Sunshine laws, 47–48
Supply side economics, 352
Supreme Court, and authority of reg-
    ulatory agencies, 136–39
Suspension, 462
System analysis, 217–22
Systems approach, four basic steps,
    224–30
Systems Development Corporation, 317
Systems structure, 317–18

T

Task behavior, 421
Task force, 318–19
Tax coordination, 356
Tax efficiency, 355–56
Tax equity, 354–55
Tax expenditures, 360, 362
Tax overlapping, 356
Tax structures, 354–56
Taxation, 352–59, 389–97
Taylor, Frederick W., 19
Technology, as strategy for improving
    productivity, 518–19
Technology assessment, 193
Technology Assessment, Office of, 192
Technology fix, 202
Telecommunications, advances in,
    502–4
Teleconferencing, 503
Tennessee Valley Authority (TVA), 65,
    414
Termination, of programs, 269–71
Testing, 450–51
Texas, budget control in, 379
Thatcher, Margaret, 123
Theory X, 410
Theory Y, 410
Theory Z, 415
Time management, 425–30
Title VII, 479
Toffler, Alvin, 327
Training, 455–59
Trait approach to leadership, 418–21
Transfer payments, 349
Treasury, Department of, 372

Trend extrapolation, 188-90
Truman, Harry S., 287, 327
Tullock, Gordon, 312 n

U
Ueberroth, Peter, 4-7
Uncontrollables in federal budget,
    372-73
Unemployment, 350
Unions, 472
    Unity of command, in military, 303-4
    Upper and lower limits of a decision;
        see Decisions
Urban management, redefined, 524-25
U.S. Code, 39-40
U.S. Conference of Mayors, 89
U.S. Steel, 66-67
United Steelworkers of America v.
    Weber (1976), 484
Urban foreign policy, 506
User fees, 355, 357

V
Vance, Cyrus R., 147, 306
Variable-sum game, 63
Vertical equity, 354
Volunteerism, 517-18

W
War on Poverty, 38
Washington, George, 417, 419
Washington v. *Davis* (1976), 484
Washington State's Department of Social
    and Health Services (DSHS), 109-13
Waterman, Alan, 61
Watson, Jack H., 101
Weber, Max, 297, 299, 300
Whistleblower, 148
Whitten, Jamie, 48
Wildavsky, Aaron
    difficulties in implementing new social
        programs, 242-43
    on implementation of programs, 245,
        247
    on politics of budgeting, 377
    on public budgets, 370
Wilson, Woodrow, 36
Word processing, 275
Wurf, Jerry, 472, 521

Y-Z
Ypsilanti, Michigan, 261
Zero-based budgeting, 366-67
Zero-sum game, 65
Zoning laws, 166

ABOUT THE AUTHOR

Grover Starling is Professor of Public Affairs and Management at the University of Houston-Clear Lake, where he has taught since 1974. Starling is a graduate of the U. S. Military Academy and holds a Ph.D. from the University of Texas at Austin. He is the author of *The Changing Environment of Business; Issues in Business and Society: Capitalism and Public Purpose;* and *Understanding American Politics.* While at UH-CL, he has been Director of Programs in Public Affairs.

Starling has served as a consultant to a number of corporations and federal agencies, including NASA, the Department of Education, and the U. S. Air Force. His research interests include the psychology of thinking, the interrelationship of business and government, and the use of historical analogy in policy analysis.

A NOTE ON THE TYPE

The text of this book was set in 10/12 Trump via computer-driven cathode-ray tube. Designed in 1950 by Georg Trump, this typeface is based on classical letterforms and is characterized by an incised, streamlined quality. The balanced weight of the letters, the large x-height, and squared curves enhance legibility. Trump was originally cut and cast by the C. E. Weber Type Foundry of Stuttgart, West Germany.

Composed by Better Graphics, Crystal Lake, Illinois.

Printed and bound by Maple Press, York, Pennsylvania.

1945   **Paul Appeleby**
Asserted that processes in government organizations *are* political — at least more than those in business organizations. Philip Selznick, Norton Long, and other writers of the late 1940s were to lend theoretical and empirical support to Appleby's most Un-Wilsonian [1887] thesis

1947   **Herbert A. Simon**
In his classic *Administrative Behavior,* Simon, like Merton [1940], attacked the principles approach to management as being often inconsistent and inapplicable. Like Barnard [1938], Simon advocated a systems approach to administration

1949   **Norbert Wiener**
          Claude Shannon
          P.M.S. Blackett
Emphasized systems analysis, operations research, and information theory in management

1955   **Herbert Kaufman**
          Fred W. Riggs
          Walter R. Sharp
First course on comparative administration introduced at Yale University. This movement, which represented a broadening of public administration to other cultures, began to wane in later years as American foreign-aid programs were scaled back

1957   **Chris Argyris**
          Douglas M. McGregor
Placed emphasis on social psychology and research in human relations in achieving a better fit between the personality of a mature adult and the requirement of a modern organization. Argyris developed an open-system theory of organization, while McGregor popularized a humanistic managerial philosophy

1959   **Charles A. Lindblom**
In his influential essay, "The Science of Muddling Through," Lindblom attacked the rational models of decision making in government. In reality, the model did not work; decision makers, therefore, depend heavily on small, incremental decisions

1961   **Aaron Wildausky**
In an article, "The Political Implications of Budgetary Reform," Wildausky developed the concept of budgetary incrementalism and its political nature that led to his landmark work, *The Politics of the Budgetary Process* (1964)

1964   **Robert R. Blake**
          Jane S. Mouton
Proposed that every leader could be categorized in terms of two variables: concern for task and concern for people. Blake and Mouton's Managerial Grid was perhaps the best known of dozens of adaptations of this idea, which could be traced back to the Ohio State University leadership studies of the 1940s